DATE DUE

NO 1'00			

DEMCO 38-296

THE BEST PLAYS OF 1998–1999

THE OTIS GUERNSEY
BURNS MANTLE
THEATER YEARBOOK

THE BEST PLAYS OF
1998–1999

EDITED BY OTIS L. GUERNSEY JR.

*Illustrated with photographs and
with drawings by* HIRSCHFELD

LIMELIGHT EDITIONS

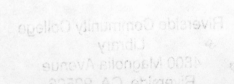

EDITOR'S NOTE

AS WE were preparing this volume for publication, Y2K—computerese for the change in the millennial digit from 1 to 2 with the arrival of the year 2000 A.D.—was a subject under discussion in every nook and cranny of our lives. The magic of this approaching number, figured from the approximate birthday of a revered individual who was "Pleased as Man with Man to dwell," got us to conjuring other numbers as they might be calculated from the lives and works of other individuals. For example, it will be the year 2525 of the theater as we know and love it, dated from the birth of that resoundingly modern playwright, Aeschylus. Our historian Thomas T. Foose informs us that it will be the year 233 of the American theater, figured from the opening in 1767 at the Southwark Theater in Philadelphia of the first play written by a native American—*The Prince of Parthia* by Thomas Godfrey—to be produced by an American company (British plays had been performed in Williamsburg, Va. since 1718). It will be the 155th year of the naturalistic theater, dated from a midpoint between the birth dates of Ibsen and Chekhov, and the 112th of the American drama's maturity, dating from Eugene O'Neill's. The year 2000 is to be the year 105 of 20th century America's great contribution to the theater art, the book musical, dating from the birth of Oscar Hammerstein II, whose *Show Boat* can be considered its first distinct flower—although, "It is generally accepted that the appearance, in 1943, of Rodgers and Hammerstein's *Oklahoma!* began what is now called the era of the modern musical," wrote the distinguished librettist Peter Stone in a *Best Plays* essay.

On the threshold of this millennium, the theater season of 1998–99 is our main concern and concentration in this volume. It is the year 80 of the *Best Plays* series of theater yearbooks begun by Burns Mantle in the 1919–20 season; and, with the addition of the three retrospective volumes dated back to 1894, the year 106 of the American theater record contained within its pages. It is the 47th year that *Best Plays* has been privileged to publish the collection of incomparably witty and perceptive Al Hirschfeld drawings of the major personalities and events of each theater season, a collection which by itself is a treasured keepsake. We are somewhere in the beginning of the 5th decade (he estimates) that Jonathan Dodd has overseen every detail of *Best Plays* publication. This is the 35th (we know only too well) go-round for the present editor and for his wife, the faithful and diligent corrector of most of his mistakes; the 7th volume published by Melvyn B. Zerman's Limelight Editions; and the 3rd in which we have changed from the selection of ten Best Plays from a single viewpoint to the detailed presentation of the major (Pulitzer, Critics,

Tony and Lortel) prizewinners, plus an occasional special citation by the *Best Plays* editors. We offer them, however, with the same detailed reporting of substance and style in the synopses of the plays by Sally Dixon Wiener, Jeffrey Sweet, David Lefkowitz (who also reports on the season's Broadway and off-Broadway happenings in our opening essay) and the editor.

Focusing on the 1998–99 twelvemonth, our program listings gather and record all available information on the flow of stage productions on and off Broadway, as well as (thanks to the energetic and comprehensive efforts of Assistant Editor Camille Dee) the further reaches of off-off-Broadway and the regional theater. The latter is well represented in our volume by the American Theater Critics Association's selections and citations of outstanding new work produced in cross-country theater, supervised by Michael Grossberg, with selections from the scripts and reviews by Grossberg, Lawrence DeVine and Misha Berson. And an important feature of our off-off-Broadway coverage is the yearly review of its highlights by Mel Gussow, with his citations of the very best of the season.

The casts of first class touring productions have been added to the annual listing of major cast replacements in holdovers on and off Broadway, prepared by the Jeffrey Finn Productions staff, and Rue E. Canvin continues to keep track of play publication and the long, long line of our theater brothers and sisters who died during the year. As the years roll by, this book maintains its character and scope thanks in very great measure to the helping hands reaching out with elements of each volume, starting with the absolutely indispensible participation of the press agents and continuing through a long list which this year includes former *Best Plays* editor Henry Hewes (Theater Hall of Fame data), Michael Kuchwara, secretary of the New York Drama Critics Circle (details of the Critics' voting for their bests of the year), Thomas T. Foose (historical footnotes), Tish Dace (Henry Hewes Design Awards), Ralph Newman of the Drama Book Shop, Markland Taylor (New England theater information), David Rosenberg (Connecticut Critics), Caldwell Titcomb (Boston's Elliot Norton Awards) and Lee Lawlor (Los Angeles Ovations). We are most particularly grateful to Robert Brill, Scott Pask and Jess Goldstein for providing samples of their Hewes Award-winning designs for *The Mineola Twins*. The New York and cross-country producers help us to record the "look" of the season's onstage action by supplying us with selections from the work of the stage photographers, including, in this volume, Jace Alexander, Catherine Ashmore, Stephanie Berger, Susan Cook, David Cooper, Michal Daniel, Henry Dirocco, T. Charles Erickson, Eric Y. Exit, Robert C. George, Hugo Glendenning, Sherman M. Howe Jr., Bruce Hubbert, Susan Johann, Ivan Kynl, Marilyn Kingwill, James Leynse, Joan Marcus, David Prittie, Carol Rosegg, Diana Segrest, Anita & Steve Shevett, Junichi Takahashi, Nigel Teare, Richard Trigg, Jay Thompson/Craig Schwartz and Bob Vergara.

What has kept the stage alive for 2,525 years and counting is the fulfilled inspiration of its authors; the dedication, talent and achievement of an Aeschylus, an Ibsen, a Chekhov, of a Shakespeare deep in the centuries, of an O'Neill, a Rodgers, a Hammerstein in this one. And—*mirabile dictu!*—the 1998–99 theater season was itself a paradigm of the theater's millennium-spanning vitality, with three of our century's most illustrious playwrights—O'Neill, Arthur Miller and Tennessee Williams—in production with a pair of outstanding revivals and a newly discovered play, right alongside an outstanding drama, *Wit,* by an author, Margaret Edson, who is brand new to the stage. In this or any other millennium, the authors generate the energy that keeps the lights burning in the playhouses. Thanks to them, those lights will not be significantly dimmed by the passage of time, the arrival of Y2K or anything else.

OTIS L. GUERNSEY Jr.

September 1, 1999

CONTENTS

EDITOR'S NOTE   vii

THE SEASON ON AND OFF BROADWAY   1
     Broadway and Off Broadway, by David Lefkowitz   3
         One-page summary of the Broadway Season   4
         One-page summary of the Off-Broadway Season   36

A GRAPHIC GLANCE BY HIRSCHFELD   49

THE PRIZEWINNING PLAYS: SYNOPSES AND EXCERPTS   79
     Side Man   81
     Wit   104
     Parade   122
     Fosse   154
     Not About Nightingales   164
     Closer   192

PLAYS PRODUCED IN NEW YORK   219
     Plays Produced on Broadway   221
     Plays Produced Off Broadway   263
     Cast Replacements and Touring Companies   307

THE SEASON OFF OFF BROADWAY   325
     Off Off Broadway, by Mel Gussow   327
     Plays Produced Off Off Broadway   333

THE SEASON AROUND THE UNITED STATES   365
     Outstanding New Plays Cited by American
         Theater Critics Association   367
     A Directory of New-Play Productions   400

xi

FACTS AND FIGURES   439
    Long Runs on Broadway   441
    Long Runs Off Broadway   444
    New York Drama Critics Circle Awards   446
    Pulitzer Prize Winners   448
    Tony Awards   450
    Lucille Lortel Awards   453
    ATCA Citations and Awards   454
    Additional Prizes and Awards   454
    Theater Hall of Fame   460
    Margo Jones Citizen of the Theater Medal   463
    1998–1999 Publication of Recently-Produced New Plays   464
    Necrology   466
    The Best Plays, 1894–1996 and the Major Prizewinners, 1997–1998   470

INDEX   493

Drawings by HIRSCHFELD

Judi Dench in *Amy's View*   51
Scott Wise, Elizabeth Parkinson, Jane Lanier and Valarie Pettiford in
    Fosse   52–53
Swoosie Kurtz in *The Mineola Twins*   54
Kevin Anderson and Brian Dennehy in *Death of a Salesman*   55
Tai Jiminez, Perry Laylon Ojeda, Robert Montano, Jesse Tyler Ferguson, Mary
    Testa, Sarah Knowlton and Lea DeLaria in *On the Town*   56–57
Bernadette Peters in *Annie Get Your Gun*   58
Jerry Herman in *An Evening With Jerry Herman*   59
Stanley Wayne Mathis, Roger Bart, Anthony Rapp, Kristin Chenoweth, Ilana
    Levine and B. D. Wong in *You're a Good Man, Charlie Brown*   60–61
Ciaran Hinds, Anna Friel, Natasha Richardson and Rupert Graves in
    Closer   62
Kevin Spacey in *The Iceman Cometh*   62
Jerry Seinfeld in *I'm Telling You for the Last Time*   64
Faith Prince and Martin Short in *Little Me*   64–65
Cathy Rigby in *Peter Pan*   66–67
Sandra Bernhard in *I'm Still Here . . . Damn It!*   68
Laurence Fishburne and Stockard Channing in *The Lion in Winter*   68–69
Paul Rudd, Philip Bosco, Max Wright, Brian Murray, Helen Hunt, Kyra Sedgwick
    in *Twelfth Night*   70–71
Joyce Van Patten, Toby Stephens, Simon Jones, Marian Seldes, Haviland Morris
    and Gretchen Egolf in *Ring Round the Moon*   72

Matthew Broderick in *Night Must Fall*   73

Zoë Wanamaker in *Electra*   74

Treat Williams and Brandon Espinoza in *Captains Courageous*   75

Margaret Edson, Christopher Durang, Patrick Marber, David Hare, Arthur
Miller, John Guare, Conor McPherson, Martin McDonagh, Eugene O'Neill and
Tennessee Williams   76–77

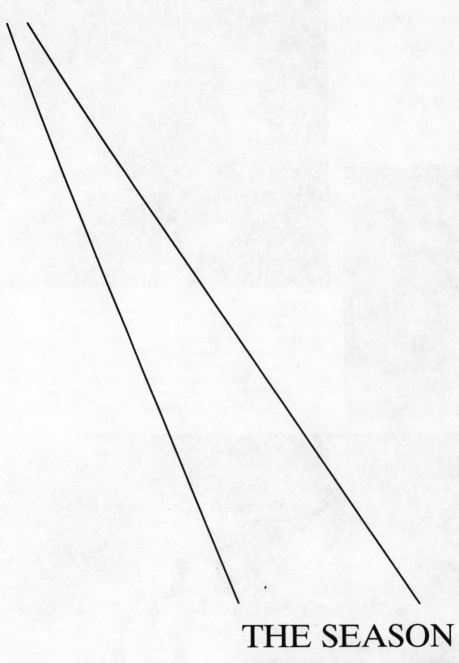

THE SEASON
ON AND OFF
BROADWAY

Broadway 1998–99:
Miller,
Williams,
O'Neill

A confluence of mighty playwrights honored Broadway this season: Arthur Miller with a revival of *Death of a Salesman* (*above,* with Brian Dennehy, Tony-winning as Willy Loman, and Kevin Anderson, Tony-nominated as Biff); Tennessee Williams with the Broadway premiere of *Not About Nightingales* (*left,* with Corin Redgrave, Tony-nominated as warden Whelan, and Sherri Parker Lee as Eva); and Eugene O'Neill with a revival of *The Iceman Cometh* (*below,* with Kevin Spacey, seated *at center,* Tony-nominated for his performance as Hickey)

O
O
O

BROADWAY AND OFF BROADWAY

O
O   *By David Lefkowitz*
O

THINK of the 1998–99 New York season as the hangover after a big party.

Broadway was heady with music and money in 1997–98, fueled by the commercial success of *The Lion King,* the artistic grandeur of *Ragtime,* the Disneyfication of 42d Street, the ceaseless runs of epic pop operas; and by a schedule so crowded, producers actually held back new shows because there were no Broadway theaters to put them in.

It was almost inevitable that 1998–99, the year after *Art, The Beauty Queen of Leenane* and *Cabaret,* would be a groggy one, reverting to a typical mid-1990s formula of flop plays by tyros *(More to Love, Getting and Spending),* return engagements *(Peter Pan, Fool Moon),* one-shot solos (Aznavour, Seinfeld, Bernhard), snob hits from the UK *(The Weir, The Blue Room),* star-driven revivals *(Little Me, The Lion in Winter, Death of a Salesman, Annie Get Your Gun, Night Must Fall, The Iceman Cometh),* pastiche revues *(Fosse, Marlene, The Gershwins' Fascinating Rhythm, Band in Berlin)* and musicals that used marketing to stay one step ahead of the critics *(Footloose,* and a re-cast, rewritten *The Scarlet Pimpernel).*

Somehow it all translated into another banner year at the Broadway bank. According to the League of American Theaters and Producers, Broadway grosses hit another new peak, reaching $588.5 million—up 5.4 percent from the record year before. It helped that 39 shows (by their count) opened, as opposed to the previous season's 33, and that the average paid admission soared to $50.45—nearly two dollars higher than the prior season ($48.58). As expected, prices for top ducats routinely hit $80, with good seats at *The Iceman Cometh* costing $100. Pundits noted that the seemingly exorbitant *Iceman* was, in fact, a 37 cents-per-minute bargain, especially when compared to Harold Pinter's *Ashes to Ashes,* which charged a dollar for each of its 45 excruciating minutes, or Jerry Seinfeld's stand-up solo, where tickets were scalped for up to $1,500 apiece, or roughly $5 a joke.

Credit where it's due: the League wasn't just hiding behind higher ticket prices for its record numbers. Broadway box office attendance rose by 200,000 humans to 11.7 million, a 1.6 percent increase from the year before. Touring attendance and revenues dipped a bit, since there were only 25 legitimate road tours (as opposed to 34 in 1997–98), but road grosses still reached $716 million. As such, between The

3

The 1998–99 Season on Broadway

PLAYS (4)

SIDE MAN
More to Love
Getting and Spending
*NOT ABOUT
NIGHTINGALES*

FOREIGN PLAYS (5)

The Blue Room
CLOSER
The Weir
Amy's View
The Lonesome West

MUSICALS (10)

The Last Empress
(return engagement)
Footloose
The Scarlet Pimpernel
(revised version)
A Christmas Carol
(return engagement)
PARADE
FOSSE
Band in Berlin
Marlene
The Civil War
The Wizard of Oz
(return engagement)

REVUES (5)

An Evening With Jerry
Herman
Riverdance
(return engagement)
Rollin' on the T.O.B.A.
(transfer)
The Gershwins' Fascinating
Rhythm
*It Ain't Nothin' But the
Blues*

REVIVALS (12)

Twelfth Night
Roundabout:
Little Me
The Lion in Winter
On the Town
Peter Pan
Electra
*You're a Good Man,
Charlie Brown*
Death of a Salesman
Annie Get Your Gun
Night Must Fall
The Iceman Cometh
Ring Round the Moon

SPECIALTIES (4)

Jerry Seinfeld: I'm Telling
You for the Last Time
Swan Lake
Radio City Christmas
Spectacular
Fool Moon

SOLO SHOWS (5)

Colin Quinn—An Irish
Wake
Mamaloshen
Aznavour on Broadway
I'm Still Here . . . Damn It!
Via Dolorosa

Categorized above are all the new productions listed in the Plays Produced on Broadway section of this volume.
Plays listed in CAPITAL LETTERS were major 1998–99 prizewinners or specially cited by *Best Plays*.
Plays listed in *italics* were still running on June 1, 1999.

Street and the streets of America, Broadway product took in $1.3 billion, with 26.5 million in attendance.

Ah, but what of "Broadway product"? By mid-season, the closest thing Broadway had to a bona fide hit musical had no lyrics at all and a score by ... Tchaikovsky. If 1997–98 rode on "The Wheels of a Dream" and 'round "The Circle of Life," 1998–99 traveled a straight and colorless line.

It didn't start out that way. Warren Leight's exceptional drama, *Side Man,* opened the season with tremendous promise. Not only was it a new American play by a previously unknown playwright, it began as an off-off-Broadway offering by Weissberger Theater Group (at the CSC space) and was picked up by the Roundabout Theater when their planned Bacharach-David revue stalled on the West Coast. A tender, wryly comic play with a truly sad undercurrent, *Side Man* proved such a winner on the Roundabout's mainstage, the show moved to the John Golden Theater in October 1998 and there played out the season.

A Pulitzer finalist and best play Tony winner, *Side Man* impressed on two fronts: milieu and character. Leight's tale of a dissolving marriage between a musician and his unstable wife occurs against the backdrop of the decline of jazz as America's popular music. It's a world of late-night diners, gigs until sunrise, unemployment lines, drugs, tenements—and a musician's gut feeling that everything worth saying in this world can be expressed in a trumpet solo.

We first meet Gene and Terry when *they* first meet, he a budding jazzman with a casual air, she a good Catholic, albeit with one failed marriage and a nervous condition already in her past. Gene settles comfortably into the life of a jazz musician, trading all-night anecdotes with his fellow side men as easily as they trade chops. That he's never home and always two paychecks away from poverty doesn't bother him much. Terry's okay with it too until, unexpectedly, they have a child (who turns out to be the grown-up narrator of the piece). The rest of *Side Man* charts Terry's mental breakdown and Gene's slow retreat from everyday life. The camaraderie among Gene's buddies that was so playful when they were younger now has an air of the pathetic; though, throughout, their dedication to the purity of jazz maintains a certain glow and nobility.

Several performers won praise for *Side Man,* notably Edie Falco as the mother driven 'round the bend by a life spent hearing " 'Round Midnight." Falco got to have her cake and eat it too. She was hailed for playing Terry at CSC but couldn't travel with the show to the Roundabout because she'd inked a deal to appear in an HBO cable mini-series, *The Sopranos* (which turned out to be wildly popular). Wendy Makkena stepped in for *Side Man*'s Broadway transfer, but when the show moved again, to the John Golden, Falco returned to the cast. (As powerfully haggard as Falco was when I saw her off Broadway, on a second view of the show, her Broadway understudy, Angelica Torn, made a gentler, more gradual—and therefore, more affecting—descent into domestic hell.)

Equally fine was Tony nominee Frank Wood, who showed how Gene allows passivity to overtake his entire personality. Robert Sella picked up a Clarence Derwent Award (given to up 'n' comers) for playing Clifford, the young man looking back with surprising fondness on his wretched parents. Of the colorful sidekicks, Kevin Geer proved most memorable as Jonesy, a raspy-voiced, sweet-natured heroin addict whose brilliant horn playing will never recover from one bad encounter with the cops.

Not a box office blockbuster (despite stints by filmdom's Christian Slater and teen TV's Scott Wolf as Clifford), *Side Man* ran the length of the season—albeit at punishingly low grosses by late spring. The horror was that by season's end, *Side Man* was the only new American play to win both acclaim and audiences on Broadway. Straight plays were plentiful, but revivals aside, the Brits wrote all the hits.

Unless you count *Not About Nightingales*, that is. So what if the playwright's been dead for 16 years, and he wrote this one in 1938, and it took a British cast to dig up this early "lost" work? *Not About Nightingales* proved an undeniable find (as Outer Critics Circle voters no doubt felt when they picked it as the year's best Broadway play). Anyone expecting a typical Tennessee Williams foray into the psyches of eccentric Southern belles and the asexual men they crave had to sit up and take notice at this harsh, moralistic and generally gripping prison melodrama.

First staged by Trevor Nunn at the Royal National's Cottesloe, the drama marked the return of Circle in the Square's Broadway space to active production. Nunn and designer Richard Hoover trisected the circular stage, with the prison barracks on one end, the warden's office at the other, and a space in the middle reserved for "Klondike," that is, the place where disobedient prisoners are sent to suffer. (The Alaskan term is horrendously ironic, as Klondike is a steambath where prisoners are locked for hours at a time and subjected to inhuman temperatures and scalding blasts.) Williams, then in his late 20s, based *Nightingales* on actual events in a Philadelphia jail involving rebellious inmates, a hunger strike and sadistic punishment.

Though containing—and occasionally hampered by—flights of poetic writing, Williams's drama did not lack for juice. "Boss" Whalen, the warden and a Southern good ol' boy, keeps a lecherous eye on his new female secretary and a sadistic thumb on his captives. His low-key assistant, inmate "Canary" Jim, endures vicious threats by his fellow prisoners for being a stoolie, while suppressing his rage at his pitiless overseer. The latter continues to pilfer money earmarked for the captives' meals, leading to chow so indigestible, a hunger strike ensues. Fearing media muckrakers, the warden gives the felons a choice: eat or face hours upon hours in Klondike.

Will Jim and the new lady clerk (they've fallen in love, of course) be able to leak word of prison conditions to the outside world and escape before it's too late? Will brash and bullying prisoner Butch O'Fallon survive temperatures hot enough to boil a potato? Will Whalen's brutality (think of him as a diabolical Big Daddy) push the inmates' bodies and spirits beyond endurance?

Admittedly, young Williams got in over his head structurally and was forced to fudge some of these answers, but with a buildup so gripping and a climax so rousing, no one in 1999 was complaining. In fact, an unintended poignancy grabbed us now and again when we realized that Williams would hardly ever be this energetic, or full of hope again.

Trevor Nunn's staging of *Nightingales,* a triumph all its own, managed to make Circle in the Square feel downright intimate. With Chris Parry's lighting often carving entire rooms and moods out of empty space, we felt discomforted by the zoo-like cells, uncomfortably near to the sleazy warden, and all too close to the tortured inmates writhing in eruptions of steam.

Like the play itself, two members of the ensemble scored Tony nominations—Finbar Lynch as "Canary" Jim and Corin Redgrave as the warden—though a half-dozen other cast members might just as easily have been recognized, notably Sherri Parker Lee as the secretary desperate enough to take a job working for Whalen but not so cynical as to turn a blind eye, and *Theater World* Award winner James Black as the Mussolini-esque O'Fallon, who menaces his fellow inmates yet ends up being crucial to their survival.

Promising kid, that Tennessee Williams. And Warren Leight seems destined for fine work in the future. But who else?

Nobody found anything to love about *More to Love,* an autobiographical comedy by Don Imus's portly radio sidekick, Rob Bartlett. The play, subtitled A Big Fat Comedy, set Bartlett's character in his garage as he sorted through forty years of family and career detritus. Dana Reeve and Joyce Van Patten served, respectively, as the comedian's supportive wife and sardonic agent. By all accounts, Bartlett tried to shoehorn his stand-up comedy act into the format of a nostalgic meditation on middle age. The shoe didn't fit, and Broadway wore it for just a week.

By contrast, the one-week run of Jerry Seinfeld's solo show, *I'm Telling You for the Last Time*, kept ticket scalpers in ermines. A "greatest hits" collection of material Seinfeld was doing before his TV show, which had ended its run three months earlier, evolved from culty urban comedy to America's favorite weekly dose of caustic angst, *Last Time* was filled with PG-rated jokes about dry cleaners, horse racing and stray hairs in the shower. As evidenced by the live HBO broadcast of the second-to-last show, Seinfeld's cruise-control demeanor and unflappable logic could be pretty darn funny: "Why do airline pilots tell us *everything* about the flight, like altitude? See the place printed on my ticket? Just get me there. Do I go to the cockpit and tell them, 'I'm having a bag of peanuts now'?"

Just to prove being a Seinfeld isn't as easy as it looks, Colin Quinn's *An Irish Wake,* a reminiscence of his Irish-Catholic Brooklyn childhood, proved surprisingly flavorful and sophisticated in its writing but drearily bland in performance. Playing a panoply of not-too-stereotyped priests, nuns, teachers, neighbors and relatives, Quinn showed a knack for bringing out details of character, as each flawed person-age proved to be, if not sympathetic, certainly understandable within the context of his lower-class urban milieu. Quinn eschewed the "dese-dem-dose" bluster that makes him a lively *Saturday Night Live* Weekend Update anchor, however, and instead played the show low key, sometimes to the point of inaudibility. Reviews were mixed-to-positive for the limited engagement, though even in the smallest the-ater on Broadway, the 499-seat Helen Hayes, *An Irish Wake* felt tiny and incon-spicuous.

The drubbing continued for American playwrights with *Getting and Spending* by Michael J. Chepiga. It wanted to be a savvy, up-to-the-minute comedy with a con-science, a plea for nouveau riche corporate traders to feel guilty about their less fortunate peers. What it was, however, was a dumbed-down sitcom with a bleeding

Bernadette Peters in her Tony-winning performance as Annie
Oakley in the revival of Irving Berlin's *Annie Get Your Gun*

heart, the tale of a button-cute corporate trader (Linda Purl) finding herself in legal
turmoil when she repents and wishes to give her ill-gotten gains to charity. From
the opening scene—in which two monks kneel in what appears to be ritual prayer,
only they're actually trading stock tips—to the relentless breast-beating of its protagonist, *Getting and Spending* thought itself oh-so-clever when, in fact, any episode
of TV's *Law & Order* or *The Practice* offered more ambiguity and moral distress.
And less overacting.

Getting and Spending ran several weeks at the Helen Hayes, mainly because co-
producer Martin Markinson also owned the theater. He'd make an even greater boo-
boo later in the season when he turned down the illustrious *Wit* (subject matter too

depressing for a mass audience) for the more commercially desirable *Band in Berlin.* But more on that snoozical later.

To be fair to producers, when they gave respected American playwrights a Broadway forum in the 1997–98 season, they got burned. Christopher Durang's *Sex and Longing*, Neil Simon's *Proposals,* Wendy Wasserstein's *An American Daughter* and David Henry Hwang's *Golden Child* all proved commercial flops (though the latter two plays deserved a better fate), while David Mamet's *The Old Neighborhood* should've been torn down and its citizens deported. Still, putting *Getting and Spending* and *More to Love* in coveted Broadway theaters is the equivalent of stocking a banquet table with Fishamajigs. When diners turn up their noses, the caterer then feels justified in importing caviar, but he might've tried a homecooked meal by Julia Child first.

Broadway Tries Three or Four Different Hare Styles

Judging by producers' tastes, David Hare turned out to be both the Le Cirque and the McDonalds of British playwrights. He had three different plays running on Broadway in 1998–99, four if you count *The Judas Kiss,* which spilled its flabby plot over from the previous season. Though no play in Hare's trio had the emotional pull of his *Skylight* or the brilliance and depth of his *Racing Demon,* he did score three different successes. *Amy's View* gave Broadway audiences both an old-fashioned mother-daughter conflict and a star turn; the monologue *Via Dolorosa* earned Hare good reviews both for his objective writing about volatile issues and his debut as a performer; and *The Blue Room* packed a box office wallop, thanks to a dash of Hollywood glamour.

Not that everyone wanted to wear Broadway's latest Hare-style. By season's end, a sufficient backlash against the playwright's Broadway dominance had already taken hold, so that none of his plays—all of which managed some level of critical acclaim and audience interest—received a best play Tony nomination. (Patrick Marber's *Closer* and Martin McDonagh's *The Lonesome West* took the other two slots.) Hare did win Drama Desk and Outer Critics Circle Awards for Outstanding Solo (*Via Dolorosa*).

The latter play seemed the least likely to succeed, especially since *Via Dolorosa*'s topic—Hare's recent visit to Jewish settlements and Arab-occupied territories in Israel—could easily offend the Jewish core of the Broadway audience. Hare's tourist-like objectivity calmed those worries, however, and audiences identified with Israelis dismayed by the stalled peace process; with settlers ready to fight for an undivided, Jewish Jerusalem; with Arab organizers who castigate Arafat's regime as corrupt and powerless; and with ordinary Arab citizens who see no end to a life of poverty and scattered revolt.

Hare's lecture-cum-travelogue stayed on safest territory when recounting the personalities encountered and their impassioned arguments. *Via Dolorosa* lost ground when its author/star felt compelled to turn metaphorical or over-explain the obvious: "Stones . . . or ideas? Stones . . . or ideas?" Nevertheless, Hare proved an engaging guide through the ideological minefield of Arab-Israeli relations, and his capturing of a sense of universal disillusionment was borne out by current events: in mid-May 1999, Israeli Prime Minister Benjamin Netanyahu was voted out in favor of Ehud Barak, the latter seen as more pro-peace and less bound by Orthodox special interest groups.

Politics and drama have long intersected in Hare's career, with the author often chastened for letting characters become mouthpieces and dialogue turn into thinly-veiled parliamentary debates. The aforementioned *Racing Demon,* about church hypocrisy, proved a turning point, wherein the characters' struggles expressed and humanized, rather than schematized, their sociological condition. *Amy's View* continued this salutary turn in Hare's writing, though the plot's shapelessness worked against its welcome dollops of sentiment. Not a lot happens in *Amy's View* (mother-daughter tussles don't tend to be action packed, unless you count screaming and bitching). Middle-aged Esme, a well-known and deeply respected stage actress, welcomes a visit from her semi-independent daughter, Amy (a compelling Samantha Bond). Mama doesn't like Amy's boyfriend, Dominic (Tate Donovan), an amiable cineaste who sees theater as an outmoded form of entertainment. It's detente for awhile, until Esme lets slip a secret she assumes will wreck Amy and Dominic's relationship. Instead, they get married and have kids, with Dominic becoming a rich and famous filmmaker.

Happy ever after? Not quite. By the mid-1980s, Dominic's work schedule makes him an absentee husband and, eventually, a philanderer. Meanwhile, Esme, who never really bothered to sort out her finances when money was readily available, discovers that not only were her investments in the Lloyd's of London "Names" program wiped out, she's liable for millions of pounds lost by other investors. In other words, no matter how much or little she earns for the rest of her life, it all goes to the government, which then doles her back a small stipend to live on. She still manages to do theater and even finds herself in an unexpected, albeit small-scale, smash. But she's also forced to act in a ridiculous television soap opera for income.

The play's most resonant scene comes 16 years after the opening. Still great but emotionally ravaged, the actress sits at a makeup table in the theater's dressing room and receives a visit from her hated son-in-law. She doesn't want his money (he offers); she doesn't want his sympathy, and we eventually learn that her tragedy has extended well beyond financial liquidation. The sequence doesn't hit us the way it should, because Hare has never decided whether *Amy's View* is about Amy or Esme, and he doesn't make clear whether the play's true thematic conflict is marriage vs. independence, "art" vs. mass entertainment or personal choice vs. sensible expectations. The dressing room scene has all the makings of a great, affecting showdown but is curiously unmoving. Or, at least it would be without the presence of Judi Dench, whose gravitas rends the heart. Until this pivotal scene, the role, and her performance, aren't all that different from the Shirley Valentine/Auntie Mame prototype of a bustling, slightly eccentric, haughty but engaging middle-aged lady dynamo. But in act three, Dench finds a well of bottomless grief in Esme. This is the opposite of weepy, histrionic sorrow; Esme has become a shell-shocked victim who presses on with life, even though she's lost absolutely everything of value except the comforts of her beloved theater. Just the way Dench's Esme, expressionless and with a deep, cracked voice, says "perhaps" is enough to connote an ocean of despair.

If, in *Amy's View,* Hare fails at milking melodrama from philosophical affrays, in *The Blue Room* it doesn't seem as though he's doing *anything* except giving us just what the world needs—another adaptation of Schnitzler's *La Ronde.* The latter's sardonic look at relationships got its kick from viewing sexual and romantic encounters as a daisy chain of dominance and submission. The man holding the cards in one scene becomes the jilted lover in the next, while the lady saying "Dear John" to him will, minutes later, be throwing herself at a disinterested cad. By using only two actors, however, *The Blue Room* neutralizes this conceit; we see the play as an exercise in versatility rather than as a series of juxtaposed manipulations.

Under any other circumstance, *The Blue Room* would have come and gone in a week or two, the victim of its sterile core and disconnected framework. Instead, Hare's play was *the* hottest ticket on Broadway all winter long, on track to gross $4 million for its limited run until lead actress Nicole Kidman bowed out a week early owing to throat trouble. Quite honestly, Kidman could have played the role mute, and patrons still would have lined up around the block. Though anyone can see her unclothed in such films as *Billy Bathgate* and Stanley Kubrick's swan song, *Eyes Wide Shut,* for some reason theatergoers went berserk over seeing 40 seconds of her naked tush live onstage. Ticket buyers pored over seating charts at the Cort Theater for the best angle to ogle Kidman during her brief, dorsal nude scene. A magnificent backside it was—and not a bad performance, either, in roles ranging from a devil-may-care actress to a slutty wannabe. Capable co-star Iain Glen showed even more flesh as well as a typically ineffectual, Brit-leading-man steadiness, but no amount of sex appeal or talent could overcome such a vacant enterprise.

Closer, the second work by U.K. wunderkind Patrick Marber, took a fishtank view of four sexy, sex-starved, very messed-up Londoners and surfaced with a lacerating look at modern-day sexual politics. Voted best foreign play by the New York Drama Critics Circle, *Closer* showed perfectly intelligent people allowing themselves to be governed by their yearnings. Marber allows us to envy these sybarites who find exhilaration in one relationship while still pursuing other objects of desire, but we're never allowed to forget the awful consequences selfishness can leave in its wake.

In *Closer,* flirtatious but accident-prone Alice picks up writer Dan, and they fast become an item. She even serves as the muse for his first book, but when it's time to take pictures for the dustjacket, Dan finds himself lusting for the photographer, Anna (Natasha Richardson). Though attracted, she repels his advances for Alice's sake. In a plot turn similar to (but more playful than) Craig Lucas's *The Dying Gaul,* Dan uses the internet to make mischief. He impersonates Anna online and arranges an erotic "date" for her with a horny dermatologist, Larry (Ciaran Hinds). This hilarious sequence was played in silence, with the two men typing at computers on opposite sides of the stage, their "dialogue" appearing on a big screen for the audience to read. It was this scene's graphic sexual references, on-the-edge humor and cheeky honesty that truly announced *Closer* as the 1990s heir to *Sexual Perversity in Chicago, The Real Thing* and other gloves-off dispatches from the male-female boxing ring.

Dan's online escapade backfires, but in a sweetly positive way—Anna and Larry end up meeting for real and hitting it off. But few other events in *Closer* are so serendipitously romantic. Dan's persistence eventually wins Anna over, while Larry lives out his lustful fantasies for Alice by becoming a client in the strip club where she works. Needless to say, the changing of partners in *Closer* often has the casual cruelty of 1990s business mergers, but the play's great strength—aside from Marber's clipped, straight-for-the-jugular dialogue, which already gripped New York in *Dealer's Choice*—is recognizing the emotional devastation wrought by these break-ups and assignations.

Though too raunchy for the blue-hair set, *Closer* used its hipness quotient and hot cast to draw crowds. Anna Friel, as the pixie-like nymph Alice, served as the show's visual icon (her photo becomes a bigger and bigger backdrop as the play progresses), while the more womanly but equally sexy Natasha Richardson served as the play's moral center (weak as her character turns out to be). Ciaran Hinds proved memorable also, as the creepy-charming, dominating-yet-desperate doctor.

Hare and Marber's treatment of characters, be they wealthy or impoverished, invariably had the tone of privileged onlookers peering in through the window; Martin McDonagh's *The Lonesome West* offered a view of Irish hell through a mouse-hole. Funnier but less rich than his *The Beauty Queen of Leenane, The Lonesome West* carried McDonagh's tit-for-tat cruelties to even greater extremes. Set like its predecessor in the wretched Galway backwater of Leenane, *West* pitches its fraternal rivalry in a so-awful-it's-funny vein that lures us into expecting homilies about brotherhood, only to turn vicious and unpleasant.

Brothers Valene and Coleman share a dingy flat—actually, share isn't quite the word. Valene has scrawled a magic marker letter "V" on every object belonging specifically to him, from the stove to religious icons lining the shelves. If his brother wants a packet of potato chips, he'd better be ready to cough up the money for them. Coleman, calmer than his sniveling sibling, simply wants to read his newspaper, nosh on crisps and not be bothered by Valene's relentless goading. It doesn't take much to get the two rolling around the floor and pummelling each other, a ritual even the good-hearted local priest can't undo.

All this is amusing in a *True West* kind of way, until we realize that Coleman, to all appearances a typical working class layabout, is also dangerously psychotic and prone to malicious violence. So hateful are his actions, in fact, that *Lonesome West* has difficulty reconciling its dark and light sides. The sweetly written opening scene of Act II, wherein Father Welsh bids a touching farewell to Girleen, a young woman with an unrequited crush on him, leads us to figure that he will, indeed, have some ameliorating effect on the boys' behavior. And sophisticated audiences are even primed for the classic comedy-sketch set-up that follows: The brothers make an attempt at detente, falling all over themselves to forgive each other's sins, only to find the catalogue of offenses piled so high, rage once again conquers all. Yet audiences were likely turned off by the final showdown, whose ugliness choked all laughter and turned an enjoyable black comedy into something nasty. Despite four Tony nominations, including best play and best director, and some excellent reviews (notably from the New York *Post*'s Donald Lyons, who called it "a tragicomedy of great power"), *The Lonesome West* had a rough time at the box office. Near the end of the run, the Lyceum Theater was 80 percent empty, making it unlikely New York will see *A Skull in Connemara,* the third play in McDonagh's "Leenane" trilogy.

Perhaps the strangest part of all this is that another Irish-themed play, Conor McPherson's *The Weir,* showed resiliency despite facing greater box office odds. *The Weir* received exceptional notices for its cast but only a couple of glowing reviews for the play itself. Worse, the Tony Awards snubbed the quiet drama completely, though actors Michelle Fairley and Jim Norton both seemed likely for nominations. Nonetheless, when close to a dozen Broadway shows shuttered in the weeks following the Tonys, *The Weir* held steady.

If only this ghost of a show were worthy of longevity! Judging by *The Weir* and the previous season's *St. Nicholas* off Broadway, McPherson certainly has the gift of gab but nary a clue as to how to shape a narrative and drive it forward. (His *This Lime Tree Bower,* late in the season at off off Broadway's Primary Stages, was a heartening step in the right direction, but even that jaunty piece put all its dramatic situations into monologues.) What's especially disheartening about *The Weir* is that McPherson defaults on what seems like the ideal premise for a good old fashioned ghost story. *The Weir* deposits us in a rustic Irish tavern with its rusted denizens, including a garrulous old geezer, a reserved homebody and a blase barkeep. These same few guys, day in day out, suddenly find themselves on their best behavior when Valerie, an attractive, middle-aged woman, arrives. It seems each dweller at the tavern has a different other-worldly experience in his past—nothing too horrific, but something years of mundane country life can't efface either. When it's Valerie's turn to spin a tale, hers is spookier and more profound than the rest put together.

Oddly, one imagines the optimal format for this sort of thing is television; think *Tales From the Crypt* meets *Northern Exposure.* Think *The X Files* meets *Cheers.* Think anything *but* the lifeless two hours McPherson dribbles out of this set-up. Each yarn spun by the barflies is so mild as to be inconsequential, while Valerie's tale, while sad, is neither supernatural nor distinctive. Her sorrowful tale supposedly draws everyone in the bar together into some kind cathartic bond, but I'd sooner wrestle with Coleman and Valene than raise a glass with this moribund crew.

In fact, one slogan for the season might be: For two hours that passed like four and a half hours, there was *The Weir;* for four and a half hours that passed like two hours, there was *The Iceman Cometh.* Eugene O'Neill's epic drama proved one of the year's major events, a painstakingly mounted, marvelously realized epic, boosted by a star performance from Kevin Spacey. Whereas Jason Robards's Hickey was reportedly an avuncular Good Time Charlie (think Willy Loman on a bender), Spacey was a coiled snake, a truly icy iceman one could imagine wheeling and dealing with Wall Street suit-and-tie types.

Whether that interpretation was enough to carry such an epic became the show's most debated element. An outcry went up when Spacey wasn't even nominated for best actor by the Drama Desk, although the theater community was less aggrieved when he was nominated but beaten out for a Tony by *Salesman*'s Brian Dennehy. While Spacey's presence ignited ticket sales, not everyone found his glad-handing sociopathy a revelation. To these eyes, the more Spacey appeared, the less he had to offer. The first time we see him in the play (after O'Neill's slow, hourlong buildup), we're primed to be electrified, and the actor doesn't disappoint. He's both the life of the party and the poison in the punchbowl. In ensuing scenes, his energy never flags, but we also don't get the feeling these people are really his friends and comrades. Not only isn't he one of them any more, it's hard to believe he was one of them even in his most debauched long weekends. In turn, that makes it tough to believe he would spend so much time desperately convincing them to drop their life-lies. When Spacey delivers Hickey's equivalent of an 11 o'clock number, a half-hour monologue that begins as a lecture and ends as a confession, he bullets through it, his torrent of words sounding more like a suburban psycho than a common man driven over the edge by crushed expectations.

Among the more memorable pipe dreamers in Harry Hope's saloon: Paul Giamatti's dissipated Jimmy Tomorrow, Clarke Peters's fierce Joe, and James Hazeldine's persuasive Harry, whose walk around the block is forever fated to boomerang back to his own front door. Michael Emerson, so memorable as Oscar Wilde in *Gross Indecency,* played the effete, posturing Willie Oban, while *Taxi*'s Tony Danza, the production's other "marquee name," proved able as Rocky the barkeep and pimp.

To be sure, more than one acquaintance of mine hailed Spacey's performance in *Iceman* as volcanic and called the production their all-time greatest experience in the theater. I acknowledge that Howard Davies's epic staging was an estimable achievement, as diligent with each minor character as it was with the obvious star turn. Still, the production did not shake my conviction that *Iceman* takes 260 minutes to tell a 200 minute story. And unlike *Long Day's Journey Into Night,* which reaches deeper into the Tyrones' psyche each time it digs into the same patch of ground, *Iceman* feels merely repetitious. "Pipe dreams" is not a phrase that rolls easily into everyday conversation, especially when used more than two dozen times in the same context.

An Enthralling Salesman *Also Cometh*

Of course, any theater season breeds competition (however meaninginless), and I freely admitted to my friends I was biased towards *Death of a Salesman.* Like the season *Six Degrees of Separation* lost the Tony to *Lost in Yonkers, Iceman* awed the intelligentsia, but *Salesman* captured the hearts of the masses. In 1998–99, those masses responded with Tonys for best revival, actor (Dennehy), featured actress (Elizabeth Franz) and director (Robert Falls), plus a special lifetime achievement nod for Arthur Miller. Adding further sentiment to this revival was its opening on February 10, 1999—50 years to the day after its 1949 Broadway debut.

Haven't we all been bludgeoned with *Salesman* since grade school, the sight of stoop-shouldered Willy Loman and his two shabby suitcases ingrained on our brains as *the* image of the 20th century everyman? And haven't we all had enough of Willy's daydreams, his crankiness, his foolish pride, his favoritism of Biff over Happy, his inability to grasp what's really going on at any given moment?

No, says Robert Falls's enthralling revival, we sure haven't. In fact, if we think of *Salesman* only from textbooks and Dustin Hoffman's pint-sized, little-man-gets-kicked-again interpretation, we've hardly appreciated the scope of it at all. When mountainous Brian Dennehy goes down, fiercely protected as he is by wife Elizabeth Franz, refuted yet honored by loafing son Kevin Anderson, and cajoled by caring neighbor Howard Witt, it's like watching the downfall of a middle-class emperor, the spearing of a mighty dinosaur. Or, as *Hollywood Reporter* critic Frank Scheck put it, "There's something about watching a big man fall."

The poeticized graveside coda still doesn't work (nor does Mark Wendland's distractingly mobile set), but otherwise five decades' passage have only made *Salesman*'s human drama even more lacerating. In the late 1990s, *Iceman*'s themes of pipe dreams and political disillusionment may still engender stimulating discussions, but *Salesman*'s issues of downsizing and domestic trauma are front page news. And here they're conveyed with immediacy by a stunning cast. Dennehy's Willy is less a bully than a bag of wind, a natural optimist who finds all his reasons to hope slowly pulled away from him. We wish he'd take Charley's job offer, or at least punch his boss in the face, but we also understand why he'd consider it a humiliating admission of defeat. And because so much of his pain is self-directed, he's just a little more sympathetic when taking Linda and Happy for granted, or expecting too much from Biff.

If Dennehy lived up to our expectations of a colossal Loman, other performances proved revelatory by blasting away vague memories of generic supporting roles—the wife, the kindly neighbor, the nerd turned conqueror. At first, we think we have Elizabeth Franz's Linda pegged; her tremulous, verge-of-tears smile and rose-tinted optimism make her a pushover, a put-upon Fifties wife dominated by her husband and fretting over her kids. But soon we realize Willy is more than her companion and provider, he's her rock, and when Biff and Happy start chipping away at what's left of him, Franz's Linda exhibits a ferocious protectiveness that would give even Antigone pause. Kevin Anderson's Biff wavers, piercingly, between wanting to be a loyal son and punishing pop for his one unpardonable sin (infidelity). Director Falls overstresses the just-wants-to-be-noticed angle of Ted Koch's Happy, but he's spot-on showing the banality of Howard's evil and simplicity of Charley's decency. As played by Chicago veteran Steve Pickering, Howard is a middle-man bureaucrat, not heartless, just exasperated by Willy's decreased productivity and unwilling (as so many of us would be) to sit down and give him a hearing. Howard Witt's Charley has a take-it-or-leave-it gravity that somehow conveys both charm and a deep reserve of ethics. He deserves having Richard Thompson's duckling-to-swan Bernard for a son.

For a son only a mother-type could love, audiences turned to *Night Must Fall*, a mediocre but surprisingly popular revival of Emlyn Williams's thriller. Matthew

*The Art
Of Scenery
And Costume
Design*

On these pages are examples of the Hewes Award-winning des[?]
The Mineola Twins, together with illustrations of how they a[?]
in this season's off-Broadway production of Paula Vogel's play[?]
is a photo of the Robert Brill-Scott Pask model for their desig[?]
luncheonette scene; *on the opposite page* is a photo of the se[?]
realized in the play, with Swoosie Kurtz as the twin Myrna ([?]
the Jess Goldstein costume whose design is pictured *below rig[?]
Julie Kavner. *At left* is Swoosie Kurtz as the twin Myra, wea[?]
Goldstein costume whose design is pictured *below left*

Broderick played Dan, the sweet-faced, Welsh handyman-cum-homicidal maniac getting on the good side of a rich, handicapped old lady (Judy Parfitt). What with Dan wandering around Essex toting a head-shaped carrying bag, *Night Must Fall* wasn't so much a whodunit as a "When will they finally realize HEdunit?" Parfitt had some fun as the snippy oldster warming to Dan's affability—and later succumbing to his bloodthirst—but John Tillinger's direction did little to make sense of the iffy motivations in Williams's potboiler. Performances roamed all over the English countryside, with some horrendous overacting by the servants and even the reliable J. Smith-Cameron was adrift in a role that called for her to be hypnotically drawn to the visitor's dark side. James Noone's black-white-grey set was eyecatching and apt, however, and *Night Must Fall* drew well enough for National Actors Theater to move it from the Lyceum to the Helen Hayes. (For his part, Broderick must have really loved the role or been well paid, since he backed out of a previous commitment at Hartford Stage—the premiere of Horton Foote's latest, *The Death of Papa*—to effectuate *Night's* commercial transfer.)

Uneven casting and direction also hurt *The Lion in Winter,* which should've been a sure thing. After all, James Goldman constructed his tale of family infighting as a series of knife-edged witticisms, a delicious concatenation of power plays that keep us guessing until the final showdown of king, queen and rotten kids. With Laurence Fishburne and Stockard Channing as the collusive sovereigns and ubiqitous golden boy Michael Mayer at the helm *(You're a Good Man, Charlie Brown, Side Man)*, *Lion* should've roared, but all Broadway got from the Roundabout mounting were grunts and chuckles. Fault not Channing; her Eleanor of Aquitaine mixed bitterness and rue with just the right tone of playful dark humor. As Henry II, Fishburne was not Channing's match, in regality or intensity. Their offspring were a mixed lot, with Neal Huff's manipulative Geoffrey coming off best. All were hampered by the production's on-the-cheap set and costumes, which reduced Goldman's life-and-death intrigues to a game of dress-up.

Another revival to come and go with decent notices and little hoopla was Jean Anouilh's *Ring Round the Moon*. Once the toast of Broadway, Anouilh's satires, which scrape away the facades of the rich, have had a difficult time competing against such swift, high concept pieces as *Art* or such sexually blunt entertainments as *The Blue Room* and *Closer*. A poorly-presented revival of his masterwork, *The Rehearsal*, a few seasons back did little to renew interest, and Lincoln Center Theater's capable mounting of *Ring Round the Moon* played like a drawing room trifle rather than an exciting discovery. Toby Stephens darted about in the lead roles of twins, one rakish, the other timorous, both causing confusion during a party at the estate of their aunt, Madame Desmermortes. The latter role was to have been played by Irene Worth, but she suffered a stroke during previews, leading the producers to replace her with Marian Seldes, who'd already been doing the matinees. Seldes's reward? Good reviews and a best-actress Tony nomination. (Oddly enough, *Ring* wasn't the only show to have a "stroke" of bad luck; Ron Taylor, a cast member and co-creator of the revue *It Ain't Nothin' But the Blues,* suffered a similar ailment that took him out of the lineup till mid-summer.)

Though in no way memorable, Gerald Gutierrez's staging of *Ring* had its felicities, mostly the wisecrack witticisms of Mme. Desmemortes, the chic costumes of the party guests, and the overall waltziness of the piece, essentially a farce without doorslams. Gretchen Egolf evoked sympathy as the poor ballerina used as a pawn by haughty twin Hugo, though her third-act histrionics proved hard to listen to. Joyce Van Patten had her best role in recent memory as Isabelle's vulgar mom, while Fritz Weaver was a welcome presence as a rich millionaire whose money has made him miserable (though more than one critic charged that *Ring's* treatment of this semi-likeable character, who sees money as the forge of all allegiances, smacked of Shylockian anti-Semitism).

Ring ran all spring, but the season's winner in the high-class froth sweepstakes was Lincoln Center's *Twelfth Night* of the previous summer. Not that Nicholas Hytner's Shakespeare was any more special than Mayer's Anouilh, but famous names brought in the bucks. Helen Hunt, a household name thanks to TV's *Mad About You,* played the masquerading Viola; Kyra Sedgwick the petulant countess Olivia, and Paul Rudd the lovesick, self-absorbed Duke Orsino. Clown roles went to such veterans as Brian Murray (Sir Toby) and Max Wright (Sir Andrew), with Philip Bosco an amusingly peeved Malvolio.

Critics faulted a mish-mash of anachronisms (take-out Chinese food??) and acting styles on view, from Murray and Bosco's classical approach to Hunt's flat American accent and Sedgwick's (often funny) hamminess. Audiences, as they did with many reviled Shakespeare-in-the-Park entries during the Papp era, arrived in droves and left with no complaints. In fact, so popular was the mounting, PBS broadcast the final performance live, and the Resmiranda CD label released a disk of the show's songs and incidental music. (That composer Jeanine Tesori would get a Tony nomination for best original score was less a function of her pleasant tunes than the season's woesome lineup of musicals. More on that anon.)

Much was made of *Twelfth Night*'s costumes and design. Hunt, shining blonde hair pulled into a ponytail, cut an appealing figure in her cream-colored men's garb (and she really looked like the equally blonde actor playing her long-lost twin brother). Sedgwick got to show off her impressive bust—in outfits that looked like cast-offs from *I Dream of Jeannie*. Bob Crowley's set, much lauded for its prettiness and its inviting inlets of water, nevertheless left pundits puzzled over what to call its Spain-meets-China motif—Deliria? Still, watching Murray's proud slob and Wright's hilariously self-abnegating nerd hold back laughing while Malvolio got his comeuppance delighted as much as any Shakespearean comic scene in recent times.

Broadway also rolled out the welcome ramp for Sophocles, courtesy of the Donmar Warehouse's spare mounting of *Electra* that premiered at the Chichester Festival in 1997 and came to New York via New Jersey's McCarter Theater. The main element of Johan Engels's set design was a wooden plank tipped seesaw-like on a rock. The rest was bleak and burnt out, meant to evoke a very modern war zone. In his program notes, director David Leveaux referred explicitly to the Balkan conflict and being influenced by an amateur documentary in which a shell-shocked young girl still "communicates" with her dead brother. Attempts to contemporize *Electra* should have stopped on that metaphorical level, but Leveaux used this as an excuse to make Sophocles's tragedy a stew of ancient masks, 1940s dress and 1990s haircuts, including a spiky 'do for Zoë Wanamaker that led New York magazine scribe John Simon to draw comparisons to both Giulietta Masina and a hedgehog.

Electra isn't the most proactive character in the canon; whether in Sophocles's original or Frank McGuinness's respectful adaptation used here, she spends most of the drama's 80 minutes sneering and grousing. In this production, she also got to roll around, stumble and wail in paroxysms of grief that, I think, were meant to imitate some kind of "birth" but came off (at least to these eyes) as an embarrassing display of hysterics. To be sure, Zoë Wanamaker secured a Tony nomination, as did the production for best revival. On the plus side, even the production's detractors had to give Claire Bloom her due. As the regal but careworn Clytemnestra, she was the epitome of grace and concealed fervor—would that we could see her as Gertrude of Denmark. As Electra's long-lost brother, Orestes, Michael Cumpsty offered his usual noble-Roman oratory; Pat Carroll's Chorus had much of Juliet's Nurse about her, and Daniel Oreskes's faceless Aegisthus deserved whatever punishment Orestes was ready to dish out.

Our historian, Thomas T. Foose, adds this comment: "As the present century nears its end, a familiarity with the Electra plays of either Sophocles or Euripides by theater audiences is a phenomenon of this century. These plays were rarely seen on our stages in the 19th century and rarely seen on London stages during either the 19th or 18th century."

In a season where incidental music could be considered an original score, and where the director and choreographer of a modern ballet could win two musical Tonys while the ballet itself wasn't actually considered a musical, little wonder shows that weren't one thing or another proliferated on the Great White Way.

For example, Sandra Bernhard's *I'm Still Here . . . Damn It!* was a typically in-your-face farrago of anecdotes, diva humor and rock n' roll posing. Her fans were in ecstasy; the rest of us cast our nets into the sea of attitude and were grateful to catch a belly laugh now and again: "Forget Caller I.D.," she ranted. "I wish they had Caller I.Q.!"

Sure, super-hip viewers laughed and whooped at every mention of Mary J. Blige, Linda Evangelista and Radiohead. Everyone else chuckled uneasily, not wanting to be left out but wishing Bernhard had taken more trouble to think up funny things *about* these 15-minute icons. Johnny Carson could tell a bad joke, wait for the punchline to flatten out, and then get a laugh by holding the moment and implying to the audience, "You know it flopped, I know it flopped. Tomorrow I'll fire the writers, but tonight, let's laugh at it anyway." When Bernhard didn't get a desired laugh, she'd pause—half-wounded, half-cocky—and insinuate that the audience wasn't hip enough to get these topical references. Her anecdotes of life as a pseudo chic, jet-setting, Kaballah-reading, lesbian mother of an infant could be amusing, but her anecdotes became so exaggerated, we wondered what parts of her stories of meeting Courtney Love, reciting doggerel at Lillith Fair, and visiting an Islamic bath house were true. Take away the gossipy angle of "did this really happen?" and the stories vanished even faster than they were told. (Comparing Bernhard's tales to those of Alexander H. Cohen in his OOB solo, *Star Billing*, made the difference clear. He embellished his reminiscences of Garbo, Burton and Chevalier with obvious jokes, but the celeb stuff fascinated because its authenticity augmented the quips.)

In *I'm Still Here,* Bernhard belted out a few rock numbers with strength and some sexiness—entertaining enough until the volume became irksome. Overmiking also detracted greatly from a limited-run solo concert by Charles Aznavour, the French-Armenian singer-composer best known to us under-40s as the guy who wrote "Yesterday When I Was Young." He sang that, and a lot of other career hits in French and English, while making charming small talk with the "Why aren't they at Westbury Music Fair?" crowd. If the shrill sound system didn't give them a headache, they got what they came for.

More welcome was Mandy Patinkin's latest Broadway stint, *Mamaloshen,* an evening of songs in Yiddish filtered through the voice, theatricality, and occasional overabundance of the *Chicago Hope* star. A fully-conceived song cycle, *Mamaloshen* offered a dozen of the world's best-known Jewish ditties ("Oyfn Pripitchik," "Raisins and Almonds"), bracketed by Paul Simon's "American Tune." The latter served as a between-song palate cleanser and a reminder of just how closely these songs are now indentified, not with Russia or Poland, but with the American immigrant experience. *Mamaloshen* (translation: "mother tongue") tried out at the Lower East Side's Angel Orensanz Center in summer 1998. A synagogue and Jewish Center, the Orensanz should have been the ideal venue for such an ethnic undertaking, but the atmosphere was neither intimate nor spiritual, and the stuffy air and comfortless chairs made even an hour's sit burdensome. Broadway's Belasco and its cushioned seats, temperate climate and more effective lighting (by Eric Cornwell) gave the uptown version a boost, as did newly-added encores, including a *freilich* "Elimelech" and more playful interaction with talented featured violinist, Saeka Matsuyama.

As if to prove not all forms of nepotism are bad, the Belasco's dark nights were given over to Patinkin's wife, Kathryn Grody, for a revival of her monologue, *A Mom's Life.* With so many shows joking up home and family, *A Mom's Life* came as a gentle refreshment, a low-key evening that was nothing more, or less, than a mother recounting the daily heartaches and miracles of raising two children. People can complain all they want about how busy they are at the office, but Grody revealed there's nothing more hectic in the universe than making lunch, calling babysitters, potty-training, dressing a two-year-old and placating a seven-year-old. *A Mom's Life* was originally produced at off Broadway's Public Theater, and, like *An Irish Wake* at the Helen Hayes, the no-frills piece felt undersized for Broadway. Response to the run was positive enough for Grody to reopen the show in the spring at the tiny ArcLight Theater where, undoubtedly, its sincerity and sweetness filled the space twice over.

By the same token, one doubted that the Broadway musical *Band in Berlin* could keep a ten-seat theater awake. Gratifying as it was to have a musical that didn't crank its amplifiers up to eleven, *B in B* was as soft in the brain as it was on the ears. This bizarrely-constructed entertainment started with a good story but picked all the wrong ways to proceed. Certainly there's drama to be found in the true tale of the Comedian Harmonists, a half-Jewish, half-Christian musical sextet (five singers and a pianist) that gained fame during Germany's Weimar years but found itself besieged once Nazism tightened its stranglehold on the region. Shortly after the Nuremberg Laws restricting Jewish rights were passed, the Harmonists held a meeting about whether to stay in Germany or leave as a group for the U.S. The non-Jews stayed, dissolving the team and, one would imagine, a number of close friendships.

A still-born lecture with music, *Band in Berlin* eschewed actual documentary footage in favor of a black and white video of an actor impersonating one of the Harmonists, accompanied by fake "home movies" of the group. As for the live material, watching the *Band in Berlin* Harmonists mix barbershop quartet and German art song with a dash of mild cavorting was like sitting through a passable Ed Sullivan act stretching their gig to 15 numbers instead of one. Two bright spots had the players vocally mimicking instruments, once for a New Orleans-style blues, the other for a truly entertaining *Barber of Seville* overture. Later came the heavy irony, as the group sang "Whistle While You Work" while photos of the death camps loomed behind them. It was hard not to be touched when works of Holocaust-inspired art accompanied a lullaby, but even these moments showed directors Pa-

Will Kemp as The Swan and Ben Wright as The Prince in
Matthew Bourne's production of Tchaikovsky's *Swan Lake*

tricia Birch and Susan Feldman artificially imposing meaning instead of revealing
what any of this meant to members of the band.

If nothing else, *Marlene,* another hybrid play-musical, tried to get at the psychology of its famed subject, actress and chanteuse Marlene Dietrich. Alas, according to Pam Gems's script, the key to understanding Dietrich lay in her sexual rec-
ollections, catty comments, neurotic mood swings and fetish for cleaning. With
nattering dialogue that made William Luce's puerile *Barrymore* look like Dostoyevsky by comparison, *Marlene* placed the diva in her dressing room, alternately
sharing stories directly with the audience or ordering around her assistant, Vivian
(Margaret Whitton). For further excitement, Marlene's other longtime helper, an
ancient Holocaust survivor (Mary Diveny), shuffled around and slept a lot.

To be fair, Gems did attempt to show the contradictions that constituted La
Marlene. As Gems saw her, Dietrich was an icon-goddess and an extremely messed

up human being; she was fiercely loyal but also took advantage of those closest to her; she mopped her own dressing room but wouldn't take the stage unless the bouquets of flowers pre-planned for her encore were distributed in just the right sequence. As displayed in *Marlene,* however, these quirks conveyed no greatness, no fascinating depth, nothing more than Gems's need to score an easy laugh line when things got dull. (Gems's previous New York contribution, *Stanley,* also used artistic temperament to excuse its protagonist's abominable behavior; but at least that piece, for all its repetitions and slow patches, explored rather than showcased Stanley Spencer's pathology.) After 90 minutes of Dietrich's self-absorption, punctuated by the occasional classic ditty, we were rewarded with a concert recreation: that is, a half-dozen songs as Marlene would have performed them.

Critics were split on the Dietrich-imitating powers of English actress Siân Phillips, best known for playing wicked Livia on *I Claudius.* Dietrich aficionados faulted her German and said Phillips captured the movements but not the essence of Marlene. She seemed fine to me, even if her reproduction of Dietrich's celebrated speech defect had a little too much Elmer Fudd in it. From the concert, one did get a strong sense of Marlene's political leanings and musical tastes. While it might strike us as bizarre for her to sing Pete Seeger's "Where Have All the Flowers Gone," that song was in Dietrich's repertoire (it's been captured on video), and Phillips reminded us how much power the diva's anti-war sentiments added to the number. Negligible as *Marlene* was, there are worse ways to spend an evening at the theater than hearing a very good Marlene impersonator doing "Lili Marlene" "La Vie en Rose" and "Falling in Love Again." The Tony Awards Administration Committee must have agreed, for they declared *Marlene* a musical (rather than a "musical play," as denoted on the Playbill) and nominated it for best book(!) and best actress in a musical. Betcha the morning after the Tonys, playwrights all over America started jamming half a dozen songs into their scripts, just to hedge their bets . . .

An All-Music Non-Musical: Swan Lake

Certainly a song or two might have helped *Swan Lake* be considered a musical, as opposed to a special, um, thingie. Matthew Bourne, artistic director of the U.K.-based Adventures in Motion Pictures company, took home Tony Awards for direction and choreography, but *Swan Lake* itself, though wall-to-wall music, did not qualify as a musical, nor could Pyotr Ilyich Tchaikovsky compete against Frank Wildhorn and Jason Robert Brown for score honors. Though it didn't quite become the *cause celebre* in the States that AMP and co-producer Cameron Mackintosh had hoped for, *Swan Lake* did make waves, its audacious uniqueness adding spark to a season that desperately needed a boost. Backed by a full orchestra (remember those?) with nary a synth in sight, *Swan Lake* was not your typical display of willowy swanoritas. Bourne's version begins in the bedroom of a spoiled Prince as he fends off the ministrations of his controlling mother and prepares for a night out with his girl friend. Things get worse for him at the Opera House, where, in a riotously funny sequence, he and his lady friend watch a ridiculous ballet about a Moth Maiden,

Butterfly Maidens and an "Evil Forest Troll." So bored is the Prince's trampy gal pal (played to perfection by Emily Piercy), she finds a dozen ways to keep busy, from snacking noisily to waving at her friends in the gallery. (Bourne cruelly split the audience's attention here; one didn't know whether to watch her antics or those of the ballet troupe trying to ignore her. Both were equally ribtickling.)

If more of *Swan Lake* were this engaging, Bourne would have pulled off a coup indeed; turning a weepy, if beautiful, dance classic into a work of vibrant, albeit wordless, musical theater. At 40 minutes into the show, however, the Prince does a rotten thing: he goes to the park and looks at swans. This turns out badly for him, since the male swan he falls in love with turns out to be his undoing. It turns out much worse for us, because we're then subjected to a half-hour of male swans in unflattering feathered tutus, fluttering about without much grace, beauty or . . . anything. Of all times for Bourne's choreographic invention to fail him!

Maybe the wunderkind felt he was making a statement by having the traditionally female swan corps played by men, but shouldn't the result be that we're as moved and impressed by the dancing as in a traditional *Swan Lake?* By the time the Prince finally exits the park, we've lost the narrative thread—not to mention our appetite for roast goose. Act II featured a good scene where a randy gay stud (is he the same swan in human form? You got me.) crashes a fancy ball and abuses all the guests, but the violent finale proved incomprehensible and the "touching" coda just ridiculous.

Those in search of pure wordless nonsense were better off catching the third go-round of *Fool Moon,* Bill Irwin and David Shiner's magnificent evening of mimed comedy. With The Red Clay Ramblers band as ever providing ideal underscoring, the rubbery Irwin and snarky Shiner trotted out the same old routines—which galloped along with the same old greatness.

No Sondheim, no Lloyd Webber, no Ahrens & Flaherty, no Maltby & Shire, no Hamlisch, no buzz. While the one-two punch of *The Lion King* and *Ragtime* was expected to make musicals *the* hot commodity on Broadway this season, the actual roster was dreary indeed, without a single new score that critics and audiences could take to heart. It didn't help that only three original scores reached The Street all year: *Parade,* by Jason Robert Brown; *The Civil War,* by Frank Wildhorn, and *Footloose,* by Dean Pitchford and Tom Snow (plus several songs from the hit film by various pop tunesmiths). All the other "new" musicals were revues of extant material: *An Evening With Jerry Herman, Fosse, The Gershwins' Fascinating Rhythm, Rollin' on the T.O.B.A.* and *It Ain't Nothin' But the Blues.* Tchaikovsky anyone?

Certainly the highest hopes went out to *Parade*, a Lincoln Center Theater mounting backed by Livent and co-conceived and staged by the one and only Harold Prince. Theater buffs worried that the subject matter—the judicial railroading and lynching of Leo Frank by an anti-Semitic Southern community—wasn't right for a musical, even a Serious-with-a-capital-S one. But naysayers were comforted by the creative team's pedigree. Brown, a relative newcomer, had worked his way up the scene as musical director and arranger for such tuners as *When Pigs Fly* and *Dinah Was.* He got his big composing break in 1995 with the generally well-received WPA

Theater staging of *Songs for a New World*. Librettist Alfred Uhry, though best known for such non-musicals as the Tony-winning *Last Night of Ballyhoo* and Pulitzer-winning *Driving Miss Daisy,* had his share of musical experience, including penning the Tony-nominated libretto for *The Robber Bridegroom*. (He lost, but his competition was *A Chorus Line, Chicago* and *Pacific Overtures*!) Lead actor Brent Carver won a whole passel of honors for *Kiss of the Spider Woman*, while choreographer Patricia Birch's resume boasted enough New York credits to lead any parade.

What all these talents came up with was an intelligent, carefully-measured, melodic show that bored critics to tears and worked like bug spray at the box office. After the first round of negative reviews, second stringers were more appreciative of *Parade*'s good points, but by then the damage was done. A planned extension was rescinded, and Broadway's musical hopes floated belly up. Even the New York Drama Critics Circle Award for best musical, Tony Awards for Uhry and Brown and a late-season announcement of a planned regional tour couldn't quash the feeling that *Parade* was a show nobody wanted except the folks who devised it.

The general complaint was that Leo Frank wasn't a terribly sympathetic character, and that by taking his innocence for granted, the show passed up a number of options to make the story more intriguing. *Parade* therefore followed a straightforward path: Frank working late at the factory, young Mary Phagan found dead, the iffy evidence pointing to Leo, Lucille Frank (Carolee Carmello) standing by her husband, the guilty verdict, Lucille crashing high society to aid her husband, the politician who helps reverse the death penalty ruling, the mob who make sure "justice" is done. Along the way, satirical stabs are taken at newshounds, right-wing preachers and a public hungry for blood lust.

Parade unquestionably had its head in the right place, but that wasn't enough for theatergoers spoiled by *Ragtime*'s intricacy and more accomplished score just a year earlier. Give Jason Robert Brown his due, though. Rather than pen a sung-through, atonal bore—as so many of his contemporaries have been doing this past decade—the composer-lyricist wrote actual *songs,* crafted in a recognizable music-theater/folk song style. Perhaps the most inspired moment had the Governor visiting a chain gang to pry more honest testimony out of the prosecution's questionable star witness, Jim Conley (a dynamic Rufus Bonds Jr.). Conley responded as if the questions were a call-and-response blues holler, both upping the ante of the scene and making it thrillingly musical. Critics unanimously appreciated a lively fantasy sequence during the trial, wherein Leo emerged from his nerdy persona to invite a chorus of factory girls to "Come Up to My Office."

Parade skidded off the track a couple of times, especially in beefing up the cliched character of a boozy journalist (a hyperactive Evan Pappas) using the Frank trial as his meal ticket. So much effort was expended on that kind of local color, there wasn't enough time to humanize Leo and Lucille's relationship, or even wrap up important secondary characters at the finale. That said, I'm not so ready to agree with my colleagues that it was a mistake to portray Leo as a model of self-righteous decency. Would they rather contradict history and give Frank a seedy side just for the sake of drama? As *Parade* told us repeatedly, sometimes an innocent man is simply that. Carver made Leo an honorable fall guy, Carmello made a strong impression as a reserved, loving wife forced by circumstance to be an outspoken public advocate for her spouse. In fact, many thought the show should have followed her journey, rather than his.

Audiences seemed to want a livelier take on historical tragedy than *Parade,* but when one did come along, they eschewed it as well. With *The Civil War,* composer Frank Wildhorn had three musicals running on Broadway, including *Jekyll & Hyde* and a revamped (and significantly improved) *The Scarlet Pimpernel.* That all three continued to lose money did little to slow the gears of the Wildhorn machine—until the usual negative reviews greeting a Wildhorn musical, combined with a Tony loss, combined with the size of the St. James Theater, conspired to kill *The Civil War* just after the Tonys. With *The Scarlet Pimpernel* shut down near season's end for yet another overhaul (this one specifically to make it cheaper to operate), the S.S. Wildhorn, for better or worse, finally hit a reef.

The queer thing about *Civil War* was that its rousing tunes converted many previous Wildhorn agnostics. Those who found *Jekyll & Hyde* overblown and *Pimpernel* hampered by a silly book had no libretto to scold in *War.* A collection of songs on the theme of Yanks versus Rebs, the piece played to Wildhorn's strength as a rousing tunesmith—as well as a marketing guru. Two CDs of the material were released *before* the show opened, one mixing songs and authentic Civil War correspondence as read and sung by celebs and pop stars, the other a Nashville disk of the more country-oriented ditties. Ironically, as of this writing, an actual original cast CD of the show has yet to be recorded. That's a shame, because ballads like "Virginia" and propulsive numbers like "That Peculiar Institution" and "Oh! Be Joyful!" would be well worth hearing again (and maybe even again and again). Other tunes, including the much-boosted "Freedom's Child," sounded a little too much like car commercials, and the non-narrative shape of the show led to some scatterbrained moments, as when, five minutes into the production, two soldiers—one blue, one grey—ran onstage. One got shot, the other turned, looked at the fallen body and shouted, "He's my brother!", allowing the dying man to sing a wrenching ballad. The action was so sudden, and the characters so unexplained, the song had no context in which to be effective. On the other hand, most of the "slave" numbers worked effectively, and a number of performers registered strongly, including Michel (*Show Boat)* Bell and Cheryl Freeman on "If Prayin' Were Horses" and Leo Burmester offering comic relief as a contemptible profiteer who steals from a corpse once too often.

And speaking of profiteers . . . hating *Footloose* would have been easy, since there was no reason on God's green earth to *do Footloose* as a stage musical except to make money and to offer yet another amusement park-ish entertainment on Broadway. When the youthful cast bounded onto the stage (shades of *Big,* another, better attempt to lure a middle-American, Stepford audience that may not actually exist), *Footloose* seemed to promise nothing but noise, phony high school wisecracking and lights shining right into our eyeballs. More than one colleague called it one of the worst musicals ever staged, so imagine my reticence to pipe up and say, "Hey, I kinda *liked* it."

Shrill and overzealous as the piece was, and unmemorable as nearly all the songs were (including the movie tunes), damned if the show didn't hook you in. The story of a happy-go-lucky visitor to a small town where dancing is banned because of a car accident years before made not a whit of sense in its plotting, but, surprisingly, its themes and emotions hit home. Other critics shook their heads at being expected to believe that a preacher would condemn an innocent dance party but allow his own daughter to dress like a tramp and accept motorcycle-riders behaving like hoodlums at the Burger Blast. Other reviewers couldn't get past the illogic of the new kid in town confessing in Act II that he needs to get a school dance going to establish his credibility, even though by then he seems not only surrounded by friends and well-wishers, he's their leader. *Footloose*'s inconsistencies were not to be ignored, but neither was the emotional soliloquy delivered by the Reverend (Stephen Lee Anderson), which did exactly what such an 11 o'clock number (actually, 10 o'clock) should: take the character into a breakthrough and move us while doing so. The marketing of *Footloose* concentrated on the energetic performers and love story between Jennifer Laura Thompson and Jeremy Kushnier—the latter an agile and appealing newcomer. The musical ultimately clicked, however, because the preacher's journey of self-discovery was both convincing and universal. At least there, *Footloose* kept one foot solidly on the ground.

Meanwhile, Cathy Rigby captured even younger crowds by staying up in the air. So popular was her Christmastime return visit as Peter Pan, she flew back again for a late season run, generally receiving the same good reviews as for her 1991 engagement. Critics were also pleased by the political correcting of the material, with the generally discomfiting "Ugg-a-Wugg" transformed into an athletic, *Stomp*-like shindig that made the Native-American crew look considerably more evolved than those three pasty English kids.

Peter Stone tried to do the same for the Injuns in *Annie Get Your Gun,* but all he came up with in his well-meaning adaptation of Herbert and Dorothy Fields's book was a stalled plot and even lamer jokes. Audiences gladly tolerated the verbal drivel, however—and the miscasting and the choreographic fiascos—and flocked to *Annie* to see Bernadette Peters do one of the signature roles in American musical theater. A half-century from now, show buffs will no doubt read this essay and gasp, "You saw Bernadette do Annie Oakley, and you *dare* criticize?" Well, yeah. She wasn't ideal for the role, and Graciela Daniele and Jeff Calhoun sabotaged the material as often as they nurtured it. No one was asking for the return of Merman, and Peters's ragamuffin sweetness was a legitimate approach. There is something to be said for a genuinely feminine Annie; Frank's romantic interest can be believably kindled, and she can be "as soft and as pink as a nursery" if she so chooses, especially on ballads. But Peters's mushy delivery and coy presence hurt many of the uptempos, especially "Doin' What Comes Nat'rally," which got so carved up by Annie and her kids, one could hardly tell it was a ribald song about coitus.

Jeremy Kushnier *(center)* and company in a scene from the Broadway musical *Footloose*

For his part, handsome and effortlessly macho Tom Wopat proved a natural choice for a kinder, gentler Frank Butler, whose sexism isn't so much about keeping a woman in her place as it is dread at being bested. Peters won Tony, Drama Desk (a tie with *Parade*'s Carmello) and Outer Critics Circle Awards; Wopat was nominated but lost in all three, though he delivered the most consistent work of the night. Heaven knows Jeff Calhoun's dancework roamed from fun to appalling, the nadir being "My Defenses Are Down," wherein Wopat's Frank gamboled with three swishy male cowpokes.

Each time this *Gun* hit a couple of bullseyes, it deliberately and cringingly misfired. Some of Tony Walton's settings looked road show tacky (e.g., ballroom chandeliers that resembled hundreds of fly eyes), and pointless subplots used up time that could have spared the excised "Colonel Buffalo Bill" and "I'm a Bad, Bad Man." So many wrong choices were made, it wasn't until the last half hour (of a nearly three-hour evening) that one could truly enjoy the romantic sparring of Annie and Frank. Peters cavorted deliciously on "An Old Fashioned Wedding," the final shooting match satisfyingly resolved a seemingly unfixable rivalry, and the ending managed to be sweetly romantic.

In fairness, the phrase "*Annie Get Your Gun* starring Bernadette Peters" comes attached to a very high set of expectations, and when those are (mostly) not met, we may feel more let down than the final result warrants. On the other hand, what does the phrase "*You're a Good Man, Charlie Brown* with a talented ensemble cast" carry with it but a shrug and a hope for the best? As such, Michael Mayer's revival of Clark Gesner's musical, starring *Rent's* Anthony Rapp, turned out to be a pleasant surprise. Courtesy of designer David Gallo, the Charles Schulzian cartoon colors looked great on a big stage and helped give the show an amplitude the material was never even meant to have. After all, the well-remembered original version ran forever *off* Broadway; when it moved uptown, it closed in a couple of weeks. Even in this artistically successful revival, to score Gesner's script joke by joke was to learn why, when blown up to Broadway size, the show landed in the dog house. (An off-Broadway Gesner revue, *The Jello Is Always Red*, closed at the York Theater after dismissive reviews.) More punchlines missed than succeeded, and even the best ones tended towards subtle irony rather than belly laughs—and Broadway musicals are more likely to thrive on the latter. Worse, other blackouts in this essentially narrative-free revue ended with a thudding finality, as one Peanuts character traipsed off the stage to silence and the audience waited for the next to say something funnier.

But Mayer's revival had a number of game-savers up its sleeve, among them Roger Bart's tirelessly chipper Snoopy, B.D. Wong's beatific Linus (his odd and distracting lisp aside) and Kristin Chenoweth's Sally, a pint-sized cross between two dolls: kewpie and Chuckie. Both Bart and Chenoweth won featured actor Drama Desk and Tony Awards, with Chenoweth really leaping to star status, courtesy of a New York *Times* rave and a Clarence Derwent newcomer prize. Hard to tell whether she was *that* good as Charlie Brown's opinionated sister, or whether this was just one of those magic, ideal-actress-for-ideal-role situations (Chenoweth also did good work in William Finn's off-Broadway musical, *A New Brain),* but hey, the role of Sally didn't even exist years ago. That she quickly became the most memorable character in this revised version was definitely a credit to the young actress. Certainly Sally's big song, "My New Philosophy," written by Andrew Lippa especially for this revival and for Chenoweth, proved a highlight. By contrast, another new tune, the ersatz gospel "Beethoven Day," sounded generic and anachronistic.

And yet, despite two Tony Awards, an overnight leap to minor stardom, an obvious target audience, a playing schedule constantly revised to accommodate school kids, a cluster of pretty good reviews and the enduring American love story with the *Peanuts* gang, *Charlie Brown* rarely managed better than 50 percent attendance and threw in the towel just after the Tony Awards, becoming the season's most unexpected flop. By contrast, the previous season's decent but far from revelatory *The Sound of Music* revival ran more than a year and even brought in a high-priced—and very well-received—Richard Chamberlain to give the show a pre-tour publicity boost in its last weeks.

Charlie Brown may have been a modest failure, but the usually savvy George C. Wolfe launched a commercial nightmare when *On the Town,* a revival of the Leonard Bernstein, Betty Comden and Adolph Green tuner, took a $5 million bath in its transfer from 1997 Central Park hit to 1998 Gershwin Theater dud. Despite a rave from Sunday *Times* critic Vincent Canby and generally good reviews elsewhere, plus the presence of ace-in-the-hole Lea DeLaria (shall we call her last year's Chenoweth?) and the charm of a show that looked at 1940s New York through the most loving of eyes, *On the Town* proved energetic but empty, an exercise in forced nostalgia. DeLaria, an essentially unknown comedienne launched to stardom when the *Times* gushed about her during the show's Central Park run, again justified the huzzahs. A brassy, belty broad who could hoist the story, the ho-hum sets and all the scrawny sailor boys on her barrel-shaped back, DeLaria made "Come Up to My Place" an unalloyed delight. Mary Testa, as voice teacher Madame Dilly, struck me as shrill, but most critics sided with *The New Yorker*'s Nancy Franklin in praising her "girdled propriety and transparent looniness." She scored a Tony nomination; DeLaria's Hildy got skunked. Few other *Town* dwellers made such an impression, though Sarah Knowlton was a fetching and melodious Claire DeLoone, and Jesse Tyler Ferguson, as Chip, was believably bowled over by Hildy's man-hungry tactics.

If the ensemble nature of *On the Town* worked against DeLaria being able to carry it, near-singlehandedly, across the finish line, Neil Simon, Cy Coleman and Carolyn Leigh's *Little Me* can, if it has the right lead, sit back and watch the jokes land, the songs bounce and the show satisfy. Now it would be great if *Little Me* could have *two* unforgettable comic turns, but for the Roundabout's mounting, it was not to be. Faith Prince, startlingly *zaftig* and less than convincing as Belle, a poor but dainty naif bumbling her way to fortune through a series of unhappy accidents (though no fault of her own, every man who gets near her has the misfortune of dying soon after), became a secondary presence in her own show, someone we tolerate while waiting for the funny guy to come back. The magical moxie of her Adelaide, the assuredness as Anna Leonowens somehow abandoned her here, leaving the field clear for her co-star, Martin Short. With the possible exceptions of Bill Irwin and David Shiner, no eyes twinkled brighter on Broadway this season, no body moved with more sheer abandon, no person cavorted with more zest than this diminutive Canadian. Whereas Sid Caesar no doubt used his boundless vigor and facility with foreign accents to milk the comic possibilities of such characters as spoiled rich boy Noble Eggleston and nightclub bon vivant Val du Val, Short was always lovable Short (okay, with a touch of "Ed Grimley" in his dance moves). Especially on the irresistible "Boom Boom," Short invited comparison to old-style pros like Bobby Clark and Ed Wynn, virtuosi who could take an agreeable musical comedy number and turn it into a treasurable moment of joy.

Revues: Collecting the Musical Collectibles

Since composers and lyricists had a tough time creating new gems, producers again Frankensteined their way through old ones, creating musicals from material by everyone from Kander and Ebb to George Gershwin to, well, Screamin' Jay Hawkins. Perhaps the season's most unlikely Broadway transfer was a revue first staged at the Denver Center and then brought to off Broadway's family-oriented New Victory Theater. When *Parade* closed sooner than Lincoln Center had hoped, a gaggle of producers joined forces to bring *It Ain't Nothin' But the Blues* to the Vivian Beaumont. *Nothin'* was nothing more, or less, than 40-odd 20th century pop tunes, all with some kind of underpinning of the blues. Though too long and, like everything else these days, over-bloody-miked, *Blues* offered a slew of nicely performed hummables, including a sexy woman's take on "I Put a Spell on You," a smokin' "Wang Dang Doodle" and a hard driving "I'm Your Hoochie Coochie Man." Conceptually, *Blues* erred on the side of inclusion, which weakened its overall effect. Jimmie Rodgers, Leadbelly and even Patsy Cline have legitimate blues roots, but calling "Good Night, Irene" and "Fever" blues numbers is pushing it. Certainly you could fill an evening with Willie Dixon, Muddy Waters, Robert Johnson, Blind Willie Johnson and their ilk without resorting to potluck pop.

In *Blues,* an ensemble of five African-American and two white performers, sometimes playing their own instruments but mostly backed by a band, ran through one catchy classic after another, occasionally stopping for chit-chat on the order of "You know, what we think of as country music also has some blues in it." "Really?" "You bet. Just listen." Somehow the Tony Nominating Committee found the libretto worthy of a nomination, though the adjudicators stood on more solid ground when recognizing such performers as *Show Boat* Tony-winner Gretha Boston and the aforementioned Ron Taylor, who suffered a stroke just two weeks after the Tony Awards. Speaking of the Tonys, a tiny tempest ensued when the ceremony, pressed for time in its two hours on CBS, cut *Blues'*s musical number, leading the show's producers to whine about mismanagement, favoritism and even racism (i.e., why was it the *black* show that got axed?). CBS tried to make good by putting the snipped number on *The Late Show with David Letterman* that week, and *Blues* ended up getting more publicity from all the angry breastbeating and damage control than it would have from simply doing its thing on the broadcast. In fact, box office grosses were strong enough for the producers to declare, midsummer, that the show would move to the Ambassador Theater in September.

Whatever the fate of *Blues,* it's already been a hundred times luckier than another off-Broadway transfer, *Rollin' on the T.O.B.A.,* which, despite a reportedly amateurish feel, generated enough good response to try for a commercial move. This musical look at black performers during the vaudeville era (the letters "T.O.B.A." officially stood for Theater Owners' Booking Association but were privately acronymed as "Tough On Black Asses") moved into the Kit Kat Klub after *Cabaret* jumped to the more capacious Studio 54 (yes, the old disco club!) to continue its wildly successful run. Although the Tony Administration Committee gave *Cabaret* official Broadway status, they would not do the same for *T.O.B.A.* Their reasoning— that the Kit Kat (nee Henry Miller's Theater) was not, of itself, a Broadway house, and that *Cabaret* merited special treatment because of its quality and the Roundabout's track record—sounded pretty arbitrary, but what isn't arbitrary in this business? Facing mixed reviews, a limited ad budget and no possible publicity or awards from the Tonys, *T.O.B.A.* soon stopped rolling.

Not that it offered much consolation to the producers of *T.O.B.A.,* but being an official Broadway show didn't help *The Gershwins' Fascinating Rhythm* fare much better. A pastiche of George and Ira ditties, *Rhythm* had a whiff of bargain basement about it that only socko reviews could deodorize. Critics were *not* kind, however,

The ensemble cast of Terrence McNally's *Corpus Christi* at Manhattan Theater Club

and declared the Mark Lamos and Mel Marvin concoction an insult to the Gershwins' exalted oeuvre. Certainly Michael Yeargan's disastrous set didn't help (think of grey Kodak camera shutters irising in and out all night), but I have to go out on a limb and say the show as a whole was misunderstood and therefore got short shrift. Theatergoers come to a Gershwin revue with a host of preconceptions, usually involving two men and two women in suits and dresses (tuxes and evening gowns in Act II), congregating around a piano and acting all coy and sophisticated for two hours. These shows usually crap out on Broadway, too, but we're so used to them, any messing with the formula feels like blasphemy. *Fascinating Rhythm* dared take George Gershwin out of the Rainbow Room and put him in the Tikki Room. Cry kitsch all you want, the show didn't give the same old songs the same old arrangements. Instead, the tunes sounded like 1970s Cy Coleman, heavy on the beat and percussion, with spunk replacing suavity as the overriding approach on nearly every song. As such, "I Love to Rhyme" became a veritable toe-tapper, and Darius de Haas worked the crowd, and his vocal dexterity, on "Little Jazz Bird." Best of all was a de Haas duet with Orfeh [sic] on "Let's Call the Whole Thing Off," sharing the season's comic showstopper honors with *Annie Get Your Gun*'s "An Old Fashioned Wedding" and *Little Me*'s "Boom Boom."

Boom went another revue, *An Evening With Jerry Herman,* which critics deferentially applauded and audiences walked around the block to avoid. It was satisfying, in a real-life fairytale way, to hear how Herman, hoping to write the score for *Hello, Dolly!,* played four hastily-written songs for David Merrick and was told by the usually sinister producer, "Kid, you've got the job." But Herman should have hired different folks for the jobs on his mummified retrospective. The composer played piano throughout, but most of the warbling was done by Florence Lacey (star of *The Grand Tour)* and the show's director, veteran musical actor-dancer, Lee Roy Reams. Lacey earned audience cheers for her second-act torch song, "Time Heals Everything" (from *Mack and Mabel),* though the profusion of her own tears stanched any that might have sprung from my eyes. While a certain gay urtext was necessary for Reams's duet with Herman on "Bosom Buddies," or when Reams donned a red boa for *La Cage aux Folles*'s "I Am What I Am," the performer's effeminacy proved embarrassing in other songs that called for something approximating a leading man. Reams also pushed too hard and gestured too broadly, calming only for two gentle numbers, "Penny In My Pocket" (a tune for Horace Vandergelder cut from *Hello, Dolly!)* and "Mrs. S. L. Jacobowsky" from *The Grand Tour.* Both were show highlights, especially since they were textbook examples of lyric writing and building a full, entertaining story from simple ideas.

Simplicity was also the key to *Fosse*'s commercial and critical success: just cobble together a host of highlights from shows directed and/or choreographed by Bob Fosse, and let the dancers strut their stuff. Like *Jerome Robbins' Broadway, Fosse* was lucky to open in a weak year for new, *original* musicals and thus trotted off with three Tonys, including orchestration and best musical. Not that the overrated *Fosse* didn't have its jewels, but when, oh when will Tony realize the inherent injustice of forcing virgin efforts to compete with beloved standards?

Directed by Richard Maltby Jr. with co-direction by Ann Reinking, who also recreated the master's dance numbers with Chet Walker, *Fosse* was a serviceable overview, filled with beautifully-sculpted, dexterous dancers but somehow missing the spark of something moving or exhilarating. One had to wonder what "Life Is Just a Bowl of Cherries" and "Mr. Bojangles" were doing in a show about a man who injected darkly sexual overtones into every leg extension and finger curl? Of course, those songs did have reasons for being in a Fosse-based revue (for example, "Cherries" was in his last Broadway show, *Big Deal;* "Bojangles" was a sequence in Fosse's influential, all-hoofing *Dancin'),* but they also made an oddly bland approach to the man whose work conveys perhaps the most alluringly dark persona of all commercial choreographers. Not that Fosse didn't have other facets to his work besides slinky hookers and gymnastic exhibitionists, but those were his lures and his specialties, and when they're paraded in a faceless, "and-then-he-dance-directed" procession, against a road-show cheesy set (by Santo Loquasto, surprisingly), the results felt like they should come with a salad bar and $20 in chips.

Much of *Fosse*'s dull first act concerned itself with dance-abstract, movement-oriented work (mostly from *Dancin'*); the second act lumped together disparate movie and commercial theater projects. Only in Act III did we sense a connective tissue, which helped make it by far the best of the three. The audience's tumultuous reaction to the just-okay "Steam Heat" mystified, though the aforementioned "Bojangles" proved an oddly welcome bit of schmaltz that had a young and agile dancer acting as the shadow of the titular, bibulous subject. A "Sing, Sing, Sing" finale proved undeniably kinetic, and a *Pippin* segment made one hanker for a full-scale revival of that tuner. Heck, if the producers are smart, they'll go one better and mount "Stephen Schwartz's *Pippin* Parade," a revue of *Pippin* highlights rearranged just enough to qualify as a new musical. From a marketing perspective, it can't miss.

Ovarian Cancer, Internet Sex and Gay Jesus

No, not a week on *Oprah,* these were the off-Broadway season's most potent topics, relating to three plays specifically: *Wit, The Dying Gaul* and *Corpus Christi. Wit,* of course, was the year's darling, snagging the Pulitzer, Lortel, Drama League, Drama Desk, Outer Critics Circle (off Broadway and John Gassner) and New York Drama Critics Circle prizes. Only the second play by Margaret Edson, a grade school teacher who'd briefly worked in hospital administration, *Wit* stunned with its Spartan language, economical storytelling, unsentimental approach to cancer and brilliant use of two other literary works to comment on the protagonist's quandary. In telling its fast-moving tale of John Donne scholar and perfectionist professor Vivian Bearing being struck down by fourth-stage ovarian cancer, *Wit* beautifully incorporated both a Donne sonnet and the children's story *The Runaway Bunny.* Not only is the sonnet an attempt to come to terms with death, which Bearing herself must do, but Bearing's students complain that the poem is intentionally arcane and obfuscated, masking its feelings behind a veil of words—something Bearing later discovers she's been doing all her life. *The Runaway Bunny,* one of Bearing's favorite books as a child (and one that kindles her desire to disappear into the complexities of language), ironically becomes the book her professor reads at Vivian's hospital bedside. In less than 90 minutes, Edson's play dissects a fascinating character, argues that too often medicine is treated as research rather than treatment, and makes an impassioned plea for the rights of patients (only a nurse listens to Vivian's request not to be revived by artificial means if her vitals flatline). Concluding his rave review of *Wit,* John Simon wrote, "Margaret Edson teaches elementary school in Atlanta. For this play alone, she should be handed the Harvard English department."

Her head shaved, her eyes burning, Kathleen Chalfant was indelible as Vivian. Hers was not a study in frailness and self pity; much like Brian Dennehy's Willy Loman, this was a towering figure succumbing to an awful force she could no longer fight. In a way, that's also the through-line of the Christ story: a great, if intractable, figure who knows what he's up against, shoulders it dutifully, but also doubts the meaning of his mission. Terrence McNally's *Corpus Christi* threw in an extra, not necessarily germane, element: what if Jesus were gay and his crucifixion the ultimate manifestation of homophobia? Despite bias crimes and anti-gay violence still pol-luting the American landscape, McNally's notion felt very 1970s, especially when the show opened with the cast introducing themselves as actors about to enact the passion play. McNally further confused the issue by neglecting to anchor the when and where of the piece; half of it was set in ancient Nazareth (I think), the other half in small-town 1950s Texas, yet it was all supposed to be one story about a gay man preaching tolerance, betrayed by one of his friends and murdered for his beliefs.

Manhattan Theater Club had been promising *Corpus Christi* for two seasons, as the author worked over rewrite after rewrite. The draft he finally came up with didn't make anybody happy, but MTC dutifully staged it for fear of losing McNally's future good will. That's when the media got hold of it, and headlines about "Gay Jesus" kissing his disciples reached the New York *Post* long before the first preview. Out came death threats from right-wing nutjobs who screamed blasphemy without having seen a word of the script. MTC, in a rare act of cowardice, canceled the production for fear of being unable to guarantee the actors' safety. This set off a firestorm from the left wing, with McNally rightfully charging MTC with self-cen-sorship, and Athol Fugard, whose *The Captain's Tiger* was also due on the theater's schedule, threatening to pull his show from the lineup. Once it became clear that the violently anti-*Corpus* corps was just a few kooks, Manhattan Theater Club re-instated McNally's drama, kept the actors' names out of the papers, set up metal detectors at the entrance and went on with the show without incident.

The greatest irony turned out to be that the play, while showing an occasional male kiss and the Jesus character sanctioning a gay marriage, turned out to be a thoughtful, even pious take on the Passion. Any worries about Last Supper orgies or Judas betraying Jesus with something raunchier than a kiss were unfounded. If anything, critics complained about the play's hesitancy and dullness—a little apos-tasy would've been welcome. (Further irony: Paul Rudnick's *The Most Fabulous Story Ever Told,* which put a gay spin on the entire Old Testament and some of the New, proved riotously heretical, yet nary a peep from the holier-than-thou crowd.)

No other off-Broadway plays caused such a fuss as *Wit* and *Corpus Christi,* but a half dozen excellent works showed playwrights grappling with the morality of their characters. Best of all was *Stop Kiss,* a nimble comedy-drama with craft, swift pacing, a sly tongue and not a little heart. It also had Jessica Hecht, out of her *Ballyhoo* ruffles and here creating an endearingly neurotic and quirkily sexy protagonist. Cal-lie (Hecht) has taken in an apartment roomie (Sandra Oh), newly arrived in New York. They become fast friends, but there's an undercurrent of romantic desire between them, even as the heterosexual Callie resists making any kind of overt move on her roommate. At long last, they're ready to take the big step, but when they do, an act of senseless urban violence greets their first tentative smooch.

Diana Son structured *Stop Kiss* cleverly—interposing scenes building up to the climactic buss with those following the brutal attack, wherein Callie's yearning for Sara moves beyond physical curiosity into deep and poignant affection. After awhile, the scene juxtapositions caused a slight seesaw effect, but the technique never smacked of gimmickry, because Son used the concurrent patterns to build suspense

The 1998–99 Season Off Broadway

PLAYS (29)

Love's Fire
Stupid Kids
Chaim's Love Song
The Dying Gaul
Playwrights Horizons:
  The Uneasy Chair
  Freedomland
  Betty's Summer Vacation
Goodnight Children Everywhere
Over the River and Through the Woods
Duet!
WIT
Manhattan Theater Club:
  Corpus Christi
  Red
Roundabout:
  Impossible Marriage
  The Mineola Twins
Killer Joe
Retribution
The Most Fabulous Story Ever Told
Far East

MUSICALS (7)

York Theater Company:
  Little By Little
  Exactly Like You
A New Brain
Nunsense A-Men
Jayson
Captains Courageous
Bright Lights Big City

REVUES (5)

The Jello Is Always Red
Unzippin' My Doodah
Forbidden Broadway Cleans Up Its Act
Rollin' on the T.O.B.A.
It Ain't Nothin' But the Blues

FOREIGN PLAYS (9)

Communicating Doors
Manhattan Theater Club:
  The Memory of Water
  The Captain's Tiger
East Is East
BAM:
  Anna Karenina
  Blue Heart
Trainspotting
Ashes to Ashes
Beautiful Thing

REVIVALS (19)

Public Theater:
  The Skin of Our Teeth
  Cymbeline
  You Never Can Tell
  Smoke on the Mountain
  Collected Stories
  Medea
The Mystery of Irma Vep
Pericles
Zora Neale Hurston
Stratford Festival:
  Much Ado About Nothing
  The Miser
BAM:
  Phedre & Britannicus
  Le Cid
Encores!:
  Babes in Arms
  Ziegfeld Follies
  Do Re Mi
That Championship Season
The Acting Company:
  Tartuffe
  Twelfth Night

SPECIALTIES (6)

Symphonie Fantastique
De La Guarda
International Festival of Puppet Theater
Culture of Desire
Mujeres y Hombres
Savion Glover: Downtown

SOLO SHOWS (9)

Lillian
Sakina's Restaurant
A Night in November
Behind the Counter With Mussolini
All Under Heaven
James Naughton
Jodie's Body
2.5 Minute Ride
The Gimmick

Categorized above are all new productions listed (with some titles abbreviated) in the Plays Produced Off Broadway section of this volume.
Play listed in CAPITAL LETTERS was a major 1998–99 prizewinner.
Plays listed in *italics* were in a continuing run June 1, 1999.

and our emotional connection to the characters. Set designer Narelle Sissons ably recreated a cluttered apartment that, like Jo Bonney's staging of this very New Yorky gem of a play, felt immediate, lived in and real.

Craig Lucas, rebounding from the execrable *God's Heart,* brought forth the acidulous *The Dying Gaul.* First staged in early summer 1998 at the Vineyard Theater, the show returned for a brief commercial run in the fall. Yet another look at Hollywood nouveau riche immorality, this one probed deeper than most, telling of a young gay screenwriter still grieving over the loss of his partner to AIDS. Soon Robert is seduced not only into cheapening his work but into sleeping with a married honcho at the studio. Here's the twist: in his spare time, Robert likes to play around in gay internet chatrooms. The studio exec's wife finds out and, as a means of revenge on this man whom she knows is sleeping with her husband, begins to impersonate the spirit of Robert's dead lover. More unsettling turns follow, with no party coming out unsullied.

The same could be said for *Snakebit,* a remarkably well-observed comedy by David Marshall Grant, best known as a baby-faced actor on TV's *thirtysomething* and in *Angels in America.* Hollywood money again plays a looming evil in *Snakebit,* though here it's more incidental to the character foibles on view. Likeable but drifting Michael (Geoffrey Nauffts), shares his L.A. beach house with Jonathan and his wife, Jenifer. Both Michael and Jenifer feel left out of things, especially since career-obsessed Jonathan (David Alan Basche), an actor, spends 24–7 worrying about a major film audition. Not much happens in *Snakebit* per se, yet somewhere along the way everyone gets betrayed, and all are forced to reevaluate their lives.

Didn't sound very promising, but author Grant's dialogue was so pointed, and the performances so polished (under Jace Alexander's direction), we listened eagerly throughout, waiting for the next hurtful aside or hint of personal crisis. And just when the second act threatened to turn too hermetic, along came a house-hunting surfer type (Michael Weston), bringing with him both laid-back humor and an unexpected plot turn.

Cut of the same cloth, almost as winningly, was *This Is Our Youth,* Kenneth Lonergan's microcosmic look at the slacker generation, its lack of ambition and oh-so-jaded 'tude. Warren (Mark Ruffalo) looks up to worldly Dennis as a kind of guru, with Dennis repaying the favor by belittling and patronizing his friend. Dennis does try to help out when Warren, having stolen a stash of cash from his dad, needs help spending the loot. Along comes Jessica (Missy Yager), a cute girl attracted to Warren's better nature but so afraid of being hurt, any wrong move sends her out the door. Set all in one day, *Youth* was most memorable when charting Jessica and Warren's half-step courtship, though its more familiar student-besting-master plot was also handled with hipness and wisdom.

A.R. Gurney turned in another of his seemingly effortless light dramas in *Far East,* the story of a Naval officer stationed in Japan during post-war rebuilding. Cocky but noble, Sparky Watts gets under the skin of his captain, a career officer who can't help feeling fatherly toward the young man. That Sparky (Michael Hayden) has to fight an attraction to the captain's fetching wife (Lisa Emery) causes less trouble than his deeper relationship with a local girl, a no-no that crosses the bounds of both race and, the captain worries, national security. Not helping matters is a blackmail scheme that makes Sparky's friend Bob (Connor Trinneer) a legitimate security risk.

All these elements could explode into something terrifying, but author Gurney backs away from that kind of emotional carnage. Faced with a fastball, Gurney's characters tend to flinch and hope the pitch is low and outside, with Gurney the pitcher-playwright often obliging. Thus, *Far East,* like many of his plays, maintains a comfortably air-conditioned tone, even when the slightest turn of events could thrust the characters' feet in the fire.

As evidenced by her Pulitzer-winning *How I Learned to Drive,* Paula Vogel has no problem letting a confrontational scene play itself fully out, but the author of *The Baltimore Waltz* also has a farcical, absurdist side, allowed to run free in *The Mineola Twins,* staged at the Roundabout's Laura Pels space. A truly zany piece with a 1950s kitsch set design to match (by Robert Brill with Scott Pask), *Twins* hit on such serious themes as reproductive rights and the changing nature of woman-hood (and wifedom) in America. It was also a tour de force for the cherishable Swoosie Kurtz, who played twins Myrna and Myra, one a bosomy but old-fashioned Fifties lady, the other a "bad" girl, embodying all the so-called vices of the era. The passage of 20 years doesn't change their values, however; by the Nixon administration, the good girl has morphed into someone who helps bomb abortion clinics, while her sister's nonconformity makes her much closer to a modern role model.

Warped perspectives were also on view in Christopher Durang's latest, *Betty's Summer Vacation,* his first full-length work since *Sex and Longing* tanked at Lincoln Center. Back when Durang was penning comedies like *'Dentity Crisis* and *Sister Mary Ignatius Explains It All for You,* it was easier to shock an audience into laughter and uncomfortable disbelief. All you had to do was release the violent side of a strict nun, or show what men and women were really thinking on a first date. Now we have the President's semen stains on the front page of the *Times* and Albanian war casualties on CNN. When the sensational becomes commonplace, a satirist's options are more limited. If you're Paul Rudnick *(The Most Fabulous Story Ever Told),* you have a store of impeccably-phrased one liners; if you're Paula Vogel *(The Mineola Twins),* you explore the way a constricted society affects exaggerated but still-human characters. If you're Chris Durang, well . . . you make a hundred sophomoric shock jokes, then you turn around and vilify the audience that (at least in your assumption) revels in the humor. On one level, *Betty's Summer Vacation,* set in a seaside timeshare, followed a classic comedy format in that a half-dozen weirdos were thrown together in one place while the straight man (here, straight woman Kellie Overbey) tries to stay sane. Durang salts this formula with tastelessness (okay, we'd expect nothing less from him), hysteria, and preachiness disguised as postmodern satire. Mystifyingly, *Betty* garnered raves from the same critics who torpedoed his long, uneven but certainly more substantial *Sex and Longing.* One hilariously rude sight gag during a charades game in *Betty* did not make up for the shrill, contemptuous tone Durang and director Nicholas Martin took throughout.

Jim Bracchitta, Dick Latessa and Marie Lillo in a scene from *Over the River and Through the Woods* by Joe DiPietro

Sordidness filled another, better play, *Killer Joe,* a cult hit in Chicago finally reaching off Broadway (OOB's 29th Street Repertory staged it, very well, in 1994) with a host of film and TV stars in various roles. Tracy Letts's sicko comedy told of a loser who hires a cop gone bad to kill his father's ex-wife for her insurance money, only to find that in order to pay off Killer Joe Cooper, he has to prostitute his mentally unstable sister, Dottie, to the hit man. Who can blame a playwright for wanting to shock jaded theatergoers out of their complacency? If it means throwing in mayhem-level violence and jaw-dropping sexual content, well, we're all adults, we can take it. Enticed by Scott Glenn and Amanda Plummer in lead roles, downtown audiences made the show a long-running hit at the Soho Playhouse. What we might have asked for from author Letts is something stronger than cheap thrills. The plot had nothing deeper in it than cynicism, and some of its sexual content— particularly the oddest fellatio sequence since the "kielbasa queen" plied her trade on Howard Stern's TV show—felt gratuitous.

By contrast, Alan Ayckbourn's *Communicating Doors,* finally making its New York debut, came on like a nasty, synthetic thriller only to swerve into farce territory before curving again into a surprisingly poignant finale. The opening was, indeed, creepy. A depraved old man and his sociopathic butler, both living in a swanky London hotel (circa 2018), hire a call girl for the night—but not for the usual reasons. Before the butler can murder her, Poopay manages to find a doorway out. Only it's not out of the room; instead, the door deposits her back in the same suite, two decades earlier. Poopay's not quite out of the woods, though, because the time travel (and another trip 20 years further back still) has given her the opportunity to avoid not only her own assassination, but to stop the butler's previous killing.

Ayckbourn's usually ingenious plotting wasn't so airtight this time, for so many rules governed the workings of the time-travel door, one sensed the author was simply adding caveats as each scene required. Logic gaps aside, *Communicating Doors* had both cat-and-mouse chills and charming humor, as the low-born, free-spirited Poopay (Mary-Louise Parker and, later in the run, Anne Bobby) developed a winning comradeship with the old man's wife, Ruella (the superb Patricia Hodges). Appealing, too, in a more sitcom way, were Peter Ackerman's *Things You Shouldn't Say Past Midnight* and Joe DiPietro's *Over the River and Through the Woods.* The former, despite brief nudity and no-holds-barred comic sex talk, proved a Neil Simonesque trifle, occasionally more dumb than funny but savvily building up to a climax (literally) wherein three partners finally table their relationship troubles long enough to shag the night away. DiPietro's *River,* a sweet bit of ethnic fluff, told of a young man forced to decide whether to take a job offer that means moving far away from his loving but overprotective Italian family. Sadly, *River* lost one of its family; co-producer James Hammerstein, son of Oscar Hammerstein II, died three months into the run.

The agreeable but inconsequential *Beautiful Thing* dealt with two boys, Jamie and Ste [sic], coping with a mutual attraction as they grow up in a rough South East London neighborhood. Throw in another neighbor who thinks she's Janis Joplin (and abuses her system the way Joplin did) and you had a coming-of-age comedy that tried to be off-kilter but was mostly standard stuff. The best character was Jamie's mom, Sandra (Kirsten Sahs), whose sexiness, short fuse and liberal attitudes made her very different from the usual cliche of an urban mother struggling to make ends meet.

Speaking of cliches, Harold Pinter's latest, *Ashes to Ashes,* made his previous inscrutable off-Broadway effort, *Moonlight,* look like *Barefoot in the Park.* The Roundabout Theater didn't even bother to come up with a double bill, going on the assumption that Pinter's one-act had enough meaning to fill an evening all by itself. Sure. *Ashes* spent 40 minutes teasing us with clues to a horror story that attractive, middle-aged heroine (Lindsay Duncan) finally allows herself to recount in the last five. Questioned by her husband (David Strathairn), she lets drop certain details— women giving their "bundles" up at a train station, streams of people disappearing like lemmings into the water—that have intimations of the Holocaust, though she's obviously English, and she keeps saying it all happened in Dorset. Could she be referring to English women sending their children to the countryside for their safety during WW2? She isn't telling, and neither is Pinter. *Ashes to Ashes* climaxed with Rebecca piecing together one thread of her biography but connecting it to nothing else—not her marriage, her former lover, her time and place, her current malaise. Actress Duncan nearly mesmerized us with Rebecca's lethargy and internal despair, but really all she had to do was change the subject every five minutes and zone into a look of anguish every ten. David Strathairn played hubby Devlin as solicitous rather than menacing, which only made him sound like an addled interviewer. (On a happier note OOB, the Atlantic Theater Company revived *The Hothouse*—penned when Pinter still wrote with exuberance, rich dark humor and a looming sense of danger. Most reviewers agreed the heat of *Hothouse* left the arid nonsense of *Ashes* in the dust.)

Arthur Miller, enjoying the plaudits for *Death of a Salesman* on Broadway, also scored a minor success off Broadway by exploring the spiritual death of a bigamist in *The Ride Down Mt. Morgan.* The provocative and entertaining piece, while not substantial enough for a two-and-a-half hour character study, reminded us anew how wrong we were to picture Miller as some stuffy classicist, best left for high school theater texts. *Mt. Morgan,* like *The Price* and other excellent "second-tier" Miller works, bubbled over with a wicked sense of humor and an understanding of how to keep an audience engaged despite having very little plot to work with. The setup: a vibrant businessman has crashed his car down a snowy mountain. When Lyman (Patrick Stewart) wakes up in hospital, he calls the nurse over and begs her to make sure two women don't visit him: his wives. Theo (Frances Conroy), the first wife, aided his rise to power, raised their daughter and ran the household with a strong Protestant backbone. Leah, younger, prettier, more sensual, more recent, is the mother of Lyman's second child and the woman he runs to when Theo's stability bores him. Too cowardly (or sybaritic) to divorce Theo and marry Leah, Lyman cheats on both, rationalizing that he's made them both happier than they would have been without him, and that he's had a more satisfying life by being able to spend it with two very different women. In essence, that's the whole story, though Miller added other elements he didn't sufficiently tie to the main story. For example, Lyman's pronouncements to his black nurse (Oni Faida Lampley) make clear he has racist leanings, yet he claims to have done a lot for minorities in his company. This should dovetail with Lyman's attraction to Leah's Jewishness, after years of denying his own background to get ahead (his last name, Felt, was shortened from Feldman). But these seemingly connected elements of Lyman's makeup don't add up to anything tangible.

As Lyman, Patrick Stewart used his brisk machismo, clarion voice and playful pupils to imbue the weaselly protagonist with picaresque charm. His two femme foils were fine, with Frances Conroy (brought in at the last minute when Blythe Danner begged off owing to a family emergency) especially notable. Not only did she do the brittle, upper-crust matron to a "t," Conroy was unexpectedly vibrant when demonstrating that Theo had more appetites and adventurousness than one would first suspect. How nice to be reminded the same held true for Arthur Miller. At season's end there was even talk of bringing *Mt. Morgan* back for a commercial run in the fall.

It would be an odd choice for a return engagement, but of this season's revivals, sometimes the oddest were the most appreciated. Donald Margulies's *Collected Stories,* a 1997 Pulitzer finalist that starred Maria Tucci off Broadway, came back just two seasons later as a vehicle for Uta Hagen, which only added further justification (as if any were needed) for her Lifetime Achievement Tony Award. For its first show at its new midtown digs, Second Stage Theater revived *That Championship*

Season, Jason Miller's Pulitzer winner about former high school basketball players now besotted by middle age, mediocrity and mendacity—potent stuff in 1972, an artifact in 1999, albeit one with a number of meaty roles. Fossilized was apparently the word for the Public Theater's Central Park mounting of *The Skin of Our Teeth* starring John Goodman, Frances Conroy and *Third Rock From the Sun's* Kristen Johnson; Andrei Serban's outdoor staging of *Cymbeline* scored an Obie Award for lead Liev Schreiber.

Musically, City Center's Encores! series offered *Babes in Arms, Ziegfeld Follies of 1936* and *Do Re Me,* with the latter's all-star cast, including Nathan Lane, Brian Stokes Mitchell and Randy Graff, receiving ecstatic notices. Critics called the 1960 musical itself a conventional bit of froth with second-act trouble—and just the kind of show they wish Broadway still knew how to do.

Solos and Singularities

On the one-person front, 1998–99 proved a quiet season, with Lisa Kron's *2.5 Minute Ride* arguably the most acclaimed and honored of the bunch. One-fifth of the Five Lesbian Brothers troupe, Kron cleverly and affectionately linked together two real-life episodes involving her father. One had the old man, a Holocaust survivor with a history of heart trouble, joining her on the "Mean Streak" roller coaster ride at a Sandusky, Ohio amusement park. In the other, the two visited Auschwitz. Occasionally too fast-talking and strident in her performance, Kron nonetheless found powerful metaphors in the material, notably during "slide show" segments where she'd point to a picture projected behind her, only the frame would be empty.

In other solo action, Aviva Jane Carlin was naked and fat in *Jodie's Body.* I'm not being mean; those were just the first two things to notice at the start of her solo. Carlin's stomach and thighs went beyond even Rodin's most clay-caked undertakings. This didn't bother Carlin, and after a few minutes, it didn't much bother us. In her meandering, 75-minute solo about the politics of the body influencing the body politic, the South African-born Carlin explained why she has always been comfortable with a body that others treat with embarrassment or even cruelty. Convincingly, she recalled the moral and physical strength of her mother, who saved a little girl's life by diving, gracefully, into the water after her. Carlin also remembered the adiposity of her mom when she blocked the doorway as Afrikaaner cops searched houses for a "troublemaker" family friend.

Also autobiographical, Dael Orlandersmith's *The Gimmick* spoke powerfully of young Dael discovering poetry as a way out of her horrific Harlem childhood. Orlandersmith's love of the written word saved her from the clutches of drugs, alcohol and illicit livelihoods running rampant through her community. Her first boy friend, an artist, was not so lucky. Given a ticket out via his gift, her swain spent his newfound money on booze and, later, drugs. No one put the spoon to his nose or the needle to his arm; even those who are inoculated with a remedy can be reinfected by a sick community. Without a shred of white-bashing, *The Gimmick* showed how a culture of decay destroys its own without any help from outside forces.

A more positive look at a tight ethnic enclave came via *Sakina's Restaurant,* featuring promising newcomer Aasif Mandvi, who crossed the facial expressions of Harpo Marx with the gleeful, tribally detailed imitations of John Leguizamo. The actor-author opened his *Restaurant* endearingly, looking in on a naive fellow leaving his Indian homeland for the wilds of New York City. After bidding his parents goodbye (including the traditional kissing of his mother's feet), the fellow finds himself working—where else?—at a restaurant on East Sixth Street. Hours are long, and the city can be overwhelming, but his boss proves wise and fair, and his boss's family form a circle of much-needed companionship. Like a more serious version of Sherry Glaser's *Family Secrets, Sakina's Restaurant* featured Mandvi as all these characters, from the restaurant owner who can't tolerate his daughter's trampy American ways, to her betrothed, who is so weighed down by exams, his pending arranged marriage, and his Islamic fundamentalist upbringing, he turns to a prostitute for relief. To Mandvi's credit, the play did more than just show off the exactness of his physical gestures (as both men and women). Each monologue told a complete short story, ever surprising us by becoming hilarious when we expected disaster and poignant when we were primed for mere spoofing.

Another solo winner, *A Night in November,* stayed mainly with one character, a Northern Irish Protestant discovering the pointlessness of bigotry. At first, Kenneth McAllister (Dan Gordon), a welfare clerk, takes pleasure in saddling his Catholic customers with belittling, bureaucratic garbage. Both Kenneth and his wife take overweening pride in his admittance to an exclusive golf club, not the least because his Catholic boss can't get in. The worm turns, however, when Kenneth's aged, cough-hacked father-in-law drags him to a World Cup qualifying soccer match between Northern and Republican Ireland teams. Ugliness reigns in the stands, as pro-Brit fans hurl insults and chant "trick or treat"—a reference to an act of terrorist slaughter committed weeks earlier on Halloween. Kenneth doesn't want to be identified with this level of hatred and is further swayed from his prejudices when he visits his boss's house in Belfast. The messiness Kenneth has always associated with poverty and poor breeding instead come to represent a personal freedom and liveliness he can't feel in his dull job and rote marriage. Act II of *A Night in November* followed Kenneth's wild and crazy decision to drop everything and follow the Republic's Irish team to New York for the World Cup. He is joined, of course, by thousands of countrymen just as desperate for a life change as he is. Marie Jones's play, though longish for a solo, plunged us into the details of each scene until we cringed when Kenneth had to lie to his wife and say that everything's fine, and we exulted when he reached Eamonn Doran's bar in Manhattan and perceived an instant sense of community with everyone around him. Dan Gordon, with a soccer player's build and a rugby player's stamina, carried the two-plus hour show, helping make *November*'s spiritual journey as inspiring as any pilgrimage, sports victory or all-night party.

Wowing the crowds in just such a fashion was *De La Guarda,* which played all season and beyond at the Daryl Roth Theater. Lucky audience members got a chance to swing from the rafters (literally) with the acrobatic *De La Guarda* troupe, who also shpritzed the spectators with water, chanted with them and generally caused an hour's worth of *Blue Man*-influenced havoc.

On the musical front, Savion Glover brought his *Downtown* show back to the Variety Arts Theater for two hours of noisy stomp-dancing, all of it lacking the context that made *Noise/Funk* such a revelation. Audiences flocked to it anyway. They also made a surprise hit out of *Symphonie Fantastique,* a performance piece utilizing a 500-gallon fishtank and various shapes passing through the water under different lighting effects. Lovely as some images were, the absence of any narrative, and the repetition of visual elements quickly wore out the novelty of Basil Twist's ingenuity. For awhile, we desperately invented mini-scenarios to go with the Berlioz music, as when a shaft of bright light flitted across the glass, then zipped off just as ominous flashes "chased" it away (to Berlioz's rumbling kettledrums). More often, pretty handkerchiefs swam, guppy-like, to our ever-decreasing amusement. All of this, even the dullest bits, would have been pleasantly watchable if the music's volume wasn't cranked high enough to make every violin note sound like nails on a chalkboard. Though puppeteer Twist worked admirably on the unforgettable *Peter and Wendy,* he hectored with his Berlioz.

And what of the off-Broadway "legit" musicals? Alas, a half dozen of them opened, each with more detractors than champions. The closest to a snob hit was William Finn's *A New Brain,* his first major work since *Falsettos.* Based on his own real-life medical scare, *A New Brain* followed the turmoil of dissatisfied gay yuppie Gordon, sick of writing for a children's show but addicted to the paycheck. Suddenly, he's faced with a brain tumor, and his world narrows to relationships with the hospital staff, his lover, his close friends and his buttinsky mother. Gordon survives the operation only to wonder what meaning his life had before it.

Unlike *Falsettos,* which had a devastating cumulative power, *A New Brain* offered a host of entertaining numbers and catchy tunes, but the whole was shapeless. For example, Gordon's mother (Penny Fuller) worries herself to distraction over her son's ill health, and she has a haunting cabaret number late in the show ("The Music Still Plays On"), but the actual relationship between her and Gordon (Malcolm Gets) is never touched. Gordon's boyfriend (Keith Byron Kirk) sings the hummable "I'd Rather Be Sailing" to explain his ambivalence about visiting his lover in the hospital, but when they do get together, their relationship feels generic, the song incidental. Though Mary Testa's singing and acting were far more ingratiating here than in *On the Town,* her character—an obnoxious bag lady—added little to the story.

A New Brain took the Outer Critics Circle Award for best off-Broadway musical, but to most, that was the equivalent of "D" winning for best fourth letter of the alphabet. By most accounts, *Captains Courageous* at Manhattan Theater Club and starring Treat Williams, was a good story turgidly told, while York Theater's *Little by Little* was a watchable but trivial love story. The major critics dismissed New York Theater Workshop's *Bright Lights Big City* as a soulless *Rent* wannabe, too literal in its lyrics, too diffuse in its storytelling, and saddled with a jejune and su-

Everett Quinton and Stephen DeRosa in a scene from
the revival of Charles Ludlam's *The Mystery of Irma Vep*

perfluous narrator. Then again, second string reviewers were more taken with the
show's indictment of 1980s self-indulgence and mindlessness, some finding it more
cohesive than the aforementioned Lower East Side musical.

Cy Coleman, who's never been shy about borrowing from his past, reworked
his Broadway flop, *Welcome to the Club,* and came up with *Exactly Like You,* an
astonishingly silly piece with a thumpy score, a few belly laughs, and perhaps the
most incoherent second act in history. Somehow, Michael McGrath and Lauren
Ward managed to stay charming as once-married lawyers representing opposite par-
ties of a high-profile, *Court TV*-style divorce. The evening's zaniest (and for some,
most tasteless) moment came during "Don't Mess Around With Your Mother-in-
Law," itself taken from *Welcome to the Club* (where a very different four-letter
word was employed instead of "Mess"). During a break in the trial, the TV commentator started interviewing people on the street about their mothers-in-law, including a family of German tourists and an Indian taxi driver. The latter, played
by McGrath, not only sang in a stereotypical Hindi accent but sniffed his armpits
for body odor.

Similarly wicked gags were employed in the latest installment of *Forbidden Broadway, Forbidden Broadway Cleans Up Its Act!,* though here they felt more at home amidst Gerard Alessandrini's sometimes malicious spoofing, including cruel but hilarious potshots at Andrew Lloyd Webber (Bryan Batt, his face pulled into a grotesque canine configuration by scotch tape), Jennifer Jason Leigh (who took lumps for her apparently pitch-imperfect Sally Bowles in *Cabaret*) and the *Side Show* twins. We also got a delicious "what if": what if *Cabaret's* Alan Cumming served as the emcee for the Von Trapps' last concert before fleeing the occupation? The joyous results featured the emcee, in bowl-cut black wig and requisite shirtless suspenders, leering at the audience and goosing the kids.

Like rising performance artist Reverend Billy, who one night hid tape recorders in the Times Square Disney store so that customers heard messages warning them of Disney's mercantilism, Alessandrini, too, attacked the Monster Mouse. Aside from an extended *Lion King* parody (featuring an hysterically funny elephant costume), the four-member cast tweaked the Disneyfication of Broadway, seeing it as the Tower of Babel in Mayor Rudolph Giuliani's campaign to G-rate all New York entertainment.

Capitol Steps would have none of that sanitizing either. Returning to New York with a better revue than their 1997 effort, the troupe titled their evening *Unzippin' My Doodah,* a dig at President Clinton's sexual exploits with Monica Lewinsky. A team since 1981, the Steps are all former Congressional staffers, now devoted to poking fun at their Washington bosses. The group rose from doing just-for-yocks gigs at local nightspots to become something of a national brand name, with CDs, television appearances, and even performances in front of four U.S. presidents (five, as the Playbill noted, "if you count Hillary"). Non-musical sketches were limited to a rather lame "who's on first" take-off, a gumshoe who talks in ribald metaphors, and two monologues loaded with naughty-sounding spoonerisms ("she socked his knocks off!"). Bread and butter for the Steps, however, were their song parodies, by Bill Strauss and Elaina Newport. One hilarious bit put the India/Pakistan nuclear race to the tune of "Chitty Chitty Bang Bang," while another showed an Orthodox Israeli warbling "Hebron, I'm in Hebron . . . dancing sheik to sheik."

Also getting a revamp this season was Dan Goggin's *Nunsense,* featuring an all-male cast. Press releases assured us the show's text hadn't changed to underline the cross-dressing and campiness, though the jokes certainly sounded more risque than I remember from years ago. A clever number about the sisters' disastrous stint in a leper colony may surprise those who think of Goggin's musical as kiddie fare about nuns romping in their habits. No, *Nunsense* isn't Finn, or Brown or Guettel or any of the up-and-coming "serious" musical makers, but playwrights and composers alike could learn from watching how *Nunsense* (or *Nunsense A-Men*) entertained an audience. Certainly a sense of looseness helped; when Mother Superior (David Titus), who has accidentally gotten high on Rush, broke up in laughter and could barely get her lines out, we were unsure whether that was the character as scripted, or if the actor had simply lost it. It didn't matter; the performer was having an awfully good time, and that bonhomie consumed the audience as well.

A similar spirit imbued Everett Quinton's hit revival of *The Mystery of Irma Vep*, Charles Ludlam's lampoon of *Rebecca*-type thrillers. Sometimes, as the characters in *Vep* discover, all it takes is a change of scenery. Lady Enid marries Lord Edgar and finds herself in the lush—but haunted—trappings of Mandacrest Manor; she then follows her new husband to an Egyptian tomb, where weird trysts ensue; and every time poor servant Nicodemus goes out to explore the grounds, he has to brave the stalkings of a wild animal. For Quinton and cohorts of the now-defunct Ridiculous Theatrical Company, however, a change of venue proved salubrious. Just a few seasons ago, Quinton, Eureka, Stephen Pell and other special talents of the Ridiculous were trotting out serviceable revivals of the troupe's campy epics. Stuck in the deteriorating confines of One Sheridan Square, however, the shows had a motheaten air, as if they were being put on for the membership of a dwindling club. With five producers chipping in, *The Mystery of Irma Vep* benefited from being in the comfy, nicely-appointed Westside Theater downstairs space. The sets (by John Lee Beatty) weren't any cleverer than the witty designs the company used to use, but they looked smarter and more vibrant on a professional-looking mainstage. The jokes got bigger laughs, too, in part because an uptown audience was having its first taste of Ludlam and Quinton's madness. Thus, although *Vep* showcased but two actors (Quinton and Stephen DeRosa), the evening felt like a full and richly comic play, even something of an off-Broadway event. All Quinton needed was a pair of enormous false teeth (as Nicodemus), or a particularly flashy dress (as Lady Enid), and he was already halfway toward the finish line of every scene. DeRosa was no slouch either, whether as a snippy maid who spars with the new lady of the house, or the husband whose brio hides a darker secret.

Perhaps the most important legacy of the Ridiculous (after the canon of plays by late co-founder Ludlam) is the approach to a play's text. Every line—every word— is played to the hilt. If there's a double-entendre to utter, an "r" to be rolled, a consonant to be snapped, a phrase that just cries for a grimace, a sneer, a tightening of the neck and a crossing of the arms, they'll all be done and then some.

The 1998–99 season as a whole could have used more of that kind of go-for-broke zeal. Or is it just that last year's grass always seems greener when you're looking too closely at this year's weeds? Pull back a bit, and the towering trees (Dennehy, Franz, Kurtz) awe us once more with their majesty, the funny-looking clumps of bushes amuse anew *(Snakebit, Vep, Most Fabulous Story)*, and the beautifully-landscaped hedges stir us with their careful mastery *(Wit, Stop Kiss, Closer, Side Man)*. The new millennium awaits; come, let us tend our garden.

A GRAPHIC GLANCE

1998–99
Drawings
By Hirschfeld

Judi Dench in *Amy's View*, her Tony-winning performance

Scott Wise, Elizabeth Parkinson, Jane Lanier and Valarie Pettiford in *Fosse*

On opposite page, Swoosie Kurtz in various aspects of her dual title role in *The Mineola Twins*

Kevin Anderson and Brian Dennehy in *Death of a Salesman*

Tai Jiminez, Perry Laylon Ojeda, Robert Montano, Jesse Tyler Ferguson, Mary Testa, Sarah Knowlton and Lea DeLaria in *On the Town*

Above, Jerry Herman in his solo show *An Evening With Jerry Herman*

On opposite page, Bernadette Peters in *Annie Get Your Gun*

Stanley Wayne Mathis as Schroeder, Roger Bart as Snoopy, Anthony Rapp as Charlie, Kristin Chenoweth as Sally, Ilana Levine as Lucy and B.D. Wong as Linus in the musical *You're a Good Man, Charlie Brown*

Above, Ciaran Hinds, Anna Friel, Natasha
Richardson and Rupert Graves in *Closer*

On opposite page, Kevin Spacey as Hickey in *The Iceman Cometh*

Below, Jerry Seinfeld on Broadway in *I'm Telling You for the Last Time*

Above, Faith Prince *(at left in drawing)* as Belle with
Martin Short in his many roles in the musical *Little Me*

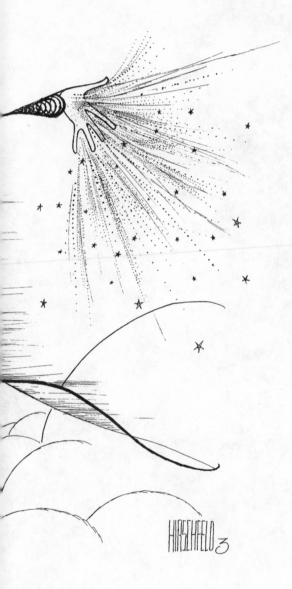

Cathy Rigby in *Peter Pan*

Sandra Bernhard in her solo show *I'm Still Here ... Damn It!*

Laurence Fishburne as Henry II with Stockard Channing as Eleanor in *The Lion in Winter*

In the drawing *at left* are Paul Rudd (Orsino), Philip Bosco (Malvolio), Max Wright (Sir Andrew Aguecheek), Brian Murray (Sir Toby Belch), Helen Hunt (Viola) and Kyra Sedgwick (Olivia) in *Twelfth Night*

Above, Joyce Van Patten, Toby Stephens, Simon Jones, Marian Seldes, Haviland Morris and Gretchen Egolf in *Ring Round the Moon*

On opposite page, Matthew Broderick as Dan in *Night Must Fa*

74

Below, Zoë Wanamaker as Electra in *Electra*

Treat Williams as Manuel and Brandon Espinoza as Harvey
E. Cheyne in the musical version of *Captains Courageous*

A SEASON OF PLAYWRIGHTS—Al Hirschfeld's vision of the great rock upon which our theater rests—the company of playwrights who made the 1998–99 New York theater season possible (along with Sophocles, Shakespeare, Molière, and a few others not shown here)—is pictured *above*. Personifying the stage's quintessential energy, *in front row,* are Margaret Edson, Christopher Durang, Patrick Marber, David Hare, Arthur Miller, John Guare, Conor McPherson and Martin McDonagh. Ensconced like gods in the clouds *above* are Eugene O'Neill and Tennessee Williams.

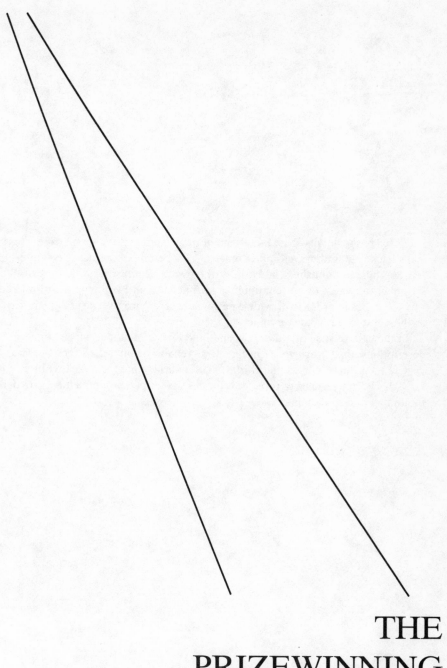

THE
PRIZEWINNING
PLAYS

Here are the details of 1998–99's major prizewinning plays—synopses, biographical sketches of authors and other material. By permission of the playwrights, their representatives, publishers, and others who own the exclusive rights to publish these scripts in full, most of our continuities include substantial quotations from crucial/pivotal scenes in order to provide a permanent reference to style and quality as well as theme, structure and story line.

In the case of such quotations, scenes and lines of dialogue, stage directions and descriptions appear *exactly* as in the stage version or published script unless (in a very few instances, for technical reasons) an abridgement is indicated by five dots (. . . . .). The appearance of three dots (. . .) is the script's own punctuation to denote the timing of a spoken line.

Tony Award

○○○
○○○
○○○
○○○
○○○
○○○

SIDE MAN

A Play in Two Acts

BY WARREN LEIGHT

Cast and credits appear on page 223

WARREN LEIGHT was born in 1957 in New York City, where he attended Fieldston High School before going on to college at early age. He graduated from Stanford in 1977 and was almost immediately involved in earning his living writing for the screen. His favorite screen achievement so far has been The Night We Never Met, *which he wrote and directed in 1994. Based continually in New York, he kept in touch with live theater by frequent work for cabaret and night club acts. His first New York production of record was the well-received cabaret musical* Mayor *(with songs and sketches based on Mayor Edward I. Koch's autobiography and with music by Charles Strouse) May 13, 1985 at Top of the Gate for 185 performances.*

Screen writing-for-hire without any control whatsoever over his work became "dispiriting," so in "self defense" Leight began contributing material, mostly one acters, to the off-off-Broadway likes of Atlantic Theater Company, Naked Angels (of which he is a member), Circle Repertory Company, Alice's Fourth Floor, the West Bank Cafe, New York Playwrights Lab and La Mama. An early production of record in that ephemeral venue was his one-acter Ceaucesceau's Dog *at Atlantic in 1992. Then along came Leight's* Side Man *which was workshopped by Naked Angels in February 1996, produced by New York Stage and Film at Vassar's Powerhouse Theater in June 1996 and then OOB at Weissberger Theater Group last season on March 11, 1998. It began attracting such attention as a Mel Gussow citation in* Best Plays *among the best OOB work of the year; three New York Drama Critics Circle votes as 1997–98's best American play; and Outer Critics and Drama Desk nominations.* Side Man *transferred to a full-sized Broadway production June 25, 1998, Leight's Broadway debut. In that incarnation, it won the best-play Tony Award as well as the 1998 Oppenheimer and George and Elisabeth Marton Awards for playwriting. Leight's stage credits have*

81

included the cabaret act High Heeled Woman, *which received an Outer Critics Award,*
The Loop *at Atlantic and* Stray Cats *at All Seasons Theater Company. Leight lives,*
as he always has, in New York City.

The following synopsis of Side Man *was prepared by Jeffrey Sweet.*

Time: 1985 to 1953
Place: New York City

ACT I

SYNOPSIS: We start in 1985. Clifford, 29, is leaving town in the morning. Tonight,
he informs the audience, he is seeing his parents.

CLIFFORD: . . . . . Both of them: Mom *and* Dad; a kind of *This Is Your Life*
bender. I'm not seeing them together, mind you. *Not* a good idea. Definitely not a
good idea. Once, long ago, this trumpet player, who I'll probably also see tonight,
told me: "The rocksh in her head fit the holesh in hish."
    Not anymore. They haven't seen each other, and I haven't seen him in—
    So, OK, it's complicated.
    Plus, if I see past all the . . . history, I sense, and this one really screws me up,
that things would have been better for them if they'd never had me. But, they did.
I'm on the scene, as my old man would say. And even though there are no clean
breaks, I swear, tomorrow morning I'm out. So tonight, before the "big reunion"
with my father, I have a farewell dinner at Mom's, in the zip code of my youth . . .

    And now we see his mother, Terry, talking to him from where she stands smoking
in her apartment. She tells him she will not be joining him at the club. She doesn't
want to hear his father, Gene, play. She mutters angrily about the husband from
whom she is separated, insisting that her alleged craziness is a product of the way
he treated her. But she can't entirely repress the old concern. She had a dream about
Gene, and he looked thin; maybe Clifford should take him some of her lasagne. She
tells her son, too, that there is a box of old stuff—photos, magazines—Clifford might
find useful for one of his projects (he makes collages).
    As Clifford steps into the Melody Lounge, a jazz hangout on New York's West
Side, Terry and her apartment fade from view, and we hear the sound of a tune
called "I Remember Clifford." A trumpet solo. Clifford (yes, he was named after
the Clifford Brown to whom the title refers) recognizes his father's voice in that
solo. He knows his old man is on the bandstand, as well as some of his father's
musician friends—guys who have played together and hung out with each other
since the 1940s when they were all playing horns in the "legendary, completely
forgotten Claude Thornhill big band." Almost nobody is here to listen to them

tonight, except for Clifford, a couple of drunks and Patsy, a woman in her late 50s whose looks still command attention.

Patsy is delighted to see Clifford, and we get the sense she's known him his whole life. Clifford tells her he's quit his job and will be taking off soon, so he stopped by to see his father. As he tries to talk to Patsy, Clifford's mother intrudes on his consciousness again ("She does this to me all the time, even when she's not here, she's here.") and asks him to relay a request to his father. She wants him to play Jerome Kern's "Why Was I Born?". Terry disappears as Patsy remembers that Clifford's parents had their first—and probably only—date here in the Melody Lounge. "Once upon a time, Clifford, we were in our prime," says Patsy. And Clifford can't help thinking of the amount of time his father and his musician buddies clocked together. Not just playing, but standing online together to sign for their unemployment check.

Flashback to Clifford eight years before, in 1977, standing in line at unemployment for the first time, his father full of pride at his son's rite-of-passage. Afterwards, with friends and fellow-musicians Al, Ziggy and Jonesy, they go to—where else—the Melody Lounge to celebrate where they all order—what else—soup. Patsy is the waitress.

We begin to get to know the guys. There's Ziggy, with a speech impediment that makes word likes "soup" come out "shoup." And there's Jonesy, a one-eyed former trombone player. And there's Al who, undeterred by the toupee they all kid him about, is the gang's perpetual Lothario.

As the five sit at the table, Jonesy admires Clifford's "rope"—a/k/a his veins. Jonesy knows from rope; he was a hardcore junkie. Talk of junk reminds them of the story of a friend who decided to become a junkie temporarily so as to beat the draft but ended up getting hooked in the process. The punchline: when he went for his army physical, it turned out that at 5'2" he was too short to be drafted anyway. None of his friends had ever noticed how short he was because he was a pianist, always sitting down. The guys howl at this story, a prime example of musicians' humor. Jonesy turns to Clifford.

JONESY: . . . . . Me though, I wasn't a junkie then so much as an addict—
AL: Ah-huh.
CLIFFORD *(to audience):* It's a subtle distinction.
JONESY: But these southern bases were so friggin' hot you had to wear short sleeves all the time, so I can't shoot into my arms, so I'm between my fingers, my toes, and then, into my eye—
ZIGGY: I would argue thish makesh him a junkie, but—
JONESY: *So* I had to shoot into my *eye.* Which only worked for a while.
AL: And that's how he got the Purple Heart—
JONESY: —and *lifetime* partial disability.
      The guys all salaam-bow to him.
ZIGGY *(to Clifford):* Even though he'sh already got dishability, he shtill comesh down every week to shign for hish unemployment check. *(Half-serious.) That'sh a work ethic.*

JONESY: *Thank you.* I told the sergeant if I had to go home to Ohio—

CLIFFORD *(to audience):* He was from the Bronx—they all were.

JONESY: —with a jaundiced, pus-leaching sore where my eye—

ZIGGY: Jeshush Chrisht. Can anyone eat with thish?

> *Al and Jonesy raise their hands.*

GENE: The eyes have it.

> *Everyone laughs. Gene winks at Clifford.*

CLIFFORD *(to audience):* These are my role models. My authority figures. My—

JONESY *(to Clifford):* Hey kid. What kind of horn do you play?

GENE *(to Jonesy):* Bite your tongue. *(To Clifford.)* Someone has to make a living in the family.

ZIGGY: I remember when you wanted lesshonsh. Your old lady shaid no shon of hersh would ever do to another woman what he *(Points to Gene.)* did to her.

AL and ZIGGY *(imitating Terry):* "The rat-bastard."

> *Everyone laughs at this.*

GENE: He's still my boy. Managed to get twenty weeks on the books—as a painter.

AL: Houses?

CLIFFORD: Collages. School job. I cut and paste these—

GENE: The kid got a scholarship to some painting school.

CLIFFORD *(to audience):* RISD. Grad school . . .

GENE: But instead, he's gonna write for TV. *(To Clifford.)* Right?

ZIGGY *(impressed):* TV? That'sh a pretty good field. Your father and I were going to do that once.

CLIFFORD: I know, I know. But it's not TV—it's advertising. Maybe. I'm up for something.

ZIGGY: TV paysh pretty good.

CLIFFORD: If I get it, yeah. Like twelve hundred a week. But it's not—*(To audience.)* The money stops the group cold.

GENE: You cop that kind of bread—you work three weeks, you can lay out the whole year.

> *Everyone agrees.*

CLIFFORD *(to audience):* You're listening to jazzonomics. The theory that—

GENE: You keep your nut small, you pay your dues, you get to blow your horn.

AL: Wait, wait, wait . . . Twelve hundred a *week?* You mean a month, right?

GENE: As long as you got a place to flop, the rest is . . . *(He spaces out.)*

CLIFFORD *(to audience):* There is no rest. From the time I was four, I knew the family was headed for financial ruin.

JONESY: You gonna finish your crackers?

> *Jonesy pockets a few cracker packets.*

CLIFFORD: From the time I was six, I, and everyone else knew, it would be up to me to save us.

The gang is already cooking up a scheme whereby Clifford works three weeks at $1,200 a week, then leaves the job. Then Gene does club dates under Clifford's name and the union doesn't know and the unemployment people are clueless, so the unemployment checks keep coming in . . . This speculation is short-circuited by Clifford's saying that he's thinking of *not* actually quitting after three weeks. He might actually keep the job. The musicians are stunned at the idea. Gene winks to the guys and says, "I have no son." Patsy arrives with five separate checks, but Gene surprises them all by insisting on picking up the entire tab—unheard of for a sideman but a measure of his pride in Clifford on this day.

CLIFFORD *(to audience):* My father covers the checks, and then, he does something else he's almost never done. He looks at me. He just stops and stares. And I think he sees something, some promise, some sadness, or . . .
>   *Gene starts to whistle the first phrase of* The Afternoon of a Faun. *Clifford waves a hand in front of his father's face: no reaction.*
He's gone now. Back to when he had no son, back to 1953—before the Beatles, before Elvis. When these guys were like ball players. On the road, written up in the papers, endorsing trumpets in *Down Beat.* Bands passing each other in the night even traded sidemen: one first trumpet player and an alto for a second trumpet and a tenor to be named later.

"Throughout the rest of the first act Clifford, when narrating, also stage manages, or plays caretaker to his parents and their friends. He hands or receives props, drinks, instruments, clothes, and even does simple set changes. He is engaged and in motion throughout." In this capacity, Clifford sets up the next scene, which tells how his parents met.

The setting is the basement of the Hotel Nevada, a "dive" where, in the old days, Gene used to stay after trips on the road and before heading up to visit his mother in the Bronx. The Nevada was particularly attractive to musicians because management allowed them to practice in the basement.

Terry—24 in this scene—is practicing her flute. The piece is the tune Gene began whistling when he zoned out with Clifford in the last scene. Terry plays a wrong note, and this pretty young woman in the late 1940s says, "Fuck." She tries again, and her playing gives her cause to say "Fuck" again. Now a sweet trumpet from somewhere unseen begins to play the phrase. The flute and trumpet play together, and then the trumpet begins to improvise on the piece and on Terry's mistakes. Irritated, Terry begins to put her flute away. Gene appears, carrying his horn. Off to the side, Clifford watches this scene from his parents' past.

Gene figures what she was playing was classical, but what was it exactly? Debussy, Terry tells him. He doesn't know classical all that well, though his mother plays classical cello. They banter a little, and then Terry takes offense at something he says and chases him away.

Clifford interrupts, reminds his mother, Terry, that isn't what happened. Reluctantly, Terry returns to the scene and plays it out the way it really went: the exchanging of names and information, including the fact that she's new in town and he's only just returned from playing with a band on the road. She shares her sandwich with him, and she accepts his invitation to see him play with Woody Herman that night. He sneaks her in through the stage door, and she stands in the wings and listens to him solo beautifully.

She goes to the band room afterwards, where she sees Gene with the younger versions of Jonesy, Al and Ziggy. His friends congratulate him on his playing, but it is clear that Gene is honestly unaware of how good he was. Jonesy and Ziggy head for the Melody Lounge. Ever on the prowl, Al suggests Terry accompany him there, but Terry announces she's with Gene. Al leaves, and Gene and Terry are alone.

Terry is curious as to why some of the guys called Gene a turtle.

GENE *(proud):* They did a contest, on the road, Krupa's band. They timed all the slow guys. How we ate, how long it took us to pack up, to shave. I had no idea this was going on. Some of the guys knew, were *trying* to go slow. But I still beat everybody.

> *She starts to help him pack. Touches the horn to put it in the case. He swiftly takes the horn away from her.*

Hey—don't touch the horn! Never touch the horn.

> *He lays it in the case, as if it were glass.*

TERRY: You sounded beautiful out there.

GENE: That guy Al, Romeo we call him, best lead player in town. Can sight-read fly shit at five hundred feet.

TERRY: But you're the one who gets to solo. You know who you sound like? *(She puffs her cheeks out.)* You sound like Dizzy.

GENE *(he covers her mouth):* Don't ever say that in front of the guys.

TERRY: There's something you do that he does.

GENE: Just an octave and a half lower.

TERRY: You don't know how good you are. You know that?

GENE: You want to go over to Charlie's? *(She nods.)* Good. Just do not mention me and Dizzy in the same sentence. I am not worthy.

They go to the Melody Lounge, joining Ziggy and Al. Patsy, waiting on them, introduces herself as Al's "piece on the side." As the scene progresses, it becomes apparent that Terry is more than a little naive. When Jonesy, having just shot up, arrives and nods at the table, Terry assumes that he's suffering from some kind of food poisoning.

This is intercut with a short scene from 1985 between Clifford and Patsy. Patsy asks after Terry, and Clifford says she has good days and bad. Patsy has tried to phone Terry, but Terry hasn't responded. Patsy is moved to tell Clifford that she never made it with Gene. Clifford's reply: "Even if you did, he wouldn't have noticed."

Patsy joins the scene back in 1953. Finished with her shift, she sits on Al's lap as he starts to pass around the joint he's just rolled. Terry thinks it's a regular cigarette.

TERRY: You roll your own? I should do that. It's much more economical.

PATSY *(to Gene while taking a hit off the joint):* Is she for real?

The joint is passed from Al, to Ziggy, to Gene, to Terry, who, thinking it's a cigarette, takes a drag. Keeps up her nervous monologue.

TERRY: I don't smoke that much. The only reason I started smoking at all was because the sisters at St. Mary's accused me of smoking all the time, so I finally figured I'd start smoking—Pall Mall Golds, 'cause that's what my brother Guy, he's a narcotics agent . . .

Ziggy, Al, Gene and even Jonesy cough on this. Terry doesn't miss a beat.

. . . smoked; although nobody ever accused him of smoking. And I've seen people roll their own in the movies, but aren't you clever for rolling your own like this. And then, the way you all share— *(Hands the joint to Gene.) Here* . . .

PATSY: What planet did you come from?

TERRY: Baltimore. Not originally. East Boston originally, but I can't go back, because my husband, Dominic Defeces, the brick-laying prick, just left me, in Baltimore. I wrote Blimpie, she's my oldest sister, there's seven others, that I had to come home, and she wrote me and told me: "Don't come back." 'Cause my mother, Italian, Catholic, thinks divorce is a sin—even though the rat-bastard got an annulment to run off with my best friend, she'll make me join a fuckin' convent in Montana, if I do. Go home. So Blimpie, Cupie, Fat Raffie and some of my other sisters pitched in and sent me a money tree with twenty-five dollars. So I came to New York. The room's eight, so now I'm down to thirteen dollars, but I can't go home. But I'm not worried because—

ZIGGY: Anybody following thish?

JONESY *(looks up from his haze):* I am.

AL: What's she saying?

JONESY: Her prick husband, a mudslinger, took her from East Boston, which is a fuckin' tough ghetto, let me tell you, and left her in Baltimore. But Italians don't divorce—so she had to come here. Good-night now.

He nods back out.

ZIGGY: You're in luck then. Jazz musiciansh divorce all the time. Patshy's on her third trumpet player.

TERRY: You and Al are married?

PATSY: No. I mean, I am, he's not. My husband's on the road.

ZIGGY: Romeo'sh what you call the relief band. Shpeaking of which, we're due downtown in oh . . . *(Looks at watch.)* twenty minutesh ago.

PATSY: And I'm back in . . .

AL: We'll hop a cab, *(To Ziggy.) your treat.*

ZIGGY *(grabbing Jonesy off the table):* I'll have to roll Joneshy. Genie, you coming?

GENE: I'll catch up with you later.

TERRY *(as the gang leaves):* Nice to meet you all. *(To Gene.)* It's amazing how economical you all are.

Terry holds the remains of the joint but since it's now roach size, and since she thinks it's a cigarette, she just puts it out in an ashtray.

It's pretty much down to the end. Here, have one of mine.

Gene watches in shock. Now Gene takes Terry's hand and leads her out of the bar, and across the stage.

As Clifford tells us, Terry went back to Gene's room, where she was impressed by the fact that he had a sink in his room and, on the wall, a picture of himself with Frank Sinatra, whom Terry has wanted to see her whole life. In order to make the scene go forward, the narrating Clifford hands his father a battered wire recorder which Gene uses to play her a choppy bootlegged recording of himself soloing behind Sinatra. And, under the influence of Sinatra, they make love. Terry stays the night.

The next morning, Terry knows her mind: they're going to live together. Gene tries to protest, but he suddenly finds himself in their new apartment, as Terry greets Ziggy, Al and Jonesy. They arrive with furniture *"from busted marriages."*

Among the stuff brought to the apartment is something that used to belong to a friend named Neon Leon: an orgone box, a device designed by Wilhelm Reich. Al explains that Reich is a renegade shrink who believes that really good sex releases positive energy in a form called orgones. This box is designed to collect orgones. Terry, unaware that she is getting stoned from what she continues to believe are ordinary cigarettes, is urged by Gene to put into the box the hand that she scraped while fixing up the apartment. As she sits there with her hand in the box, the guys sorrowfully discuss Leon's situation.

JONESY: I can't believe Leon's old lady won't let him keep his box.

GENE: His old lady's moving him to Massachusetts.

ZIGGY: Who'sh he gonna play with in Masha, Mashaschu—fuck it, Boshton.

AL: What play? She wants him out of the business.

JONESY: Leon? Neon Leon? Tell me he could get a job other than playing trumpet.

TERRY: Who's Neon Leon?

GENE: Neon Leon. I told you about him. The one Benny Goodman fired because he peed on stage.

JONESY *(as Leon, stage whispers):* "Benny, Benny—I gotta go."

AL *(as Benny Goodman):* "That's not my problem, Neon, you knew about this gig weeks ago."

JONESY: "Benny, what am I supposed to do?"

AL: "You can pee on the stage for all I care."

ZIGGY: Sho he did.

AL: He's a motherfucker though. Let's face it, he's a motherfucker.
    The guys all agree, he's a motherfucker.

JONESY: Total motherfucker.

TERRY: Is motherfucker good or bad?

JONESY *(gently explaining):* G's above high C, all night long.

GENE: What a waste, chops like that, going to law school.

ZIGGY: We oughtta have a wake: Requiem for a Motherfucker.

> *Lights dim on them, lights up on Clifford, as a funeral march, Louis Armstrong's "St. James Infirmary," plays.*

CLIFFORD *(to audience):* A moment of silence. For Leon. Since he's leaving the business, in effect, he's passed away. Over the years there'd be more and more of these moments. Guys would O.D., or go to jail, or worse get married and have to work nine to five. By the time I was on the scene, these guys were sort of an underground railroad to the straight world. We got our eyeglasses from a former tenor player, car insurance from an alto, and of course that box, from Leon.

> *Back to the living room, music out.*

JONESY: How's your hand?

TERRY: What?

JONESY: Your hand.

> *She takes it out of the box. Stares at it.*

TERRY: Holy shit. It's better. It's almost healed.

JONESY: HALLELUJAH.

TERRY *(scared):* What the fuck is in there?

ZIGGY and AL *(spooky-voice):* Orrrr-gooones.

GENE: Don't ever tell anyone we have one of these things. They're illegal. They're chasing Reich all over the country.

TERRY: You guys are fuckin' weird. I don't want that thing in my house. Get it out.

GENE: Calm down, Terry. It's harmless.

TERRY: I'm serious, get it out.

ZIGGY: Wait 'til she shees the resht of Leon's shtuff.

> *Terry, very quickly, loses it. She starts to beat Gene's chest with her hands. He grabs them.*

TERRY: Don't tease me. I hate when you all do that.

GENE: Terry, no one is doing anything to you.

TERRY *(embarrassed, calming down):* OK—still, get it out of the house.

Sensitive to their need for privacy, the guys leave Gene and Terry alone. Gene continues to promise to get rid of the orgone box.

Together in the Melody Lounge, Terry tells Patsy about the box, which Patsy recognizes as having belonged to Leon. It turns out Leon is one of Patsy's many exes—the first one she actually married. Patsy is philosophical about being a serial divorcee. "They get easier. After a while, it's like falling off a bicycle." Terry, still bruised from being dumped by her "rat-bastard" ex, Dominic, doesn't think she could survive another bust-up. Patsy tries to reassure Terry about Gene—not only did she never have an affair with Gene, he's the designated non-junkie in the group, "the one they all call when their cars break down." As Clifford notes, "This was some sort of code, 'cause these guys' cars always break . . . . . and half of them don't even have cars."

Clifford hands Gene and Terry the props for another domestic scene from the early days of their relationship. They're having dinner at home.

Edie Falco as Terry and Frank Wood (winner of the Tony for best featured performance in a play) as Gene in *Side Man* by Warren Leight

TERRY: Patsy says these doo-wop groups don't even use horns.

GENE: She's married three trumpet players in a row, so she must think there's some future in it.

TERRY: She says the big bands are gone for good. And a lot of the clubs are—

GENE: Terry, trust me, it's nothing to worry about. I'm a professional. Like a doctor, or a lawyer. And here in New York, with all the TV and radio here. You can't ask for a more secure field—every station will have to have its own band. Honest.

TERRY: Then why is Patsy's husband getting out?

GENE: That's her *ex*-husband. The second one. Stu. Not Bernie. Bernie's a motherfucker—he's out on the road sixty weeks a year. When he comes back to town, Charlie Barnett's gonna add him to the band, and we'll record.

TERRY: Then why is Stu getting out?

GENE: Stu's a lead player. Great chops, but he can only work the big bands. But I'm a true sideman—I can solo, back up a singer—

TERRY: Or fake Deboosy—

GENE: And harmony. Three part. Four part. I'm a . . . a—

TERRY: A jack-of-all-trades.

GENE: Bingo.

> *They kiss, then she pulls back.*

TERRY: Wait—it wasn't just Stu—Al too. She said he hasn't even had a Saturday night this month.

GENE: That won't happen. To me. I mean, look: if there ever comes a Saturday night when I'm not booked, just one Saturday night, then—I promise, I'll get out of the business, OK?

TERRY: You don't have to say that.

GENE: But I can. It's the easiest promise I could ever make.

> *She kisses him.*

TERRY: Are you going to be on the road a lot?

GENE: I used to think I was. But you came in and . . . *(Looks around.)*

TERRY: You like it?

GENE: I've never had a home in my life—I like it a lot.

TERRY: Patsy's gonna get me a job waitressing soon, at Charlie's. So you won't have to—

GENE: No. I don't want you working. I'm a little behind now—with the car breaking down, and the rent—but we're almost out of the woods. And, *(Looks straight into her eyes.)* I promise you. I'm going to take care of us, *(Kisses her.)* you won't ever have to work at all.

> *Terry stands.*

TERRY *(yelling to a kitchen's short-order window):* BLT please, whiskey down.

Despite Gene's assurances, Terry ends up working as a waitress at the Melody Lounge with Patsy. Patsy has news: she and Al are getting married. Which means that Patsy is divorcing Bernie, which means that Terry and Gene get Bernie's busted marriage stuff, which they put into their rent-controlled, ninth-floor apartment. As just about everybody else has moved to the suburbs, Terry and Gene's place becomes hang-out central in the city for the musicians. And, as more and more of the guys' various relationships and marriages fall apart, the apartment gets more and more furnished. Clifford, looking at a photo of the gang dating from those days, observes, "From what I understand, EVERYONE WAS HAPPY BEFORE I WAS BORN."

We pick up the gang watching TV in Gene and Terry's apartment. Elvis Presley is performing on the *Ed Sullivan Show*. Jonesy can see the writing on the wall: "That kid will do to horn players what talkies did to Buster Keaton." That night, Jonesy gets arrested and consequently loses his cabaret card, without which he can't work in New York. Jonesy moves to Las Vegas, and Gene and Terry acquire his coffee table.

Terry tells Gene of a card they got from Jonesy telling him they should move to Vegas, too. But Gene thinks there's no future in Vegas. And he is also certain that, though some TV is moving to L.A., New York will always be where the work is. "Gene was sort of an anti-psychic," Clifford comments from the side. But Terry didn't challenge him.

Gene and Ziggy decide to try to write some sample scripts, trying to get on staff for Sid Caesar's TV show. The excerpt we hear from one of their sketches does not suggest that's where their talents lie. In any case, they never do anything with the scripts.

Shift to Patsy handing Clifford a drink in the Melody Lounge in 1977 to celebrate his first unemployment check. Having gotten the idea (from Gene) that Clifford is off to try his hand at TV, she gives Clifford some of Gene and Ziggy's old scripts. But Gene told her wrong; Clifford's going to train for a job in advertising. It's a job that would pay really well.

PATSY: You don't need money, you're a kid.
CLIFFORD: *I* don't need anything, but Gene's so far behind on his credit cards—
PATSY: Genie is always behind—
CLIFFORD: And Mom's not doing so well, lately. Her health . . .
    Patsy, very sober all of a sudden, looks at Clifford.
PATSY: Why do you think that is?
CLIFFORD: I'm sorry?
PATSY: Clifford, when you were about to go away to college, the same thing happened.
CLIFFORD: It's a good thing I didn't go away to college. Can you imagine Genie handling the—
PATSY: Clifford, listen to me: I don't care what you do, or where you go—just get the hell out of here.

Back to the days when Gene and Terry were still shacking up together: Terry is two months late. Gene says, "Al knows someone who can take care of it." Yes, Terry's pregnant. And, as Clifford watches the flashback, Gene makes the case for aborting the baby who will grow up to be him. Terry passionately refuses to consider the idea. Even if the child is born a bastard, she's going to have the baby. Gene says that the baby won't be born a bastard. This is how he proposed.

Gene starts to talk about a big wedding with caterers. More realistic, Terry says, "We can't afford that. I can cook a lasagne—" And, despite Gene's protestations, two weeks later she makes the lasagne and they get married in their apartment. None of her Catholic family show up. The post-ceremony celebration is held (of course) at the Melody Lounge, where most of the action centers on who is going to play with whom in the band. The only person Terry dances with that night is Jonesy, newly returned from Vegas.

TERRY: How come he doesn't dance with me? On his wedding night?
JONESY: Trumpet players don't dance.

TERRY: How come you dance?

JONESY: I play trombone. Patsy taught me. After she left Al . . . before she went back to her second husband.

TERRY: Bernie?

JONESY: No. Bernie was number three. She wouldn't leave me and Al for Bernie, because Bernie still plays. Greatest lead player in America. She went back to Stu— number two, if you're keeping score. Which in Patsy's case is almost impossible to do.

TERRY: Stu the foot doctor?

JONESY *(to himself):* Stu the foot doctor. *(To Terry.)* He used to be a good player. He came by 52nd Street one night, saw us all play. He started to cry. Ziggy looks at him and says: "Podiatrisht, heel thyshelf."

> *The ballad ends. Jonesy and Terry applaud. She motions for Gene to come join her. Instead, the band starts another tune: like "Daahoud," an up-tempo, undanceable, hard-bop number.*

TERRY: How do you dance to this?

JONESY: You don't. You drink to it. That's another reason why jazz is dying. Let's go to the bar.

> *He steers her to the bar.*

TERRY: I'll have a Shirley Temple.

JONESY: Terry, you marry a musician, you're gonna have to learn to drink hard stuff. Start with a Tom Collins.

> *Clifford serves Terry her first drink. She and Jonesy listen to the band.* Gene sounds pretty good tonight.

TERRY: He told me never to tell anyone, but I think he sounds like Dizzy.

JONESY: In a way. Nicer tone than Dizzy. But he does those same long lines. Every solo has a beginning, middle, and end when he plays.

TERRY: Do you think he'll make it?

JONESY: Honey. He's made it. This is it.

> *Terry looks around, lets this sink in. Then:*

TERRY: What about that record he did . . . with Charlie Barnett's band?

JONESY: He's a player, Terry. He's not a hustler.

TERRY: But he played really well on it.

JONESY: Didn't he tell you what happened?

TERRY: No.

JONESY: Ask him about the review.

Jonesy goes off to score a fix. An hour goes by, and Jonesy still hasn't returned. Terry is worried about him, but Gene tells her not to be. The party is breaking up. Tonight, Patsy is going home with Ziggy. Al is not happy with her new sleeping arrangements and leaves after expressing his displeasure. Patsy's response—"That stage should be over by now." As they leave the Melody Lounge, they see a police car across the street. Sitting in it with his hands cuffed behind his back is Jonesy. As Clifford relates, Terry and Gene spend the rest of their wedding night waiting with Ziggy in night court. Terry is still ignorant of Jonesy's junk problem.

Gene assures Terry that Jonesy's going to be all right (though it's evident that they don't have the resources to put up his bail). Now Terry remembers to ask Gene about the review Jonesy told her about. Gene reluctantly tells her that a major French jazz critic reviewed the Charlie Barnett record he played on. The critic liked the band, but most of his enthusiasm was for Gene's trumpet solos which he termed "the best in the last decade." There's only one problem, the critic got the name of the soloist wrong, and Bernie got the credit. So there's no way for Gene to capitalize on the review. And, truth to tell, he doesn't seem to care much. "You know, Bernie's a great player, and he deserves a good review." "NOT FOR YOUR FUCKING SOLOS HE DOESN'T," says an enraged Terry. She wants him to write to the magazine and get a correction, but Gene won't humiliate Bernie by doing that. Besides, people in the business know his playing.

Ultimately, they turn to Leon (who's now a Harvard-trained lawyer) to try to help Jonesy with his legal troubles. But Jonesy's troubles have gotten worse when Gene gets to visit him. It seems that Jonesy agreed to a deal with the cops to name his supplier in return for a fix. Having gotten his fix, Jonesy told them where he got his stuff: "I look them right in the eye, and I tell them the truth: *(Pause.)* General MacArthur." The cops didn't appreciate that. They worked him over pretty badly, breaking three of his teeth. Jonesy cries, "I don't know if I'll ever be able to play." He ends up being sentenced to eight years. Terry tries to keep in touch with him in prison, sending him care packages, but Jonesy never replies.

A drink in hand (she's grown to like Tom Collinses), Terry confronts Gene.

TERRY *(to Gene):* You lied to me. When Jonesy was arrested the first time, it wasn't disorderly conduct, was it? It was for junk, wasn't it?

GENE: I guess—I mean, he's not really a junkie junkie. More of an addict. He never misses a gig.

TERRY: He told me he doesn't have any gigs.

GENE: It's a little slow right now. No one works in September—the Jewish holidays.

TERRY: Patsy says it's all over. Elvis. TV. L.A. Jazz is—

GENE: Patsy is just pissed off because she can't get Al or Bernie or Ziggy to quit, so she had to go back to Stu, who spends his day touching people's feet. Is that what you want me to do?

TERRY: That's the same Bernie who got credit for your solos, isn't it?

GENE: Most likely. So *what.*

TERRY: Why don't you send out those scripts you and Ziggy wrote?

GENE: They're not ready.

TERRY: Do you want me to help?

GENE: Honey, you can barely speak English; no one understands a word you say. How the hell are you going to help with the scripts?

TERRY: Fuck you.

GENE: What? Oh don't get upset. I'm just saying. Ziggy and I went to college. We know what we're doing. As soon as those scripts are ready—they're going out.

TERRY: Do you have a gig for tonight?

GENE: Not yet.

TERRY and GENE: Huh.

GENE: It happens. What's the big deal.

TERRY: It's Saturday night.

GENE: The Jewish holidays. No one's working.

TERRY: But it's Saturday night.

GENE: Terry, I've got my twenty weeks in, I subbed at the Copa twice last week, what's so goddamn important about Saturday night. Jesus—a gig is a gig.

TERRY: You said if you ever weren't booked for a Saturday night, you'd quit the business.

GENE: Oh, come on. I never said that.

> *She stares at him in disbelief, then anger.*

TERRY: You lying motherfucker—

GENE: Terry—

> *She walks away from him.*

TERRY: You lying motherfucker—

> *Terry doesn't see Gene as he moves toward her.*

GENE: Terry, get a hold of your—

> *He is suddenly next to her. She bats him away.*

TERRY: Get your hands off of me, Dominic—

GENE: I'm Gene.

TERRY: I don't care who you are. All of you. Stay away. I can't take this bullshit. All of you lie. All of you fucking lie.

GENE: STOP IT. Stop it.

> *She snaps back to reality. Calms a bit.*

TERRY: What time is it?

GENE: Nine.

TERRY: You have until midnight. If that phone doesn't ring, and you stay in the business, I'll fuckin' kill you. And I'll kill the baby.

> *She takes her drink and walks past Gene to the bedroom, as Clifford sits.*

I swear to God, I'll kill you both.

> *She slams the bedroom door behind her. Curtain.*

ACT II

"Same apartment, ten years later, with ten more years of inherited furniture, broken lamps, tchotchkes. Every surface is piled high; every inch of space below the couch or tables is crammed full as well." Clifford returns and tells us of the circumstances of his birth. Terry was supposed to spend the evening seeing Gene accompanying Sinatra at the Copa. Then came contractions. It was the last time Gene played with Sinatra, so Terry never got to see Sinatra live. Angry at fate, instead of naming the baby Francis Albert, she let Gene choose a name, which is how Clifford ended up

being named after Clifford Brown, a legendary trumpet player who died in a car accident at age 25. Not an easy name for a kid to carry, especially when, by virtue of being very bright and having skipped two grades, he didn't mix comfortably with other kids.

Clifford now introduces key scenes from his childhood. (The stage directions note that *"when Clifford interacts with his family, he does so as a child; when he talks to the audience, he finds a middle ground between the manner of a child and the ironic detachment of the adult Clifford."*)

It's 1967. A ten-year-old Clifford wakes his father, who has been asleep on the couch in his tux. It's time for Gene to get ready for the evening's gig, a date playing for Lester Lanin's society band. Gene loathes Lanin—his lack of musicianship, his meanness and the tone-deaf people who hire him, "people couldn't swing if you hung them." As he tells Clifford stories illustrating how appalling Lanin is, Clifford tries to act as a buffer between him and Terry. Gene still looks pretty much the same. But years of alcohol and despair have taken their toll on Terry. Drunk and filled with a never-abating rage, she wanders in and out of the room hurling invective at her passive husband. She reminds him to come back with cigarettes and her "medicine." He checks his wallet and realizes he doesn't have enough to get a fifth, so (behind Terry's back and against her strict injunction) he borrows five from Clifford.

Gene wants to warm up before going to the gig, but Terry hates his practicing. Why didn't he practice before she got home from her job? Because he got hung up (as he always does) running errands and dealing with the car. Terry brings out the dinner, in the process stumbling around the room. At one point, she accidentally knocks over the table. Gene, protecting the suit he's going to have to wear to work, automatically leaps to his feet. "Sure," says Terry. "Now you move. You mother-fucker. Nothing gets you. Nothing gets you."

She slams into the bedroom. Gene and Clifford try to eat and talk, but they are interrupted every other breath by Terry opening the door and yelling something that always includes the word "motherfucker," punctuated by slamming the door. Finally, in a rage, she pops out, an empty cup in her hand. She hurls it at Gene, but her aim is off, and it hits the wall and smashes.

CLIFFORD *(to Gene):* She broke Bakelite. NICE, MA, I didn't think that was possible.
> *Gene tries to quiet Clifford.*
TERRY: DON'T GET CUTE WITH ME.
GENE: He wasn't getting cute with—
> *She grabs his trumpet case, shakes it, AND THE HORN GOES CRASH-ING TO THE FLOOR.*
CLIFFORD: Ma!
> *Terry SLAMS the door behind her. Gene rushes to his horn as if it were his child. Checks it carefully. It's OK. Now tuxedo neat, trumpet case in hand:*

GENE: OK kiddo . . . thanks for cleaning up. I'd better get going. Try and get her to eat something.

CLIFFORD *(nonchalant):* OK. See you later.

Gene leaves. Clifford picks up. To audience:

It's good for a family to have rituals. This was ours. Once, twice, three times a month. He'd screw up. She'd flip out. He'd leave for work. I'd clean up. She'd hide in the room. I'd bring her something to eat. She'd have a few drinks. Fall asleep. He'd sneak in around four A.M. Every once in a while she'd put furniture in front of the door. I'd wait until she'd fall asleep, and I'd move it so he could get in. If you got through the night without the cops coming, things were usually fine in the morning.

Gene arrives at the gig at the Metropolitan Club to find he's going to be playing with Ziggy and Al. They commiserate over being reduced to playing for Lanin. As they are about to warm up, the blare of a bad rock band is heard. The rock is for the kids, and the guys are set to be sandwiched between their noise to play three sets for "the old farts." The guys complain about the treatment—not only are they not getting dinner, the club has a rule that the employees can't use the guests' bathroom, and the employees' john isn't working, so they'll have to scuttle to a diner across the street to answer nature's call. As Ziggy says, "If we were black, they couldn't get away with thish." They trade stories of the bad old days working at the Copa, one of the places they closed together. Come to think of it, in the last 20 years, together they've closed an awful lot of places.

Meanwhile, back at home Clifford enters his mother's bedroom with dinner to find her sitting halfway out her window, threatening suicide. And it's all Gene's fault. Clifford tries to say how badly Gene feels, but Terry isn't buying it. Clifford edges toward her, and she relents and comes back in. "You shouldn't have to do this," she tells him, weeping in her boy's arms. "He should do this. Not you."

Back at the Metropolitan Club, the gig has been a killer. They compare Lanin's sadism with that of the circus playing Madison Square Garden, whose arrangements require horns to play so many screaming high notes that the job is actually a health risk. And, of course, there's no help from the union that's supposed to represent their interests.

As the guys pack up, Al tells them that Jonesy's returned to town. He's back at the Melody Lounge, playing piano now. (After being worked over by that cop, he never could pick up a trombone again.) Jonesy gave Al a copy of a precious tape, which Al wants to share with his friends. And Al pulls out a cassette player and plays them a tape of Clifford Brown playing, on the night that he died. This is the stuff of legend. Brown and some others were playing in the back room of a music store in Philadelphia, and some guy happened to be there with a wire recorder and captured Brown's solo on "Night in Tunisia." "Just listen," says Al, "you're not going to believe this."

Al hits the play button on Clifford Brown's last recording of "A Night in Tunisia." After a few notes:

ZIGGY: That'sh Clifford!
> *Now, chorus after inventive chorus. It is one thing to listen to this unbelievable recording. It is another thing entirely to watch three lifelong jazz trumpet players listen to this fabled lost masterpiece for the first time. Every turn Brownie takes causes them to shake their heads, laugh, murmur. They listen and react to every nuance of this solo with an intensity and passion that is otherwise not part of their lives.*

ZIGGY: Can you believe—

AL: Wait wait wait.
> *They are astonished by his level of musicianship. It brings tears to their eyes. The swiftness of their reactions, and the depth of their understanding of what Brownie is playing, tells us something about these three musicians as well. For all their joking and fucking up, they have a profound connection to their music, one they can only share with each other. Every time Ziggy and Gene think Clifford Brown has reached a musical climax, Al says:*

AL: Wait wait wait.
> *Brownie plays through the turn around. Plays another chorus . . . Gene in particular laughs at every quote within the solo. He smiles at the way Clifford threads his long melodic lines through the chords. Ziggy nudges Al to watch how Gene takes in the nuances. Each phrase builds on the one before it. Brownie takes another chorus, and the musicians are staggered.*

AL: Motherfucker. That is one motherfucker.
> *Gene is mute in ecstasy. Finally, Clifford all but ignites.*

ZIGGY: That'sh it. I quit.

Gene returns to the apartment late to find Clifford still up in front of the TV. Clifford tells him Terry is asleep in the bedroom, so he should be safe if he wants to go in. Gene tells him about the tape Al played. Clifford doesn't need his father to repeat the story of his namesake's last night, ten years ago. For a second, Gene spaces out, struck by the idea that it has indeed been ten years. Returning to the present, Gene pulls out the tape and starts to play it for his son, who *"laughs in the same spots Al and Ziggy did."* Even at his young age, Clifford knows what he is listening to. They begin to lose themselves in the music, when an awakened Terry slams in and turns off the player.

In response to her demand for an explanation, Gene says he hung out with the boys after the gig. Terry wonders if Patsy was hanging with him, too. Gene dismisses what she is implying. Terry has a more pressing concern, so Gene opens his case and hands her a bottle. But it's sherry—not what she wanted at all. She hasn't touched sherry for two years.

GENE: What difference does it make, booze is booze, Terry.
TERRY: What the fuck is that supposed to mean?

Scott Wolf (*foreground,* as Clifford) and Michael Mastro (Ziggy), Angelica Torn
(Patsy), Frank Wood (Gene), Edie Falco (Terry), Joseph Lyle Taylor (Al) and
Kevin Geer (Jonesy) in a scene from *Side Man*

GENE *(to Clifford):* Poison is poison.

TERRY: And you're so fucking clean, Gene. A monk. Gene's so sweet. Gene is
so clean. Bullshit. Fifteen years of your bullshit and lies: "It's just slow right now.
Wait until this record comes out. Every TV station will have a band. We'll go on
vacation next year. You shouldn't be tired, you're a waitress, not a doctor. We'll get
our own furniture." YOU AND YOUR FUCKING LIES. *(To Clifford.)* Your father hasn't touched me in ten years. I'VE HAD IT. DO YOU HEAR ME. ALL
OF YOU.

> *She takes the sherry and pours it over the living room. She soaks the rug.
> She starts to light her cigarette. She looks at the match. Then at the rug.
> She throws the match on the rug.*

CLIFFORD: Ma!

TERRY: Francis, you stay out of this.

> *She lights another, and another. Flings them at the rug, at Gene; she fails
> to start a fire and finally throws the whole box of matches to the floor.*

Get away from me. Get away from me. Goddamn it. You got the wrong booze. If you'd gotten bourbon this whole fucking place would be on fire by now.

Now narrating in an adult voice, Clifford tells us that this evening led to Terry being institutionalized the first of many times. Sometimes he would have to call to have her taken away, sometimes she would call herself. This pattern continued for years, and her reliance on him kept Clifford in the neighborhood even after he had managed to move out after college. When a phone call would come in the middle of the night, he'd know it was Terry in trouble again. Like the time she was found naked on Amsterdam Avenue and told the officers she wanted to be put on a bus and sent to a convent out west.

We pick up Clifford in an emergency room with his mother. She pours out her grievances against Gene, many of them legitimate and most of them based on Gene's obliviousness to everything but his music. Clifford insists that Gene does try, even if it doesn't seem that way. But what doesn't need to be said is that Gene's tries fall far short of the effectual.

TERRY: I used to tell your father, it wasn't right, that you had to do this. You know what your father said: "That's why you have kids, Terry, so they'll take care of you." You never should have saved me, Clifford. I've been dead for thirty years anyway.

    Terry exits.

CLIFFORD *(to audience):* I went to work; I was two hours late. No one noticed. I spent the morning writing ads. At lunchtime, I went into a stairwell and cried. For the first time in twenty years. I finished the afternoon, like nothing happened.

    Clifford, now with Gene, who's more spaced-out than usual.

Couldn't you tell that she was losing it, before she—

GENE: How can you tell? It's irrational.

CLIFFORD: You ran out of insurance. They want to send her upstate.

GENE: She'll talk her way out of it.

CLIFFORD: They won't let her come home if you're here.

GENE: You know, she drinks.

CLIFFORD: *Really?*

GENE: After she flipped out, I found bottles all over the place.

CLIFFORD: What?

GENE: Things just got . . . the boozing, the flip outs—I just thank God it started after you left home.

CLIFFORD: Are you *serious?*

GENE: It didn't get bad till the last couple of years.

CLIFFORD: Dad, you're nuts. That's just not . . . she's had a drinking problem since I can remember.

GENE: Clifford, I think I would know that.

CLIFFORD: I don't.

GENE *(changing the subject):* So what do you want to do?

CLIFFORD: What do *you* want to do? She's your wife.

GENE: She won't talk to me when she's like this. She's completely irrational. You know that.

CLIFFORD: Why does it have to be up to me?

GENE: You're the son. She's your mother. Who else is there?

CLIFFORD: Dad, what the fuck is your problem, she's your wife. SHE'S YOUR WIFE and if we don't do something, she's gone. Do you get it? *DO YOU UNDERSTAND WHAT'S GOING ON?*

> *Gene spaces out.*

Are you listening to me?

GENE: There's no reason to get upset. You always figure something out. You're the RED CROSS.

> *Gene stares into space. There is a long, awkward pause.*

CLIFFORD: OK, get your horn, you're out.

GENE: I'm sorry?

CLIFFORD: Get your fuckin' horn, and get out.

GENE: What are you talking about?

CLIFFORD: Dad, she can't live with you. She can't get a place on her own. I'm not letting them send her upstate. You're out. It's over.

GENE: Clifford.

CLIFFORD: It's over. As of tonight. Call Ziggy. Call Al. I don't give a fuck. Call someone. You're out of here.

> *He packs the horn, gives it to Gene.*

Dad, she's coming, you're going. You two are done.

GENE: I don't think it's that bad.

CLIFFORD: You don't think, Dad. You don't know. YOU DON'T HAVE A FUCKING CLUE.

> *He pushes the case into Gene.*

You don't have a fucking clue.

> *Gene stares at Clifford, completely in shock. Gene walks out. Clifford steps forward, to audience.*

Before that night, I had never yelled at my father. And yelling at him . . . if my mom couldn't get through to him in thirty years, I wasn't going to either. That night, at midnight, I drove him over to Ziggy's. I don't think he had any idea what was going on. It was like moving a cat.

In effect, Clifford engineered his parents' de facto divorce. Terry returned home. Clifford stayed with her a bit. When he left, she started drinking again. Meanwhile, Ziggy got a taste of Gene's spaciness when they roomed together, and it drove him nuts, too.

A few years pass. Terry keeps drinking till she finds herself in a coma with a bum liver and lung cancer. And somehow she comes out of it! But the scare had an effect,

Clifford reports. "Quit drinking, denies ever having had a drinking problem. And still smokes three packs a day. She still makes a decent lasagne. And Genie ... I haven't seen him in five years ... "

And now we're back to the Melody Lounge in 1985, Clifford standing with Patsy, listening to Gene play "I Remember Clifford." "Genie on a ballad, break your heart every time," says his son. Patsy tells him that Gene plays it every night. This registers with Clifford Brown's namesake.

This set over, Gene and Ziggy enter the bar. Ziggy has to point out Clifford's presence to Gene—"Turtle, your shon ish here." Now Gene sees him. An awkward moment. Clifford tells his father how good he sounded, but Gene shrugs the compliment off. He's sure he's lost it. And, of course, he hasn't. But what does Gene know? Gene and Clifford join Ziggy and Patsy in the booth, and they are joined by Al and Jonesy. *The gang is all there, but much the worse for wear.*" Jonesy greets Clifford as "Frankie." He's the one who remembers that Terry wanted to name him after Sinatra. He's also the one who wistfully asks after Terry. Clifford avoids answering.

News: Patsy's husband Stu retired with the intention of coming back to music, but died before he could do it. And Bernie is dying of cancer in Germany. The halting way Al speaks is evidence to the mini-stroke that took him away from the trumpet (he's playing drums now), and of course Jonesy is on piano. Yes, it's the old gang, or what's left of them.

The guys get up and head for the bandstand. Patsy is going to sing with them. Clifford tells them Terry had a request, and Jonesy and Patsy correctly guess, "Why Was I Born?". The others having exited, Clifford and Gene are alone together.

CLIFFORD: Dad ... *(They look at each other.)* It's been a while.

GENE: You're busy. Work. Your job's—

CLIFFORD: I quit.

GENE: You quit? Are you gonna be able to collect—

CLIFFORD: I'm gonna go west—work on the ... painting stuff. I was hoping you'd look in on her once in a while.

> *Gene thinks about this.*

GENE: You were always good with those collages, you know.

> *Clifford can't believe his father noticed.*

CLIFFORD: Huh?

GENE: Not just me—your mother always thought that's what you were gonna do.

CLIFFORD: It's just cut and paste ... see how it goes. How've you—

GENE: You'll be fine—keep your nut small, pay your dues, as long as you have a place to paint ...

> *They look at each other.*

How's she look?

CLIFFORD: OK, so-so ... she gave me some lasagne, to give you.

GENE *(thinks about Terry):* Terry. She . . . *(Gene is suddenly overwhelmed. An instant later he seals it up.)* OK kiddo. Thanks for . . .

> *They have an awkward choice: to hug goodbye or to shake hands. They stop. Start. Finally, Gene just turns and goes up toward the bandstand.*

CLIFFORD: Dad—"Why Was I Born?".

GENE: I'll play it. Two tunes in. Good to see you, kiddo.

CLIFFORD: If you think of it, call her in the morning, say thanks.

> *Gene heads up onto the bandstand.*

He's not going to remember to call her. But I have to ask, same way I ask Mom to come and hear him play.

> *Lights up on Terry in her bedroom doorway, smoking a cigarette, alone.*

TERRY: Leave your poor old lady alone, Clifford. I'm not going over there to hear that rat-bastard play. Thirty years he never took me out. *(She stops.)* And besides, if I hear him play—I get all . . . *(She starts to cry.)* You go. Godspeed, *caro figlio.*

> *Lights out on Terry.*

CLIFFORD: So long, Ma. *(To audience.)* Like I said: No clean breaks.

> *Clifford crosses to the bar, listens to Gene onstage as he starts to play "It Never Entered My Mind." We see a silhouette of Gene playing behind a scrim.*

When he's up there, blowing, he's totally in touch with everything that's going on around him. Ziggy bends a note, he echos it instantly. A car horn sounds outside, he puts it into his solo, or harmonizes under it, a second later. I used to wonder how he could sense everything while he was blowing, and almost nothing when he wasn't. Now I just wonder how many more chances will I have to hear him blow. If I have kids . . .

These guys are not even an endangered species any more. It's too late. There are no more big bands, no more territory bands. No more nonets, or tentets. No more sixty weeks a year on the road. No more jam sessions 'til dawn in the Cincinnati Zoo. When they go, that'll be it.

No one will even understand what they were doing. A fifty year blip on the screen. Men who mastered their obsession, who ignored, or didn't even notice, anything else. They played not for fame, and certainly not for money. They played for each other. To swing. To blow. Night after night, they were just burning brass. Oblivious.

> *The lights come down on the Melody Lounge as the music comes up. Curtain.*

Pulitzer, Lortel, Critics Awards

OOO
OOO
OOO
OOO
OOO
OOO **WIT**

A Full Length Play in One Act

BY MARGARET EDSON

Cast and credits appear on page 282

MARGARET EDSON was born in Washington, D.C. in 1961. Before penning her first play, Wit, *in 1995, Edson seemed destined for a career in academia, having earned degrees in history (at Smith College) and literature (a Masters at Georgetown University). Nevertheless, she had a variety of occupations, including pouring drinks in a rural Iowa bar and serving as a sales clerk in a D.C. cycle shop.*

After spending a year living in a Dominican convent in Rome, Edson began working in the oncology/AIDS unit of a research hospital, serving as a physical therapy aide and unit clerk. Though low-level jobs, they accorded Edson the opportunity to watch the way nurses interacted with patients and to see once-mighty people brought low by disease. She told the New York Times, *"Because I had no skills, I could see the whole exchange. And so being useless is really the key here to any kind of insight."*

Wit *premiered at South Coast Repertory, where it received six 1995 Los Angeles Drama Critics Awards, including best production, writing, direction (Martin Benson), lead performance (Megan Cole), lighting and the Ted Schmitt Award for a world premiere. The off-Broadway production began life at Connecticut's Long Wharf Theater, opening there on Halloween 1997. Three Connecticut Critics Circle Awards followed, including best actress, direction and play. That production, staged by Derek Anson Jones (a high school classmate of Edson) and starring Kathleen Chalfant, reached off off Broadway's MCC (Manhattan Class Company) Theater September 17, 1998. Exceptional reviews allowed the play to shift to an off-Broadway schedule October 6 and to move to the larger Union Square Theater January 7. The producers had wanted to try Broadway's Helen Hayes Theater, but the theater owners worried that such a darkly-themed work might scare away audiences and opted for* Band in Berlin *instead. When that musical quickly closed, speculation again rose as to whether*

Wit *would make the Broadway jump. The producers decided to remain at the Union Square Theater but nevertheless petitioned the Tony Administration Committee to consider* Wit *for a nomination. The request was denied.*

Though excited about Wit's *success, Edson tries not to let it interfere with her day job: first grade teacher at Centennial Place Elementary School in Atlanta.*

According to a New York Times *interview, Edson moved to Atlanta in 1997 because her partner, Linda Merrill, accepted a curator's job at the High Museum of Art. Another Edson play,* Satisfied, *about country-gospel radio in Kentucky, has not yet been produced. Edson has been quoted as saying she has no intention of writing another play after* Wit.

Concluding his rave review of Wit, *John Simon wrote, "Margaret Edson teaches elementary school in Atlanta. For this play alone, she should be handed the Harvard English Department."*

The following synopsis was prepared by David Lefkowitz.

Place: *Most of the action, but not all, takes place in a room of the University Hospital Comprehensive Cancer Center*

SYNOPSIS: The stage is empty, and furniture is rolled on and off by the Technicians. There is no break between scenes and no intermission. When we first see Vivian Bearing, Ph.D., she has a central venous access catheter over her left breast, the tubing connected to an IV pole. Vivian is *"50, tall and very thin, barefoot and completely bald. She wears two hospital gowns ... one tied in front and one tied in the back ... a baseball cap, and a hospital ID bracelet."*

VIVIAN *(in false familiarity, waving and nodding to the audience):* Hi. How are you feeling today? Great. That's just great. *(In her own professorial tone.)* This is not my standard greeting, I assure you.

I tend toward something a little more formal, a little less inquisitive, such as, say, "Hello."

But it is the standard greeting here.

There is some debate as to the correct response to this salutation. Should one reply "I feel good," using "feel" as a copulative to link the subject, "I," to its subjective complement, "good"; or "I feel well," modifying with an adverb the subject's state of being?

I don't know. I am a professor of seventeenth-century poetry, specializing in the Holy Sonnets of John Donne.

So I just say, "Fine."

Of course it is not very often that I do feel fine.

I have been asked, "How are you feeling today?" while I was throwing up into a plastic washbasin. I have been asked as I was emerging from a four-hour operation with a tube in every orifice, "How are you feeling today?"

I am waiting for the moment when someone asks me this question and I am dead. I'm a little sorry I'll miss that.

It is unfortunate that this remarkable line of inquiry has come to me so late in my career. I could have exploited its feigned solicitude to great advantage: as I was distributing the final examination to the graduate course in seventeenth-century textual criticism—"Hi. How are you feeling today?"

Of course I would not be wearing this costume at the time, so the question's *ironic significance* would not be fully apparent.

As I trust it is now.

Irony is a literary device that will necessarily be deployed to great effect.

I ardently wish this were not so. I would prefer that a play about me be cast in the mythic-heroic-pastoral mode; but the facts, most notably stage-four metastatic ovarian cancer, conspire against that. *The Faerie Queene* this is not.

And I was dismayed to discover that the play would contain elements of . . . humor.

I have been, at best, an *unwitting* accomplice. *(She pauses.)* It is not my intention to give away the plot, but I think I die at the end.

After invoking Shakespearean verse to comment on her predicament, Bearing recalls the moment she was told by her doctor, Harvey Kelekian, that she had advanced metastatic ovarian cancer.

KELEKIAN: Now it is an insidious adenocarcinoma, which has spread from the primary adnexal mass—

VIVIAN: "Insidious"?

KELEKIAN: "Insidious" means undectectable at an—

VIVIAN: "Insidious" *means* "treacherous."

KELEKIAN: Shall I continue?

VIVIAN: By all means.

While Dr. Kelekian continues with a run of technical medical jargon, Vivian vows to read about her disease and gather further information. One thing her doctor has been clear about: Vivian will need to undergo an in-patient cycle of treatments, followed by another battery of tests. The two momentarily banter about how they emphasize thoroughness when teaching their students.

VIVIAN: My students read through a text once—*once!*—and think it's time for a break.

KELEKIAN: Mine are blind.

VIVIAN: Well, mine are deaf.

KELEKIAN *(resigned, but warmly):* You just have to hope . . .

VIVIAN *(not so sure):* I suppose. *(Pause.)*

The physician informs Bearing her eight months of aggressive chemotherapy will mean being unable to teach the following semester. He adds that "It will make a significant contribution to our knowledge." He hands her a consent form to sign, asking if she wants him to explain her situation to a family member.

VIVIAN *(signing):* That won't be necessary.

KELEKIAN: Good. The important thing is for you to take the full dose of chemo-therapy. There may be times when you'll wish for a lesser dose, due to the side effects. But we've got to go full-force. The experimental phase has got to have the maximum dose to be of any use. Dr. Bearing—

VIVIAN: Yes?

KELEKIAN: You must be very tough. Do you think you can be very tough?

VIVIAN: You needn't worry.

KELEKIAN: Good. Excellent.

Kelekian and the desk exit as Vivian stands and walks forward.

VIVIAN *(hesitantly):* ..... I have stage-four metastatic ovarian cancer. There is no stage five. Oh, and I have to be very tough. It appears to be a matter, as the saying goes, of life and death . . . . .

And I know for a fact that I am tough. A demanding professor. Uncompromising. Never one to turn from a challenge. That is why I chose, while a student of the great E.M.Ashford, to study Donne.

Professor E.M. Ashford appears at her desk. An "eager and intimidated" Vivian, age 22, awaits the assessment of her essay.

E.M.: Please sit down. Your essay on Holy Sonnet Six, Miss Bearing, is a melo-drama, with a veneer of scholarship unworthy of you—to say nothing of Donne. Do it again.

VIVIAN: I, ah . . .

E.M.: You must begin with a text, Miss Bearing, not with a feeling.

Vivian has apparently missed the point of *Death Be Not Proud* because she's used "an edition of the text that is inauthentically punctuated." E.M. insists that Vivian must treat every line of the poem with the highest critical standards, including those pertaining to punctuation.

E.M.: The sonnet begins with a valiant struggle with death, calling on all the forces of intellect and drama to vanquish the enemy. But it is ultimately about overcoming the seemingly insuperable barriers separating life, death, and eternal life.

In the edition you chose, this profoundly simple meaning is sacrificed to hysterical punctuation.

And Death—*capital D*—shall be no more—*semi-colon!*
Death—*capital D*—*comma*—thou shalt die—*exclamation point!*

If you go in for this sort of thing, I suggest you take up Shakespeare.

E.M. then refers to *the* accepted scholarly source for the sonnet, where the line reads, "And death shall be no more, Death thou shalt die."

E.M.: Nothing but a breath—a comma—separates life from life everlasting. It is very simple really. With the original punctuation restored, death is no longer something to act out on a stage, with exclamation points. It's a comma, a pause.

This way, the *uncompromising* way, one learns something from this poem, wouldn't you say? Life, death. Soul, God. Past, present. Not insuperable barriers, not semicolons, just a comma.

VIVIAN: Life, death . . . I see. *(Standing.)* It's a metaphysical conceit. It's wit! I'll go back to the library and rewrite the paper—

E.M. *(standing, emphatically):* It is *not wit,* Miss Bearing. It is truth.

Ashford advises her not to go back to the library, but to take some fresh air and socialize a bit. Vivian gives it a try but can't reconcile "simple human truth" with "uncompromising scholarly attitudes." She chose the latter.

Vivian arrives at the hospital and encounters a whirlwind of activity. "The attention was flattering," she says, "for the first five minutes. Now I know how poems feel."

Tests are administered, suggested by lighting and sound cues. When a technician gives her a chest x-ray, Vivian informs him that she's a Ph.D. and an important literary scholar. He seems interested only in the procedure. Technician 2 is equally oblivious. Asked her name, Vivian tells him she's "Lucy, Countess of Bedford." The med tech replies that he doesn't see that name on his printout.

Left alone, Vivian continues filling the audience in on her background. She spent an invaluable three years studying under E.M. Ashford, alphabetizing her index cards for a study of Donne's *Devotions Upon Emergent Occasions.* Vivian's own first article was then published in a surprisingly prestigious journal. The success of her second published article—on *Death Be Not Proud*—led to a university press request for a book on the twelve Holy Sonnets. "My book, entitled *Made Cunningly,* remains an immense success, in paper as well as cloth," Vivian tells the audience. "I devote one chapter to a thorough examination of each sonnet, discussing every word in extensive detail . . . . . I summarize previous critical interpretations of the text and offer my own analysis. It is exhaustive."

As Technician 3 positions Bearing for a CT scan, Vivian tells us the salient characteristic of the Holy Sonnets is wit.

VIVIAN: To the common reader—that is to say, the undergraduate with a B-plus or better average—wit provides an invaluable exercise for sharpening the mental faculties, for stimulating the flash of comprehension that can only follow hours of exacting and seemingly pointless scrutiny . . . . . To the scholar, to the mind comprehensively trained in the subleties of seventeenth-century vocabulary, versification, and theological, historical, geographical, political and mythological allusions, Donne's wit is . . . a way to see how good you really are.

After twenty years, I can say with confidence, no one is quite as good as I.

Susie Monahan, the primary nurse, positions Vivian on the exam table and introduces Dr. Jason Posner, a clinical fellow in oncology. He tells her he took her course as a biochemistry undergraduate . . . and scored an A-minus. This time, however, it's her turn to be examined. Bearing protests that Dr. Kelekian has already examined her. Jason replies that Kelekian wanted him to examine her as well. She complies, and Jason begins the case history.

JASON: How old are you?
VIVIAN: Fifty
JASON: Are you married?
VIVIAN: No.
JASON: Are your parents living?
VIVIAN: No.
JASON: How and when did they die?
VIVIAN: My father, suddenly, when I was twenty, of a heart attack. My mother, slowly, when I was forty-one and forty-two, of cancer. Breast cancer.
JASON: Cancer?
VIVIAN: Breast cancer.
JASON: I see. Any siblings?
VIVIAN: No.
JASON: Do you have any questions so far?
VIVIAN: Not so far.

More questions about Vivian's medical history follow, though aside from a tonsillectomy she has not suffered any mental or physical ailment prior to the cancer. She first felt the pain a few months ago—"like a cramp, but not the same." Vivian elaborates on the symptoms, telling the doctor she'd be teaching and then feel a "sharp and sudden pain." She'd also undergo periods of exhaustion. Her gynecologist referred her to an internist, who then referred her to Kelekian.

Jason puts her legs in stirrups and is about to begin the physical part of the exam when he remembers he has to have a woman present. He exits to find Susie, the primary nurse, while Vivian muses, "I wish I had given him an A." To pass the time, she first recites the times table, then a section of *Death Be Not Proud*. During the pelvic exam, Jason informs Susie that he had once been a student of Vivian's.

SUSIE: Yeah, I wish I had taken some literature. I don't know anything about poetry.

JASON *(trying to be casual):* Professor Bearing was very highly regarded on campus. It looked very good on my transcript that I had taken her course. *(Silence.)* They even asked me about it in my interview for med school— *(He feels the mass and does a double take.)* Jesus! *(Tense silence. He is amazed and fascinated.)*

SUSIE: What?

VIVIAN: What?

JASON: Um. *(He tries for composure.)* Yeah. I survived Bearing's course. No problem.

Flustered, the doctor quickly finishes the exam and exits, leaving Susie to clean up. Vivian climbs off the table.

VIVIAN *(walking downstage to audience):* That . . . was . . . hard. That . . . was . . .

One thing can be said for an eight-month course of cancer treatment: it is highly educational. I am learning to suffer.

Yes, it is mildly uncomfortable to have an electrocardiogram, but the . . . agony . . . of a proctosigmoidoscopy sweeps it from memory. Yes, it was embarrassing to have to wear a nightgown all day long—two nightgowns!—but that seemed like a positive privilege compared to watching myself grow bald. Yes, having a former student give me a pelvic exam was thoroughly *degrading*—and I use the term deliberately—but I could not have imagined the depths of humiliation that—Oh God—

Vivian runs across the stage to throw up in a washbasin. She lies down on a bed, then throws up again. She remarks that if she ended up barfing her brains out, her colleagues would first jockey for her position, then put out a volume of John Donne essays in her memory. "Published *and* perished," Vivian jokes.

Vivian rings a bell, which brings Susie into the room.

SUSIE: You okay all by yourself here?

VIVIAN: Yes.

SUSIE: You're not having a lot of visitors, are you?

VIVIAN *(correcting):* None, to be precise.

SUSIE: Yeah, I didn't think so. Is there somebody you want me to call for you?

VIVIAN: That won't be necessary.

SUSIE: Well, I'll just pop my head in every once in a while to see how you're coming along. Kelekian and the fellows should be in soon. *(She touches Vivian's arm.)* If there's anything you need, you just ring.

VIVIAN *(uncomfortable with kindness):* Thank you.

Susie exits. After a moment, Vivian begins to consider how heavily time hangs for her at the hospital.

We flash forward to Grand Rounds, with Kelekian offering his diagnoses for the benefit of four Fellows following him from patient to patient. Simultaneously with

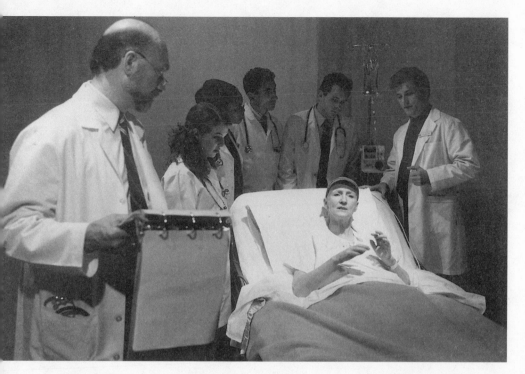

Kathleen Chalfant *(center)* as Vivian Bearing with Walter Charles *(left)* as Dr. Kelekian,
Alec Phoenix as Jason Posner and members of the company in *Wit* by Margaret Edson

his negative findings (including "full lymphatic involvement" and the removal, during first-look surgery, of Vivian's ovaries, fallopian tubes and uterus), Vivian considers the derivation of the term "Grand Rounds." "It is just like a graduate seminar.
With one important difference: in Grand Rounds, *they* read *me* like a book. Once I
did the teaching; now I am taught. This is much easier. I just hold still and look
cancerous. It requires less acting every time."

Kelekian then quizzes his Fellows on the findings, with Jason Posner, who is
resented by the others for his smarts, answering first.

JASON: The kidneys are designed to filter out impurities in the bloodstream. In
trying to filter the chemotherapeutic agent out of the bloodstream, the kidneys shut
down.

KELEKIAN: Intervention.

JASON: Hydration.

KELEKIAN: Monitoring.

JASON: Full recording of fluid intake and output, as you see here on these graphs,
to monitor hydration and kidney function. Totals monitored daily by the clinical
fellow, as per the protocol.

KELEKIAN: Anybody else. Side effects.

FELLOW 1: Nausea and vomiting.
KELEKIAN: Jason.
JASON: Routine.
FELLOW 2: Pain while urinating.
JASON: Routine. *(The Fellows are trying to catch Jason.)*
FELLOW 3: Psychological depression.
JASON: No way.

Kelekian eggs the other Fellows on to think of further relevant side effects, but they're stumped.

KELEKIAN *(to the Fellows):* Use your eyes. *(All Fellows look closely at Vivian.)* Jesus God. Hair loss.
FELLOWS *(all protesting. Vivian and Kelekian are amused):*
    —Come on.
    —You can see it.
    —It doesn't count.
    —No fair.
KELEKIAN: Jason.
JASON: Hair loss after first cycle of treatment.

The rounds being over, the Fellows exit. Jason nearly joins them, but he's stopped by Kelekian and reminded to be "clinical" and thank Vivian for her cooperation, which he does, perfunctorily. As all except Vivian exit, she comments on playing her part, noting that she'd rather know all that's wrong with her than be ignorant. She even looks up all the medical terms, which brings back her childhood fascination with word derivations. After undergoing the full treatment, Vivian feels better and is sent home.

We're transported back to Bearing's fifth birthday, with her father reading a newspaper as she explores a pile of six little white books. Tolerant but not wanting to be bothered, Mr. Bearing listens as Vivian starts reading from *The Tale of the Flopsy Bunnies.* When she comes to a tough word—"soporific"— he advises sounding it out. She does, and he explains it as something that makes you sleepy. He goes back to his newspaper, but she's had a revelation.

VIVIAN: The little bunnies in the picture are asleep! They're sleeping! Like you said, because of *soporific!*
        She stands up and Mr. Bearing exits.
The illustration bore out the meaning of the word, just as he had explained it. At the time, it seemed like magic.

So imagine the effect that the words of John Donne first had on me: ratiocination, concatenation, coruscation, tergiversation.

Medical terms are less evocative. Still, I want to know what the doctors mean when they . . . anatomize me. And I will grant that in this particular field of endeavor they possess a more potent arsenal of terminology than I. My only defense is the acquisition of vocabulary.

Vivian has returned to the hospital, owing to a serious fever. Susie runs to get Jason and a cold drink for Vivian, who worries that, in her haste to reach the hospital, she's left all the lights on in her house. Jason arrives and asks for Vivian's "vitals."

SUSIE: Temp thirty-nine point four. Pulse one hundred twenty. Respiration thirty-six. Chills and sweating.

JASON: Fever and neutropenia. It's a "shake and bake." Blood cultures and urine, stat. Admit her. Prepare for reverse isolation. Start with acetaminophen. Vitals every four hours. *(He starts to leave.)*

SUSIE *(following him):* Jason—I think you need to talk to Kelekian about lowering the dose for the next cycle. It's too much for her like this.

JASON: Lower the dose? No way. Full dose. She's tough. She can take it. Wake me up when the counts come from the lab.

Jason exits. Susie washes Vivian's face with a washcloth. The next morning, Kelekian arrives to check on the patient. He tells her she's making progress but must continue in isolation for another couple of days. Jason enters, a bit taken aback—and crabby—at having to don a paper gown, mask and gloves just to check Vivian's charts. He scans her I & O sheets, reminding himself to be "clinical" and actually interact with the patient. For her part, Vivian knows her immune system has been wiped out, and that, in her present condition, "every living thing is a health hazard." She also realizes the isolation isn't so much about her cancer as her cancer *treatment.* She appreciates the paradox and briefly fantasizes how powerful a lecture she could give regarding these ironies.

With that, Vivian disconnects her IV and treats the audience to a lecture on Donne's use of wit: "In his poems, metaphysical quandaries are addressed, but never resolved. Ingenuity, virtuosity, and a vigorous intellect that jousts with the most exalted concepts: these are the tools of wit."

Donne's Holy Sonnet Five is projected on a screen with asterisks marking several phrases, about which she makes numerous comments. She explains that in the poem's 14 lines, the protagonist goes from being a brilliant intellectual questioning God's motives to melodramatic pleading.

VIVIAN: Where is the hyperactive intellect of the first section? Where is the histrionic outpouring of the second? When the speaker considers his own *sins,* and the inevitability of God's *judgement,* he can conceive of but one resolution: to *disappear.* *(Vivian moves away from the screen.)*

Doctrine assures us that no sinner is denied *forgiveness,* not even one whose sins are overweening intellect or overwrought *dramatics.* The speaker does not need to *hide* from God's *judgment,* only to accept God's *forgiveness.* It is very simple. Suspiciously simple.

We want to correct the speaker, to remind him of the assurance of salvation. But it is too late. The poetic encounter is over. We are left to our own consciences. Have we outwitted Donne? Or have we been outwitted?

Susie interrupts the discourse to bring Vivian another medical procedure. The patient refuses, cross at being denied these satisfying mental gymnastics for yet another test. Of course, she has no choice. Afterwards, she quotes another Donne sonnet from 1609:

> This is my playes last scene, here heavens appoint
> My pilgrimages last mile; and my race
> Idly, yet quickly runne, hath this last pace,
> My spans last inch, my minutes last point,
> And gluttonous death will instantly unjoynt
> My body, 'and soule.

Vivian tells us she'd always liked that poem—until it started hitting too close to home. She's now extremely, terminally ill. She's survived eight full-dose chemo treatments, which will mean more to her doctors and their medical journals than to her own health. She observes, "My next line is supposed to be something like this: 'It is such a relief to get back to my room after these infernal tests.' This is hardly true. It would be a *relief* to be a cheerleader on her way to Daytona Beach for Spring Break. To get back to my room after those infernal tests is just the next thing that happens."

Jason comes by to check her condition and points out, patronizingly, how pleasantly surprised he is the treatments haven't shut down her kidney functions. Vivian makes a wry comment about his bedside manner; he responds, obliviously, that it's a required med school course and "a colossal waste of time for researchers."

VIVIAN: I was just wondering: why cancer?

JASON: Why cancer?

VIVIAN: Why not open-heart surgery?

JASON: Oh yeah, why not *plumbing*. Why not run a *lube rack,* for all the surgeons know about *homo sapiens sapiens*. Cancer's the only thing I ever wanted.

VIVIAN *(intrigued):* Huh.

JASON: No, really. Cancer is . . . *(Searching.)*

VIVIAN *(helping):* Awesome.

JASON *(pause):* Yeah. Yeah, that's right. It is. Awesome.

Jason goes on to explain that normal cells multiply at a brisk rate but ultimately "conk out," whereas cancer cells "just keep replicating forever." Vivian is more interested, however, in the way Jason deals with patients as people.

JASON: Everybody's got to go through it. All the great researchers. They want us to be able to converse intelligently with the clinicians. As though researchers were the impediments. The clinicians are such troglodytes. So smarmy. Like we have to hold hands to discuss creatinine clearance. Just cut the crap, I say.

VIVIAN: Are you going to be sorry when I— Do you ever miss people?

JASON: Everybody asks that. Especially girls.

VIVIAN: What do you tell them?

JASON: I tell them yes.

VIVIAN: Are they persuaded?

JASON: Some.

VIVIAN: Some. I see. *(With great difficulty.)* And what do you say when a patient is . . . apprehensive . . . frightened.

JASON: Of who?

VIVIAN: I just . . . Never mind.

Jason instantly steers the conversation back to technical doctor-patient ex-changes, then exits. Getting out of bed without her IV, Vivian notes, "The young doctor, like the senior scholar, prefers research to humanity. At the same time the senior scholar, in her pathetic state as a simpering victim, wishes the young doctor would take more interest in personal contact."

Suddenly we're back in a classroom situation, Vivian calling on a student to pick out the principal poetic device of a sonnet. Receiving no answer, Vivian offers an ultimatum: come to the class prepared, or excuse yourself from the course—and the college—altogether. A second student questions why Donne has to make everything so complex.

VIVIAN *(to the audience):* You know, someone asked me that every year. And it was always one of the smart ones. What could I say? *(To student 2.)* What do you think?

STUDENT 2: I think it's like he's hiding. I think he's really confused. I don't know, maybe he's scared, so he hides behind all this complicated stuff, hides behind this *wit.*

VIVIAN: *Hides* behind *wit?*

STUDENT 2: I mean, if it's really something he's sure of, he can say it more sim-ple—simply. He doesn't have to be such a brain, or such a performer. It doesn't have to be such a big deal.

Vivian counters that Donne might be suspicious of something that appears too simple. Yet she wants to draw the student out further, perhaps eliciting some true insight. The student sees Donne as running away from the big questions, which intrigues Vivian further. As Vivian warns us, however, the undergraduate brain can take only so much real thought, and the student gets lost trying to advance his argument. Vivian also reacts glumly when overhearing several carefree students making fun of poetry and of her, for she can appreciate wit only when it's meticu-lously applied, rather than spontaneous.

The first, unprepared student returns to talk to her after class about an extension on his paper.

VIVIAN: Don't tell me. Your grandmother died.
STUDENT 1: You knew.
VIVIAN: It was a guess.
STUDENT 1: I have to go home.
VIVIAN: Do what you will, but the paper is due when it is due.

This short meeting leaves Vivian with an unsettled feeling she can't put into words.

Vivian is then back at the hospital during the graveyard shift. Feeling lonely, she pinches her IV tubing, which brings Susie scurrying in to check on her. Susie apologizes for the occlusion and calls her patient "sweetheart"—a word Vivian ordinarily wouldn't tolerate, but this time it's okay. Vivian confesses she's confused and unable to sleep.

VIVIAN: I can't figure things out. I'm in a . . . *quandary,* having these . . . *doubts.*
SUSIE: What you're doing is very hard.
VIVIAN: Hard things are what I like best.
SUSIE: It 's not the same. It's like it's out of control, isn't it?
VIVIAN *(crying, in spite of herself):* I'm scared.
SUSIE *(stroking her):* Oh, honey, of course you are.
VIVIAN: I want . . .
SUSIE: I know. It's hard.
VIVIAN: I don't feel sure of myself any more.
SUSIE: And you used to feel sure.
VIVIAN *(crying):* Oh, yes, I used to feel sure . . . . .
SUSIE: Vivian, there's something we need to talk about, you need to think about.
          Silence.
VIVIAN: My cancer is not being cured, is it.
SUSIE: Huh-uh.
VIVIAN: They never expected it to be, did they.
SUSIE: Well, they thought the drugs would make the tumor get smaller, and it has gotten a lot smaller. But the problem is that it started in new places too. They've learned a lot for their research. It was the best thing they had to give you, the strongest drugs. There just isn't a good treatment for what you have yet, for advanced ovarian. I'm sorry. They should have explained this—
VIVIAN: I knew.
SUSIE: You did.
VIVIAN: I read between the lines.

The unthinkable being thought, Susie then brings up Vivian's "code status," that is, what to do if her heart stops. Two options face Vivian: "full code" (if the heart stops, the Code Team tries to resuscitate her in intensive care) or "do not resuscitate" (DNR). Susie notes that Doctors Kelekian and Posner invariably opt for "full code," since it's their business to save lives, and the longer the patient endures, the more research can be carried out. Vivian appreciates that scholarly angle, which Susie takes as a request for "full code."

VIVIAN: No, don't complicate the matter.
SUSIE: It's okay. It's up to you—
VIVIAN: Let it stop.
SUSIE: Really?
VIVIAN: Yes.
SUSIE: So if your heart stops beating—
VIVIAN: Just let it stop.
SUSIE: Sure?
VIVIAN: Yes.

Vivian makes Susie promise she will still be her nurse and take care of her. Susie reassures her, and exits.

VIVIAN: That certainly was a *maudlin* display . . . . . "Sweetheart?" I can't believe my life has become so . . . *corny*. But it can't be helped. I don't see any other way. We are discussing life and death, and not in the abstract, either; we are discussing *my* life and *my* death, and my brain is dulling, and poor Susie's was never sharp to begin with, and I can't conceive of any other . . . *tone*.

(Quickly.) Now is not the time for verbal swordplay, for unlikely flights of imagination and wildly shifting perspectives, for metaphysical conceit, for wit. And nothing would be worse than a detailed scholarly analysis. Erudition. Interpretation. Complication. *(Slowly.)* Now is a time for simplicity. Now is a time for, I dare say it, kindness. *(Searchingly.)* I thought being extremely smart would take care of it. But I see that I have been found out. Ooohhh. I'm scared. Oh, God. I want . . . I want . . . No. I want to hide. I just want to curl up in a little ball. *(She dives under the covers.)*

Vivian wakes in horrible pain. She is tense, agitated, fearful. Slowly she calms down and addresses the audience.
VIVIAN *(trying extremely hard):* I want to tell you how it feels. I want to explain it, to use *my* words. It's as if . . . I can't . . . There aren't . . . I'm like a student and this is the final exam and I don't know what to put down because I don't understand the question and I'm *running out of time.*

Writhing in agony, Vivian rings for Susie, who tells her about an analgesic pump which dispenses medication whenever the patient pushes a button—but Susie can't authorize it herself. The doctors rush in, Kelekian asking the moaning Vivian if she's in any pain.

VIVIAN *(sitting up, unnoticed by the staff):* Am I in pain? I don't believe this. Yes, I'm in goddamn pain. *(Furious.)* I have a fever of a hundred and one spiking to a hundred and four. And I have bone metastases in my pelvis and both femurs. *(Screaming.)* There is cancer eating away at my goddamn bones, and I did not know there could be such pain on this earth.
(She flops back on the bed and cries audibly to them.) Ooh, God.

Kelekian orders a morphine drip, though Susie suggests the aforementioned patient-controlled analgesic. She is overruled. They all leave after Kelekian assures her they'll help her through this.

VIVIAN *(weakly, painfully, leaning on her IV pole, she moves to address the audience):* Hi. How are you feeling today? *(Silence.)* These are my last coherent lines. I'll have to leave the action to the professionals.
It came so quickly, after taking so long. Not even time for a proper conclusion.
> *Vivian concentrates with all her might, and she attempts a grand summation, as if trying to conjure her own ending.*

And Death—*capital D*—shall be no more—semicolon.
Death—*capital D*—thou shalt die—*ex-cla-mation point!*

> *She looks down at herself, looks out at the audience and sees that the line doesn't work. She shakes her head and exhales with resignation.*

I'm sorry.

Vivian gets back into bed, as Susie arrives with the morphine and injects it into the IV. Deliberately, Vivian lies back, closes her eyes and folds her arms over her chest.

VIVIAN: I trust this will have a soporific effect.
SUSIE: Well, I don't know about that, but it sure makes you sleepy.
> *This strikes Vivian as delightfully funny. She starts to giggle, then laughs out loud. Susie doesn't get it.*

What's so funny? *(Vivian keeps laughing.)* What?
VIVIAN: Oh! It's that—"Soporific" *means* "makes you sleepy."
SUSIE: It does?
VIVIAN: Yes. *(Another fit of laughter.)*
SUSIE *(giggling):* Well, that was pretty dumb—
VIVIAN: No! No, no! It was *funny.*
SUSIE *(starting to catch on):* Yeah, I guess so. *(Laughing.)* In a dumb sort of way. *(This sets both of them laughing again.)* I never would have gotten it. I'm glad you explained it.
VIVIAN *(simply):* I'm a teacher.

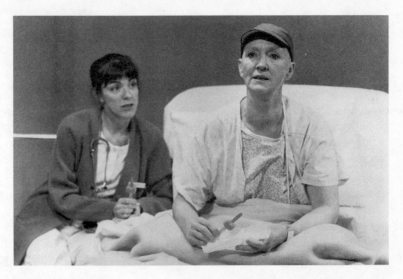

Paula Pizzi *(left)* as Susie Monahan with Kathleen Chalfant in *Wit*

Susie leaves, and then, after a long silence, she reenters with Jason, who checks the sleeping Vivian's charts. Jason admires both his former teacher's toughness at getting through the treatment they've dished out to her—eight cycles, each at full dosage—and the impressive scholarship he witnessed at first hand while taking her course.

Susie expresses surprise that a poetry teacher like Vivian would be so tough-minded. Jason compares her class to boot camp but also explains that John Donne would intentionally make his poems complicated. Jason recalls a term he coined for Donne's method in his term paper: "Salvation Anxiety."

JASON: You're this brilliant guy, I mean, brilliant—this guy makes Shakespeare sound like a Hallmark card. And you know you're a sinner. And there's this promise of salvation, the whole religious thing. But you just can't deal with it.

SUSIE: How come?

JASON: It just doesn't stand up to scrutiny. But you can't face life without it, either. So you write these screwed-up sonnets. Everything is brilliantly convoluted. Really tricky stuff. Bouncing off the walls. Like a game, to make the puzzle so complicated.

A catheter is inserted, and Susie puts things away, while wondering whether Donne ever gets through his form of anxiety, or whether Vivian's students ever get to solve the puzzle of his writings. Jason's answer is no to both questions, but examining this kind of enigma was good training for a future in research. There was nothing sentimental about 17th century poetry, Jason adds, and *"Enzyme Kinetics* was more poetic than Bearing's class. Besides, you can't think about that *meaning-of-life* garbage all the time, or you'd go nuts."

Jason exits. Susie rubs baby oil on Vivian's hands and then leaves.

Vivian then receives a guest: Professor E.M. Ashford, now 80, in town to visit her great-grandson. E.M. comforts Vivian, as Vivian breaks down and cries.

The professor volunteers to recite a Donne sonnet, but Vivian moans "Nooooooo." Instead, E.M. retrieves a book she'd gotten for her great-grandson: *The Runaway Bunny* by Margaret Wise Brown. E.M. reads this bedtime tale of a little bunny who wants to run away, but no matter what animal he chooses to become, the mommy bunny will be there for him.

E.M.: "If you run after me," said the little bunny, "I will become a fish in a trout stream, and I will swim away from you."

"If you become a fish in a trout stream," said his mother, "I will become a fisherman, and I will fish for you."

(Thinking out loud.) Look at that. A little allegory of the soul. No matter where it hides, God will find it. See, Vivian?

VIVIAN *(moaning.):*   Uhhhhhh.

E.M. finishes the book, which ends with the little bunny deciding it makes the most sense to remain exactly where he is. "Have a carrot," the mother bunny suggests.

Vivian has fallen asleep. Before leaving, E.M. kisses her maternally and quotes *Hamlet:* "And flights of angels sing thee to thy rest."

Jason strides in, not even looking at Vivian but going straight to her chart. Her kidneys have shut down.

JASON *(looks at Vivian):* Professor Bearing? Highly unresponsive. Wait a second— *(Puts his head down to her mouth and chest to listen for heartbeat and breathing.)* Wait a sec—Jesus Christ! *(Yelling.)* CALL A CODE!
> *Jason throws down the chart, dives over the bed and lies on top of her body as he reaches for the phone and punches in the numbers.*

Jason calls a Code Blue and waits for the staff to help resuscitate the patient. He starts CPR. Susie runs in and asks why he called a code, reminding him that Vivian is DNR, do not resuscitate. Jason pushes her away, saying, "She's Research!"

Susie grabs Jason and hurls him off the bed. He tries to get up; she uses the phone to try to have the code cancelled. There is a frenzy of activity as the Code Team arrives, each of them pushing Susie out of the way and ignoring her pleas to cancel the code.

The members of the Code Team *"throw Vivian's body up at the waist and stick a board underneath for CPR. In a whirlwind of sterile packaging and barked commands, one team member attaches a respirator, one begins CPR and one prepares the defibrillator. Susie and Jason try to stop them but are pushed away. The loudspeaker in the hall announces, "Cancel code, Room 707. Cancel code, Room 707."*

Both Jason and Susie try to stop the Code Team, but they do not pay attention, even when she holds up a chart that reads: "Do Not Resuscitate. Kelekian." They continue to administer electric shocks until Jason yells, "I MADE A MISTAKE!"

SUSIE: No code! Patient is no code.
CODE TEAM HEAD: Who the hell are you?
SUSIE: Sue Monahan, primary nurse.
CODE TEAM HEAD: Let me see that goddamn chart. CHART!
CODE TEAM (*slowing down*):
—What's going on?
—Should we stop?
—What's it say?
SUSIE (*pushing them away from the bed*): Patient is no code. Get away from her!
CODE TEAM HEAD (*reading*): "Do Not Resuscitate. Kelekian." Shit.

The Code Team stops working. The members argue about who screwed up on the DNR. Meanwhile, Susie lifts Vivian's blanket, allowing her to step out of bed and away from the scene. Suddenly very much alive and vital, Vivian walks toward a shining light. She removes her cap and hospital bracelet.

> *She loosens the ties, and the top gown slides to the floor. She lets the second gown fall. The instant she is naked and beautiful, reaching for the light—Lights out. Curtain.*

Critics Award

○○○
○○○
○○○
○○○
○○○
○○○ # PARADE

A Musical in Two Acts

BOOK BY ALFRED UHRY

MUSIC AND LYRICS BY JASON ROBERT BROWN

CO-CONCEIVED BY HAROLD PRINCE

Cast and credits appear on pages 243–245

ALFRED UHRY (book) was born in Atlanta in 1936. His father was a furniture dealer and by avocation an artist whose paintings are now hung in museums. Uhry can't remember when he didn't write—he didn't care much for the novel he wrote at age 9, so he immediately switched to writing for the theater, partly inspired by family visits to see such shows as South Pacific *and* Kiss Me Kate. *At Brown University, from which he graduated in 1958, he won the competition to write the book and lyrics for the varsity shows (Robert Waldman wrote the music). His first New York production of record, a 1968 Broadway musical version of* East of Eden *entitled* Here's Where I Belong, *written with Waldman and Alex Gordon, closed after only 1 performance, but Uhry was taken under the broad wing of Frank Loesser, and soon his work was appearing on all three TV networks and on various stages. For the latter, he wrote the musical* The Robber Bridegroom *(music by Waldman), produced OOB in 1974 at St. Clements, on Broadway in 1975 for 15 performances by* The Acting Company, *winning Tony and Drama Desk nominations, and returning to Broadway the following season for 145 more performances. He also provided a new adaptation of* Little Johnny Jones *for Broadway in 1982 (but again for only 1 performance);* America's Sweetheart *in 1985 for the Hartford Stage Company, and five reconstructions of period musicals for the Goodspeed Opera House.*

Uhry's Driving Miss Daisy, *his first non-musical play, opened off Broadway at Playwrights Horizons April 15, 1987, collected the 1987 Pulitzer Prize, was named a Best Play of its season and remained for 1,195 performances.*

In its Southeastern debut at Atlanta's Alliance Studio Theater it ran for 20 months and then toured Russia and China. Uhry wrote the screen play for the movie version, collecting a Writers Guild Award and an Oscar. His second Best Play, The Last Night of Ballyhoo, *premiered at the Alliance Studio Theater and then moved on to Broadway February 27, 1997 for 557 performances, carrying off the best-play Tony Award. Uhry's next was the book for the Broadway musical* Parade, *with music and lyrics by Jason Robert Brown, which opened December 17, 1998 at Lincoln Center's Vivian Beaumont Theater, attracting more critical kudos than it did audiences. Soon after its closing on February 28, it collected the award as the season's best musical from the New York Drama Critics Circle, so that it is included in synopsis herewith as one of 1998–99's major prizewinners, and from the Drama Desk voters. And the Tony voters gave their 1999 best-book and best-score awards to Uhry and his collaborator, Jason Robert Brown, for* Parade.

Uhry's screen credits include Mystic Pizza *and* Rich in Love. *He is married, with four daughters, and lives in New York City, where he has been active in Dramatists Guild affairs as a member of its council since 1988 and president of its Young Playwrights Inc. since 1992. He is also a patron of British Performing Arts Labs.*

JASON ROBERT BROWN (music and lyrics) is making his Broadway composing and writing debut with Parade. *He was born June 20, 1970 in Ossining, N.Y. where his father was in sales and his mother was an English teacher. There is no special musical tradition in his family, but he remembers that at age 7 he begged his parents for a piano—there was one in his grandfather's cellar which they dusted off and put in place for him. He must have made good use of it, because at age 18 and 19 he was studying at Eastman School of Music in Rochester, N.Y. with ambition to become a rock star, writing songs which he meant to perform himself. Stardom has eluded him so far, but not success as an orchestrator, arranger, musical director and composer. Audra McDonald has performed two of his songs on her album* Way Back to Paradise. *His musical* Songs for a New World *was produced OOB at WPA Theater October 26, 1995 under the direction of Daisy Prince, Harold Prince's daughter.* Parade *won Brown this season's Tony for best musical score (recorded in a cast album by RCA Victor). For various other activities on New York musical stages he won the 1996 Gilman and Gonzalez-Falla Musical Theater Award. He lives in New York City.*

HAROLD PRINCE (co-conceiver, director) has had such a distinguished career in 20th century theater as director and producer, beginning with the Tony-winning The Pajama Game *in 1954, that only a full-scale biography could possibly convey its true dimensions. He was born in New York City on January 30, 1928 and educated at the University of Pennsylvania (B.A. 1948), and no mere biographical sketch could outline the creative, the entertaining, the effulgent consequences of his subsequent presence for more than 45 years on the Broadway musical theater scene. He has won 20 Tony Awards, and 13 of his productions have been cited as Best Plays of their seasons in these volumes:* Fiorello *(Pulitzer Prize, Critics Award),* Fiddler on the Roof *(Critics Award),* Poor Bitos, She Loves Me, Superman, Zorba, Company *(Critics Award),* A Little Night Music *(Critics Award),* Pacific Overtures *(Critics Award),* Follies

(Critics Award), Sweeney Todd *(Critics Award),* The Phantom of the Opera *and* Kiss of the Spider Woman *(Critics Award).*

Parade *now becomes Prince's 14th featured production in* Best Plays, *this time by virtue of its Critics Award for best musical, the 9th such honor for his shows.* Parade *is special in another way, too: it is only the second time that he has accepted any kind of authorship credit on the record—as "co-conceiver"—although it is certain that he has made many, many creative contributions to his dozens of shows. His first authorship credit was as the adapter (from Sean O'Casey's autobiographies) as well as the director of the play* Grandchild of Kings *off Broadway February 16, 1992 for 97 performances.*

Harold Prince received Kennedy Center Honors in 1994. He has served as a member of the NEA's National Council of the Arts and the League of American Theaters (past president) and as a trustee of the New York Public Library.

ACT I

Scene 1

SYNOPSIS: As a sort of prologue, there are *"military drums in the distance, then an explosive clang from the orchestra, and the lights rise on a verdant field in the small town of Marietta, Georgia, 20 miles from Atlanta. A picturesque and glorious field with beautiful red hills far off behind it. There is also a large, full oak tree occupying much of stage left. This is a significant tree, and a significant field in our play, but we will not see Marietta again until the second to last scene.*

"The year is 1862. A Confederate Young Soldier stands alone in the field, facing us. He is newly enlisted, his uniform is crisp, his pack is full. He stands still."

YOUNG SOLDIER *(sings "The Old Red Hills of Home"):*
    Fare well, my Lila—
    I'll write every evening.
    I've carved our names
    In the trunk of this tree
    Fare well, my Lila—
    I miss you already,
    And dream of the day
    When I'll hold you again
    In a home safe from fear,
    When the Southland is free

    I go to fight for these old hills behind me
    These old red hills of home.
    I go to fight, for these old hills remind me
    Of a way of life that's pure—
    Of the truth that must endure—

In a town called Marietta
In the old red hills of home.

A drumburst summons a crowd of townspeople running onstage and settling in, their backs to the audience, to get a good view of an approaching parade.

Fifty one years later—on April 26, 1913—The lights come up on Peachtree Street, Atlanta, on an overcast Confederate Memorial Day.*"This is the heart of industrial Georgia, and this frenetic city is as far removed as possible from the gentility of Marietta and the antebellum South."* The Young Soldier moves downstage, where an Aide and his Assistant are placing an armchair. The Young Soldier makes no reply when the Aide addresses him as "Captain" and comments that it's not a very nice day for a parade.

ASSISTANT: I guess he's hard of hearing. I wonder how he lost that leg?
AIDE *(ignoring her; to the Soldier):* I said we're supposed to escort.
> *The Old Soldier is revealed, wearing the same uniform as his young counterpart, but he is a grizzled, bitter man, worn down and missing his right leg. The Young Soldier fades from view.*
OLD SOLDIER: Quit hollerin'! I'm old, not deaf.
AIDE: Your men from the fifty-fifth will be ridin' on their own float in the parade!
OLD SOLDIER: Me and my boys marched into Chickamauga fifty years ago, and we'll march down Peachtree Street today.
AIDE: I guess they can march. But you are ridin' in the parade!
OLD SOLDIER: Quit hoverin'!

As the Aide and Assistant depart, the Soldier, once young, now old, struggles up out of the chair to address his Lila and remember the sacrifices made in defense of the old red hills once more in song, while the parade passes by, seen *"from the viewpoint of someone standing five feet deep in a crowd"* as a procession of massed Confederate flags and the tops of musical instruments. The Townspeople join the Soldier in song. They continue to sing after he exits, "We'll sing 'Dixie' once again/ For the men of Marietta/For the fathers of Atlanta/Who gave everything for Georgia/And the old red hills of home!"

The crowd freezes as the lights go down.

Scene 2

In the bedroom of Leo and Lucille Frank, *"decorated with stodgy, heavy furniture,"* Lucille, 20, *"the quintessential Southern wife, deferential and well-mannered,"* is putting up her hair. Leo, *"some years older . . . . . reserved, a bit stiff—wearing thick glasses, a three-piece suit, watch chain across his chest,"* comes into the room. He is on his way to work, although Lucille had hoped they could go on a picnic to celebrate the holiday.

LEO: Confederate Memorial Day is asinine. Why would anyone want to celebrate losing a war?

LUCILLE *(flirting):* I guess that's what I get for marryin' a Yankee.

LEO *(not flirting):* You dropped a pin.

LUCILLE: Minnie will get it when she cleans up.

> *This irritates him. He picks up the hairpin and puts it on the vanity.*

I was just sure today would be a day off.

LEO: Not for the superintendent.

LUCILLE: Superintendent! Honestly, the way you slave yourself down there, a person'd think you owned that old pencil factory.

LEO: Don't be such a meshuggeneh!

LUCILLE: Why do you use words like that?

LEO: Because they're Jewish words and I'm Jewish.

LUCILLE: Well, I am too, but it doesn't mean I have to speak a foreign language!

Leo protests that he's working extra hard to save up enough money so that they can finally "procreate." He leaves for work as Lucille continues fixing her hair.

Scene 3

The lights come up on the Townspeople still watching a parade that is going full blast. They sing their city anthem.

TOWNSPEOPLE *(sing "Dream of Atlanta"):*
> Ever more lives the dream of Atlanta
> Ever more Her eternal Pride!
> Strong and sure is the dream of Atlanta
> When Her Brothers are unified!
> And the sound of Her Voice is clearer
> When Her People are proud and free!
> Not a star to the sky could be nearer
> Than my heart is, Atlanta, to thee!

Standing on a float, Hugh Dorsey, the district attorney, introduces Governor John Slaton, accompanied by his wife Sally, to the cheering throng. Speaking into a microphone, Slaton asserts that the men and women of Georgia were never defeated, though they suffered greatly in defending their homeland.

Leo Frank is seen trying to make his way very cautiously through the crowd. He has a dream, too—he often dreams that he is back in Brooklyn with people like himself.

LEO *(sings "How Can I Call This Home?"):*
> These people make me tense
> I live in fear they'll start a conversation

These people make no sense:
They talk and I just stare and shut my mouth.
It's like a foreign land
I didn't understand
That being Southern's not just being in the South!
When I look out on all this,
How can I call this home?

Even his fellow Jews "are not like Jews," Leo sings, continuing to pick his way very carefully through a crowd that is listening to Governor Slaton express his pride in his city and his state. Leo finally exits, while Slaton's float moves off to vigorous applause.

The crowd opens up, revealing Frankie Epps, 16, *"with the air of a know-it-all."* He boards a street car and joins Mary Phagan, almost 14, *"dressed up to beat the band in a fancy white dress with lavender sash and matching parasol."* They embark upon a teenage flirtation, as at first she pretends not to notice him, then Frankie calls attention to himself by pulling her hair ribbon and inviting her to go to the movies with him in the song "The Picture Show." Mary's mother won't let her accept such an invitation until after she turns 16, she answers Frankie, as she moves away from him to a seat scross the aisle. Frankie offers her a look at the book he is carrying, and chewing gum, but she will have none of either. He crosses to sit next to her and insinuates that he might invite Iola Stover, whose mother is more liberal. "I hope you do," sings Mary, as she stands up to leave the streetcar.

FRANKIE: Where you goin'?
MARY: To the factory. I didn't get my pay this week.
FRANKIE: Okay. I'll see you at the parade.
MARY: Or at the picture show.
FRANKIE: What? I thought your mama wouldn't let you.
MARY: She will with Essie and Betty Jean. Just not with you!

"Bye, Sunshine," Frankie calls, as they get off the streetcar. Frankie issues an invitation to Iola, as the crowd closes in and the lights go down.

Scene 4

The crowd, still watching the parade and singing, moves apart to reveal the National Pencil Factory with Leo sitting at his desk, checking figures in an account book and concluding, in the song "Leo at Work," that something is wrong, they don't add up as they should. At the same time, back at the Frank home, Lucille has her own song, "What Am I Waiting For?", recalling Leo's courtship and her reaction to it. Leo was everything she wanted, but she hesitated.

Brent Carver as Leo Frank and Christy Carlson Romano as Mary Phagan in the
musical *Parade,* with book by Alfred Uhry and score by Jason Robert Brown
(both Tony Award winners), under Harold Prince's direction

LUCILLE *(sings):*
   Didn't my wishes come true for me
   The day he walked through the door?
   Isn't he all that I knew he'd be?
   Brilliant and filled with humility?
   Loyal and stable as any tree?
   So why do I wait for more?
   What am I waiting for?

Mary Phagan appears in the office doorway, startling Leo, who doesn't see her
at first. She has come to pick up her pay. Leo counts it out, puts it in an envelope
and enters it in the ledger.

LEO: Twelve hours, ten cents an hour. One dollar and twenty cents. Here you
are.
MARY: Thank you, sir.
         He nods, goes back to his bookkeeping. She walks toward the door, then
         turns. The drums of the parade are becoming audible through the window.
Mr. Frank?
         He finishes a sum at his ledger, looks up.
LEO: What is it?
MARY: Happy Memorial Day.

Lights linger on Mary and Leo, he at his desk, she in her finery at the door. Neither moves. Lights down.

TOWNSPEOPLE *(singing from offstage):*

Not a star to the sky could be nearer

Than my heart is, Atlanta, to thee!

We see dimly the street level front entrance of the factory featuring an impressive staircase leading to the second floor and Leo's office. More apparently, under the staircase, Jim Conley, a black janitor, is asleep while his broom sits idly beside him. Blackout.

Scene 5

The doorbell rings and the lights come up on the Frank home, with Lucille wearing a wrapper as she opens the door to two men, Starnes and Ivey, asking for Leo. Leo is wearing trousers and is buttoning his shirt as he enters, clearly upset. The men identify themselves as policemen and require Leo to come with them immediately. Leo fears that something has gone wrong at the factory—a fire, maybe, but he is only told that "A tragedy has occurred." His reaction is, "A tragedy? What? Is somebody dead? Is somebody dead?"

"Starnes and Ivey exchange looks," as the scene blacks out.

Scene 6

A bright light shines on Newt Lee, who is chained hand and foot and is undergoing some kind of interrogation in what appears to be a police station. *"A single note repeats insistently in the bass,"* as he gives his testimony.

NEWT *(sings "I Am Trying to Remember . . . "):*

I am tryin' to remember . . .

I was checkin' roun' the fact'ry,

And I went into the basement,

Down the stairs into the basement

And I shine my light around here,

In the corners and the ceiling,

And I'm 'bout to check the washroom

When my light, it kinda catches

On this pile of rags in the middle of the room . . .

Lights up on the factory basement, and we see the body covered with a dirty cloth. Starnes and Ivey bring in Leo, who is very nervous. Starnes whips the cloth off the body.

LEO *(trembling, nearly fainting):* Oh my God! Oh my God! Oh my God!

STARNES: Do you know who this is, Mr. Frank?

LEO: Oh God! It's the little girl I paid yesterday. She came up to my office.

IVEY: Can you give us her name, sir?

LEO *(extremely emotional):* I-I-I can't think! Farrell? No. Oh God! Faley? Pha-gan? The name is Phagan—P–H–A–G–A–N.

STARNES *(writing it down):* Phagan.

NEWT *(sings):*

>I ain't seen no pile o' rags there before,
>So I go over and I kick it,
>And I shine down my light and Lord,
>Lord, ain't no pile of rags at all . . .

LEO: Will this be in the newspapers?

IVEY: Does that bother you, sir?

LEO: Well, of course it bothers me! How does it look for the company to have a child killed in the basement?

STARNES: Was she killed in the basement, Mr. Frank?

LEO: I would assume so, I—Who did it? Do you know who did it yet?

>*No response from the detectives.*

NEWT *(sings):*

>This small white body
>With her tongue stickin' out,
>This pretty little child
>With her eyes wide open . . .

LEO: Oh no. You don't think it was my night watchman?

>*No answer.*

Newt? Newt Lee? You think it was Newt?

>*Silence.*

NEWT *(sings):*

>So I ran to the phone
>And I called Mr. Frank,
>But the phone kep' ringin',
>So I called y'all to help me—
>Mr. Frank, he didn't answer . . .
>And that's all I can remember.

LEO: Oh God! Oh my God! You think—you think—that's absurd! It's prepos-terous. I was at home all night! I didn't even know this child. I only remembered her name because she was in my office yesterday. How could you possibly—

>*Panicked, he starts taking off his clothes, tearing at them, the jacket, the shirt, the undershirt, the trousers, opening the union suit as he speaks.*

Look! Look! No marks on me! Write that down! Where are the scratches? Where are the bruises? Look! Nothing! I want you to write it down. Look at me! What do you see? Nothing!

IVEY: Put your clothes on, Mr. Frank.

LEO: Can I go home now and have my breakfast?

IVEY: No, sir, I'm 'fraid you can't do that.

Mrs. Phagan, *"a pretty but faded country woman in her early 30s,"* is seen coming toward the factory with her sister Lizzie, in search of her daughter Mary. Inside the factory, Starnes suggests to Leo that he'll need a lawyer, and Leo names one Nathan Rosenblatt. Mrs. Phagan enters and asks the policeman about her daughter, as the scene blacks out.

Scene 7

Toward sunrise the next day, Britt Craig, *"middle 20s, inebriated, disheveled and still good looking and absolutely charming,"* tries to get his friend MacDaniel to let him into his closed saloon for a drink but is turned down. Walking along, in the song "Big News," Craig complains that the Atlanta stories a reporter like himself is assigned to cover are so trivial.

CRAIG *(sings):*
You got a kitten up a tree?
Well, come to me! And I'll see
It makes it on the front page!
The Mayor's mother broke her toe?
They gotta know!
Stop the press—it's a mess!
It's the scandal of the age!!
Hell, it's big news!
Another shock to rock Atlanta!
Another information feast
From the gateway to the whole Southeast!

But Craig runs into Starnes and Ivey, who inform him they have something that might interest him as a newspaperman. Craig pulls himself together, neatens himself up and joins a group of reporters in the Municipal Builiding. He hears District Attorney Dorsey *("in his 40s—intense, driven—a man on his way up")* announce that two suspects—the Negro watchman Ludie Newton Lee and the superintendant Leo Max Frankel—are being held "for further questioning" regarding the murder of Mary Phagan. Craig comments that they must have a strong reason for detaining a white man like Leo Frank.

Scene 8

In his cell, Leo curtly refuses the greasy food brought by the Guard. Lucille comes in to see him. He believes his lawyer will arrange for his release today. She has brought him a package of toilet articles, etc., which he doesn't think he'll need. Leo, extremely upset and frightened by his predicament, shies away from Lucille's attempt to touch him and orders the Guard to show her out.

Scene 9

District Attorney Dorsey and Governor Slaton are conferring in Slaton's office.

SLATON: Good people of Georgia been raisin' hell about children bein' forced to work in fact'ries. Now they gonna read in their newspapers 'bout a thirteen-year-old girl fastenin' erasers to pencil caps—200 caps an hour, ten hours a day, six days a week. And not only that, she got herself killed doin' it! Know who they're gonna blame?

DORSEY: Well, certainly not you, Governor!

SLATON: Damn right they'll blame me. And you. And ev'rybody else holdin' public office. We gotta get to the bottom of this one fast.

DORSEY: Well, they're holdin' two suspects over yonder at the Fulton Tower.

SLATON: Good for them. It's up to you to convict one of 'em.

DORSEY: Done.

SLATON: Done my ass! You got a lousy conviction record, Hughie. How long you think they're gonna keep you in office if you let this one wriggle off the hook?
    Lights down.

Scene 10

The Mourners at Mary Phagan's funeral sing a traditional hymn, "There Is a Fountain": "There is a fountain filled with blood/Drawn from Immanuel's veins . . . . . /And sinners plunged beneath that flood/Lose all their guilty stains." Craig sees that Frankie Epps, Mary Phagan's teen-aged suitor, is taking her death very hard.

FRANKIE: *(sings "It Don't Make Sense"):*
    Did you ever hear her laugh?
    When she laughed, you swore you'd never cry again.
    Did you ever see her smile?
    Her smile was like a glass of lemonade.
    And she said funny things,
    And she wore pretty dresses,
    And she liked to see the pictures at the VFW hall,
    And she loved ridin' swings,
    And she liked cotton candy,
    But I think she liked the pictures best of all . . . . .

    God forgive me what I wish right now.
    I don't know the coward's name.
    I don't know the bastard's face.
    But I swear right now to God
    He ain't never gonna git away with what he done to Mary!

Tom Watson, the editor and publisher of the *Jeffersonian*, a paper he says "speaks for every right thinking Christian in this state," greets Slaton and introduces himself to Slaton's wife Sally, who clearly is not pleased to meet him. Watson kneels by Mary's coffin while the Slatons depart, Sally commenting that Watson is a dangerous man, Slaton that Watson is merely a buffoon.

The lights change to show Newt Lee being interrogated by Dorsey in the presence of Ivey and Starnes. The District Attorney, trying to persuade Newt to confess, suggests that it might have been merely an accident, Newt was the victim of an irresistable, impulsive force. Newt merely shakes his head and recites his prayers. Finally Dorsey gives up and tells the policemen to release Newt, commenting, "Hangin' another Nigra ain't enough this time. We gotta do better. Let him go."

At the grave, Watson is singing "Watson's Lullaby": "Sleep, sleep, little angel . . . . . /Never you cry/Justice is nigh!/Soon Armageddon comes."

Scene 11

Dorsey is telling the policemen he has decided that Leo Frank is the murderer. The evidence is in Leo's looks and behavior.

DORSEY *(sings "Somethin' Ain't Right"):*
  It's in his hands:
  See how he rubs 'em both together
  Like he's tryin' to get 'em clean?
  It's in his eyes:
  Wonder why he stares at the floor
  And won't look you straight in the face?
  Somethin' ain't right.
  I can tell, somethin' ain't right.
  I can see it in his eyes, boys.

It would be good to have an eyewitness, Starnes remarks. Dorsey orders the policemen to go out and find one.

Scene 12

Craig sings that his career has now taken a leap forward with "Real Big News": "Take this superstitious city, add one little Jew from Brooklyn/Plus a college education, and a mousy little wife/And big news! Real big news!/That poor sucker saved my life!"

Leo Frank is now the only suspect, and Craig goes out to interview people on the subject. Everybody has an accusatory tale to tell or a wild rumor to pass on about Leo's behavior and wealth.

Scene 13

Leo is in his cell, dressed now in prison garb, reading a newspaper fabrication about how he was supposed to have gotten a high school girl pregnant. Luther Z. Rosser *("an unkempt whale of a man with stains on his jacket, a rumpled shirt, frayed collar, etc.")* comes in and introduces himself as Leo's lawyer, sent to him by Nathan Rosenblatt.

LEO: Why isn't he here?

ROSSER: Cause he knows I'll represent you better. A drunk shouldn't defend another drunk. A Jew shouldn't defend another Jew. Makes sense, don't it? Can you see without those specs?

LEO: No.

ROSSER: Get rid of 'em anyway.

LEO: Why?

ROSSER: Because you look like a goddam chicken hawk blinkin' at me behind those things. And that hair. Who cut it? An undertaker? Problem is you don't look a lot like a real person, Leo. No wonder everybody thinks you tore into that little girl. I kinda think so myself.

LEO: Now just a minute!

ROSSER: You wanna walk outa here?

LEO: Of course.

ROSSER: Then act more like a good ol' boy.

LEO: Be specific.

ROSSER: Okay. Don't say things like "specific."

Rosser gives Leo further advice about changing his style. And he wants Leo to arrange a conjugal visit and get his wife pregnant.

In his office, Dorsey is interviewing Jim Conley *("black, in his late 20s—muscular, self assured, quick-witted and dressed in 'street people' hand-me-downs. He manages to be charming, even sexy in a dangerous way")*. Conley (whom we have glimpsed sleeping under the stairs at the pencil factory) was hired about a year ago for janitorial duties. Conley has noticed that Leo wrings his hands a lot. Dorsey suggests that Conley might have seen Leo asking the factory girls into his private office.

Back at the jail, Rosser continues to advise Leo.

ROSSER: We're gonna hafta get some of your mama's recipes for the ladies' page, long as they ain't too Yankee-fied or peculiar. Potato salad, that's always a good one. Jews do eat potato salad, don't they?

LEO: May I be honest with you?

ROSSER: You gotta be.

LEO: I don't like you. In fact, I dislike you intensely.

ROSSER: You know, I'm gettin' a feelin' 'bout you, Leo. And when I get a feelin', I work up a strategy. And when I work up a strategy, I win. Ev'ry goddamn time. You don't like me? Fine, I don't like you either. But I swear to God and Jesus and ev'rybody else that I'm gonna win this case, and send you home.

LEO: You're growing on me.

They shake hands.

Dorsey reviews Conley's record of arrests for disorderly conduct and notes that once Conley simply walked away from a chain gang. "You know what that makes you? An escaped convict," Dorsey says. "Now, what should we do about that?" Conley replies, "Now what was that you asked me about Mr. Frank?" The two exchange smiles—Dorsey has found his "eyewitness." Reporters are soon singing out the news that Leo Frank has been indicted on a murder charge to be prosecuted by Dorsey at a trial scheduled about a month in the future.

Scene 14

Lucille has refused all interviews, but reporters harass her until she spills a basket of laundry and is reduced to tears. After the others leave, Craig stays to help her pick things up.

LUCILLE *(sings "You Don't Know This Man")*:
    You don't know this man.
    You don't even try.
    When a man writes his mother every Sunday,
    Pays his bills before they're due,
    Works so hard to feed his family—
    There's your murderer for you—
    And you stand here spitting words
    That you know aren't true.

Craig comments, "You're sayin' he's decent, you're sayin' he's honest, but you're not sayin' he's innocent." Lucille picks up her laundry basket and walks away.

Scene 15

Leo and Lucille are separated by a partition and observed by the Guard in the prison's visitors' room. Leo is worried about the bills being paid on time, as they won't let him have his check book to do it himself. Lucille assures him she'll take care of it. But she wants to go away and visit her aunt in Savannah. She doesn't think she can endure going through the trial, being stared at while terrible things are said about her husband. "You have to be there!" Leo insists, "You have to be there!" The lights fade as Lucille exits.

Scene 16

Outside the Atlanta Courthouse, a throng is peering into the windows while the musical number "It Is Time Now" begins with Fiddlin' John standing on a crate and accompanying himself with his violin. He sings, "People of Atlanta/Swear that some-one's/Gonna pay." Tom Watson joins him with "I have come/To see the Devil/Get his just/And true reward!"

Inside, Judge Roan *("an unwell and elderly Southern gentleman")* presides. The courtroom is stifling hot despite its electric fans, crowded with *"the whole range of citizenry"* as spectators. Fiddlin' John exhorts them.

FIDDLIN' JOHN *(sings):*
    People of Atlanta,
    Better bow your heads in shame.

    There's a man who came
    And spit on your fine city's name.

    People of Atlanta,
    All are victims of this crime!
    It is time now!
WATSON *(sings):*
    It is time now!
ALL *(sing):*
    It is time!

Leo enters with Rosser—he hasn't taken his lawyer's advice about altering his appearance. Lucille's chair is conspicuously empty. Judge Roan gives the signal for the trial to begin. Dorsey rises and addresses the jury.

DORSEY *(sings "Twenty Miles From Marietta"):*
    There is a farmhouse in Marietta,
    Kinda battered and forlorn,
    And in that farmhouse, fourteen years ago,
    A girl named Mary was born.
    And she would dance in fields of cotton.
    She had a tree where she could play,
    But when her daddy died, two years ago,
    Mary and her mama moved away.
    It's only twenty miles from Marietta
    To a fact'ry in the center of this town,
    And twenty miles was all it took
    To strike that sweet girl down.

Lucille enters the courtroom, eyes down, not even looking at Leo as she takes her seat. The District Attorney continues, "People of Atlanta fought for freedom to their graves/And now their city is a fact'ry and their children are its slaves," arousing the jeers of the crowd as he points to Leo.

Judge Roan bangs his gavel, and now Frankie Epps is on the witness stand remembering the meeting with Mary on the streetcar. A vision of Mary dressed as she was the day of the parade appears in the courtroom, so that Frankie's testimony is presented as a scene between the two teenagers. Mary tells him she's uneasy about going to Leo's office because he always looks at her in a strange way.

FRANKIE: What does he do?
MARY *(sings):*
   He calls my name,
   I turn my head,
   He got no words to say.
   His eyes get big,
   My face gets red,
   And I want to run away,
   And he looks . . .
   And I wait . . .
   And he smiles . . .
FRANKIE: You better tell on him.
MARY: Tell who? He's the boss.
FRANKIE: He do the other girls that way?
MARY: I guess. Some of 'em.

In the courtroom, Frankie blurts out to Leo that he wishes he'd accompanied Mary to the office and "broke your damn face!", to the crowd's approval. Rosser declines to cross-examine Frankie, a decision Leo can't understand. In explanation, Rosser says, "Forget about him. I got us a strategy." And in spite of Leo's questions, Rosser refuses to reveal what that strategy is.

Iola, Essie and Monteen take the witness stand in the song "The Factory Girls" and give similar testimony about Leo's behavior, passing too close to them in the hall, staring at them until they blush and feel uncomfortable in his presence. Their representation of Leo as a philanderer is portrayed as Mary's was, in imaginary action, with Leo joining the girls, singing and dancing and acting out a caricature of himself.

LEO *(sings "Come Up to My Office"):*
   Why don'tcha come up to my office?
   Got a couple o' things you might like to see.
   Why don'tcha come up to my office,
   About two-fifteen till a quarter to three?
   If you could maybe swing by, honey,

Well, you know it'd be okay with me
If you came, if you came, if you came
If you came to my office . . . . .
> *Leo continues dancing, while the girls, in fear, stare straight forward, avoiding his glance.*

GIRLS *(sing):*
He calls my name
I turn my head
He got no words to say . . .
His eyes get big,
My face gets red,
And I want to run away.
> *And now Leo is still, staring at Iola, rubbing his hands slowly together. The other girls take their seats.*

IOLA *(sings):*
And he looks,
And I wait,
And he smiles.
> *Leo sits at the defense table, still facing forward. Lucille is in her chair behind him, each in their own light.*

LEO: She's lying!

ROSSER: Sit down, Leo. And shut up. I'm not just sittin' on my ass here. I'm workin' out a strategy. We're gonna be fine.

LEO: Tell me!

ROSSER: When it's time, I will.

LEO: Somebody told them to say all that. They were coached! They were coached!

Now it's Newt Lee's turn to take the stand. He is led by Dorsey's questioning, somewhat reluctantly, to testify that he saw Leo looking through the doorway of the girls' dressing room while they were in there changing clothes. Leo cries "Shame!" at Newt, whom he has always treated well, and Rosser commands him to shut up.

Next comes Mrs. Phagan, who describes the outfit her daughter Mary was wearing on Memorial Day. Dorsey holds up *"a small pile of torn, ruined clothes,"* and the courtroom explodes in anger. Then all freeze as *"delicate waltzing music can be heard,"* and Mrs. Phagan rises to sing "My Child Will Forgive Me" for not having protected her and paid more attention to her needs.

MRS. PHAGAN *(sings):*
My child will be safe in the arms of the Lord,
And as pure as the day of her birth.
My child will be cozied and blessed and adored
As she never could be here on Earth.
And my child will be watchin' me, givin' me faith

In *Parade*'s courtroom scene, Lucille Frank (Carolee Carmello, *front row center* of spectators) watches her husband Leo *(standing, at right)* and his lawyer Luther Rosser (J.B. Adams, *seated*)

In a future that's golden and new.
My Mary will teach me to open my heart,
And so I forgive you,
Jew.

> *She sings the word right to Leo, who is shaken.*

Next to testify is Jim Conley, now an impressive presence, neatly dressed. The crowd wonders what Conley can have to say about the murder. Conley soon satisfies their curiosity.

CONLEY *(sings "That's What He Said"):*
He tol' me to watch the door
"Watch the door"—That's what he said.
That's what he said—I should make sure
No one came and interrupted.

I'd say once or twice a month,
He'd tell me, "Jim you watch the door—
I got a lady comin'.
I got a lady comin'."
Like I said, once or twice a month,
There'd be a lady come to call
And he'd say, "Jim, you watch the door,"
That's what he said.
And once, I remember it was two ladies. Another time, there was a black gentleman
from Chicago.
ROSSER: Objection!
JUDGE ROAN: Mr. Dorsey, will you instruct your witness to answer only the questions put to him?
DORSEY: Jim, do you understand the man?
CONLEY: Yessir.

Dorsey then asks Conley to describe the events of Memorial Day morning. Continuing to do so in song, Conley testifies that Leo told him he expected a visit from a girl named Mary. She arrived, and after a while Conley heard Leo calling out, went to investigate and found the little girl *"crumpled in the corner"*—the result of a game they were playing that went wrong, Leo told him. Leo thought she was just hurt, but Conley ascertained that she was dead. Ordered by Leo, who gave him a hundred dollars, Conley wrapped the body in a gunny sack and deposited it in the basement. Then Leo said (Conley finishes in song), "There ain't no reason I should hang/You got money in your pocket and there's plenty more o' that/I got wealthy friends an' family, and a wife who's dumb and fat/I got rich folks out in Brooklyn if I need somewheres to go/And these stupid rednecks never gonna know!"

Rosser shouts "Objection! Goddammit, objection!" but the crowd has been whipped into a frenzy of anger and demands "Hang the killer!" The Judge points out that under Georgia law the defendant in a murder trial cannot testify in his own defense but is permitted to make a statement at this time. Leo initially declines to make a statement, but Rosser insists. Leo says, "I'm not prepared!" And Rosser responds, "I know. That's my strategy." Leo nervously rises to take the stand.

LEO (sings "Hard to Speak My Heart"):
    It's hard to speak my heart.
    I'm not a man who bares his soul.
    I let the moment pass me by—
    I stay where I am in control.
    I hide behind my work,
    Safe and sure of what to say ...
    I know I must seem hard,
    I know I must seem cold.
    I never touched that girl—

You think I'd hurt a child yet?
I'd hardly seen her face before—
I swear—I swore we'd barely met.
These people try to scare you
With things I've never said.
I know it makes no sense.
I swear I don't know why . . .
  Lights go down on everything but Leo and Lucille.
You see me as I am—You can't believe I'd lie—
You can't believe I'd do these deeds—
A little man who's scared and blind,
Too lost to find the words he needs.
I never touched that child—
God—I never raised my hand!
I stand before you now . . .
Incredibly afraid.
I pray you understand.

Leo and Lucille lock and hold eyes—it is clear that she now knows he is innocent. In his summation, Rosser tells the jury, "Gentlemen, I have just taken the biggest gamble of my entire career. I forced Leo Frank to speak to you. I did not coach him or rehearse him or have any idea what he was going to say. Why would I do such a dangerous thing? Because I knew in the marrow of my bones that he was innocent. Because I knew you would recognize simon-pure truth when you heard it. Gentlemen, look Leo Frank in the eye. Look hard. Don't be afraid of what you see. Because it is the truth, and Leo Frank is innocent."

Dorsey begins his summation and once again waves aloft Mary's bloody clothing and demands a verdict of guilty. The jury is swayed and, to the crowd's delight, brings in a guilty verdict. As one after another of the jury is polled and the city's noon bells ring out, *"Leo looks at Lucille as the voices drone on and the bells chime. She reaches out her hand to touch his face . . . . . They embrace each other, terrified."* Curtain.

ACT II

Scene 1

Judge Roan declares Leo's appeal rejected and sets the date for his execution by hanging. Another year's Memorial Day parade is seen in progress, *"but a little slower than the first time. Discordant."* One of the spectators is Craig, and he turns to face us and update us on the situation.

CRAIG *(sings "It Goes On and On"):*
> We got a murder—that ain't enough.
> We got a trial—that ain't enough.
> Poor Mary died one year ago an'
> Still this story keeps on growin'!
> It goes on and on and on . . .
>
> He keeps on fightin'—he files appeals.
> He gets rejected—tries making deals.
> I got a plaque and a citation
> From the Press Association
> And it goes on and on and on . . .

In fact, Craig is now famous from coast to coast for his coverage of this case, which is aiming for Washington after denial of appeal by the Georgia Supreme Court.

In his cell, Leo is poring over law books when Rosser comes in to tell him that the Supreme Court is about to rule on one of his appeals, and he is preparing another one. He is surpised to see Leo reading the law himself from books Lucille has brought him.

ROSSER: Now, listen here. You just leave all the legal doo-wacka-doo to me.

LEO: And what'll you do when they reject this appeal like they did the first one?

ROSSER: Who says they will?

LEO: You know what? I'm all those evil things Hugh Dorsey keeps saying I am. I'm a Yankee, and I'm college educated, and I have an extensive vocabulary. Oh, and I'm a Jew of course! And you know what us Jews are, don't you? Smart!
  He goes back to the law book.
Malice. Mandamus. Quo Warranto. Statute of Limitations. Subpoena.

ROSSER: Stay with me, Leo.

LEO: And do what? End up on the wrong end of a rope? Here. Get this to that Craig fellow at the newspaper.
  He hands him a stack of letters.
And this one goes to Mr. Adolph Ochs at the New York *Times.* And this one is to the Chief Justice of the Supreme Court.

ROSSER: Have you lost your mind completely?

LEO: While you were sitting in that courtroom developing that brilliant strategy of yours, Hugh Dorsey was getting away with murder. My murder! I read in this book that the prosecution in a murder case carried the burden of proof. He proved nothing. I was railroaded by redneck savages, and people need to know that.

ROSSER: Come on, Leo. People know ev'rything there is to know about your case.

LEO: I don't mean Southern people. I mean real people. Oh, and one more thing.

ROSSER: What's that?

LEO: You're fired.
> *Blackout.*

Lights come up on Craig at the parade, informing us, "Leo's gonna prove they got the verdict all wrong/Stirrin' up emotions that can get pretty strong—", so that there is no end to public controversy over this tragedy—it goes on and on and on and on. Craig exits.

Lights are up on a black couple downstage. Riley is polishing shoes and Angela is ironing the wash, as they sing "A Rumblin' and a Rollin' " to describe the public energy that is coming down from the North, generated by interest in the imminent hanging of a white man.

RILEY *(sings):*
> They're gonna yell, "Set that man free!"
>> *We see Newt Lee carrying his lantern through the factory, making his rounds.*

NEWT *(sings):*
> Well, they sure ain't talkin' 'bout me.

ALL THREE *(sing):*
> Now there's a rumblin' and a rollin'
> Here comes the Yankee Brigade!

NEWT *(sings):*
> They gonna come through this town—
> We better keep our heads down—

RILEY and NEWT *(sing):*
> We better start mumblin' and a-shufflin'

ALL THREE *(sing):*
> We better polish our smiles.
>> *The light from Newt's lantern has fallen on Conley, lying on his cot in the factory basement.*

CONLEY *(sings):*
> Old Black Joe at your service,
> Won't do nothin' that'll make you nervous.
> Won't do nothin' worth a look or a mention

ALL FOUR *(sing):*
> And they won't never pay attention!

CONLEY *(sings):*
> They'll never say, "My! My! My!"

RILEY *(sings):*
> They gonna say, "Bring me my boots!"

ANGELA *(sings):*
> "Bring me my tea!"

NEWT *(sings):*
> I betcha thought the slaves were free . . .

ANGELA *(sings):*
    Mister Frank, good for you.
    Lotta folks comin' to get you through.
    Mister Frank, ain't that grand?
    Lotta folks comin' to take a stand.
    Mister Frank, knock on wood,
    Ain't gonna do you no goddam good!

The song continues: the Atlanta hotels wouldn't be full if it'd been a little black girl who was attacked, or a black man who was going to be executed. "There's a black man swingin' in every tree," Conley observes, and they never give that a lot of attention. The lights fade on the singers.

Scene 2

Lucille visits Leo in jail, bringing him some more law books and papers. Trying to help him, she has told a Detroit reporter about his plan to prepare a document proving that all the evidence given against him was false. Leo didn't want this to get out until he'd finished writing it, and he tells Lucille not to talk to any more reporters. Leo appreciates her much-needed and well-meaning efforts to help him—"But keep my stupid mouth shut," Lucille adds.

LUCILLE *(sings "Do It Alone"):*
    Do it alone, Leo—do it all by yourself.
    You're the only one who matters after all.
    Do it alone, Leo—Why should it bother me?
    I'm just good for standing in the shadows
    And staring at the walls, Leo . . . . .
    No, do it alone, Leo—now there's the right idea:
    Make me feel as useless as you always have.
    Do it alone, Leo—what could a woman do?
    After all, so many people love you,
    They're dancing in the streets, Leo . . . . .
    Look at me now, Leo.
    I can be more . . .
    I can bring you home, Leo.
    We can bring you home, Leo.
    I want you to come home.
            The light fades.

Scene 3

At Governor Slaton's mansion, a tea party is in full swing. The Governor is dancing with his wife. Rosser laces his tea from a flask of whiskey and approaches Dorsey, telling him he should have a guilty conscience for prosecuting Leo so ardently, because "You know damn well Leo Frank couldn't even manage to step on a red ant at a Sunday School picnic!"

Watson approaches the District Attorney and calls attention to the pro-Dorsey editorial he is publishing in this week's *Jeffersonian*, characterizing Leo Frank in a grotesque manner. Dorsey is uncomfortable with Watson's fanatical views, even though Watson intends to support Dorsey for governor.

Meanwhile, the Governor is singing the song "Pretty Music" into his wife's ear.

SLATON *(sings):*
>   Don't ya think that's pretty music?
>   Those fellas sure can play.
>   That beat was really made for dancin'.
>   Yes Ma'am, that's pretty music.
>   I could dance the night away.
>   You can hear that song's so sweet and true,
>   But truth to tell, not half as sweet as you.

The Governor comes off the floor with Sally, and they approach Dorsey. Slaton wants to warn the District Attorney that a large volume of mail about the Leo Frank case is coming in, not just inspired by Jewish money, as Dorsey would have it, but from people like Thomas Edison and Henry Ford.

Slaton invites a female guest onto the floor for more dancing to "Pretty Music." When he takes this lady back to her place, there is a line of ladies forming for a turn with the Governor—"a regular dancin' fool," Dorsey comments—and Lucille is one of the women in line. When Lucille's turn comes and she introduces herself as "Mrs. Leo Frank," everything stops, including the music. She insists that she must talk to Slaton even though he's in the middle of hosting a party. Slaton accompanies her to a corner of the ballroom, and the dancing resumes.

Slaton assures Lucille that he knows how she must feel in this situation, and Lucille points out that he's the Governor, he could do something about it. Slaton tries to get her back to dancing, and when she refuses he turns away from her in jovial conversation with a couple from Valdosta. Lucille persists, asking him, "Don't you have at least one small question about the way my husband's trial was conducted?" Slaton lays it on the line: "Your husband was tried and found guilty by a jury of his peers, Ma'am, and that's good enough for me." "Then you are either a fool or a coward," Lucille declares and exits.

The Governor takes his wife to the floor. *The dance seems to pick up speed and is abruptly stopped by a chord in the orchestra which tears the two-step in half. Blackout.*

Scene 4

A nurse brings pen and paper to Judge Roan, now in a wheelchair, so that he can write to Governor Slaton, to tell him that he's having misgivings about the Leo

Frank sentence: maybe it is right to go along with the people crying for justice and more blood, and maybe not.

> JUDGE ROAN (*sings "Letter to the Governor"*):
> With hatred in the air,
> How is any man to know
> What is or isn't fair.
> I left it up to fate.
> It now may be too late . . .
> They'll be calling out to you, Gov'nor.
> You will know what's right to do.

Scene 5

In the prison, the phone is answered by the Guard, who then calls to Leo that it was Lucille with the cryptic message, "Guess who is going to re-examine guess what." The Guard doesn't realize what this means, but it sends Leo into ecstasies of joy— and admiration for Lucille.

> LEO (*sings "This Is Not Over Yet"*):
> It means cancel all your parties.
> Forget your big parade.
> It means the crowds will not be cheering,
> So despite what you've been hearing,
> You can lay down your spade.
> It means my mother can stop crying,
> My rabbi's eulogy can wait.
> I means that Dorsey can stop beaming,
> And my cousin can stop dreaming
> Of his portion of my estate.
>
> It means, no! This isn't over!
> No, the date's not set!
> No, I won't wake up tomorrow
> Drowning in my sweat!
> It means I've got the greatest partner
> Any man can get!
> It means I'll never ever ever
> Underestimate that woman,
> 'Cause this is not over yet!

As the song continues, Lucille joins Leo in rejoicing that they now have reason to hope. They must make sure that the Governor interviews the factory girls and gets the truth out of them.

Scene 6

Iola, Monteen and Essie try to repeat and confirm their testimony, but under closer questioning by Slaton and Lucille, they admit that Leo came into their changing room only because they were taking too long a break, and he wanted them back at work.

LUCILLE: Did he touch you?
IOLA: Not exactly.
SLATON: Then he didn't touch you.
LUCILLE: Did he touch any of you?
SLATON: He ever touch any of you? The truth.
    There is no answer.
I see. Now you all testified that Mr. Frank tried to get you to come to his office.
    The girls look at one another. No one speaks.
Who did that happen to?
MONTEEN: Well, Hattie Hoover said that Corinthia Wilson told her that . . .
SLATON: He asked this Corinthia Wilson to his office?
ESSIE: Yes sir.
LUCILLE: Then why didn't she testify?
IOLA *(uncomfortable):* She wouldn't.
SLATON: Why not?
ESSIE: She said it never happened.
MONTEEN: But everybody knows Corinthia is a big fibber, and Mr. Dorsey said it didn't matter anyway, long as we . . .
    Iola pokes her. She stops talking.
SLATON: As long as you what?
IOLA: All told the same thing

Newt Lee also elaborates on his testimony for the Governor and Lucille. He told the truth . . . Leo Frank "looked at those ladies funny" . . . but he wasn't allowed to go on and tell the whole truth: Leo Frank looked at *everybody* funny. The District Attorney cut Newt off, and the defense attorney never asked him anything.

Lucille suggests that the Governor now has enough new information to take action, but Slaton has another stop to make. This time, he tells Lucille, he can't take her along with him: "But I'll try not to behave like a fool or a coward."

Scene 7

Conley is on a chain gang breaking rocks, doing time as an accessory because of the tale he told in court about helping Leo Frank move the body. When the Governor comes to see him, Conley immediately knows what the visit is about and teases Slaton by pretending to admit a mistake in his testimony, but the "mistake" is totally irrelevant.

Another matter is not, though: Conley testified that he carried the dead body from the second floor to the basement. But the coroner's report stated that there was sawdust in the dead girl's lungs. The only sawdust at the factory is in the basement, so she must have been alive (Slaton concludes) when she was taken there.

This discrepancy casts doubt on Conley's testimony, but he won't change it, and he defies the Governor to prove anything in court. Slaton has heard enough. He departs, leaving Conley and the members of the chain gang breaking rocks and singing the blues in "Feel the Rain Fall."

CONLEY and CHAIN GANG MEN *(sing):*
  Yeah! (Yeah!)
  I get a high fever! (Yeah . . .)
  When I hear her call! (Yeah . . .)
  She gonna cool my fever—(Yeah . . .)
  I gonna take that woman! (Yeah . . .)
  We gonna ride like lightnin'
  We gonna roll, roll, roll like thunder
  And feel the rain fall . . . (Feel the rain fall . . .)
  Yeah . . . (Yeah . . .)
  Hey yeah . . . (Hey yeah . . .)
    They continue to sing as the lights fade.

Scene 8

Slaton and his wife Sally are preparing to go out, when he confesses to her that he is going to take an action that may jeopardize their promising political future. "I'd a whole lot rather be wife to a fine ex-governor than first lady to a chicken," is her reaction.

They proceed to a gallows, where a group of reporters is waiting and wondering what Slaton is up to, calling a meeting here at this time. They soon find out, as Slaton addresses the assembled crowd: "Two thousand years ago, another governor washed his hands and turned a Jew over to a mob. Ever since then, that governor's name has been a curse. If today another Jew went to his grave because I failed to do my duty, I would all my life find his blood on my hands. I have reviewed all the evidence in the case of the State of Georgia against Leo Frank, and I have decided to commute his sentence from the death penalty to imprisonment for life."

Slaton asks the citizens of Georgia to withold judgement of this development until they have heard and digested all the facts. But the crowd is clearly angry. A torchlight parade develops, and the publisher Watson becomes a center of attention as he aggravates the situation in song.

WATSON *(sings "Where Will You Stand When the Flood Comes?"):*
  Will you beg for the Jew's reward
  Or walk with us at the side of the Lord?

Put your soul in the devil's hand?
Well, where will you stand when the flood comes?
>   *Dorsey watches the furious crowd . . . . .*

WATSON and ENSEMBLE *(sing):*
Where will you stand?

DORSEY: With you, Mr. Watson. I'll be proud to stand with you!

WATSON: God bless the next governor of Georgia!
>   *They join together—Craig watches, horrified.*

DORSEY *(sings):*
Yes, I see through the fog and the dust,
So let the mob do whatever they must,
Slaton jumps at the Jew's command—

DORSEY and WATSON *(sing):*
Well, where will you stand when the flood comes?
Where will you stand?
>   *And now the whole company has gathered onstage, among them Mrs.*
>   *Phagan, Frankie and Fiddlin' John, who saws away . . . . .*

ALL *(sing):*
See them laugh when an angel dies
See them tell all their Jew-loving lies!
But they'll run on the judgement day!
Someone's gonna pay when the flood comes!

See the blood as a city grieves!
See the stain that the Jew-money leaves!
Traitors won't keep the mobs at bay!
Someone's gonna pay when the flood comes!

The angry mob now includes three men in hoods and robes brandishing a picture of Mary. Slaton and Sally confront Watson and Dorsey for a moment, as Guards assist the Governor and his wife to exit through the hostile crowd.

Scene 9

Lucille comes to visit Leo in his cell in *"a minimum security prison"* in Milledge-ville. She has come well ahead of her time for the appointment, but the guard, Peavy, doesn't seem to mind letting the rules bend a little. She has brought a picnic hamper and proceeds to lay out its contents. She notices a bandage on Leo's neck and learns that one of his fellow convicts attacked him in the shower with a razor.

Lucille had to bribe the Warden with a job for his daughter in an Atlanta drug store to get permission for this "picnic," and now she proceeds to bribe Peavy with a bottle of whiskey to leave them alone in the cell. *"Peavy takes the bottle, goes back to sit by his post, which suddenly becomes our oak tree. He disappears behind the tree."*

Brent Carver and Carolee Carmello in *Parade*

As Lucille pretends that they are picnicking on the grass, *"The jail has disappeared. They are in the country on a perfect August afternoon."* She is sure that Leo will get a full pardon eventually, when the public furor dies down. Leo wonders how he could have been so lucky as to have such a one as Lucille on his side..

LEO *(sings "All the Wasted Time"):*
    I will never understand
    What I did to deserve you.
    Or how to be the man
    That I'm supposed to be.
    I will never understand
    If I live a thousand lifetimes
    Why you did the things you did for me.

    Just look at you—
    How could I not be in love with you?
    What kind of fool could have taken you
    For granted for so long?

    All the wasted time
    All the million hours,

Pushing you away,
Building up my wall;
All the days gone by
To glare, to pout, to push you out,
And I never knew anything at all . . .
I never knew anything at all.
LUCILLE *(sings):*
I will never understand
How all the world misjudged you
When I have always known
How lucky I must be.
I will never understand
How I kept from going crazy
Just waiting there till you came home to me.
Now look at me
Now that you're finally here with me—
Now that I know I was right to wait
And everyone else was so wrong
For so long . . .
All the wasted time.
LEO *(sings):*
All the wasted time . . .

They kiss and make love. The oak tree casts a green and gold shadow until it takes over the whole stage.

When Peavy tells them it's time for Lucille to go, the lights return to normal, showing them half dressed and putting on the rest of their clothes. They exchange "I love you" and "See you Sunday," and Lucille exits.

Scene 10

Both Leo and Peavy are asleep. The sound of a distant snare drum is heard, as a line of automobile lights advances in the darkness. Men masked with kerchiefs over their faces enter and knock Peavy senseless. They unlock Leo's cell and take him from it, dressed in his nightshirt, never even giving him a chance to put on his pants. The snare drum is heard again as a line of automobile tail lights moves away in the distance.

At the oak tree, at first light, a rope has been thrown over a low-hanging limb with a chair beneath it. Leo is led in manacled, barefoot and in his nightshirt but with demeanor that is *"stoic and with great dignity."* Men take the kerchiefs off their faces and reveal themselves to be the Old Soldier, Starnes, Ivey, Frankie and the original prison Guard.

The Old Soldier declares their intention of carrying out the court's sentence. Leo understands this and simply declares his innocence. Frankie is prevented from attacking Leo, who asks for something to cover his nakedness. The Guard tying a burlap sack around Leo's waist begins to wish they didn't have to go through with this, and Ivey suggests they might let Leo go if he would confess his guilt and say he's sorry. Frankie and Starnes are adamant, but even the Old Soldier begins to have second thoughts.

OLD SOLDIER: Just tell us, sir. That's all we ask.

LEO: All right. I will. I believe God has a plan in all this. And I believe He chose me for a reason. So all this time I've considered and I've pondered and I've prayed, but for the life of me I can't seem to come up with what that reason is. I do know this, though. I haven't gone through the last two years just to stand here now and tell you a bald faced lie. That is not part of God's plan for me.

GUARD: He didn't do it!

STARNES: Shut up.

OLD SOLDIER: Mr. Frank, for the last time, did you kill Mary Phagan?

LEO: I did not.

STARNES: Let's get this over.

LEO: Wait!

STARNES: Jesus! Now what?

LEO: I want my wedding ring to go to my wife.

> The Old Soldier nods—the prison Guard slides the ring from Leo's finger—someone else ties a blindfold around his eyes. They lift him to the chair and place the noose around his neck. From behind the tree Tom Watson appears silently, wearing his homburg, to observe from the periphery.

OLD SOLDIER: Anything else, Mr. Frank?

LEO (*Quietly begins singing a prayer in Hebrew—a simple prayer with a simple melody*):

Sh'ma Yisroel, Adonai elohainu,

Adonai echod.

Baruch sheym k'vod malchuso l'olam va-ed.

FRANKIE (*while Leo sings*): Mary! This is for you!

> He races forward and kicks the chair out from under Leo. Simultaneously, Ivey has broken from the vigilantes and crossed the stage by himself, turning his back on the hanging. Blackout on Leo. Furious chimes ring. All that is left is a light on Frankie and the rest of the men in tableau watching, Ivey with his back to the hanging. The bells cry out again and again. We watch forever, until finally, abruptly, everything stops and the lights black out.

Scene 11

Weeks later, Lucille, in mourning, receives Craig, who has come to deliver a small package. Lucille opens it and finds that it is Leo's wedding ring. As she stares at it,

Craig assures her of his support if she ever needs anything. But he's heard that she's moving up North.

LUCILLE: No. I'm not leavin' home.

CRAIG: But after all this . . .

LUCILLE: I'm a Georgia girl. I always will be.

CRAIG: Well, I'm sorry, ma'am. Sorry for your loss.

LUCILLE: Sorry? That won't do, Mr. Craig. You'd better hurry.

CRAIG: What?

LUCILLE: It's Memorial Day, don't you have a parade to cover?

Craig leaves Lucille turning the wedding ring *"over and over in her hand."* In the distance, Leo and Mary are seen reenacting the scene in which she came to the factory to get her pay.

As Lucille fingers the wedding ring, another Memorial Day parade is in progress. She sings "Leo, oh Leo/I know He'll protect you/And don't be afraid/I'll be fine here—you'll see," as the scene at the factory ends and Leo and Mary disappear.

Frankie emerges from the parade to sing the Young Soldier's song about going to fight for "the Old Red Hills of Home," and the Ensemble sings praise for those who have fought to defend Georgia's honor. *"The parade continues, including a float carrying the new governor of Georgia, Hugh Dorsey, along with Tom Watson and the Old Soldier. A final tableau of the proud citizens of Georgia, as Lucille crosses the stage, putting the wedding ring on her finger."* Blackout. Curtain.

Tony Award

○○○
○○○
○○○
○○○
○○○
○○○ FOSSE

A Dance Musical in Three Acts

CHOREOGRAPHY BY ROBERT FOSSE

CONCEIVED BY RICHARD MALTBY JR.,
CHET WALKER AND ANN REINKING

Cast and credits appear on pages 245–248

BOB FOSSE (choreographer) is the principal "author" of this book-less, Tony Award-winning, all-dancing musical, with a score collected from shows and movies for which he created and/or performed the choreography (a detailed listing of these sources appears with the cast-and-credits entry of Fosse *in this volume). He was born Robert Louis Fosse in Chicago on June 23, 1927. In 1938, at age 11, he was a member of the Riff Brothers vaudeville team and at 14 was also appearing in cabaret. He was educated at Amundsen High School in Chicago and studied at the American Theater Wing for two years (1947–48) in New York City. In 1948 and 1949 he made his entrance into the musical theater in touring companies of* Call Me Mister *and* Make Mine Manhattan. *His first appearance on the New York stage was on January 20, 1950 in the revue* Dance Me a Song *at the Royale Theater for 35 performances. The first Broadway show he choreographed was* The Pajama Game *at the St. James Theater, a 1,063-performance hit, thanks in no small measure to Fosse's contribution.*

It would be impossible to encapsulate in a mere biographical sketch a career as brilliantly distinguished as Fosse's, as it flowered all over show business from stage to screen. But a good deal of it is recorded in the abovementioned list of scenes and musical numbers in his 1999 Tony Award-winning musical, which opened at the Broadhurst Theater January 14 and continues as a highlight of the turn-of-the-century Broadway scene. The summary of his many honors in the biographical sketch in the Fosse *program begins with the fact that in 1973 he became the only person in history*

154

to win Tony, Oscar and Emmy Awards in the same year, these for his direction of Pippin, *the movie* Cabaret *and* Liza With a Z *on TV. He was showered with Tony Awards for choreography for* The Pajama Game, Damn Yankees, Redhead, Little Me, Sweet Charity, Dancin' *and* Big Deal. *His movie version of* Cabaret *won seven Oscars including the one for best director, and his* All That Jazz—*which he wrote, directed and choreographed—won at the Cannes Film Festival. He received three Emmy Awards as director-choreographer including the one for* Liza With a Z.

Fosse *choreographed a ballet,* Magic Bird of Fire, *and was a member of the Society of Stage Directors and Choreographers, which he served as treasurer. He was married three times, and his widow is the Broadway star Gwen Verdon, the mother of his daughter Nicole. Bob Fosse died in 1987, leaving for all theatergoers a treasure not only of delightful memories of his performances and those of others under his direction, but also of inspired choreography on the permanent record, as per this season's staged collection of his work.*

RICHARD MALTBY JR., CHET WALKER *and* ANN REINKING (*co-conceivers) are credited with various aspects of the creation and development of* Fosse. *Maltby is no stranger to authorship, having contributed the lyrics and other material to* Miss Saigon, *a 1991 Best Play, and the conception as well as the direction of the Tony and Drama Critics Award-winning* Ain't Misbehavin' *in 1978. He was born in Ripon, Wisconsin, the son of an orchestra leader and arranger, and educated at Phillips Exeter and Yale, where he wrote two undergraduate shows with a classmate, David Shire. After their graduation in 1959, the Maltby-Shire collaboration has continued through many Broadway and off-Broadway musicals. Maltby's major credits also list director and co-lyricist for* Song and Dance, *director and lyricist for* Starting Here, Starting Now; Baby *and* Closer Than Ever, *lyricist for* Big—*and he directed (for which he was Tony-nominated) as well as co-conceived* Fosse. *For 25 years Maltby has been associated with the Manhattan Theater Club in New York. He is married, with five children.*

Chet Walker *re-created Fosse choreography for* Fosse, *a project which he originally conceived together with Bob Fosse himself in 1986. Prior to the present project, he had also re-created the Fosse choreography for national and international productions of* Sweet Charity. *As a performer, he has appeared in four Broadway musicals. His major creative work has included direction and choreography for the 10th anniversary tour of* La Cage aux Folles, *and choreographing productions of* Annie Get Your Gun, A Funny Thing Happened on the Way to the Forum, Pal Joey *(Joseph Jefferson Award),* Chita From Broadway to Belles Artes *(for Chita Rivera) and* The Best Little Whorehouse in Texas *(Drama-Logue Award).*

Ann Reinking *was born in Seattle on November 10, 1949, was educated at Bellevue High School and trained for three years with the San Francisco Ballet Company. As every theatergoer knows, as an actress and dancer she is a Broadway star who made her debut in 1969 as a replacement in the role of Lulu in* Cabaret *and has proceeded through a flourishing career, Tony-nominated for* Dancin' *and* Good Time Charlie. *Her choreography for the 1997 revival of* Chicago *won her the Tony, Drama Desk,*

Outer Critics and Astaire Awards, and she served as co-choreographer and co-director (Tony-nominated) of Fosse.

The *"script" of* Fosse *is its choreography and direction, so we celebrate it in these pages with a sampling of the show's action in photographs by Catherine Ashmore and Joan Marcus of performances in Toronto (where it opened July 16, 1998) and New York (where it opened January 14, 1999), generously provided by the show's producer, Livent (US) Inc., through their press agents Mary Bryant and Wayne Wolfe. These photos depict typical examples of Bob Fosse's choreography as re-created in this production by Chet Walker and co-choreographed by Ann Reinking, as directed by Richard Maltby Jr. and co-directed by Ann Reinking, with the artistic advice of Gwen Verdon and with scenery and costumes by Santo Loquasto and lighting by Andrew Bridge. And we offer our special thanks to Nicole Fosse Greiner for helping us to identify her late father's names for some of the elements of his work.*

Right, the Toronto company in "Fosse's World"

ACT I

Right, Brad Musgrove in a typical Fosse attitude in "Fosse's World," the opening number of *Fosse.* Bob Fosse referred to this position of the hand as "teacup fingers"

Hand positions are a feature of the dancers' performance (the one *above* is called "squidgie"), as Valarie Pettiford (facing camera, *above,* and *in center, below*) leads the *Fosse* company through the "Bye Bye Blackbird" number, which originated in the TV special *Liza With a Z*

Above, Rachelle Rak, Mary MacLeod, Dede LaBarre, Dana Moore, Valarie Pettiford and Jane Lanier as the "broken dolls" in "Big Spender" from *Sweet Charity; left,* Desmond Richardson, Elizabeth Parkinson and others in "Crunchy Granola Suite," a number from Fosse's *Dancin'*

ACT II

Above, the New York company in the "Shoeless Joe From Hannibal, Mo" ballet from *Damn Yankees; below,* Scott Wise *(center)* in "I Love a Piano," a selection from the director-choreographer-dancer's night club material

Left, Lisa Gajda—arms in the "Blake's angels" position—with Brad Musgrove and Andy Blankenbuehler in "Rich Man's Frug" from *Sweet Charity.* Fosse often drew choreographic inspiration from poses, like this one, which he admired in sculpture and paintings

The New York company, hands in the "soft boiled egg" position, in "Rich Man's Frug"

In another ensemble effect from "Rich Man's Frug," the Toronto company
strikes a pose the dancers called the "slope clump" and Fosse called "zonk"

ACT III

Left, Valarie Pettifo
"Mein Herr" from the m
picture version of *Caba*

Left, Sergio Trujillo and Desmond Richardson in "Mr Bojangles" from *Dancin'*

Below, "Benny Goodman's 'Sing Sing Sing'" from *Dancin'*, the *Fosse* finale, which its choreographer sometimes called "popcorn"

Special Citation

○○○
○○○
○○○
○○○
○○○
○○○

NOT ABOUT NIGHTINGALES

A Play in Three Acts

BY TENNESSEE WILLIAMS

Cast and credits appear on pages 249–250

TENNESSEE WILLIAMS was born Thomas Lanier Williams in Columbus, Miss. on March 26, 1911 and died in New York City on February 25, 1983 in his 72d year, one of the most distinguished playwrights not only of his generation but of this century.

Williams's biographical sketch in the Playbill for Not About Nightingales *records as his earliest published work an essay,* Can a Wife Be a Good Sport?, *at age 16 in* Smart Set *magazine. He attended the Universities of Missouri, Washington and Iowa, where he enrolled in the famous E.P. Conkle–E.C. Mabie playwriting class (his first produced play,* Cairo! Shanghai! Bombay! *had already been put on by Memphis Garden Players in 1935). After receiving his B.A. from Iowa in 1938, he worked as a shoe clerk, elevator operator, waiter, movie usher, etc. He was encouraged to devote himself to the theater by the St. Louis Mummers (for whom he had written* Candles in the Sun, *presented as a curtain raiser in 1936), and Williams's* Not About Nightingales *was put on by the Mummers in 1939, according to a 1972* Best Plays *biographical sketch. In 1940 the Theater Guild produced his* Battle of Angels *in a Boston tryout (it later came to New York as* Orpheus Descending), *and his* Stairs to the Roof *was produced by the Pasadena, Calif. Playbox during the 1944–45 season.*

Then, with the New York opening of Williams's The Glass Menagerie *(Best Play, Critics Award) on March 31, 1945, his soaring skyrocket of a playwriting career took on the visibility of a 561-performance Broadway hit. The list of Tennessee Williams plays and prizes includes the following:* You Touched Me! *(1945, in collaboration with Donald Windham),* A Streetcar Named Desire *(1947, Best Play, Critics Award, Pulitzer Prize),* Summer and Smoke *(1948),* The Rose Tattoo *(1951, Best Play, Tony Award),* Camino Real *(1953),* Cat on a Hot Tin Roof *(1955, Best Play, Critics Award, Pulitzer Prize),* Orpheus Descending *(1957, Best Play),* Garden District *(1958, a program of one acters including* Suddenly Last Summer), Sweet Bird of Youth *(1959, Best Play),* Period of Adjustment *(1960, Best Play),* The Night of the Iguana *(1961, Best Play, Critics Award),* The Milk Train Doesn't Stop Here Anymore *(1963, Best Play),* Slapstick Tragedy *(1966),* The Seven Descents of Myrtle *(1968),* In the Bar of a Tokyo Hotel *(1969) and* Small Craft Warnings *(1972, Best Play). Now we have the 1999 London and New York incarnation of the Tony-nominated* Not About Nightingales *which was retrieved from obscurity by Corin and Vanessa Redgrave's Moving Theater, staged by Trevor Nunn for his Royal National Theater, brought to America for a production at the Alley Theater, Houston and premiered on Broadway February 25. It receives Williams's 11th Best Plays citation, tying him with Moss Hart in the all-time list. Only Maxwell Anderson (19), George S. Kaufman (18), Neil Simon (15) and Eugene O'Neill (12) have more.*

The Tennessee Williams career marches through the 1970s to the early 1980s with Out Cry *(1973, a.k.a.* The Two-Character Play), 27 Wagons Full of Cotton *(1976, on a bill with Arthur Miller's* A Memory of Two Mondays), The Red Devil Battery Sign *(1975, closed in tryout),* Vieux Carré *(1977) and* Clothes for a Summer Hotel *(1980) for Broadway; and, off Broadway,* A Lovely Sunday for Creve Coeur *(1979) and* a/k/a Tennessee *(1982, compiled from his writings). The ten of his many one acters which were showcased by the Acting Company off Broadway in 1986 were* The Lady of Larkspur Lotion, Talk to Me Like the Rain and Let Me Listen, Portrait of a Madonna, The Unsatisfactory Supper, The Long Goodbye, Auto-Da-Fé, The Strangest Kind of Romance, A Perfect Analysis Given by a Parrot, This Property Is Condemned *and* I Can't Imagine Tomorrow. *Among his other one acters are* Something Unspoken, The Purification *and* I Rise in Flame, Cried the Phoenix. *Among his screen plays are those for his own* Suddenly Last Summer *and* The Fugitive Kind. *His published works include collections of poetry and* The Roman Spring of Mrs. Stone.

Williams was a member of the Dramatists Guild and ASCAP. In additon to his 11 Best Play citations, four Critics Awards, two Pulitzers and one Tony, he was the recipient of the Brandeis University Creative Arts Medal (1965), the National Arts Club Medal of Honor for Literature and the National Institute of Arts and Letters Gold Medal for Drama (1969).

We are most grateful to those who retrieved, designed, mounted and performed Not About Nightingales *for providing us with this opportunity to enjoy still another Tennessee Williams play, when we presumed we had seen them all. Best Plays cites it among this and any other New York theater season's outstanding accomplishments, in particular for the playwright's ability to understand what a play is and should be— and to construct it effectively, and with clear-cut characterizations, even around such a familiar theme as a prison conflict between a sadistic warden and his longsuffering charges. We enjoy watching a real playwright at work in these scenes, and his talent shines through the simplicities of the dialogue and brutalities of the action.*

The following synopsis of Not About Nightingales *was prepared by Sally Dixon Wiener.*

Time: July/August 1938

Place: A large American prison

ACT I

SYNOPSIS: The theater's playing area is dominated on one side by a towering grillwork of labyrinthine passageways with entrances off right and left. A catwalk is in the upper forefront, and below more gates open into the cellblocks from a lower passageway. The repeated clash of metal on metal punctuates the transformation of the scene from one part of the prison to another—the cells with their three-tiered cots and dingy bedding, the dining area, the basement with the steam radiators and the prison yard.

In the area directly opposite the cage-like grillwork is the prison warden's office with its grayed-down desks, chairs, telephone, radio, lamp and filing cabinets. There is a huge opaque window above the office area, and nearby a set of steps leads down to an unseen room below the office. The relentlessly drab monochromatic gunmetal atmosphere is perhaps best exemplified by an American flag with gray stripes instead of red.

In between the warden's office and the grillwork wall, metal grills crisscrossing the floor add to the monotonous cacophony. Here there are benches that serve as a waiting room for visitors to the warden's office and as the dining facilities for the prisoners. The theater aisles are also used for entrances and exits.

We hear a voice on a loudspeaker from an excursion steamer that is passing by the prison.

LOUDSPEAKER: Yeah, this is the Lorelei excursion steamer. All-day trip around Sandy-Point. Leaves eight A.M., return at midnight, sightseeing, dancing. Magnificent skyline of the city against the early morning sunlight. It's still a little misty around the tops of them big towers downtown. Hear them bells ringing? It's eight o'clock sharp. Sun's bright as a dollar, swell day, bright, warm, makes you mighty proud to be alive. Yes, Ma'am! There it is! You can see it now, folks. That's the Island. Sort of misty still. See them big stone walls. Dynamite-proof, escape-proof! Thirty-five hundred men in there, folks, and lots of 'em'll never get out! Oh, oh!! There goes the band, folks! Dancing on the upper deck! Dancing, folks! Lorelei Lee and her eight Lorelights! Dancing on the upper deck—dancing!—dancing!—dancing . . . *(Fade.)*

Episode 1

We see the first of the periodic announcements flashing briefly across the upper part of the set, telling us it is the afternoon of July 25, 1938, and that Miss Eva Crane is applying for a job. Mrs. Bristol, *"a worn matron in black,"* with a covered basket, is seated on the bench outside the warden's office as Eva Crane, pretty, young and blonde, modestly but smartly dressed, with a pert little hat, comes on nervously clutching her handbag. To Mrs. Bristol's surprise, Eva reveals she's come hoping to get a job. It wouldn't be depressing, as Mrs. Bristol suggests, because it's an unusual prison. Eva's read about it in the Sunday supplement—it's a model institution, "They've got experts—in psychology and sociology and things like that, you know!"—and social rehabilitation has replaced the idea of punishment of crime.

Jim Allison—a tense, clean-cut, dark-haired young man—crosses the area. Eva asks him if she may see the warden. Jim tells her the warden isn't here yet, goes into the office and shuts the door.

Mrs. Bristol is here about her son Jack, a former sailor, who's in this prison because of some trouble over a woman—"a common slut!"—she reveals to Eva. His most recent letter sounded "feverish" to her. He said he'd been sent down to a place called Klondike. Both the women had supposed Klondike was part of Alaska, but Jack wrote that it was very hot, and he couldn't have written his mother about it unless he'd been able to get someone to sneak the letter out.

Eva goes into the office to find out how she can get to see the warden. Jim tells her the warden is inspecting the grounds, which is sometimes "an idiomatic expression for having a couple of beers in the back room at Tony's . . . . . His actions are pretty unpredictable." Jim likes that word—it has five syllables. He gets big words out of a big dictionary because he is "one of the exhibition pieces."

JIM: I'm supposed to tell you that when I came in here I was just an ordinary grifter. But look at me now. I'm reading Spengler's *Decline of the West,* and I'm editor of the prison monthly. Ask me what is an archaeoptryx.

EVA: What is it?

JIM: An extinct species of reptile-bird. Here's our latest issue.

EVA *(more and more confounded):* Of—what?

JIM: The Archaeoptryx. Our monthly publication.

EVA: Why do you call it that?

JIM: It sounds impressive. Do you know what an amaranth is?

EVA: No. What is it?

JIM: A flower that never dies. *(Lifts book.)* I came across it in here. One of the classical poets compares it to love. What's your opinion of that?

EVA: Well, I—what's yours?

JIM: I wouldn't know. I started my present career at the age of sixteen.

EVA: That early.

JIM: Yes, the usual case of bad influences And at that age of course—love is something you dream about and blush when you look at yourself in the mirror next morning!

   Laughs. Eva looks away in slight confusion.
Say, d'you know that song?

EVA: What song?

JIM *(giving a sour imitation):* "Ah, tis love alone the world is seeking!" A guy sang it in chapel last night—Is that on the level?

EVA: Well, I—not exactly.

JIM: You're inclined to admit a few qualifications?

EVA: Yes. For instance, what I'm seeking is a job. And a new pair of stockings.

JIM: They look good to me.

EVA: They're worn to shreds!

JIM: Well, perhaps I'm prejudiced!

> *Eva clears her throat, Jim clears his.*

EVA *(picking up paper):* "Prison: The Door to Opportunity!"

JIM: Yes, that's one of my best editorials. I got ten years of copper for writing that.

EVA: Copper?

JIM: Time off your sentence for good behavior. I've got ten years of copper stashed away in the files, and most of it's for extolling the inspirational qualities of prison life.

Their conversation is interrupted by Mrs. Bristol, telling Jim who she is and inquiring if Mr. Whalen, the warden, is in yet. Jim admits to knowing her son Jack slightly but can't give out information about him. He suggests she see Mr. Whalen the next morning. Mrs. Bristol leaves her basket and asks that it be given to Jack before the contents get stale, then exits.

Eva wonders why Jim couldn't have said something to Mrs. Bristol to put her mind at ease. Jim tells her Sailor Jack has gone "stir-bugs," cracked up, "an occupational disease" among prisoners. The Sunday supplement had given Eva a rosier picture of prison life (it was Jim and the warden whom they interviewed for the story). That's why she's applying for a job here—also, her landlady's brother-in-law, McBurney, is a guard here—and a good one, Jim admits.

Jim is handing Eva one of the prison's sample menus, claiming it's comparable to those at a good boarding school, when the warden appears: Bert "Boss" Whalen, *"a powerful man, but with coarse good looks."* He takes a good look at Eva, tosses his coat to Jim, belches, excuses himself to "do a strip-tease" because the weather's so hot and passes around cookies from Mrs. Bristol's basket. He takes Eva for a newspaper reporter and begins to deny reports about pellagra in the prison, until Eve informs him she's there seeking a job. She cites her college education and three years' business experience, but she is so nervous that she spills her handbag's contents and confesses she's been down on her luck lately, and if she doesn't get work soon she'll—"Go off the deep end?" Whalen suggests, pointing to the big window, without bars because it's over the Bay. Then the warden orders Jim to explain the one prerequisite for a job in this office—"The ability to keep your mouth shut except when you're given specific instructions to speak""—and Eva realizes that Whalen is going to hire her. Jim instructs her to come over on the 7:45 boat the next morning. After she leaves,Whelan sums her up: "Dizzy as hell—But she's got a shape on her that would knock the bricks out of a Federal Pen!"

Finbar Lynch as Canary Jim Allison, Sherri Parker Lee as Eva Crane
and Corin Redgrave as "Boss" Whalen in a scene from *Not About
Nightingales* by Tennessee Williams

Episode 2

The evening of the same day, in the cell block, Sailor Jack—visibly a bloody
mess—is singing "Auprès de Ma Blonde" and talking in a rambling way. His cellmates—cock-of-the-walk tough guy Butch O'Fallon, curly-haired Joe and The
Queen, a black homosexual—are returned to their cell by Schultz, a beefy uni-
formed guard. Sailor Jack goes on mindlessly singing after Schultz has blown the
whistle for lights out. Schultz warns Sailor that if he earns another trip to Klondike,
he won't survive to come back. Butch defends Sailor, arguing that it was Klondike

that put Sailor into this state in the first place. Sailor takes up the song again, and to prevent his being punished, Butch knocks Sailor senseless. When a more sympathetic guard, McBurney, comes on duty, Butch persuades him to have Sailor taken to isolation for his own good.

The sound of bird calls among the prisoners tips Butch off that Jim Allison is returning to his adjoining cell—Jim is considered a canary, or stool pigeon.

BUTCH: Hey, Canary! Allison!

JIM: What do you want, Butch?

> *He is shown removing shirt and shoes.*

BUTCH: Next time you're in a huddle with the boss, tell him the Angels in Hall C have put another black mark on his name for Sailor Jack.

JIM: I'll tell him that.

BUTCH: Tell him some day we're going to appoint a special committee of one to come down there an' settle up the score—You hear me, Stool?

JIM: I hear you.

BUTCH: Just think—I used to be cellmates with him. I lie awake at night regrettin' all the times I had a chance to split his guts—but didn't!

JOE: Why didn'tcha?

BUTCH: That was before he started workin' for the boss. But now he's number three on the Angel's Records. First Whalen, then Schultz and then the Stool! You hear that Stool?

JIM: Yes, I hear you, Butch.

The orchestra from the Lorelei can be heard playing "Roses of Picardy," making Butch wish he could have a dance with an old flame named Goldie. He is reminded that there's a window in the warden's office looking out over the Bay, which would come in handy for an escape route after, say, killing the warden. But (Joe reminds him) nobody's ever swum to freedom yet. Besides, Butch is scared of water. The Queen complains that his manicure kit is missing, and that he has been persecuted all his life for being refined.

Episode 3

The next morning, July 26, Boss Whelan is studying the racing form when Mrs. Bristol comes in to inquire about her son. Jim is told to get out Bristol's card, but he's stalling.

BOSS: Jim, that card?

JIM *(coming slowly forward with card from files):* You'd better look at it yourself.

BOSS: Read it, read it! We running a social service bureau?

> *Jim looks uncertainly at Mrs. Bristol, who raises a clenched hand to her breast.*

MRS. B *(softly):* If anything's gone wrong I'd like to know.

JIM *(reading huskily):* Jack Bristol. Larceny. Convicted May, 1936. Sentenced three years. *(Looks up.)* He slacked his work. Spent three days in Klondike.

BOSS *(sharply):* Is that on the card?

JIM: No, but I want to explain to this lady what happened.

MRS. B *(rising slowly):* What happened?

JIM: You see, Ma'am—

BOSS *(sharply):* Read what's on the card, that's all!

JIM: Came May 1938. Came up before the lunacy commission. July 15, transferred to the psychopathic ward. Violent delusions. Prognosis—dementia praecox.

MRS B: That isn't—Jack—my boy!

BOSS: Now see here—I . . . *(Motions Jim to get her out.)* I know how you feel about this. I got all the sympathy in the world for you women that come in here, but this is a penal instate-union, and we simply can't be taking time out from our routine business for things like this.

MRS. B *(overlap):* My boy, not what you said! Anything, but not that! Say he's dead, say you killed him, killed him! but don't tell me that . . .

She knows about Klondike from her son's letters and accuses Whelan of torturing him until he was driven insane. When she begins sobbing, the warden orders Jim to take her out, then picks up the phone and tells his bookie to put twenty bucks on Windy Blue to show.

Episode 4

Late that night, Jim's cellmate Ollie is kneeling in prayer by his bunk. Butch is eavesdropping from the adjoining cell.

OLLIE *(in audible whisper):* Oh, Lawd, de proteckter an preserbation ob all, remembuh dis nigguh. Remembuh his wife Susie an his six chillun, Rachel, Rebekkah, Solomon, Moses, Ecclesiastics an' Deuteronomy Armsted. You look out fo' dem while I'se in jail. An ah'd git out fo' de cole weathuh sets in cause Susie's gonna have another baby, Lawd, n' she can't git aroun't' gather kindlin' wood. God bless my ole woman an' daddy an Presiden' Roosevelt an' de W.P.A. in Jesus Chris' name—Amen. *(Rises stiffly.)*

BUTCH *(grinning):* Hey, Ollie, yuh better have 'em reverse the charges on that one!

OLLIE: It don' co' nothin.

BUTCH: It ain't worth nothin.

OLLIE: De Lawd remembuhs who remembuhs Him.

BUTCH: Hawshit!

The usual bird calls precede Jim's arrival at the cell. He takes off his shirt and asks Ollie to rub his back with linament, while Butch continues scoffing at them both. Ollie wonders how Jim got his purple scars. Butch replies that " 'Dr. Jones' is the guy gave Canary Jim his singin' lessons" and hints at how he'd like to finish the job if he could only get at Jim.

OLLIE: Don't pay him no mind.

JIM: Naw. There's a wall between him an' me.

BUTCH: You bet there is. Or you'd be a dead canary. There'd be yellow feathers floating all over Hall C!

JIM *(exhaling smoke as he speaks—a la Jules Garfield):* There's a wall like that around ev'ry man in here an' outside of here, Ollie.

OLLIE: Outside? Naw.

JIM: Sure there is. Ev'ry man living is walking around in a cage. He carries it with him wherever he goes and don't let it go till he's dead.

> *Butch grins delightedly. He nudges Joe; describes circle with finger and points at Jim's cell: They both crouch, grinning, listening on the bench by wall . . . . .*

But sometimes I think, Ollie, a guy don't have to wait till he's dead to get outside of his cage.

OLLIE: Yuh mean he should bump himself off?

JIM: No. A guy can use his brain two ways. He can make it a wall to shut him in from the world or a great big door to let him out. *(Musingly.)* Intellectual emancipation!

OLLIE: Huh?

> *Butch gives a long whistle.*

What's that?

JIM: Couple of words I came across in a book.

OLLIE: Sound like big words.

JIM: They *are* big words. So big that the *world* hangs on 'em. They can tell us what to read, what to say, what to do—but they can't tell us what to *think!* And as long as man can think as he pleases, he's never exactly locked up anywhere. He can think himself outside of all their walls and boundaries and make the world his place to live in—It's a swell feeling, Ollie, when you've done that. It's like being alone on the top of a mountain at night with nothing around you but stars. Only you're not alone, though, cause you know that you're part of everything living, and everything living is part of you. Then you get an idea of what God is. Not Mr. Santie Claus, Ollie, dropping answers to prayers down chimneys.

OLLIE: Naw?

JIM: No, not that. But something big and terrible as night is, and yet—

OLLIE: Huh?

JIM: And yet—as soft as a—woman. Y'see what I mean?

BUTCH: I see whatcha mean—it's kind of a—sticky feeling!

> *Butch and Joe laugh. Jim looks resentfully at wall.*

JIM: You guys don't get what I'm talking about.

OLLIE *(musingly):* Naw, but I do. Thinkin's like prayin', excep' that prayin' yuh feel like yuh've got someone on the other end a th'line . . .

JIM *(smiling):* Yeah.

Joe, moaning and twisting with a stomach ache, threatens to stop eating if the food isn't more digestible. Butch picks up on this and thinks a hunger-strike might be a good idea—they'd get in the newspapers, and there'd be an investigation, and they'd get better food. Klondike is what they'd get, Joe believes. Butch has been there and calls it "a little suburb of hell," but he thinks they could beat it.

Episode 5

The next morning, July 27, Eva enters the office for her first day of employment, and Jim admits it's a privilege for a con to be close to a person of the opposite sex. Eva's predecessor was "sort of a cow." She was Whalen's wife's second cousin, and she would accompany him to a room on the floor below "to relax after ground-inspection."

Jim admits that life inside here is not all it was blown up to be in the Sunday supplement. The sample menu, for example, is a hoax. "Y'know they take normal sex-life away from convicts, they take profitable work away from them—they take everything away from them but food—and when they make *that* so darned monotonous that you feel like puking at the sight of it ... " And the climate here is "the practical equivalent of Mount Vesuvius," with the mid-August heat threatening to overwhelm them and wipe everybody out.

They hear a brass band practicing. Impulsively, Jim clasps Eva in an embrace. She breaks away with "Not in the warden's office!" and attends to her chores.

Episode 6

That evening after supper, Schultz arrives with a new prisoner, a track star who once held the state record for the 220 and whose nickname is Swifty. The newcomer's complaints about the accommodations are soon silenced by Butch, who assigns him to the upper bunk and explains to him who's boss: "In Germany it's that monkey wit' the trick mustache!—But in here it's Butch O'Fallon! And Butch O'Fallon is me!" Swifty has been sentenced to five years for stealing, but he expects his lawyer to get him out soon and hopes he can get permission from the warden to run in the yard, so he can keep in shape.

BUTCH: Naw.
SWIFTY: Why not?
BUTCH: Because you're a con.
SWIFTY: But a con's a human being. He's got to be treated like one.
BUTCH: A con ain't a human being. A con's a con.
    Lights fade on others and concentrate on Butch.
He's stuck in here, and the world forgot him. As far as the world is concerned he doesn't exist any more. What happens to him in here—them people outside don't know, they don't care. He's entrusted to the care of the State. The State? Hell! The

State turns him over to a guy called a warden and a bunch of other guys called guards. Who're they? Men who like to boss other men. Maybe they could've been truck drivers or street cleaners or circus clowns. But they didn't wanta be none a them. Why? Cause they've got a natural instinct for swinging a shillelagh! They like to crack heads, make sausage out of human flesh! And so they get to be guards. That sounds like "gods"—which ain't so much a coincidence either, because the on'y diff'rence between "guards" and "god" is that "guards" has got an "r" in it, an' the "r" stands for "rat!"—That's what a guard is, accordin' to my definition—A rat who thinks that he's GOD!—You better not forget that.

Butch also warns Swifty against becoming friendly with a stool pigeon like Allison. He goes on to tell the others that he is thinking over the possiblity of staging a hunger-strike.

Episode 6A

That night, Butch dreams that Goldie comes to him, with "Roses of Picardy" heard faintly in the background. Butch remembers how special their love-making seemed, and Goldie assures him she's still waiting for him. But when he reaches toward her she fades away, and Butch awakens with a heartfelt "God-damn!"

Episode 7

On Friday afternoon, July 29, "Boss" Whalen is in his office inflating a rubber duck he's bought for his little daughter. Jim comes in and reports that the complaints about the food are getting louder. There were seven cases of ptomaine poisoning after supper Wednesday, and Jim declares that the meatballs were fit only "for buzzards at the zoo." Whalen thinks Jim is talking too uppity, showing off for Eva, but Jim believes he can be useful only if he gives his honest opinion. Whelan studies Jim for a moment, then agrees that he is "a good boy." He orders Jim to turn to show Eva his profile, looking as though it had been carved out of rock. Whelan once tried to break Jim by giving him 50 lashes with a rubber hose every morning for two weeks.

BOSS: Remember, that, Jim?
JIM *(face barely tightening):* Yes, sir.
BOSS: When I seen I couldn't break him, I said to myself, Hey, Bert, here's a man you could use! So I did. Jim's a trusty now, a stool pigeon—Canary Jim—That's what the other cons all call him! Ain't that so, Jim?
JIM: Yes, sir.
BOSS: Keeps me posted on conditions among the men. That's what makes him valuable to me!—But the men don't like him. They hate your guts, don't they Jim?
JIM *(almost a whisper):* Yes, Sir.
BOSS: Take off your shirt, Jim.
JIM: Yes, Sir.
BOSS: Show Eva your back.

Jim obeys with curious, machine-like precision. Diagonally across his shoulders down to the waist are long scars which ten years could not obliterate.

See them scars, Eva? He got them ten years ago. Pretty sight he was then. Raw meat. The skin hung down from his back like pieces of red tissue paper! The flesh was all pulpy, beat up, the blood squirted out like juice from a ripe tomato ev'ry time I brung the whip down on him—Had enough, Jim? Ready to go back to that embossing machine?—Naw, says Jim—Not till it's fixed!—He defied me like that for fourteen days.

Eva nearly faints at the sight of Jim's scars but manages to pull herself together. The warden sends Jim out to talk to Butch, to tell the cons in Hall C he's tired of them complaining about the food. Whelan tells Eva that Jim's a good boy but needs to be reminded of his old friend "Dr. Jones" periodically. He hopes she realizes the position he's in, in charge of 3,500 men "that would knife their own mothers for the price of a beer."

Episode 8

It's Friday evening, and the tension in the cells is increasing because the word is out that it's going to be cold beans for supper again. Butch suggests that maybe the boss is trying to call their hand. The warden has an ace in the hole, they know—Klondike. But Butch claims they have one too—hunger-strike.

Episode 8A

Bird calls signal the arrival of Jim, who has something to tell Butch and dares to enter his cell only after he makes sure that the guard McBurney is on duty. Jim tells Butch he has never deliberately ratted on anybody. Butch is impressed with Jim's daring to come into the cell but wants him to say his say and get out.

JIM: I know what you've got in mind.
BUTCH: What?
JIM: Hunger-strike.
BUTCH: What of it?
JIM: I don't recommend it, Butch.
BUTCH: Did Whalen tell you to say that?
JIM: Naw, this is on the level, Butch.
BUTCH: Yeah, about as level as the Adirondacks.
JIM: I'll admit I've made myself useful to him. But I haven't forgotten two weeks we spent in the hole together, and those visits he paid every morning to inquire about our health. He was even more solicitous about mine than yours, Butch. Things like that make a common bond between men that nothing afterwards can ever—
BUTCH: Come to the point!
JIM: All right. I'm coming up for parole next month.
BUTCH *(rising):* You are, huh?

James Black (Butch O'Fallon), Finbar Lynch (Canary Jim), Daniel Freedom Stewart (Krause), Alex Giannini (Joe) and Dion Graham (Ollie) in *Not About Nightingales*

JIM: There's a chance I might get it. And if I do, I'm going to justify my reputation as a brilliant vocalist, Butch. I'm going to sing as loud and so high that the echo will knock these walls down! I know plenty from working in the office. I know all the pet grafts. I know about the intimidation of employees and torture of convicts, I know about the hole, about the water-cure, about the over-coat—about Klondike! You wait a month! That's all! When I get through, Whalen will be where he belongs—in the psychopathic ward with Sailor Jack! And I promise you things will change in here—look—here's an article about the Industrial Reformatory in Chillicothe—that's the kind of place this'll be!

BUTCH *(throwing paper aside):* I don't want no articles!—Allison, you're full a shit.

JIM: The boss'll throw the bunch of you in Klondike. Do yourself a favor. Work with me. We can case the jug. But not if we keep going opposite ways—Give me your hand on it, Butch.

BUTCH: Fuck you!

JIM: It's no dice, huh? What do you say, Joe? Swifty?

BUTCH: They say what I say! Now git out before I lose my last ounce a' restriction!

JIM: Okay. *(He goes out.)*

Maybe Jim was on the level, Joe suggests. In Butch's opinion, Jim will be on the level only when he's in his coffin. Swifty feels sick and doesn't want to go to supper, but Butch needs him to help make noise.

Episode 8B

The men from Hall C march in to the dining area, take places at table and sit. When the order to start eating comes, Butch calls out "Don't eat it!" McBurney orders them to eat, but gradually a chorus of "Don't eat, don't eat, don't eat" begins. It builds and culminates in a chorus of "Ain't gonna eat, ain't gonna eat/They're gonna give us hell when we/Ain't gonna eat." Schultz blows the whistle and tells McBurney to get Hall C back into their cells. They're gonna learn a lesson, Schultz hollers, and he selects some from each cell—Ollie, Shapiro, Mex and Swifty—to spend two weeks in the hole on bread and water. Butch protests, "I started the noise." Schultz knows this but has other plans for Butch. The men march out, The Queen commenting that the hole will kill Swifty, already sick and off his feed from lack of exercise.

Episode 9

Ten days later, the evening of August 9, Whelan and Eva are in the office, she concerned about $600 missing in the commissary report, he unconcerned and on the make for her.

BOSS: What color's that blouse you got on?
EVA *(sensing nervously his approach)*: Chartreuse.
BOSS *(half-extending his hand)*: It's right Frenchy-looking.
EVA: Thank you. *(Types rapidly.)*
BOSS: Why don't you drop that formality stuff? *(Crosses to her.)* How do I look to you? Unromantic? Not so much like one of the movie stars?—Well, it might surprise you to know how well I go over with some of the girls! *(Seats himself on corner of the desk.)* I had a date not so long ago—Girl works over at the Cattle and Grain Market—'bout your age, build, ev'rything— *(Licks his lips.)* When I got through loving her up, she says to me—"Do it again, Papa, do it again!"— *(Roars with laughter, slaps the desk.)* Why? Because she *loved* it, that's why!

Whelan wants Eva to go with him to the room below the office. She won't. He's a married man, and she isn't that sort of a girl. He protests, he laughs, and she wants to know if she still has her job. He assures her she does, continuing to laugh as he grabs her. She is enduring his "fumbling embrace" as Jim enters, apologetically, and Whelan's fumbling ceases.

Whalen tells Jim to deal with the commissary report discrepancies. Jim observes that the men of Hall C are "too quiet." Whelan guesses they're scared, but Jim thinks they're probably planning a hunger-strike. The mention of this scares the warden, because it always causes a public sensation. Improving the food would avoid it, Jim argues, but Whalen thinks that the sight of the bunch of men who have been down in the hole might teach them a lesson and put them off. If not, there's always the heat, Whalen remarks, calling to Schultz as he moves out of the office.

Eva tells Jim that Whelan tried to get her to go to the room below with him, but she refused. She has a mark on her arm where he pinched her.

JIM: Were you scared?

EVA: Terribly scared—and at the same time—something else. If I told you, you'd be disgusted with me.

JIM: Attracted?

EVA: Yes, in a way. I knew that if he touched me I wouldn't have been able to move.

JIM: In the wood-pulps they call it fascinated horror.

EVA: Yes. Or a horrible fascination.

JIM: So you're convinced it's no place for a lady.

EVA: I'm not going to quit. Not yet. I've got a favorite nightmare, Jim, about finding myself alone in a big empty house. And knowing that something or some-body was hidden behind one of those doors, waiting to grab me—but instead of running out of the house, I always go searching through it; opening all of the closed doors—even when I come to the last one.

JIM: And what do you find?

EVA: I don't know. I always wake up just then.

JIM: So you're going to try the same thing here?

EVA: Something like that.

JIM: I guarantee you won't be disappointed.

As they work on the commissary report, Eve challenges Jim to open the door he's hiding behind, come out and trust her. It's repression that's making his hands shake, pent-up power all going to waste, getting bigger, accomplishing nothing. She promises him that the ten years of waiting here in prison have made him strong, and when the parole he hopes for comes through next month, nothing will stand in his way.

Whalen enters, followed by the guards escorting the hole prisoners, *"barely able to stand—some with heads bloody, others with clotted, shredded shirts."* Swifty has been in a straitjacket for five days and can barely stand. When Jim comments that Swifty has had enough, Whalen wants to know if Jim would like to take his place and, if not, to stay quiet. Ollie didn't think he'd make it through last night and is sentenced to two more nights for complaining. He is taken out, chanting his prayers, and the others are taken back to Hall C.

There is a sound of a disturbance, and Jim goes to investigate, returning imme-diately with the news that Ollie has killed himself by bashing his head against the wall. Whalen issues orders for Eva to fill out a card: Oliver Armsted, 26, black; sentence, three years for stealing a crate of canned goods from a truck to feed his family; cause of death, stomach ulcers and severe hemorrhages.

Disturbing noises are beginning to penetrate the office. The prison grapevine is in action with the news of Ollie's death, and the sounds are coming from all the Halls now. Whalen, alarmed, directs Schultz to ready the Klondike radiators. In sudden darkness, whispers escalate in volume and pitch. Then the lights go up on Butch in the cell.

BUTCH *(shouts it through the bars):* They killed Ollie!

SHAPIRO: Ollie's dead!

ALL: They killed Ollie!

JOE: What are we going to do about it?

BUTCH: Quit eating! *(Shouts through the bars.)* QUIT EATING!

CHORUS: Quit eating! Quit eating!

ALL *(sing):* Ain't gonna eat, ain't gonna, etc. . . .

BUTCH: HUNGER-STRIKE! . . . . .

WHISPERS: What does Butch say?—Butch says to quit eating—hunger-strike?—Yeah, hunger-strike!—Butch says HUNGER-STRIKE!—Hunger-strike—quit eating—quit eating—HUNGER-STRIKE!

SCHULTZ *(picks up intercom):* The men in Hall C have quit eating!

KRAUSE: Hunger-strike in Hall C!

NEWSBOY: *Morning Star!* Paper! *Morning Star!* Paper! Read about the big hunger-strike!

WOMAN'S VOICE: It is reported that some of the men in the state prison have gone on a hunger-strike!

      Sound: Click of telegraph.

VOICE: Associated Press Bulletin—Hunger-strike at Monroe City Penitentiary! Men rebel against monotonous diet!

VOICE: Columbia Broadcasting System!

BOSS: Hunger-strike denied.

VOICE: Commissioners promise an investigation of alleged starvation in state penitentiary . . . !

VOICE: Warden denies hunger-strike!

VOICE: Hunger-strike reported.

ALL: HUNGER-STRIKE! HUNGER-STRIKE! HUNGER-STRIKE! HUNGER-STRIKE!

      Traffic noises, sirens, bells. Curtain.

ACT II

Episode 1

The evening of Saturday, August 13, the sixth day of the hunger-strike, the atmosphere is tense. Eva is alone in the office, when the Chaplain appears—a decent-looking and unassuming man with a dignified presence—worried about danger "aggravated by the fact that Mr. Whalen apparently won't recognize it." Jim enters; he has been hurt when he got too close to one of the cages, but he won't tell who did it. The Chaplain, before going off, expresses the hope that the next month will be the end of the bad years for Jim.

Jim is worried that Eva may be in danger because she knows a lot she could tell. Eva admits it, but she's not ready to leave yet—maybe next month they can both go. He informs her that the boiler room pipes have been reinforced; Jim realizes that he probably ought to tell all he knows himself right now, but doing so would cost him his chance of getting out soon.

JIM: It's funny—

EVA: What?

JIM: Nothing has quite so much value as the skin our own guts are wrapped in.
> *Takes a book and sits down at window. Eva resumes typing. Jim suddenly tears a page out and throws it on the floor in disgust.*

Christ!

EVA: What did you do that for?

JIM: I didn't like it.

EVA: What was it?

JIM: A little piece of verbal embroidery by a guy named Keats.

EVA: What's wrong with it?

JIM: It's sissy stuff—*Ode to a Nightingale!* Don't those literary punks know there's something more important to write about than that? They ought to spend a few years in stir before they selected their subjects!

EVA: Why don't you show them, then?

JIM: I'd give my right arm for the chance.

EVA: You have the chance.

JIM: Not in here I don't, if I wrote what I wanted to write. I'd stay in here till Klondike becomes an ice-plant! But maybe next month—

EVA: Yes. Next month—

JIM: Maybe then I'll start writing—but not about nightingales!

Eva informs him that Keats "didn't have a very good time of it" and died at 26. "He wanted to live. Terribly." She reads Jim another of Keats's poems, one he'll like, she thinks, the sonnet beginning "When I have fears that I may cease to be." Keats's writing about beauty was a form of escape, she tells him. Jim claims his form of escape would be "blowing things wide open," destruction, yes. She's sorry he's so bitter. He wonders why she'd be sorry about anything, except possibly losing her job. It's because she likes him, she insists.

Whelan comes in and sends Jim off to drop the word that they got the temperature in Klondike up to 150 degrees in a test. The Chaplain comes in to talk about Ollie's death—"Too many suicides, drownings, hangings, so-called accidents," he tells Whalen, and now it looks like a mass-suicide in Hall C is possible. Whalen demands to know who's running the prison, "You or me?" The Chaplain answers him by describing the universe as a set of blocks, the little one fitting into the big one, bigger one over that one, till the biggest of all fits on top of the others—and the biggest block, which he represents, is the Kingdom of God. Whalen suggests that the Chaplain's work at the prison is interfering with his higher duties, and he wants the Chaplain up there on the top, leaving him alone down here on his little block.

CHAPLAIN: I could leave here gladly if it wasn't for what I have to take with me.

BOSS: You're taking nothing with you but the shirt on your back.

CHAPLAIN: I'm taking much more than that.

BOSS: Aw. Maybe I'd better have you frisked on the way out.

CHAPLAIN: You could strip me naked, and I'd still have these.

BOSS: These what?

CHAPLAIN: Memories—shadows—ghosts! Things I've seen that I can't forget. Men tortured, twisted, driven mad. Death's the least of it. It's the *life* in here that's going to stay with me like an incurable disease.

BOSS: Ahhhhhh! *(Lifts phone.)* Git me Atwater 277.

CHAPLAIN: By God, Whelan, and that's not profanity. I won't rest easy until I've seen these walls torn down, stone by stone, and others put in their place that let the air in!

BOSS: Hello. Reverend? This is Warden Whalen. Our chaplain's just resigned.

CHAPLAIN: Goodnight! *(Goes out quickly.)*

BOSS: I want you to come over and talk to me—might be a steady job in it for you. Yes, siree! You be over here in time for our Sunday service ... *(Hangs up.)* Memories, shadows, ghosts! What a screwball! *(Pours himself a drink.)*

Episode 2

Sunday morning, August 14, in Hall C Butch is describing Klondike to The Queen and Joe. There are radiators all around the windowless walls. Steam comes out of the valves, so thick you can't see, "like breathin' fire in yer lungs." The floor is too hot to stand on, but there's nowhere else to stand. There's one air hole, but the people panic and fight over it, and the weak ones die, "Unless the Boss takes 'em out. And when you beat Klondike you beat everything they've got to offer in here. It's their ace of spades."

Episode 3

That afternoon, Whalen is interviewing the Reverend Hooker, "*a nervous, precise little man with a prodigious anxiety to please.*" Whelan wants to assure himself that the man is "adjustable" to conditions, and that he doesn't have any theories about a set of blocks. He hopes the Reverend is good at speaking extemporaneously, because it's almost time for the service to begin, and his job will depend on his bringing these three subjects into his talk: food, heat and Klondike.

Sound of hymn ending.

REV: Yes—uh—very good afternoon to you all. *(Clears his throat; beams.)* I hope that you enjoyed your Sunday dinner as much as I did mine—

VOICE: We don't eat spaghetti and meatballs!

Chorus of booing. Schultz: warning whistle. Silence.

REV *(nervously):* Food is such a familiar blessing that—uh—we sometimes forget to be properly grateful for it. But when I read about the horrible conditions in famine-stricken portions of Europe and Asia—tch, tch!—I feel that I am indeed very fortunate to have a full stomach!

Booing. Schultz whistles.

When one thinks of food—uh—one also thinks by a natural association of ideas— about—uh—the marvelous blessing of—uh—*heat!* Heat—uh—that makes food possible—wonderful *heat!* Heat of all kinds! The heat of the sun that warms the earth's atmosphere and permits the growth of the vegetables and the grains *(Slow stomping of feet.)* and the—uh—fruits—uh—the heat of the—uh—body—uh . . . *(Wipes his forehead.)* heat, universal heat—At this time of the year some of us find heat oppressive—uh—But that is ungrateful of us, extremely ungrateful. *(Raising his voice.)* For all living matter depends on the presence of heat—northward and southward from the equator to the twin poles—even to far Alaska—even in *Klondike* . . . *(Stomping louder.)* What would Klondike be without heat? A frozen wasteland.

The Reverend scrubs his forehead and glances nervously about. A hymnal is hurled: furious stomping.)

The Reverend tries to go on, but is bombarded. There are whistles, shouting and a siren. Whalen is on the phone in his office calling for all guards on duty. The men from Hall C are to be locked in. The Reverend rushes in, claiming he needs medical attention. Whelan soothes him with a few dollars, then orders Schultz to tell the men they have one more chance: if they don't eat supper, they're in Klondike.

Episode 4

Late that afternoon, Jim, who isn't locked up in Hall C like his fellow inmates, joins Eva in the office. *"His chronic tension has now risen to the point of breaking."* Eva too is torn between her desperate need for this job and her knowledge that "thirty-five hundred animals are being starved to death and threatened with torture," and she ought to tell somebody about it. Jim, deciding to take action even though it will cost him his parole, picks up the phone, but Eva stops him. She'll go to the newspaper office herself, this evening, on the way home. Jim tells her not to do it.

Eva is getting her hat when Whelan enters and tells her he needs her back here after supper. After she exits, Jim asks Whelan about the status of his "ten years of copper" and his upcoming parole. Whelan is angry at Jim for bringing it up at a time like this, threatening him with Klondike if he doesn't drop the subject. He orders

Jim to return later and goes off to get his own supper. *"Jim covers his face with a strangled sob."*

Episode 5

There is *"an undercurrent of desperation"* later that evening in Hall C, but Butch is gamely singing "I'm Forever Blowing Bubbles," Goldie's favorite. Shultz returns Swifty from the hole to the cell, reminding the others that "The hole is just a small dose compared to Klondike!" Swifty is coughing and sobbing and slowly collapses. The Queen tries to comfort him as the others begin chorusing, "Where's Ollie?" Schultz threatens them again before going off: "Just one of you finicky lads leave a little spaghetti on his plate tonight an' see what happens!!"

Butch raps on the bars for attention.

BUTCH: Cut the cackle, all of yuz! ..... Lissen here now!—Anybody in Hall C that eats is gonna pay for his supper in Kangaroo Court—I'll assess the maximum fine, you know what!—You're scared of Klondike? I say, let 'em throw us in Klondike!—Maybe some of you weak sisters will be melted down to grease-chunks. But not all twenty-five of us! Some of us are gonna beat Klondike! And Klondike's deir las' trump card, when you got that licked, you've licked everything they've got to offer in here! You got 'em over the barrel for good! So then what happens? They come up to us, and they say, "You win! What is it you want?"—We say, "Boss Whalen is out! Git us a new warden! Git us decent livin' conditions! No more overcrowdin', no more bunkin' up wit' contajus diseasus, fresh air in the cell-blocks, fumigation, an' most of all—WE WANT SOME FOOD THAT'S FIT TO PUT IN OUR BELLIES!" *(Applause.)* ..... Maybe when we git through housecleaning, this place'll be like the Industrial Reformatory they got at Chillicothe! A place where guys are learnt how to make a livin' after they git outta stir! Where they teach 'em trades an' improve their ejication! Not just lock 'em up in dirty holes an' hope to God they'll die so as to save the state some money!! *(Fierce yammering.)* —Tonight we go to Klondike!—Dere's three compartments! One of 'em's little hell, one of 'em's middle-sized hell, and one of 'em's BIG HELL!—You know which one Butch O'Fallon is gonna be in!—So if I ain't yellow, boys, don't you be neither!—That's all I got to say.

VOICE: Okay, Butch.
KRAUSE: We're witcha!
SHAPIRO: We'll beat Klondike!
VOICE: You bet we'll beat it—
QUEEN: Put Whalen over a barrel—
      Nervous laughter and applause. Voices die abruptly under a shadow of fear.

Episode 6

Later in the evening, Eva joins Jim in the office. Jim is morosely defining life as "a gradual process of dying"—at least in here it is. He believes he'll be turned down for parole. It was bad timing, bringing it up to Whelan. He's feeling "out of control."

The warden looks over the prisoners in their cellblock, a section of Richard Hoover's Tony Award-winning set for *Not About Nightingales*

JIM *(his fear visible):* If I get turned down again this time, I'll never get another chance.

EVA: Why not?

JIM: Because I'll blow up!—Crack to pieces! I'm drawn as tight as I can get right now!

EVA: Don't be a fool, Jim.

JIM: You don't know what it's been like. Hated like poison for ten years by everybody but him. Working for him and all the time hating him so that it made me sick at the guts to look at him even! Ten years of being his stooge. Jimmy boy, do this, do that! Yes Sir, yes, Mr. Whalen!—My hands aching to catch that beefy red neck of his and choke the breath out of it! That's one reason why they shake so much—and here's another. Standing here at this window, looking out, seeing the streets. the buildings, the traffic moving, the lights going off and on, and me being penned up in here, in these walls, locked in 'em so tight it's like I was buried under the earth in a coffin with a glass lid that I could see the world through! While I felt the worms crawling inside me . . .

EVA: No. Don't be a fool. There's a carnival on South Gay. I ran in like a kid and took a ride on the zebra!

JIM: Yes?

EVA: There's two seats on the zebra, Jim. One in front, one in back—Next month we'll ride him together!

JIM *(suddenly breaking):* Eva! Eva! *(Covers his face.)*

EVA *(running to him):* I love you!

     Pause.

JIM *(his voice choked):* What is this place? What's it for? Why, why! The judges say guilty. But what is guilty? What does that word mean, anyhow? It's funny, but I don't know. Look it up in Webster's Dictionary. What's it say? "Responsible for the commission of crime." But why responsible? What's responsible mean? Who's ever been given a choice? When they mix up all the little molecules we're made out of, do they ask each other one politely which he will be—rich man, poor man, beggar man, thief? God, no! It's all accidental. And yet the judge says, "Jim, you're guilty."

     Tosses dictionary to floor.

This book's no good any more. We need a new one with a brand new set of definitions.

EVA: Don't say any more—I—

     Kisses him.

Jim wonders how this thing happened between himself and Eva, it's a dirty trick because they can never have each other. Eva insists they can. She doesn't know how, but she believes it because of her love for him. They cling to each other until Jim has to answer the phone. It's Schultz calling—supper's not being eaten, and Hall C will be in Klondike by 10 o'clock.

Whelan enters and sends Jim downstairs with a message for the bulletin board. We hear Schultz's whistle signaling that the prisoners from Hall C are on their way to Klondike. They are chanting, "Devil come to meet us an' he rang on a bell/ Twenty-five men got a ticket to hell!/Turn on the heat, turn on the heat/They're gonna give us hell when they turn on the heat!"

Episode 6A

The next morning, August 15, Whelan informs Eva that he should have told her to bring her things with her—"Your little silk nightie and stuff"—because he's put the prison under quarantine restrictions. Is there an epidemic? "Twenty-five cases are going to be running a pretty high fever tonight." Nobody is allowed on or off the island without the warden's permission, and no outside phone calls are permitted.

Whelan is drinking. He notices that Eva is upset and wonders why she seems to be afraid of him. Eva's reaction is, "Don't touch me! Please don't!" He knows all about this "Don't touch me stuff," his wife gets that way, too. When she does, he runs his fingers along her throat, very gently, until the stiffness is gone. His voice is hypnotic, and the nervously-exhausted Eva's eyes are closing. "And then I—" he goes on, but the phone rings. He answers, then takes his coat and leaves, telling the semi-conscious Eva he'll be right back.

When the door slams, Eva comes to; then, as it opens again, she screams. It's Jim, and she pleads hysterically for him to get her out of here. He calms her down, and she tells him what has happened: She is virtually a prisoner here herself. Whelan frightened her the way he was looking at her, and his voice had kind of put her to sleep. She would have gone out the window if Jim hadn't come.

Jim promises Eva she'll get away, and they'll be together. He tells her to meet him in the southwest corner of the yard at 9:30 that night. They'll be safe there, Jim assures her, "It's dark. Nobody could see us." *Curtain.*

ACT III

Episode 1

"During the following episodes the theater is filled almost constantly with the soft hiss of live steam from the pipes." As of 8 a.m. Monday morning, the men have been in Klondike for ten hours. Whalen wants the temperature raised to 130 degrees and in Butch's compartment to 135.

In the clouded atmosphere of Klondike, *"The men are sprawled on the floor, breathing heavily . . . . . skin shiny with sweat."* Swifty and The Queen are sick. Butch is trying to tell old jokes, then wants them to sing. Joe tries but bends double coughing. Swifty sobs for water.

At 2 p.m. Whalen is told the men were singing and orders the temperature up again so they have something to sing about. There is the *"loud shrill hiss of steam as more pressure is turned on."* The Queen is terrified. Butch demands that they go on singing. They are fighting over the one air-hole. They have to take turns, so many seconds per man, but if somebody flips out he'll have to be pushed out of the line, Butch pronounces. Some of them will beat it, though, Joe swears. They try to get Swifty to the air hole, but it's no good. "I guess he's—beating a cinder track— around the stars now," Butch surmises.

Episode 2

It is 7 p.m. Swifty is dead. As the pipes hiss, Butch warns the others to keep down close to the floor. He reveals to Joe that he's got his razor with him. "That's one way out," Joe notes, but Butch hopes to find it useful if the Boss or Schultz or the Canary come down here. Butch hears the lock-up bell and figures they'll only be in here for 12 more hours.

JOE: How d'you know how long it will be?

BUTCH: They don't want to kill us!

JOE: Why don't they? *(Coughs.)* Your turn, Butch.

BUTCH: Yeah, git moving, Queenie!

QUEEN: Naw! Lemme breathe!

> *Butch tears him away from air-hole. Shapiro shouts something in Yiddish. The Queen rises and staggers.*

I got to get out of here! I can't breathe! Lemme out, lemme out, lemme out!

> *Pounds at wall, staggers blindly toward the pipes.*

BUTCH: Stay away from the pipes!

> *The Queen staggers directly into cloud of steam—screams—falls to floor.*

He's scalded himself. *(The Queen screams and sobs.)* Stop it! Goddam yuh!

> *Grasps The Queen's collar and cracks his head against the floor.*

There now!

JOE: Butch—you killed him.

BUTCH: Someone shoulda done him that favor a long time ago.

The lights fade on Klondike as Butch resumes telling a joke to keep his companions going, and a spotlight comes up on Whelan's office. The warden orders Schultz to keep the heat at 150 in Butch's compartment until further notice.

In Klondike, Shapiro, The Queen and Swifty are lying dead, while Butch and Joe are at the air hole. Joe begs Butch to use the razor on him.

JOE: I'm chokin' t'death. I can't stand it.

BUTCH: Breathe!

JOE: There ain't no air comin' in now, Butch.

BUTCH: There's air—breathe it, Joe.

JOE: Naw . . .

BUTCH *(raises his face, shakes him; hoarsely):* Goddam yuh, don't chicken-out! Stay with me, Joe. We can beat Klondike! *(Joe laughs deliriously. Butch springs up.)* Turn off them fuckin' pipes!! Turn the heat off, Goddam yuh, turn it off! *(Staggers toward pipes.)* Stop it, y'hear me? Quit that SSSSS! SSSSS! *(Imitates sound.)* I'll turn yuh off, yuh sonsa-bitches!

> *Springs on pipes and grapples with them as though with human adversary—tries to throttle steam with hands—is scalded—screams with agony—breaks away, his face contorted, wringing hands.*

With Joe at the air-hole, Butch imitates the sound of the steam and, maddened with pain, demands that his companions, the living and the dead, raise their voices in song: "I'm Forever Blowing Bubbles . . . "

Episode 2A

Butch hallucinates Goldie dancing with him, as he confesses to her that he never could find the right words to tell her how he really felt about her. She knew he loved her, though, without being told. And she is still true to him, waiting for him, alone in her half-empty bed.

Episode 3

At 9:45 p.m. in the southwest corner of the yard, Eva tells Jim she is upset because Whalen's wife has left the island, and she just can't bear the thought of staying "in that place" alone with the warden. As Jim begins to undress Eva, a light is moving above them. He warns her to keep down and be quiet. The light disappears, and Eva mentions that he's never said he loves her. "I love you. Now!" he responds. The light reappears and circles down, stopping directly above them. Jim whispers, "Crawl" and "Quick!" But the light comes right in on Eva's face, causing her to scream. There are sirens and bells and an offstage voice laughing and ordering, "O.K., we've got them, keep them in the light."

Episode 4

Jim and Eva have been brought to the office by a Guard who explains to Whelan that "Canary's turned into a love-bird." He'd heard a girl's voice in the corner of the yard, put the light on, and there they were!—and they "weren't picking daisies."

Whelan is angry—Eva had been hysterical with him but has behaved "like a bitch in heat" with Jim. Eva declares that she asked Jim to meet her in the yard because she was frightened of being locked in this place, and she demands that she be let out of here immediately. Whelan orders the Guard to hold onto Eva. Jim tries to intervene, and Whelan lashes him and knocks him to the floor. The warden orders the Guard to take Jim out and throw him into Klondike with Butch O'Fallon.

Alone with Eva, Whelan changes his tactics and apologizes to her, pleading that he's been under a strain.

BOSS: It's not easy to be the head of an institution like this. I've handled it like I would handle everything else. The best I knew how. Sometimes—I'm telling you the truth, girl—I've been so sick at heart at things I've had to do and see done— that it hurt me to look into my own little girl's face and hear her call me—Daddy!
        Pours himself a drink.
Here. You take one, too. (*He is breathing heavily and for the moment is perfectly earnest.*) Maybe it's done something to me in here. (*Touches head.*) Sometimes I don't feel quite the same any more. Awful, awful! Men down there now being sub-jected to awful torture! But what can I do about it? I got to keep discipline—dealing with criminals—there's no other way.

Eva takes the offered drink and asks Whelan what it is he wants from her. He wants what any man wants, and what she gave Jim—he wants sympathy. She gave it because she loves him, Eva asserts, and she wants to know what Whelan is going to do about Jim's upcoming parole. The warden has already prepared a letter recommending Jim's release, but he won't send it now. Eva wonders if he would change his mind and send the letter if she offered him the kind of sympathy he longs for. "Why not?" Whalen smiles. "You see how easy it is to straighten things out!" There is still time tonight to get the letter into the mail on the 11:45 boat, Eva points out, assuring him, "Don't worry. I won't back out. I'm not afraid of you now." Whelan calls for the Guard and hands him a letter to be posted immediately.

Episode 5

At 10 p.m. in Klondike, Butch, lying by the air hole, hears voices and lifts his head. When the door opens he pretends to be unconscious. When the flashlight is turned on, Schultz and McBurney see the dead bodies. McBurney is horrified that they've been roasted alive. Schultz has started a body count, when Butch springs up and grabs him by the throat, and at the same time Jim attacks McBurney. A shot is fired. Jim takes possession of the revolver and orders Schultz to put up his hands and Butch—who is astonished to find the Canary on his side—to get hold of Schultz's keys. Butch obliges, grins and goes to release all the men. Schultz threatens, but Jim tells him he's the one who's going to sweat. Jim backs out the door and slams it, leaving Schultz inside Klondike.

Episode 6

At 10:30 p.m. a siren's wail is heard in Whalen's office as Jim bursts in, bloodied, armed with the revolver, announcing, "Sometimes even hell breaks open and the damned get loose!" There's no point in pushing the buzzer, Jim tells Whalen, there's nobody at the other end. Everyone has broken out of Klondike, Jim informs him, except the four dead men and Schultz, and the other guards are locked into the cell block.

Jim asks for Eva. She's not there, Whelan lies. The other prisoners are just outside, waiting to come in here. Jim wanted to make sure Eva was out of the way before he let them in. Eva is heard calling to Jim from the next room. She comes in to tell Jim not to let the men in, the warden has already sent the letter recommending Jim's parole, because . . . Looking at them, Jim surmises the meaning of that "because." He orders Eva back into the other toom and locks the door.

Whelan can't believe Jim would give up his parole and put himself at risk of the electric chair. Jim thinks it's worth it. He hasn't forgotten the 14 days in the hole at the mercy of Whelan and "Dr. Jones." Whelan pleads that he was Jim's friend afterward and good to him. But Jim still has Whelan's signature on his back, and now a new whipping-boss is waiting—Butch O'Fallon.

> *Jim has gone out. Roar of men rises as doors are opened. Boss gasps and darts behind desk— men enter like a pack of wolves and circle about the walls.*

BUTCH *(lunges through):* Where is he?

BOSS: Butch. Butch!

BUTCH *(his eyes blinded):* There! I've caught the smell of him now!

> *The two rulers face each other for the first time. Outside there is scattered gunfire, and a flickering light is thrown through the windows like the reflection of flames.*

It's been you an' me for a long time—you in here—me out there—But now it's— together at last—It's a pleasure, Pig Face, to make your acquaintance.

BOSS: Look here now, boys—O'Fallon—Jim—I'll make a deal with you all—

BUTCH *(laughing and coming toward him):* Where's the Doctor?

CONVICT: Here!

> *Snatches rubber hose from wall and hands it to Butch.*

BUTCH: Yeah!

BOSS: Naw! Think of the consequences. Don't be fools. *(Cowers to floor.)* Stop! I'm a family man. I've got a wife! A daughter! A little girl.

BUTCH: This is for Ollie, Sailor Jack, Joe, Shapiro, Queenie.

> *The final words turn into a scream of anguish, as Butch crouches over him . . . . . beating him with demoniacal fury till he is senseless.*

The sound of a siren signals the imminent landing of a gunboat full of troopers. Butch calls for the lights to be turned off. The men, growing panicky, leave the room. The siren's wail goes on and on. Butch has thrown Whelan's "blubbering carcass" out the window into the Bay, and Jim says they have a chance that way— but Butch doesn't know how to swim. Jim decides he'll try it, while Butch will stay and fight it out. He holds out his hand to Jim, wishes him luck and admits he'd figured him wrong. He takes off a ring, gives it to Jim to give to a girl named Goldie who used to be at the Paradise Dance Hall on Brook Street west of the ferry—if he should ever meet her—and tell her Butch'd kept it all these years.

There is the sound of gunfire as Butch exits and Jim unlocks the door to let Eva out. She learns what has become of Whelan and what Jim plans to do. She doesn't think he'll have a chance. Jim hears the music of the Lorelei cruise boat—he'll "swim out and catch a ride." Eva warns that they'd just bring him back to prison. They won't see him, Jim insists.

EVA: Why?

JIM: Don't ask me why! There'll be a rope or something hanging overside. Or if she doesn't ride too high I'll grab the rail! How! Don't ask me how! Now is the time for unexpected things, for miracles, for wild adventures like the story-books!

EVA: Oh, Jim, there's not a chance that way!

JIM: Almost a chance! I've heard of people winning on a long shot. And if I don't—at least I'll be outside!

EVA: Oh, Jim, I would have liked to live with you outside. We might have found a place where searchlights couldn't point their fingers at us when we kissed. Quick love is hard. It gives us so little pleasure. We should have had long nights together with no walls. Or no stone walls—I know that place! A tourist camp beside a highway, Jim, with all night long the great trucks rumbling by—but only making shadows through the blinds! I'd touch the stone you're made of, Jim, and make you warm, so warm your love would burn a scar upon my body that no length of time could heal! We could forget all this as something dreamed!—Where shall it be? When, Jim? Tell me before you go . . . . .

JIM *(climbing to sill):* Watch the personal columns!

Eva calls goodbye as Jim, his shoes off, plunges from the window. The music from the Lorelei grows louder. We hear shouting, and three Troopers come into the office. Eva is recognized as the warden's secretary. The Troopers assure her she's all right, but she's in a daze and unable to speak.

TROOPER ONE: What's that she's got?

TROOPER THREE: A pair of—shoes!

TROOPER ONE: What's she doing with them?

TROOPER TWO: Whose are they?

EVA *(facing window with a faint smile):* I picked them up somewhere. I can't remember.

> *Music from the Lorelei rises to a crescendo as a string of colored lights slides past the window.*

LOUDSPEAKER: Aw, there it is! Y'can see it now, folks. That's the Island! Sort of misty tonight on account of the moon's gone under. Them walls are *escape-proof,* folks. Thirty-five hun'erd men locked in there an' some of them gonna stay there till Doomsday . . . *(Music.)* Ah, 's music again! Dancing on the upper deck, folks, dancing—dancing . . .

> *Light fades except spot on Eva clutching shoes. Curtain.*

Critics Award

○○○
○○○
○○○
○○○
○○○
○○○ CLOSER

A Play in Two Acts

BY PATRICK MARBER

Cast and credits appear on pages 254–255

PATRICK MARBER was born in London in 1965 to a middle class Jewish family in Wimbledon. Though he's written only two plays at this point, the awards and plaudits have been mounting steadily.

An Oxford English literature graduate in 1986, Marber tried his hand at stand-up comedy for a few years, an occupation he called "lonely." "I was a very dark version of Pee-wee Herman," he told a New York Magazine *scribe. He quit in 1992 and got work as a writer and performer on satirical television programs in the U.K. His directing assignments have included David Mamet's* The Old Neighborhood *at the Royal Court in June 1998.*

Marber's first play, Dealer's Choice, *debuted at the Royal National Theater's Cottesloe auditorium in February 1995. A transfer to the Vaudeville Theater soon followed, as did the* Evening Standard *Award for best comedy and the Writers Guild Award for best West End play. The play had its American premiere at the Long Wharf Theater, New Haven, October 16, 1996 (where it won the Connecticut Critics Circle Award for best production of a play). It reached New York's Manhattan Theater Club April 8, 1997 and won praise for its focused, intense and verbally astute look at a high-stakes weekly poker game among co-workers at a restaurant. In his review of the MTC mounting, Clive Barnes lauded John Tillinger's direction and wrote, "It is remarkable how well Marber maintains the interest and tension—especially in the crucial second act, which is little more than a succession of poker hands."*

In creating Dealer's Choice, *Marber certainly followed the famous bit of playwriting advice, "Write what you know." He'd been in Gamblers Anonymous for several years. Pool and poker are still occasional vices for him. The show was invited to Atlanta as part of a cultural festival surrounding the Olympics. One night, the all-*

male group went out after the performance to a nearby strip club, which set Marber to thinking about the identities of the women who work there—hence the origin of Closer.

Marber's strong suit of crisp, no-holds-barred banter would again dominate in his second play. Closer *opened at the Cottesloe in May 1997. Directed by Marber, it moved to the Royal National's Lyttelton Theater and gave the author his second* Evening Standard *Award for best comedy. He also took home the* Time Out *Award for best West End play, the London Critics Circle Award for best play and the Laurence Olivier Award for best new play. The Broadway production, again staged by Marber and featuring Anna Friel, Natasha Richardson, Ciaran Hinds and Rupert Graves, opened March 25 at the Music Box. The New York Drama Critics Circle hailed it with best-foreign-play honors, and a best-play Tony nomination followed.*

Interviewed by Time Out New York, *Marber no doubt made a host of other playwrights jealous by saying, "I approach my writing with all the vanity and egomania of an artist, but the way I make a work of art is through craft . . . . . I just don't feel there's anything particularly mysterious about writing. It's hard work, and you have to use your brain, and you have to be brave and skillful." As for his writing style, Marber told the Los Angeles* Times, *he remains influenced by his years doing standup: "If you're not quick and interesting, the audience will be gone. There's no point setting up a joke for five minutes before you deliver the punch line. [So] you write a joke, add to it, and it becomes a routine. From one line it becomes twenty minutes of material. Work it up, and you have a scene."*

Crediting Mamet's Glengarry Glen Ross *as an influence on* Dealer's Choice *and Harold Pinter's* Betrayal *for* Closer, *Marber told the Los Angeles* Times, *"I hope I'm beginning to develop my own voice, but for now I'm a playwright whose influences are visible. I'm not ashamed of that. One frightening thing about success with your first two plays is, you aren't given time to find your voice. You arrive fully formed, but I don't feel fully formed as a writer. Nor should I be."*

The following synopsis of Closer *was prepared by David Lefkowitz. This synopsis is based on the script as performed on Broadway this season, not upon the final published version authorized by the playwright.*

Time and Place: The play is set in London in the 1990s

ACT I

SYNOPSIS: The play's 12 scenes span approximately five years. Scene 1 begins in the waiting room of a hospital, where Alice, *"a girl from the town,"* sits awaiting medical help. *"She is wearing a black leather coat. She has a duffle bag by her side. Also a brown leather briefcase. She has a cut on her leg. Quite bloody. She looks at it. She picks some grit from the wound."*

Alice takes out her cigarette pack—it is empty. She looks into the briefcase and takes an apple from it. As she begins to eat, Dan, *"a man from the suburbs,"* enters carrying two styrofoam cups. He stops and watches her, then hands her one of the hot drinks. Alice apologizes for going through his briefcase in search of a cigarette.

DAN: Didn't fancy my sandwiches?
ALICE: I don't eat fish.
DAN: Why not?
ALICE: Fish piss in the seas.
DAN: So do children.
ALICE: I don't eat children either. What's your work?
DAN: I'm a . . . sort of journalist.
ALICE: What *sort.*
     Beat.
DAN: I write obituaries.
ALICE: Do you like it . . . in the dying business?
DAN: It's a living.

Dan helps Alice put her leg up; it's clear her injury isn't all that serious. Nevertheless, during their flirtation, Dan asks her why she stepped into the road without looking.

ALICE: I never look where I'm going.
DAN: We stood at the lights, I looked into your eyes, and then you . . . stepped into the road.
ALICE: Then what?
DAN: You were lying on the ground, you focused on me, you said, "Hallo, stranger."
ALICE: What a tart.
DAN: I noticed your leg was cut.
ALICE: Did you notice my legs?
DAN: Maybe.

Dan recounts to Alice how he and the cabdriver who hit her brought her, disoriented, into the hospital. Alice explains that she'd just come out of a club near the meat market at Blackfriars Bridge, followed by a walk in Postman's Park—"a tiny park . . . it's a graveyard too," with a memorial to people who died saving the lives of others, and a statue of a Minotaur. This triggers a memory for Dan: sitting in the same park with his father on the afternoon of his mother's death.

The topic quickly brings them back to Dan's job writing obituaries, "the Siberia of journalism."

DAN: Well . . . we call it "the obits page." There's three of us: Me, Harry and *Graham.* When I get to work, without fail Graham will say, "Who's on the slab?" Meaning, did anyone important die overnight—are you *sure* you want to know?
ALICE: Yes.

DAN: Well, if someone "important" did die, we go to the "deep freeze," which is a computer containing all the obituaries, and we'll find the dead person's life.

ALICE: People's obituaries are written while they're still alive?

DAN: Some people's. If no one important has died, then Harry—he's the editor—decides who we lead with, and we check facts, make calls, polish the prose. At six, we stand round the computer and read the next day's page, make final changes, put in a few euphemisms to amuse ourselves . . .

ALICE: Such as?

DAN: "He was a convivial fellow," meaning he was an alcoholic. "He valued his privacy"—gay. "He *enjoyed* his privacy"—raging queen.

> *Alice gently strokes Dan's face. He is unnerved but not unwilling.*

ALICE: What would *your* euphemism be . . .

DAN: "He was *reserved.*"

ALICE: And mine?

DAN: "She was—*disarming.*"

A doctor finally enters the room. He has no intention of staying but is held there by Alice's pretty face. He examines her leg and notices a long scar, commenting on the poor stitch job. Alice replies, cryptically, "In America. A truck . . . . . I was in the middle of nowhere." Before he exits, the doctor, Larry, *"a man from the city,"* gives a grateful Alice a cigarette. Non-smoker Dan is tempted to have a drag, but he's more interested in what brought Alice to the middle of nowhere. She replies that she'd been traveling with a guy but ran away.

DAN: Where?

ALICE: New York.

DAN: Just like that?

ALICE: It's the only way to leave. "I don't love you any more. Goodbye."

DAN: Suppose you do still love them?

ALICE: You don't leave.

DAN: You never left someone you still love?

ALICE: No.

Further conversation reveals that Alice has worked as a stripper, about which she's nonchalant, saying, "I know what men want . . . Men want a girl who looks like a boy. They want to protect her, but she must be a survivor, And she must *come*—like a train—but with *elegance.*" When Dan asks her what *she* wants, she replies, "To be loved."

Dan, who already has a girl friend, wants to meet Alice after work, but she convinces him to take the day off. As the scene ends, they exchange their full names: his, Daniel Woolf; hers, Alice Ayres. Her nickname for him, though, is "Buster."

A year and a half later, Anna, *"a woman from the country,"* is photographing Dan in her studio. During a break, Dan lights a cigarette but stubs it out when Anna disapproves. Shooting resumes, as does their chit-chat.

ANNA: I liked your book.

DAN: Thank you.

ANNA: When's it published?

DAN: Next year. How come you read it?

ANNA: Your publisher sent me a manuscript, I read it last night. You kept me up till four.

DAN: I'm flattered.

ANNA: Is your anonymous heroine based on someone real?

DAN: She's . . . someone called Alice . . .
>   *Beat.*

ANNA: How does she feel about your stealing her life?

DAN: *Borrowing* her life. I've dedicated the book to her, she's pleased.

Dan then asks Anna about her work; she tells him she'll be exhibiting a series of portraits the following summer. As Anna adjusts his hair for the next shot, Dan tells her she's beautiful. "No I'm not," she counters. He then asks if she found the content of his book obscene. She replies that she found it honest about sex and love but thinks a better title would be *The Aquarium,* which Dan reminds her refers to a particularly risque scene.

DAN: You like Aquariums?

ANNA: Fish are therapeutic.

DAN: Hang out in Aquariums, do you?

ANNA: When I can.

DAN: Good for picking up "strangers?"

ANNA: *Photographing* strangers. I took my first picture in the one at London Zoo.

DAN: Come here.
>   *He gently strokes her arm, she looks at him.*

ANNA: I don't kiss strange men . . .

DAN: Neither do I.

A kiss leads Anna to enquire whether Dan lives with Alice. He concedes as much. She tells him she's married but separated, no kids. Dan checks his watch and realizes Alice will be arriving here to meet him momentarily.

ANNA: Why are you wasting her time?

DAN: I'm not. I'm grateful to her . . . she's . . . completely lovable and completely unleavable.

ANNA: And you don't want someone else to get their dirty hands on her?

DAN: Maybe.

ANNA: Men are crap.

DAN: But all the same.

ANNA: They're still crap. *(The door buzzer goes.)* Your muse . . .

DAN *(looks at Anna):* You've ruined my life.
ANNA: You'll get over it.

Dan goes to open the door for Alice, who has arranged to meet him here, and introduces the two women to each other. Alice asks Anna if Dan has been a well-behaved and photogenic subject. "Did you steal his soul?" she jokes. Anna laughs and offers tea, but Alice requests only directions to the rest room. When she's off, Dan begs to see Anna again. Anna declines.

Alice reenters and asks if Anna will take a photo of her—on condition that Dan not be in the room. All agree, and Dan heads to the local pub, leaving the women alone. As the photo session starts, Anna comments, "I read Dan's book, you've had . . . quite a life." Alice grills Anna about her personal life, learning that her husband, who left for a younger woman, was a stockbroker type.

ALICE: We used to get those in the clubs. Wall Street boys.
ANNA: So . . . those places were quite . . . up-market?
ALICE: Some of them, but I preferred the dives.
ANNA: Why?
ALICE: The poor are more generous.
ANNA *(looks back into the camera):* You've got a great face. *(Focuses.)* How do you feel about Dan using your life, for his book?
ALICE: None of your fucking business.
     Beat.
When he let me in . . . downstairs, he had . . . this . . . "look." I just listened to your . . . *conversation.*
     Pause.
ANNA: I don't know what to say.
ALICE: Take my picture.
     Beat.
ANNA: I'm not a thief, Alice.

The photo session resumes, with both women regarding each other warily.

The next scene splits the stage, with Dan in his apartment sitting at his computer table, and Larry, the doctor from the first scene, staring at the computer in his office. Between them is a large screen on which the audience can read their typed, internet instant messages. Neither know who the other is. Larry makes believe he's never been in an on-line chat room before. Dan makes believe he's Anna.

LARRY: Nice 2 meet U.
DAN: I love COCK.
     Pause.
LARRY: Youre v.forward
DAN: And UR chatting on "LONDON FUCK." Do U want sex?
LARRY: yes. describe u.

DAN: Tall, blonde 30s, dirty mouth, Epic Tits.
LARRY: define epic
DAN: 36DD
LARRY: Nice arse?
DAN: Y
LARRY: Becos i want 2 know.
DAN *(smiles):* No, "Y" means "Yes!"
LARRY: O
DAN: Sit on my face Fuckboy.

This continues, with Dan (as Anna) convincing Larry to unzip. Before he can start masturbating, Larry is distracted, as his business phone rings. After taking a medical call, he hurries back to the keyboard, worried that "Anna" has left. Dan (as Anna) asks him what he thinks of when he masturbates. Larry replies, "Ex girl friends."

DAN: Tell me your sex-ex fantasy . . .
LARRY: Hotel room . . . they tie me up—tease me—won't let me come. They fight over me, 6 tonges on my cock, balls, perineum et cetera.
DAN: All hail the Sultan of Twat? *(Larry laughs.)*

Larry asks what "Anna" imagines when she wanks, leading to a response so filthy, even he's taken aback. His business phone rings again. He picks up and hangs up instantaneously, then takes the phone off the hook.

DAN: Wait, have to type with 1 hand . . . I'm cumming right now . . . ohohoh-ohohohohohohohohohohohohohohohohohohohohohohohohohohohohohohoh . . . . .
LARRY: Was it good?
DAN: No!

Dan (as Anna) begs to meet Larry in person. The latter demurs because he has to do rounds, but they agree to meet the next day, at 1 p.m., at the Aquarium in the London Zoo.

That's where the next scene occurs, with the real Anna spending her lunch hour at the Aquarium, as is her wont. She notices this man in a white lab coat staring at her.

LARRY *(smiles):* I'm Larry . . . *(Dirty.)* "The Doctor."
ANNA: Hallo, Doctor Larry.
LARRY: Feel free to call me . . . "The Sultan."
ANNA: Why?
LARRY: I can't believe these things actually *happen.* I thought . . . if you turned up, you'd be a bit of a trout . . . but you are bloody gorgeous.
ANNA: Thank you.

Pause.
LARRY: You mentioned a hotel.

Larry doesn't want to rush things, but he is due in surgery at 3. Anna is surprised to discover he really is a doctor. Anna assures him she's *not* the "Nymph of the Net" he chatted with the day before. She'd been at a cafe with her friend Alice at the time she was supposedly cybering. He assumes she's simply playing dumb because she's not interested in him, now that they've met face to face. But he presses on, leading Anna to conclude someone was pretending to be her—that someone being Daniel Woolf.

LARRY: Who?
ANNA: He's Alice's boy friend. She told me yesterday that he plays around on the Net. It's *him.*
LARRY: No, I was talking to a woman.
ANNA: How do you know?
LARRY: Believe me, she was a woman, I got a huge . . . she was a woman.
ANNA: No she wasn't.
LARRY: She wasn't, was she.
ANNA: No.

Feeling great embarrassment, Larry enquires about this Daniel person. Anna fills in the details, with Larry remarking that he hopes Dan's book, *The Aquarium,* "sank without a trace." Anna replies that that's exactly what it's doing but also acknowledges that Dan is interested in her, and she finds him "interesting." Still, they hardly know each other. Larry senses a sadness in Anna and learns it's her birthday and she's come to the Aquarium to lament a bit. She takes his picture, and they have a moment of connection.

Five months later we're at a gallery showing an exhibition of Anna's photographs. Alice is there, staring at a huge picture of herself. Dan can't take his eyes off the photo, leading Alice to remind him that she's also there, in the flesh.

ALICE: I'm waiting for *you.*
DAN: To do what?
        Beat.
ALICE: Leave me . . .
DAN *(concerned):* I'm not going to leave you. I totally love you. What is this?
ALICE: Please let me come. *(Dan turns away.)* I want to be there for you. Are you ashamed of me?
DAN: No. I've told you, I want to be alone.
ALICE: Why?
DAN: To *grieve,* to think.
ALICE: I love you, why won't you let me?
DAN: It's only a weekend.

ALICE: Why won't you let me *love* you?
DAN: I do. *(Silence.)*

Dan then mentions that a newspaper co-worker has invited him to come back and write obits—a tempting offer, since he and Alice need the money. The issue isn't resolved as Dan hurries off to say goodbye to Anna and catch a cab to the station. Nearly colliding with Dan on the way out is a well-dressed and sanguine Larry.

Larry stands by Alice, and both regard her photo. He asks why she looks so sad in the picture; she replies, "Life."

LARRY: I know it's *vulgar* to discuss "The Work" at an opening of "The Work," but *someone's* got to do it. Serious, what do you think?
ALICE: It's a lie. It's a bunch of sad strangers photographed beautifully, and all the rich fuckers who appreciate *art* say it's beautiful because that's what they want to see. But the people in the photos are sad and alone, but the pictures make the world *seem* beautiful. So the exhibit is reassuring, which makes it a lie, and everyone loves a Big Fat Lie.
LARRY: I'm the Big Fat Liar's boy friend.
ALICE: Bastard.
LARRY: Larry.
ALICE: Alice. *(She moves toward him.)* You're Anna's boy friend.
LARRY: A princess can kiss a frog.
ALICE: How long have you been seeing her?
LARRY: Four months. We're in the first flush, it's *paradise,* all my nasty habits amuse her . . .

Larry cautions Alice not to smoke, which triggers her recognition of him as the doctor who looked at her in the hospital room. She smokes anyway, which makes ex-smoker Larry envious. "Pleasure and self-destruction—the perfect poison," he says.

Larry then asks about Dan's book, which Alice says wasn't so truthful about her. They notice Dan is still talking to Anna. Larry asks a flirtatious Alice more about her past, and she reminds him he'd asked those questions when they met before. Still, he presses on about her and the scar on her leg.

ALICE: A mafia hit man broke my leg.
LARRY: Really?
ALICE: Absolutely.
LARRY: Doesn't look like a break . . .
ALICE: What does it look like?
LARRY: Like something went into it. *(Tentatively.)* A knife, maybe . . .
ALICE: When I was eight . . . some metal went into my leg when my parents' car crashed . . . when they died. Happy now?

Ciaran Hinds as Larry and Anna Friel as Alice in the
photo exhibition scene of *Closer* by Patrick Marber

Larry apologizes, and she asks, "Is it nice being good?" He moves closer and
admits, "I'm not good." She lets him stroke her face. They depart, separately.
Dan appears, Anna shortly thereafter. He asks her about her boy friend.

DAN: So, he's a *dermatologist.* Can you get more boring than that?
ANNA: Obituarist?
DAN: Failed novelist, please.
ANNA: I was sorry about your book.

DAN: Thanks, I blame the title . . . . . Talk to *Doctor Larry* about photography, do you? Is he a fan of Man Ray or Karsh? He'll *bore* you.

ANNA: No he won't—he *doesn't,* actually.

DAN *(exasperated):* I cannot believe I made this happen. What were you *doing* at the Aquarium anyway? *(Joking.)* Thinking of me?

ANNA: Hardly. How's Alice?

DAN: She's fine. Do you love him?

ANNA: Yes, very much.

Dan cautions her not to marry Larry—then begs her to marry him. She accuses him of stalking her outside her studio. "I didn't *stalk* . . . I . . . *lurked,*" he replies. He then invites her to come with him for the weekend. She declines.

DAN: Anna, you want to believe he's . . . "the one" . . . it's not *real* . . . . .

ANNA: I love him.

DAN: *Why?*

ANNA: Any number of reasons.

DAN: Name one.

ANNA: He's kind.

DAN *(ferocious):* Don't give me "kind." "Kind" is dull, "kind" will kill you. Alice is *kind,* even *I'm* "kind," anyone can be fucking "kind."

ANNA: Shhh!

DAN *(gentle):* I cannot live without you.

ANNA: You can. You *do.*

The conversation continues in this vein, with Dan pleading and Anna increasingly intrigued. They then notice Larry looking at them. Dan exits. Larry joins Anna, who asks if he'd been spying. "Lovingly observing," he replies, making disparaging comments on Dan's physique. As a pleasant joke, they refer to Dan as "Cupid," since in his weird way he brought them together.

LARRY: I had a chat with young Alice.

ANNA: Fancy her?

LARRY: 'Course. Not as much as *you.*

ANNA: Why?

LARRY: You're a woman . . . she's a girl. She has the moronic beauty of youth, but she's . . . devious.

ANNA: She seems very open to me.

LARRY: That's how she wants to seem. You forget you're dealing with a clinical observer of the human carnival.

Larry changes the subject, remarking that he'd just met Anna's dad in the gallery. Both note that their families approve of their respective matches. Says Anna, "Your mother's got such a . . . kind face."

It's a year later, and the stage is split once again, this time between two apartments. Anna lounges in her flat; Alice, eating an apple dipped in honey, sits on a small sofa in Dan's. Dan comes home, Alice asks why he's late. First he lies, then he confesses he's just been with Anna: "We've been seeing each other for a year." Alice leaves the room.

In the other apartment, Larry enters, suitcase in hand. He tells Anna, "Don't move. I want to remember this moment; the first time I walked through the door, returning from a business trip, to be greeted by my *wife*. I have, in this moment, become an adult."

Anna then asks about his trip to New York for the Dermatological Conference. Larry raves about the craziness of Manhattan, "a twenty-four-hour pageant called 'Whatever You Want.' " He offers Anna "a friendly poke," but she declines, saying she's just had a bath. This leads to a brief conversation about their guilt at being able to afford such an opulent bathroom, until Larry notices that Anna is dressed, even though she's just bathed. He senses something amiss.

In the other flat, Alice reappears, wearing the same coat and carrying the same duffle bag she had in the begnning of the play.

ALICE: I'm going.
DAN: I'm sorry.
ALICE: Irrelevant. What are you sorry for?
    Beat.
DAN: Everything
    Beat.
ALICE: Is it because she's clever?
DAN: No, it's because . . . she doesn't need me.
    Pause.
ALICE: Do you bring her here?
DAN: Yes.
ALICE: She sits here?
DAN: Yes.
    Beat.
ALICE: Didn't she get married?
DAN: She stopped seeing me.
    Beat.
ALICE: Is that when we went to the country? To celebrate our third anniversary?
DAN: Yes.
ALICE: At least have the guts to look at me . . . . .
DAN *(looks at her):* Deception is brutal, I'm not pretending otherwise.
ALICE: How . . . How can you do this to someone?
    Silence.
DAN: I don't know.
ALICE: Not good enough, I'm going.
DAN: It's late, it's not safe out there.

ALICE: And it's safe in here?
DAN: What about your things?
ALICE: I don't need "things."
DAN: Where will you go?
ALICE: I'll disappear.

The other flat. Larry, in a dressing gown, presents Anna with a gift, a pair of shoes. He also mentions he saw the book of her photographs on sale at the Museum of Modern Art. An "artsy student with a ridiculous little beard" even bought a copy.

Alice and Dan. She asks if she can still see him. He replies, "If I see you, I'll never leave you." He admits he still loves her but can't deny he thinks he'll be happier with Anna. Says Alice, "Why isn't love enough? I'm the one who leaves. I'm supposed to leave *you*. I'm the one who leaves." She kisses him and asks him to make some tea. He goes off to do so.

Anna and Larry. Larry is fully dressed again.

ANNA: Why are you dressed?
LARRY: Because I think you might be about to leave me, and I didn't want to be wearing a bathrobe. I slept with someone in New York. A whore. I'm sorry.
        Beat.
ANNA: Why?
LARRY: For sex. I wanted sex. I wore a condom . . .
        Beat.
ANNA: Was it . . . good?
LARRY *(huffs and puffs):* . . . Yes.

A few more details follow, and Larry senses something else is wrong. (During the exchange, in the other apartment Alice takes her things and leaves.)

LARRY: Are you leaving me? *(She nods.)* Why?
ANNA: Dan . . .
LARRY: Cupid? He's our joke.
ANNA: I love him.
        Beat.
LARRY: You're seeing him now . . . ?
ANNA: Yes.
LARRY: Since when?
ANNA: Since my opening, last year. I'm disgusting.
        Beat.
LARRY: You're phenomenal. . . . you're so . . . *clever.* Why did you marry me?
ANNA: I stopped seeing him, I wanted us to work.
LARRY: Why did you tell me you wanted children?
ANNA: Because I did.

LARRY: And now you want children with him?

ANNA: Yes—I don't know—I'm so sorry.

Anna confesses she's going to live with Dan. Anger rises in Larry, though he's disappointed. Anna fears he's the type who might hit her. "I've been hit before," she tells him. "But not by me," he counters.

Larry does ask for the details of her sex with Dan. She allows that Dan is gentler in bed, and simply different. Larry warns her she's making a mistake. Seething again, he asks for more details about what they did in his apartment. He gestures to the chaise longue.

LARRY: We had our first fuck on this. Think of me? When? When did you do it here? ANSWER THE FUCKING QUESTION.

> *Beat.*

ANNA *(scared):* This evening.

> *Pause.*

LARRY: Did you come?

ANNA: Why are you doing this?

LARRY: Because I want to know.

> *Beat.*

ANNA: Yes, I came.

LARRY: How many times?

ANNA: Twice.

LARRY: How?

ANNA: First he went down on me, and then we fucked . . . Why is the sex so important?

LARRY: BECAUSE I'M A FUCKING CAVE MAN. Did you touch yourself while he fucked you?

ANNA: Yes.

LARRY: You wank for him?

ANNA: Sometimes.

LARRY: And he does?

ANNA: We do everything that people who have sex do.

LARRY: You like sucking him off?

ANNA: Yes.

LARRY: You like his cock?

ANNA: I love it.

LARRY: You like him coming in your face?

ANNA: Yes.

LARRY: What does it taste like?

ANNA: It tastes like you but sweeter.

LARRY: That's the spirit. Thank you. Thank you for the *honesty*. Now fuck off and die. You fucked up slag.

> *Blackout. Curtain.*

ACT II

Three months later, we're in the Paradise Suite at a tapdance club. *"Larry is sitting. He is wearing a smart suit. He had a big, fat line of cocaine 15 minutes ago. Alice is standing. She is wearing a short dress and high heels. She is wearing a wig. She has a garter round her thigh. There is cash in the garter. They are in a private room. Music in the distance."*

Larry tells Alice he loves her. Paid to be nice to the customers, she thanks him. He tells her, "I went to a place like this in New York. This is *swish*. Pornography has gone up-market—Bully for England." He also recalls coming to this same venue back when it was a punk club, but this only reminds them both of their age differences.

LARRY: You have the face of an angel.
ALICE: Thank you.
LARRY: What does your cunt taste like?
ALICE: Heaven
    Beat.
LARRY: How long have you been doing this?
ALICE: Three months.
LARRY: Straight after he left you?
ALICE: No one left me.
    Beat.
LARRY: Does it turn you on?
ALICE: Sometimes.
LARRY: Liar. You're telling me it turns you on because you think that's what I want to *hear*. You think I'm turned on by it turning you on.
ALICE: The thought of me creaming myself when I strip for strangers doesn't turn you on?
LARRY: Put like that . . . yes.

After a bit more of this, Larry tries to touch her, but that's against the rules; if he persists, she'll call Security, and he will have to leave. She cautions that they're behind a two-way mirror, and there are cameras in the ceiling. He wants to meet her later, but each time he gets personal—or asks about her split with Dan—she escapes into her new persona.

LARRY: Why are you calling yourself *Jane?*
ALICE: Because it's my name.
LARRY: We both know it isn't. You're all protecting your identities. The girl in there who calls herself "Venus." What's her real name?
ALICE: Pluto.

LARRY: You're cheeky . . . . . There's another one in there (judging by the scars, a recent patient of Doctor Tit), she calls herself "Cupid." Who's going to tell her Cupid was a bloke?

ALICE: He wasn't a bloke, he was a little boy.

LARRY: I'd like you to tell me your name. Please.

Larry keeps giving her 20-pound notes for her to answer the question. She keeps replying that it's Jane, even as he gives her 500 pounds.

ALICE: Thank you. My name is Plain . . . Jane . . . Jones.

LARRY: I may be rich, but I'm not stupid.

ALICE: What a shame, Doc, I love 'em rich and stupid.

LARRY: DON'T FUCK AROUND WITH ME.

ALICE: I apologize.

LARRY: Accepted. All the girls in this hell-hole; the pneumatic robots, then coked-up baby dolls—and you're no different—you all use stage names to con yourselves you're someone else so you don't feel ashamed when you show your cunts and arseholes to Complete Fucking Strangers. I'm trying to have a conversation here.

ALICE: You're out of cash, Buster.

Larry begs Alice to talk to him "in real life." "I love your scar," he tells her, "I love everything about you that hurts." She remains cold, and it is Larry who breaks down, still upset over losing Anna. He pleads with her to come home with him; Alice pointedly disagrees that she needs his money, his safety or his looking after. When he asks for some of the loot he's given her, for his cab fare, she refuses.

ALICE: Company policy, you give *us* the money.

LARRY: And what do we get in return?

ALICE: We're nice to you.

LARRY: "And We Get To See You Naked."

ALICE: It's beautiful.

LARRY: *Except* . . . you think you haven't given us anything of yourselves. You think because you don't love us or desire us or even *like* us, you think you've *won*.

ALICE: It's not a war.

     Larry laughs for some time.

LARRY: But you *do* give us something of yourselves: you give us . . . *imagery*. And we do with it what we will. If you women could see one minute of our Home Movies—the shit that slops through our minds every day—you'd string us up by our balls, you really would.

Larry makes one more attempt to establish some kind of truth and intimacy with Alice. No go. So he orders her to strip and touch the floor. As she starts to undress, the scene changes to a restaurant, a month later. Dan sits, nursing a drink, smoking.

Anna arrives and apologizes for her lateness. She'd just come in from a final lunch with Larry.

ANNA: Are you angry I saw him?

DAN: No, no, I just . . . I haven't seen Alice.

ANNA: You can't see Alice, you don't know where she is.

DAN: I haven't tried to find her.

ANNA: He's been begging me to see him for months, you know why I saw him, I saw him so he'd . . . *sign.*

DAN: So he signed?

ANNA: Yes,

DAN: Congratulations. You are now a divorcee—double divorcee. Sorry.
    Dan takes her hand.
How do you feel?

ANNA: Tired.

Dan leaves to use the rest room. We then flash back to Anna's meeting with Larry, also in a restaurant (the same table is used). Almost as soon as they sit down, Larry is exhorting her to come back. She spreads out the divorce papers and forces a pen into his hand. Larry tells her, "I'll sign it on one condition; we skip lunch, we go to my sleek little surgery, and we christen the patients' bed with our final fuck. I know you don't want to. I know you think I'm sick for asking—but that's what I'm asking. For old times sake, because I'm obsessed with you, because I can't get over you unless you . . . because I think on some small level you owe me *something,* for deceiving me so . . . *exquisitely.*

Larry promises not to bother her again if she complies. He heads to the bar while she thinks about the deal.

Dan returns, bringing us back to the previous scene. He looks at Anna closely and realizes she's slept with Larry.

DAN: What do you expect me to do?

ANNA *(pleading):* Understand, hopefully?
    Beat.

DAN: Why didn't you lie to me?

ANNA: We said we'd always tell each other the truth.

DAN: What's so great about the *truth?* Try lying for a change—it's the currency of the world.

ANNA: Dan, I did what he wanted, and now he will leave us alone. I love *you.* I didn't give *him* anything.

DAN: Your body?
    Dan reaches for his cigarettes.

ANNA: If Alice came to you . . . desparate . . . with all that love still between you, and said she needed you to want her so that she could get over you, you would do it. I wouldn't like it either, but I would forgive you. It's . . . kindness.

DAN: No, it's *cowardice.* You don't have the guts to let him hate you.

With this, Dan begins questioning Anna about the details of that last tryst with Larry. When she tells him she faked orgasm to make Larry think she enjoyed it, he questions whether she fakes it for him, too.

ANNA: *Occasionally* . . . I have faked it. It's not important, you don't *make* me come. I *come* . . . you're . . . "In the area" . . . providing valiant assistance.

DAN: You make *me* come.

ANNA: You're a man, you'd come if the tooth fairy winked at you . . . . . Dan, please be bigger than . . . *jealous.* Please, be bigger.

DAN: What could be bigger than jealousy?
             Pause.

ANNA: Why don't you kiss me when we're making love? Why don't you like it when I say I love you? I'm on your side. Talk to me.

DAN: It hurts . . . I'm ashamed . . . I know it's illogical and I do understand, but I hate you. I love you, and I don't like other men fucking you, is that so weird?

ANNA: No. YES. It was only *sex.*

DAN *(hard):* If you can still fuck him, you haven't left him. *(Soft.)* It's gone . . . we're not innocent any more.

ANNA: Don't stop loving me . . . I can see it draining out of you. Dan, I do understand . . .

DAN *(laughs):* No . . . *he* understands. *(He looks at her.)* All I can see is him all over you. He's clever, your *ex*-husband . . . I almost admire him.

Anna wonders aloud whether Dan really loves her or is simply driven by sexual compulsion. Dan can't shake the need to know what Anna really felt when she was sleeping with Larry. She suggests if he's so curious, he should just ask Larry himself.

Larry then returns to the table, so both men are there at the same time, though the scenes are still separate. Dan thinks better of his venality; Anna assures him she didn't want to hurt him. They kiss, and Dan leaves to call a cab. Anna tells Larry she pities him; he tells her he forgives her—and signs the documents.

The next scene takes place in a museum, where Alice, wearing Larry's black cashmere sweater, stares at a life-size model of a Victorian child. Larry enters, late. She hands him a package for his birthday and promises another surprise. As she goes off, Larry opens the package and smiles. Enter Anna, of all people.

ANNA: What are *you* doing here?

LARRY: I'm . . . lazing on a Sunday afternoon. You?

ANNA: I'm meeting Alice.

LARRY *(never heard of her):* Who?

ANNA: Dan's Alice—Dan's *ex*-Alice. She phoned me at the studio this morning . . . she wants her negatives . . .

LARRY: Right . . .

Anna, remembering, wishes Larry a happy birthday. She notices the present—a Newton's Cradle (swinging metal balls that clack into each other in rhythm). Larry tells her it's from his dad, then tells the truth.

LARRY: It's from *Alice.* I'm fucking her. She's set us up, I had no idea you were meeting her.
       Pause.
ANNA: You're old enough to be her ancestor.
LARRY: Disgusting, isn't it.
ANNA: You should be ashamed.
LARRY *(smiling):* Oh, I am.

Larry fills in the details of how he met Alice at a strip club. He asks how Dan took the news of their pre-divorce shag. "Like . . . a *Man,*" she replies, but he sees through it.

ANNA: Please don't hate me.
LARRY: It's easier than loving you. *(He looks at her.)* Me and Alice . . . it's nothing.
ANNA: Nice nothing?
LARRY: Very. *(They look at each other.)* Since we're talking, could you have a word with your lawyer? I'm still waiting for confirmation of our divorce, if that's what you want.

Alice reappears, which is Larry's cue to make himself scarce.

ANNA: How did you get so brutal?
ALICE: I lived a little. How's Dan?
ANNA: Fine.
ALICE: Did you tell him you were seeing me?
ANNA: No . . . . . What are you doing with Larry?
ALICE: *Everything.* I like your bed. You should come round one night, come and watch your husband blubbering into his pillow—it might help you develop a conscience.
ANNA: I know what I've done.
ALICE: His big thing at the moment is how upset his family are. God knows why, but they all worship you, they can't understand why you had to ruin everything. He spends hours staring up my arsehole like there's going to be some answer there. Any ideas, Anna? Why don't you go back to him?
ANNA: And then Dan would go back to you?
ALICE: Maybe.
ANNA: Ask him.
ALICE: I'm not a beggar . . . . .
ANNA: I don't want a fight.

ALICE: SO GIVE IN. Why did you do this?

ANNA *(tough):* I fell in love with him, Alice.

ALICE: That's the most stupid expression in the world. "I fell in love"—as if you had no *choice.* There's a moment, there's always a moment; I can do this, I can give in to this or I can resist it. I don't know when your moment was, but I bet there was one.

ANNA: Yes, there was.

ALICE: You didn't fall in love, you gave in to temptation.

ANNA: Well, *you* fell in love with him.

ALICE: No, I chose him. I looked in his briefcase and I found this . . . *sandwich* . . . and I thought, "I will give all my love to this charming man who cuts off his crusts." I didn't *fall* in love, I chose to.

ANNA: You still want him, after everything he's done to you?

ALICE: You wouldn't understand, he . . . buries me. He makes me invisible.

Anna admits to acting selfishly, leading Alice to admit that she behaved the same way when stealing Dan from his previous girl friend. They briefly discuss who's better in bed, Larry or Dan. It's something of a draw.

ANNA: They spend a lifetime fucking and never know how to make love.
    Pause.

ALICE: I've got a scar here, Larry's mad about it. He licks it like a dog. Any ideas?

ANNA *(shrugs):* Dermatology? God knows, this is what we're dealing with; we arrive with our . . . "baggage," and for awhile they're brilliant, they're baggage handlers. We say, "Where's your baggage?" They deny all knowledge of it . . . "they're *in love*" . . . they have none. Then . . . just as you're relaxing . . . a Great Big Juggernaut arrives . . . with *their* baggage. It Got Held-up. One of the greatest myths men have about women is that we overpack. They love the way we make them feel, but not "us." They love dreams.

ALICE: So do we. You should lower your expectations.

Alice entreats Anna to "do the right thing," and then exits.

The next scene, a month later, occurs in Larry's office. Dan is there, distraught: he wants Anna back.

DAN: If you love her, you'll let her go so she can be . . . happy.

LARRY: She doesn't want to be "happy."

DAN: *Everyone* wants to be happy.

LARRY: Depressives don't. They want to be *unhappy* to confirm they're depressed. If they were *happy,* they couldn't be depressed any more, they'd have to go out into the world and *live,* which can be . . . *depressing.*

DAN: Anna's not a depressive.

LARRY: Isn't she?

DAN: I love her.

LARRY: Boo hoo, so do I. You don't love Anna, you love yourself.

DAN: You're wrong, I don't love myself.

LARRY: Yes you do, and you know something; you're winning—you selfish people—it's your world. Nice, isn't it?

DAN: It's you who's selfish—you don't even want Anna, you want revenge. She's gone back to you because she can't bear your *suffering.* You don't know who she is, you love her like a dog loves its owner.

LARRY: And the owner loves the dog for so doing. Companionship will always triumph over "passion."

DAN: You'll hurt her. You'll never forgive her.

LARRY: Of course I'll forgive her—I have forgiven her. Without forgiveness, we're savages.

Larry saves the worst sting for last: Anna never even sent the divorce papers to her lawyer. He promises to kill Dan if Dan ever goes near Anna again. Dan then brings up the time Anna had sex with Larry just before signing the papers.

DAN: You're an animal.

LARRY: YES. What are *you?*

DAN: You think love is simple? You think the heart is like a diagram?

LARRY: Ever *seen* a human heart? It looks like a fist wrapped in blood. GO FUCK YOURSELF . . . you . . . WRITER. You LIAR . . . . . You don't even know . . . Alice. *(Dan looks at him.)* Consider her scar, how did she get that?

DAN: When did you meet Alice?

   Pause.

LARRY: Anna's exhibition. You remember. A scar in the shape of a question mark, solve the mystery.

DAN: She got it whan her parents' car crashed.

LARRY: . . . . . I think she mutilated herself. It's fairly common in children who lose their parents young, they blame themselves, they're disturbed.

Dan objects, but Larry reiterates how fragile and vulnerable Alice is, someone who just wants to be loved. Dan begins to sob and admits he'd go back to Alice if he could, but he doesn't know where she is. Larry tells Dan he found Alice "by accident" at the strip club, and that she still loves Dan "beyond comprehension." He admits they talked and that he saw her naked, but he didn't have intercourse with her. He then writes down the club address on a prescription pad and hands it to Dan, saying, "Go to her."

Before a grateful Dan exits, he and Larry make small talk about his writing career. Dan has been made obit editor (the previous one died) at the paper but hasn't got a subject for his next book. "Don't tell me you haven't got a subject, every human life is a million stories," Larry tells him. "Thank God life ends—we'd never survive it. From Big Bang to weary shag, the history of the world. Our flesh is ferocious ... our bodies will kill us ... our bones will outlive us." Off-handedly, Larry also mentions that he lied; he and Alice did have sex that night at the club. "I'm sorry for telling you," Larry gloats. "I'm just ... not big enough to forgive you. *Buster.*"

In the next scene, Dan and Alice are in a hotel, Alice desiring yet another shag. A tired Dan declines, more interested in the special "holiday surprise" trip to new York Alice has arranged.

DAN: Did you remember to pack my passport?
ALICE: Yes, it's with my passport.
DAN: And where's that?
ALICE: In a place where you can't look. No one sees my passport photo. Did you know that when we get on the plane, we'll have been together four years. Happy anniversary ... Buster.

Dan then playfully starts quizzing Alice on details of the first time they met, at the hospital. He's impressed by her memory, though she doesn't recall the doctor who looked at her leg. Dan can't help wondering if Larry and Anna are happy; Alice "couldn't give a toss." In bed, Dan holds Alice and strokes her leg.

DAN: How *did* you get this?
ALICE: You know how ...
DAN: How?
ALICE: I fell off my bike because I refused to use stabilizers.
DAN *(disbelieving):* Really?
ALICE: You know how I got it.
     Beat.
DAN: Did you do it yourself?
ALICE: No.
     Beat.
DAN: Show me your passport.
ALICE: No I look ugly.
     Beat.
DAN: When are you going to stop stripping?
ALICE: Soon.

Dan can't stop himself from asking about what really happened when Larry came to the club. Alice manages to change the subject back to the first time she and Dan met ... but not for long.

DAN: You're not trusting me. I'm in love with you. You're safe. If you fucked him, you fucked him. I just want to know.
ALICE: Why?

Rupert Graves as Dan with Anna Friel as Alice in *Closer*

DAN *(tenderly):* Because I want to know everything because ... I'm insane. Tell me ...
>   *He strokes her face. Pause.*

Alice tells him nothing happened that night in the club, but he won't believe her. "You and the truth are known strangers," he scowls, putting his trousers on to go out for cigarettes.

DAN: When I get back, please tell me the truth.
ALICE: Why?
DAN: Because I'm addicted to it. Because without it, we're animals. Trust me, I love you. *(He looks at her. Beat.)* What?
>   *Beat.*
ALICE: I don't love you any more.
DAN: Look ... I'm sorry ...
ALICE: No, I've changed the subject. I don't love you any more.
DAN: Since when?
ALICE: Now ... Just now. I don't want to lie and I can't tell the truth, so it's over.
DAN: You're leaving me?
>   *She rummages in her duffle bag and hands him his passport.*
ALICE: I've left. I've gone. I don't love you any more. Goodbye.
DAN: Why don't you tell me the truth?
ALICE: So you can hate me? I fucked Larry, many times, I enjoyed it, I came, I prefer you. Now go.

Pause.

DAN: I knew that, he told me.

ALICE: You knew?

DAN: I needed *you* to tell me . . . . .

ALICE: But why test me?

DAN: Because I'm an idiot.

ALICE: Yeah, you are. I would've loved you forever. Now, please go.

Dan apologizes and says he loves her, but Alice can't see or feel this love; it's just words to her. She threatens to call Security; Dan reminds her she's not at the club and throws her on the bed, demanding she tell him why she copulated with Larry.

ALICE: He asked me nicely.

DAN: You're a liar.

ALICE: So?

DAN: WHO ARE YOU?

ALICE: I'M NO-ONE
Alice spits in his face. He grabs her by the throat, one hand.
Go on, hit me. That's what you want. Hit me, you fucker.
Dan hits her. Silence.
Do you have a single original thought in your head?
Blackout.

The final scene occurs six months later, on a summer day in Postman's Park. Anna, holding a guide book, gazes at a memorial to an 1880s heroine who tried to save a child from a runaway horse. Larry enters carrying his white lab coat and two styrofoam cups.

ANNA: How's Polly?

LARRY: Polly's great.

ANNA: I always knew you'd end up with a pretty nurse.

LARRY: Yeah? How?

ANNA: I just thought you would.
Beat.
Is she . . . "the one?"

LARRY: I don't know. *(He looks at Anna.)* No. Everyone learns, nobody changes.

ANNA: *You* don't change.

LARRY: You . . . seeing anyone?

ANNA: No. Thank you . . . . .

LARRY: You look fantastic.

ANNA: Don't start. *(She looks at him.)*

LARRY: How's work?

ANNA: I'm having a break. I'm taking the dog to the country, we're going to go for long walks . . .

LARRY: Don't become . . . a sad person.

ANNA: I won't. I'm not. Fuck off.

They look out at the memorial.

LARRY: How did she die?

ANNA: I don't know. When he phoned, he said it happened last night in New York. He's flying out today, and he wanted to see us before he left.

LARRY: So they weren't together?

ANNA: They split up in January.

Beat.

LARRY: Did he say why?

ANNA: No.

Beat.

LARRY: How did they contact him?

ANNA: Maybe she wrote his name in her passport as next of kin. You're still in mine . . . in the event of death. I must remove you.

Larry takes her guide book and looks up the entry for the memorial in this park. He reads: " 'Alice Ayres, daughter of a bricklayer's laborer, who by intrepid conduct saved three children from a burning house in Union Street, Borough, at the cost of her own young life . . . . . April Twenty-fourth, Nineteen Fifty Five.' She made herself up."

By his own admission, Larry isn't good at grief and doesn't want to commiserate with Dan, so he bids Anna farewell. Just as Larry exits, Dan enters, bearing flowers.

DAN *(to Anna):* You look well.

ANNA: I am well. *(Dan looks out at the memorial.)* Dan . . . *(She gestures for him to sit.)*

DAN: This is where we sat.

ANNA: Who?

DAN: Me and my father, didn't I tell you?

ANNA: No, wrong girl, you told Alice.

Beat.

DAN: Jane. Her name was Jane Jones. The police phoned me . . . they said that someone I know, called Jane, had died . . . they found her address book. I said there must be a mistake . . . they had to describe her. There's no one else to identify the body . . . She was knocked down by a car . . . on Forty-third and Madison. When I went to work today . . . Graham said, "Who's on the slab?" I walked out to the fire escape and just cried like a baby. I covered my face . . . why do we do that? . . . . . The phone rang. It was the police . . . they said there's no record of her parents' death . . . they said they were trying to trace them. She said she fell in love with me because . . . I cut off my crusts . . . but it was just . . . it was only that day . . . because the bread broke in my hands.

Changing the subject, Dan tells Anna he bumped into his previous girl friend last week. She's now married—to a Spanish poet—a mom, and pregnant again.

Looking at the flowers in his hand, Dan is reminded he has to place them at Blackfriars Bridge before he catches his plane. He says goodbye to Anna, and "they exit separately."

Fade. Curtain.

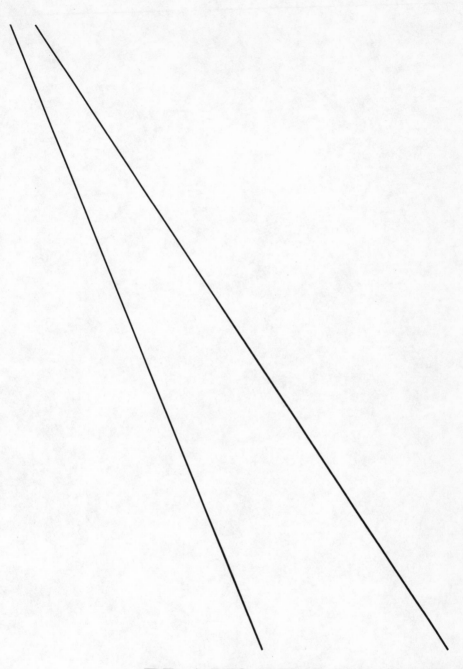

PLAYS PRODUCED
IN NEW YORK

PLAYS PRODUCED
ON BROADWAY

Figures in parentheses following a play's title give number of performances. These figures do not include previews or extra non-profit performances. In the case of a transfer, the off-Broadway run is noted but not added to the figure in parentheses.

Plays marked with an asterisk (*) were still in a projected run June 1, 1999. Their number of performances is figured through May 31, 1999.

In a listing of a show's numbers—dances, sketches, musical scenes, etc.—the titles of songs are identified wherever possible by their appearance in quotation marks (").

HOLDOVERS FROM PREVIOUS SEASONS

Broadway shows which were running on June 1, 1998 are listed below. More detailed information about them appears in previous *Best Plays* volumes of the years in which they opened. Important cast changes since opening night are recorded in the Cast Replacements section of this volume.

*Cats (6,950; longest running show in Broadway history). Musical based on *Old Possum's Book of Practical Cats* by T.S. Eliot; music by Andrew Lloyd Webber; additional lyrics by Trevor Nunn and Richard Stilgoe. Opened October 7, 1982.

*Les Misérables (5,031). Musical based on the novel by Victor Hugo; book by Alain Boublil and Claude-Michel Schönberg; lyrics by Herbert Kretzmer; original French text by Alain Boublil and Jean-Marc Natel; additional material by James Fenton. Opened March 12, 1987.

*The Phantom of the Opera (4,762). Musical adapted from the novel by Gaston Leroux; book by Richard Stilgoe and Andrew Lloyd Webber; music by Andrew Lloyd Webber; lyrics by Charles Hart; additional lyrics by Richard Stilgoe. Opened January 26, 1988.

*Miss Saigon (3,373). Musical with book by Alain Boublil and Claude-Michel Schönberg; music by Claude-Michel Schönberg; lyrics by Richard Maltby Jr. and Alain Boublil; additional material by Richard Maltby Jr. Opened April 11, 1991.

*Beauty and the Beast (2,138). Musical with book by Linda Woolverton; music by Alan Menken; lyrics by Howard Ashman and Tim Rice. Opened April 18, 1994.

*Smokey Joe's Cafe (1,772). Musical revue with words and music by Jerry Leiber and Mike Stoller. Opened March 2, 1995.

Bring in 'da Noise Bring in 'da Funk (1,130). Transfer from off Broadway of the musical performance piece based on an idea by Savion Glover and George C. Wolfe; conceived by George C. Wolfe; choreography by Savion Glover; book by Reg E. Gaines; music by Daryl Waters, Zane Mark and Ann Duquesnay. Opened November 15, 1995 off Broadway where it played 85 performances through January 28, 1996; transferred to Broadway April 25, 1996. (Closed January 10, 1999)

*__Rent__ (1,289). Transfer from off Broadway of the musical with book, music and lyrics by Jonathan Larson. Opened off off Broadway January 26, 1996 and off Broadway February 13, 1996 where it played 56 performances through March 31, 1996; transferred to Broadway April 29, 1996.

*__Chicago__ (1,059). Revival of the musical based on the play by Maurine Dallas Watkins; book by Fred Ebb and Bob Fosse; music by John Kander; lyrics by Fred Ebb; original production directed and choreographed by Bob Fosse. Opened November 14, 1996.

The Last Night of Ballyhoo (557). By Alfred Uhry. Opened February 27, 1997. (Closed June 28, 1998)

Titanic (804). Musical with story and book by Peter Stone; music and lyrics by Maury Yeston. Opened April 23, 1997. (Closed March 28, 1999)

The Life (465). Musical based on an original idea by Ira Gasman; book by David Newman, Ira Gasman and Cy Coleman; lyrics by Ira Gasman; music by Cy Coleman. Opened April 26, 1997. (Closed June 7, 1998)

*__Jekyll & Hyde__ (872). Musical based on the novella *The Strange Case of Dr. Jekyll and Mr. Hyde* by Robert Louis Stevenson; conceived by Steve Cuden and Frank Wildhorn; book and lyrics by Leslie Bricusse; music by Frank Wildhorn. Opened April 28, 1997.

Forever Tango (453). Dance musical created by Luis Bravo. Opened June 19, 1997. (Closed August 1, 1998)

*__Roundabout Theater Company. 1776__ (333). Revival of the musical based on a concept of Sherman Edwards; book by Peter Stone; music and lyrics by Sherman Edwards. Opened August 14, 1997. (Closed June 14, 1998) **A View From the Bridge** (251). Revival of the play by Arthur Miller. Opened December 14, 1997. (Closed August 29, 1998) *__Cabaret__ (461). Revival of the musical based on the play by John Van Druten and stories by Christopher Isherwood; book by Joe Masteroff; music by John Kander; lyrics by Fred Ebb. Opened March 19, 1998.

The Scarlet Pimpernel (373). Musical based on the novel by Baroness Orczy; book and lyrics by Nan Knighton; music by Frank Wildhorn. Opened November 9, 1997. (Closed October 3, 1998). Reopened November 4, 1998 in a revised version; see its entry elsewhere in this section of this volume.

*__The Lion King__ (649). Musical adapted from the screen play by Irene Mecchi, Jonathan Roberts and Linda Woolverton; book by Roger Allers and Irene Mecchi; music by Elton John; lyrics by Tim Rice; additional music and lyrics by Lebo M, Mark Mancina, Jay Rifkin, Julie Taymor and Hans Zimmer. Opened November 13, 1997.

The Diary of Anne Frank (221). Revival of the play by Frances Goodrich and Albert Hackett; newly adapted by Wendy Kesselman. Opened December 4, 1997. (Closed June 14, 1998)

The Sunshine Boys (230). Revival of the play by Neil Simon. Opened December 8, 1997. (Closed June 28, 1998)

*__Ragtime__ (570). Musical based on the novel by E.L. Doctorow; book by Terrence McNally; music by Stephen Flaherty; lyrics by Lynn Ahrens. Opened January 18, 1998.

Freak (145). Solo performance by John Leguizamo; written by John Leguizamo. Opened February 12, 1998. (Closed July 5, 1998)

*Art (521). By Yasmina Reza; translated by Christopher Hampton. Opened March 1, 1998.

*The Sound of Music (509). Revival of the musical suggested by *The Trapp Family Singers* by Maria Augusta Trapp; book by Howard Lindsay and Russel Crouse; music by Richard Rodgers; lyrics by Oscar Hammerstein II. Opened March 12, 1998.

The Chairs (75). Revival of the play by Eugene Ionesco; translated by Martin Crimp. Opened April 1, 1998. (Closed June 13, 1998)

Wait Until Dark (97). Revival of the play by Frederick Knott. Opened April 5, 1998. (Closed June 28, 1998)

The Beauty Queen of Leenane (372). Transfer from off Broadway of the play by Martin McDonagh. Opened April 23, 1998. (Closed March 14, 1999)

Honour (57). By Joanna Murray-Smith. Opened April 26, 1998. (Closed June 14, 1998)

High Society (144). Musical with book by Arthur Kopit based on the play *The Philadelphia Story* by Philip Barry and the motion picture *High Society;* music and lyrics by Cole Porter; additional lyrics by Susan Birkenhead. Opened April 27, 1998. (Closed August 30, 1998)

The Judas Kiss (110). By David Hare. Opened April 29, 1998. (Closed August 2, 1998)

PLAYS PRODUCED JUNE 1, 1998–MAY 31, 1999

*Roundabout Theater Company. 1997–98 schedule concluded with ***Side Man** (318). Transfer from off off Broadway of the play by Warren Leight. Produced by Weissberger Theater Group, Jay Harris producer, Peter Manning and Roundabout Theater Company (see note), Todd Haimes artistic director, Ellen Richard general manager, in the Weissberger Theater Group production at Criterion Center Stage Right. Opened June 25, 1998.

Clifford	Robert Sella	Al	Joseph Lyle Taylor
Terry	Wendy Makkena	Ziggy	Michael Mastro
Patsy	Angelica Torn	Jonesy	Kevin Geer
Gene	Frank Wood		

Understudies: Messrs. Mastro, Wood, Geer—Geoffrey P. Cantor; Messrs. Taylor, Sella, Mastro—Jeff Binder; Miss Torn— Marissa Matrone.

Directed by Michael Mayer; scenery, Neil Patel; costumes, Tom Broecker; lighting, Kenneth Posner; sound, Raymond D. Schilke; founding director, Gene Feist; casting, Jim Carnahan, Matt Messinger; production stage manager, Andrea J. Testani; stage manager, Brendan Smith; press, Boneau/Bryan-Brown, Adrian Bryan-Brown, Erin Dunn (see note).

Time: 1985 to 1953. Place: New York City. The play was presented in two parts.

A trumpet-player's son recalls and reflects on his troubled growing-up within the special milieu of the dedicated jazz musician. Previously produced 3/11/98 by Weissberger Theater Group. Winner of the 1998–99 Tony Award for best play; see its entry in the Prizewinning Plays section of this volume.

Christian Slater replaced Robert Sella 10/20/99. Edie Falco replaced Wendy Makkena 1/8/99. Robert Sella replaced Christian Slater 3/2/99. Scott Wolf replaced Robert Sella 5/28/99.

Note: James Cushing and Jean Stein joined the group of this show's producers and its press was taken over by Springer/Chicoine Public Relations when it tranferred to the Golden Theater 11/8/98.

Lincoln Center Theater. 1997–98 schedule concluded with **Twelfth Night** (53). Revival of the play by William Shakespeare. Produced by Lincoln Center Theater under the direction of

Andre Bishop and Bernard Gersten in association with Lincoln Center Festival 98 at the Vivian Beaumont Theater. Opened July 16, 1998. (Closed August 30, 1998)

Orsino	Paul Rudd	Sir Andrew Aguecheek	Max Wright
Curio	Steven Ochoa	Feste	David Patrick Kelly
Valentine	Daniel Sunjata	Malvolio	Philip Bosco
Viola	Helen Hunt	Sebastian	Rick Stear
Sea Captain	Paul O'Brien	Antonio	Julio Monge
Olivia	Kyra Sedgwick	Fabian	Skipp Sudduth
Maria	Amy Hill	Priest	Jack Davidson
Sir Toby Belch	Brian Murray		

Officers—Matte Osian, Adam Dannheisser, Kevin Daniels. Lords in Orsino's Household—Kevin Daniels, Adam Dannheisser, John Michael Gilbert, Matte Osian. Ladies in Olivia's Household—Kim Awon, Ryan Dunn, Robin Weigert.

Understudies: Mr. Rudd—Daniel Sunjata; Messrs. Ochoa, Kelly—Adam Dannheisser; Miss Hunt—Robin Weigert; Messrs. O'Brien, Sunjata, Davidson, Monge—Kevin Daniels; Miss Sedgwick—Kim Awon; Mr. Murray—Jack Davidson; Miss Hill—Ryan Dunn; Mr. Wright—John Michael Gilbert; Mr. Stear—Steven Ochoa; Mr. Bosco—Paul O'Brien; Mr. Sudduth—Matte Osian.

Orchestra: Kimberly Grigsby musical director, conductor, keyboards; Rick Bassett orchestrator; Seymour Red Press musical coordinator; Marshall Coid violin, counter-tenor; Norbert Goldberg percussion; Anik Oulianine cello; Steven Silverstein woodwinds; Mark Stewart guitar.

Directed by Nicholas Hytner; scenery, Bob Crowley; costumes, Catherine Zuber; lighting, Natasha Katz; original music, Jeanine Tesori; sound, Scott Stauffer; dance sequences, Joey McKneely; fight direction, Steve Rankin; special effects, Gregory Meeh; casting, Daniel Swee; stage manager, Erica Schwartz; press, Philip Rinaldi.

The last major New York revival of *Twelfth Night* was in the touring repertory of The Acting Company at the Public Theater 5/23/94 for 4 performances. The play was presented in two parts.

An Evening With Jerry Herman (28). Musical revue of songs by Jerry Herman. Produced by Manny Kladitis and Jon Wilner at the Booth Theater. Opened July 28, 1998. (Closed August 23, 1998)

CAST: Jerry Herman piano, vocals; Lee Roy Reams vocals; Florence Lacey vocals; Jered Egan bass. Standby: Mr. Reams, Miss Lacey—Alix Korey.

Directed by Lee Roy Reams; scenery, Kenneth Foy; lighting, Ken Billington; sound, Peter J. Fitzgerald; music coordinator, William Meade; produced in association with Magicworks Entertainment and PACE Theatrical Group, Inc.; production stage manager, Jim Semmelman; stage manager, Marci Glotzer; press, Cromarty & Co., Peter Cromarty, Alice C. Herrick, Philip Thurston.

Musical reminiscence of Jerry Herman's distinguished song writing and performing career. Previously produced at the Coconut Grove Playhouse, Arnold Mittelman producing artistic director.

ACT I

From *Milk and Honey,* 1961
  "Shalom" .... Florence Lacey, Lee Roy Reams
From *Hello, Dolly!,* 1964
  "Put On Your Sunday Clothes," "It Only Takes a Moment,"
    "Before the Parade Passes By" .... Reams
  "So Long, Dearie," "Ribbons Down My Back," "Dancing" .... Lacey
  "Penny in My Pocket" .... Reams
  "Hello, Dolly!" .... Lacey, Reams, Jerry Herman
From *Mame,* 1966
  "It's Today" .... Reams
  "Gooch's Song" .... Herman
  "We Need a Little Christmas" .... Lacey, Herman
  "If He Walked Into My Life" .... Lacey
  "Mame" .... Lacey, Reams, Herman

ACT II

From *Dear World*, 1969
"I Don't Want to Know" .... Lacey
From *Mack & Mabel*, 1974
"Movies Were Movies" .... Lacey, Reams, Herman
"I Won't Send Roses" .... Reams
"Hundreds of Girls" .... Herman
"Time Heals Everything" .... Lacey
"Tap Your Troubles Away" .... Reams
"Movies Were Movies" (Reprise) .... Lacey, Reams, Herman
From *The Grand Tour*, 1979
"I Belong Here" .... Lacey
"Mrs. S.L. Jacobowsky" .... Reams
"I'll Be Here Tomorrow" .... Herman
From *La Cage aux Folles*, 1983
"La Cage aux Folles" .... Reams
"Song on the Sand" .... Lacey
"I Am What I Am" .... Reams
"The Best of Times" .... Lacey, Reams, Herman
From *Mrs. Santa Claus*, 1996
"The Best Christmas of All" .... Lacey, Reams

Jerry Seinfeld: I'm Telling You for the Last Time (10). Performance piece by Jerry Seinfeld. Produced by A Contemporary Prods Inc. and HBO at the Broadhurst Theater. Opened August 5, 1998. (Closed August 9, 1998)

CAST: Jerry Seinfeld, Kevin Meany, the Don Miller Orchestra.
Special benefit standup comedy performances by the TV star, presented without intermission.

The Last Empress (24). Return engagement of the musical with book conceived and written by Mun Yol Yi, based on his book *Fox Hunt;* adapted by Kwang Lim Kim; music by Hee Gab Kim; lyrics by In Ja Yang; translation by Ha Yun Jung, Jun Taek Jun, Hee Hwan Lee. Produced in the Korean language with English supertitles by Arts Communications (A-Com) at the New York State Theater. Opened August 4, 1998. (Closed August 23, 1998)

Korean Cast:
Queen .... Wonjung Kim,
                Taewon Yi Kim (alternating)
Taewongun .... Sung Hoon Lee
King Kojung .... Hee Sung Yu
Inoue .... Hee Jung Lee
Itoh Hirobumi, Prime Minister
    of Japan .... Young Jae Choi
Gen. Kye Hun Hong .... Min Soo Kim
Miura Goroh .... Sung Ki Kim
Yuan Shi Kai .... Sung Ho Lee

Jinryonggun .... Hyun Dong Kim
Court Lady Park .... Young Joo Jeong
Court Lady Kim .... Hyo Jung Moon
Prince .... Jae Wean Kim, Jung Hoon Woo
American Cast:
German Envoy .... Peter Marinos
Lady Sontag .... Mary Jo Todaro
French Envoy .... Paul Taylor
Lady Underwood .... Marci Reid
Weber; Russian Envoy .... Al Bundonis

Chorus, Dancers: So Youn An, Ji Soo Choi, So Young Choi, Jeong Ju Doh, Eun Kyoung Han, Mi Kyung Jung, Do Hoon Kim, Do Hyeong Kim, Tai Hyun Kim, Ho Jin Kim, Sang Jin Kim, Young Ju Kim, Sun Mi Kim, Hak Muk Kim, Bong Soo Kim, So Yeoun Kim, So Young Kim, Yu Lim Kwak, Ji Eun Lee, Jae Gu Lee, Soo Hyoung Lee, Kyoung Woo Lee, Ji Youn Lee, Sang Ho Park, Yong Park, Sang Ryu, Beom Seok Seo, Eun Kyoung Yoon, Chan Yun.

Directed by Ho Jin Yun; choreography, Byung Goo Seo, Jin Wook Jung; musical direction, Kolleen Park; scenery, Dong Woo Park; costumes, Hyun Sook Kim; lighting, Hyung O Choi; sound, Ki Young Kim; orchestrations, Peter Casey, Hyuk Soon Kwon; additional music, Peter Casey; executive producer, Young Hwan Kim; associate producers, Sang Ryul Lee, Su Mun Lee, Young Il Yang, Mun Yol Yi, Hee Hwan Lee,Woo Jong Lee; production stage manager, Seok Yong Ryu; press, Tony Origlio Publicity, Tony Origlio, Karen Greco, David Lotz.

VIA DOLOROSA—British Playwright David Hare had four of his works performed on Broadway this season: *The Judas Kiss* held over from last year, *The Blue Room, Amy's View* and his solo performance, *as above,* portraying characters he met on his travels in the Near East

The life and death of Queen Min (Myungsung), a matriarch of the Chosun Kingdom who influenced her society in the direction of the 20th century but was assassinated by the Japanese in 1895 at the age of 45.

ACT I

Prologue
   "Japan Has Chosen" .... Miura Goroh, Japanese Assassins
Scene 1
   "The Day We Greet the New Queen" .... Regent, King, Queen, Company
Scene 2
   "Regency of the King's Father" .... Regent, Subjects
   "Soft Is the Spring Breeze" .... King, Court Ladies
   "Your Highness Is So Beautiful" .... Court Ladies
   "There Is a Star in My Heart" .... Queen
   "The Examination for State Military Service" .... Gen. Hong, Regent,
                                                                                    King, Applicants
   "A Wish for a Prince" .... Queen, King, Regents, Court Ladies, Subjects
   "Shaman Rite" (for Child Bearing) .... Jinryonggun, Shamans
Scene 3
   "Open Up the Door" .... Regent, Foreigners
   "Song of the Soldiers" .... Soldiers, People

Scene 4
    "Grow Big and Strong, Dear Prince" .... Court Ladies
    "You Are the King of Chosun" .... Queen, King, Court Ladies
    "Until the World Needs Me Again" .... Regent
Scene 5
    "Kojong's Imperial Conference" .... King, Subjects
    "It's All a Scheme" .... Queen
    "Seven Foreign Envoys" .... Foreign Envoys
Scene 6
    "New Army Unit, Old Army Unit" .... Soldiers, Japanese Merchants
    Military Mutiny of 1882 (Instrumental)
    "Back at the Seat of Power" .... Regent
    "I Miss You, My Dear Queen" .... King
    "We Shall Return to the Palace" .... Queen, King, Gen. Hong
Scene 7
    "Regent and Chinese" .... Regent, Yuan Shi Kai
    "Inoue Threatens King Kojong" .... Inoue
    "Queen Min's Return" .... Company
    "We Shall Rise Again" .... Queen, King, Gen. Hong, Company
    "Meeting on Japan's Chosun Policy" .... Prime Minister, Miura Goroh,
                                                               Japanese Cabinet Ministers

ACT II

Scene 8
    Dance at the Grand Banquet (Instrumental)
    "Come Celebrate Our Reforms" .... Queen, King
    "Queen Elizabeth of Chosun" .... Wives of Foreign Envoys
    "Negotiations at the Grand Banquet" .... Inoue, Queen, Foreign Envoys
    "The Sun Is Rising in Chosun" .... Company
    "Isn't It Strange, Snowflakes Are Falling" .... Child
Scene 9
    "You Shall Drink the Wine Offered by Miura" .... Inoue, Queen
    "Triple Intervention and the Atami House Conspiracy" .... Queen, King,
                       Russian, French and German Envoys, Miura Goroh, Assassins
    "Isn't It Strange, Snowflakes Are Falling" (Reprise) .... Child
Scene 10
    "New Era for the Prince" .... Royal Tutor, Prince, Queen, King
    "Miura's Audience With the King" .... Miura Goroh, Queen, King
Scene 11
    "The Situation Has Quickly Been Changed" .... Miura Goroh
    "The Queen Is Studying French Today" .... Sontag
    "By the Time This Drink Gets Cold" .... Miura Goroh, Assassins
    "Welcome" .... Wives of the Foreign Envoys, Queen
    Ritual for "Fox Hunt" (Instrumental)
Scene 12
    "The Prince and Queen" .... Prince, Queen
    "Where Was It That We Met?" .... Queen, Gen. Hong
    "You Are My Destiny" .... Gen. Hong
    "Thunder and Lightning" .... Prince, Queen
    "Light Up My Darkest Night" .... Queen
Scene 13
    "Do Not Harm the Queen" .... Regent, Japanese Military Officer
    "The Last of Gen. Hong" .... Gen. Hong
    "The Queen Is Hunted Down" .... Queen Min, Court Lady Park
    "Find the Queen, Kill the Fox" .... Assassins, Court Ladies
    "How Will I Live From Now On?" .... Prince
Epilogue
    "Rise, People of Chosun" .... Queen, Company

Colin Quinn—An Irish Wake (22). Solo performance by Colin Quinn; written by Colin Quinn and Lou DiMaggio. Produced by Delsener Slater/Lorne Michaels at the Helen Hayes Theater. Opened August 27, 1998. (Closed September 19, 1998)

Directed by Bobby Moresco; design, Eugene Lee; lighting, Roger Morgan; associate producer, Bobby Spillane; consulting producer, Michael Shoemaker; press, Fourfront, John Wimbs.

Colin Quinn of TV's *Saturday Night Live* portraying a number of characters remembered from his growing-up in a Brooklyn neighborhood in the 1970s, in material revised and expanded from a 1994 off-off-Broadway production at the Irish Arts Theater entitled *Sanctifying Grace.* The play was presented without intermission.

Riverdance. (23) Return engagement of the dance and music revue with music and lyrics by Bill Whelan. Produced by Radio City Productions in association with Abhann Productions, Moya Doherty producer, Julian Erskine executive producer, at Radio City Music Hall. Opened September 24, 1998. (Closed October 11, 1998).

With Eileen Martin, Pat Roddy.

Riverdance Irish Dance Troupe: Andrea Curley (dance captain), Dearbhail Bates (assistant dance captain), Sarah Barry, Tara Barry, Natalie Biggs, Lorna Bradley, Martin Brennan, Rachel Byrne, Zeph Caissie, Melissa Convery, Marty Dowds, Jo Ellen Forsyth, Susan Ginnety, Paula Goulding, Sinéad Green, Gary Healy, Donnacha Howard, Sean Kelliher, Nicola Leonard, Matt Martin, Sorcha McCaul, Jonathan McMorrow, Paula McNelis, Joe Moriarty, Niall Mulligan, Aoibheann O'Brien, Ursula Quigley, Katie Regan, Ann Ryan, Lisa Ryan, Sheila Ryan, Anthony Savage, Anthony Sharkey, Ryan Sheridan, Claire Usher, Leanda Ward.

Moscow Folk Ballet Company: Serguei Iakoubov, Svetlana Kossoroukova, Olena Krutsenko, Tatiana Nedostop, Iouri Oustiougov, Iouri Shiskine, Ilia Streltsov, Marina Taranda.

Singers: Katie McMahon (soloist), Cathal Synnott (choir leader), Derek Byrne, Derek Collins, Patrick Connolly, Jennifer Curran, Tony Davoren (soloist, "Oscail an Doras"), Joanna Higgins, Maire Lang, Denise O'Cain.

Drummers: Abraham Doron, Vinny Ozborne, Darren Smith, David Tilly.

Understudies: Tara Barry, Susan Ginnety, Sorcha McCaul, Martin Brennan, Donnacha Howard.

Orchestra: Eoghan O'Neill musical director, bass guitar; Eileen Ivers fiddle; Brian O'Brian, uilleann pipes, low whistle; Kenneth Edge soprano and alto saxophones; Nikola Parov gadulka, kaval, gaida; Eilis Egan accordion; Des Moore electric and acoustic guitars; Noel Heraty percussion; Desi Reynolds drums, percussion; Jim Higgins bodhrán, darrabukkas, dunbeg, ouida; Pete Whinnett keyboards.

Directed by John McColgan; scenery, Robert Ballagh; costumes, Jen Kelly, original design, Margaret Crosse; lighting, Rupert Murray; sound, Michael O'Gorman; projections, Chris Slingsby; orchestrations, Nick Ingman, Bill Whelan; poetry, Theo Dorgan, narrated by John Kavanagh; press, Merle Frimark.

Choreography: Reel Around the Sun, Thunderstorm—Michael Flatley; Women of Ireland—Jean Butler; Shivna, Russian Dervish—Moscow Folk Ballet Company; Firedance—Maria Pagés, Colin Dunne; Riverdance—Mavis Ascott, Michael Flatley (Irish Step Dance choreography), Jean Butler (lead female solo choreography); American Wake—Michael Flatley, Paula Nic Cionnaith (set dance consultant); Trading Taps—Colin Dunne, Tarik Winston; Oscail an Doras—Tara Little; Heartbeat of the World—Maria Pagés, Colin Dunne; Andalucia—Maria Pagés; Heartland—Michael Flatley, Colin Dunne, Jean Butler.

Extravaganza featuring Irish step dancers as well as choral and solo songs and dances by European performers. A foreign show previously produced in Dublin and London and at the Music Hall 4/13/96 for 8 performances and 10/2/96 for 21 performances and 10/12/97 for 23 performances.

SCENES, DANCES AND MUSICAL NUMBERS, ACT I: Introduction. Scene 1: Reel Around the Sun (Corona, The Chronos Reel, Reel Around the Sun). Scene 2: "The Heart's Cry." Scene 3: Women of Ireland (The Countess Cathleen, Women of the Sidhe). Scene 4: "Caoineadh Chú Chulainn" (lament). Scene 5: Thunderstorm. Scene 6: "Shivna." Scene 7: Firedance (with Nuria Brisa, Marta Jiménez, Arantxa Jurado). Scene 8: Slip Into Spring—The Harvest (Eileen Ivers fiddle). Scene 9: Riverdance ("Cloudsong," The Dance of the Riverwoman, Earthrise, Riverdance).

ACT II: Introduction. Scene 10: American Wake (Nova Scotia Set, "Lift the Wings"). Scene 11: The Harbour of the New World; I—"Heal Their Hearts—Freedom" (with Charles Gray), II—Trading Taps (with Robert Reed, Toby Harris, Donnell A. Russell), III—Morning in Macedonia (The Russian Dervish), IV—Oscail an Doras (Open the Door), V—Heartbeat of the World—Andalucia (with Nuria Brisa, Marta Jiménez Luis, Arantxa Jurado). Scene 12: "Home and the Heartland" (Eileen Ivers fiddle). Scene 13: Riverdance International (reprise; story by Bill Whelan, Moya Doherty and John McColgan; music and lyrics by Bill Whelan).

Swan Lake (124). Dance performance piece directed and choreographed by Matthew Bourne; music by Peter Ilyich Tchaikovsky. Produced by Adventures in Motion Pictures, Katharine Doré producing director, and Cameron Mackintosh at the Neil Simon Theater. Opened October 8, 1998. (Closed January 23, 1999)

Swan	Adam Cooper	Prince's Girlfriend	Emily Piercy
Prince	Scott Ambler	Private Secretary	Barry Atkinson
Queen	Fiona Chadwick, Isabel Mortimer	Young Prince	Andrew Walkinshaw

Others: Detlev Alexander, Jacqueline Anderson, Sarah Barron, Wilson A. Batista, Graham Bowen, Theo Clinkard, Andrew Corbett, Saranne Curtin, Matthew Dalby, Darren Ellis, Vicky Evans, Ramon Flowers, Valentina Formenti, Christopher Freeman, Jeffrey Lane Freeze, Fred Gehrig, Nina Goldman, Gino Grenek, Heather Habens, Ben Harley, Floyd Hendricks, Will Kemp, Hans-Werner Klohe, Martin Lofsnes, Michela Meazza, Sam Meredith, Mark Mitchell, Neil Penlington, Arthur Pita, Colin Ross-Waterson, Ruthlyn Salomons, Tom Searle, Kirsty Tapp, Alan Vincent, Tom Ward, Ewan Wardrop, Ben Wright, William Yong.

Orchestra: David Frame conductor; Jack Buckhannan associate conductor, keyboard II; Erica Kiesewetter concertmaster; Robert Zubrycki, Conway Kuo, Phil Spletzer, Basia Danilow violin; Sarah Adams violin, viola; David Cerutti, Richard Brice viola; Wolfram Koessel cello; Jordan Frazier double bass; Diva Goodfriend-Koven flute, piccolo; Brian Greene oboe; Anthony Brackett clarinet, flute; Tom Sefcovic bassoon; Ken De Carlo trumpet I; John Sheppard trumpet II; Javier Gandara, French horn I; Nancy Billmann, French horn II; Lisa Albrecht trombone; Pablo Rieppi tympany, percussion; David Rozenblatt percussion; Rob Mukulski keyboard I; Ann Fornara keyboard II.

Musical direction, David Frame; scenery and costumes, Lez Brotherston; lighting, Rick Fisher; sound, Mark Menard; orchestrations, David Cullen; production stage manager, Kate Elliott; press, The Publicity Office, Marc Thibodeau, Bob Fennell.

The performance was presented in two parts.

A version of the 1895 ballet *Swan Lake* story, told in dance and mime, of a Prince, dominated by his mother, looking for love amid a flock of male swans.

Mamaloshen (28). Concert performance by Mandy Patinkin in the Yiddish language. Produced by Dodger Endemol Theatricals at the Belasco Theater. Opened October 13, 1998. (Closed November 7, 1998)

Paul Ford, Eric Stern, Lawrence Yurman piano; Saeka Matsuyama violin.

Musical arrangements, Paul Ford, Eric Stern; scenery, Eric Renschler; lighting, Eric Cornwell; sound, Otts Munderloh; press, Boneau/Bryan-Brown.

Program of Yiddish and American songs, with some Yiddish versions of American lyrics. The show was presented without intermission.

Note: The solo show *A Mom's Life,* written and performed by Kathryn Grody—Jack Hofsiss creative consultant, Eric Cornwell lighting, Otts Munderloh sound, Lee Kahrs stage manager—was presented at this theater on four Monday evenings 10/19 to 11/7.

MUSICAL NUMBERS: "Rozhinkes Mit Mandlen" (Raisins and Almonds) by Abraham Goldfaden, Henry Lefkowitch and Stanley Lionel; "Mayn Mirl" (Maria) by Leonard Bernstein and Stephen Sondheim; "Yome, Yome . . . " (traditional), "Belz . . . " by Alexander Olshanetsky and Jacob Jacobs; "Tsen Koikes" (Ten Kopeks, traditional); "Supercalifragilisticexpialidocious" by Richard M. Sherman and Robert B. Sherman; "The Hokey Pokey" by Charles Mack, Taft Baker and Roland LaPrise; "Papirosin" (Cigarettes) by Herman Yablokoff; "Motl Der Opreyter . . . " by Chaim Towber and H. Solomonson; "Ynter Dayne Vayse Shtern" (Under Your White Stars) by Abraham Sutzkever and Abraham Bruno;

"Lid Fun Titanic" (Song of the Titanic) by Joshua Rayzner; "Hey, Tsigelekh" (Hey, Little Goats) by Mordecai Gebirtig; "Take Me Out to the Ball Game" by Jack Norworth and Albert von Tilzer; "God Bless America" by Irving Berlin; "Der Alter Tzigayner" (The Old Gypsy) by Abraham Ellstein and Jacob Jacobs; "White Christmas" by Irving Berlin; "Oyfn Pripetshik … " by Mark M. Warshawsky; "American Tune … " by Paul Simon.

More To Love (4). By Rob Bartlett. Produced by Mitchell Maxwell, Mark Balsam, Jim Russek, Gary Grant, Dede Harris, Bob Cuillo, Alvin and Karen Moss, Fred H. Krones and Victoria Maxwell at the Eugene O'Neill Theater. Opened October 15, 1998. (Closed October 17, 1998)

Rob	Rob Bartlett	Maxine	Joyce Van Patten
Alice	Dana Reeve		

Understudy: Misses Reeve, Van Patten—Kay McClelland.

Directed by Jack O'Brien; scenery, David Gallo; costumes, Ann Hould-Ward; lighting, Michael Lincoln; sound, Peter J. Fitzgerald; songs, Rob Bartlett, Michael Pagano; casting, Jay Binder; production stage manager, Robert Mark Kalfin; stage manager, Dana Williams; press, Cromarty & Company, Peter Cromarty, Alice Cromarty, Philip Thurston.

Time: Saturday morning, two days before Rob's 40th birthday. Place: Long Island, N.Y. The play was presented without intermission.

Subtitled A Big Fat Comedy, an overweight stand-up comedian on the verge of an HBO television deal talks it over with his wife (real) and his agent (in fantasy).

Aznavour on Broadway (24). Concert performance by Charles Aznavour. Produced by Delsener Slater/SFX Entertainment, by special arrangement with Levon Sayan, at the Marquis Theater. Opened October 20, 1998. (Closed November 15, 1998)

Musical direction, Russell Kassoff.

The noted French singer, at 74, in a program of songs, some in French, others in English and Spanish. The show was presented in two parts.

Footloose (253). Musical based on the original screen play by Dean Pitchford; adapted by Dean Pitchford and Walter Bobbie; music by Tom Snow; lyrics by Dean Pitchford; additional song credits are noted in the list of musical numbers below. Produced by Dodger Endemol Theatricals at the Richard Rodgers Theater. Opened October 22, 1998.

Ren McCormack	Jeremy Kushner	Wendy Jo	Rosalind Brown
Ethel McCormack	Catherine Cox	Chuck Cranston	Billy Hartung
Rev. Shaw Moore	Stephen Lee Anderson	Lyle	Jim Ambler
Vi Moore	Dee Hoty	Travis	Bryant Carroll
Ariel Moore	Jennifer Laura Thompson	Cop; Country Fiddler	Nick Sullivan
Lulu Warnicker	Catherine Campbell	Betty Blast; Irene	Robin Baxter
Wes Warnicker	Adam Lefevre	Willard Hewitt	Tom Plotkin
Eleanor Dunbar; Doreen	Donna Lee Marshall	Principal Clerk; Saloon Keeper	John Deyle
Coach Dunbar	John Hillner	Jeter; Cowboy Bob	Artie Harris
Rusty	Stacy Francis	Bickle	Hunter Foster
Urleen	Kathy Deitch	Garvin	Paul Castree

Ensemble: Billy Angell, Angela Brydon, Paul Castree, Hunter Foster, Kristen Leigh Gorski, Artie Harris, Sean Haythe, Lori Holmes, Daniel Karaty, Katharine Leonard, Mark Myars, JoAnna Ross, Serena Soffer, Ron Todorowski.

Orchestra: Doug Katsaros conductor, keyboard; Joseph Baker associate conductor, keyboard; John Benthal, Bob Rose guitar; Clint de Ganon drums; Vince Fay bass; Tim Ries reeds; Kenny Kosek violin; Stephanie Cummins cello; Mark Sherman percussion; John Miller music coordinator.

Understudies: Messrs. Kushner, Hartung—Hunter Foster, Jim Ambler; Mr. Anderson—John Hillner, Rick Crom; Miss Hoty—Susan Bigelow, Donna Lee Marshall; Misses Thompson, Deitch—Katharine Leonard, Janine Meyers; Mr. Plotkin—Artie Harris, Paul Castree; Miss Francis—Lori Holmes, Orfeh; Miss Brown—Orfeh, Kristen Leigh Gorski; Misses Cox, Campbell, Marshall—Susan Bigelow,

Janine Meyers; Miss Baxter— Donna Lee Marshall, Orfeh; Messrs. Lefevre, Deyle—Rick Crom, Nick Sullivan; Mr. Hillner—Rick Crom, Hunter Foster; Messrs. Carroll, Ambler—Ben Cameron, Jamie Gustis; Mr. Sullivan—Rick Crom, Sean Haythe.

Directed by Walter Bobbie; choreography, A.C. Ciulla; scenery, John Lee Beatty; costumes, Toni-Leslie James; lighting, Ken Billington; sound, Tony Meola; orchestrations, Danny Troob; music supervision and vocal arrangements, Doug Katsaros; dance music arrangements, Joseph Baker; music coordinator, John Miller; executive producers, Dodger Management Group, Tim Hawkins; associate producer, The John F. Kennedy Center for the Performing Arts; casting, Julie Hughes, Barry Moss; production stage manager, Steven Beckler; stage manager, Dale Kaufman; press, Boneau/Bryan-Brown, Adrian Bryan-Brown, Susanne Tighe.

Time: In the recent past. Place: Somewhere in the heartland of America.

Small-town minister wrestles with the "evils" of rock 'n' roll.

ACT I

Scene 1: City of Chicago
"Footloose" .... Ren, Company
    (music by Kenny Loggins; lyric by Dean Pitchford and Kenny Loggins)
Town of Bomont-Church
"On Any Sunday" .... Rev. Moore, Company
Scene 2: Church Yard
Scene 3: Burger Blast Restaurant
"The Girl Gets Around" .... Chuck, Ariel, Travis, Lyle
    (music by Sammy Hagar)
Scene 4: High school hallway
"I Can't Stand Still" .... Ren
Scene 5: Street corner, Principal's office, Warnicker house
"Somebody's Eyes" .... Rusty, Wendy Jo, Urleen, Company
Scene 6: Moore home
"Learning To Be Silent" .... Vi, Ethel
Scene 7: Burger Blast Restaurant
"Holding Out for a Hero" .... Ariel, Rusty, Wendy Jo, Urleen
    (music by Jim Steinman)
Scene 8: Plains of Bomont
Scene 9: Moore home
"Somebody's Eyes" (Reprise) .... Rusty, Wendy Jo, Urleen
"Heaven Help Me" .... Rev. Moore
Scene 10: High school gymnasium
"I'm Free"/"Heaven Help Me"/"On Any Sunday" .... Ren, Rev. Moore, Company

ACT II

Scene l: The Bar-B-Q Country & Western Bar
"Let's Make Believe We're in Love" .... Irene, Country Kickers
"Let's Hear It for the Boy" .... Rusty, Company
Scene 2: Moore home
"Can You Find It in Your Heart?" Vi
Scene 3: Lot behind the Feed and Fuel
"Mama Says" .... Willard, Boys
Scene 4: The Potawney Bridge
"Almost Paradise" .... Ren, Ariel
    (music by Eric Carmen)
Scene 5: Bomont Town Hall
"Dancing Is Not a Crime" .... Ren, Boys
Scene 6: Church
"I Confess" .... Rev. Moore
"On Any Sunday" (Reprise) .... Company
Scene 7: Church yard
"Can You Find It in Your Heart?" (Reprise) .... Rev. Moore
High school gymnasium
"Footloose" (Reprise) .... Company

Getting and Spending (41). By Michael J. Chepiga. Produced by Martin Markinson, Elsa Daspin Haft, Allen M. Shore, Norma Langworthy and Sheilah Goldman at the Helen Hayes Theater. Opened October 25, 1998. (Closed November 29, 1998)

Brother Thaddeus;		Elizabeth Panelli	Deirdre Lovejoy
Judge Keefe	MacIntyre Dixon	Charles Humboldt	Jack Gilpin
Brother Alfred	Derek Smith	Victoria Phillips	Linda Purl
Richard O'Neill	David Rasche	Mary Phillips	Debra Mooney

Understudy: Messrs. Dixon, Gilpin, Smith—Tom Fitzsimmons.

Directed by John Tillinger; scenery, James Noone; costumes, Michael Krass; lighting, Kevin Adams; sound, Jeff Ladman; casting, Elissa Myers, Paul Fouquet; production stage manager, Kelley Kirkpatrick; stage manager, Kirstin Mooney; press, The Pete Sanders Group, Pete Sanders, Clint Bond Jr., Glenna Freedman.

Time: The present. Place: Various places in Kentucky and New York. The play was presented in two parts.

Male lawyer is disillusioned with the world of high finance but is persuaded to defend a female investment banker from a charge of insider trading.

Previously produced in regional theater by the Old Globe Theater, San Diego.

The Scarlet Pimpernel (239). Revised version of the musical based on the novel by Baroness Orczy; book and lyrics by Nan Knighton; music by Frank Wildhorn. Produced by Radio City Entertainment and Ted Forstmann with Pierre Cossette, Bill Haber, Hallmark Entertainment and Kathleen Raitt, Tim Hawkins executive producer, at the Minskoff Theater. Opened November 4, 1998. (Suspended performances May 30, 1999; scheduled to reopen 9/10/99)

Marguerite	Rachel York	Jessup	James Dybas
Chauvelin	Rex Smith	Ben	Ken Land
Percy	Douglas Sills	Hastings	William Thomas Evans
Marie	Elizabeth Ward	Neville	Stephen Hope
Armand	James Bohanek	Leggett	Douglas Storm
Tussaud	Philip Hoffman	Hal	Michael Hance
Coupeau	Timothy Eric Hart	Robespierre;	
Mercier	Jeff Gardner	Prince of Wales	David Cromwell
Ozzy	Harvey Evans	Lady Digby	Sandy Rosenberg
Elton	Russell Garrett	Lady Llewellyn	Pamela Burrell
Farleigh	Tom Zemon	Jailer	T. Doyle Leverett
Dewhurst	James Judy		

French Mob, Soldiers, Dancers, British Guests, Servants: Stephanie Bast, Nick Cavarra, Michael Halling, Marine Jahan, John Lathan, Alison Lory, Mark McGrath, Katie Nutt, Jessica Phillips, Terry Richmond, Craig Rubano, Cynthia Sophiea, Charles West.

Orchestra: Ron Melrose conductor; Wendy Bobbitt associate conductor, keyboards; Andrew Wilder assistant conductor, keyboards; Michael Roth concertmaster; Laura Oatts, Britt Swenson, Lisa Matricardi, Ashley Horne violin; Liuh-Wen Ting, Leslie Tomkins viola; Daniel D. Miller, Sarah Hewitt cello; Richard Sarpola bass; Edward Joffe, James Roe, Andrew Sterman woodwinds; Gilbert Dejean bassoon, contra bassoon; Chris Gekker trumpet; Mike Christianson trombone; Chris Komer, Kelly Dent, French horn; Robert Gustafson keyboards; John Meyers, Benjamin Herman percussion.

Standby: Mr. Sills—Nat Chandler. Understudies: Mr. Sills—William Thomas Evans; Miss York—Jessica Phillips, Elizabeth Ward; Mr. Smith—Timothy Eric Hart, Mark McGrath, Tom Zemon; Mr. Bohanek—Nick Cavarra, Craig Rubano; Mr. Cromwell—James Dybas, James Van Treuren; Messrs. Evans, Judy, Zemon—Stephen Hope, Ken Land, James Van Treuren; Miss Ward—Jessica Phillips, Terry Richmond; Misses Rosenberg, Burrell—Sarah Knapp, Cynthia Sophiea; Swings—Drew Geraci, Stephen Hope, Sarah Knapp, James Van Treuren.

Directed and choreographed by Robert Longbottom; musical direction and vocal arrangements, Ron Melrose; scenery, Andrew Jackness; costumes, Jane Greenwood; lighting, Natasha Katz; sound, Karl Richardson; fight direction, Rick Sordelet; special effects, Jim Steinmeyer; orchestrations, Kim Scharnberg; musical supervision, Jason Howland; music coordinator, John Miller; assistant choreographers, Tom Kosis, Darlene Wilson; dance arrangements, David Chase; originally choreographed by Adam

THE SCARLET PIMPERNEL—Douglas Sills (Percy), Rachel York (Marguerite) and Rex Smith (Chauvelin) in the revised version of the Nan Knighton-Frank Wildhorn musical

Pelty; casting, Julie Hughes, Barry Morse; production stage manager, Bonnie L. Becker; stage manager, Jack Gianino; press, Boneau/Bryan-Brown, Adrian Bryan-Brown, Steven Padla.

Time: May into July, 1794. Place: England and France.

A brave Englishman pretends to be a fop, as he leads a League of his countrymen rescuing French aristocrats from the guillotine, as in Baroness Orczy's novel and co-authored play produced on Broadway 10/24/10, a musical version produced off Broadway 1/7/64 for 3 performances, the movie starring Leslie Howard and last season's version of this musical which opened 11/9/97 and played 373 performances through 10/3/98.

ACT I

"Storybook" .... Marguerite, French Ensemble
"Madame Guillotine" .... Chauvelin
"You Are My Home" .... Percy, Marguerite
Wedding Dance .... Ensemble
"Prayer" .... Percy
"Into the Fire" .... Percy, The League
The Rescue .... Ensemble
"Falcon in the Dive" .... Chauvelin
"When I Look at You" .... Marguerite
"Where's the Girl?" .... Chauvelin

"You Are My Home" (Reprise) .... Marguerite, Armand
"The Creation of Man" .... Percy, The League
"The Riddle" .... Chauvelin, Marguerite, Percy, Company

ACT II

"The Scarlet Pimpernel" .... Percy, Marguerite, Ball Guests
"They Seek Him Here" .... Percy, Company
The Gavotte .... Ensemble
"She Was There" .... Percy
"Storybook" (Reprise) .... Marguerite, French Girls
"Where's the Girl?" (Reprise) .... Chauvelin
"Into the Fire" (Reprise) .... The League
"I'll Forget You" .... Marguerite
The Duel .... Percy, Chauvelin, Marguerite
"When I Look at You" (Reprise) .... Percy, Marguerite
"Into the Fire" (Reprise) .... Company

I'm Still Here ... Damn It! (51). Solo performance by Sandra Bernhard. Produced by Contemporary Productions and Arielle Tepper at the Booth Theater. Opened November 5, 1998. (Closed January 3, 1999)

The Band: Mitchell Kaplan keyboards, special material; Denise Fraser drums, percussion; Dan Petty guitar; Michael Stanzilis bass guitar; Soumaya Akaaboune gembe, vocals.

Artistic consultant, Marty Callner; scenic consultant, Paul Holt; lighting consultant, Allen Branton; sound consultant, Nelson & O'Reilly Productions; press, The Publicity Office, Marc Thibodeau, Bob Fennell, Michael S. Borowski.

Barbed stand-up comedy, much of it aimed at celebrities and show business, presented without intermission.

Radio City Christmas Spectacular (202). Holiday spectacle including *The Living Nativity* pageant originally conceived by Robert F. Jani. Produced by Radio City Productions, Howard Kolins executive producer, at Radio City Music Hall. Opened November 6, 1998. (Closed January 3, 1999)

		Elves:	
Narrator	George Hearn		
Santa Claus	Charles Edward Hall	Tinker	Kristoffer Elinder
Mrs. Claus	Mary Stout, Lynn Eldridge	Thinker	Adam Brown
Clara	Ann Brown, Pamela Elaine Otterson	Tannenbaum	Lisa Blanchard
Skaters	Laurie Welch and Randy Coyne,	Bartholomew	Marty Klebba
	Jeb Rand and Jennifer Bayer	Thumbs	Leslie Stump-Vanderpool
Young Boy	Alex Bowen, Blaine Horton		

Understudy: Mr. Hall—Paul Gallagher. Elf Swings—Steven Babiar, Margarita Fernandez.

Radio City Rockettes: Melanie Allen, Abby Arauz, Leslie Barlow, Linda Beausoleil-Baldwin, Kiki Bennett, Elizabeth Charney-Sprei, Jennifer Clippinger, Renee Collins, Jacqueline Collins, Lillian Colon, Helen Conklin, Katherine Corp, Kimberly Corp, Cheryl Hebert Cutlip, Susanne Doris, Jenny Eakes, Ashlee Fife, Vanessa Foley, Michelle Gaudette, Prudence Gray-Demmler, Leslie Guy, Julie Harkness, Susan Heart, Vicki Hickerson, Ginny Hounsell, Danielle Jolie-Archer, Pamela Jordan, Temple Kane, Donna Kapral, Louisa Kendrick, Natalie King, Debby Kole, Amy Krawcek, Judy Little, Melissa Rae Mahon, Jean Marie, Setsuko Maruhashi, Mindy Mason, Lisa Matsuoka, Mary McCatty, Patrice McConachie, Julie McDonald, Lori Mello, Dottie Belle Meyman, Hayley Nathan, Rhonda Notary, Michelle O'Steen, Kerri Pearsall, Renee Perry-Lancaster, Allison Richy, Ivy Risser, Megan Schenck, Jennifer Leigh Schwerer, Maryellen Scilla, Genia Sherwood-Moss, Tamlyn Shusterman, Jane Silane, Debra Smith, Amber Snow, Alyssa Stec, Katherine Steers, Leslie Stroud, Lynn Sullivan (Rockette Captain), Karyn Tomzak, Kristin Tudor, Brooke Wendle, Darlene Wendy, Jaime Windrow, Elaine Winslow, Eileen Woods, Beth Woods-Nolan, Deborah Yates.

Ensemble: Barbara Angeline, Robert Armitage, Alan Bennett, Michelle Chase, Eric Clausell, Michael Clowers, Kelly Cole, Laurie Crochet, Jason Davies, John Dietrich, Bill Disbennett, Caroline Doherty, Byron Easley, Timothy Farley, Cynthia Goerig, Aldrin Gonzalez, Jamie Harris, Selena Harris, Susannah Israel, Lesley Jennings, Tom Kosis, Shawn Ku, Richard Lewis, Michelle Lynch, Troy Magino, Melanie Malicote, Joanne Manning, Richie Mastascusa, Marty McDonough, Corinne McFadden, Hannah Meadows, Stephanie Michels, Mayumi Miguel, Ginger Norman, Carolyn Ockert, Sean Palmer, Wes Pope, Chesley Powell, Jermaine R. Rembert, Jim T. Ruttman, Tim Santos, Joni Michelle Schenck, Rebecca Sherman-Morcelo, Megan Sikora, Michael Susko, James Tabeek, Jim Testa, David Underwood, Karl Wahl, Greg Zane.

Radio City Orchestra: Grant Sturiale conductor; Larry Yurman associate conductor; Mary L. Rowell concertmaster; Andrea Andros, Eric De Gioia, Carmen DeLeo, Michael Gillette, Nannette Levi, Susan Lorentsen, Samuel Marder, Holly Ovenden violin; Barbara H. Vaccaro, Richard Spencer viola; Frank Levy, Sarah Carter cello; Dean Crandall bass; Kenneth Emery flute; Gerard J. Niewood, Richard Oatts, John M. Cippola, Joshua Siegel, Kenneth Arzberger reeds; Daniel Culpepper, Russ Rizner, French horn; Richard Raffio, Hollis Burridge, Zachary Shnec trumpet; John D. Schnupp, Thomas B. Olcott, Mark Johansen trombone; Andrew Rodgers tuba; Thomas J. Oldakowski drums; Mario DeCiutiis, Maya Gunji percussion; Anthony Cesarano guitar; Susanna Nason, Henry Aronson piano; Jeanne Maier harp; George Wesner, Fred Davies organ.

Directed and choreographed by Robert Longbottom; musical director, David Chase; associate musical director, Grant Sturiale; lighting, Ken Billington, Jason Kantrowitz; assistant director, Tom Kosis; assistant choreographers, Michael Clowers, John Dietrich, Tom Kosis, Lynn Sullivan; vocal arrangements, David Chase, Don Pippin, Bryan Louiselle; original orchestrations, Elman Anderson, Douglas Besterman, Michael Gibson, Don Harper, Arthur Harris, Phillip J. Lang, Dick Lieb, Don Pippin, Danny Troob, Jonathan Tunick, Jim Tyler; dance music arrangements, David Chase, Peter Howard, Mark Hummel, Marvin Laird; musical routines, Tony Fox, Bob Krogstad, Don Pippin, Don Smith; "Silent Night" arrangement by Percy Faith; production stage manager, John Bonanni; 1st assistant stage managers, Kathy J. Hoovler, Carey Lawless; stage managers, David Hyslop, Peggy Imbrie, Joseph Oronato, Nichola Taylor, Karl Thompson; press, Michael P. Taylor, Kate Schroeder.

Original music: "Santa's Gonna Rock and Roll" and "I Can't Wait Till Christmas Day" music by Henry Krieger, lyrics by Bill Russell, arrangements by Bryan Louiselle; "What Do You Want for Christmas" music by Larry Grossman, lyrics by Hal Hackady; "It's Christmas in New York" written by Billy Butt.

66th edition of Radio City Music Hall's Christmas show, starring the Rockettes and including the traditional Nativity pageant, presented without intermission.

SCENES: Overture—Radio City Orchestra (arrangement, Don Pippin; film score arrangement, Bryan Louiselle).

Scene 1: Santa's Gonna Rock and Roll—Santa, Rockettes (choreography, Robert Longbottom; scenery, Michael Hotopp; costumes, Gregg Barnes; Rockette dance arrangement, Peter Howard).

Scene 2: The Nutcracker—A Little Girl's Dream (choreography, Robert Longbottom; scenery, Michael Hotopp; costumes, Gregg Barnes)

Scene 3: The Parade of the Wooden Soldiers—Rockettes (choreography, Russell Markert; restaged by Violet Holmes; scenery, Charles Lisanby; costumes, Vincente Minnelli).

Scene 4: Here Comes Santa Claus—Santa (choreography, Robert Longbottom; scenery, Michael Hotopp; costumes, Gregg Barnes; dance music arrangement, David Chase).

Scene 5: Christmas in New York—Rockettes, Radio City Orchestra, Company (choreography, Marianne Selbert; Rockette choreography, Violet Holmes; scenery, Charles Lisanby; gowns and Rockette costumes, Pete Menefee).

Scene 6: Ice Skating in the Plaza

Scene 7: Santa and Mrs. Claus: In Concert (choreography, Robert Longbottom; scenery, Michael Hotopp; costumes, Gregg Barnes; dance music arrangement, David Chase).

Scene 8: Carol of the Bells—Rockettes, Company (choreography, Scott Salmon; scenery, Charles Lisanby; costumes, Pete Menefee).

Scene 9: Santa's Toy Fantasy—Santa, Mrs. Claus, Elves (choreography, Scott Salmon, Linda Haberman; scenery, Charles Lisanby; costumes, Pete Menefee; Elves costumes, Gregg Barnes).

Scene 10: The Living Nativity with One Solitary Life—"Silent Night," "O Little Town of Bethlehem," "The First Noel," "We Three Kings," "O Come All Ye Faithful," "Hark, the Herald Angels Sing" (restaged by Linda Lemac; scenery, Charles Lisanby; costumes, Frank Spencer).

Jubilant: Joy to the World—Organ, Company.

Roundabout Theater Company. Schedule of two programs. **Little Me** (101). Revival of the musical based on the novel by Patrick Dennis; book by Neil Simon; music by Cy Coleman; lyrics by Carolyn Leigh. Opened November 12, 1998. (Closed February 7, 1999) **The Lion in Winter** (93). Revival of the play by James Goldman. Opened March 11, 1999. (Closed May 30, 1999) Produced by Roundabout Theater Company, Todd Haimes artistic director, Ellen Richard managing director, Julia C. Levy executive director of external affairs, at the Criterion Center Stage Right.

LITTLE ME

CAST: Belle—Faith Prince; Momma, Mrs. Eggleston—Ruth Williamson; Ramona—Andrea Chamberlain; Bruce, Bernie Buchsbaum, Bert, German Soldier, Yulnick—Michael McGrath; Cerine, Kitty—Cynthia Onrubia; Noble Eggleston, Amos Pinchley, Benny Buchsbaum, Val du Val, Fred Poitrine, Otto Schnitzler, Prince Cherney, The Drunk—Martin Short; Greensleeves, Sergeant, Movie "King"—Michael McEachran; Maid, Miss Kepplewhite, Christine, Army Nurse, Secretary, Casino Woman—Christine Pedi; Lucky—Michael Park; Pinchley Junior, Steward, Assistant Director, Doctor—Brooks Ashmanskas; Nurse—Kimberly Lyon; Kleeg, Attorney, Maitre D', Preacher, General, Captain, Victor—Peter Benson; Newsboy—Michael Arnold; Newsboy, 2d Sailor, Justice—Jeffrey Hankinson; Colette, Roxane—Roxane Barlow; Suzie—Joanne McHugh; Soldier; Justice—Denis Jones.

Belle's Boys, Chain Gang—Michael Arnold, Jeffrey Hankinson, Ned Hannah, Denis Jones. Boom Boom Girls—Kimberly Lyon, Joanne McHugh, Cynthia Onrubia. Party Guests, Rich Kids, Drifter's Row Townspeople, Courtroom Dancers, Skylight Roof Patrons, Nurses, Soldiers, Medics, Passengers, Biblical Slaves, Casino Patrons, Mourners—Company.

Orchestra: David Chase conductor, keyboards; Robert Berman associate conductor, keyboards; Danny Cahn, Glenn Drewes trumpet; Jack Schatz trombone, tuba; Dan Willis, Frank Santagata woodwinds; Ray Grappone drums; Leon Maleson bass; Dave Yee percussion.

Standby: Miss Prince—Jennifer Allen. Understudies: Mr. Short—Michael McGrath; Mr. Benson—Michael McEachran; Mr. McGrath—Josh Prince; Mr. Park—Denis Jones; Miss Pedi—Courtney Young; Miss Williamson—Christine Pedi; Mr. Ashmanskas—Josh Prince. Swings—Joey Pizzi (Dance Captain), Josh Prince, Courtney Young.

Directed and choreographed by Rob Marshall; musical direction, David Chase; scenery, David Gallo; costumes, Ann Hould-Ward; lighting, Kenneth Posner; sound, Brian Ronan; orchestrations, Harold Wheeler; dance music arrangements, David Krane; music coordinator, John Miller; projections, Jan Hartley; associate director and choreographer, Cynthia Onrubia; founding director, Gene Feist; casting, Jim Carnahan; production stage manager, Perry Cline; stage manager, David Sugarman; press, Boneau/Bryan-Brown, Adrian Bryan-Brown, Erin Dunn.

Time & place: The present—Southampton, 1962; The past—Venezuela, Illinois, Chicago, somewhere in France, on the North Atlantic, Hollywood, Monte Carlo, a principality in Middle Europe.

The last major New York revival of *Little Me* took place on Broadway 1/21/82 for 36 performances.

ACT I

"Little Me"	Belle, Belle's Boys
"The Other Side of the Tracks"	Belle
"Rich Kids Rag"	Rich Kids, Noble
"I Love You"	Noble, Belle, Company
"The Other Side of the Tracks" (Reprise)	Belle
"Deep Down Inside"	Belle, Pinchley, Company
"Be a Performer"	Benny & Bernie Buchsbaum, Belle
"Dimples"	Belle, Chain Gang
"Boom Boom"	Val du Val, Boom Boom Girls
"I've Got Your Number"	Lucky
"Real Live Girl"	Fred Poitrine
"Real Live Girl" (Reprise)	Fred, Soldiers
Finale, Act I	Belle

ACT II

"I Love Sinking You"	Belle, Noble, Company
"Poor Little Hollywood Star"	Belle

"Goodbye" .... Prince Cherney, Yulnick, Company
"Here's to Us" .... Belle, Company

THE LION IN WINTER

Henry II	Laurence Fishburne	Richard Lionheart	Chuma Hunter-Gault
Alais	Emily Bergl	Eleanor	Stockard Channing
John	Keith Nobbs	Philip	Roger Howarth
Geoffrey	Neal Huff		

Servants—Jeff Croteau, Dan Maceyak, Benjamin Nurick.

Standbys: Mr. Fishburne—Jonathan Peck; Miss Channing—Patricia Hodges. Understudies: Messrs. Hunter-Gault, Howarth—Reuben Jackson; Miss Bergl—Lauren Stamile; Messrs. Nobbs, Huff—Brian Ibsen.

Directed by Michael Mayer; scenery, David Gallo; costumes, Michael Krass; lighting, Kenneth Posner; sound, Mark Bennett; associate artistic director, Scott Ellis; casting, Jim Carnahan; production stage manager, Gary Mickelson; stage manager, Becky Garrett.

Time: Christmas 1183. Place: Henry's castle at Chinon, France. The play was presented in two parts. *The Lion in Winter* was first produced on Broadway 3/3/66 for 92 performances and was designated a Best Play of its season. The play was presented in two parts.

On the Town (65). Transfer from off Broadway of the revival of the musical based on a concept by Jerome Robbins; book and lyrics by Betty Comden and Adolph Green; music by Leonard Bernstein. Produced by The Joseph Papp Public Theater/New York Shakespeare Festival, George C. Wolfe producer, Rosemarie Tichler artistic producer, Mark Litvin managing director, at the Gershwin Theater. Opened November 19, 1998. (Closed January 17, 1999)

Workman	Gregory Emanuel Rahming	Mr. S. Uperman;	
Ozzie	Robert Montano	Master of Ceremonies	Blake Hammond
Chip	Jesse Tyler Ferguson	Hildy Esterhazy	Lea DeLaria
Gabey	Perry Laylon Ojeda	Waldo Figment	Tom Aulino
Flossie	Linda Mugleston	Claire DeLoone	Sarah Knowlton
Flossie's Friend	Chandra Wilson	Primitive Man &	
Subway Bill Poster;		Woman	Stephen Campanella,
Rajah Bimmy	John Jellison		Judine Richard
Little Old Lady;		Pas de Deux Dancers	Kristine Bendul,
Mme. Maude P. Dilly	Mary Testa		Darren Gibson
Miss Turnstiles Announcers	Nora Cole,	Pitkin W. Bridgework	Jonathan Freeman
	Gregory Emanuel Rahming	Lucy Schmeeler	Annie Golden
Ivy Smith	Tai Jiminez	Diana Dream; Dolores Dolores	Nora Cole
Policeman	Christopher F. Davis		

Quartet—Tom Aulino, Christopher F. Davis, Blake Hammond, John Jellison. Mannequins—Dottie Earle, Jennifer Frankel, Amy Heggins, Judine Richard. Women of Carnegie Hall—Nora Cole, Linda Mugleston, Chandra Wilson. Diamond Eddie's Girls—Kristine Bendul, Jennifer Frankel, Amy Heggins, Keenah Reid, Judine Richard. New Sailors in Town—Brad Aspel, Stephen Campanella, Christopher F. Davis. The People of New York—Tom Aulino, Blake Hammond, John Jellison, Linda Mugleston, Gregory Emanuel Rahming, Chandra Wilson.

Dance Ensemble: Brad Aspel, Kristine Bendul, Stephen Campanella, R.J. Durell, Dottie Earle, Jennifer Frankel, Edgard Gallardo, Darren Gibson, Amy Heggins, Darren Lee, Keenah Reid, Judine Richard.

Swings: Kim Craven, Sloan Just, Wes Pope, Rommy Sandhu, Scott Spahr.

Orchestra: Kevin Stites conductor; Jeffrey Harris associate conductor, piano; Kenneth G. Adams, Dennis Anderson, William Blount, Roger Rosenberg, Eddie Salkin, Edward Zuhlke woodwinds; Kamau Adilifu, Christian Jaudes, Larry Lunetta trumpet; Randall T. Andos, Lawrence Farrell, Joel Shelton trombone; Theresa MacDonnell, Roger Wendt, French horn; Brian O. Grice drums; Eric Kivnick percussion; Peter Donovan bass.

Standbys: Messrs. Rahming, Jellison, Hammond, Aulino—David Lowenstein; Miss Jiminez—Dana Stackpole. Understudies: Mr. Montano—Brad Aspel; Mr. Ferguson—Brad Aspel, Darren Lee; Mr.

Ojeda—Stephen Campanella, Darren Lee; Misses DeLaria, Testa—Linda Mugleston; Messrs. Freeman, Rahming—John Jellison; Miss Golden—Chandra Wilson; Miss Cole—Judine Richard; Miss Mugleston—Jennifer Frankel; Miss Wilson—Keenah Reid; Messrs. Davis, Campanella, Aspel—Wes Pope, Rommy Sandhu, Scott Spahr; Miss Richard—Kim Craven, Sloan Just; Miss Bendul, Mr. Gibson—Kim Craven, R.J. Durell, Dana Stackpole.

Directed by George C. Wolfe; musical direction, Kevin Stites; choreography, Keith Young; scenery, Adrianne Lobel; costumes, Paul Tazewell; lighting, Paul Gallo; sound, Jon Weston; orchestrations, Bruce Coughlin; music coordinator, Seymour Red Press; associate producer, Wiley Hausam; casting, Jordan Thaler, Heidi Griffiths; stage managers, Karen Armstrong, Kenneth J. McGee, Donna A. Drake; press, Carol R. Fineman, Thomas V. Naro, Bill Coyle.

Time: 1944—wartime. Place: New York City.

The last major New York revival of *On the Town* took place in this Joseph Papp Public Theater/ New York Shakespeare Festival production 8/1/97 off Broadway at the Delacorte Theater for 25 performances.

ACT I

Overture
Scene 1: The Brooklyn Navy Yard
"I Feel Like I'm Not Out of Bed Yet" .... Workman, Quartet
"New York, New York" .... Ozzie, Chip, Gabey, Company
Scene 2: A subway train in motion
Scene 3: A New York Street
"Gabey's Coming" .... Ozzie, Chip, Gabey, Mannequins
Scene 4: Presentation of Miss Turnstiles
"Presentation of Miss Turnstiles" .... Announcers, Ivy Smith, Dance Ensemble
Scene 5: A taxicab
"Come Up to My Place" .... Hildy, Chip
Scene 6: The Museum of Natural History
"Carried Away" .... Claire, Ozzie, Primitive Man & Woman
Scene 7: A busy New York City street
"Lonely Town" .... Gabey, Dance Ensemble
Scene 8: A corridor and studio in Carnegie Hall
"Carnegie Hall Pavane" .... Ivy, Mme. Dilly, Women of Carnegie Hall
Scene 9: Central Park
"Lucky To Be Me" .... Gabey, Ensemble
Scene 10: Claire's and Hildy's apartments
"I Understand" .... Pitkin
"I Can Cook Too" .... Hildy

ACT II

Scene 1A: Diamond Eddie's Club
"So Long, Baby" .... Diamond Eddie's Girls
"I Wish I Was Dead" .... Diana Dream
Scene IB: The Congacabana
"I Wish I Was Dead" .... Dolores Dolores
"Ya Got Me" .... Hildy, Claire, Ozzie, Chip
Scene IC: The Slam Bang Club
"I Understand" .... Pitkin, Lucy
Scene 2: The subway train to Coney Island
"Subway Ride" .... Gabey, People of New York
Scene 3: The dream Coney Island
"Imaginary Coney Island" .... Gabey, Ivy, Dance Ensemble
Scene 4: Subway platform
"Some Other Time" .... Claire, Hildy, Ozzie, Chip
Scene 5: The real Coney Island
"The Real Coney Island" .... Rajah Bimmy
Scene 6: The Brooklyn Navy Yard
"I Feel Like I'm Not Out of Bed Yet" (Reprise) .... Workman
"New York, New York" (Reprise) .... Company

Fool Moon (49). Performance piece created by Bill Irwin and David Shiner. Produced by James B. Freydberg, Jeffrey Ash, Dori Berinstein and CTM Productions at the Brooks Atkinson Theater. Opened November 22, 1998. (Closed January 3, 1999)

CAST: David Shiner, Bill Irwin, the Red Clay Ramblers.

Scenery, Douglas Stein; costumes, Bill Kellard; lighting, Nancy Schertler; sound, Tom Morse; flying effects, Foy; producing associate, Nancy Harrington; associate poroducer, Sammi Rose Cannold; stage manager, Julie Baldauff; press, Boneau/Bryan-Brown, Chris Boneau, Jackie Green.

The unique Irwin-Shiner mixture of comedy and acrobatics last produced in New York 10/29/95.

*Peter Pan (104). Revival of the musical version of the play by J.M. Barrie; music by Moose Charlap; lyrics by Carolyn Leigh; additional lyrics by Betty Comden and Adolph Green; additional music by Jule Styne. Produced by McCoy Rigby Entertainment, The Nederlander Organization and La Mirada Theater for the Performing Arts, in association with Albert Nocciolino, Larry Payton and J. Lynn Singleton at the Marquis Theater. Opened November 23, 1998. (Closed January 3, 1999 after 48 performances) Reopened April 7, 1999.

Mrs. Darling; Mermaid;	Curly .... Alon Williams
Wendy (Grown-Up) .... Barbara McCulloh	lst Twin .... Janet Higgins
Wendy Darling .... Elisa Sagardia	2d Twin .... Doreen Chila
John Darling .... Chase Kniffen	Slightly .... Scott Bridges
Michael Darling .... Drake English	Tootles; Jane .... Aileen Quinn
Liza; Tiger Lily .... Dana Solimando	Mr. Smee .... Michael Nostrand
Nana; Bill Jukes; Crocodile .... Buck Mason	Cecco .... Tony Spinoza
Mr. Darling; Capt. Hook .... Paul Schoeffler	Gentleman Starkey .... Sam Zeller
Peter Pan .... Cathy Rigby	Noodler .... Randy Davis

Pirates and Indians: Kim Arnett, Randy Davis, Jeffrey Elsass, Casey Miles Good, Buck Mason, Brian Shepard, Roger Preston Smith, Tony Spinoza, Sam Zeller.

Orchestra: Craig Barna conductor; Michael Rice assistant conductor, keyboard II; Bruce Barnes associate conductor, keyboard I; Sylvia D'Avanzo, Margaret Jones, Heidi Stubner, Maura Giannini violin; Roger Shell, Deborah Assael cello; Laura Sherman harp; David Wechsler, Phil Chester, Tuck Lee, Tom Christensen, Mike Migliore reeds; Larry Pyatt, Jon Owens, Joe Reardon trumpet; Jason Ingram, Bill Whitaker trombone; Richard Tremarello, French horn; Tom Mendel bass; Ed Shea percussion; Tod Barnard, Steve Bartosik drums.

Standbys and understudies: Miss Rigby—Janet Higgins; Mr Schoeffler—Sam Zeller; Miss McCulloh—Kim Arnett; Mr. Nostrand—William Alan Coates, Roger Preston Smith; Miss Sagardia—Aileen Quinn; Messrs. Kniffen, Bridges—Doreen Chila; Mr. English—Michael Kirsch; Miss Solimando—Kim Arnett; Miss Quinn—Elisa Solimando; Miss Solimando—Kim Arnett, Doreen Chila; Mr. Zeller—Jeffrey Elsass; Mr. Mason—William Alan Coates. General understudy: Michelle Berti. Swing: William Alan Coates.

Directed by Glenn Casale; choreography, Patti Colombo; musical direction, vocal arrangements and new dance music, Craig Barna; original Broadway production conceived, directed and choreographed by Jerome Robbins; scenery, John Iacovelli; costumes, Shigeru Yaji; lighting, Martin Aronstein; sound, Francois Bergeron; flying illusions, ZFX Inc.; new orchestrations, Craig Barna, Kevin Farrell, M. Michael Fauss, Brian Tidwell; "Ugg-a-Wugg" orchestrations, Craig Barna, Steve Bartosik; casting, Julia Flores; production stage manager, Michael McEowen; stage manager, Nevin Hedley; press, The Pete Sanders Group, Pete Sanders, Glenna Freedman.

The last major New York revival of this musical *Peter Pan* took place on Broadway 12/13/90 for 45 performances, with a return engagement 11/27/91 for an additional 48 performances.

Barry Cavanagh replaced Chase Kniffen 4/7/99.

ACT I

Scene 1: The nursery of the Darling residence

"Tender Shepherd" .... Mrs. Darling, Wendy, John, Michael
"I Gotta Crow" .... Peter
"Neverland" .... Peter
"I'm Flying" .... Peter, Wendy, John, Michael

ACT II

Scene 1: Neverland
"Pirate March" .... Hook, Pirates
"A Princely Scheme" .... Hook, Pirates
"Indians!" .... Tiger Lily, Indians
"Wendy" .... Peter, Boys
"I Won't Grow Up" .... Peter, Wendy, Boys
"Another Princely Scheme" .... Hook, Pirates
Scene 2: Marooner's Rock
Scene 3: The home underground
"Ugg-a-Wugg" .... Peter, Tiger Lily, Wendy, Boys, Indians
"Distant Melody" .... Wendy, Peter

ACT III

Scene 1: The Pirate Ship
"Hook's Waltz" .... Hook, Pirates
"I Gotta Crow" (Reprise) .... Peter, Company
Scene 2: The nursery of the Darling residence
"Tender Shepherd" (Reprise) .... Wendy, John, Michael
"I Won't Grow Up" (Reprise) .... The Darling Family, Lost Boys
Scene 3: The nursery many years later
"Neverland" (Reprise) .... Peter

A Christmas Carol (69). Return engagement of the musical based on the story by Charles
Dickens; book by Mike Ockrent and Lynn Ahrens; music by Alan Menken; lyrics by Lynn
Ahrens. Produced by American Express at the Theater at Madison Square Garden. Opened
November 27, 1998. (Closed December 27, 1998)

Beadle .... Del-Bourree Bach
Mr. Smythe .... Chris Vasquez
Grace Smythe; Want .... Tavia Rivee Jefferson,
                                Netousha Harris
Scrooge .... Roger Daltrey
Cratchit .... Todd Gross
Old Joe; Mr. Hawkins .... Kenneth McMullen
Mrs. Cratchit .... Rachel Black
Tiny Tim .... Anthony Blair Hall,
                              Christian Valiando
Poulterer; Judge .... Roland Rusinek
Sandwichboard Man;
  Ghost of Christmas Present .... Roz Ryan
Jonathon .. Adam Barruch, Kennedy Kanagawa
Lamplighter;
  Ghost of Christmas Past .... Ken Jennings
Blind Hag; Scrooge's Mother ... Debra Cardona

Fred .... John Sloman
Mrs. Mopps .... Marilyn Pasekoff
Ghost of Jacob Marley .... Paul Kandel
Scrooge at 8; Ignorance ... Dennis Michael Hall,
                              Stephen Scarpulla
Scrooge's Father; Undertaker .... Wayne
                                     Schroder
Scrooge at 12 .... Jesse McCartney,
                              Gabriel Millman
Fan .... Dana Chechile, Carissa Farina
Fezziwig .... Daniel Marcus
Scrooge at 18 .... Joe Cassidy
Young Marley; Undertaker .... Ken Barnett
Mrs. Fezziwig .... Joy Hermalyn
Emily .... Kristin Huxhold
Sally .... La Tanya Hall
Ghost of Christmas
  Yet-To-Be .... Christine Dunham

Charity Men: David Aron Damane, Roland Rusinek, Wayne Schroder.
Street Urchins: Dana Chechile, Carissa Farina, Dennis Michael Hall, Jesse McCartney, Gabriel Mill-
man, Stephen Scarpulla.
Lights of Christmas Past: Matthew Baker, Ronald Cadet Bastine, Keith Fortner, Michael Lomeka.
The Cratchit Children: Dana Chechile, Carissa Farina, Jesse McCartney, Gabriel Millman.
Business Men, Gifts, Ghosts, People of London: Lori Alexander, Del-Bourree Bach, Matthew Baker,
Ken Barnett, Ronald Cadet Bastine, Hayes Bergman, Rachel Black, Liam Burke, Joe Cassidy, Debra
Cardona, Candy Cook, David Aron Damane, Juliet Fischer, Keith Fortner, Peter Gregus, La Tanya
Hall, Joy Hermalyn, Kristin Huxhold, Carrie Kenneally, Kate Levering, Michael Lomeka, Daniel Mar-
cus, Kenneth McMullen, Marilyn Pasekoff, Gail Pennington, Meredith Patterson, Pamela Remler, Ro-
land Rusinek, Yasuko Tamaki, Vikki Schnurr, Wayne Schroder, John Sloman, Chris Vasquez. Swings:

Ron Bagden, Jane Brockman, Ann Kittredge, Robin Lewis, Angela Piccinni, Scott Taylor, Cynthia Thole, Jeff Williams.

Angels: Terrill Middle School Broadway Chorus; P.S/M.S. 330 Glee Club; South Side Middle School Select Chorus; Eastwood International Children's Choir.

Red Children's Cast: Adam Barruch, Carissa Farina, Anthony Blair Hall, Dennis Michael Hall, Netousha Harris, Gabriel Millman. Green Children's Cast: Dana Chechile, Kennedy Kanagawa, Tavia Riveé Jefferson, Jesse McCartney, Stephen Scarpulla, Christian Valiando. Swings: Barry Cavanagh, Bret Fox, Chloe Zeitounian.

Orchestra: Paul Gemignani conductor; Mark C. Mitchell assistant conductor, keyboard; Aloysia Friedmann concertmaster; Karl Kawahara, Ann Labin, Sebu Serinian violin; Monica Gerard, Adria Benjamin viola; Clay Ruede cello; Charles Bergeron bass; David Weiss, Kenneth DyBisz, Alva Hunt, Daniel Wieloszynski, John Winder woodwinds; Ronald Sell, French horn; Stu Sataloff, Phil Granger, Dominic Derasse trumpet; Bruce Eidem, Dean Plank trombone; Janet Aycock keyboard; Jennifer Hoult harp; Michael Berkowitz drums; Glenn Rhian percussion.

Standby: Messrs. Daltrey, Kandel—Patrick Page.

Directed by Mike Ockrent; choreography, Susan Stroman; musical direction, Paul Gemignani; scenery, Tony Walton; costumes, William Ivey Long; lighting, Jules Fisher, Peggy Eisenhauer; sound, Tony Meola; projections, Wendall K. Harrington; flying, Foy; orchestrations, Michael Starobin, Douglas Besterman; dance arrangements and incidental music, Glen Kelly; associate director, Steven Zweigbaum; associate choreographer, Chris Peterson; executive producer, Dodger Endemol Theatricals; producer, Tim Hawkins; casting, Julie Hughes, Barry Moss; production stage manager, Steven Zweigbaum; stage manager, Rolt Smith; press, Cathy Del Priore.

Time: 1880. Place: London. The play was presented without intermission.

This is the fifth annual production of this musical version of *A Christmas Carol,* which was presented without intermission.

SCENES AND MUSICAL NUMBERS

Scene 1: The Royal Exchange
"A Jolly Good Time" .... Charity Men, Smythe Family, Business Men, Wives, Children
"Nothing to Do With Me" .... Scrooge, Cratchit
Scene 2: The street
"You Mean More to Me" .... Cratchit, Tiny Tim
"Street Song (Nothing to Do With Me)" .... People of London, Scrooge, Fred,
                                    Jonathon, Sandwichboard Man, Lamplighter, Blind Hag, Grace Smythe
Scene 3: Scrooge's house
"Link by Link" .... Marley's Ghost, Scrooge, Ghosts
Scene 4: Scrooge's bedchamber
"The Lights of Long Ago" .... Ghost of Christmas Past
Scene 5: The law courts
"God Bless Us, Everyone" .... Scrooge's Mother
Scene 6: The factory
"A Place Called Home" .... Scrooge at 12, Fan, Scrooge
Scene 7: Fezziwig's Banking House
"Mr. Fezziwig's Annual Christmas Ball" .... Fezziwig, Mrs. Fezziwig, Guests
"A Place Called Home" (Reprise) .... Emily, Scrooge at 18, Scrooge
Scene 8: Scrooge and Marley's
"The Lights of Long Ago" (Part II) .... Scrooge at 18, Young Marley, Emily,
                                                                  People From Scrooge's Past
Scene 9: A starry night
"Abundance and Charity" .... Ghost of Christmas Present, Scrooge, Christmas Gifts
Scene 10: All over London
"Christmas Together" .... Tiny Tim, The Cratchits, Ghost of Christmas Present, Fred,
                                                         Sally, Scrooge, People of London
Scene 11: The graveyard
"Dancing on Your Grave" .... Ghost of Christmas Yet-To-Be, Monks, Business Men,
                                                    Mrs. Mopps, Undertakers, Old Joe, Cratchit
"Yesterday, Tomorrow and Today" .... Scrooge, Angels, Children of London
Scene 12: Scrooge's bedchamber
"London Town Carol" .... Jonathon

ELECTRA—Zoë Wanamaker in the title role
of Frank McGuinness's adaptation of Sophocles

Scene 13: The street, Christmas Day
"Nothing to Do With Me" (Reprise) .... Scrooge
"Christmas Together" (Reprise) .... People of London
"God Bless Us, Everyone" (Finale) .... Company

Electra (115). Revival of the play by Sophocles; adapted by Frank McGuinness. Produced by
Eric Krebs, Randall L. Wreghitt, Anita Waxman, Elizabeth Williams and Lawrence Horowitz
in the McCarter Theater/Donmar Warehouse and Duncan C. Weldon Production at the Ethel
Barrymore Theater. Opened December 3, 1998. (Closed March 21, 1999)

Servant to Orestes	Stephen Spinella	Chorus of Mycenae	Pat Carroll
Orestes	Michael Cumpsty	Chrysothemis	Marin Hinkle
Pylades	Ivan Stamenov	Clytemnestra	Claire Bloom
Electra	Zoë Wanamaker	Aegisthus	Daniel Oreskes
Chorus	Mirjana Jokovic,		
	Myra Lucretia Taylor		

Directed by David Leveaux; scenery and costumes, Johan Engels; lighting, Paul Pyant; sound, Fergus
O'Hare; movement direction, Jonathan Butterell; associate producers, Marcia Roberts, Lauren Doll,

June Curtis, Lynne Peyser; production stage manager, Robert L. Cohen; stage manager, Emily N. Wells; press, James LL Morrison.

The last major New York production of this Sophocles play took place off Broadway in the Greek language 9/25/96 for 6 performances. This season's production is presented without intermission and was previously staged at the Chichester Festival Theater, the Donmar Warehouse and the McCarter Theater in Princeton, N.J.

The Blue Room (81). Freely adapted from Arthur Schnitzler's *La Ronde* by David Hare. Produced by The Shubert Organization, Scott Rudin, Robert Fox, Roger Berlind and ABC, Inc. in the Donmar Warehouse production at the Cort Theater. Opened December 13, 1998. (Closed February 25, 1999)

CAST: The Girl, The Au Pair, The Married Woman, The Model, The Actress—Nicole Kidman; The Cab Driver, The Student, The Politician, The Playwright, The Aristocrat—Iain Glen.

Directed by Sam Mendes; design, Mark Thompson; lighting, Hugh Vanstone; original music, Paddy Cunneen; sound, Scott Myers; production stage manager, David Hyslop; stage manager, Sally J. Jacobs; press, Boneau/Bryan-Brown, Adrian Bryan-Brown, John Barlow.

Time: The present day. Place: One of the great cities of the world. The play was presented without intermission.

The last major New York staging of Schnitzler's interlocking sexual adventures was by Lincoln Center off Broadway 1/20/94 for 65 performances in a musical version entitled *Hello Again.* A foreign play previously produced in London.

*Lincoln Center Theater. Schedule of three programs. **Parade** (85). Musical with book by Alfred Uhry; music and lyrics by Jason Robert Brown; co-conceived by Harold Prince; produced in association with Livent (U.S.) Inc. Opened December 17, 1998. (Closed February 28, 1999) ***Via Dolorosa** (85). Solo performance by David Hare; written by David Hare; presented in the Royal Court Theater production, Ian Rickson artistic director. Opened March 18, 1999. ***Ring Round the Moon** (38). Revival of the play by Jean Anouilh; adapted by Christopher Fry. Opened April 28, 1999. Produced by Lincoln Center Theater under the direction of Andre Bishop and Bernard Gersten, *Parade* at the Vivian Beaumont Theater, *Via Dolorosa* at the Booth Theater, *Ring Round the Moon* at the Belasco Theater.

Note: Lincoln Center Theater also co-produced **It Ain't Nothin' But the Blues.** Musical revue based on an original idea by Ron Taylor; written by Charles Bevel, Lita Gaithers, Randal Myler, Ron Taylor and Dan Wheetman; music by various authors; presented in the Crossroads Theater Company production, Ricardo Kahn artistic director, in association with San Diego Repertory Theater, Sam Woodhouse artistic director, and Alabama Shakespeare Festival, Kent Thompson artistic director. Opened April 26, 1999 at the Vivian Beaumont Theater; see its entry in this section of this volume.

PARADE

Young Soldier; Fiddlin' John	Jeff Edgerton	Officer Ivey	Tad Ingram
Aide; Mr. Peavy	Don Stephenson	Newt Lee	Ray Aranha
Assistant	Melanie Vaughan	Prison Guard	Randy Redd
Old Soldier; Judge Roan	Don Chastain	Mrs. Phagan	Jessica Molaskey
Lucille Frank	Carolee Carmello	Lizzie Phagan	Robin Skye
Leo Frank	Brent Carver	Floyd MacDaniel; Luther Rosser ...	J.B. Adams
Hugh Dorsey	Herndon Lackey	Britt Craig	Evan Pappas
Gov. Slaton	John Hickok	Tom Watson	John Leslie Wolfe
Sally Slaton	Anne Torsiglieri	Angela	Angela Lockett
Frankie Epps	Kirk McDonald	Riley	J.C. Montgomery
Mary Phagan	Christy Carlson Romano	Nurse	Adinah Alexander
Iola Stover	Brooke Sunny Moriber	Monteen	Abbi Hutcherson
Jim Conley	Rufus Bonds Jr.	Essie	Emily Klein
J.N. Starnes	Peter Samuel		

Ensemble: Adinah Alexander, Duane Boutté, Diana Brownstone, Thursday Farrar, Will Gartshore, Abbi Hutcherson, Tad Ingram, Emily Klein, Angela Lockett, Megan McGinnis, J.C. Montgomery, Brooke Sunny Moriber, Randy Redd, Joel Robertson, Peter Samuel, Robin Skye, Don Stephenson, Bill Szobody, Anne Torsiglieri, Melanie Vaughan, Wysandria Woolsey.

Orchestra: Eric Stern conductor; Henry Aronson associate conductor; Rick Dolan concertmaster; Karen Milne, Mia Wu violin, viola; Sarah Carter, Chungsun Kim cello; Chuck Wilson, Rick Heckman, Ed Matthew, Mark Thrasher woodwinds; Terry Szor, Alex Holton trumpet; Vernon Post tenor trombone; Ron Raffio string bass, tuba; John David Smith, Jill Williamson, French horn; Jack Cavari guitar; Tom Partington drums; Dean Thomas percussion; Henry Aronson keyboards.

Understudies: Messrs. Edgerton, McDonald—Will Gartshore, Randy Redd; Mr. Chastain—Peter Samuel, Tad Ingram; Miss Carmello—Jessica Molaskey, Anne Torsiglieri; Mr. Carver—Don Stephenson, Jeff Edgerton; Messrs. Lackey, Wolfe, Hickok—Peter Samuel, Don Stephenson; Miss Torsiglieri—Robin Skye, Diana Brownstone; Miss Romano—Brooke Sunny Moriber, Abbi Hutcherson; Messrs. Bonds, Aranha—J.C. Montgomery, Duane Boutté; Miss Molaskey—Adinah Alexander, Melanie Vaughan; Mr. Pappas—Randy Redd, Jeff Edgerton; Miss Lockett—Thursday Farrar; Mr. Montgomery—Duane Boutté; Mr. Adams—Tad Ingram, Joel Robertson; Messrs. Ingram, Samuel, Stephenson, Ensemble—Joel Robertson; Mr. Redd—Will Gartshore; Misses Moriber, Hutcherson, Klein, Ensemble—Megan McGinnis; Misses Alexander, Skye, Vaughan, Ensemble—Wysandria Woolsey, Megan McGinnis; Swing, Dance Captain—Rob Ashford.

Directed by Harold Prince; choreography, Patricia Birch; musical supervision and direction, Eric Stern; scenery, Riccardo Hernandez; costumes, Judith Dolan; lighting, Howell Binkley; sound, Jonathan Deans; orchestrations, Don Sebesky; music coordinator, John Miller; assistant to Harold Prince, Brad Rouse; assistant choreographer, Rob Ashford; associate producer, Ira Weitzman; casting, Beth Russell, Mark Simon; production stage manager, Clayton Phillips; press, Philip Rinaldi, Brian Rubin, Amy Hughes.

The tragic fate of a young Jew, Leo Frank, falsely accused of the murder of a 13-year-old, abducted from jail and lynched by an Atlanta mob in 1915. Winner of the 1998–99 New York Drama Critics Circle Award for best musical; see its entry in the Prizewinning Plays section of this volume.

ACT I

Prologue: "The Old Red Hills of Home"	Young Soldier, Old Soldier, Ensemble
Anthem: "The Dream of Atlanta"	Ensemble
"How Can I Call This Home?"	Leo Frank, Ensemble
"The Picture Show"	Frankie Epps, Mary Phagan
"Leo at Work"/"What Am I Waiting For?"	Leo Frank, Lucille Frank
Interrogation: "I Am Trying to Remember ... "	Newt Lee, Mrs. Phagan
"Big News!"	Britt Craig

"There Is a Fountain" (traditional hymn by William Cowper and Lowell Mason)

incorporated with "It Don't Make Sense"	Frankie Epps, Ensemble
"Watson's Lullaby"	Tom Watson
"Somethin' Ain't Right"	Hugh Dorsey
"Real Big News"	Britt Craig, Reporters, Ensemble
"You Don't Know This Man"	Lucille Frank

The Trial (Finale Act I)

I: "It Is Time Now"	Fiddlin' John, Tom Watson, Ensemble
II: "Twenty Miles From Marietta"	Hugh Dorsey
III: Frankie's Testimony	Frankie Epps, Mary Phagan, Watson, Ensemble
IV: "The Factory Girls"/"Come Up to My Office"	Iola, Essie, Monteen, Leo Frank
V: Newt Lee's Testimony	Newt Lee, Ensemble
VI: "My Child Will Forgive Me"	Mrs. Phagan
VII: "That's What He Said"	Jim Conley, Ensemble
VIII: Leo's Statement: It's Hard to Speak My Heart	Leo Frank
IX: Closing Statements & Verdict	Ensemble

ACT II

"It Goes On and On"	Britt Craig
"A Rumblin' and a Rollin'"	Riley, Angela, Newt Lee, Jim Conley
"Do It Alone'	Lucille Frank
"Pretty Music"	Gov. Slaton

"Letter to the Governor" .... Judge Roan
"This Is Not Over Yet" .... Leo Frank, Lucille Frank, Factory Girls, Newt Lee
Blues: "Feel the Rain Fall" .... Jim Conley, Ensemble
"Where Will You Stand When the Flood Comes?" .... Tom Watson, Hugh Dorsey, Ensemble
"All the Wasted Time" .... Leo Frank, Lucille Frank
Finale .... Ensemble

VIA DOLOROSA

Directed by Stephen Daldry; scenery, Ian MacNeil; lighting, Rick Fisher; sound, Paul Arditti; stage manager, Karen Armstrong; press, Philip Rinaldi, Brian Rubin, Amy Hughes.

The playwright, David Hare, remembers in characterization some of the Arabs and Jews he met during a visit to the West Bank and their emotional relationships there. The play was presented without intermission. A foreign play previously produced in London.

RING ROUND THE MOON

Joshua	Richard Clarke	Messerschmann	Fritz Weaver
Hugo; Frederic	Toby Stephens	Romainville	Simon Jones
Diana Messerschmann	Haviland Morris	Isabelle	Gretchen Egolf
Lady India	Candy Buckley	Isabelle's Mother	Joyce Van Patten
Patrice Bombelles	Derek Smith	The General; Footman	John Newton
Madame Desmermortes	Marian Seldes	Footman	Philip Hoffman
Capulat	Frances Conroy		

Understudies: Messrs. Clarke, Weaver—John Newton; Mr. Stephens—Josh Mosby; Misses Morris, Egolf—Melinda Page Hamilton; Misses Buckley, Conroy, Van Patten—Nancy Opel; Messrs. Smith, Jones—Philip Hoffman; Messrs. Newton, Hoffman—Lee Coleman, David Fitzgerald.

Directed by Gerald Gutierrez; scenery, John Lee Beatty; costumes, John David Ridge; lighting, Natasha Katz; sound, Aural Fixation; music, Francis Poulenc; music supervisor, Tom Fay; choreography, Kathleen Marshall; casting, Daniel Swee; stage manager, Frank Hartenstein.

Time: The spring of 1912. Place: The winter garden of Mme. Desmermortes' chateau in France. Act I, Scene 1: Morning. Scene 2: The same evening, before the ball. Act II: The same evening, the ball. Act III, Scene 1: The same evening, after supper. Scene 2: Dawn.

The last major New York revival of *Ring Round the Moon* was by Equity Library Theater off Broadway in the 1959–60 season.

*Fosse (165). Dance revue with choreography by Bob Fosse; conceived by Richard Maltby Jr., Chet Walker and Ann Reinking; artistic advisor, Gwen Verdon; music and lyrics by various authors (see listing below). Produced by Livent (U.S.) Inc., Roy Furman chairman and chief executive officer, Todd Haimes artistic director, David Maisel president, at the Broadhurst Theater. Opened January 14, 1999.

Julio Agustin	Shannon Lewis
Brad Anderson	Mary MacLeod
Andy Blankenbuehler	Dana Moore
Bill Burns	Brad Musgrove
Marc Calamia	Sean Palmer
Holly Cruikshank	Elizabeth Parkinson
Eugene Fleming	Michael Paternostro
Lisa Gajda	Valarie Pettiford
Kim Morgan Greene	Rachelle Rak
Scott Jovovich	Josh Rhodes
Christopher R. Kirby	Desmond Richardson
Dede LaBarre	Lainie Sakakura
Mary Ann Lamb	Alex Sanchez
Susan LaMontagne	Sergio Trujillo
Jane Lanier	J. Kathleen Watkins
Deborah Leamy	Scott Wise

Orchestra: Patrick S. Brady conductor; Ethyl Will associate conductor, synthesizer; Ed Joffe, Dale Kleps, Bill Easley, Walt Weiskopf, Allen Won woodwinds; Craig Johnson, Scott Wendholt, Don Downs, Glenn Drewes trumpet; Jim Pugh, Keith O'Quinn trombone; Jeff Nelson trombone, tuba; Jon Werking, Seth Farber synthesizer; David Spinozza guitar; Mike Hall bass; Perry Cavari drums; Jim Saporito percussion.

Swings: Bill Burns, Susan LaMontagne, Deborah Leamy, Sean Palmer, Josh Rhodes, J. Kathleen Watkins.

Directed by Richard Maltby Jr.; co-directed and co-choreographed by Ann Reinking; choreography recreated by Chet Walker; musical direction, Patrick S. Brady; scenery and costumes, Santo Loquasto; lighting, Andrew Bridge; sound, Jonathan Deans; musical arrangements and supervision, Gordon Lowry Harrell; orchestrations, Ralph Burns, Douglas Besterman; casting, Arnold J. Mungioli; production stage manager, Mary Porter Hall; stage managers, Lori Lundquist, Brad Musgrove; press, Mary Bryant, Wayne Wolfe.

Program recreating Bob Fosse dances choreographed and often performed by him. Winner of the 1998–99 Tony Award for best musical; see its entry in the Prizewinning Plays section of this volume.

ACT I

Prologue

"Life Is Just a Bowl of Cherries" .... Valarie Pettiford
    From *Big Deal* (1986); music and lyrics by Lew Brown and Ray Henderson
Fosse's World .... Brad Musgrove, Jane Lanier, Company
    Music by G. Harrell including *Calypso;* and "Snake in the Grass" by Frederick Loewe from the motion picture *The Little Prince* (1974); staged by Ann Reinking; dance elements inspired by *The Little Prince* and signature Fosse styles which appeared in *The Little Prince, Damn Yankees, Redhead, New Girl in Town, Little Me, Sweet Charity, How to Succeed in Business Without Really Trying, Cabaret, Chicago.*
"Bye Bye Blackbird" .... Pettiford, Julio Agustin, Andy Blankenbuehler, Marc
                                Calamia, Holly Cruikshank, Lisa Gajda, Scott Jovovich, Dede
                                LaBarre, Mary Ann Lamb, Shannon Lewis, Mary MacLeod, Dana
                                Moore, Elizabeth Parkinson, Michael Paternostro, Rachelle Rak,
                                Desmond Richardson, Lainie Sakakura, Sergio Trujillo
    From the TV special *Liza With a Z* (1972); music by Ray Henderson; lyrics by Lew Brown

Part I

"From the Edge" .... Brad Anderson, Christopher R. Kirby, Alex Sanchez
    From *Dancin'* (1978); music by G. Harrell
"Percussion 4" .... Desmond Richardson
    From *Dancin'*; music by G. Harrell
"Big Spender" .... Pettiford, Lanier, Kim Morgan Greene, LaBarre, Lamb, Lewis, MacLeod,
                                                                    Moore, Parkinson, Rak
    From *Sweet Charity* (1966); music by Cy Coleman; lyrics by Dorothy Fields
"Crunchy Granola Suite" .... Agustin, Calamia, Cruikshank, Gajda, Jovovich,
                    Christopher R. Kirby, LaBarre, Lamb, Lewis, MacLeod, Parkinson, Paternostro,
                    Richardson, Sakakura, Sanchez; Singers: Anderson, Eugene Fleming
    From *Dancin'*; music and lyrics by Neil Diamond

Part II

Transition: "Hooray for Hollywood"
    Music by Richard Whiting; lyrics by Johnny Mercer
"From This Moment On" .... Lamb (matinees, Sakakura), Blankenbuehler
    From the movie *Kiss Me Kate* (1953); lst 45 seconds of film choreography by Bob Fosse; originally danced by Bob Fosse and Carol Haney
"Alley Dance" .... Scott Wise (matinees, Brad Musgrove), Jovovich
    From the movie *My Sister Eileen* (1955); words and music by Jule Styne, Leo Robin; originally danced by Bob Fosse and Tommy Rall
Transition .... Company
    Dance elements inspired by *Redhead* (1959); "Walking the Cat" music by Patrick S. Brady; staged by Ann Reinking
"I Wanna Be a Dancin' Man" .... Fleming, Pettiford, Lanier, Wise, Anderson,
                    Blankenbuehler, Calamia, Gajda, Greene, Kirby, Lewis, MacLeod, Moore,
                    Musgrove, Parkinson, Sanchez, Trujillo
    From *Dancin'*; music by Harry Warren; lyrics by Johnny Mercer

ACT II

Part III
"Shoeless Joe From Hannibal, Mo" Ballet .... Agustin, Anderson, Blankenbuehler,
Calamia, Fleming, Kirby, Sanchez, Trujillo, Paternostro, Wise
    Pitcher .... Alex Sanchez
    Batters .... Anderson, Wise
    Bunter .... Agustin
        From *Damn Yankees* (1955); music and lyrics by Richard Adler and Jerry Ross
Transition .... Sanchez
    Dance elements inspired by *New Girl in Town* (1958)
Nightclubs
    "Dancing in the Dark"
        Music by Arthur Schwartz; lyrics by Howard Dietz
    "I Love a Piano" .... Wise, Parkinson, Jovovich, Sakakura, Blankenbuehler,
        Lanier, Paternostro, Sanchez, Agustin, Anderson, Calamia,
        Cruikshank, LaBarre, Lamb, McLeod, Trujillo. Singers: Lewis, Rak
    Music and lyrics by Irving Berlin; staged by Ann Reinking; music arranged by Patrick S.
    Brady; dance elements inspired by the dance team of Bob Fosse and Mary Ann Niles or
    Fosse appearances on such television shows as *Your Hit Parade* (1950), *The Morey Amster-
    dam Show* (1949), *The Colgate Comedy Hour* (1951), *The Burns and Allen Show* (1950),
    Cavalcade of Stars (1951), *The Ed Sullivan Show* (1956) and the movie *The Affairs of Dobie
    Gillis* (1953)
"Steam Heat" .... Lanier, Patterson, Sanchez
    From *The Pajama Game* (1954); music and lyrics by Richard Adler and Jerry Ross
"I Gotcha" .... Lewis, Musgrove, Kirby
    From *Liza With a Z;* music and lyrics by Joseph Arrington Jr.
"Rich Man's Frug" .... Gajda, Musgrove, Blankenbuehler, Agustin, Anderson,
        Calamia, Cruikshank, Jovovich, Kirby, LaBarre, Lewis,
        MacLeod, Rak, Sakakura, Trujillo
    From *Sweet Charity;* music by Cy Coleman. Part I: The Aloof. Part II: The Heavyweight.
    Part III: The Big Finish.
Transition
    "Silky Thoughts" music by Patrick S. Brady
"Cool Hand Luke" .... Parkinson, Richardson, Kirby
    From *The Bob Hope Special* (1968); music by Lalo Schifrin; choreographed for Gwen Verdon
    with Lee Roy Reams and Buddy Vest
Transition
    "Big Noise From Winnetka"
        From *Dancin';* music by Ray Bauduc and Bob Haggart; lyrics by Bob Crosby and Gil Rodin
    "Dancin' Dan" ("Me and My Shadow") .... Fleming, Greene, Moore
        From *Big Deal* (1986); music by Dave Dreyer and Al Jolson; lyrics by Billy Rose
    "Nowadays" and "The Hot Honey Rag" .... Pettiford, Lanier
        From *Chicago* (1975); music by John Kander; lyrics by Fred Ebb

ACT III

Part IV
"Glory" .... Kirby, Agustin, Anderson, Blankenbuehler, Calamia, Jovovich, Lamb,
        Musgrove, Parkinson, Paternostro, Sakakura, Sanchez. Singer: Fleming
    From *Pippin* (1972); music and lyrics by Stephen Schwartz
"Manson Trio" .... Fleming, LaBarre, MacLeod
    From *Pippin;* music and lyrics by Stephen Schwartz
"Mein Herr" .... Pettiford, Cruikshank, Gajda, Greene, Lewis, Moore, Rak
    From the movie *Cabaret* (1962); music by John Kander; lyrics by Fred Ebb
"Take Off With Us—Three Pas de Deux" .... Calamia and Sakakura, Lamb and Parkinson,
        Musgrove and Richardson
    From the movie *All That Jazz* (1979); music by Stanley R. Lebowsky; lyrics by Frederick K.
    Tobias
"Razzle Dazzle" .... Wise, Greene, Moore
    From *Chicago;* music by John Kander; lyrics by Fred Ebb

"Who's Sorry Now?" .... Cruikshank, Gajda, LaBarre, Lamb, Lewis,
MacLeod, Parkinson, Rak, Sakakura
From *All That Jazz;* music by Harry Ruby; lyrics by Ted Snyder and Bert Kalmar
"There'll Be Some Changes Made" .... Lanier, Greene, Moore
From *All That Jazz;* music by W. Benton Overstreet; lyrics by Billy Higgins
"Mr. Bojangles"
Mr. Bojangles .... Trujillo
The Spirit .... Richardson
Singer .... Blankenbuehler
From *Dancin';* music and lyrics by Jerry Jeff Walker
Part V: Finale
Benny Goodman's "Sing, Sing, Sing" .... Company
Drums .... Perry Cavari
Bass .... Mike Hall
Trombone Solo .... Jim Pugh
Danced by Cruikshank, Kirby, Richardson
Trumpet Solo .... Glenn Drewes
Danced by Parkinson
Clarinet Solo .... Walt Weiskopf
Danced by Pettiford, Lanier, MacLeod, Moore, Greene, Lamb, Rak, Agustin, Anderson,
Calamia, Kirby, Sanchez, Trujillo, Paternostro
Piano Solo .... Jon Werking
Danced by Wise, Fleming

*You're a Good Man, Charlie Brown (136). Revival of the musical based on the comic strip
Peanuts by Charles M. Schulz; book, music and lyrics by Clark Gesner. Produced by Michael
Leavitt, Fox Theatricals, Jerry Frankel, Arthur Whitelaw and Gene Persson at the Ambassador Theater, Opened February 4, 1999.

Sally	Kristin Chenoweth	Snoopy	Roger Bart
Schroeder	Stanley Wayne Mathis	Lucy	Ilana Levine
Linus	B.D. Wong	Charlie Brown	Anthony Rapp

The Band: Kimberly Grigsby conductor, piano, keyboard; Lynne Shankel associate conductor; Jill
Jaffe violin, viola; Mary Ann McSweeney bass; Joseph Mowatt percussion; Christine MacDonnell reeds.
Standbys: Messrs. Rapp, Wong, Mathis—Doan Mackenzie; Messrs. Rapp, Bart, Mathis—Mark
Price; Misses Levine, Chenoweth—Kirsten Wyatt.
Directed by Michael Mayer; choreography, Jerry Mitchell; musical direction, Kimberly Grigsby;
musical supervision, arrangements and additional material, Andrew Lippa; scenery, David Gallo; costumes, Michael Krass; lighting, Kenneth Posner; orchestrations, Michael Gibson; produced in association
with Larry Payton; casting, Jay Binder; production stage manager, James Harker; stage manager, Allison
Sommers; press, Richard Kornberg & Associates, Jim Byk, Don Summa, Rick Miramontez.
Time: An average day in the life of Charlie Brown.
You're a Good Man Charlie Brown was first produced (without a comma in its title) off Broadway
3/7/67 for 1,597 performances and was named a Best Play of its season. This is its first major New York
revival.

ACT I

"You're a Good Man, Charlie Brown" .... Company
(additional material by Andrew Lippa)
"Schroeder" .... Lucy, Schroeder
"Snoopy" .... Snoopy
"My Blanket and Me" .... Linus
"The Kite" .... Charlie Brown
"The Doctor Is In" .... Lucy, Charlie Brown
"Beethoven Day" .... Schroeder, Company
(music and lyrics by Andrew Lippa)
"Rabbit Chasing" .... Sally, Snoopy
"Book Report" .... Charlie Brown, Lucy, Linus, Schroeder

ACT II

"The Red Baron" .... Snoopy
"My New Philosophy" .... Sally, Schroeder
   (music and lyrics by Andrew Lippa)
"T.E.A.M. (The Baseball Game)" .... Charlie Brown, Company
"Glee Club Rehearsal" .... Company
"Little Known Facts" .... Lucy, Linus, Charlie Brown
"Suppertime" .... Snoopy
"Happiness" .... Company

*Death of a Salesman (126). Revival of the play by Arthur Miller. Produced by David Rich-
enthal, Jujamcyn Theaters, Allan S. Gordon and Fox Theatricals, in association with Jerry
Frankel, by special arrangement with the Roundabout Theater Company, in the Goodman
Theater production, Robert Falls artistic director, Roche Edward Schulfer executive director,
at the Eugene O'Neill Theater. Opened February 10, 1999.

Willy Loman	Brian Dennehy	Uncle Ben	Allen Hamilton
Linda	Elizabeth Franz	Howard Wagner	Steve Pickering
Biff	Kevin Anderson	Jenny	Barbara eda-Young
Happy	Ted Koch	Stanley	Kent Klineman
Bernard	Richard Thompson	Miss Forsythe	Stephanie March
The Woman	Kate Buddeke	Letta	Chelsea Altman
Charley	Howard Witt		

Understudies: Miss Franz—Barbara eda-Young; Messrs. Anderson, Koch—David Mogentale;
Messrs. Witt, Hamilton—Philip LeStrange; Mr. Pickering—Kent Klineman; Messrs. Thompson, Klineman, Koch—Steve Cell; Misses Buddeke, March, eda-Young, Altman—Nina Landey.

Directed by Robert Falls; scenery, Mark Wendland; costumes, Birgit Rattenborg Wise; lighting,
Michael Philippi; original music and sound, Richard Woodbury; associate producer, PACE Theatrical
Group; casting, Bernard Telsey, Tara Lonzo; production stage manager, Joseph Drummond; stage man-
ager, Robert Kellogg; press, Richard Kornberg & Associates, Don Summa, Rick Miramontez, Jim Byk.

Time: The late 1940s. Place: Willy Loman's house and yard, and various places in New York and
Boston. The play was presented in two parts.

The last major New York revival of *Death of a Salesman* took place on Broadway 3/29/84 for 158
performances, with Dustin Hoffman as Willy Loman.

*Not About Nightingales (109). By Tennessee Williams. Produced by Carole Shorenstein
Hays, Stuart Thompson, Marsha Garces Williams, Kelly Gonda, the Royal National Theater,
Trevor Nunn director, the Alley Theater, Gregory Boyd artistic director and the Moving
Theater, Corin Redgrave, Vanessa Redgrave, Kika Markham artistic directors, at Circle in
the Square. Opened February 25, 1999.

Voice of the Lorelei	Mark Heenehan	Joe	Alex Giannini
Mrs. Bristol;		McBurney	J.P. Linton
Goldie	Sandra Searles Dickinson	Oliver Armsted (Ollie)	Dion Graham
Eva Crane	Sherri Parker Lee	Shapiro	Joel Leffert
Jim Allison (Canary Jim)	Finbar Lynch	Jeremy Trout (Swifty)	Mark Dexter
Bert "Boss" Whalen	Corin Redgrave	Mex	Chico Andrade
Jack Bristol		Krause	Daniel Freedom Stewart
(Sailor Jack)	Matthew Floyd Miller	Alberts; Rev. Hooker	Noble Shropshire
Schultz	Richard Ziman	Tom; Chaplain	Tom Hodgkins
Butch O'Fallon	James Black	Chick	Bruce Kirkpatrick
The Queen	Jude Akuwudike		

Guards, Convicts, Troopers—Chico Andrade, Tom Hodgkins, Bruce Kirkpatrick, Matthew Floyd
Miller, Daniel Freedom Stewart.

Understudies: Mr. Redgrave—J.P. Linton; Mr. Lynch—Mark Dexter; Messrs. Black, Linton, Kirkpatrick—Michael Pemberton; Misses Lee, Dickinson—Tina Benko; Messrs. Miller, Dexter—Daniel

THE WEIR—Kieran Ahern, Brendan Coyle, Dermot Crowley, Michelle
Fairley and Jim Norton in a scene from the play by Conor McPherson

Freedom Stewart; Mr. Ziman—Bruce Kirkpatrick; Mr. Leffert—Chico Andrade; Messrs. Akuwudike,
Graham—Gregory Simmons; Messrs. Giannini, Andrade, Stewart—Philip Anthony; Messrs. Shropshire, Hodgkins—Joel Leffert.

Directed by Trevor Nunn; scenery, Richard Hoover; costumes, Karyl Newman; lighting, Chris Parry;
sound, Christopher Shutt; associate director, Stephen Rayne; music, Steven Edis; fights, Malcolm Ranson; associate producer, Phyllis Wattis; casting, Liz Woodman; production stage manager, Michael Brunner; press, Philip Rinaldi, Barbara Carroll.

Time: July/August 1938. Place: A large American prison. The play was presented in two parts.

1930s-style prison melodrama, sympathetic to inmates suffering under a brutal warden. A newly
discovered, very early Williams play previously produced in London and in regional theater at the Alley
Theater, Houston. A special *Best Plays* citation; see its entry in the Prizewinning Plays section of this
volume.

*Annie Get Your Gun (101). Revival of the musical with book by Herbert and Dorothy Fields
as revised by Peter Stone; music and lyrics by Irving Berlin. Produced by Barry and Fran
Weissler in association with Kardana, Michael Watt, Irving Welzer and Hal Luftig at the
Marquis Theater. Opened March 4, 1999.

Buffalo Bill	Ron Holgate	Annie Oakley	Bernadette Peters
Frank Butler	Tom Wopat	Jessie Oakley	Cassidy Ladden
Dolly Tate	Valerie Wright	Nellie Oakley	Mia Walker
Tommy Keeler	Andrew Palermo	Little Jake	Trevor McQueen Eaton
Winnie Tate	Nicole Ruth Snelson	Eagle Feather	Carlos Lopez
Mac the Propman; Running Deer;		Dining Car Waiter	Brad Bradley
Messenger	Kevin Bailey	Sleeping Car Porter	Patrick Wetzel
Charlie Davenport	Peter Marx	Band Leader	Marvin Laird
Foster Wilson; Pawnee Bill	Ronn Carroll	Mrs. Schyler Adams	Julia Fowler
Chief Sitting Bull	Gregory Zaragoza	Sylvia Potter-Porter	Jenny-Lynn Suckling

Ensemble: Shaun Amyot, Kevin Bailey, Brad Bradley, Randy Donaldson, Madeleine Ehlert, Julia Fowler, Kisha Howard, Adrienne Hurd, Keri Lee, Carlos Lopez, Desiree Parkman, Eric Sciotto, Kelli Bond Severson, Timothy Edward Smith, Jenny-Lynn Suckling, David Villella, Patrick Wetzel.

Orchestra: Nicholas Archer associate conductor, synthesizer; Bruce Samuels synthesizer programmer; Chris Jaudes trumpet I; Joe Mosello trumpet II; Larry Lunetta trumpet III; Dale Kirkland tenor trombone; Morris Kianuma bass trombone, tuba; Roger Wendt, French horn; William Ellison bass; Ed Hamilton guitar, banjo; Beth Ravin percussion; Cubby O'Brien drums; Les Scott woodwinds I; Morty Silver woodwinds II; Ken DyBisz woodwinds III; Terrence Cook woodwinds IV; John Campo woodwinds V; Todd Reynolds concertmaster I, stage solo; Victor Schultz violin II; Heidi Stubner violin III; Nina Simon violin IV; Richard Clark violin, viola; Clay Ruede cello I; Marisol Espada cello II.

Standbys and Understudies: Mr. Wopat—Christopher Councill, Kevin Bailey; Miss Peters—Valerie Wright; Miss Wright—Jenny-Lynn Suckling; Mr. Palermo—Carlos Lopez, Shaun Amyot; Miss Snelson—Keri Lee, Kisha Howard; Mr. Marx—Brad Bradley, Patrick Wetzel; Mr. Holgate—Christopher Councill; Messrs. Zaragoza, Carroll—Kevin Bailey, Patrick Wetzel; Misses Walker, Eaton—Blair Goldberg; Mr. Eaton—Mia Walker; Hoop Dance—David Villella; "The Girl That I Marry" Dancer—Leasen Beth Almquist; Swings—Leasen Beth Almquist, Patti D'Beck, Rick Spaans.

Directed by Graciela Daniele; choreography, Graciela Daniele, Jeff Calhoun; supervising musical director and vocal and incidental music arrangements, John McDaniel; musical direction and dance music arrangements, Marvin Laird; scenery, Tony Walton; costumes, William Ivey Long; lighting, Beverly Emmons; sound, G. Thomas Clark; orchestrations, Bruce Coughlin; musical coordinator, John Monaco; associate choreographer, Patti D'Beck; associate producers, Alecia Parker, Judith Ann Abrams; casting, Betsy D. Bernstein, Howie Cherpakov; stage managers, Richard Hester, Jim Woolley; press, the Pete Sanders Group, Miguel Tuason, Bill Coyle, Glenna Freedman.

The last major New York revival of *Annie Get Your Gun* took place on Broadway 9/21/66 for 78 performances, with Ethel Merman as Annie Oakley.

ACT I

"There's No Business Like Show Business"	Frank, Company
"Doin' What Comes Natur'lly"	Annie, Kids, Foster Wilson
"The Girl That I Marry"	Frank, Annie
"You Can't Get a Man With a Gun"	Annie
"There's No Business Like Show Business" (Reprise)	Frank, Buffalo Bill, Charlie, Annie
"I'll Share It All With You"	Tommy, Winnie, Company
"Moonshine Lullaby"	Annie, Kids, Ensemble Trio
"There's No Business Like Show Business" (Reprise)	Annie
"They Say It's Wonderful"	Annie, Frank
"My Defenses Are Down"	Frank, Young Men
The Trick	Annie, Company
Finale: "You Can't Get a Man With a Gun" (Reprise)	Annie

ACT II

Entr'acte: "The European Tour"	Annie, Company
"Lost in His Arms"	Annie
"Who Do You Love, I Hope"	Tommy, Winnie, Company
"I Got the Sun in the Morning"	Annie, Company
"An Old Fashioned Wedding'	Annie, Frank

"The Girl That I Marry" (Reprise) .... Frank
"Anything You Can Do" .... Annie, Frank
"They Say It's Wonderful" (Reprise) .... Annie, Frank, Company
Finale Ultimo .... Company

Band in Berlin (16). Musical co-conceived by Susan Feldman, Patricia Birch and Wilbur Pauley; written by Susan Feldman. Produced by Robert V. Straus, Jeffrey Ash, Randall L. Wreghitt, Gayle Francis and Marcia Roberts in association with DLT Entertainment/ZDF Enterprises and by special arrangement with Arts at St. Ann's and American Music Theater Festival at the Helen Hayes Theater. Opened March 7, 1999. (Closed March 21, 1999)

Roman Cycowski .... Herbert Rubens
Hudson Shad:
   Ari Leshnikoff; lst Tenor .... Mark Bleeke
   Erich Collin;
      2d Tenor .... Timothy Leigh Evans
   Harry Frommermann;
   Lyric Baritone .... Hugo Munday

Young Roman Cycowski;
   Baritone .... Peter Becker
Robert Biberti; Bass .... Wilbur Pauley
Erwin Bootz;
   Pianist .... Robert Wolinsky

Understudies: Messrs. Bleeke, Evans—John Easterlin; Messrs. Munday, Becker—Eric Edlund; Mr. Pauley—Seth Malkin.

Co-directed by Susan Feldman and Patricia Birch; choreography, Patricia Birch; musical direction and English translations, Wilbur Pauley; scenery, Douglas W. Schmidt; costumes, Jonathan Bixby, Gregory Gale; lighting, Kirk Bookman; sound, David Schnirman; media design, Richard Law; filmmakers, Anthony Chase, Eric Rodine; puppet design, Stephen Kaplin; keyboard arrangements, Robert Wolinsky; assistant director-choreographer, Jonathan Stuart Cerullo; associate producers, Marsha Dubrow, Gilford/Freeley, Kathleen O'Grady, Geoffrey Shearing, Joseph S. Steinberg; casting, Johnson-Liff Associates; production stage manager, Robert Mark Kalfin; stage manager, Debora Porazzi; press, James LL Morrison Associates.

Time and place: Memories of Germany, 1927–1935. The play was presented without intermission.

The true story of the Comedian Harmonists, a German musical troupe of singers and a pianist, internationally popular in the 1920s but eventually broken up by Hitler and their music banned.

MUSICAL NUMBERS—Overture: "Goodnight, Sweetheart" (by Noble/Lohner and Beda). Prologue: "A New Spring Will Come to the Homeland" (by Engel/Berger/Rotter).

The Beginning: "Dearest Isabella From Castille" (by Bootz/Karlick), "My Little Green Cactus" (by Dorian/Horda), "Stormy Weather" (by Kohler/Arlen).

The Rise: "Happy Days Are Here Again" (by Ager/Yellen), "The Spring Is Here" (by Jurmann/Rotter), "Village Music" (by Fryberg/von Donop/Kirsten), "Tea for Two" (by Youmans/Caesar).

World Tour: "What's Happening in Lisbon?" (by Bochman/Lenow), "It Don't Mean a Thing if It Ain't Got That Swing" and "Creole Love Call (by Ellington), *The Barber of Seville* Overture (by Rossini).

Performing Under the Third Reich: "Night and Day" (by Porter), "A New Spring Will Come to the Homeland" (Reprise), "A Little Spring Melody" (by Dvorak/Langsfelder), "Uncle Bumba From Columba Dances the Rhumba" (by Hupfeld/Rotter/Robinson).

Swansong Tour: "Whistle While You Work" (by Churchill/Morley), "Love Comes, Love Goes" (by Kreisler/Marischka), "Baby" (by Hollander/Mehring), "The Old Cowboy, The Last Roundup" (by Hill/Walter).

Epilogue: "Auf Wiederseh'n, My Dear" (by Hoffman/Goodheart/Nelson/Ager/Amberg).

*Night Must Fall (96). Revival of the play by Emlyn Williams. produced by National Actors Theater, Tony Randall founder and artistic director, at the Lyceum Theater. Opened March 8, 1999.

Mrs. Bramson .... Judy Parfitt
Olivia Grayne .... Pamela J. Gray
Nurse Libby .... Jennifer Wiltsie
Hubert Laurie .... Michael Countryman
Mrs. Terence .... Patricia Kilgarriff

Dora Parkoe .... Seana Kofoed
Inspector Belsize .... Peter McRobbie
Dan .... Matthew Broderick
Man .... David Dartley

Standby: Mr. Broderick—Kevin Shinick; Understudies: Messrs. Countryman, McRobbie—Kevin Shinick; Misses Parfitt, Kilgarriff—Paddy Croft; Miss Gray—Seana Kofoed; Misses Wiltsie, Kofoed—Anita Dashiell.

Directed by John Tillinger; scenery, James Noone; costumes, Jess Goldstein; lighting, Brian MacDevitt; sound, Aural Fixation; executive producer, Manny Kladitis; casting, Deborah Brown; production stage manager, Anne Keefe; stage manager, Cynthia Bauer-Espinosa; press, Springer/Chicoine Public Relations, Gary Springer, Susan Chicoine.

Place: The sitting room of Mrs. Bramson's house in Essex, England. Act I, Scene 1: A fine Sunday in October, 1935. Scene 2: An afternoon 12 days later. Act II, Scene 1: Late afternoon, two days later. Sunday again. Scene 2: Immediately afterwards. Scene 3: A few minutes later. Night.

Night Must Fall had its American premiere on Broadway 9/28/36 for 64 performances with the author in the role of Dan. The most recent of its several off-Broadway revivals was by Equity Library Theater 3/29/69 for 9 performances.

Rollin' on the T.O.B.A. (14). Transfer from off Broadway of the musical revue conceived by Ronald "Smokey" Stevens and Jaye Stewart; featuring excerpts from *The Simple Stories* by Langston Hughes; additional material by Irvin S. Bauer. Produced by John Grimaldi, Ashton Springer and Frenchman Productions, Inc. at the Kit Kat Klub at Henry Miller's Theater. Opened March 24, 1999. (Closed April 4, 1999)

Stewart .... Ronald "Smokey" Stevens   Bertha Mae Little .... Sandra Reaves-Phillips
Stevens .... Rudy Roberson

Understudies: Messrs. Stevens, Roberson—Jackie Jay Patterson; Miss Reaves-Phillips—Alyson Williams.

Directed and choreographed by Ronald "Smokey" Stevens and Leslie Dockery; musical direction and arrangements, David Alan Bunn; scenery, Larry W. Brown; costumes, Michele Reisch; lighting, Jon Kusner; sound, Shabach Audio; associate producers, Martin Shugrue, Carriene Nevin; stage manager, Femi S. Heggie; press, The Jacksina Company, Judy Jacksina, Ed Ku.

Time: 1931. Place: On the Theater Owners' Booking Association circuit.

A performance tribute to the last days of black vaudeville, originally presented by the AMAS Musical Theater, Rosetta LeNoire founder and artistic director.

ACT I

Overture
    "Rollin' on the T.O.B.A." .... Stevens, Stewart, Bertha Mae
        (by Ronald "Smokey" Stevens, Sandra Reaves-Phillips, Chapman Roberts, Benny Key and David Alan Bunn)
Scene 1: On the Train
    Toast to Harlem .... Stevens, Stewart
        (by Langston Hughes)
Scene 2: Monogram Theater
    Bill Robinson Walk .... Stevens
        (by Bill "Bojangles" Robinson)
    "Evolution"/"Ugly Chile" .... Stevens, Stewart
        (by Miller & Lyles/Clarence Williams)
Scene 3: Bertha's phone call
    "Travelin' Blues" .... Bertha Mae
        (by Ronald "Smokey" Stevens and Sandra Reaves-Phillips)
Scene 4: Dressing room
    Lincoln West/The Liar (Staggolee) .... Stevens, Stewart
        (by Gwendolyn Brooks and Terrence Cooper)
Scene 5: Royal Theater
    Fish Fry .... Stevens, Stewart
        (by Ellis Walsh and Louis Jordan)
Scene 6: Bertha's letter/On the train
    "St. Louis Blues" .... Bertha Mae
        (by W.C. Handy)

Scene 7: Booker T. Theater
The Poker Game .... Stevens
    (by Bert Williams; "Black & Tan Fantasy" music by Duke Ellington)
Nobody .... Stevens
    (by Bert Williams)
"Huggin' & Chalkin'" .... Stewart
    (by Kermit Goell and Clancey Hayes)
"Sexy Blues"/"You've Taken My Blues and Gone" .... Bertha Mae
    (by Sandra Reaves-Phillips, Chapman Roberts and Ronald "Smokey" Stevens/Langston
    Hughes)
The Car Crash and Broken Dialog .... Stevens, Stewart
    (by Miller & Lyles)
Conversationalization .... Stevens, Stewart
    (by Miller & Lyles)
"Let the Good Times Roll" .... Company
    (by Sam Theard and Fleecie Moore)

ACT II

Entr'acte
Piano Interlude .... David Allen Bunn
Scene 1: Regal Theater
"Hop Scop Blues" .... Stevens
    (by Clarence Williams)
The Chess Game .... Stevens, Stewart
    ("Funeral March of the Marionettes" music by Charles Gounod)
Scene 2: Bertha's Show/The Regal Theater
"Take Me As I Am" .... Bertha Mae
    (by Sandra Reaves-Phillips)
"One Hour Mama" .... Bertha Mae
    (by Porter Grainger)
"Million Dollar Secret" .... Bertha Mae
    (by Helen Humes and Jules Bihari)
Freddie and Flo .... Bertha Mae, Stewart
    (by Butterbeans and Suzie)
"A Good Man Is Hard to Find" .... Bertha Mae
    (by Eddie Green)
"Take Me As I Am" (Reprise) .... Bertha Mae
Scene 3: On the train
Simple on Integration .... Stevens, Stewart
    (by Langston Hughes)
Soul Food .... Company
    (by Langston Hughes)
Scene 4: On the train
Banquet in Honor .... Stevens, Stewart
    (by Langston Hughes)
"I'm Still Here"/"Trouble in Mind" .... Company
    (by Langston Hughes/Richard Jones)
"Rollin' on the T.O.B.A." (Reprise) .... Company

*Closer (77). By Patrick Marber. Produced by Robert Fox, Scott Rudin, Roger Berlind, Carole
Shorenstein Hays, ABC Inc. and The Shubert Organization in the Royal National Theater
production, Trevor Nunn director, at the Music Box. Opened March 25, 1999.

Alice .... Anna Friel   Larry .... Ciaran Hinds
Dan .... Rupert Graves   Anna .... Natasha Richardson

Understudies: Miss Richardson—Natacha Roi; Mr. Graves—Joseph Murphy; Miss Friel—Dagmara Dominczyk; Mr. Hinds—J. Tucker Smith.

Directed by Patrick Marber; scenery and costumes, Vicki Mortimer; lighting, Hugh Vanstone; original music, Paddy Cunneen; sound, Simon Baker; casting, Ilene Starger; production stage manager, R. Wade Jackson; stage manager, Deirdre McCrane; press, Boneau/Bryan-Brown, Adrian Bryan-Brown, John Barlow.

Time: The l990s. Place: London. The play was presented in two parts.

Pitfalls of sex and evanescence of love, with two couples. A foreign play previously produced in London. The play was presented in two parts. Winner of the 1998–99 New York Drama Critics Circle Award for best foreign play; see its entry in the Prizewinning Plays section of this volume.

*The Weir (70). By Conor McPherson. Produced by Thomas Viertel, Richard Frankel, Steven Baruch, Marc Routh, Jujamcyn Theaters, Manhattan Theater Club and Turnstyle/Ambassador Theater Group in the Royal Court Theater production, Ian Rickson artistic director, at the Walter Kerr Theater. Opened April 1, 1999.

Jack	Jim Norton	Finbar	Dermot Crowley
Brendan	Brendan Coyle	Valerie	Michelle Fairley
Jim	Kieran Ahern		

Understudies: Messrs. Norton, Crowley—Gerard Doyle; Miss Fairley—Fiana Toibin.

Directed by Ian Rickson; scenery and costumes, Rae Smith; lighting, Paule Constable; sound, Paul Arditti; associate producers, James D. Stern, Judith Marinoff, Nancy Myers; U.K. casting, Lisa Makin; U.S. casting, Ciaran O'Reilly, Charlotte Moore; production stage manager, Brian Meister; stage manager, Pamela Edington; press, Helene Davis Publicity.

Time; Present day. Place: A small bar in a rural part of Ireland, Northwest Leitrim or Sligo. The play was presented without intermission.

Irish locals and a visitor reveal their inner natures while drinking Guiness and telling ghost stories in a country pub. A foreign play previously produced in London.

*The Iceman Cometh (53), Revival of the play by Eugene O'Neill. Produced by Allan S. Gordon, Bill Haber, Ira Pittelman, Elan McAllister, Trigger Street Productions and Emanuel Azenberg at the Brooks Atkinson Theater. Opened April 8, 1999.

Rocky Pioggi	Tony Danza	Pat McGloin	Richard Riehle
Larry Slade	Tim Pigott-Smith	Ed Mosher	Jeff Weiss
Hugo Kalmar	Stephen Singer	Margie	Catherine Kellner
Willie Oban	Michael Emerson	Pearl	Dina Spybey
Harry Hope	James Hazeldine	Cora	Katie Finneran
Joe Mott	Clarke Peters	Chuck Morello	Skipp Sudduth
Don Parritt	Robert Sean Leonard	Theodore Hickman (Hickey)	Kevin Spacey
Cecil Lewis (The Captain)	Patrick L. Godfrey	Moran	Steve Ryan
Piet Wetjoen (The General)	Ed Dixon	Lieb	Ned Van Zandt
James Cameron			
(Jimmy Tomorrow)	Paul Giamatti		

Understudies: Messrs. Hazeldine, Singer, Godfrey, Riehle, Weiss—Jarlath Conroy; Messrs. Godfrey, Riehle, Weiss, Pigott-Smith, Dixon—Julian Gamble; Misses Finneran, Kellner, Spybey—Teri Lamm; Messrs. Emerson, Leonard, Danza—Matthew Mabe; Messrs. Sudduth, Danza, Dixon—Steve Ryan; Messrs. Giamatti, Singer, Ryan—Ned Van Zandt; Messrs. Van Zandt, Peters—Isiah Whitlock Jr.

Directed by Howard Davies; scenery and costumes, Bob Crowley; lighting, Mark Henderson; original music, Paddy Cunneen; sound, John A. Leonard; associate director, Jonathan Bernstein; associate producer, Ginger Montel; casting, Jay Binder; production stage manager, Steven Zweigbaum; stage manager, Rolt Smith; press, Boneau/Bryan-Brown, Adrian Bryan-Brown, Michael Hartman.

Place: Downtown West Side of New York City. Act I: Harry Hope's bar before dawn, 1912. Act II: Near midnight of the same day. Act III: Morning of the following day. Act IV: The next day, 1:30 A.M. The play was presented in three parts with intermissions after Acts I and III.

The last major New York revival of *The Iceman Cometh* took place on Broadway with Jason Robards as Hickey 9/29/85 for 55 performances. The present revival is based on a production by the Almeida Theater Company in London.

Marlene (25). Musical play by Pam Gems. Produced by Ric Wanetik and Frederic B. Vogel at the Cort Theater. Opened April 11, 1999. (Closed May 2, 1999)

Mutti	Mary Diveny	Marlene Dietrich	Siân Phillips
Vivian	Margaret Whitton		

Newsreader Voiceover—Edward Hibbert. Standby: Miss Phillips—Lucy Martin. Understudies: Misses Whitton, Diveny—Becky London.

Musicians: Kevin Amos piano; Mary Rowell violin; Peter Donovan bass.

Directed by Sean Mathias; musical direction, Kevin Amos; scenery, John Arnone; costumes, David C. Woolard; lighting, Mark Jonathan; sound, Peter J. Fitzgerald; associate producers, Alice Chebba Walsh, Mary Ellen Ashley, Anne L. Bernstein, Kimberly Vaughn, Richard Samson, Jennifer Lee, Herb Goldsmith Productions; casting, Ilene Starger; production stage manager, Arthur Gaffin; stage manager, David Sugarman; press, James LL Morrison Associates.

Time: 1969. Place: A theater in Paris.

Homage to Marlene Dietrich, played by Siân Phillips, as she reviews some of the events of her life. A foreign play previously produced in England and on tour.

MUSICAL NUMBERS, ACT I: "You Do Something to Me" (by Cole Porter), "Look Me Over Closely" (by Terry Gilkyson); "Illusions," "Jonny" and "Lola" (by F. Hollaender); "I Wish You Love" (music by Charles Louis Trenet, lyrics by Albert Askew Beach).

ACT II: "Mein Blondes Baby" (by Peter Kreuder and Fritz Rotter), "Warum," "The Laziest Girl in Town" (by Cole Porter), "The Boys in the Back Room" (by F. Hollaender and Frank Loesser), "Lili Marlene" (by Schultz, Leip, Conner and Phillips), "Honeysuckle Rose" (by Andy Razaf and Thomas "Fats" Waller), "Where Have All the Flowers Gone" (by Pete Seeger), "La Vie en Rose" (by Louiguy and Edith Piaf), "Falling in Love Again" (by F. Hollaender and S. Lerner).

*Amy's View (53). By David Hare. Produced by Robert Fox, Scott Rudin, Roger Berlind, Joan Cullman, ABC Inc. and The Shubert Organization in the Royal National Theater production, Trevor Nunn director, at the Ethel Barrymore Theater. Opened April 15, 1999.

Dominic Tyghe	Tate Donovan	Frank Oddie	Ronald Pickup
Amy Thomas	Samantha Bond	Toby Cole	Maduka Steady
Evelyn Thomas	Anne Pitoniak	Stage Manager	Willis Sparks
Esme Allen	Judi Dench		

Understudies: Miss Dench—Jennifer Harmon; Miss Bond—Melissa Bowen; Messrs. Donovan, Steady—Willis Sparks; Mr. Pickup—Herb Foster; Miss Pitoniak—June Gibbons.

Directed by Richard Eyre; scenery and costumes, Bob Crowley; lighting, Mark Henderson; music, Richard Hartley; sound, Scott Myers, projections, Wendall K. Harrington; U.S. casting, Daniel Swee; production stage manager, Susie Cordon; stage manager, Thom Widmann; press, Boneau/Bryan-Brown, Adrian Bryan-Brown, John Barlow.

Place: Near Pangbourne and in London. Act I: 1979. Act II: 1985. Act III: 1993. Act IV: 1995. The play was presented in two parts with the intermission following Act II.

Sixteen years in the life of a dedicated actress facing emotional conflicts with her adult daughter and with the late 20th century society of which she is a part. A foreign play previously produced in London.

*The Civil War (45). Musical with book and lyrics by Frank Wildhorn, Gregory Boyd and Jack Murphy; music by Frank Wildhorn. Produced by Pierre Cossette, PACE Theatrical Group/SFX Entertainment, Bomurwil Productions, Kathleen Raitt and Jujamcyn Theaters at the St. James Theater. Opened April 22, 1999.

Union Army:		Sgt. Patrick Anderson	Rod Weber
Capt. Emmett Lochran	Michael Lanning	Sgt. Byron Richardson	Royal Reed

Capt. William McEwen .... Gilles Chiasson
Pvt. Conrad Bock .... Ron Sharpe
Pvt. Elmore Hotchkiss .... Bart Shatto
Pvt. Nathaniel Taylor .... John Sawyer
Confederate Army:
Capt. Billy Pierce .... Gene Miller
Sgt. Virgil Franklin .... Dave Clemmons
Cpl. John Beauregard .... Mike Eldred
Cpl. Henry Stewart .... David M. Lutken
Pvt. Darius Barksdale .... Anthony Galde
Pvt. Cyrus Stevens .... Jim Price
Pvt. Sam Taylor .... Matt Bogart
Frederick Douglass .... Keith Byron Kirk

Clayton Toler .... Michel Bell
Bessie Toler .... Cheryl Freeman
Benjamin Reynolds .... Lawrence Clayton
Exter Thomas .... Wayne W. Pretlow
Harriet Jackson .... Capathia Jenkins
Liza Hughes .... Cassandra White
Autolycus Fell .... Leo Burmester
Auctioneer's Assistant .... Dave Clemmons
Sarah McEwen .... Irene Molloy
Violet; Nurse .... Hope Harris
Mabel; Mrs. Bixby .... Beth Leavel
Voice of President Lincoln .... David M. Lutken

Pit Singers: David Michael Felty, Hope Harris, Monique Midgette, Raun Ruffin.

Musicians: Jeff Lams conductor, piano; John Korba associate conducto, keyboard; Scott Kuney, John Herington, Gordon Titcomb guitar; Bill Holcomb bass; Warren Odze drums; Michael Rubin harmonica; Birch Johnson trombone; Wayne duMaine trumpet; Charlie Pillow woodwinds; Carol Sharar violin; Laura Bontrager cello; Roger Squitero percussion.

Understudies: Messrs Lanning, Burmester—David M. Lutken, Jim Price; Mr. Chiasson—Mike Eldred, Ron Sharpe; Mr. Miller—Eldred, Royal Reed; Mr. Bogart—Reed, Sharpe; Miss Freeman—Capathia Jenkins, Monique Midgette: Messrs. Kirk, Bell, Clayton—Wayne W. Pretlow, Raun Ruffin; Miss Jenkins—Cassandra White, Midgette; Miss Molloy—Kristine Fraelich, Hope Harris; Misses Harris, Leavel—Fraelich, Harris.

Directed by Jerry Zaks; musical staging, Luis Perez; musical direction, Jeff Lams; scenery, Douglas W. Schmidt; costumes, William Ivey Long; lighting, Paul Gallo; sound, Karl Richardson; projections, Wendall K. Harrington; battles, David Leong; orchestrations, Kim Scharnberg; musical supervision, Jason Howland; vocal direction, casting, Dave Clemmons; music coordinator, John Miller; executive producer, Gary Gunas, PACE Theatrical Group; associate director, BT McNicholl; associate producers, I.W. Marks, Michael Skipper, Chris Edgecomb; stage manager, Rick Steiger; press, Echo New York, Norman Zagier.

Typical individuals who fought or lived though the Civil War characterized in examples of the episodes which they endured. Commissioned and previously produced by the Alley Theater, Houston, Gregory Boyd artistic director.

ACT I

"A House Divided" .... Citizens
"Freedom's Child" .... Frederick Douglass, Abolitionists
"By the Swords/Sons of Dixie" .... Armies
"Tell My Father" .... Pvt. Taylor
"The Peculiar Institution" .... The Enslaved
"If Prayin' Were Horses" .... Clayton Toler, Bessie Toler
"Greenback" .... Autolycus Fell, Mabel, Violet
"Missing You (My Bill)" .... Sarah McEwen
"Judgment Day" .... Capt. Pierce, Capt. Lochran; Pvt. Taylor; Armies
"Father, How Long?" .... Clayton Toler
"Someday" .... Harriet Jackson, Bessie Toler, Others
"I'll Never Pass This Way Again" .... Cpl. Stewart
"How Many Devils?" .... Armies

ACT II

"Virginia" .... Capt. Pierce
"Candle in the Window" .... Harriet Jackson
"Oh! Be Joyful" .... Autolycus Fell, Sgt. Richardson, Pvt. Bock, Pvt. Hotchkiss
"The Hospital" .... Mrs. Bixby, Nurse, Union Soldiers, Clayton Toler
"If Prayin' Were Horses" (Reprise) .... Clayton Toler, Bessie Toler
"River Jordan" .... Benjamin Reynolds, Others
"Sarah" .... Cpl. McEwen

THE CIVIL WAR—Gene Miller *(second from right)* and Confederate soldiers in the "Sons of Dixie" number in the Frank Wildhorn-Gregory Boyd-Jack Murphy musical

"The Honor of Your Name" .... Sarah McEwen
"Greenback" (Reprise) .... Autolycus Fell, Violet
"Northbound Train" .... Capt. Lochran
"Last Waltz for Dixie" .... Capt. Pierce, Confederate Soldiers
"The Glory" .... Capt. Lochran, Frederick Douglass, Benjamin Reynolds, Company

The Gershwins' Fascinating Rhythm (17). Musical revue conceived for the stage by Mark Lamos and Mel Marvin from source material by Deena Rosenberg; music and lyrics by George Gershwin and Ira Gershwin. Produced by Music Makers Inc., Columbia Artists and Manny Kladitis at the Longacre Theater. Opened April 25, 1999. (Closed May 9, 1999)

Michael Berresse	Karen Lifshey
Darius de Haas	Jill Nicklaus
Chris Ghelfi	Orfeh
Tim Hunter	Sara Ramirez
Adriane Lenox	Patrick Wilson

Swings: Brian J. Marcum, Kenya U. Massey.
Orchestra: Cynthia Kortman conductor; Paul J. Ascenzo associate conductor, keyboard II; Paul Hostetter assistant conductor, percussion; Dennis Anderson reed I; Ed Salkin reed II; Frank Santagata

reed III; Danny Cahn trumpet I; Bud Burridge trumpet II; Randy Andos trombone; Mark Berman keyboard I; Greg Skaff guitar; Jeff Hanz bass; Gary Seligson drums.

Directed by Mark Lamos; choreography, David Marques; musical direction and supervision, Cynthia Kortman; scenery, Michael Yeargan; costumes, Paul Tazewell; lighting, Peggy Eisenhauer; sound, Abe Jacob; orchestrations, Larry Hochman; musical and vocal arrangements, Mel Marvin; additional arrangements, Paul J. Ascenzo, Joseph Church; music coordinator, Michael Keller; associate producers, Magicworks/SFX Entertainment, Jerry Frankel; casting, Bernard Telsey; production stage manager, Alan Hall; stage manager, Ruth E. Rinklin; press, Boneau/Bryan-Brown, Chris Boneau, Amy Jacobs.

Contemporary musical styles and tastes applied to the Gershwin classics. The show was presented without intermission.

MUSICAL NUMBERS: "Fascinating Rhythm"—Company. "I've Got a Crush on You"—Sara Ramirez, Michael Berresse. "Oh, Lady, Be Good!" (arranged by Paul J. Ascenzo)—Darius de Haas. "High Hat"—Patrick Wilson, Ramirez. "Clap Yo' Hands"—Orfeh, Company. "Cousin in Milwaukee"/"The Lorelei"—Adriane Lenox, Orfeh. "The Man I Love"/"Soon"—Ramirez, Wilson. "Love Is Here to Stay" pas de deux (arranged by Paul J. Ascenzo)—Jill Nicklaus, Berresse. "Little Jazz Bird" (arranged by Paul J. Ascenzo)—de Haas. "Isn't It a Pity"—Ramirez, Karen Lifshey. "I Love to Rhyme," "Blah, Blah, Blah," "I Got Rhythm"—Berresse, Company. "Embraceable You"—Wilson, Chris Ghelfi, Tim Hunter, Lifshey, Nicklaus. "Let's Call the Whole Thing Off"—de Haas, Orfeh. "Nice Work if You Can Get It"—Lenox. "But Not for Me"—Wilson. "Just Another Rhumba" (arranged by Joseph Church)—Ramirez, Berresse. "Someone to Watch Over Me"—de Haas, Lifshey, Orfeh, Ramirez, Wilson. "The Half of It, Dearie, Blues" (arranged by Paul J. Ascenzo)—Lenox. "How Long Has This Been Going On?"—Wilson. "Home Blues"—Ramirez, Wilson. "Who Cares?"—Berresse, Company. "They Can't Take That Away From Me"—Company. "Hang on to Me"—Company.

*It Ain't Nothin' But the Blues (40). Transfer from off Broadway of the musical revue based on an original idea by Ron Taylor; written by Charles Bevel, Lita Gaithers, Randal Myler, Ron Taylor and Dan Wheetman; music by various authors (see listing below). Produced by Eric Krebs, Jonathan Reinis, Lawrence Horowitz, Anita Waxman, Elizabeth Williams, CTM Productions and Anne Squadron, in association with Lincoln Center Theater, in the Crossroads Theater Company production, Ricardo Kahn artistic director, in association with San Diego Repertory Theater, Sam Woodhouse artistic director, and Alabama Shakespeare Festival, Kent Thompson artistic director, at the Vivian Beaumont Theater. Opened April 26, 1999.

Charles Bevel	Gregory Porter
Gretha Boston	Ron Taylor
Carter Calvert	Dan Wheetman
Eloise Laws	

The Band: Kevin Cooper bass; Jim Ehinger keyboards; Debra Laws backup vocals; Tony Mathews guitar; Daryll Whitlow percussion; Charlie Rhythm saxophone, horns.

Understudy: Misses Boston, Calvert, Eloise Laws—Debra Laws.

Directed by Randal Myler; musical direction, Dan Wheetman; movement, Donald McKayle; vocal direction, Lita Gaithers; scenery, Robin Sanford Roberts; lighting, Don Darnutzer; sound, Edward Cosla; producing associate, Ron Taylor; associate producers, Electric Factory Concerts, Adam & David Friedson, Richard Martini, Marcia Roberts, Murray Schwartz; production stage manager, Doug Hosney; press, James LL Morrison & Associates, James LL Morrison, Tom D'Ambrosio.

History represented by visual projections of events and intertwined with songs from African chants to American blues. Previously produced off Broadway 3/17/99 by The New 42nd Street Inc. at the New Victory Theater for 16 performances.

MUSICAL NUMBERS, ACT I: "Odun De" (traditional)—Company; "Niwah Wechi" (traditional)—Eloise Laws, Company; "Blood Done Signed My Name" (traditional)—Ron Taylor, Gretha Boston; "Raise Them Up Higher" (traditional)—Charles Bevel; "Danger Blues" (traditional)—Laws; "Black Woman" (traditional)—Gregory Porter; "I'm Gonna Do What the Spirit Says Do" (traditional)—Boston; "I've Been Living With the Blues" (by Sonny Terry)—Company; "Blues Man" (by Z.Z. Hill)—Taylor; "My Home's Across the Blue Ridge Mountains" (traditional)—Carter Calvert; " 'T' for Texas" (by Jimmie Rogers)—Dan Wheetman; "Who Broke the Lock?" (traditional)—Porter Bevel;

"My Man Rocks Me" (traditional)—Laws; "St Louis Blues" (by W.C. Handy)—Boston; "Now I'm Gonna Be Bad" (by Dan Wheetman)—Calvert; "Walkin' Blues" (by Robert L. Johnson)—Bevel; "Come on in My Kitchen" (by Robert L. Johnson)—Porter; "Cross Road Blues" (by Robert L. Johnson)—Bevel; "I Know I've Been Changed" (traditional)—Boston; "Child of the Most High King" (traditional, arranged by Ron Taylor)—Taylor, Men; "Children, Your Line Is Dragging" (traditional, arranged by Fisher Thompson Sr.)—Porter; "Catch on Fire" (traditional, arranged by Lita Gaithers)—Company.

ACT II: "Let the Good Times Roll" (by F. Moore and S. Theard)—Taylor; "Sweet Home Chicago" (by Robert L. Johnson)—Porter, Bevel; "Wang Dang Doodle" (by Willie Dixon)—Boston, Calvert, Laws; "Someone Else Is Steppin' In" (by Denise LaSalle)—Laws; "Please Don't Stop Him" (by Herb J. Lance and John Wallace)—Boston; "I'm Your Hoochie Coochie Man" (by Willie Dixon, arranged by Ron Taylor)—Taylor; "Crawlin' King Snake" (by John Lee Hooker)—Porter; "Mind Your Own Business" (by Hank Williams Sr.)—Wheetman; "Walking After Midnight" (by Don Hect and Alan Block)—Calvert; "I Can't Stop Lovin' You" (by Don Gibson)—Bevel; "The Thrill Is Gone" (by Roy Hawkins and Rick Darnell)—Taylor; "I Put a Spell on You" (by Jay Hawkins)—Laws; "Fever" (by John Davenport and Eddie Cooley)—Calvert; "Candy Man" (traditional)—Wheetman; "Good Night, Irene" (by Huddie Ledbetter)—Bevel, Wheetman; "Strange Fruit" (by Lewis Allan)—Boston; "Someday We'll All Be Free" (by Donny Hathaway and Edward Howard, arranged by Charles Bevel)—Bevel, Porter; "Members Only" (by Larry Addison)—Company; "Let the Good Times Roll" (Reprise)—Company.

*The Lonesome West (40). By Martin McDonagh. Produced by Randall L. Wreghitt and Steven M. Levy, in association with Norma Langworthy, Gayle Francis, Dani Davis & Jason Howland, Joan Stein & Susie Dietz and Everett King, in the Druid Theater Company/Royal Court Theater production, at the Lyceum Theater. Opened April 27, 1999.

Coleman Connor	Maeliosa Stafford	Father Welsh	David Ganly
Valene Connor	Brian F. O'Byrne	Girleen Kelleher	Dawn Bradfield

Directed by Garry Hynes; scenery and costumes, Francis O'Connor; lighting, Tharon Musser; music, Paddy Cunneen; sound, Paul Arditti; special effects, Gregory Meeh; associate producer, Robert E. Lang; casting, Maureen Hughes; production stage manager, Matthew Silver; stage manager, Dan da Silva; press, Boneau/Bryan-Brown, Chris Boneau, Susanne Tighe.

Place: Leenane, a small town in County Galway. The play was presented in two parts.

Running family quarrel between two ill-matched and abrasive brothers. A foreign play previously produced in Galway, Ireland and London.

The Wizard of Oz (22). Musical based on the novel by L. Frank Baum and the M-G-M motion picture; adapted by Robert Johanson; music and lyrics of the motion picture score by Harold Arlen and E.Y. Harburg; background music by Herbert Stothart. Produced by Radio City Entertainment and the Dime Savings Bank at the Theater at Madison Square Garden. Opened May 6, 1999. (Closed May 16, 1999)

In Kansas:

Dorothy Gale	Jessica Grové	Mayor of Munchkinland	Eugene Pidgeon
Toto	Plenty	Barristers	Wendy Coates, Wendy Watts
Aunt Em	Judith McCauley	Coroner	Bill Rolon
Uncle Henry	Tom Urich	Wicked Witch of the West	JoAnne Worley
Hunk	Casey Colgan	Scarecrow	Casey Colgan
Hickory	Dirk Lumbard	Tin Man	Dirk Lombard
Zeke	Francis Ruivivar	Cowardly Lion	Francis Ruivivar
Almira Gulch	JoAnne Worley	Wizard of Oz	Mickey Rooney
Professor Marvel	Mickey Rooney	Nikko	Martin Klebba

In Oz:

Glinda	Judith McCauley
Winkie General	Tom Urich

Lollipop Guild—Ethan Crough, Martin Klebba, David Steinberg. Crows—Shauna Markey, Mary Ruvolo, Martin Klebba. Crow Voices—Lenny Daniel, Trent Armand Kendall, Danny Vaccaro. Apple

Trees—Lenny Daniel, Bill Rolon, Danny Vaccaro. Apple Tree Voices—Karen Babcock, Gail Cook Howell, Christi Moore.

Munchkins, Poppies, Citizens of Oz, Jitterbugs, Flying Monkeys, Winkies: Karen Babcock, Steve Babiar, Bill Brassea, Alvin Brown, Wendy Coates, Ethan Crough, Lenny Daniel, Gail Cook Howell, Trent Armand Kendall, Martin Klebba, Cindy Marchionda, Shauna Markey, Caroline McMahon, Christi Moore, Eugene Pidgeon, Allison Queal, Bill Rolon, Mary Ruvolo, David Steinberg, Danny Vaccaro, Wendy Watts, Deborah Y. Wilson. Swings—Ron Gibbs (Dance Captain), Kevin Steele, Jamie Waggoner, Emily Westhafer.

Orchestra: Jeff Rizzo conductor; Maggie Torre associate conductor, keyboards; Rick Dolan concertmaster; Heidi Modr, Peter Martin Weimar violin; Maxine Roach viola; Chungsun Kim cello; Leon Maleson bass; Svjetlana Kabalan flute; Lynne Cohen oboe; Mark Thrasher, Eddie Salkin, Donn McGeen woodwinds; Katie Dennis, Kelly Dent horns; Tony Kadleck, Liesl Whitaker trumpet; Mike Christianson trombone; Richard Rosenzweig drums; Lou Oddo percussion; Nina Kellman harp; Madelyn Rubinstein keyboard.

Understudies: Miss Grové—Cindy Marchionda, Caroline McMahon; Plenty—Ashley; Miss Mc-Cauley—Gail Cook Howell, Jamie Waggoner; Mr. Urich—Lenny Daniel; Messrs. Colgan, Lumbard—Kevin Steele, Danny Vaccaro; Mr. Ruivivar—Trent Armand Kendall; Miss Worley—Karen Babcock, Christi Moore; Mr. Rooney—Tom Urich; Mr. Pidgeon—Ethan Crough; Mr. Rolon—Ron Gibbs; Mr. Klebba—David Steinberg.

Directed by Robert Johanson; musical staging, Jamie Rocco; musical direction and additional orchestrations, Jeff Rizzo; scenery, Michael Anania; costumes, Gregg Barnes; lighting, Steve Cochrane; sound, David Paterson, Mark Menard; orchestrations, Larry Wilcox; dance and vocal arrangements, Peter Howard; animals, William Berloni; special effects, Ian O'Connor; flying, Foy; associate choreographer, Donna Drake; assistant director, Ron Gibbs; music coordinator, John Miller; executive producer, Tim Hawkins; casting, Julie Hughes, Barry Moss; production stage manager, Bill Roberts; stage manager, Paul J. Smith; press, Cathy Del Priore.

This is the third annual presentation of this musical at the Theater at Madison Square Garden. It was first produced by the Paper Mill Playhouse, Angelo Del Rossi executive producer. The play was presented without intermission.

SCENES AND MUSICAL NUMBERS

Overture .... Orchestra
Scene 1: The Gales' farm in Kansas
  "Over the Rainbow" .... Dorothy
Scene 2: Professor Marvel's wagon
Scene 3: The Gales' farm
  "The Cyclone"
Scene 4: Munchkinland
  "Come Out, Come Out" .... Glinda, Dorothy, Lollipop Guild, Munchkins
  "Ding Dong the Witch Is Dead!" .... Glinda, Mayor, Barristers, Coroner, Munchkins
  "Follow the Yellow Brick Road" .... Dorothy, Munchkins
Scene 5: A cornfield
  "If I Only Had a Brain" .... Scarecrow, Dorothy, Crows
  "We're Off to See the Wizard" .... Dorothy, Scarecrow
Scene 6: An apple orchard
  "If I Only Had a Heart" .... Tin Man, Dorothy, Scarecrow, Apple Trees
  "We're Off to See the Wizard" .... Dorothy, Scarecrow, Tin Man
Scene 7: A wild forest
  "Lions, Tigers and Bears" .... Dorothy, Scarecrow, Tin Man
  "If I Only Had the Nerve"/"We're Off to See the Wizard" .... Cowardly Lion, Dorothy,
                                                                          Tin Man, Scarecrow
Scene 8: A field of poppies
  "Poppies/Optimistic Voices" ..... Glinda, Dorothy, Scarecrow, Tin Man, Cowardly Lion, Wicked
                                                                          Witch, Poppies
Scene 9: Outside the gates of the Emerald City
  "Optimistic Voices" .... Female Chorus
Scene 10: Inside the Emerald City
  "The Merry Old Land of Oz" .... Dorothy, Scarecrow, Tin Man,
                                                      Cowardly Lion, Guard, Citizens of Oz
  "King of the Forest" .... Cowardly Lion, Dorothy, Tin Man, Scarecrow

Scene 11: The Wizard's chamber
Scene 12: The Haunted Forest
  "March of the Winkies" .... Winkies
  "The Jitterbug" .... Wicked Witch, Dorothy, Cowardly Lion,
                                                          Scarecrow, Tin Man, Jitterbugs
Scene 13: Inside the Witch's castle
  "Ding Dong the Witch Is Dead!" (Reprise) .... Winkies, Dorothy,
                                                     Cowardly Lion, Scarecrow, Tin Man
Scene 14: The Wizard's chamber
Scene 15: Inside the Emerald City
  "Over the Rainbow" (Reprise) .... Glinda
Scene 16: The Gales' farm in Kansas
  Finale .... Company

PLAYS PRODUCED OFF BROADWAY

Some distinctions between off-Broadway and Broadway productions at one end of the scale and off-off-Broadway productions at the other end are blurred in the New York Theater of the 1990s. For the purposes of *Best Plays* listing, the term "off Broadway" signifies a show which opened for general audiences in a mid-Manhattan theater seating 499 or fewer and 1) employed an Equity cast, 2) planned a regular schedule of 8 performances a week in an open-ended run (7 a week for solo shows) and 3) offered itself to public comment by critics after a designated opening performance.

Occasional exceptions of inclusion (never of exclusion) are made to take in visiting troupes, borderline "showcase" presentations and nonqualifying productions which readers might expect to find in this list because they appear under an off-Broadway heading in other major sources of record.

Figures in parentheses following a play's title give number of performances. These numbers do not include previews or extra non-profit performances.

Plays marked with an asterisk (*) were still in a projected run on June 1, 1999. Their number of performances is figured from opening night through May 31, 1999.

Certain programs of off-Broadway companies are exceptions to our rule of counting the number of performances from the date of the press coverage. When the official opening takes place late in the run of a play's regularly-priced public or subscription performances (after previews), we sometimes count the first performance of record, not the press date, as opening night—and in any such case in the listing we note the variance and give the press date.

In a listing of a show's numbers—dances, sketches, musical scenes, etc.—the titles of songs are identified wherever possible by their appearance in quotation marks (").

HOLDOVERS FROM PREVIOUS SEASONS

Off-Broadway shows which were running on June 1, 1998 are listed below. More detailed information about them appears in previous *Best Plays* volumes of appropriate date. Important cast changes since opening night are recorded in the Cast Replacements section of this volume.

*The Fantasticks (16,188; longest continuous run of record in the American Theater). Musical suggested by the play *Les Romanesques* by Edmond Rostand; book and lyrics by Tom Jones; music by Harvey Schmidt. Opened May 3, 1960.

*Perfect Crime (5,002). By Warren Manzi. Opened October 16, 1987.

*Tony 'n' Tina's Wedding (3,857). By Artificial Intelligence. Opened February 6, 1988.

*Tubes (3,544). Performance piece by and with Blue Man Group. Opened November 17, 1991.

*Stomp (2,210). Percussion performance piece created by Luke Cresswell and Steve Mc-Nicholas. Opened February 27, 1994.

Grandma Sylvia's Funeral (1,360). Transfer from off off Broadway of the environmental theater piece conceived by Glenn Wein and Amy Lord Blumsack; created by Glenn Wein, Amy Lord Blumsack and the original company. Opened October 4, 1994. (Closed June 20, 1998)

*I Love You, You're Perfect, Now Change (1,179). Musical revue with book and lyrics by Joe DiPietro; music by Jimmy Roberts. Opened August 1, 1996.

When Pigs Fly (840). Musical revue conceived by Howard Crabtree and Mark Waldrop; sketches and lyrics by Mark Waldrop; music by Dick Gallagher. Opened August 14, 1996. (Closed August 15, 1998)

*Late Nite Catechism (841). By Vicki Quade and Maripat Donovan. Opened October 3, 1996.

Forbidden Broadway Strikes Back (850). Musical revue created and written by Gerard Alessandrini. Opened October 17, 1996. (Closed September 20, 1998)

Gross Indecency: The Three Trials of Oscar Wilde (534). Transfer from off off Broadway of the play by Moisés Kaufman. Opened June 5, 1997. (Closed September 13, 1998)

*Secrets Every Smart Traveler Should Know (649). Musical revue with songs and sketches by Douglas Bernstein, Francesca Blumenthal, Michael Brown, Barry Creyton, Lesley Davison, Addy Fieger, Stan Freeman, Murray Grand, Glen Kelly, Barry Kleinbort, Jay Leonhart and Denis Markell. Opened October 30, 1997.

Visiting Mr. Green (354). By Jeff Baron. Opened December 17, 1997. (Closed November 22, 1998)

*Hedwig and the Angry Inch (495). Transfer from off off Broadway of the musical with book by John Cameron Mitchell; music and lyrics by Stephen Trask. Opened February 14, 1998.

R & J (385). Transfer from off off Broadway of the Joe Calarco adaptation of *Romeo and Juliet* by William Shakespeare. Opened March 3, 1998. (Closed January 3, 1999)

Savion Glover/Downtown (51). Performance piece by the cast. Opened May 19, 1998. (Closed June 6, 1998) Reopened July 8, 1998. (Closed July 25, 1998)

Manhattan Theater Club. Power Plays (252). Program of three one-act plays: *The Way of All Fish* and *In and Out of the Light* by Elaine May and *Virtual Reality* by Alan Arkin. Opened May 21, 1998. (Closed January 3, 1999) Labor Day (58). By A.R. Gurney. Opened June 1, 1998. (Closed July 22, 1998)

Dinah Was (242). Transfer from off off Broadway of the musical by Oliver Goldstick. Opened May 28, 1998. (Closed January 3, 1999)

PLAYS PRODUCED JUNE 1, 1998–MAY 31, 1999

*Symphonie Fantastique (353). Transfer from off off Broadway of the puppet show created by Basil Twist; music by Hector Berlioz. Produced by the Here Arts Center at the Dorothy B. Williams Theater. Opened June 5, 1998.

CAST: Basil Twist, Oliver Dalzell, Sam Hack, Chris Hymas, Eric Jacobson, Jessica Chandlee Smith.
Producer, Barbara Busackino; lighting, Andrew Hill; production stage manager, Greg Stillman; press, Shirley Herz Associates, Sam Rudy.
Puppetry performed entirely under water and set to the music of Berlioz's *Symphonie Fantastique* in its five movements: 1, Reveries, Passions; 2, A Ball; 3, Scene in the Country; 4, March to the Scaffold; 5, Dream of a Witches' Sabbath.
The show was presented without intermission.

York Theater Company. Schedule of four programs. **The Jello Is Always Red** (22). Musical revue of songs and sketches by Clark Gesner. Opened June 11, 1998. (Closed June 28, 1998) **Little by Little** (41). Musical with story by Annette Jolles and Ellen Greenfield; music by Brad Ross; lyrics by Ellen Greenfield and Hal Hackady. Opened January 21, 1999. (Closed February 21, 1999) **Exactly Like You** (31). Musical with book by A.E. Hotchner; music by Cy Coleman; lyrics by Cy Coleman and A.E. Hotchner; presented in association with Stuart Zimberg, Judith Ann Abrams and David Day. Opened April 14, 1999. (Closed May 9, 1999) And *After the Fair.* Musical with book and lyrics by Stephen Cole, music by Matthew Ward, scheduled to open 7/15/99. Produced by the York Theater Company, James Morgan artistic director, Joseph V. De Michele managing director, at the Theater at St. Peter's Church.

THE JELLO IS ALWAYS RED

Celia Gentry   Neal Young
Clark Gesner

Directed by James Morgan; musical direction, Winston Clark; costumes, John Carver Sullivan; lighting, Brian Haynsworth; production stage manager, Alan Bluestone; press, Keith Sherman & Associates.
Program of cabaret songs and sketches by the author of the musical *You're a Good Man Charlie Brown.*

MUSICAL NUMBERS AND SKETCHES, ACT I: "The Jello Is Always Red"—Clark Gesner; "Hey, There, Let's All Have a Little Fun"—Company; "You're the One I'm Four"—Gesner; "Resolution"— Neal Young; "Reflection"—Celia Gentry; "Everything I Buy Was Made in China"—Gesner; "There Is Always Some More Toothpaste in the Tube"—Company; The Diner—Company; "By the Sea"—Gesner; "It's Very Warm in Here"—Gentry; Humpty Doo—Gesner, Young; "If I Could"—Young; "The Peanut Butter Affair"—Company; Roses—Gesner; "Hey, Buckaroo"—Gentry, Young; "Where Do the Chickens All Come From"—Gesner.
ACT II—"Bird's Song (I Like Them)"—Bird; "Beautiful Song"—Young; Baby—Company; "A Proposal for Our Time"—Neal; "I'm No Sure"—Gentry; "You Are"—Gesner; The Agent Returns—Gesner, Young; "I Love a Lad"—Gentry; "Cool"—Gesner; From *Animal Fair* "The Chipmunk"—Young, "A Bird in a Cage"—Gentry, "A Dog Outside a Store"—Gesner, "Alligators"—Company; "The Ending"—Company.

LITTLE BY LITTLE

Woman I .... Liz Larsen   Man .... Darrin Baker
Woman II .... Christiane Noll

Directed by Annette Jolles; musical direction, Vincent Trovato; scenery, James Morgan; costumes, John Carver Sullivan; lighting, Mary Jo Dondlinger; vocal direction, Joel Fram; musical and vocal ar-

THE JELLO IS ALWAYS RED—Clark Gesner, whose musical *You're a Good Man, Charlie Brown* was a feature of the Broadway season, is pictured *above, center* flanked by Neal Young and Celia Gentry in his off-Broadway revue at York Theater Company

rangements, Wendy Bobbitt, Joel Fram, Brad Ross; casting, Liz Lewis; production stage manager, Jason Cohen; press, Keith Sherman & Associates, Kevin Rehac.

Sweetly conceived love triangle, performed entirely in song. The play was presented without intermission.

MUSICAL NUMBERS: "Little by Little I," "Friendship and Love," "Homework," "Tag," "Little by Little II," "Life and All That," "Starlight," "Popcorn," "Just Between Us," "I'm Not," "Little by Little III," "A Little Hustle," "Rainbows," "Nocturne," "Little by Little IV," "Yes," "The Schmooze," "Take the World Away," "Okay," "If You Only Knew," "Little by Little V," "If You Loved Me," "I'm Not" (Reprise), "Tell Me," "I Ought to Cry," "Little by Little VI," "So It Goes," "Popcorn II," "I'm a Rotten Person," "A Journey That Never Ends."

EXACTLY LIKE YOU

TV Commentator	Tony Hastings	Martin Murphy	Michael McGrath
Judge Maximilian Meltzer	Doug Katsaros	Winona Shook	Blair Ross
Kevin Bursteter	Edward Staudenmayer	Aaron Bates	Robert Bartley
Priscilla Vanderhosen	Susan Mansur	Stenographer	Donya Lane
Eve Bursteter	Kate Levering	Lamarr	Frank Gravis
Arlene Murphy	Lauren Ward	Juror	Donna Kelly

Musicians: Doug Katsaros conductor, keyboards; Donya Lane 2d keyboard; Frank Gravis bass; Donna Kelly drums, percussion.

Directed and choreographed by Patricia Birch; musical direction, Doug Katsaros; scenery, James Morgan; costumes, Richard Schurkamp; lighting, Kirk Bookman; sound, Peter Hylenski; vocal and dance arrangements, Cy Coleman, Doug Katsaros; orchestrations, Doug Katsaros; assistant director/choreographer, Jonathan Cerullo; casting, Warren Pincus; production stage manager, Barnett Feingold; press, Keith Sherman & Associates, Kevin Rehac.

Place: In and around a courtroom.

Subtitled A Romantic Musical Comedy, four couples with mother-in-law and other family problems mix it up with lawyers and jurors.

ACT I

Overture .... Band
"Courtroom Cantata" .... Ensemble
"Southern Comfort" .... Winona, Bates, Ensemble
"Thanks to Mom" .... Eve, Ensemble
"Why Did You Have To Be a Lawyer?" .... Arlene, Martin
"I Get Tired" .... Lamarr, Winona
"That's a Woman" .... Bates
"Cottage by the Sea" .... Kevin
"In the Name of Love" .... Arlene, Martin
"I Want the Best for Him" .... Priscilla
"Don't Mess Around With Your Mother-in-Law" .... Ensemble

ACT II

"Good Day" .... TV Commentator
"She Makes Me Laugh" .... Bates
"Rio" .... Kevin, Martin, Ensemble
"At My Side" .... Kevin, Eve
"No Further Questions, Please" .... Arlene
"You're Good for Me" .... Judge, Priscilla
"Guilty" .... Winona
"Ain't He Cute?" .... Arlene
"Ain't She Cute?" .... Martin
"Exactly Like You" .... Ensemble

The Joseph Papp Public Theater/New York Shakespeare Festival. Schedule of two outdoor programs. **The Skin of Our Teeth** (27). Revival of the play by Thornton Wilder. Opened June 12, 1998. (Closed July 12, 1998) **Cymbeline** (24; see note). Revival of the play by William Shakespeare. Opened August 4, 1998. (Closed August 30, 1998) Produced by The Joseph Papp Public Theater/New York Shakespeare Festival, George C. Wolfe producer, Rosemarie Tichler artistic producer, Mark Litvin managing director, at the Delacorte Theater in Central Park with the cooperation of the City of New York, Rudolph W. Giuliani mayor, Peter F. Vallone speaker of the City Council, Schuyler Chapin commissioner, Department of Cultural Affairs, Henry J. Stern commissioner, Department of Parks & Recreation.

ALL PLAYS: Margaret M. Lioi senior director of external affairs; Wiley Hausam, Bonnie Metzgar associate producers; Brian Kulick artistic associate; casting, Jordan Thaler, Heidi Griffiths; press, Carol R. Fineman, Thomas V. Naro, Bill Coyle.

THE SKIN OF OUR TEETH

Dancer; Dinosaur .... Michael H. Fielder	Doctor; Chair Pusher;
Dancer; Mammoth .... Maria Torres	Fred Bailey .... Thomas Ikeda
Annoucer; Broadcast Official .... J.R. Horne	Professor .... Robert Alexander Owens
Sabina .... Kristen Johnson	Judge; Mr. Tremayne .... Herb Foster
Ms. Fitzpatrick .... Lola Pashalinski	Homer; Chair Pusher .... Paul Kielar
Mrs. Antrobus .... Frances Conroy	Miss E. Muse .... Maria Elena Ramirez
Telegraph Boy .... Matthew Soursourian	Miss T. Muse; Hester .... Tina Johnson
Gladys .... Brienin Bryant	Miss M. Muse .... Rashmi
Henry .... John Ortiz	Miss P. Muse; Ivy .... Monique Holt
Mr. Antrobus .... John Goodman	Fortune Teller .... Novella Nelson

Homeless People, Conveeners, Atlantic City Revelers—Michael H. Fielder, Herb Foster, Tina Johnson, Andrew McGinn, Robert Alexander Owens, Maria Elena Ramirez, Rashmi, Matthew Soursourian, Adam Stein, Maria Torres.

Understudies: Messrs. Goodman, Foster—Robert Alexander Owens; Misses Conroy, Pashalinski, Nelson—Maria Elena Ramirez; Miss Johnston—Tina Johnson; Messrs. Ortiz, Kielar—Adam Stein; Misses Bryant, Johnson, Holt, Mr. Soursourian—Rashmi; Messrs. Horne, Ikeda, Kielar—Andrew McGinn.

Directed by Irene Lewis; scenery, John Conklin; costumes, Candice Donnelly; lighting, Mimi Jordan Sherin; sound, Dan Moses Schreier; choreography, Willie Rosario; fight direction, J. Allen Suddeth; production stage manager, James Latus.

Time: The present and the 1940s, the first preview of a revival of *The Skin of Our Teeth*. Place: The Delacorte Theater and New Jersey. The play was presented in two parts.

The last major New York revival of this Wilder play was by the Classic Stage Company 11/9/86 for 28 performances.

CYMBELINE

Storyteller; Cornelius .... George Morfogen	Lady .... Wendy Rich Stetson
Child .... Jacob Smith	Helen .... Mia Yoo
Queen .... Hazelle Goodman	Messenger .... Jeffrey Fracé
Posthumus Leonatus .... Michael Hall	Caius Lucius .... Thom Sesma
Imogen; Ghost of Posthumus's	Belarius .... Randall Duk Kim
Mother .... Stephanie Roth Haberle	Guiderius; Ghost of Posthumus
Cymbeline; Ghost of Sicilius	Brother .... Adam Greer
Leonatus .... Herb Foster	Arviragus; Ghost of Posthumus
Pisanio .... Philip Goodwin	Brother .... Andrew Garman
Lord .... Andrew McGinn	Lord .... David Snider
Cloten .... Robert Stanton	Roman Captains .... Anson Mount, Jeremy
Lord .... Sam Catlin	Shamos
Lady .... Holly Natwora	British Lord .... George Drance Jr
Iachimo; Jupiter .... Liev Schreiber	British Captains .... Jimmie D. Woody,
Philario; Philharmonous .... Frank Raiter	Christopher Jean
Frenchman .... Anson Mount	Jailers ...... Sam Catlin, Charles Anthony Burks

Singers: George Drance Jr., David Snider, Christopher Jean, Jeremy Shamos. Vision Singers: George Drance Jr., Christopher Jean, Jeremy Shamos, Wendy Rich Stetson, Mia Yoo.

Musicians: Michael Friedman, Bill Ruyle.

Understudies. Mr. Morfogen (Cornelius)—Charles Anthony Burks; Messrs. Foster, Raiter—George Drance Jr.; Messrs. Kim, Mount, Greer—Jeffrey Fracé; Mr. Garman—David Snider; Mr. Goodwin—Christopher Jean; Mr. Hall—Andrew McGinn; Mr. Schreiber—Anson Mount; Miss Goodman—Holly Natwora; Mr. Stanton—Jeremy Shamos; Mr. Morfogen (Storyteller), Miss Yoo—Wendy Rich Stetson; Mr. Sesma—Jimmie D. Woody; Miss Haberle—Mia Yoo.

Directed by Andrei Serban; scenery, Mark Wendland; costumes, Marina Draghici; lighting, Michael Chybowski; sound, Jeffrey Carlson; composer, Elizabeth Swados; fight direction, J. Steven White; production stage manager, Buzz Cohen; stage manager, Michael Sisolak.

The last major New York revival of *Cymbeline* was in Royal Shakespeare Company repertory at the Brooklyn Academy of Music 6/3/98 for 5 performances.

Note: Press date for *Cymbeline* 8/15/98.

Playwrights Horizons. 1997–98 schedule concluded with **Lillian** (24). Solo performance by David Cale; written by David Cale. Produced by Playwrights Horizons, Tim Sanford artistic director, Leslie Marcus managing director, at Playwrights Horizons Studio Theater. Opened June 15, 1998. (Closed July 5, 1998)

Directed by Joe Mantello; scenery, Robert Brill; lighting, Beverly Emmons; production stage manager, Peter D. Waxdal; press, James LL Morrison & Associates.

Middle-aged woman's passionate love affair with a younger man. The play was presented without intermission.

*De La Guarda (400). Spectacle devised by De La Guarda (Pichon Baldinu, Diqui James, Gabriel Kerpel, Fabio D'Aquila, Tomas James, Alejandro Garcia, Augustina James, Gabriella Baldini); produced by Kevin McCollum, Jeffrey Seller, David Binder and Daryl Roth at the Daryl Roth Theater. Opened June 16, 1998.

CAST: Valeria Alonso, Pichon Baldinu, Gabriela Barberio, Martin Bauer, Mayra Bonard, Carlos Casella, Fabio D'Aquila, Julieta Dentone, Rafael Ferro, Ana Frenkel, Alejandro Garcia, Diqui James, Tomas James, Gabriel Kerpel, Maria Ucedo.

Creator-directors and production designers, Pichon Baldinu, Diqui James; composer and musical direction, Gabriel Kerpel; costumes, De La Guarda, Cecilia Alassia; lighting De La Guarda, Charles Trigueros; sound, De La Guarda; stage manager, Tomas James; press, Richard Kornberg & Associates, Richard Kornberg, Don Summa.

Airborne combination of theatrical and acrobatic effects. A foreign show originially produced in Buenos Aires and previously titled *Villa Villa.*

Lincoln Center Theater. 1997–98 season concluded with **A New Brain** (78). Musical with book by William Finn and James Lapine; music and lyrics by William Finn. Produced by Lincoln Center Theater, under the direction of Andre Bishop and Bernard Gersten, at the Mitzi E. Newhouse Theater. Opened June 18, 1998. (Closed August 23, 1998)

Gordon Michael Schwinn	Malcolm Gets	Richard	Michael Mandell
Lisa	Mary Testa	Dr. Jafar Berensteiner	John Jellison
Rhoda	Liz Larsen	Minister	Keith Byron Kirk
Waitress; Nancy D.	Kristin Chenoweth	Roger Delli-Bovi	Christopher Innvar
Mr. Bungee	Chip Zien	Mimi Schwinn	Penny Fuller

Orchestra: Ted Sperling conductor; Seymour Red Press musical coordinator; Laura Bontrager cello; Alva F. Hunt Jr. woodwinds; Philip Reno synthesizer; Glenn Rhian percussion; Roger K. Wendt, French horn.

Understudies: Messrs. Gets, Kirk—Danny Gurwin; Misses Larsen, Chenoweth—Lovette George; Messrs. Zien, Mandell, Jellison—Stephen Berger; Mr. Innvar—Mark Hardy; Misses Testa, Fuller— Lauren Mufson.

Directed and choreographed by Graciela Daniele; musical direction and additional vocal arrangements, Ted Sperling; scenery, David Gallo; costumes, Toni-Leslie James; lighting, Peggy Eisenhauer; sound, Tony Meola; orchestrations, Michael Starobin; vocal arrangements, Jason Robert Brown; associate producer, Ira Weitzman; casting, Alan Filderman; stage manager, Bonnie Panson; press, Philip Rinaldi, Miller Wright, Brian Rubin.

Composer faces possibility of imminent death from a brain tumor. The play was presented without intermission.

MUSICAL NUMBERS: "Prologue," "The Specials Today," "911 Emergency," "I Have So Many Songs," "Heart and Music," "There's Trouble in His Brain," "Mother's Gonna Make Things Fine," "Be Polite to Everybody," "I'd Rather Be Sailing," "Family History," "Gordo's Law of Genetics," "And They're Off," "Roger Arrives," "Just Go," "Operation Tomorrow," "Poor, Unsuccessful and Fat," "Sitting Becalmed in the Lee of Cuttyhunk," "Craniotomy," "An Invitation to Sleep in My Arms," "Change," "Yes," "In the Middle of the Room," "I Am the Nice Nurse," "Throw It Out," "A Really Lousy Day in the Universe," "Brain Dead," "Whenever I Dream," "Eating Myself Up Alive," "Music Still Plays On," "Don't Give In," "You Boys Are Gonna Get Me in Such Trouble," "The Homeless Lady's Revenge," "Time," "Time and Music," "I Feel So Much Spring."

Smoke on the Mountain (79). Revival of the Gospel musical comedy conceived by Alan Bailey; written by Connie Ray; musical numbers by various authors (see credits below). Produced by

Carolyn Rossi Copeland and Marie B. Corporation at the Lamb's Theater. Opened June 18, 1998. (Closed September 12, 1998)

Vera Sanders	Constance Barron	June Sanders	Jonah Marsh
Dennis Sanders	Sean Dooley	Pastor Mervin Oglethorpe	Robert Olsen
Denise Sanders	Dionne McGuire Gardner	Burl Sanders	Bobby Taylor
Stanley	John Griffith		

Directed by Alan Bailey; musical direction, John Foley; scenery, Peter Harrison; costumes, Pamela Scofield; lighting, Mary Jo Dondlinger; musical arrangements, Mike Craver, Mark Hardwick; associate producer, Nancy Nagel Gibbs; production stage manager, Erika Feldman; stage manager, Dyanne McNamara; press, David Rothenberg Associates, David J. Gersten.

Time: A Saturday night, June 1938. Place: Mount Pleasant Baptist Church, Mount Pleasant, N.C. The play was presented in two parts.

Smoke on the Mountain was originally produced in regional theater by the McCarter Theater, Princeton, N.J. in July 1988 and off Broadway by the Lambs Theater Company 8/14/90 for 332 performances.

MUSICAL NUMBERS (as listed in *Best Plays* for the original production): "Wonderful Time Up There" by Lee Roy Abernathy, "No Tears in Heaven" by Robert S. Arnold, "Christian Cowboy" by Cindy Walker, "The Filling Station" by April Ann Nye, "I'll Never Die (I'll Just Change My Address)" by J. Preston Martinez, "Jesus Is Mine" by Wally Fowler and Virginia Cook, "I'll Live a Million Years" by Lee Roy Abernathy, "I Wouldn't Take Nothing for My Journey Now" by Charles Goodman and Jimmy Davis, "I'm Using My Bible for a Roadmap" by Don Reno and Charles Schroeder, "I'm Taking a Flight" by Kathryn Boyington, "I'll Walk Every Step of the Way" by Mike Craver and Mark Hardwick, "Smoke on the Mountain" by Alan Bailey, "I'll Fly Away" by Albert E. Brumley.

Roundabout Theater Company. 1997–98 schedule concluded with **You Never Can Tell** (81). Revival of the play by George Bernard Shaw. Produced by Roundabout Theater Company, Todd Haimes artistic director, Ellen Richard general manager, at the Laura Pels Theater. Opened June 21, 1998. (Closed August 30, 1998)

Dolly	Catherine Kellner	Crampton	Simon Jones
Valentine	Robert Sean Leonard	M'Comas	Nicholas Kepros
Parlor Maid	Sarah Rafferty	Waiter	Charles Keating
Philip	Saxon Palmer	Bohun	Jere Shea
Mrs. Clandon	Helen Carey	Jo	Greg Keller
Gloria	Katie Finneran	Louis	Phil Tabor

Understudies: Misses Kellner, Finneran—Sarah Rafferty; Miss Carey—Joan Rosenfels; Messrs. Jones, Keating—Julian Gamble; Messrs. Kepros, Shea—Murphy Geyer; Mr. Leonard—Phil Tabor; Mr. Palmer—Greg Keller.

Directed by Nicholas Martin; scenery, Allen Moyer; costumes, Michael Krass; lighting, Frances Aronson; sound and original music, Mark Bennett; casting, Jim Carnahan, Julie Tucker; production stage manager, Julie Baldauff; press, Boneau/Bryan-Brown.

Time: A fine August day at the turn of the century. Place: The coast of Torbay in England. Act I, Scene 1: A dentist's office in a furnished lodging. Scene 2: A terrace at the Marine Hotel, noon. Act II, Scene 1: The Marine Hotel, later in the day. Scene 2: The same, that evening.

The last major New York revival of *You Never Can Tell* was by Circle in the Square on Broadway 10/9/86 for 125 performances.

Love's Fire (32). Program of seven one-act plays inspired by sonnets of William Shakespeare: *Bitter Sauce* by Eric Bogosian; *Hydraulics Phat Like Mean* by Ntozake Shange; *140* by Marsha Norman; *Terminating, or Lass Meine Schmertzen Nicht Verloren Sein, or Ambivalence* by Tony Kushner; *Painting You* by William Finn; *Waiting for Philip Glass* by Wendy Wasserstein; *The General of Hot Desire* by John Guare. Produced by The Acting Company, Margot Harley producing director, at the Estelle R. Newman Theater in The Joseph Papp Public Theater. Opened June 22, 1998. (Closed July 19, 1998)

Bitter Sauce

Sonnet 118 .... Heather Robison
Rengin .... Heather Robison
Herman .... Daniel Pearce
Red .... James Farmer
　　Black comedy, a fiancee tells her future husband about an affair with a biker.

Hydraulics Phat Like Mean

Sonnet 128 .... Jason Alan Carvell
Female Player .... Lisa Tharps
Male Player .... Jason Alan Carvell
　　Original music, Chico Freeman; choreography, Dyane Harvey.
　　Carnal love expressed in dance.

140

Sonnet 140 .... Stephen DeRosa,
　　　　　　　　　　　　　　 Heather Robison
Wife .... Jennifer Rohn
David .... Daniel Pearce
Jackie .... Lisa Tharps
Roland .... Hamish Linklater
Roland's New Lover .... James Farmer
Roland's Lover's
　　New Lover .... Heather Robison
Roland's New Lover's
　　Lover .... Jason Alan Carvell
Lover .... Stephen DaRosa
Lover .... Erika Rolfsrud
　　A round of sexual betrayal.

Terminating, or Lass Meine Schmertzen Nicht Verloren Sein, or Ambivalence

Sonnet 75 .... Daniel Pearce, Lisa Tharps,
　　　　　　　　　　　　　　 Hamish Linklater
Hendryk .... Stephen DeRosa
Esther .... Erika Rolfsrud
Dymphna .... Lisa Tharps
Billygoat .... Hamish Linklater
　　Farcical treatment of the emotional entanglements of a psychiatrist, her patient and their lovers.

Painting You

Sonnet 102 .... James Farmer
Painter .... Stephen DeRosa
Subject .... Jason Alan Carvell
　　Musicians: Jason Robert Brown piano, synthesizer; Mia Wu violin, viola; Sal Spicola woodwinds; Dean Thomas percussion.
　　Original music, William Finn; orchestration and arrangement, Jason Robert Brown.
　　With musical accompaniment, a painter celebrates his lover in his art.

Waiting for Philip Glass

Sonnet 94 ... Jason Alan Carvell, Jennifer Rohn
Holden .... Erika Rolfsrud
Spencer .... Jennifer Rohn
Harry .... Stephen DeRosa
Laura .... Heather Robison
Gerry .... James Farmer
Rina .... Lisa Tharps
Joe .... Daniel Pearce
　　A celebrity-studded party going amiss.

The General of Hot Desire

Sonnet 153 .... Erika Rolfsrud
Sonnet 154 .... James Farmer
Michael .... Hamish Linklater
God .... Stephen DeRosa
Adam; Solomon .... James Farmer
Eve .... Jennifer Rohn
Cain .... Heather Robison
Abel; King of Sheba .... Jason Alan Carvell
Seth .... Daniel Pearce
Seth's Children .... Erika Rolfsrud, Lisa Tharps
Sheba .... Lisa Tharps
　　Also inspired by *The Golden Legend* by Jacobus de Voragine; original music, Adam Guettel; musical direction, Kimberly Grigsby.
　　A group of students, challenged to make the sonnets into a play, comes up with a reworking of Biblical stories.

ALL PLAYS: Directed by Mark Lamos; scenery, Michael Yeargan; costumes, Candice Donnelly; lighting, Robert Wierzel; sound, John Gromada; choreography, Dyane Harvey; produced in association with Ira Pittelman and Jonathan C. Herzog; casting, Bernard Telsey; production stage manager, Jennifer Rae Moore; press, Springer/Chicoine Public Relations, Gary Springer, Susan Chicoine.
　　The program was presented in two parts with the intermission following *Terminating, etc.*

Nunsense A-Men! (231). Revised version of the musical *Nunsense* with an all-male cast; book, music and lyrics by Dan Goggin. Produced by The Nunsense Theatrical Company in association with Joseph Hoesl, Bill Crowder and Jay Cardwell at the 47th Street Theater. Opened June 23, 1998. (Closed January 3, 1999)

Sister Mary Regina .... David Titus
Sister Mary Hubert .... Lothair Eaton
Sister Robert Anne .... Danny Vaccaro
Sister Mary Amnesia .... Greg White
Sister Mary Leo .... Doan Mackenzie
Sister Mary Immaculata .... Tom Dwyer

Musicians: Leo P. Carusone conductor, piano; Daniel Harris synthesizer.
Understudy: Tom Dwyer.
Directed by Dan Goggin; musical staging and choreography, Felton Smith; musical direction, Leo P. Carusone; scenery, Barry Axtell; lighting, Richard Latta; production stage manager, John W. Calder III; press, Pete Sanders Group, Pete Sanders, Glenna Freedman.
Time: The present. Place: Mt. Saint Helen's School auditorium.
The last major New York revival of *Nunsense* took place off Broadway 11/17/95.

ACT I

Welcome .... Regina
"Nunsense Is Habit Forming" .... Company
Opening Remarks .... Regina, Hubert
"A Difficult Transition" .... Company
The Quiz .... Amnesia
"Benedicite" .... Leo
"The Biggest Ain't the Best" .... Hubert, Leo
"Playing Second Fiddle" .... Robert
Taking Resposibility .... Regina
"So You Want To Be a Nun" .... Amnesia
A Word From the Reverend Mother .... Regina
"Turn Up the Spotlight" .... Regina
"Lilacs Bring Back Memories" .... Regina, Hubert, Leo, Amnesia
An Unexpected Discovery .... Regina
"Tackle That Temptation With a Time Step" .... Company

ACT II

Robert to the Rescue .... Robert
"Growing Up Catholic" .... Robert, Leo, Hubert, Amnesia
"We've Got to Clean Out the Freezer" .... Company
A Minor Catastrophe .... Company
"Just a Coupl'a Sisters" .... Regina, Hubert
"Soup's On" (The Dying Nun Ballet) .... Leo
Baking with the BVM .... Sister Julia, Child of God
"Playing Second Fiddle" (Reprise) .... Robert
"I Just Want To Be a Star" .... Robert
"The Drive In" .... Robert, Amnesia, Leo
A Home Movie .... Company
"I Could've Gone to Nashville" .... Amnesia
"Gloria in Excelsis Deo" .... Company
Closing Remarks .... Regina, Company
"Holier Than Thou" .... Hubert, Company
"Nunsense Is Habit Forming" (Reprise) .... Company

The American Place Theater. 1997–98 season concluded with **Sakina's Restaurant** (190). Solo performance by Aasif Mandvi; written by Aasif Mandvi. Produced by The American Place Theater, Wynn Handman artistic director, Carl H. Jaynes general manager, at The American Place Theater. Opened June 24, 1998. (Closed January 3, 1999)

Directed and developed by Kim Hughes; scenery, Tom Greenfield; lighting, Ryan E. McMahon; sound, David Wright; stage managers, Richard A. Hodge, Hurvey Morris; press, Springer/Chicoine Public relations, Gary Springer, Susan Chicoine.
A young immigrant from India learns to live in New York.

Jayson (44). Musical with book by Jeff Krell based on his comic strip; music and lyrics by Ron Romanovsky and Paul Phillips. Produced by Ignite! Entertainment Corp. at the 45th Street Theater. Opened July 10, 1998. (Closed August 16, 1998)

Jayson Callowhill .... Brian Cooper
Arena Stage .... Susan Agin
Robyn Ricketts .... Craig Dawson
Eduardo Rivera; Mr. Feldman ...... Mark Haen

Bertha Callowhill; Stella Stage .... Jane Smulyan
Armistice Callowhill; Stan Stage; Phelps;
Rabbi; Riverdale; DiCerchio .... Kenny Morris
Ensemble ...... D. Matt Crabtree, Alicia Litwin

Understudies: Male Characters—D. Matt Crabtree; Female Characters—Alicia Litwin.

Directed by Jay Michaels; musical direction and arrangements, Simon Deacon; choreography, Kyle Craig; scenery, Jim McNicholas; costumes, Julia N. Van Vliet; lighting, Roger Formosa; conductor, Simon Deacon; assistant choreographer, Lee Wilkins; production stage manager, Joseph Mauro; press, Zeisler Group.

Place: A cartoon world, remarkably similar to our own, in Jayson's apartment, Robyn's apartment, various offices, a movie theater and a temple. The play was presented in two parts.

Love and friendship in the world of the gays.

ACT I

"I May Not Be Much" .... Jayson
"A Friend Like Me" .... Arena
"I'm Here!" .... Robyn
"Video Boys" .... Jayson, Arena
"My Mother's Clothes" .... Robyn, Jason, Arena
"Always a Friend (Never a Lover)" .... Arena, Robyn
"Baby, Take Advantage of Me" .... Jayson
"All We Have to Do" .... Jayson, Arena

ACT II

"The Promise of Love" .... Company
"Authentic" .... Robyn, Jayson, Eduardo
"All You Had to Do" .... Arena
"Dr. Love" .... Eduardo, Company
"He Wasn't Talking to Me" .... Jayson
"Let's Do Lunch" .... Robyn, Company
"Follow Your Heart" .... Jayson, Arena
"Success" .... Jayson, Arena, Robyn

Unzippin' My Doodah and Other National Priorities (46). Revue conceived and written by Bill Strauss and Elaina Newport, with contributions from the cast. Produced by Eric Krebs in association with Capitol Steps at the John Houseman Theater. Opened July 15, 1998. (Closed September 5, 1998)

Mike Carruthers
Andy Clemence
Janet Davidson Gordon
Mike Loomis
Elaina Newport
Ann Margaret Schmitt

Bill Strauss
Mike Thornton
Mike Tilford
Brad Van Grack
Delores King Williams
Jamie Zemarel

Pianists: Howard Breitbart, Lenny Williams.

Directed by Bill Strauss and Elaina Newport; scenery, R.J. Matson; costumes, Robyn Scott; lighting, Marina Bridges; sound, Jill Duboff; press, Jeffrey Richards Associates, Caral Craig, Irene Gandy, Brett Kristofferson.

Political satire, 1998 version, by the group known as Capitol Steps, performing nightly in material which keeps up with events on the political scene. The show was performed without intermission.

Collected Stories (232). Revival of the play by Donald Margulies. Produced by Chase Mishkin, Sonny Everett, Steven M. Levy, Leonard Soloway, by special arrangement with Lucille Lortel, in the HB Playwrights Foundation production at the Lucille Lortel Theater. Opened August 13, 1998. (Closed February 28, 1999)

Ruth .... Uta Hagen
Lisa .... Lorca Simons

THE MOST FABULOUS STORY EVER TOLD—Alan Tudyk, Juan Carlos Hernandez, Becky Ann Baker, Kathryn Meisle, Orlando Pabotoy, Peter Bartlett, Lisa Kron (who also appeared this season at the Public Theater in her solo stint *2.5 Minute Ride*) and Joanna P. Adler in a scene from the play by Paul Rudnick at New York Theater Workshop

Directed by William Carden; scenery, Ray Recht; costumes, Mirenda Rada; lighting, Chris Dallos; sound, Robert Auld; associate producer, Skylight Productions; casting, Adrienne Stern; production stage manager, Pamela Edington; press, Jeffrey Richards Associates, Caral Craig, Irene Gandy, Brett Kristofferson.

Time: 1990 to 1996. Place: Ruth's apartment in Greenwich Village. Act I, Scene 1: September 1990. Scene 2: May 1991. Scene 3: August 1992. Act II, Scene 1: December 1994. Scene 2: October 1996. Scene 3: Later that night.

Collected Stories was previously produced in regional theater by South Coast Repertory, Costa Mesa, Calif. and off Broadway by Manhattan Theater Club 5/20/97 for 80 performances.

Communicating Doors (175). By Alan Ayckbourn. Produced by Harriet Newman Leve and James D. Stern at the Variety Arts Theater. Opened August 20, 1998. (Closed January 3, 1999)

Julian	Gerrit Graham	Ruella	Patricia Hodges
Poopay	Mary-Louise Parker	Harold	David McCallum
Reece	Tom Beckett	Jessica	Candy Buckley

Understudies: Misses Parker, Hodges, Buckley—Judith Lightfoot Clarke; Messrs. McCallum, Beckett, Graham—Jonathan Bustle.

Directed by Christopher Ashley; scenery, David Gallo; costumes, Jess Goldstein; lighting, Donald Holder; original music and sound, John Gromada; fight direction, B.H. Barry; casting, Stuart Howard, Amy Schecter; production stage manager, Kate Broderick; press, The Publicity Office, Bob Fennell, Marc Thibodeau, Michael S. Borowski, Brett Oberman.

Time: 2018, 1998, 1978. Place: A suite in the Regal Hotel, London WC2. The play was presented in two parts.

Comedy mystery involving 20-year-old murder, with time-travelling joining it to the present. A foreign play previously produced in London.

Anne Bobby replaced Mary-Louise Parker 11/98.

Stupid Kids (48). By John C. Russell. Produced by WPA Theater, The Shubert Organization, ABC Inc., Scott Rudin, Roger Berlind and Robert Fox at the Century Theater. Opened August 25, 1998. (Closed October 4, 1998)

Judy Noonan	Shannon Burkett	John "Neechee" Crawford	Keith Nobbs
Jim Stark	James Carpinello	Jane "Kimberly" Willis	Mandy Siegfried

Understudies: Messrs. Carpinello, Nobbs—Danny Seckel; Misses Burkett, Siegfried—Alexandra Johnes.

Directed by Michael Mayer; musical staging, Ken Roberson; scenery, David Gallo; costumes, Michael Krass; lighting, Kevin Adams; sound, Laura Grace Brown; casting, Jim Carnahan; production stage manager, Bradley McCormick; press, James LL Morrison & Associates, James LL Morrison, Tom D'Ambrosio.

Time: First through eighth periods, rest of the day, day in, day out. Place: The 'burbs. The play was presented without intermission.

The world of suburban teenagers represented by two couples: the most admired and most misfit pairs. Previously produced off off Broadway by WPA Theater, Kyle Renick artistic director, Lori Sherman managing director.

MUSIC CREDITS: "Radio Song" by Bill Berry, Peter Buck and Mike Mills; "How Soon Is Now?", "Is It Really So Strange?", "The Headmaster Ritual" by John Marr annd Steven Morrissey; "Wave of Manhattan" by Black Francis; "Lust for Life" by Iggy Pop and David Bowie; "Fall in Love With Me" by Iggy Pop, Hunt Sales and Tony Sales; "Kimberly" by Patti Smith, Ivan Kral and Allen Lanier; "Good Guys and Bad Guys," "Jerry's Daughter" by David Lowery, Jonathan Segel, Victor Krummenacher, Greg Lisher, Chris Molla and Chris Pederson; "Take the Skinheads Bowling" by David Lowery, Chris Molla, Victor Krummenacher and Jonathan Segel; "I Don't See You" by David Lowery, Chris Molla and Eric Laing; "Stupid Kids" by Dan Sezman, Elizabeth Cox, Michael Cudahy and Peter Rutigliano.

Chaim's Love Song (177). By Marvin Chernoff. Produced by The American Renegade Theater in association with Leslie deBeauvais, Edmund Gaynes and David Billotti at the Raymond J. Greenwald Theater. Opened August 26, 1998. (Closed February 14, 1999)

Kelly Burke	Kathleen Marshall	Tzawrah Shotsky	Alice Spivak
Chaim Shotsky	Allen Bloomfield	Stage Manager; Boarder;	
Oscar Birnbaum	Arnold Weiss	Reporter	Jeff Kronson
Reuben Shotsky	Ian Kahn	Pearl Brisistky; Raizel Bokash	Mary Tahmin
Rachel Shotsky	Wendy Axelrod		

Directed by David A. Cox; scenery and lighting, Mark Bloom; costumes, Erica Thomas; production stage manager, Duff Dugan; press, David Rothenberg Associates.

Time: The 1980s, early in October. Place: A very small city park in Brooklyn. Act I, Scene 1: Monday, 8 a.m. Scene 2: Tuesday, 8 a.m. Scene 3: Wednesday, 8 a.m. Act II, Scene 1: Wednesday, 8:25 a.m. Scene 2: Thursday, 8:19 a.m. Scene 3: Three weeks later.

Retiree and young woman rendezvous romantically in their neighborhood park.

International Festival of Puppet Theater. 191 performances of 28 puppet productions from 16 countries, performed by 166 artists with 498 puppets. Produced by The Jim Henson Foundation, Cheryl Henson executive producer, Leslee Asch producing director, Anne Dennin associate producer, in 14 New York City venues (see note). Schedule included 6 off-Broadway programs for adults hosted by the Joseph Papp Public Theater. **UBU & The Truth Commission** (5). Written by Jane Taylor. Opened September 9, 1998. (Closed September 13, 1998) **Tinka's New Dress** (5). Solo performance by Ronnie Burkett; created by Ronnie Burkett. Opened September 9, 1998. (Closed September 13, 1998) **The House of Horror,** solo performance by Paul Zaloom, written by Paul Zaloom, and **Bubbly Beds,** devised by Liz Walker and Gavin Glover (5). Double bill opened September 9, 1998. (Closed September 13, 1998) **Wayang Listrik/Electric Shadows** (7). Shadow theater conceived by I Wayan Wija, Larry Reed and I Dewa Barata. Opened September 15, 1998. (Closed September 20, 1998) **Salomé** (5). Solo performance by Neville Tranter conceived by Neville Tranter; written by Luk van Meerbeke. Opened September 15, 1998. (Closed September 19, 1998) **Short Stories** (6). Created by Ines Pasic and Hugo Suarez. Opened September 15, 1998. (Closed September 20, 1998)

UBU & THE TRUTH COMMISSION

Presented by the Handspring Puppet Company, South Africa, in association with The Kennedy Center African Odyssey Program.

Pa Ubu .... Dawid Minnaar
Ma Ubu .... Busi Sokufa

Puppet Characters—Basil Jones, Adrian Kohler, Louis Seboko.
Directed by William Kentridge; choreography, Robyn Orlin; design, Adrian Kohler, William Kentridge; costumes, Adrian Kohler; lighting, Wesley France; sound, Wilbert Schübel; music, Brendan Jury, Warrick Sony; puppet master, Adrian Kohler; stage manager, Kim Gunning; press, Cromarty & Co., Peter Cromarty, Sherri Jean Katz.
A combination of animation, live actors, puppetry and documentary footage, as a villainous couple testify before The Truth Commission about their part in apartheid.

TINKA'S NEW DRESS

Presented by Ronnie Burkett Theater of Marionettes, Canada.
Music and sound, Cathy Nosaty; choreography, Denise Clarke; marionettes, scenery and costumes, Ronnie Burkett; stage manager, Terri Gillis.
Cast of 37 marionettes in performance by Ronnie Burkett in a fable based on Czech underground shows put on by puppeteers during the Nazi occupation.

THE HOUSE OF HORROR and BUBBLY BEDS

THE HOUSE OF HORROR: Researched and presented by Paul Zaloom, United States.
Design, Joseph John, Paul Zaloom; lighting, Lori A. Dawson; puppet heads, Paul Zaloom; puppet bodies, Barbara Pollitt; puppet costumes, Donna Langman.
Long Island dream house turns into a disaster for the family in residence. An Obie Award-winner previously produced off off Broadway by Dance Theater Workshop and Vineyard Theater.
BUBBLY BEDS: Presented by Faulty Optic, United Kingdom.
Performed by Liz Walker and Gavin Glover.
Design, Gavin Glover; sets and puppets, Liz Walker, Gavin Glover, Martin Smith; music, Hugh Nankivell; video operator, Steve Tiplady.
A family copes with a flooded basement, performing onstage in a fish tank with live feed video.

WAYANG LISTRIK/ELECTRIC SHADOWS

Presented by ShadowLight Productions, Indonesia and United States.
Shadowcasters: I Wayan Wija, Larry Reed, I Nyoman Catra, Ramon Abad, Matthew Antaky, I Made Moja, I Made Sidia, Tim Smith, I Made Sukadana, Emiko Saraswati Susilo.
Musicians: I Dewa Putu Berata, Miguel Frasconi, I Dewa Ketut Alit, I Made Subandi, Sarah Willner.

Directed by Larry Reed and I Wayan Wija; choreography, I Nyoman Catra; scenery, I Dewa Berata, I Made Moja; music and sound, I Dewa Berata, Miguel Frasconi.

Dramatizing the battle between mind and matter.

SALOME

Presented by Stuffed Puppet Theater, Netherlands.

Directed by Luk van Meerbeke; puppets, Neville Tranter; choreography consultant, Lisa Marcus; music, Ake Danielson; costumes, Neville Tranter, Carin Eilers; lighting, Matthias Vogels.

Salomé, Jokanaan, Herod Atipas, Herodias, The Executioner Naaman and Big John portrayed by Neville Tranter in the Biblical story.

SHORT STORIES

Presented by Teatro Hugo & Ines, Peru.

Performed by Ines Pasic and Hugo Suarez.

Mime artistry self-described as "a picturesque parade of amusing characters which, in their brief moments of existence on the scene, seek to catch those poetic moments that are hidden in daily life."

Note: Details of International Festival of Puppet Theater programs for adults presented in off-off-Broadway venues appear in the Plays Produced off off Broadway section of this volume.

New York Theater Workshop. Schedule of four programs. **Culture of Desire** (24). Performance piece conceived by Anne Bogart; created by the Siti Company; presented in the Siti Company, City Theater and Portland Stage production. Opened September 14, 1998. (Closed October 4, 1998). **The Most Fabulous Story Ever Told** (198). By Paul Rudnick. Opened December 10, 1998. (Closed May 2, 1999) **Bright Lights Big City** (31). Musical based on the novel by Jay McInerney; book, music and lyrics by Paul Scott Goodman. Opened February 24, 1999. (Closed March 21, 1999) **The Gimmick** (23). Solo performance by Dael Orlandersmith; written by Dael Orlandersmith. Opened May 5, 1999. (Closed May 23, 1999) Produced by New York Theater Workshop, James C. Nicola artistic director, at New York Theater Workshop.

CULTURE OF DESIRE

CAST: Kelly Maurer, Akiko Aizawa, J. Ed Araiza, Ellen Lauren, Jefferson Mays, Karenjune Sanchez, Stephen Webber.

Understudies: Susan Hightower, Barney O'Hanlon.

Directed by Anne Bogart; scenery, Neil Patel; costumes, James Schuette; lighting, Mimi Jordan Sherin; sound, Darron L. West; company stage manager, Megan Wanlass; stage manager, Charles Means; press, Richard Kornberg.

Diana Vreeland conducts the shade of Andy Warhol through an inferno demonstrating the over-development of the acquisitive instinct in the modern materialistic world. The play was presented without intermission

THE MOST FABULOUS STORY EVER TOLD

Stage Manager .... Amy Sedaris	Shreve Pomfret; Peter; Dad #1; Pharoah;
Adam .... Alan Tudyk	Trey Pomfret .... Peter Bartlett
Steve .... Juan Carlos Hernandez	Cheryl Mindle; Fluffy; Mom #2;
Father Joseph; Bugs; Rhino; Dad #2; Brad;	Peggy .... Joanna P. Adler
Kevin Markham .... Orlando Pabotoy	Jane .... Becky Ann Baker
Miriam Miller; Babe; Mom #1; Ftatateeta;	Mabel .... Kathryn Meisle
Rabbi Sharon .... Lisa Kron	

Directed by Christopher Ashley; scenery, Michael Brown; costumes, Susan Hilferty; lighting, Donald Holder; sound, Darron L. West; choreography, Joey Pizzi; casting, Bernard Telsey; production stage manager, Charles Means; press, Richard Kornberg & Associates.

Biblical tales and modern values juxtaposed and viewed from oblique angles. The play was presented in two parts. Previously produced in regional theater at the Williamstown Theater Festival.

BRIGHT LIGHTS BIG CITY

Writer .... Paul Scott Goodman
Jamie .... Patrick Wilson
Tuff Babe #1; Sally;
  Mary O'Brien McCann .... Carla Bianco
Tuff Babe #2; Theresa; Vicky ..... Natascia Diaz
Drug Girl; Coma Baby; Elise .... Liza Lapira
Tad .... Jerry Dixon
Pinkie; Megan .... Kerry O'Malley

Amanda .... Napiera Daniele Groves
Statue of Liberty; Clara ...... Jacqueline Arnold
Yasu; Michael;
  Drug Dealer #1 .... John Link Graney
Alex; Drug Dealer #2;
  Mad Person .... Ken Marks
Elaine; Mom .... Annmarie Milazzo

Musicians: Joe McGinty conductor, keyboards; Clem Waldmann drums; Paul Ossola bass; Ivan Julian guitar; Lisa Haney cello; Claudia Chopek violin;

Direction and musical staging by Michael Greif; musical direction, Richard Barone; scenery, Paul Clay; costumes, Angela Wendt; lighting, Blake Burba; sound, Jon Weston; orchestrations, Richard Barone; vocal arrangements, Annmarie Milazzo; casting, Bernard Telsey; associate choreographer, Lisa Shriver; production stage manager, Martha Donaldson.

Frustrated writer and husband seeks to find himself in the night spots and other Manhattan diversions of the 1980s.

ACT I

Saturday night/Sunday morning
  Prologue .... Writer
  "Bright Lights Big City" .... Jamie, Company
  "I Love Drugs" .... Jamie, Drug Girl
  "1984/Heartbreak" .... Tad, Jamie, Company
  "Missing" .... Mary O'Brien McCann
  "Beautiful Sunday" .... Jamie, Amanda, Writer
  "Bright Lights Big City" .... Statue of Liberty, Company
Monday
  "Coma Baby/Gotham Magazine" .... Writer, Jamie, Company
  "Can I Come Over Please" .... Sally, Megan, Yasu
  "Fact and Fiction" .... Clara, Alex, Sally, Megan, Yasu, Jamie
  "You Don't Show Me Your Stories Anymore" .... Alex, Jamie
  "I Hate the French" .... Jamie, Co-Workers
  "Brother" .... Michael
  "Monstrous Events" .... Tad, Jamie, Sally, Megan, Yasu, Clara, Alex
Monday night
  "Odeon/Club Crawl" .... Elaine, Theresa, Company
  "I Wanna Have Sex Tonight" .... Tad, Jamie, Company
Tuesday
  "Forest Hills 9 A.M." .... Elise, Jamie
  "Happy Birthday Darling" .... Mom
  "Coma Baby/Missing" .... Jamie, Mary O'Brien McCann, Company
  "Fact and Fiction" .... Alex, Megan, Yasu, Sally, Jamie
  "New Literature" .... Alex
  "Walk" .... Jamie, Writer, Drug Dealer
  "To Model" .... Amanda, Jamie
  "So Many Little Things" .... Jamie, Company

ACT II

Tuesday night
  "It's Great To Be Back in the City" .... Tad, Company
  "Monstrous Events" .... Jamie, Tad
  "Thinkers and Drinkers/Kindness" .... Vicky
  "Perfect Feeling" .... Jamie, Vicky, Company
  "Tonight I Am Happy" .... Jamie
Wednesday
  "You Couldn't Handle It, Jamie" .... Clara

"Come On" .... Writer, Jamie
"Wednesday" .... Writer, Jamie, Company
"Heart and Soul" .... Michael, Vicky, Company
"The Letter" .... Jamie
Wednesday night
"Bad Blow" .... Jamie, Tad
Thursday
"Camera Wall" .... Amanda, Models, Jamie
"Fact and Fiction" .... Co-Workers
"How About Dinner at My Place" .... Megan, Jamie
Thursday night
"My Son" .... Megan, Jamie
Friday
"Missing" .... Mary O'Brien McCann
"Brother 2" .... Michael, Jamie
"Mummies at the Met" .... Jamie, Company
"Are You Still Holding My Hand?" .... Mom
Saturday night/Sunday morning
"Monstrous Events" .... Tad
"Stay in My Life" .... Jamie, Vicky, Company
"Bright Lights Big City" .... Jamie
"Wordfall" .... Writer, Jamie, Company

THE GIMMICK

Directed by Chris Coleman; created and originally directed by Peter Askin; scenery and costumes, Scott Pask; lighting, Matthew Frey; sound, Kurt Kellenberger; production stage manager, Martha Donaldson.

Dael Orlandersmith dramatizes the dreams and sufferings of children growing up severely disadvantaged and neglected in East Harlem, but clinging to great aspirations. Previously produced in regional theater at the McCarter Theater, Princeton, N.J. and the Long Wharf Theater, New Haven, Conn.

The Dying Gaul (39). Transfer from off off Broadway of the play by Craig Lucas. Produced by Vineyard Theater, Douglas Aibel artistic director, Barbara Zinn Krieger executive director and founder, Jon Nakagawa managing director, at the Gertrude and Irving Dimson Theater. Opened September 18, 1998. (Closed October 25, 1998)

Robert .... Tim Hopper   Elaine .... Linda Emond
Jeffery .... Cotter Smith   Foss .... Robert Emmett Lunney

Directed by Mark Brokaw; scenery, Allen Moyer; costumes, Jess Goldstein; lighting, Christopher Akerlind; original music and sound, David Van Tieghem; casting, Janet Foster; production stage manager, Amy Patricia Stern; press, Shirley Herz Associates, Sam Rudy.

Time: 1995. Place: Los Angeles, Calif. The play was presented in two parts.

Triangular tension among a young screen writer, a producer who wants to film his script and the producer's wife. Previously produced off off Broadway last season by Vineyard Theater.

Medea (6). Revival of the play by Euripides; modern Greek translation by Yorgos Heimonas. Produced by ICM Artists Ltd. in association with Kritas Productions Inc. in the National Theater of Greece production, Nikos Kourkoulos artistic director, in the Greek language with English supertitles. Opened September 23, 1998. (Closed September 27, 1998)

Nurse .... Melina Vamvaka   King Aegeus .... Aristotellis Aposkitis
Tutor .... Meletis Georgiadis   Messenger .... Maria Katsiadaki
Medea .... Karyofyllia Karabeti   Prosopeion;
Creon .... Kostas Triantafyllopoulos   Vocal Improvisations .... Savina Yannatou
Jason .... Lazaros Georgakopoulos

Chorus Leaders: Viki Kambouri, Frezi Machaira, Zacharoula Oikonomou, Martha Tomboulidou, Foteini Tsantili, Anni Tsolakidou, Betty Nikolessi. Chorus: Evgenia Apostolou, Vasiliki Demou, Dimitra Zerva, Eleftheria Koutsavlaki, Pari Korahai.

Directed by Niketa Kontouri; scenery and costumes, Yorgos Patsas; lighting, Lefteris Pavlopoulos; music, Savina Yannatou; choreography, Vasso Barbousi; press, James LL Morrison & Associates, Candi Adams, Tom D'Ambrosio, Miguel Tuason, Faith Wilson.

The last major New York revival of *Medea* took place on Broadway 4/7/94.

*The Mystery of Irma Vep (300). Revival of the play by Charles Ludlam. Produced by Steve Asher, Richard Frankel, Thomas Viertel, Steven Baruch and Marc Routh at the Westside Theater. Opened October 1, 1998.

CAST: Jane Twisden, Lord Edgar Hillcrest, Intruder—Stephen DeRosa; Nicodemus Underwood, Lady Enid Hillcrest, Alcazar, Pev Amri—Everett Quinton; Irma Vep—Unspecified.
Understudy: Mike Finesilver.
Directed by Everett Quinton; scenery, John Lee Beatty; costumes, William Ivey Long; lighting, Paul Gallo; original music, Peter Golub; sound, One Dream Sound; casting, Stuart Howard, Amy Schecter; stage manager, Julia P. Jones; press, Helene Davis.
Act I: Mandacrest, on the moors. Act II: Various places in Egypt. Act III: Mandacrest. The play was presented in two parts.
Subtitled A Penny Dreadul, *The Mystery of Irma Vep* was first produced by The Ridiculous Theatrical Company 10/2/84. This is its first major New York revival.

A Night in November (81). Solo performance by Dan Gordon; written by Marie Jones. Produced by Anita Waxman, Edward Burke, Georganne Heller and Elizabeth Williams at the Douglas Fairbanks Theater. Opened October 4, 1998. (Closed December 13, 1998)

Directed by Pam Brighton; scenery and costumes, Robert Ballagh; lighting, Brian McDevitt; press, Boneau/Bryan-Brown,
Dan Gordon as a Belfast Protestant transformed by his realization and disgust at the extent of his bigotry, playing all the parts including wife, children, friends and neighbors.

*Playwrights Horizons. Schedule of four programs. **The Uneasy Chair** (25). By Evan Smith. Opened October 4, 1998. (Closed October 25, 1998) **Freedomland** (23). By Amy Freed. Opened December 16, 1998. (Closed January 3, 1999) **Betty's Summer Vacation** (41). By Christopher Durang. Opened March 14, 1999. (Closed April 18, 1999) ***Goodnight Children Everywhere** (7). By Richard Nelson. Opened May 26, 1999. Produced by Playwrights Horizons, Tim Sanford artistic director, Leslie Marcus managing director, Lynn Landis general manager, at Playwrights Horizons.

THE UNEASY CHAIR

Capt. Josiah Wickett	Roger Rees	Mr. John Darlington	Paul Fitzgerald
Miss Amelia Pickles	Dana Ivey	Edward Cagebee; Others	Michael Arkin
Miss Alexandrina Crosbie	Haviland Morris		

Directed by Richard Cottrell; scenery, Derek McLane; costumes, Jess Goldstein; lighting, Peter Kaczorowski; sound, JR Conklin; casting, James Calleri; production stage manager, Laurie Goldfeder; press, James LL Morrison & Associates, Candi Adams, Tom D'Ambrosio.
Time: The 19th century. Place: London. The play was presented in two parts.
Victorian confrontation between a boarding house keeper and the tenant whom she is suing for breach of promise.

FREEDOMLAND

Sig	Veanne Cox	Polly	Carrie Preston
Titus	Jeff Whitty	Noah	Dakin Matthews

Claude .... Robin Strasser   Lori .... Heather Goldenhersh
Seth .... Jeffrey Donovan

Directed by Howard Shalwitz; scenery, Loy Arcenas; costumes, Candice Donnelly; lighting, Christopher Akerlind; original music and sound, Johnna Doty; fight direction, Allen Suddeth; casting, James Calleri; production stage manager, Amanda M. Sloan.

Time: Around now. Place: An urban artist's studio. An old house somewhere in upstate New York. The play was presented in two parts.

Retired professor's rambunctious offspring intrude on his quiet life in a family reunion. Previously produced in regional theater at South Coast Repertory, Costa Mesa, Calif. and the Woolly Mammoth Theater Company, Washington, D.C.

BETTY'S SUMMER VACATION

Betty .... Kellie Overbey   Mr. Vanislaw .... Guy Boyd
Trudy .... Julie Lund   Voice No. 1 .... Jack Ferver
Keith .... Nat DeWolf   Voice No. 2 .... Geneva Carr
Mrs. Siezmagraff .... Kristine Nielsen   Voice No. 3 .... Godfrey L. Simmons Jr.
Buck .... Troy Sostillio

Directed by Nicholas Martin; scenery, Thomas Lynch; costumes, Michael Krass; lighting, Kevin Adams; sound, Kurt B. Kellenberger; original music, Peter Golub; casting, James Calleri; production stage manager, Kelley Kirkpatrick.

Time: Now. Place: Seashore. The play was presented in two parts.

A black-comedy group of ill-assorted characters turns a summer rental into a haunted house of horrors.

GOODNIGHT CHILDREN EVERYWHERE

Betty .... Robin Weigert   Peter .... Chris Stafford
Ann .... Kali Rocha   Hugh .... John Rothman
Vi .... Heather Goldenhersh   Rose .... Amy Whitehouse
Mike .... Jon DeVries

Directed by Richard Nelson; scenery, Thomas Lynch; costumes, Susan Hilferty; lighting, James F. Ingalls; sound, Raymond D. Schilke; produced by special arrangement with Gregory Mosher and Arielle Tepper; casting, James Calleri; production stage manager, Marjorie Horne.

Time: Late spring, 1945. Place: The living room of a flat in Clapton, South London, England.

In the aftermath of World War II, four teenagers, reunited in their now parentless home in London, set about rebuilding their lives.

*Over the River and Through the Woods (271). By Joe DiPietro. Produced by Jonathan Pollard, Bernie Kukoff, Tony Converse and James Hammerstein at the John Houseman Theater. Opened October 5, 1998.

Nick Cristano .... Jim Bracchitta   Nunzio Cristano .... Dick Latessa
Frank Gianelli .... Val Avery   Emma Cristano .... Marie Lillo
Aida Gianelli .... Joan Copeland   Caitlin O'Hare .... Marsha Dietlein

Understudies: Mr. Bracchitta—Paul Urcioli; Messrs. Avery, Latessa—Herbert Rubens; Misses Copeland, Lillo—Elaine Kussack; Miss Dietlein—Kate Hampton.

Directed by Joel Bishoff; scenery and lighting, Neil Peter Jampolis, Jane Reisman; costumes, Pamela Scofield; music, Jimmy Roberts; casting, Julie Hughes, Barry Moss; stage manager, Megan Schneid; press, Bill Evans & Associates, Jim Randolph.

Time: Most of the play takes place several years ago. Place: Hoboken, New Jersey. The play was presented in two parts.

Comedy, grandparents conspire to prevent their beloved grandson from moving across the country. Previously produced in regional theater at American Stage Company and Berkshire Theater Festival.

Kay Ballard replaced Joan Copeland 4/6/99.

Duet! (87). By Gregory Jackson and Erin Quinn Purcell. Produced by Adobe Theater Company, Jeremy Dobrish artistic director, at the Actors' Playhouse. Opened October 6, 1998. (Closed December 20, 1998)

Exotica Dancer .... Beau Ruland	Lud; Stump; Cop;	
Noam Pearlstein .... Henry Caplan	Supervisor .... Frank Ensenberger	
Lydia Fishback .... Kathryn Langwell	Shadow; Mrs. Wolf; Woody;	
Marcia .... Erin Quinn Purcell	Boss; Doctor .... Derin Basden	
Mike .... Gregory Jackson		

Percussionist: Chris Klimkoski.

Understudies: Misses Ruland, Langwell—Jacqui Malouf; Miss Purcell—Kathryn Langwell.

Directed by Gregory Jackson and Erin Quinn Purcell; co-director, Jeremy Dobrish; scenery, Steven Capone; costumes, Daryl A. Stone; lighting, Paul Ziemer; sound, Chris Todd; original songs, Michael Garin; production stage manager, Sarah Bittenbender; press, Jeffrey Richards Associates.

Subtitled A Romantic Fable, *Duet!*, previously produced off off Broadway, lampoons the traditional values of the boy-meets-girl story. The play was presented without intermission.

*Wit (227). Transfer from off off Broadway of the play by Margaret Edson. Produced by MCC Theater, Robert LuPone and Bernard Telsey executive directors; the Long Wharf Theater, Doug Hughes artistic director, Michael Ross managing director; and Daryl Roth, with Stanley Shopkorn, Robert G. Bartner and Stanley Kaufelt at MCC Theater. Opened October 6, 1998.

Vivian Bearing .... Kathleen Chalfant	Jason Posner .... Alec Phoenix	
Harvey Kelekian;	Susie Monahan .... Paula Pizzi	
Mr. Bearing .... Walter Charles	E.M. Ashford .... Helen Stenborg	

Lab Technicians—Brian J. Carter, Daniel Sarnelli, Alli Steinberg, Lisa Tharps.

Understudies: Misses Chalfant, Stenborg—Tanny McDonald; Mr. Charles—James Shanklin; Mr. Phoenix—Daniel Sarnelli; Miss Pizzi—Lisa Tharps.

Directed by Derek Anson Jones; scenery, Myung Hee Cho; costumes, Ilona Somogyi; lighting, Michael Chybowski; original music and sound, David Van Tieghem; associate producer, Lorie Cowen Levy; casting, Bernard Telsey; production stage manager, Katherine Lee Boyer; press, Boneau/Bryan-Brown, Erin Dunn.

Place: Most of the action, but not all, takes place in a room of the University Hospital Comprehensive Cancer Center. The play was presented without intermission.

Study of the indignities, pains and courage of a woman dying of cancer. Previously produced in regional theater by South Coast Repertory, Costa Mesa, Calif, and Long Wharf Theater, New Haven, Conn., and off off Broadway by and at MCC Theater 9/17/98, adopting a regular off-Broadway schedule starting 10/6/98. Winner of the 1998–99 Pulitzer Prize, and the New York Drama Critics Circle and Lucille Lortel Awards for best play; see its entry in the Prizewinning Plays section of this volume.

*The Joseph Papp Public Theater/New York Shakespeare Festival. Schedule of six programs. **Pericles** (48). Revival of the play by William Shakespeare. Opened October 13, 1998; see note. (Closed November 22, 1998) **The Ride Down Mt. Morgan** (40). By Arthur Miller. Opened October 27, 1998; see note. (Closed November 29, 1998) **Stop Kiss** (40). By Diana Son. Opened November 17, 1998; see note. (Closed December 20, 1998) **Everybody's Ruby** (56). By Thulani Davis. Opened February 23, 1999; see note. (Closed April 11, 1999) **Tongue of a Bird** (40). By Ellen McLaughlin; co-produced with the Mark Taper Forum, Gordon Davidson artistic director/producer. Opened March 16, 1999; see note. (Closed April 18, 1999) ***2.5 Minute Ride** (86). Solo performance by Lisa Kron; written by Lisa Kron. Opened March 17, 1999; see note. Produced by The Joseph Papp Public Theater/New York Shakespeare Festival, George C. Wolfe producer, Rosemarie Tichler artistic producer, Mark Litvin managing director, at the Joseph Papp Public Theater (see note).

ALL PLAYS: Margaret M. Lioi senior director of external affairs; Wiley Hausam, Bonnie Metzgar associate producers; Brian Kulick artistic associate; press, Carol R. Fineman, Thomas V. Naro, Bill Coyle.

The 1998–99 season at The Joseph Papp Public Theater/New York Shakespeare Festival included a production of Shakespeare's *Pericles,* directed by Brian Kulick, with *(above)* Miriam A. Laube as Marina and Jay Goede in the title role; the world premiere of *Stop Kiss* by Diana Son, directed by Jo Bonney, with *(left)* Jessica Hecht; and the New York premiere of Arthur Miller's *The Ride Down Mt. Morgan,* directed by David Esbjornson, with *(below)* Patrick Stewart and Frances Conroy

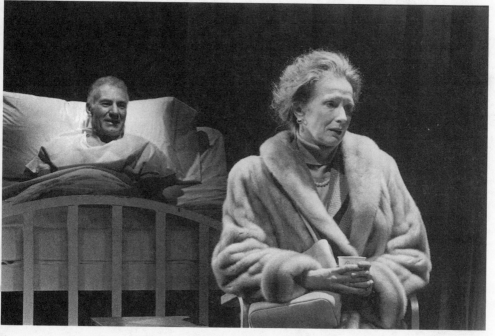

PERICLES

CAST: Gower, Helicanus, 1st Fisherman, Pandar—Philip Goodwin; Antiochus, Simonides, Cerimon—Sam Tsoutsouvas; Pericles—Jay Goede; Antiochus's Daughter, Thaisa—Gail Grate; Thaliard, Knight, Leonine—Francis Jue; Messenger, Knight, Lysimachus—Julio Monge; Cleon, Knight—Geoffrey Owens; Dionyza, Diana—Vivienne Benesch; Messenger, 3d Fisherman, Knight, Boult—Torquil Campbell; 2d Fisherman, Lychorida, Bawd—Viola Davis; Marina—Miriam A. Laube.

Directed by Brian Kulick; scenery, Mark Wendland; costumes, Anita Yavich; lighting, Mimi Jordan Sherin; music, Mark Bennett; sound, JR Conklin; choreography, Naomi Goldberg; casting, Jordan Thaler, Heidi Griffiths; production stage manager, Lisa Iacucci; stage manager, Laura Steib.

Place: In and around the Mediterranean and Aegean Seas. The play was presented in two parts.

The last major New York production of *Pericles* took place in The Joseph Papp Public Theater/New York Shakespeare Festival Shakespeare Marathon 11/5/91 for 56 performances.

THE RIDE DOWN MT. MORGAN

Lyman	Patrick Stewart	Leah	Meg Gibson
Nurse Logan	Oni Faida Lampley	Tom	John C. Vennema
Theo	Frances Conroy	Pianist	Glen Pearson
Bessie	Kali Rocha		

Directed by David Esbjornson; scenery, John Arnone; costumes, Elizabeth Hope Clancy; lighting, Brian MacDevitt; sound and original music, Dan Moses Schreier; casting, Jordan Thaler, Heidi Griffiths; production stage manager, Erica Schwartz.

Time: The present. Place: Elmira, N.Y. and New York City. The play was presented in two parts.

Prominent, commanding middle-aged husband and father involved in a publicity-generating sex scandal.

STOP KISS

Callie	Jessica Hecht	Martha; Nurse	Saundra McClain
Detective Cole	Saul Stein	George	Kevin Carroll
Sara	Sandra Oh	Peter	Rick Holmes

Directed by Jo Bonney; scenery, Narelle Sissons; costumes, Kaye Voyce; lighting, James Vermeulen; sound and original music, David Van Tieghem; casting, Jordan Thaler, Heidi Griffiths; production stage manager, Buzz Cohen.

Time: The Present. Place: New York City. The play was presented without an intermission.

Affection between two New York women grows to the point of a kiss which brings on an act of anti-gay violence.

EVERYBODY'S RUBY

Zora Neale Hurston	Phylicia Rashad	White Citizen; Prosecutor; Suit; Store Owner	James Shanklin
Dr. C. Leroy Adams	Beau Gravitte		
Ruby McCollum	Viola Davis	Black Citizen; Bartender Mechanic	Chuck Patterson
Marie; Waitress; Receptionist	Crystal Fox		
Judge; Pharmacist	Bernie McInerney	Black Citizen; Carpenter	Ron Cephas Jones
Deputy Sherriff Barkley	Raynor Scheine	Librarian Logan "Beau" Shipp	Bryan Webster
White Citizen; Defense Attorney; Suit	J.R. Horne		
White Citizen; Clerk; Mrs. X	Peggy Scott	Barber; Sam McCollum	Bill Nunn
White Citizen; William Bradford Huie	Tuck Milligan		

Directed by Kenny Leon; scenery, Marjorie Bradley Kellogg; costumes, Mariann Verheyen; lighting, Tom Sturge; sound, Jeffrey Carlson; original music, Dwight Andrews; casting, Jordan Thaler, Heidi Griffiths; production stage manager, Lisa Porter.

Time: 1952. Place: Live Oak, Florida.

Dramatization of a real-life Florida murder case in which a much-abused black woman killed her white lover. The play was presented in two parts.

2.5 MINUTE RIDE

Directed by Mark Brokaw; scenery, Allen Moyer; costumes, Jess Goldstein; lighting, Kenneth Posner; sound, Darron L. West; production stage manager, Bess Marie Glorioso.

Lisa Kron's script and performance contrasts two family visits, one to Auschwitz and one to an Ohio amusement park.

TONGUE OF A BIRD

Maxine	Cherry Jones	Evie	Sharon Lawrence
Dessa	Melissa Leo	Charlotte	Julia McIlvaine
Zofia	Elizabeth Wilson		

Directed by Lisa Peterson; scenery, Rachel Hauck; costumes, Candice Cain; lighting, Mary Louise Geiger; original music and sound, Gina Leishman; casting, Jordan Thaler/Cindy Tolan, Stanley Soble; production stage manager, Nancy Elizabeth Vest.

Time: Winter. Place: The Adirondacks. The play was presented in two parts.

Aviatrix on a search-and-rescue mission is haunted by memories of her own past.

Note: Press date for *Pericles* was 11/1/98, for *The Ride Down Mt. Morgan* was 11/16/98, for *Stop Kiss* was 12/6/98, for *Everybody's Ruby* was 3/9/99, for *2.5 Minute Ride* was 3/28/99, for *Tongue of a Bird* was 4/4/99.

Note: In The Joseph Papp Public Theater there are many auditoria. *Pericles* and *Tongue of a Bird* played Martinson Hall, *The Ride Down Mt. Morgan* played the Estelle R. Newman Theater, *Stop Kiss* and *2.5 Minute Ride* played the Susan Stein Shiva Theater, *Everybody's Ruby* played the Florence Anspacher Theater.

*Manhattan Theater Club. Schedule of seven programs. **Corpus Christi** (56). By Terrence McNally. Opened October 13, 1998. (Closed November 29, 1998) **The Memory of Water** (32). By Shelagh Stephenson. Opened November 10, 1998. (Closed December 6, 1998) **The Captain's Tiger: A Memoir for the Stage** (25). By Athol Fugard. Opened January 19, 1999. (Closed February 8, 1999) **Captains Courageous, the Musical** (56). Musical based on the Rudyard Kipling novel and the movie, courtesy of Turner Entertainment Co.; book and lyrics by Patrick Cook; music by Frederick Freyer. Opened February 16, 1999. (Closed April 4, 1999) **Red** (40). By Chay Yew; produced in association with Long Wharf Theater, Doug Hughes artistic director, Michael Ross managing director. Opened March 23, 1999. (Closed April 25, 1999) ***East Is East** (8). By Ayub Khan-Din; produced in association with The New Group, Scott Elliott artistic director, Claudia Catania executive producer. Opened May 25, 1999. And *La Terrasse* by Jean-Claude Carrière, American adaptation by Mark O'Donnell, scheduled to open 6/8/99. Produced by Manhattan Theater Club, Lynne Meadow artistic director, Barry Grove executive producer, *Corpus Christi, Captains Courageous* and *East Is East* at City Center Stage I, *The Memory of Water, The Captain's Tiger* and *Red* at City Center Stage II.

ALL PLAYS: Associate artistic director, Michael Bush; general manager, Victoria Bailey; director of musical theater program, Clifford Lee Johnson III; press, Boneau/Bryan-Brown, Chris Boneau, Andy Shearer,

CORPUS CHRISTI

James, et al.	Sean Dugan	Matthew, et al.	Drew McVety
Thomas, et al.	Christopher Fitzgerald	Joshua	Anson Mount
Peter, et al.	Michael Hall	Bartholomew, et al.	Jeremy Shamos
John, et al.	Michael Irby	Simon, et al.	Ben Sheaffer
James the Less, et al.	Ken Leung	Thaddeus, et al.	Troy Sostillio
Judas	Josh Lucas	Andrew, et al.	Greg Zola
Philip, et al.	Matthew Mabe		

Understudies: Messrs. Mount, Irby—Corey Behnke; Messrs. Sheaffer, Hall, Zola, McVety—Erik Jensen; Messrs. Fitzgerald, Shamos, Dugan, Sostillio—Josh Perilo.

Directed by Joe Mantello; scenery, Loy Arcenas; costumes, Jess Goldstein; lighting, Brian Mac-Devitt; sound, David Van Tieghem; original music and arrangements, Drew McVety; additional musical staging, Jerry Mitchell; casting, Nancy Piccione; production stage manager, James Fitzsimmons.

Group of young actors performs the drama of an imaginary gay Messiah, a Christ-like figure with his twelve apostles in a New Testament-like parable of tolerance.

THE MEMORY OF WATER

Mary	J. Smith-Cameron	Catherine	Seana Kofoed
Vi	Robin Moseley	Mike	David Hunt
Teresa	Suzanne Bertish	Frank	Peter McRobbie

Directed by John Tillinger; scenery, James Noone; costumes, Jess Goldstein; lighting, Donald Holder; sound, Aural Fixation; casting, Nancy Piccione; production stage manager, Leila Knox.

Time: The present. Place: Yorkshire, England.

Three sisters react in different fashions to the death of their mother. The play was presented in two parts. A foreign play previously produced in London.

THE CAPTAIN'S TIGER:
A MEMOIR FOR THE STAGE

The Author	Athol Fugard	Betty	Felicity Jones
Donkeyman	Tony Todd		

Understudies: Mr. Todd—Regi Davis; Mr. Fugard—Bill Largess; Miss Jones—Carol Monda.

Directed by Athol Fugard and Susan Hilferty; scenery and costumes, Susan Hilferty; lighting, Dennis Parichy; original music, Lulu Van Der Walt; casting, Bernard Telsey; production stage manager, Susie Gordon.

Time: 1952. Place: Number Four Hatch of the S/S Graigaur. The play was presented without intermission.

Writer, on a tramp steamer, struggles with a novel about his mother as a young woman. A foreign play previously produced in South Africa and in regional theater at the McCarter Theater, Princeton, N.J.

CAPTAINS COURAGEOUS, THE MUSICAL

Harris	Erick Buckley	Long Jack	Michael X. Martin
Evans; Eliot	Dick Decareau	Capt. Troop	Michael Mulheren
Mr. Cheyne; Peters	Michael DeVries	Murphy; Attendant 2	Gary Schwartz
Harvey E. Cheyne	Brandon Espinoza	Simon; Teacher	Dan Sharkey
Ollie	J. Lee Flynn	Tom Platt; Attendant 1	Daniel Siford
Hemans; Parent	Pete Herber	Dan	Jim Stanek
Walters	George Kmeck	Stephens; Principal	Erik Stein
Doc	Norm Lewis	Manuel	Treat Williams

Orchestra: Robert Gustafson conductor, keyboard; Antony Geralis associate conductor, keyboard, accordion; Alva Hunt flute, clarinet, piccolo; Elizabeth Kieronsky oboe, English horn; Peter T. Simmons bassoon; Stu Satalof trumpet; Peter J. Gordon, French horn; Robert Lawrence violin; Richard Brice viola; Scott D. Ballantyne cello; Louis Bruno bass; Thad J. Wheeler drums, percussion.

Standby: Mr. Williams—Rich Hebert. Understudies: Mr. Lewis—J. Lee Flynn; Mr. Stanek—Daniel Siford; Mr. Espinoza—Reed Van Dyk. Swings: Jody Ashworth, Jason Opsahl.

Directed by Lynne Meadow; musical staging, Jerry Mitchell; musical direction, Robert Gustafson; scenery, Derek McLane; costumes, Catherine Zuber; lighting, Brian MacDevitt; sound, Otts Munderloh; orchestrations, Jonathan Tunick; music advisor, Paul Bogaev; music coordinator, Seymour Red Press; casting, Nancy Piccione; production stage manager, Ed Fitzgerald; stage manager, John J. Harmon.

Time: 1928, over the course of three months; Act II begins two weeks after the end of Act I. Place: Various spots on the North Atlantic and in the port of Gloucester, Mass.

Spoiled young son of a wealthy father falls overboard from an ocean liner, is rescued by a Portuguese fisherman and is exposed to the finer values of character and friendship by the captain and crew of a Gloucester fishing schooner.

ACT I

"Out on the Sea"	Captain, Crew
"Little Fish"	Manuel
"I'm Harvey Ellsworth Cheyne"	Harvey, Captain
"Not So Bad"	Manuel
"I Married a Woman"	Simon
"I Make Up This Song"	Manuel, Harvey
"A Hundred Years Ago"	Crew
"Goodnight, Sweet Molly"	Evans
"She Waits for Me"	Tom, Captain
"That's Where I'm Bound"	Captain, Crew
"Jonah"	Long Jack, Crew
"You Never Saw"	Harvey

ACT II

"Song of the Sea"	Dan, Manuel, Crew
"Grand Banks Sequence/Not This Year"	Captain, Harvey, Crew
"Regular Fellas"	Manuel, Harvey
"I'm Home"	Manuel, Harvey
"I Make Up This Song" (Reprise)	Harvey
"Song of the Sea" (Reprise)	Crew

RED

Sonja	Jodi Long	Ling	Liana Pai
Hua	Ric Young	Opera Actor	Jamie H.J. Guan

Understudy: Messrs. Young, Guan—Mel Duane Gionson.

Directed by David Petrarca; scenery, Michael Yeargan; costumes, Anita Yavich; lighting, James F. Ingalls; original music and sound, Rob Milburn, Michael Bodeen; Beijing opera consultant, Jamie H.J. Guan; casting, Nancy Piccione; production stage manager, Leila Knox.

Place: New York and Shanghai.

Novelist doing research in China is caught up in events of the Cultural Revolution.

EAST IS EAST

George Khan	Edward A. Hajj	Saleem	Gregory J. Qaiyum
Ella Khan	Jenny Sterlin	Meenah	Purva Bedi
Their Children:		Sajit	Rishi Mehta
Abdul	Dariush Kashani	Auntie Annie	Christine Child
Tariq	Rahul Khanna	Dr. Mehta	Sendhil Ramamurthy
Maneer	Amir Sajadi	Mr. Shah	Ajay Mehta

Understudy: Mr. Hajj—Ajay Mehta.

Directed by Scott Elliott; scenery, Derek McLane; costumes, Mattie Ullrich; lighting, Brian Mac-Devitt; sound, Red Ramona; fight direction, J. Allen Suddeth; casting, Nancy Piccione, Judy Henderson; production stage manager, Barnaby Harris.

Time: 1971. Place: Salford, England. The play was presented in two parts.

Family portrait of a mixed marriage, a Pakistani fish-and-chips shop owner and his British wife, with many children and conflicts. A foreign play previously produced by London's Royal Court Theater.

Roundabout Theater Company. Schedule of four programs. **Impossible Marriage** (95). By Beth Henley. Opened October 15, 1998. (Closed January 3, 1999) **Ashes to Ashes** (78). By

Harold Pinter. Opened February 7, 1999. (Closed April 25, 1999) **The Mineola Twins** (117). By Paula Vogel. Opened February 18, 1999. (Closed May 30, 1999) And *Hurrah at Last* by Richard Greenberg scheduled to open 6/3/99. Produced by Roundabout Theater Company, Todd Haimes artistic director, Ellen Richard general manager, Julia C. Levy executive director of external affairs; founding director, Gene Feist; associate artistic director, Scott Ellis; *Impossible Marriage* and *The Mineola Twins* at the Laura Pels Theater, *Ashes to Ashes* at the Gramercy Theater.

IMPOSSIBLE MARRIAGE

Sidney Lunt .... Daniel London
Floral Whitman .... Holly Hunter
Kandall Kingsley .... Lois Smith
Jonsey Whitman .... Jon Tenney
Pandora Kingsley .... Gretchen Cleevely
Rev. Jonathan Larence .... Alan Mandell
Edvard Lunt .... Christopher McCann

Understudies: Miss Smith—Brenda Currin; Messrs. Tenney, McCann, Mandell—Kevin Hogan; Misses Hunter, Cleevely—Monique Vukovic; Mr. London—Leo Kittay.

Directed by Stephen Wadsworth; scenery, Thomas Lynch; costumes, Martin Pakledinaz; lighting, Peter Kaczorowski; sound, Dan Wojnar; founding director, Gene Feist; casting, Julie Tucker; production stage manager, Jay Adler; press, Boneau/Bryan-Brown, Adrian Bryan-Brown, Erin Dunn.

Place: Kandall Kingsley's garden on her country estate outside of Savannah. The play was presented in three parts without intermission.

Southern family's reactions to an impending, undesirable marriage.

ASHES TO ASHES

Rebecca .... Lindsay Duncan
Devlin .... David Strathairn

Standbys: Miss Duncan—Kate Skinner; Mr. Strathairn—Kent Broadhurst.

Directed by Karel Reisz; scenery and costumes, Tony Walton; lighting, Richard Pilbrow; sound, Tom Clark; casting, Jim Carnahan; production stage manager, Jay Adler.

Place: A university town outside of London. The play was presented without intermission.

A marriage in trouble. A foreign play previously produced in London.

THE MINEOLA TWINS

Myrna/Myra .... Swoosie Kurtz
Jim; Sarah .... Mo Gaffney
Kenny; Ben .... Mandy Siegfried
Man No. 1 .... Daniel Sherman
Man No. 2 .... Jimmy Holder

Standby: Miss Kurtz—Ellen Foley. Understudies: Ms. Gaffney, Mr. Siegfried—Drew Richardson; Messrs. Sherman, Holder—Matthew Montelongo.

Directed by Joe Mantello; scenery, Robert Brill, Scott Pask; costumes, Jess Goldstein; lighting, Kevin Adams; sound, David Van Tieghem; musical staging, Ken Roberson; casting, Jim Carnahan, Amy Christopher; production stage manager, James FitzSimmons; stage manager, Andrew Bryant.

Time: Scenes 1 and 2 take place during the Eisenhower administration. Scenes 3 and 4 take place at the beginning of the Nixon administration. Scenes 5 and 6 take place during the Bush administration. The play was presented in two parts with the intermission following Scene 3.

Lives of two sisters greatly differing in personality and values add up to a reflection of American suburbia over the past four decades. The play was presented in two parts.

Julie Kavner replaced Mo Gaffney 3/30/99.

*Killer Joe (265). By Tracy Letts. Produced by Darren Lee Cole and Scott Morfee in association with 29th Street Rep at the Soho Playhouse. Opened October 18, 1998.

Chris Smith .... Mike Shannon
Sharla Smith .... Amanda Plummer
Ansel Smith .... Marc A. Nelson
Dottie Smith .... Sarah Paulson
Killer Joe Cooper .... Scott Glenn

Understudies: Messrs. Nelson, Shannon, Glenn—Allyn Burrows; Misses Plummer, Paulson—Mary Hammett.

Directed by Wilson Milam; scenery, George Xenos; costumes, Jana Stauffer; lighting, Greg Mac-Pherson; sound, Hired Gun/One Dream; fight staging, J. David Brimmer; production stage manager, Richard Hodge; press, Shirley Herz Associates, Shirley Herz, Vanessa Meza.

Time: The present. Place: The Smiths' trailer on the outskirts of Dallas, Texas. The play was presented in two parts.

Brutal results of a dysfunctional trailer-park family's scheming hostilities. It is a new play on the off-Broadway scene but was previously produced off off Broadway by 29th Street Rep and in Edinburgh.

Paul Dillon replaced Scott Glenn and Jan Leslie Harding replaced Amanda Plummer 1/99. Lori Petti replaced Jan Leslie Harding 3/99.

Retribution (29). By Mark R. Shapiro; based on the novel *Who Shall Live, Who Shall Die* by Daniel Stern. Produced by Jadbro Productions at the Lamb's Theater. Opened October 24, 1998. (Closed November 11, 1998)

Carl Walkowitz	Dennis Christopher	Larry Elgin	Stuart Zagnit
Judah Kramer	Jack Laufer	Paul Rovic	Paul Stolarsky
Marianne Kramer	Jenna Stern	Joe Quinn	Walter Hudson

Understudies: Messrs. Laufer, Zagnit, Hudson, Stolarsky—Curt Hostetter; Miss Stern—Linnea Pyne; Mr. Christopher—Walter Hudson.

Directed by Michael Unger; scenery, Narelle Sissons; costumes, Candice Donnelly; lighting, Christopher J. Landy; sound, David Lynd; casting, Cindi Rush; production stage manager, Marci A. Glotzer; stage manager, Dan Zittel; press, Susan L. Schulman.

Time: The winter of 1965. Place: New York City. Act I, Scene 1: Kramer apartment, morning. Scene 2: Theater, the next afternoon. Scene 3: Kramer apartment, that night. Act II, Scene 1: Kramer apartment, afternoon, one month later. Scene 2: Theater, same afternoon. Scene 3: Kramer apartment, that night. Act III, Scene 1: Kramer apartment, four days later. Scene 2: Theater, same afternoon. Scene 3: Backstage, that night. Scene 4: Theater, half hour later. Scene 5: Outside cemetery, two days later. The play was presented in two parts.

The revenge of a Holocaust survivor on a onetime fellow-prisoner in a concentration camp.

Zora Neale Hurston (51). Revival of the play by Laurence Holder; produced by The American Place Theater, Wynn Handman artistic director, Carl H. Jaynes general manager, in association with the National Black Touring Circuit, Woodie King Jr. producer, at The American Place Theater. Opened October 29, 1998. (Closed December 13, 1998)

Zora Neale Hurston .... Elizabeth Van Dyke
Herbert Sheen, Langston Hughes, Alain Locke, Richard Wright .... Joseph Edward

Directed by Wynn Handman; design, Ryan E. McMahon; production stage manager, Wendy Ouellette; press, Springer/Chicoine Public Relations, Gary Springer, Susan Chicoine, Ann Guzzi, Charlie Siedenberg.

Time: Christmas Eve, 1949; Place: A bus station, New York City.

The last major New York production of this biographical play about "The Queen of the Harlem Renaissance" was by American Place 4/29/92 for 60 performances.

Second Stage Theater. Schedule of four programs. **This Is Our Youth** (240). By Kenneth Lonergan; presented by special arrangement with Barry and Fran Weissler and The New Group. Opened November 3, 1998. (Closed May 2, 1999) **That Championship Season** (14). Revival of the play by Jason Miller. Opened April 21, 1999. (Closed May 2, 1999) And *Gemini* by Albert Innaurato scheduled to open 6/16/99; and *Jar the Floor* by Cheryl West scheduled to open 8/11/99. Produced by Second Stage Theater, Carole Rothman artistic director, Carol Fishman managing director, Alexander Fraser executive director, at the Second StageTheater.

THIS IS OUR YOUTH

Dennis Ziegler .... Mark Rosenthal   Jessica Goldman .... Missy Yager
Warren Straub .... Mark Ruffalo

Directed by Mark Brokaw; scenery, Allen Moyer; costumes, Michael Krass; lighting, Mark Mc-Cullough; sound, Robert Murphy; fight direction, Rick Sordelet; production stage manager, William H. Lang; press, Richard Kornberg, Don Summa.

Parental abuse, thievery and drugs among post-adolescents of New York's Upper West Side. Previously produced off off Broadway by The New Group.

THAT CHAMPIONSHIP SEASON

Tom Daley .... Michael O'Keefe   Phil Romano .... Dennis Boutsikaris
George Sikowski .... Ray Baker   Coach .... James Gammon
James Daley .... Dylan Baker

Directed by Scott Ellis; scenery, Allen Moyer; costumes, Jennifer von Mayrhauser; lighting, Kenneth Posner; sound, Kurt B. Kellenberger; fight direction, David Leong; casting, Jim Carnahan; production stage manager, Lori M. Doyle; stage manager, Michael Sisolak; press, Richard Kornberg, Don Summa.

Time: 1972. Place: The Coach's house, somewhere in the Lackawanna Valley, Pennsylvania. The play was presented without intermission.

That Championship Season was first produced off Broadway 5/2/72 for 144 performances and transferred to Broadway 9/14/72 for an additional 700 performances. It was named a Best Play of the 1971–72 season, also winning the Critics Award for best play regardless of category. Following its transfer, it won the 1972–73 Pulitzer Prize and best-play Tony. This is its first major New York revival of record.

Behind the Counter With Mussolini (39). Solo performance by Marco Greco; written by Marco Greco and Dante Albertie. Produced by Myrna E. Duarte and Behind the Counter Productions at the Theater at Saint Peter's Church. Opened November 11, 1998. (Closed December 13, 1998)

Directed by Stephen Adly Guirgis; scenic consultant, James Morgan; lighting, Zdenek Kriz; associate producer, Dan Dzindzihashvili; production stage manager, Jason Cohen; press, The Zeisler Group, Ellen Zeisler.

Subtitled An Italian-American Folk Tale, a lad in the process of growing up, working in his dictatorial father's Italian deli. The play was presented in two parts.

Brooklyn Academy of Music. Schedule of six programs. **Anna Karenina** (6). Adapted by Helen Edmundson from the novel by Leo Tolstoy; presented in the Shared Experience production, Nancy Meckler artistic director, Polly Teale associate director. Opened November 11, 1998. (Closed November 15, 1998) **Phèdre** (10), new version by Ted Hughes of the play by Jean Racine, opened January 5, 1999; and **Britannicus** (4), new version by Robert David Macdonald of the play by Jean Racine, opened January 8, 1999; presented in repertory in the Almeida Company productions, Jonathan Kent and Ian McDiarmid joint artistic directors. (Repertory closed January 17, 1999) **Blue Heart** (23) Program of two one-act plays by Caryl Churchill in the Out of Joint production, Graham Cowley producer: *Heart's Desire* and *Blue Kettle.* Opened January 30, 1999. (Closed February 21, 1999) **Le Cid** (7). Revival of the play by Pierre Corneille in the French language with English surtitles; presented in the Festival d'Avignon production. Opened April 6, 1999; see note. (Closed April 10, 1999) And *The Image Makers* by Per Olov Enquist scheduled to open 6/4/99. Produced by Brooklyn Academy of Music, Bruce C. Ratner chairman of the board, Harvey Lichtenstein president and executive producer, at the Majestic Theater.

ANNA KARENINA

CAST: Stiva, Bailiff, Petritsky—Simeon Andrews; Dolly, Countess Vronsky—Karen Ascoe; Anna—Teresa Banham; Princess Betsy, Agatha, Governess, Railway Widow—Katharine Barker; Kar-

THIS IS OUR YOUTH—Missy Yager and Mark Ruffalo in a
scene from Kenneth Lonergan's play at Second Stage Theater

enin, Priest—Ian Gelder; Levin—Richard Hope; Kitty, Seriozha—Pooky Quesnel; Vronsky, Nikolai—
Derek Riddell.

Peasants, Muffled Figures—Members of the company.

Directed by Nancy Meckler; design, Lucy Weller; lighting, Chris Davey; music, Peter Salem; casting,
Toby Whale; press, Susan Yung.

Time: The 1870s. Place: Russia.

Tolstoy's drama of a woman's passion and despair, with the Levin-Kitty characters and story brought
into prominence as a companion piece to the central Anna-Vronsky affair. A foreign play previously
produced at the Theater Royal, Winchester, England.

PHEDRE and BRITANNICUS

Performer	*Phèdre*	*Britannicus*
David Bradley	Theramene	Burrus
Holly de Jong	Panope	
Avril Elgar	Ismene	
John Fairfoul	Guard	Guard
Julian Glover	Theseus	Narcissus
Colin Haigh		Guard
Barbara Jefford	Oenone	Albina
Kevin McKidd		Britannicus
Diana Rigg	Phèdre	Agrippina
Joanna Roth	Aricia	Julia
Toby Stephens	Hippolytus	Nero

Undersudies: Holly de Jong, John Fairfoul, Colin Haigh, Seána Montague.

BOTH PLAYS: Directed by Jonathan Kent; design, Maria Björnson; lighting, Mark Henderson; music, Jonathan Dove; sound, John A. Leonard; casting, Wendy Brazington; company stage manager, Rupert Carlile; American stage manager, Kim Beringer. *Phèdre* filmmaker, Tony Palmer.

Both plays were presented without intermission. Foreign plays previously produced in England.

The last major New York production of *Phèdre* took place off Broadway in a new translation by William Packard 2/10/66 for 100 performances. The last major New York production of *Britannicus* was in the Comédie Française production .at New York City Center 3/2/61 for 4 performances.

BLUE HEART

Performer	*Heart's Desire*	*Blue Kettle*
Gabrielle Blunt		Mother
Bernard Gallagher	Brian	Mr. Vane
Mary Macleod	Maisie	Mrs. Oliver
Doreen Mantle		Mrs. Vane
Pearce Quigley	Lewis	Derek
Alexandra Roberts	Young Australian Woman	
Sally Rogers	Susy	Enid
June Watson	Alice	Mrs. Plant
Anna Wing		Miss Clarence

Directed by Max Stafford-Clark; scenery and costumes, Julian McGowan; lighting, Johanna Town; sound, Paul Arditti; stage manager, Kim Beringer.

In *Heart's Desire,* parents and an aunt await the return of a daughter who has been away for years. In *Blue Kettle,* a 40-year-old man pretends to be a son given up for adoption many years ago. Foreign plays previously produced in London.

LE CID

Infanta of Castile	Sandrine Attard	Don Alonse	Nicolas Ducron
Don Diegue	Michel Baumann	Prince	Benjamin Dupé
Don Gomes	Philippe Blancher	Chimene	Sarah Karbasnikoff
Leonor	Odile Cointepas	Don Rodrigue	William Nadylam
Elvire	Josephine Derenne	Don Fernand	Patrick Rameau
Don Arias	Laurent Desponds	Don Sanche	Yaneck Rousselet

Directed by Declan Donnellan; scenery, Philippe Marioge; costumes, Jacques Perdiguès; lighting, Judith Greenwood; music, Benjamin Dupé; stage manager, Kim Beringer.

The last major New York revival of *Le Cid* was the Comédie Française production in French on Broadway 2/11/66 for 5 performances.

Note: Press date for *Le Cid* was 4/7/99.

Stratford Festival. Repertory of two revivals. **Much Ado About Nothing** (11). By William Shakespeare. Opened November 12, 1998. **The Miser** (8). By Molière. Opened November 14, 1998. Produced by Stratford, Canada Festival, Richard Monette artistic director, Judith E. Daykin president and executive director, at the City Center. (Repertory closed November 12, 1998)

MUCH ADO ABOUT NOTHING

The Household:

Leonato	William Hutt		Guests: Victoria Adilman, Michelle Giroux, Ngozi Paul, Laurel Thomson.
Hero	Jennifer Gould		
Beatrice	Martha Henry	The Visitors:	
Antonio	Joseph Shaw	Don Pedro	James Blendick
Margaret	Chick Reid	Don John	Tom McCamus
Ursula	Sandi Ross	Benedick of Padua	Brian Bedford
Maid	Claire Jullien	Claudio of Florence	Tim MacDonald

Borachio .... Jeffrey Renn
Conrade .... Ian Deakin
Messenger .... Shawn Campbell
Balthasar .... Jonathan W. Munro
Boy .... Michael Therriault
    Soldiers: Evan Buliung, Bradford Farwell,
Rory Feore, Anthony McLean.
The Town:

Dogberry .... Stephen Ouimette
Verges .... Brian Tree
Sexton .... David Glass
George Seacole .... Michael Therriault
Hugh Oatcake .... Shawn Campbell
Richard Cowley .... Bradford Farwell
Robert Armin .... Rory Feore
Friar Francis .... John Gilbert

Musicians: Berthold Carrière conductor, keyboards; Christophe Chiasson violin; Ian Harper flute, piccolo, clarinet and soprano, alto and tenor saxophone; Holly Shepard trumpet; Patricia Mullen cello; Jerry Johnson trombone; Don MacDonald guitar, banjo; Kevin Muir bass; David Campion percussion.

Standby: Miss Henry—Chick Reid. Understudies: Miss Gould—Victoria Adilman; Messrs. Munro, Deakin—Evan Buliung; Messrs. Blendick, Renn, Farwell—Shawn Campbell; Messrs. Bedford, Gilbert—Ian Deakin; Messrs. Shaw, Tree, Glass, Campbell—Bradford Farwell; Messrs. MacDonald, Therriault—Rory Feore; Mr. Hutt—John Gilbert; Miss Jullien—Michelle Giroux; Mr. McCamus—Anthony McLean; Miss Ross—Ngozi Paul; Messrs. Ouimette, Campbell, Feore—Michael Therriault; Miss Reid—Laurel Thomson.

Directed by Richard Monette; scenery, Guido Tondino; costumes, Ann Curtis; lighting, Michael J. Whitfield; sound, Jim Neil; composer, Berthold Carrière; fight direction, James Binkley; choreography, Valerie Moore; production stage manager, Nora Polley; press, Philip Rinaldi.

The last major New York revival of *Much Ado About Nothing* took place last season 3/25/98 for 13 performances at the Brooklyn Academy of Music. The play was presented in two parts.

THE MISER

Harpagon .... William Hutt
Elise .... Michelle Giroux
Cleante .... Michael Therriault
Valere .... David Glass
Mariane .... Victoria Adilman
La Fleche .... Richard Curnock
Master Simon;
    Seigneur Anselm .... Joseph Shaw

Frosine .... Martha Henry
Jacques .... Brian Tree
Justice of the Peace .... Jeffrey Renn
Clerk to the Justice .... Ian Deakin
1st Servant .... Bradford Farwell
2d Servant .... Jonathan W. Monro

Musicians: Berthold Carrière conductor, keyboards; Christophe Chiasson violin; Sharon Kahan flute; Donna-Claire McLeod oboe; Patricia Mullen cello; Marilyn Dallman harpsichord; Jennifer Gould soprano.

Understudies: Messrs. Therriault, Renn—Evan Buliung; Mr. Curnock—Ian Deakin; Messrs. Glass, Tree—Bradford Farwell; Miss Adilman—Jennifer Gould; Miss Giroux—Claire Jullien; Messrs. Shaw, Farwell, Deakin—Anthony Mclean; Mr. Monro—Ngozi Paul; Miss Henry—Laurel Thomson; Mr. Hutt—Brian Tree.

Directed by Richard Monette; scenery and costumes, Meredith Caron; lighting, Michael J. Whitfield; sound, Peter McBoyle; composer, Berthold Carrière; production stage manager, Nora Polley.

Time: 1668. Place: Paris—a day in the household of Monsieur Harpagon. The play was presented in three parts.

The last major New York revival of *The Miser* was by Circle in the Square on Broadway 10/11/90 for 93 performances.

The Primary English Class (9). By Israel Horovitz. Produced by Ron Kastner at the Minetta Lane Theater. Opened November 15, 1998. (Closed November 22, 1998)

Smiednik .... Edward Furs
Patumiera .... Mark Lotito
LaPoubelle .... Charles Stransky
Mulleimer .... Kenneth Garner
Mrs. Pong .... Diane Cheng

Yoko Kuzukago .... Nami Hirayanagi
Debbie Wastba .... Didi Conn
Male Translator .... Daniel Whitner
Female Translator .... Jurian Hughes

Standby: Miss Conn—Jurian Hughes. Understudies: Messrs. Furs, Whitner—Buzz Roddy; Messrs. Lotito, Stransky, Garner—Thomas A. Hays; Misses Cheng, Hughes—Jade Wu; Miss Hirayanagi—Kimmy Zuzuki.

Directed by Gerald Gutierrez; scenery, Derek McLane; costumes, Catherine Zuber; lighting, Peter Kaczorowski; sound, Aural Fixation; fight direction, Rick Sordelet; casting, Stuart Howard, Amy Schecter; production stage manager, Michael Brunner; press, Philip Rinaldi, Barbara Carroll, Brian Rubin.

Black comedy of a teacher out of tune with herself and her non-English-speaking pupils, previously staged in New York's tributary theater in the 1970s, but with no production of record.

*Forbidden Broadway Cleans Up Its Act! (224). Musical revue created and written by Gerard Alessandrini. Produced by John Freedson, Harriet Yellin and Jon B. Platt at the Stardust Theater. Opened November 17, 1998.

Bryan Batt   Edward Staudenmayer
Lori Hammel   Kristine Zbornik

Understudies: Messrs. Batt, Staudenmayer—William Selby; Misses Hammel, Zbornik—Ellen Margulies.

Directed by Phillip George and Gerard Alessandrini; choreography, Phillip George; musical direction, Matthew Ward; costumes, Alvin Colt; lighting, Marc Janowitz; produced in association with Steve McGraw, Nancy McCall, Peter Martin, Gary Hoffman, Jerry Kravat and Mazakazu Shibaoka; scenery, Bradley Kaye; production stage manager, Jim Griffith; press, The Pete Sanders Group, Pete Sanders, Glenna Freedman.

Newest edition of the revue parodying the current New York Theater scene. The show was presented in two parts.

Trainspotting (17). By Harry Gibson; adapted from the novel by Irvine Welsh. Produced by Columbia Artists and Arielle Tepper, Aldo Scrofani executive producer, at the Players Theater. Opened November 15, 1998. (Closed November 29, 1998)

CAST: June, Girl in Pub, Alison, Lizzie—Tessa Auberjonois; Tommy, Sick Boy, Drunkard—Josh Peace; Franco, Johnny, Mother—Sebastian Roché; Mark, Boy in Pub—Seth Ullian.

Directed by Harry Gibson; scenery, Joe Robinson; costumes, Julie Robbins; lighting, Jeffrey Koger; sound, Raymond D. Schilke; production stage manager, Christine Catti: press, The Publicity Office, Bob Fennell.

Lower levels of the drug-addicted set in today's Edinburgh. A foreign play previously produced in Glasgow in 1994 and as a movie in 1996.

All Under Heaven (65). Solo performance by Valerie Harper; written by Dyke Garrison with Valerie Harper. Produced by Randolph-Macon Woman's College and Tony Cacciotti at the Century Theater. Opened November 16, 1998. (Closed January 10, 1999)

Directed by Rob Ruggiero; scenery, Michael Schweikardt; costumes, Peg Carbonneau; lighting, John Wade; sound, Ron Barnett; production stage manager, Christina Massie; press, David Rothenberg Associates, David J. Gersten.

Act I: The afternoon of May 24, 1972 in Pearl Buck's office in her home in Danby, Vermont. Act II: Moments later.

A biographical study, with Valerie Harper as the Nobel Prizewinning author Pearl S. Buck at 79 and other characters who took part in challenging events of her life.

Far East (168). By A.R. Gurney. Produced by Lincoln Center Theater under the direction of Andre Bishop and Bernard Gersten at the Mitzi E. Newhouse Theater. Opened January 10, 1999. (Closed June 6, 1999)

Stagehands	Mia Tagano,	James Anderson	Bill Smitrovich
	Toshiro Akira Yamamoto	Julia	Lisa Emery
Reader	Sonnie Brown	Bob Munger	Connor Trinneer
Sparky Watts	Michael Hayden		

Musician: Carlos Valdez.
Understudies: Stagehands—Ariel Estrada; Miss Brown—Mia Tagano; Messrs. Hayden, Trinneer—Barnaby Carpenter; Mr. Smitrovich—Bill Cwikowski; Miss Emery—Susan Wilder.

FAR EAST—Lisa Emery, Michael Hayden and *(top right)* Sonnie Brown in the Lincoln Center production of A.R. Gurney's play

Directed by Daniel Sullivan; scenery, Thomas Lynch; costumes, Jess Goldstein; lighting, Rui Rita; original music and sound, Dan Moses Schreier; casting, Daniel Swee; stage manager, Roy Harris; press, Philip Rinaldi.

Time: July 1954–October 1955. Place: Japan. The play was presented in two parts.

Young American stationed in Japan during the Korean War tries to absorb the unfamiliar culture, in the midst of a love affair with a Japanese woman.

*A Couple of Blaguards (213). By Frank and Malachy McCourt. Produced by Howard Platt, Steve McGraw, Nancy McCall and Peter Martin at the Triad Theater. Opened January 13, 1999.

Malachy McCourt .... Shay Duffin
Frank McCourt .... Mickey Kelly

Directed by Howard Platt; scenery and costumes, Gloria Parker; lighting, Matt Berman; associate producers, Lawrence Kelly, Dan Conway; stage manager, Alan Fox; press, Philip Rinaldi, Miller Wright.

Brothers remember the youthful escapades of growing up in Ireland and in Brooklyn.

Malachy McCourt replaced Shay Duffin.

Rollin' on the T.O.B.A. (45). Musical revue conceived by Ronald "Smokey" Stevens and Jaye Stewart; featuring excerpts from *The Simple Stories* by Langston Hughes; additional material by Irvin S. Bauer. Produced by John Grimaldi, Ashton Springer and Frenchman Productions, Inc. at the 47th Street Theater. Opened January 28, 1999. (Closed March 7, 1999 and transferred to Broadway; see its entry in the Plays Produced on Broadway section of this volume)

Stewart .... Ronald "Smokey" Stevens   Bertha Mae Little .... Sandra Reaves-Phillips
Stevens .... Rudy Roberson

Understudies: Messrs. Stevens, Roberson—Jackie Jay Patterson; Miss Reaves-Phillips—Alyson Williams.

Directed and choreographed by Ronald "Smokey" Stevens and Leslie Dockery; musical direction and arrangements, David Alan Bunn; scenery, Larry W. Brown; costumes, Michele Reisch; lighting, Jon Kusner; sound, Shabach Audio; associate producers, Martin Shugrue, Carriene Nevin; stage manager, Juliana Hannett; press, The Jacksina Company, Judy Jacksina, Ed Ku.

Time:1931. Place: On the Theater Owners' Booking Association circuit.

A performance tribute to the last days of black vaudeville, originally presented by the AMAS Musical Theater, Rosetta LeNoire founder and artistic director.

ACT I

Overture
"Rollin' on the T.O.B.A." .... Stevens, Stewart, Bertha Mae
    (by Ronald "Smokey" Stevens, Sandra Reaves-Phillips, Chapman Roberts, Benny Key and David Alan Bunn)
Scene 1: On the Train
Toast to Harlem .... Stevens, Stewart
    (by Langston Hughes)
Scene 2: Monogram Theater
Bill Robinson Walk .... Stevens
    (by Bill "Bojangles" Robinson)
"Evolution"/"Ugly Chile" .... Stevens, Stewart
    (by Miller & Lyles/Clarence Williams)
Scene 3: Bertha's phone call
"Travelin' Blues" .... Bertha Mae
    (by Ronald "Smokey" Stevens and Sandra Reaves-Phillips)
Scene 4: Dressing room
Lincoln West/The Liar (Staggolee) .... Stevens, Stewart
    (by Gwendolyn Brooks and Terrence Cooper)
Scene 5: Royal Theater
Fish Fry .... Stevens, Stewart
    (by Ellis Walsh and Louis Jordan)
Scene 6: Bertha's letter/On the train
"St. Louis Blues" .... Bertha Mae
    (by W.C. Handy)
Scene 7: Booker T. Theater
The Poker Game .... Stevens
    (by Bert Williams; "Black & Tan Fantasy" music by Duke Ellington)
Nobody .... Stevens
    (by Bert Williams)
"Huggin' & Chalkin'" .... Stewart
    (by Kermit Goell and Clancey Hayes)
"Sexy Blues"/"You've Taken My Blues and Gone" .... Bertha Mae
    (by Sandra Reaves-Phillips, Chapman Roberts and Ronald "Smokey" Stevens/
    Langston Hughes)
The Car Crash and Broken Dialog .... Stevens, Stewart
    (by Miller & Lyles)
Conversationalization .... Stevens, Stewart
    (by Miller & Lyles)

"Let the Good Times Roll" .... Company
    (by Sam Theard and Fleecie Moore)

ACT II

Entr'acte
Piano Interlude .... David Allen Bunn
Scene 1: Regal Theater
  "Hop Scop Blues" .... Stevens
    (by Clarence Williams)
  The Chess Game .... Stevens, Stewart
    ("Funeral March of the Marionettes" music by Charles Gounod)
Scene 2: Bertha's Show/The Regal Theater
  "Take Me As I Am" .... Bertha Mae
    (by Sandra Reaves-Phillips)
  "One Hour Mama" .... Bertha Mae
    (by Porter Grainger)
  "Million Dollar Secret" .... Bertha Mae
    (by Helen Humes and Jules Bihari)
  Freddie and Flo .... Bertha Mae, Stewart
    (by Butterbeans and Suzie)
  "A Good Man Is Hard to Find" .... Bertha Mae
    (by Eddie Green)
  "Take Me As I Am" (Reprise) .... Bertha Mae
Scene 3: On the train
  Simple on Integration .... Stevens, Stewart
    (by Langston Hughes)
  Soul Food .... Company
    (by Langston Hughes)
Scene 4: On the train
  Banquet in Honor .... Stevens, Stewart
    (by Langston Hughes)
  "I'm Still Here"/"Trouble in Mind" .... Company
    (by Langston Hughes/Richard Jones)
  "Rollin' on the T.O.B.A." (Reprise) .... Company

James Naughton: Street of Dreams (69). Solo performance by James Naughton; conceived by James Naughton. Produced by Mike Nichols at the Promenade Theater. Opened February 4, 1999. (Closed April 11, 1999)

The Band: John Oddo piano; Dave Pietro saxophone; Jay Azzolina guitar; Steve Laspina bass; Ray Marchica drums.

Musical direction, John Oddo; producers, Julian Schlossberg, Chase Mishkin, David Stone; scenery, John Lee Beatty; lighting, Tharon Musser; sound, Domonic Sack; associate producers, The Araca Group, Meyer Ackerman; production stage manager, Karen Moore; press, Boneau/Bryan-Brown, Chris Boneau, Jackie Green.

Concert of jazz and popular songs with monologues including excerpts of Larry Gelbart dialogue from the Broadway musical *City of Angels*. The show was presented without intermission.

Encores! Great American Musicals in Concert. Schedule of three musical revivals presented in limited concert engagements. **Babes in Arms** (5). Musical with book by Richard Rodgers and Lorenz Hart; music by Richard Rodgers; lyrics by Lorenz Hart. Opened February 11, 1999. (Closed February 14, 1999) **Ziegfeld Follies of 1936** (6). Musical revue with sketches by David Freedman and Ira Gershwin; music by Vernon Duke; lyrics by Ira Gershwin. Opened March 25, 1999. (Closed March 29, 1999) **Do Re Mi** (5). Musical with book by Garson Kanin; music by Jule Styne; lyrics by Betty Comden and Adolph Green. Opened May 7, 1999. (Closed

May 9, 1999) Produced by City Center, Kathleen Marshall artistic director, Rob Fisher musical director, Judith E. Daykin president and executive director, at the City Center.

BABES IN ARMS

Emma Blackstone	Priscilla Lopez	Lee Calhoun	Shaun Powell
Nat Blackstone	Thommie Walsh	Beauregarde Calhoun	Matthew Ballinger
Marshall Blackstone	Perry Laylon Ojeda	Dolores Reynolds	Jessica Stone
Mazie LaMar	Donna McKechnie	Peter	Kevin Cahoon
Dan LaMar	Don Correia	Irving de Quincy	Scott Irby-Ranniar
Val LaMar	David Campbell	Ivor de Quincy	Cartier Anthony Williams
Billia Smith	Erin Dilly	Baby Rose	Melissa Rain Anderson
Sheriff Reynolds	Richard Riehle	Rene Flambeau	Matt McGrath
Gus Fielding	Christopher Fitzgerald	Phil McCabe	Michael McCormick

Quartet: Chris Hoch, Mark Lanyon, Daniel C. Levine, Ben Saypol. Dancing Girls: Pamela Jordan, Tina Ou, Amanda Paige, Amber Stone. Dancing Boys: Justin Geer, Josh Prince, Noah Racey, James Tabeek. Singing Girls: Kate Baldwin, Sharon Richards.

The Coffee Club Orchestra: Rob Fisher conductor; Red Press flute, piccolo; Robert Ingliss oboe, English horn; David Tofani alto saxophone, clarinet, flute, piccolo; Lino Gomez alto saxophone, clarinet; Alva Hunt tenor saxophone, clarinet; Paul Gallo clarinet, bass clarinet, bassett horn; John Frosk, Robert Millikan, Kamau Adilifu trumpet; Jack Gale trombone; Joseph Thalken, Mark Mitchell piano; Glenn Rhian drums, percussion; Suzanne Ornstein concert mistress; Belinda Whitney-Barratt, Maura Giannini, Martin Agee, Christoph Franzgrote, Mineko Yajima, Eric De Gioia, Ashley Horne, Rebekah Johnson violin; Jeanne LeBlanc, Lanny Paykin cello; John Beal acoustic bass.

Directed and choreographed by Kathleen Marshall; script consultant, John Guare; scenic consultant, John Lee Beatty; costume coordinator, Toni-Leslie James; lighting, Peter Kaczorowski; sound, Scott Lehrer; original orchestrations, Hans Spialek; musical coordinator, Seymour Red Press; associate choreographer, Robert Ashford; casting, Jay Binder; production stage manager, Maximo Torres; stage manager, Daniel S. Rosokoff; press, Philip Rinaldi.

The last major New York revival of *Babes in Arms* was by Equity Theater off Broadway 10/20/67 for 15 peformances.

ACT I

Overture .... Orchestra, Priscilla Lopez, Thommie Walsh, Donna McKechnie, Don Correia
The Kitchen of the Lamars' house, Seaport, L.I.
  "Where or When" .... David Campbell, Erin Dilly
  "Babes in Arms" .... Perry Laylon Ojeda, Campbell, Dilly, The Gang
The Oscar W. Hemingway Post of the American Legion
  "I Wish I Were in Love Again" .... Christopher Fitzgerald, Jessica Stone
  "Babes in Arms" (Reprise) .... Richard Riehle, The Gang
A clubhouse
  "Light on Their Feet" .... Scott Irby-Ranniar, Cartier Anthony Williams
The Calhouns' living room
  "Way Out West" ...... Melissa Rain Anderson, Chris Hoch, Mark Lanyon, Daniel C. Levine, Ben Saypol
The LaMars' house
  "My Funny Valentine" .... Dilly
The stage of the Old Barn Theater
  "Johnny One-Note" .... Anderson, The Gang

ACT II

Entr'acte .... Orchestra
A stable on the work farm
  "Imagine" .... Anderson, Hoch, Lanyon, Levine, Saypol
  "All at Once" .... Campbell, Dilly
Ballet: Peter's Journey .... Kevin Cahoon, Gang

The LaMars' field
"The Lady Is a Tramp" .... Dilly
"You Are So Fair" .... Fitzgerald, Stone
"The Lady Is a Tramp" (Reprise) .... Dilly
A bedroom in the LaMars' house
The Oscar W. Hemingway Post of the American Legion
Finale .... Company

ZIEGFELD FOLLIES OF 1936

Roles originated by Rodney McLennan .... Howard McGillin
Roles originated by Fanny Brice .... Mary Testa
Specialty Trio .... Bob Walton, Jim Walton, Karen Ziemba
Roles originated by Eve Arden .... Christine Ebersole
Roles originated by Bob Hope .... Peter Scolari
Sketch Comics .... Stanley Bojarski, Kevin Chamberlin
Roles originated by Josephine Baker .... Stephanie Pope
Roles originated by Gertrude Niesen .... Ruthie Henshall
Ballet Soloists .... Jenifer Ringer, Jonathan Sharp, Jock Soto

Show Girls: Dottie Earle, Jennifer Frankel, Amy Heggins, Pamela Jordan, Aixa M. Rosario Medina, Tamlyn Brooke Shusterman, Wendy Waring, Deborah Yates. Dancers: Stephen Campanella, Angelo Fraboni, Aldrin Gonzalez, Peter Gregus, Jeffrey Hankinson, Jack Hayes, Wes Pope, Rocker Verastique. Varsity Eight: Timothy Breese, Tony Capone, Nat Chandler, Will Gartshore, Chris Hoch, Damon Kirsche, Eric van Hoven, Joseph Webster.

The Coffee Club Orchestra: Rob Fisher conductor; Red Press alto saxophone, flute, piccolo, clarinet; Al Regni alto saxophone, clarinet; Rick Heckman tenor and alto saxophone, oboe, clarinet, English horn; Lawrence Feldman tenor saxophone, clarinet, bass clarinet; John Frosk, Glenn Drewes, Kamau Adilifu trumpet; Jack Gale trombone; John Redsecker drums; Erik Charlston percussion; Leslie Stifelman, Joe Thalken piano; Suzanne Ornstein concert mistress; Belinda Whitney-Barratt Maura Giannini, Martin Agee, Christoph Franzgrote, Xin Zhao, Rebekah Johnson, Katherine Livolsi-Stern, Mineko Yajima, Lisa Matricardi violin; Jill Jaffe, Richard Brice, David Blinn, Kenneth Burward-Hoy viola; Clay Ruede, Lanny Paykin cello; John Beal bass.

Directed and adapted by Mark Waldrop; choreography, Thommie Walsh; ballet choreography, Christopher Wheeldon; scenery consultant, John Lee Beatty; costume coordinator, Gregg Barnes; lighting, Peter Kaczorowski; sound, Scott Lehrer; projections, Eyewash, Inc.; original orchestrations, Robert Russell Bennett, Conrad Sallinger, Hans Spialek, Don Walker; musical coordinator, Seymour Red Press; original performance material reconstructed by Mark Trent Goldberg; original orchestrations restored by Steven D. Bowen; vocal arrangements, Rob Fisher; casting, Jay Binder; production stage manager, Arturo E. Porazzi; stage manager, Casey Rafter.

This *Ziegfeld Follies* opened at the Winter Garden 1/30/36 and played 115 performances. It returned as *Ziegfeld Follies of 1936–37* for 112 additional performances 9/14/36.

ACT I

Overture .... Orchestra
"Time Marches On" .... Howard McGillin, Varsity Eight, Show Girls
"He Hasn't a Thing Except Me" .... Mary Testa
"My Red-Letter Day" .... Karen Ziemba, Bob Walton, Jim Walton
Of Thee I Spend
Miss Gherkin .... Christine Ebersole   John D. Littlefeller .... Kevin Chamberlin
Rexford Givewell .... Peter Scolari   Charles G. Clawes .... Stanley Bojarski
"Island in the West Indies" .... Ebersole, Stephanie Pope, McGillin,
Varsity Eight, Show Girls, Dancers
Psychoanalysis
Phoebe .... Mary Testa   Dr. Fradler .... Peter Scolari
Nurse .... Karen Ziemba
"Words Without Music" .... Ruthie Henshall, Jenifer Ringer, Jonathan Sharp, Jock Soto

"The Economic Situation" .... Ebersole, Show Girls
"Fancy, Fancy" (by Ira Gershwin)
Sir Henry .... Kevin Chamberlin   Zuleika .... Mary Testa
Sir Robert .... Peter Scolari
"Night Flight" .... Ringer
The Reading of the Play
Flyde Twitch .... Stanley Bojarski   Warren Bruce .... Tony Capone
Mlle. Leonore .... Christine Ebersole   Pierre .... Timothy Breese
Armand .... Nat Chandler   Alphonse .... Eric van Hoven
Producer .... Kevin Chamberlin
"Maharanee" .... McGillin, Pope, Varsity Eight, Dancers
"The Gazooka," a super-special musical photoplay (by David Freedman and Ira Gershwin)
Conductor .... Tony Capone   Casting Agent .... Jim Walton
Father .... Kevin Chamberlin   Producer .... Howard McGillin
Mother .... Stanley Bojarski   Dolores Del Morgan .... Ruthie Henshall
Bing Powell .... Peter Scolari   Director .... Bob Walton
Aviator .... Will Gartshore   Large Supporting Cast
Ruby Blondell .... Mary Testa   of Featured Players .... Company

ACT II

Entr'acte .... Orchestra
"That Moment of Moments" .... Henshall, McGillin, Company
"Sentimental Weather" .... Ziemba, Bob and Jim Walton
Baby Snooks Goes Hollywood
Director .... Peter Scolari   Joan Crawford .... Ruthie Henshall
Mrs. Higgins .... Christine Ebersole   Grip .... Kevin Chamberlin
Baby Snooks .... Mary Testa   Official .... Stanley Bojarski
Clark Gable .... Howard McGillin   Newsreel Man .... Joseph Webster
"5 A.M." .... Pope, Ringer, Soto, Dancers
The Petrified Elevator
Operator .... Peter Scolari   Pickpocket .... Jim Walton
Doctor .... Peter Gregus   Allan .... Bob Walton
Actress .... Ruthie Henshall   Husband .... Howard McGillin
Banker .... Kevin Chamberlin   Old Woman .... Christine Ebersole
Anxious Girl .... Karen Ziemba   Author .... Jack Hayes
Evangelist .... Stanley Bojarski   Quiet Woman .... Jennifer Frankel
Tax Collector .... Jonathan Sharp
"Modernistic Moe" .... Testa
"I Can't Get Started" (by Ira Gershwin) .... Scolari, Ebersole.
"Dancing to the Score" .... McGillin, Company

DO RE MI

Kay Cram .... Randy Graff   Photographer .... John Herrera
Hubert Cram .... Nathan Lane   Reporter .... Patricia Ben Peterson
Waiter .... Blake Hammond   Marsha Denkler .... Marilyn Cooper
John Henry Wheeler ..... Brian Stokes Mitchell   Irving Feinberg .... Gerry Vichi
M.C. .... Brad Oscar   Gretchen Mulhausen .... Tovah Feldshuh
Fatso O'Rear .... Lee Wilkof   Tilda Mullen .... Heather Headley
Brains Berman .... Lewis J. Stadlen   Moe Shtarker .... Michael Mulheren
Skin Demopoulos .... Stephen DeRosa   Chief Counsel .... Michael X. Martin

The Swingers: Leslie Castay, Colleen Fitzpatrick, Ann Kittredge. The Animal Girls: Amy Heggins, Nancy Lemenager, Carol Lee Meadows, Michelle O'Steen, Greta Martin, Tamlyn Brooke Shusterman. The Dancers: Brad Aspel, Vince Pesce, Josh Prince, Noah Racey. The Singers: Leslie Castay, Colleen Fitzpatrick, Blake Hammond, Dale Hensley, John Herrera, Ann Kittredge, Michael X. Martin, Brad Oscar, Patricia Ben Peterson, Gerry Vichi.

Orchestra: Paul Gemignani guest conductor; Mark Mitchell associate conductor, piano; Red Press flute, piccolo, alto flute, clarinet, alto saxophone; Al Regni flute, piccolo, clarinet, alto saxophone; Dennis Anderson oboe, English horn, clarinet, tenor saxophone; David Tofani tenor saxophone, clarinet, bass clarinet; John Campo baritone saxophone, clarinet, bass clarinet, bassoon; John Frosk, Stu Satalof, Kamau Adilifu trumpet; Jack Gale, Bruce Eidem trombone; Jack Schatz bass trombone; Mike Berkowitz drums; Erik Charlston percussion; Andy Schwartz acoustic & electric guitar; Suzanne Ornstein concert mistress; Martin Agee, Christoph Franzgrote, Maura Giannini, Rebekah Johnson, Robert Lawrence, Laura Seaton, Belinda Whitney-Barratt, Mineko Yajima violin; Clay Ruede, Lanny Paykin cello; John Beal acoustic bass.

Directed by John Rando; choreography, Randy Skinner; musical direction, Paul Gemignani; scenery consultant, John Lee Beatty; costume coordinator, David C. Woolard; lighting, Ken Billington; sound, Bruce Cameron; concert adaptation, David Ives; original orchestration, Luther Henderson; musical coordinator, Seymour Red Press; production stage manager, Arturo E. Porazzi.

Do Re Mi was first produced on Broadway 12/26/60 for 400 performances. This is its first major New York revival.

ACT I

Overture .... Orchestra
The Casacabana
   "Waiting" .... Randy Graff
   "All You Need Is a Quarter" .... Leslie Castay, Colleen Fitzpatrick, Ann Kittredge
Hubie and Kay's apartment
   "Take a Job" .... Nathan Lane, Graff
   "Waiting" (Reprise) .... Graff
Fatso's Ice Cream Parlor
   "All You Need Is a Quarter" .... Castay, Fitzpatrick, Kittredge, Dancers
   "It's Legitimate" .... Lane, Lee Wilkof
The Music Enterprise Associates, Inc. office
   "It's Legitimate" .... Lane, Wilkof, Lewis J. Stadlen, Stephen DeRosa, Men
John Henry Wheeler's office
   "I Know About Love" .... Brian Stokes Mitchell
The Music Enterprise Associates, Inc. office
   The Auditions .... Marilyn Cooper, Gerry Vichi, Tovah Feldshuh
The Zen Pancake Parlor
   "Cry Like the Wind" .... Heather Headley
   "Ambition" .... Lane, Headley
All over town
   Juke Box Montage .... Lane, Headley, Singers, Dancers
A recording studio
   "Fireworks" .... Mitchell, Headley
The Imperial Room
   "What's New at the Zoo" .... Headley, Animal Girls
   "Asking for You" .... Mitchell
   "The Late, Late Show" .... Lane

ACT II

Entr'acte .... Orchestra
Hubie and Kay's apartment
   "Adventure" .... Lane, Graff
John Henry Wheeler's office
   "Make Someone Happy" .... Mitchell, Headley
The Music Enterprise Associates, Inc. office
   "Adventure" (Reprise) .... Graff
The city
   Investigation—Prelude: Trouble .... Michael Mulheren, Singers, Dancers
A hearing room in the Senate Office Building
   Investigation—"Who Is Mr. Big?" .... Wilkof, Stadlen, DeRosa, Singers, Dancers

IT AIN'T NOTHIN' BUT THE BLUES—Gretha Boston and Ron Tayor in the musical revue which came from cross-country theater to the New Victory Theater for its New York premiere, thence to the Vivian Beaumont and a Tony nomination as best musical

Investigation—"He's a V.I.P." .... Lane, Singers, Dancers
"All of My Life" .... Lane
Finale .... Graff, Lane, Company

*Beautiful Thing (120). By Jonathan Harvey. Produced by Roy Gabay and Ron Kastner in The Famous Door Theater Company production, Dan Rivkin artistic director, at the Cherry Lane Theater. Opened February 14, 1999.

Jamie	Matt Stinton	Ste	Daniel Eric Gold
Leah	Susan Bennett	Tony	Kurt Brocker
Sandra	Kirsten Sahs		

Directed by Gary Griffin; scenery, Robert G. Smith; costumes, Kari Beth Rust; lighting, Jeff Pines; sound, Lindsay Jones; production stage manager, Shawn Senavinin; press, Sam Rudy/Shirley Herz Associates.

Time: May 1993. Place: Thamesmead, South East London. The play was presented in two parts.

Distressed teen-agers find and love each other against the odds in a working-class neighborhood. A foreign play previously produced in London.

***Jodie's Body** (112). Transfer from off off Broadway of the solo performance by Aviva Jane Carlin; written by Aviva Jane Carlin. Produced by The ArcLight Theater Company, Julian Schlossberg artistic director, William Repicci managing director, and Gloria Steinem, Chris Groenewold and Meyer Ackerman at the ArcLight Theater. Opened February 18, 1999.

Directed by Kenneth Elliott; scenery, B.T. Whitehill; lighting, Vivien Leone; Diana K. Roesch associate producer; production stage manager, Chris Groenewold; press, Jeffrey Richards & Associates.
Time: April 29, 1994. Place: London.The play was presented without intermission.
Aviva Jane Carlin as a model who poses in the nude for art students.

***Snakebit** (104). Transfer from off off Broadway of the play by David Marshall Grant. Produced by Hal Luftig, Daryl Roth and Ted Snowdon in association with Roy Gabay in The Naked Angels production at the Century Theater for the Performing Arts. Opened March 1, 1999.

Jonathan	David Alan Basche	Michael	Geoffrey Nauffts
Jenifer	Jodie Markell	Young Man	Michael Weston

Understudies: Messrs. Basche, Nauffts—Patrick Boll; Miss Markell—Claire Beckman; Mr. Weston—Drew Starlin.
Directed by Jace Alexander; scenery, Dean Taucher; costumes, Elizabeth Roles; lighting, Renee Molina; sound, Raymond D. Schilke; production stage manager, Kimberly Ann Berdy; press, Richard Kornberg, Don Summa, Rick Miramontez, Jim Byk.
Place: Los Angeles. Act I: Monday. Act II, Scene 1: Wednesday. Scene 2: Thursday morning.
Tensions among a gay social worker, his wife and his best childhood friend, an actor up for a major movie role.

The New 42nd Street Inc. Schedule of two programs. **Mujeres y Hombres** (5). Flamenco dance program presented in the Flamenco Vivo production, Carlota Santana artistic director. Opened March 17, 1999. (Closed March 21, 1999) **It Ain't Nothin' But the Blues** (16). Musical revue based on an original idea by Ron Taylor; written by Charles Bevel, Lita Gaithers, Randal Myler, Ron Taylor and Dan Wheetman; music by various authors (see listing below); presented in the Crossroads Theater Company production, Ricardo Kahn artistic director, in association with San Diego Repertory Theater, Sam Woodhouse artistic director, and Alabama Shakespeare Festival, Kent Thompson artistic director. Opened March 26, 1999. (Closed April 11, 1999 and transferred to Broadway; see its entry in the Plays Produced on Broadway section of this volume) Produced by The New 42nd Street Inc., Cora Cahan president, at the New Victory Theater.

MUJERES Y HOMBRES

Carmen's Sisters

La Gitana	Clara Mora	The Wife	Elena Andujar
The Maiden	Tania Garcia	The Mother	Esperanza Montes

Created and choreographed by Clara Mora; directed by Seret Scott; music, David Serva; guitarist, David Serva.
Flamenco expressions of the gypsy life cycle.

Bailaor

With Antonio Hidalgo, Rodrigo Alonso, Pedro Blasquez.
Musicians: Roberto Castellón guitar, Terence Butler flute. Singer: El YiYi.
Choreographed by Antonio Hidalgo; music, Roberto Castellón.
The evolution of male dancing from the end of the last century until today.

Ask for Me
    With Carlota Santana, Antonio Hidalgo.
    Choreographed by Antonio Hidalgo.
Finale—Entire Company.

    ALL DANCES: Lighting, Annmarie Duggan; stage manager, Frank Ramirez; press, Lauren
Daniluk.

IT AIN'T NOTHIN' BUT THE BLUES

Charles Bevel	Gregory Porter
Gretha Boston	Ron Taylor
Carter Calvert	Dan Wheetman
Eloise Laws	

    The Band: Kevin Cooper bass; Jim Ehinger keyboards; Debra Laws backup vocals; Tony Mathews
guitar, Daryll Whitlow percussion; Charlie Rhythm sax, horns.
    Understudy: Misses Boston, Calvert, Eloise Laws—Debra Laws.
    Directed by Randal Myler; musical direction Dan Wheetman; musical staging, Donald McKayle;
vocal direction, Lita Gaithers; scenery, Robin Sanford Roberts; costumes, Dione H. Lebhar; lighting,
Don Darnutzer; sound, Edward Cosla; production stage manager, Linda Harris.
    History represented by visual projections of events and intertwined with songs from African chants
to American blues.

    MUSICAL NUMBERS, ACT I: "Odun De" (traditional)—Company; "Niwah Wechi" (tradi-
tional)—Eloise Laws, Company; "Blood Done Signed My Name" (traditional)—Ron Taylor, Gretha
Boston; "Raise Them Up Higher" (traditional)—Charles Bevel; "Danger Blues" (traditional)—Laws;
"Black Woman" (traditional)—Gregory Porter; "I'm Gonna Do What the Spirit Say Do" (traditional)—
Boston; "I've Been Living With the Blues" (by Sonny Terry)—Company; "Blues Man" (by Z.Z. Hill)—
Taylor; "My Home's Across the Blue Ridge Mountains" (traditional)—Carter Calvert; "'T' for Texas"
(by Jimmie Rogers)—Dan Wheetman; "Who Broke the Lock?" (traditional)—Porter, Bevel; "Ga-
brielle" (by Dan Wheetman)—Wheetman, Taylor; "Goin' to Lousianne" (by Ron Taylor)—Taylor;
"My Man Rocks Me" (traditional)—Laws; "St Louis Blues" (by W.C. Handy)—Boston; "Now I'm
Gonna Be Bad" (by Dan Wheetman)—Calvert; "Walkin' Blues" (by Robert L. Johnson)—Bevel;
"Come on in My Kitchen" (by Robert L. Johnson)—Porter; "Crossroad Blues" (by Robert L. Johnson)—Bevel; "Children, Your Line Is Dragging" (traditional, arranged by Fisher Thompson Sr.)—
Porter; "How Can I Keep From Singing" (traditional)—Calvert; "I Know I've Been Changed" (tradi-
tional)—Boston; "Go Tell It on the Mountain" (traditional)—Laws; "Child of the Most High King"
(traditional, arranged by Ron Taylor)—Taylor, Men; "Catch on Fire" (traditional, arranged by Lita
Gaithers)—Company.
    ACT II: "Let the Good Times Roll" (by F. Moore and S. Theard)—Taylor; "Sweet Home Chicago"
(by Robert L. Johnson)—Porter, Bevel; "Wang Dang Doodle" (by Willie Dixon)—Boston, Calvert,
Laws; "Someone Else Is Steppin' In" (by Denise LaSalle)—Laws; "Please Don't Stop Him"/"Blues
Medley" (by Herb J. Lance and John Wallace, additional lyrics and arrangements by Lita Gaithers)—
Boston; "I'm Your Hoochie Coochie Man" (by Willie Dixon, arranged by Ron Taylor)—Taylor; "Craw-
lin' King Snake" (by John Lee Hooker)—Porter; "Mind Your Own Business" (by Hank Williams Sr.)—
Wheetman; "Walking After Midnight" (by Don Hect and Alan Block)—Calvert; "I Can't Stop Lovin'
You" (by Don Gibson)—Bevel; "The Thrill Is Gone" (by Roy Hawkins and Rick Darnell)—Taylor;
"I Put a Spell on You" (by Jay Hawkins)—Laws; "Fever" (by John Davenport and Eddie Cooley)—
Calvert; "Candy Man" (traditional)—Wheetman; "Good Night, Irene" (by Huddie Ledbetter)—Bevel,
Wheetman; "Strange Fruit" (by Lewis Allan)—Boston; "Someday We'll All Be Free" (by Donny Hath-
away and Edward Howard, arranged by Charles Bevel)—Bevel, Porter; "Members Only" (by Larry
Addison)—Company; "Let the Good Times Roll" (Reprise)—Company.

    *Savion Glover: Downtown (49). Performance piece created by the cast. Produced by Dodger
Theatricals in association with Maniactin Productions Inc. at the Variety Arts Theater. Opened
April 20, 1999.

With Savion Glover and the NYOTs (Not Your Ordinary Tappers)—Ayodele Casel, Omar Edwards, Abron Glover, Jason Samuels.

Poetry—Reg E. Gaines.

Musicians: Eli Fountain percussion; Gregory Jones bass; Tommy James keyboards; Patience Higgins saxophone, flute.

Directed and choreographed by Savion Glover; musical direction, Eli Fountain; costumes, Virginia Webster; lighting, Mike Baldassari; sound, John Shivers, Bob Harari; stage manager, Thomas McMorrow Jr.; press, Boneau/Bryan-Brown, Adrian Bryan-Brown, Amy Jacobs.

Combination of impromptu and scheduled musical performances featuring tap dancing and including selections from the program listed here.

MUSICAL NUMBERS: "Love of Money"—Savion Glover, Company; "Thievery!"—Savion, Company; "Milestones"—Savion; "Quick Thoughts From AG!"—Abron Glover; "Bof Booof"—Savion, Company; "At This Moment"—Ayodele Casel; "Sentimental Mood"—Savion; "The Track"—Savion, Company; "Sheik & E"—Savion, Company; "Air Jordans"—Savion, Reg E. Gaines; "All Blues Jam"—Savion, Company; "Murder"—Jason Samuels; "Caravan"—Savion; "Some Killa Sh*"—Gaines; "Silk Suits"—Savion, Company; "Incog-Negroes"—Savion, Company; "Swing a Li'l Funk Into Gang Gang"—Savion, Company; "Ain't Nobody"—Savion, Company; "Forget . me . knots"—Gaines, Savion, Company.

*2 1/2 Jews (32) Transfer from off off Broadway of the play by Alan Brandt. Produced by Do Gooder Productions, Mark Robert Gordon founding artistic/executive director, at the Raymond J. Greenwald Theater. Opened May 5, 1999.

Nathan	Richard M. Davidson	Marc	Tyagi Schwartz
Morris	Sam Gray		

Directed by Joe Brancato; scenery, David Harwell; lighting, Jeff Nellis; sound, Johnna Doty; stage manager, Denise Pera.

Prominent attorney's stressful relationship with his father and fledgling lawyer son. The play was presented in two parts.

*Things You Shouldn't Say Past Midnight (22). By Peter Ackerman. Produced by Good Friends LLC, Jeffrey Richards/Michael Rothfield, Jean Donmanian, Ted Snowdon, Steven M. Levy and Leonard Soloway at the Promenade Theater. Opened May 13, 1999.

Nancy	Erin Dilly	Grace	Clea Lewis
Ben	Mark Kassen	Mark	Andrew Benator
Gene	Jeffrey Donovan	Mr. Abramson	Nicholas Kepros

Understudies: Messrs. Kassen, Benator, Donovan—Ian Kahn; Mr. Kepros—Robert Levine.

Directed by John Rando; scenery, Rob Odorisio; costumes, Tom Broecker; lighting, Donald Holder; sound, Peter J. Fitzgerald; casting, Jay Binder; production stage manager, Karen Moore; press, Jeffrey Richards Associates, Caral Craig, Brett Kristofferson.

Comedy of three couples sexually involved. The play was presented without intermission.

The Acting Company. Repertory of two programs. **Tartuffe** (11). Revival of the play by Molière; translated by Richard Wilbur. Opened May 20, 1999. **Twelfth Night** (4). Revival of the play by William Shakespeare. Opened May 25, 1999. Produced by The Acting Company, Margot Harley producing director, at the Playhouse at St. Clements. (Repertory closed May 29, 1999)

Performer	*Tartuffe*	*Twelfth Night*
Tim Barker	Valere	Sebastian
Anne Bates	Mariane	Lady-in-Waiting
Clark Scott Carmichael	Damis	Captain; Officer; Priest
Rayme Cornell	Elmire	Olivia
Kristen Gass	Dorine	Lady-in-Waiting
Christopher Jean	Tartuffe	Feste

Charity Jones	Flipote	Viola
John Kinsherf	Monsieur Loyal; Guard	Sir Toby Belch
Andrew McGinn	Orgon	Malvolio
Garrett McKechnie	Guard	Antonio
Dana Slamp	Mme. Pernell	Maria
Jonathan Uffelman	Officer	Valentine; Fabian
Kevin Varner	Cleante	Sir Andrew Aguecheek
Michael Wiggins	Laurent	Orsino

BOTH PLAYS: Lighting based on original design by Matthew Frey; fight direction and movement, Felix Ivanov; casting, Liz Woodman; production stage manager, Jennifer Rae Moore; press, Springer/Chicoine Public Relations, Gary Springer, Susan Chicoine.

TARTUFFE: Party Guests, Beggars—Company.

Understudies: Messrs. Jean, Uffelman—Michael Wiggins; Mr. McGinn—Kevin Varner; Messrs. Barker, Wiggins, Carmichael—Garrett McKechnie; Messrs. Varner, Kinsherf—Jonathan Uffelman; Misses Cornell, Slamp—Charity Jones; Misses Bates, Gass—Dana Slamp.

Directed by Mark Ax, based on the original production by Garland Wright; scenery, Troy Hourie; costumes, Susan Hilferty.

The last major New York revival of *Tartuffe* took place on Broadway 5/30/96 for 29 performances.

TWELFTH NIGHT: Understudies: Miss Cornell—Anne Bates; Messrs. Kinsherf, McKechnie—Clark Scott Carmichael; Mr. Barker—Garrett McKechnie; Messrs. Varner, Jean, McGinn—Jonathan Uffelman; Miss Slamp, Mr. Uffelman—Kristen Gass; Mr. Wiggins—Tim Barker; Miss Jones—Dana Slamp.

Directed by Penny Metropulos; scenery, Michael Vaugh Sims; costumes, Jeff Fender; original music, Kim D. Sherman; sound, Fabian Obispo.

The last major New York revival of *Twelfth Night* took place this season 7/16/98 for 53 performances.

CAST REPLACEMENTS
AND TOURING COMPANIES

Compiled by Jeffrey Finn Productions

The following is a list of the major cast replacements of record in productions which opened in previous years, but were still playing in New York during a substantial part of the 1998–99 season; and other New York shows which were on a first-class tour in 1998–99.

The name of each major role is listed in *italics* beneath the title of the play in the first column. In the second column directly opposite appears the name of the actor who created the role in the original New York production (whose opening date appears in *italics* at the top of the column). In shows of the past five years, indented immediately beneath the original actor's name are the names of subsequent New York replacements, together with the date of replacement when available. In shows that have run longer than five years, only this season's or the most recent cast replacements are listed under the names of the original cast members.

The third column gives information about first-class touring companies. When there is more than one roadshow company, #1, #2, etc., appear before the name of the performer who created the role in each company (and the city and date of each company's first performance appears in *italics* at the top of the column). Their subsequent replacements are also listed beneath their names in the same manner as the New York companies, with dates when available.

ART

	New York 3/1/98
Marc	Alan Alda
	Brian Cox 9/1/98
	Judd Hirsch 12/22/98
	Buck Henry 5/11/99
Serge	Victor Garber
	Henry Goodman 9/1/98
	Joe Morton 12/22/98
	George Segal 5/11/99
Yvan	Alfred Molina
	David Haig 9/1/98
	George Wendt 12/22/98
	Wayne Knight 5/11/99

BEAUTY AND THE BEAST

	New York 4/18/94	*Minneapolis 11/7/95*
Beast	Terrence Mann	Frederick C. Inkley
	Jeff McCarthy	Roger Befeler
	Chuck Wagner	
	James Barbour	
	Steve Blanchard	

Casts
of
Art

Two of the several casts which have performed on the Broadway stage in Yazmina Reza's three-character play are pictured here: *above,* Joe Morton, George Wendt and Judd Hirsch; *at right,* Buck Henry, George Segal and Wayne Knight

Belle

Susan Egan
Sarah Uriarte
Christianne Tisdale
Kerry Butler
Deborah Gibson

Kim Huber
Erin Dilly 2/11/98

	Kim Huber	
	Toni Braxton	
	Andrea McArdle	
Lefou	Kenny Raskin	Dan Sklar
	Harrison Beal	Jeffrey Schecter
	Jamie Torcellini	Aldrin Gonzalez
	Jeffrey Schecter	
Gaston	Burke Moses	Tony Lawson
	Marc Kudisch	
	Steve Blanchard	
	Patrick Ryan Sullivan	
Maurice	Tom Bosley	Grant Cowan
	MacIntyre Dixon	
	Tom Bosley	
	Kurt Knudson	
	Tim Jerome	
Cogsworth	Heath Lamberts	Jeff Brooks
	Peter Bartlett	
	Gibby Brand	
	John Christopher Jones	
Lumiere	Gary Beach	Patrick Page
	Lee Roy Reams	David DeVries
	Patrick Quinn	Gary Beach
	Gary Beach	David DeVries
	Meschach Taylor	
	Patrick Page	
Babette	Stacey Logan	Leslie Castay
	Pamela Winslow	Mindy Paige Davis 2/15/97
	Leslie Castay	Heather Lee
	Pam Klinger	
Mrs. Potts	Beth Fowler	Betsy Joslyn
	Cass Morgan	Barbara Marineu 7/2/97
	Beth Fowler	

THE BEAUTY QUEEN OF LEENANE

	New York 4/23/98
Maureen Folan	Marie Mullen
	Kate Burton 1/5/99
Pato Dooley	Brian F. O'Byrne
	Stevie Ray Dallimore 1/5/99
Ray Dooley	Tom Murphy
	Christopher Murphy Carley 1/5/99

BRING IN 'DA NOISE BRING IN 'DA FUNK

	New York 4/25/96	*Detroit 9/30/97*
'Da Beat	Savion Glover	Derick K. Grant
	Baakari Wilder 7/1/97	Jimmy Tate
	Savion Glover 12/8/98	Sean C. Fielder

Performer	Baakari Wilder	Jimmy Tate
	Dulé Hill 7/1/97	
Performer	Jimmy Tate	Christopher A. Scott
	Jason Samuels 7/1/97	
Performer	Vincent Binghamon	Dominique Kelley
	Omar A. Edwards 2/4/97	
'Da Voice	Jeffrey Wright	Thomas Silcott
	Curtis McClarin 8/5/97	
'Da Singer	Ann Duquesnay	Vickilyn Reynolds
	Lynette G. DuPre 8/5/97	Debra Byrd
Drummer	Jared Crawford	David Peter Chapman
Drummer	Raymond King	Dennis J. Dove
The Kid	Dulé Hill	B. Jason Young
	Jason Samuels 7/1/97	Christopher Scott
	Marshall L. Davis Jr. 9/16/97	

CABARET

	New York 3/19/98	*Los Angeles 2/99*
Emcee	Alan Cumming	Norbert Leo Butz
	Robert Sella 9/17/98	
	Alan Cumming 12/1/98	
Sally Bowles	Natasha Richardson	Teri Hatcher
	Jennifer Jason Leigh 8/4/98	
	Mary McCormack 3/2/99	
Clifford Bradshaw	John Benjamin Hickey	Rick Holmes
	Boyd Gaines 3/2/99	
Ernst Ludwig	Denis O'Hare	Andy Taylor
	Michael Stuhlbarg 5/4/99	
Fraulein Schneider	Mary Louise Wilson	Barbara Andres
	Blair Brown 8/20/98	
	Carole Shelley 5/4/99	
Fraulein Kost	Michele Pawk	Jeanine Morick
	Victoria Clark 5/4/99	
Herr Schultz	Ron Rifkin	Dick Latessa
	Laurence Luckinbill 5/4/99	

CATS

	New York 10/7/82	National tour 1/94
Alonzo	Hector Jaime Mercado	William Patrick Dunne
	Hans Kriefall 4/24/95	Scott Carlyle 9/8/98
		Alan Bennett 10/10/98
		Matt Rivera 3/23/99
Bustopher	Stephan Hanan	Richard Poole
	Daniel Eli Friedman 4/14/97	Kelly Briggs 3/16/99

Bombalurina	Donna King Marlene Danielle 1/9/84	Helen Frank Parisa Ross 9/1/98
Cassandra	Rene Ceballos Meg Gillentine	Laura Quinn Carrie Kenneally 2/1/99 Jennifer Paige Chambers 3/2/99 Naomi Kakuk 4/6/99
Demeter	Wendy Edmead Amanda Watkins	N. Elaine Wiggins Amy Hamel 5/11/99
Grizabella	Betty Buckley Linda Balgord	Mary Gutzi Linda Balgord 9/22/98 Jessica Hendy 10/20/98 Jodie Langel
Jellylorum	Bonnie Simmons Jean Arbeiter	Patty Goble Kris Koop 2/1/99
Jennyanydots	Anna McNeely Carol Dilley 8/22/94	Alice C. DeChant
Mistoffeles	Timothy Scott Christopher Gattelli	Christopher Gattelli Brian Barry 6/9/98 Julius Sermonia 2/1/99
Mungojerrie	Rene Clemente Roger Kachel 5/11/92	Gavan Palmer David Petro 4/19/99
Munkustrap	Harry Groener Michael Gruber Abe Sylvia	Robert Amirante Kip Driver 6/23/98 Bobby Miranda 1/12/98 Paul Clausen 2/1/99
Old Deuteronomy	Ken Page Jimmy Lockett	John Treacy Egan Craig A. Benham 5/19/98
Plato/Macavity	Kenneth Ard Steve Geary	Steve Bertles Chadwick T. Adams 2/23/99
Pouncival	Herman W. Sebek Joey Gyondla	Joey Gyondla Jon-Erik Goldenberg 3/16/99
Rum Tum Tugger	Terrence Mann Stephen Bienskie	Ron Seykell Kevin Loreque 4/27/99
Rumpleteazer	Christine Langner Tesha Buss	Jennifer Cody Renee Bonadio 1/12/99
Sillabub	Whitney Kershaw Maria Jo Ralabate 4/1/96	Lanene Charters Claci Miller 3/23/99
Skimbleshanks	Reed Jones Owen Taylor	Carmen Yurich Michael Etzwiler 5/5/98 Ryan Shepherd 3/16/99
Tumblebrutus	Robert Hoshour Patrick Mullaney	Joseph Favolora Angelo Rivera 1/6/98
Victoria	Cynthia Onrubia Missy Lay Zimmer	Tricia Mitchell Jessica Dillan 1/12/99

Note: Only this season's or the most recent cast replacements are listed above under the names of the original cast members. For previous replacements, see previous volumes of *Best Plays*.

CHICAGO

	New York 11/14/96	*#1 Cincinatti 3/25/97* *#2 Ft. Myers, Fla. 12/12/97*

Velma Kelly	Bebe Neuwirth
	Nancy Hess
	Ute Lemper
	Mamie Duncan-Gibbs
	Ruthie Henshall 5/25/99
		#1 Jasmine Guy
		    Janine LaManna
		    Jasmine Guy
		    Donna Marie Asbury
		    Stephanie Pope
		    Jasmine Guy 7/7/98
		    Stephanie Pope 7/14/98
		    Mamie Duncan-Gibbs 1/12/99
		    Deidre Goodwin 2/16/99
		    Ruthie Henshall 4/22/99
		    Deidre Goodwin 5/18/99
		#2 Stephanie Pope
		    Jasmine Guy
		    Stephanie Pope
		    Khandi Alexander 8/4/98
		    Donna Marie Asbury 9/29/98
		    Stephanie Pope 2/2/98
		    Ute Lemper 2/19/99

Roxie Hart	Ann Reinking
	Marilu Henner
	Karen Ziemba
	Belle Calaway
	Karen Ziemba
	Charlotte d'Amboise
		#1 Charlotte d'Amboise
		    Belle Calaway
		    Ann Reinking 4/22/99
		    Belle Calaway 5/18/99
		#2 Karen Ziemba
		    Nancy Hess
		    Charlotte d'Amboise
		    Amy Spranger 11/10/98
		    Charlotte d'Amboise 11/24/98
		    Amy Spranger 12/1/98
		    Chita Rivera 2/2/99

Amos Hart	Joel Grey
	Ernie Sabella
	Tom McGowan
	P.J. Benjamin
		#1 Ron Orbach
		    Michael Tucci
		    Bruce Winant 12/22/98
		#2 Ernie Sabella
		    Tom McGowan
		    Ron Orbach
		    Tom McGowan
		    Ron Orbach
		    P.J. Benjamin 11/10/98
		    Joel Grey 12/1/98
		    P.J. Benjamin 12/29/98
		    Ernie Sabella 2/2/99

Matron "Mama" Morton	Marcia Lewis
	Roz Ryan
		#1 Carol Woods
		    Lea DeLaria
		    Carol Woods 8/4/98
		#2 Avery Sommers
		    Marcia Lewis 2/2/99

Billy Flynn	James Naughton	#1 Obba Babatunde
	Gregory Jbara	Alan Thicke
	Hinton Battle	Michael Berresse 8/18/98
	Alan Thicke	Alan Thicke 8/25/98
	Michael Berresse	Destin Owens 10/13/98
	Brent Barrett	Alan Thicke 10/27/98
		Destin Owens 1/26/99
		Adrian Zmed 2/16/99
		#2 Brent Barrett
		Michael Berresse 11/3/98
		Brent Barrett 11/24/98
		Michael Berresse 12/1/98
		Ben Vereen 2/19/99
Mary Sunshine	D. Sabella	#1 M.E. Spencer
	J. Loeffenholz	D.C. Levine
	R. Bean	M.E. Spencer 7/7/98
		R. Bean 7/28/98
		A. Saunders 10/13/98
		R. Bean 10/20/98
		J. Maldonado 10/27/98
		J. Roberson 2/9/99
		#2 D.C. Levine
		M.E. Spencer

DINAH WAS

New York 5/28/98

| *Dinah Washington* | Yvette Freeman |
| | Lillias White 8/10/88 |

THE FANTASTICKS

New York 5/3/60

El Gallo	Jerry Orbach
	John Savarese 10/7/97
Luisa	Rita Gardner
	Gina Schuh-Turner 10/7/97
Matt	Kenneth Nelson
	Eric Meyersfield

Note: Only this season's or the most recent replacements are listed above under the names of the original cast members. For previous replacements, see previous volumes of *Best Plays*.

FOOTLOOSE

	New York 10/22/98	*Cleveland 12/15/98*
Reverend Shaw Moore	Stephen Lee Anderson	Daren Kelly
Wendy Jo	Rosalind Brown	Katie Harvey
Lulu Warnicker	Catherine Campbell	Tina Johnson
Ethel McCormack	Catherine Cox	Marsha Waterbury
Urleen	Kathy Deitch	Andrea McCormack

Chuck Cranston	Billy Hartung	Richard H. Blake
Vi Moore	Dee Hoty	Mary Gordon Murray
Ren McCormack	Jeremy Kushnier	Joe Machota
Wes Warnicker	Adam LeFevre	Steve Luker
Willard Hewitt	Tom Plotkin	Christian Borle
Ariel Moore	Jennifer Laura Thompson	Niki Scalera

HEDWIG AND THE ANGRY INCH

New York 7/14/98

Hedwig Schmidt   John Cameron Mitchell
Michael Cerveris 1/4/99

I LOVE YOU, YOU'RE PERFECT, NOW CHANGE

New York 8/1/96

Jordan Leeds
Danny Burstein 10/1/96
Adam Grupper 8/22/97
Gary Imhoff 2/9/98
Adam Grupper 4/1/98
Jordan Leeds 3/17/99

Robert Roznowski
Kevin Pariseau 5/25/98

Jennifer Simard
Erin Leigh Peck 5/25/98

Melissa Weil
Cheryl Stern 2/16/98

JEKYLL & HYDE

New York 4/28/97

Sir Danvers Carew   Barrie Ingham

Dr. Henry Jekyll;   Robert Cuccioli
Edward Hyde   Robert Evan (alt.)
Robert Evan 1/5/99
Joseph Mahowald (alt.)

Emma Carew   Christiane Noll
Anastasia Barzee

Lucy   Linda Eder
Luba Mason

LES MISERABLES

	New York 3/12/87	*Tampa 11/18/88*
Jean Valjean	Colm Wilkinson	Gary Barker
	Fred Inkley 9/8/98	Colm Wilkinson 7/15/98
		Ivan Rutherford 1/19/99

Javert	Terrence Mann
	  Philip Hernandez 10/27/98
		Peter Samuel
		  Todd Alan Johnson 3/31/97

Fantine	Randy Graff
	  Alice Ripley 9/8/98
	  Susan Gilmour 3/9/99
	  Alice Ripley 3/23/99
		Hollis Resnik
		  Susan Gilmour 6/2/98
		  Joan Almedilla 3/2/99

Enjolras	Michael Maguire
	  Gary Mauer 12/8/98
	  Stephen R. Buntrock 4/6/99
		Greg Zerkle
		  Matthew Shepard 12/8/98
		  Kevin Earley 1/19/99

Marius	David Bryant
	  Peter Lockyer 3/12/97
		Matthew Porretta
		  Tim Howar

Cosette	Judy Kuhn
	  Tobi Foster 11/6/98
		Jacquelyn Piro
		  Regan Thiel

Eponine	Frances Ruffelle
	  Megan Lawrence 6/19/98
	  Kerry Butler 12/11/98
	  Megan Lawrence 2/25/99
		Michele Maika
		  Sutton Foster 1/19/99

Note: Only this season's or the most recent cast replacements are listed above under the names of the original cast members. For previous replacements, see previous volumes of *Best Plays*.

THE LION KING

	New York 11/13/97
Rafiki	Tsidii LeLoka Thuli Dumakude 11/11/98
Mufasa	Samuel E. Wright
Sarabi	Gina Breedlove Meena T. Jahi 8/4/98
Zazu	Geoff Hoyle Bill Bowers 10/21/98
Scar	John Vickery Tom Hewitt 10/21/98
Banzai	Stanley Wayne Mathis Keith Bennett 9/30/98
Shenzi	Tracy Nicole Chapman
Ed	Kevin Cahoon Jeff Skowron 10/21/98
Timon	Max Casella Danny Rutigliano 6/16/98
Pumba	Tom Alan Robbins
Simba	Jason Raize

Nala	Heather Headley
	  Mary Randle 7/7/98
	  Heather Headley 12/8/98

MISS SAIGON

	New York 4/11/91	*Seattle 3/16/95*
The Engineer	Jonathan Pryce Luoyong Wang 10/2/95	Thom Sesma Joseph Anthony Foronda 4/22/97
Kim	Lea Salonga Joan Almedilla Deedee Lynn Magno 7/21/97 Lea Salonga 1/18/99	Deedee Lynn Magno Elizabeth Paw Kristine Remigio Kim Hoy 1/19/99
Chris	Willy Falk Matt Bogart 1/12/98 Will Chase 7/20/98	Matt Bogart Will Chase 4/16/96 Steve Pasquale 6/30/97 Greg Stone 1/19/99

Note: Only this season's or the most recent cast replacements are listed above under the names of the original cast members. For previous replacements, see previous volumes of *Best Plays*.

THE PHANTOM OF THE OPERA

		#1 *Los Angeles 5/31/90* #2 *Chicago 5/24/90* #3 *Seattle 12/13/92*
	New York 1/26/88	
The Phantom	Michael Crawford Hugh Panaro 2/1/99	#1 Michael Crawford Frank D'Ambrosio 3/28/94 #2 Mark Jacoby Davis Gaines 8/98 #3 Frank D'Ambrosio Ted Keegan 3/31/99
Christine Daae	Sarah Brightman Sandra Joseph 1/27/98 Adrienne McEwan (alt.) 10/26/98	#1 Dale Kristien Lisa Vroman 12/2/93 Karen Culliver (alt.) 6/3/97 #2 Karen Culliver Marie Danvers 6/98 Susan Facer (alt.) 6/98 #3 Tracy Shane Megan Starr-Levitt (alt.) 1/21/98 Rebecca Pitcher 3/31/99
Raoul	Steve Barton Ciaran Sheehan 10/13/98 Gary Mauer 4/19/99	#1 Reece Holland Christopher Carl 7/2/96 #2 Keith Buterbaugh Lawrence Anderson 7/98 #3 Ciaran Sheehan Jason Pebworth 7/22/98 Richard Todd Adams 3/31/99

Note: Only this season's or the most recent cast replacements are listed above under the names of the original cast members. For previous replacements, see previous volumes of *Best Plays*.

MISS SAIGON—Will Chase as Chris and Deedee Lynn Magno as Kim in the long-running Claude-Michel Schön-berg-Alain Boublil-Richard Maltby Jr. musical

POWER PLAYS

New York 5/21/98

De Recha, Dr. Kesselman   Alan Arkin
                                    Richard Benjamin 9/22/98

Mrs. Asquith, Sue   Elaine May
                                    Paula Prentiss 9/22/98

RAGTIME

	New York 1/18/98	Washington, D.C. 4/29/98
Father	Mark Jacoby John Dossett 4/99	Chris Groenendaal
Mother	Marin Mazzie Donna Bullock 1/99	Rebecca Eichenberger
Mother's Younger Bro.	Steven Sutcliffe Scott Carollo 1/99	Aloysius Gigl
Coalhouse Walker Jr.	Brian Stokes Mitchell Alton Fitzgerald White 1/99	Alton Fitzgerald White Lawrence Hamilton 12/28/98
Sarah	Audra McDonald LaChanze 1/99	Darlesia Cearcy
Tateh	Peter Friedman John Rubinstein 1/99	Michael Rupert
Harry Houdini	Jim Corti	Bernie Yvon
Henry Ford	Larry Daggett David Masenheimer 9/98 Larry Daggett 3/99	Larry Cahn
Emma Goldman	Judy Kaye	Theresa Tova
Evelyn Nesbit	Lynette Perry Janine LaManna 8/98	Melissa Dye

RENT

	New York 4/29/96	#1 Boston 11/18/96 #2 La Jolla 7/1/97
Roger Davis	Adam Pascal Nobert Leo Butz Richard H. Blake (alt.) Manley Pope	#1 Sean Keller Manley Pope 3/14/97 Christian Anderson Dean Balkwill #2 Christian Mena Cary Shields Christian Mena
Mark Cohen	Anthony Rapp Jim Poulos	#1 Luther Creek Christian Anderson Trey Ellet #2 Neil Patrick Harris Kirk McDonald Scott Hunt
Tom Collins	Jesse L. Martin Michael McElroy	#1 C.C. Brown Mark Leroy Jackson #2 Mark Leroy Jackson Dwayne Clark
Benjamin Coffin III	Taye Diggs Jacques C. Smith	#1 James Rich Dwayne Clark Brian Love #2 D'Monroe Brian Love Carl Thornton

Joanne Jefferson	Fredi Walker	#1 Sylvia MacCalla
	Gwen Stewart	Kamilah Martin
	Alia León	#2 Kenna J. Ramsey
	Kenna J. Ramsey	Monique Daniels
		Danielle Lee Greaves
Angel Schunard	Wilson Jermaine Heredia	#1 Stephan Alexander
	Wilson Cruz	Shaun Earl
	Shaun Earl	Evan D'Angeles
	Jose Llana	Shaun Earl
	Jai Rodriguez	#2 Wilson Cruz
		Andy Senor
		Pierre Bayuga
Mimi Marquez	Daphne Rubin-Vega	#1 Simone
	Marcy Harriell 4/5/97	Laura Dias
	Krysten Cummings	Daphne Rubin-Vega
		Sharon Leal
		#2 Julia Santana
Maureen Johnson	Idina Menzel	#1 Carrie Hamilton
	Sherie Scott	Amy Spanger 6/5/97
	Kristen Lee Kelly	Erin Keaney
	Tamara Podemski	#2 Leigh Hetherington
		Carla Bianco
		Leigh Hetherington
		Christina Fadale

THE SCARLET PIMPERNEL

	New York 11/9/97
Percy Blakeney	Douglas Sills
Chauvelin	Terrence Mann
	Rex Smith
Marguerite St. Just	Christine Andreas
	Rachel York

1776

	New York 12/3/97
Abigail	Linda Emond
	Carolee Carmello 3/3/98
Rutledge	Gregg Edelman
Lee	Merwin Foard
Franklin	Pat Hingle
	David Huddleston 3/3/98
Livingston	Daniel Marcus
Adams	Brent Spiner
	Michael McCormick 3/3/98
Jefferson	Paul Michael Valley
Martha	Lauren Ward

SMOKEY JOE'S CAFE

	New York 3/2/95
Ken	Ken Ard
Adrian	Adrian Bailey
Brenda	Brenda Braxton
Victor	Victor Trent Cook
	James Beeks 6/8/97
	Victor Trent Cook 10/6/98
B.J.	B.J. Crosby
	D'Atra Hicks 1/3/98
	B.J. Crosby 10/6/98
Pattie	Pattie Darcy Jones
DeLee	DeLee Lively
Michael	Michael Park
	Jerry Tellier 9/9/97
Fred	Frederick B. Owens

THE SOUND OF MUSIC

	New York 3/12/98
Maria	Rebecca Luker
	Laura Benanti
Captain Von Trapp	Michael Siberry
	Dennis Parlato 11/4/98
	Richard Chamberlain 3/10/99
Max	Fred Applegate
	Patrick Quinn
	Lenny Wolpe
Mother Abbess	Patti Cohenour
	Jeanne Lehman
Rolf	Dashiell Eaves
	Ben Sheaffer
Friedrich	Ryan Hopkins
	Lou Taylor Pucci
	Christopher Trousdale
Louisa	Natalie Hall
	Nora Blackall
	Rachel Beth Levenson
Kurt	Matthew Ballinger
	Marshall Pallet
	Christopher Cordell
Gretl	Ashley Rose Orr
	Christiana Anbri
	Ashlee Keating

TITANIC

	New York 4/23/97	*Los Angeles 1/5/99*
Capt. E.J. Smith	John Cunningham	William Parry

1st Officer William Murdoch	David Costabile Danny Burstein	David Pittu
Frederick Barrett	Brian d'Arcy James Clarke Thorell Stephen R. Buntrock	Marcus Chait
Harold Bride	Martin Moran Don Stephenson	Dale Sandish
Henry Etches	Allan Corduner Henry Stram	Edward Conery
Thomas Andrews	Michael Cerveris Matthew Bennett Joseph Kolinski	Kevin Gray
Isidor Straus	Larry Keith	S. Marc Jordan
Ida Straus	Alma Cuervo	Taina Elg
Edgar Beane	Bill Buell	David Beditz
Alice Beane	Victoria Clark	Liz McConahay
Kate McGowen	Jennifer Piech	Melissa Bell
Jim Farrell	Clarke Thorell Christopher Wells	Richard Roland

A VIEW FROM THE BRIDGE

	New York 12/14/97
Eddie	Anthony LaPaglia Tony Danza
Catherine	Brittany Murphy Chelsea Altman
Beatrice	Allison Janney Karen Browning
Rodolpho	Gabriel Olds David Berry Grey

OTHER NEW YORK SHOWS
ON FIRST CLASS TOURS IN 1998–99

ALMOST LIKE BEING IN LOVE—
THE LERNER AND LOEWE SONGBOOK

	Englewood, NJ 11/5/98
Diahann	Diahann Carroll
David	David Bedella
Jonathan	Jonathan Dokuchitz
Jordan	Jordan Leeds
David	David White

ANNIE

	Houston 11/29/96
Annie	Joanna Pacitti Brittny Kissinger 2/25/97
Miss Hannigan	Roz Ryan Nell Carter 1/3/97 Sally Struthers
Grace Farrell	Colleen Dunn Lisa Gunn Kay Story 7/30/98
Oliver Warbucks	John Schuck
Rooster Hannigan	Jim Ryan Laurent Girouy
Lily	Karen Byers Blackwell

FAME

	Toronto 11/17/98
Serena Katz	Jennifer Gambatese Erika Shannon
Miss Greta Bell	Kim Cea Christia Leigh Mantzke
Iris Kelly	Nadine Isenegger Jennifer Cohen

HIT ME WITH A HOT NOTE!— THE DUKE ELLINGTON SONGBOOK

	Englewood, NJ 2/6/99
Marilyn	Marilyn McCoo
Billy	Billy Davis Jr.
Stacie	Stacie Precia Angela Robinson 3/25/99
Cindy	Cindy Marchionda Kyla Grogan 3/25/99
Abe	Abe Clark
Chad	Chad Borden

PETER PAN

	Seattle 11/28/97
Wendy Darling	Elisa Sagardia
John Darling	Michael LaVolpe Chase Kniffen 4/20/98 Barry Cavanagh 3/2/99

Mrs. Darling	Barbara McCulloh
Michael Darling	Paul Tiesler
	Drake English 2/2/98
Peter Pan	Cathy Rigby
Captain Hook	Paul Schoeffler

SHOW BOAT

#1 Los Angeles 11/12/96
#2 Detroit 3/11/97

Cap'n Andy	#1 George Grizzard
	Tom Bosley 2/97
	Len Cariou 4/97
	Dean Jones 9/30/97
	#2 Tom Bosley
Parthy	#1 Cloris Leachman
	Karen Morrow 2/97
	Cloris Leachman 4/97
	#2 Karen Morrow
Magnolia	#1 Teri Hansen
	Gay Willis 1/13/98
	#2 Sarah Pfisterer
Gaylord Ravenal	#1 J. Mark McVey
	Hugh Panaro 4/97
	Stephen Bogardus 6/22/97
	Keith Buterbaugh 1/13/98
	#2 John Ruess
	Alex Sharp
Julie	#1 Valarie Pettiford
	Karen-Angela Bishop 5/97
	#2 Debbie DeCoudreaux
Frank	#1 Keith Savage
	#2 Kirby Ward
Ellie	#1 Jacquey Maltby
	Kerri Clarke
	Tari Kelly
	#2 Beverly Ward
Queenie	#1 Anita Berry
	Jo Ann Hawkins White
	#2 Gretha Boston
	Janelle Robinson 2/23/98
Steve	#1 Todd Noel
	Kip Wilborn 3/29/96
	Ross Neill 5/97
	#2 John Clonts
	Craig Ashton 3/6/98
Joe	#1 Dan Tullis Jr.
	Michel Bell
	#2 Andre Solomon-Glover

SUNSET BOULEVARD

	Pittsburgh 12/1/98
Norma Desmond	Petula Clark
Joe Gillis	Lewis Cleale
Max von Mayerling	Allen Fitzgerald
Betty Schaefer	Sarah Uriarte Berry
Cecil B. DeMille	George Merner
Artie Green	Michael Berry

THE WHO'S TOMMY

	Wilmington, Del. 3/19/99
Tommy	Michael Seelbach
Capt. Walker	Christopher Monteleone
Mrs. Walker	Lisa Capps
Uncle Ernie	Paul Dobie
Gypsy	Virginia Woodruff
Young Tommy	Ross Ramone Zachary Freed (alt.)
Cousin Kevin	Michael Gruber
Sally Simpson	Dennis Summerford

VICTOR/VICTORIA

	Reno, NV 9/98
Carroll Todd	Jamie Ross
Henri Labisse	Dominic Cuskern
Victoria Grant	Toni Tennille
Andre Cassell	John-Charles Kelly Kenn Christopher
Norma Cassidy	Dana Lynn Mauro
King Marchan	Dennis Cole
Squash (Mr. Bernstein)	A.J. Irvin

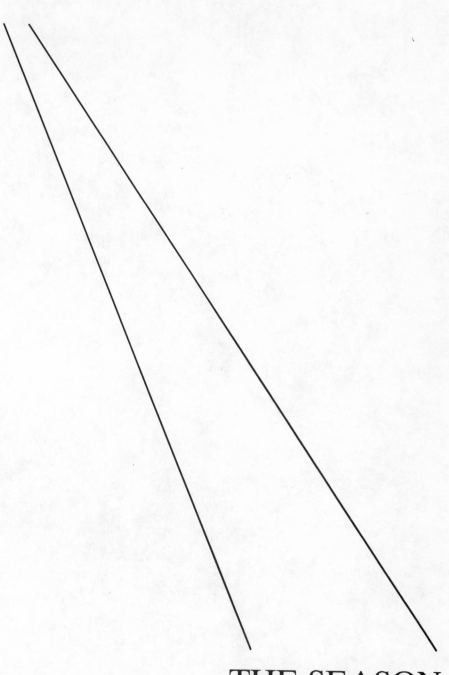

THE SEASON
OFF OFF BROADWAY

OFF OFF BROADWAY

By Mel Gussow

THE DIVIDING LINES between the various sectors of the New York theater are increasingly blurred, at least partly because uptown producers are becoming more alert to what's happening in non-commercial arenas. More and more plays move from off off Broadway to off Broadway and even to Broadway. Margaret Edson's *Wit,* the best play to be presented off off Broadway this season, had a long run off Broadway after its OOB premiere at MCC Theater and turned out to be the best play anywhere, as certified by the Pulitzer and other prizes. In a similar fashion, Warren Leight's *Side Man,* given an OOB citation last season, eventually moved to Broadway and won a Tony Award this season as best new play. Quality shines, no matter what the venue.

In previous years, the Vineyard Theater gave a first New York staging to Edward Albee's *Three Tall Women* and Paula Vogel's *How I Learned to Drive,* both of which went on to win Pulitzer Prizes, as did *Rent,* which shifted to Broadway after opening at the New York Theater Workshop. This year the Workshop raised its programs to full off-Broadway status but tripped with a musical version of the novel *Bright Lights Big City,* then recovered with Paul Rudnick's *The Most Fabulous Story Ever Told,* a broadly amusing spoof of Genesis, and with Dael Orlandersmith's solo show *The Gimmick,* a kind of cross between Ntozake Shange and Anna Deavere Smith tracing a portrait of a young woman on the streets (and in the libraries) of Harlem. As actress and author, Orlandersmith commanded the stage with authority and grace. One of the most notable events of this season—and an outstanding OOB production—was *Snakebit,* which opened at the enterprising Naked Angels company and then had a long run off Broadway. This first play by David Marshall Grant, an actor best known previously for his role in Tony Kushner's *Angels in America,* was a shrewdly observant look at love and the limits of friendship—and the stressful self-interest of a movie actor seeking a livelihood. Grant skewers Hollywood egos while reserving his sympathy for those who give the most to the neediest. At the same time, this is a play for actors, with admirable contributions from Geoffrey Nauffts, David Alan Basche and Jodie Markell under the astute direction of Jace Alexander.

Another important sign of this movement—or symbiosis—was the latest incar-

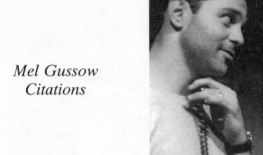

*Mel Gussow
Citations*

Above, Drew McVety, Thomas Lyons and T.R. Knight in Conor
McPherson's *This Lime Tree Bower* at Primary Stages: "A series
of monologues which, taken together, offered a portrait of robbery, violence, drinking . . . and sensitivity;" *Right,* Kei Arita
and Jun Kim in Bat Theater Company's *Benten Kozo* by Kawatake Mokuami: "An opera-sized venture blending diverse
dramatic traditions . . . new life in an old Kabuki"

nation of Second Stage. For years this off-off company has operated on a minuscule
budget in a tiny upstairs space on upper Broadway, presenting often worthy revivals
of overlooked plays as well as occasional premieres. The company has furthered the
careers of, among others, Tina Howe, Michael Weller and Lanford Wilson. On its
20th anniversary, Second Stage, under the artistic direction of Carole Rothman,
opened a splendid new theater designed by Rem Koolhaas near Broadway on West

43d Street. The new theater was inaugurated with revivals of Jason Miller's *That Championship Season* and Albert Innaurato's *Gemini,* with Second Stage—like New York Theater Workshop—now operating in its first year of full off-Broadway status. And both plays had made their own earlier journey from non-profit to Broadway.

Casey Childs's Primary Stages, which also operates near Broadway (on West 45th Street), has opened its doors to new English and American plays of value. While Conor McPherson, a young Irish playwright, was making his Broadway debut with his luminous barroom play *The Weir,* Primary Stages presented his earlier *This Lime Tree Bower.* With pungency and humor McPherson trails three young men in a day and night on the town near Dublin. This outstanding OOB play was a series of monologues which, taken together, offered a portrait of robbery, violence, drinking—and sensitivity. Although the New York version was not of the caliber of the original London production at the Bush Theater, the play itself further confirms McPherson's formidable talent, which was first demonstrated in New York the previous season with the monodrama *St. Nicholas* (starring Brian Cox), also at Primary Stages.

The Signature Theater, which defines itself by presenting an entire season of work by one playwright (Edward Albee, Horton Foote and last year Arthur Miller), turned its attention to John Guare with revivals of the futuristic *Marco Polo Sings a Solo* and *Bosoms and Neglect* (a bitterly sardonic family comedy, with Mary Louise Wilson's performance the highlight of the Guare series). The two were followed by the premiere of *Lake Hollywood,* a double barreled, generational look at a marriage and a divisive family. The Signature's theater is itself an example of the new comfort and conviviality that one often finds off off Broadway today. It is a handsome space with good sightlines and a wide stage, far west on 42d Street. Downtown in Soho is the Here Theater, a multi-theater complex, complete with a bar and art gallery. Playing in the downstairs theater was the long-running *Symphonie Fantastique,* Basil Twist's whirl-in-fishbowl puppet show, and on other stages there was a continually shifting variety of plays and performance events. Several streets south is the Flea Theater, which became an elegant drawing room for Bat Theater Company's *Cher Maitre,* a stylish exchange of literary letters between George Sand (Irene Worth) and Gustave Flaubert (Peter Eyre).

The Flea was the home for various experimental excursions, including Jim Simpson's *Benten Kozo,* an opera-sized venture blending diverse dramatic traditions and cited as an outstanding OOB production. Simpson, best known as a director of works by Mac Wellman and others, found new life in an old Kabuki, taking a step into the authorial ring with this kinetic extravaganza based on an 1862 play by Kawatake Mokuami. One of the most imaginative shows of the year, *Benten Kozo* scurried back and forth between cultures and centuries. The theatrical equivalent of fusion cooking (an amalgam of food identities), it told a story of con men and samurai in which every character seemed to have a second and even a third identity. A vast cast (with an especially funny performance by Stacie Hirsch) rocked merrily through this epic, which began with a terrible poem but sharpened its image as it proceeded to a crazy quilt of an ending. Assets included the colorful costumes by Moe Schell and sets by Kyle Chepulis. During its run at the Flea, the show was paired with a late-night revival of Mac Wellman's *Cleveland,* a shaggy mother-and-daughter problem comedy from 1986. Wellman himself is a vital force off off Broadway, with several plays, old and new, every season.

Mandy Patinkin staked out a former synagogue on the Lower East Side with a mono-musical, *Mamaloshen,* an evening of Yiddish (and Yiddishized) songs, including "Take Me Out to the Ball Game." After a sold-out run, Patinkin shifted his musicale to Broadway for a brief engagement. At Here, Lyn Austin's Music-Theater Group presented *Running Man,* an experimental jazz oratorio about a young man who is defeated, not by society or racism, but by his family: an abusive father and an overly possessive mother. Diedre Murray's score had ragged edges, but there were evocative performances by Roberta Gumbel as the mother, Darius de Haas as the title character and Chris Rustin as his younger alter ego; points, too, for the onstage band and Myung Hee Cho's set design. Another chamber musical, *Dream True: My Life With Vernon Dexter* at the Vineyard, was also exploratory but far less interesting. This show followed the misfortunes of a disturbed child who, to no one's surprise, grows up to be a very disturbed adult. The music by Ricky Ian Gordon, one of several promising new theatrical composers (others include Adam Guettel and Jeanine Tesori), had its moments. The lyrics, however, by the talented Tina Landau, struck obvious notes, and her book seemed adrift in a quandary.

One of the most highly anticipated works was *The Cider House Rules,* adapted by Peter Parnell from the John Irving novel. In a style somewhat reminiscent of the Royal Shakespeare Company's historic reinvention of *The Life and Adventures of Nicholas Nickleby,* Parnell condensed the Irving novel to two full evenings of theater with actors stepping forward, Story Theater style, to deliver narrative as well as dialogue. After productions at the Seattle Repertory Theater and the Mark Taper Forum in Los Angeles, Parnell and his collaborators (Tom Hulce and Jane Jones who conceived and directed the project), brought *Part I: Here in St. Cloud's* to the Atlantic Theater Company. The adaptation was ambitious and well-intentioned, but unfulfilled, especially for those who admire the novel, which is buoyed by Irving's gift for narrative and character. Presumably the film version would be able to capture more completely the vastness of the original. Nevertheless, there were strong performances by Josh Hamilton and Colm Meaney in the leading roles, and it was provocative to see a play on an important subject, in this case abortion and adoption. One hopes that *The Cider House Rules, Part II,* previously the winner in regional theater of the American Theater Critics Association New Play Award, will eventually come to New York. The Atlantic also offered a revival of Harold Pinter's *The Hothouse,* a madhouse farce that the playwright had written early in his career and had shelved after the failure in London of his first full-length play, *The Birthday Party.* When *The Hothouse* was finally presented in the early 1980s, it became an established part of Pinter's body of work. Perhaps closer in spirit to Joe Orton than to other plays by Pinter, it has a limberness and spontaneity as well as an off-the-wall humor, a great deal of which was captured in Karen Kohlhaas's production, and especially in the performances by Larry Bryggman and Jordan Lage.

One of the other revivals of note was the Irish Repertory Theater's production of *The Shaughraun,* a rambunctious 19th century comedy by Dion Boucicault about an irrepressible rogue in a small Irish community. In contrast to the large-scale revival some seasons ago at London's National Theater, Charlotte Moore's version was intimate—and endearing. Daniel Gerroll was outstanding as an English officer who falls in love with a local lass.

Two highly promising young playwrights, Jessica Goldberg and Brooke Berman, both of them protegees of Marsha Norman in her playwriting class at the Juilliard School, were introduced. Goldberg, who was this year's winner of the Susan Smith Blackburn Prize for her unproduced play *Refuge,* was represented by *Stuck* at the Rattlestick company. Two young women are trapped in small town America where they share language, dreams, illusions and fears. The plot spun away, but the dialogue was incisive, and Goldberg is very much a talent to watch. Equally so for Berman, who was a winner of the Actors Theater of Louisville 10 Minute Play competition. She was represented (at Here) by *The Liddy Plays,* a sensitive triptych of vignettes in the life of a woman searching for self-direction. Rattlestick also did Travis Baker's *The Weatherbox,* a chaotic play about a supremely dysfunctional family.

Richard Foreman, the mind behind the Ontological-Hysteric Theater, took an unusual turn, plunging into erotica with *Paradise Hotel,* which was Foremanized Feydeau, uninhibited in the extreme, with a cast led by Tony Tom. The Brooklyn Academy of Music, in the final season (much of it presented at the off-Broadway level) under the direction of Harvey Lichtenstein, was highlighted by Diana Rigg in *Phèdre* and *Britannicus; Monsters of Grace,* a 3D dreamlike opera by Philip Glass and Robert Wilson; Caryl Churchill's *Blue Heart,* two surreal one-act comedies about the depletion of language; and Declan Donnellan's shapely, minimalist production of Corneille's classic, *Le Cid.* The Ensemble Studio Theater, Curt Dempster's outpost on West 52d Street, had two fine plays in its 22d annual Marathon of one-acts: *Deaf Day,* a poignant monologue written by Leslie Ayvazian about a mother (Kaitlyn Kenney) and a deaf child; and *Goodbye Oscar,* Romulus Linney's imaginative exploration of the last days of Oscar Wilde, as touchingly recreated by Jack Gilpin. Earlier in the season, the EST offered *Step In and Stand Clear: A City Slam,* a delightful little revue about some of the traumas of New York life, such as apartment hunting and noises on and off the street. The show was created by its company of actors, a sprightly collective that included Geneva Carr and India Cooper, who was also the director.

Highly accomplished actors continued to find a home—and a challenge—away from the mainstream, including, this season, the prodigious Brian Murray (in *Spread Eagle*), Theodore Bikel (in *The Gathering*) and Phyllis Newman and Randall Duk Kim (in a revival of Leonard Spigelgass's *A Majority of One*), the last two shows at the Jewish Repertory Theater. John Turturro and Tony Shalhoub starred in Andrei Belgrader's earnest production of *Waiting for Godot* at the Classic Stage Company, also the setting for Martin Crimp's outlandish adaptation of *The Misanthrope,* which wrestled Molière into the 1990s. Heading the cast were Roger Rees and Uma Thurman. Frances Sternhagen was at the center of *The Exact Center of the Universe* by Joan Vail Thorne. This formulaic play creaked with cliches but earned a measure of charm from Sternhagen as a domineering mother. There was charm in abundance in *Tennessee Williams Remembered,* a staged memoir in which Eli Wallach and Anne Jackson looked back fondly on their long career with the playwright. In their show, they reminisced and also reenacted scenes from *Camino Real, Summer and Smoke* and other plays. They recalled that they had met when they were the entire cast of the Williams one-act *This Property Is Condemned.*

As always, monologuists abounded. Leslie Nipkow, an actress turned author, offered *Guarding Erica,* the very amusing story of her days in a soap opera as a prison guard (later in the season she was represented by her first full-length play, *The Moment of Aha).* Danny Hoch, Aviva Jane Carlin and Margaret Cho appeared as singles on other stages. *The Pitchfork Disney,* presented by the Blue Light Theater Company, was a case of sub-Orton, a hermitic black comedy about twins barricading themselves against the world. Leslie Lyles's *A Lifetime of Reasons* was a rambling, un-Chekhovian look at three nutty sisters over an extended period of years. In any summary of a season there should be room for a worst play, and, unequivocally, that honor goes to *F@UST: Version 3.0* by La Fura dels Baus, a Spanish company appearing at the Lincoln Center Festival. Unbearably pretentious and gratuitously violent, it rattled chains (really and metaphorically) and sent theatergoers scurrying to the exit at intermission. Fortunately, it was offset at the Festival by the return of the tantalizing Théâtre de Complicité with *Street of Crocodiles.*

PLAYS PRODUCED
OFF OFF BROADWAY

AND ADDITIONAL N.Y.C. PRODUCTIONS

Compiled by Camille Dee

Here is a comprehensive sampling of off-off-Broadway and other experimental or peripheral 1998–99 productions in New York. There is no definitive "off-off-Broadway" area or qualification. To try to define or regiment it would be untrue to its fluid, exploratory purpose. The listing below of hundreds of works produced by more than 100 OOB groups and others is as inclusive as reliable sources will allow, however, and takes in all leading Manhattan-based, new-play producing, English-language organizations.

The more active and established producing groups are identified in **bold face type,** in alphabetical order, with artistic policies and the names of the managing directors given whenever these are a matter of record. Each group's 1998–99 schedule, with emphasis on new plays and with revivals of classics usually omitted, is listed with play titles in CAPITAL LETTERS. Often these are works-in-progress with changing scripts, casts and directors, sometimes without an engagement of record (but an opening or early performance date is included when available.)

Many of these off-off-Broadway groups have long since outgrown a merely experimental status and are offering programs which are the equal in professionalism and quality (and in some cases the superior) of anything in the New York theater, with special contractual arrangements like the showcase code, letters of agreement (allowing for longer runs and higher admission prices than usual) and, closer to the edge of the commercial theater, a so-called "mini-contract." In the list below, all available data on opening dates, performance numbers and major production and acting credits (almost all for Equity members) is included in the entries of these special-arrangement offerings.

A large selection of lesser-known groups and other shows that made appearances off off Broadway during the season appears under the "Miscellaneous" heading at the end of this listing.

AMAS Musical Theater. Dedicated to bringing people of all races, creeds, colors, religious and national origins together through the performing arts. Rosetta LeNoire founder, Donna Trinkoff producing director.

ROLLIN' ON THE T.O.B.A.: A TRIBUTE TO THE LAST DAYS OF BLACK VAUDEVILLE (16). Conceived by Ronald "Smokey" Stevens and Jaye Stewart; additional material from Langston Hughes's *The Simple Stories.* July 23, 1998. Director, Ronald "Smokey" Stevens; scenery, Larry W. Brown; lighting, Melody Beal; costumes, Joey Hooks; musical direction, David Alan Bunn. With

Sandra Reaves-Phillips, Rudy Roberson, Ronald "Smokey" Stevens. Transferred to off Broadway; see its entry in the Plays Produced Off Broadway section of this volume.

DELPHI OR BUST (16). Book and lyrics, Michael Colby; music, Gerald Jay Markoe. December 3, 1998. Direction and choreography, Christopher Scott; scenery, Michael Schweikardt; lighting, Deborah Constantine; costumes, Michele Reisch. With Jody Ashworth, Darren Lee Frazier, Jill Geddes, Kimberly Harris, Colleen Hawkes, John Simeone, Ken Prymus, Tia Riebling.

REUNION: A CIVIL WAR EPIC IN MINIATURE (46). Book, Jack Kyrieleison; traditional music arranged by Michael O'Flaherty. April 5, 1999. Director, Ron Holgate; scenery, Doug Huszti; lighting, Stephen Petrilli; costumes, Jan Finnell; choreography, Karen Azenberg; musical direction, Robert Lamont. With Joe Barrett, Don Burroughs, Donna Lynne Champlain, Harriett D. Foy, Jonathan Hadley, Michael A. Shepperd.

American Place Theater. Issue-oriented and community-focused plays in their world premieres. Wynn Handman artistic director, Carl Jaynes general manager.

SAKINA'S RESTAURANT. Written and directed by Aasif Mandvi. June 24, 1998; see its entry in the Plays Produced Off Broadway section of this volume.

DREAMING IN CUBAN: RHYTHM, RUM, CAFÉ CON LECHE AND NUESTROS ABUELOS. Adapted from Cristina Garcia's novel and directed by Wynn Handman. April 26, 1999. Scenery, Manuel Vega; lighting, Ryan E. McMahon. With Eileen Galindo, Michael John Garces.

American Theater of Actors. Dedicated to providing a creative atmosphere for new American playwrights, actors and directors. James Jennings artistic director.

Schedule included:

DELIVERING DAD. By Lee Richard Lawing. June 3, 1998. Director, Douglas Mercer. With Devin McLean, Josh Miller, J. Richey Nash.

THE JEW OF BLEECKER STREET. By Norman Rhodes. June 3, 1998. Director, Marc Sabin. With Mort Forrest, James J. Gerber, Kristin Karayan, Jeanne LaSala.

BETWEEN THE AGES. By Betty Brito. June 10, 1998. Director, Maninder K. Saini. With Patricia McCurdy, Abby Ross, Ronnie Siegel.

TOGETHER AGAIN. Written and directed by James Jennings. June 24, 1998. With Ernest Lean, Jenifer Shaw.

THE EVIL THAT MEN DO. By Frank Barth. June 24, 1998. Director, Richard Bach. With Ariana Berman, Pascale Roger, John Justin Whitney.

TROILUS AND CRESSIDA. By William Shakespeare. July 8, 1998. Director, Jeff Sult. With Paul James Bowen, Campbell Bridges, Peter Chaskes, Mark Gordon.

LOVE IN THE AGE OF DION. By Philip Cioffari. July 22, 1998. Director, Kirk Vichengrad. With Lisa Dodd, Brent Erdy,Tom Reid, Mark Schmetterer.

ION. By Euripides. August 12, 1998. Director, James Jennings. With Cary Patrick Martin, Marie Thomas, J.C. Islander, Michael Medori.

PERMISSION TO BE NICK. By Ralph Cozzarelli and Mike Frensly. August 12, 1998. Director, Joe Pellegrino. With Ralph Cozzarelli, Mike Frensly, Veronica Bero, Amy Korb.

MURMURS OF CALIFORNIA. By Robert Vivian. August 19, 1998. Director, Harriet Spitzer. With Mort Forrest, Sharon Katz, Eric Pass, Brian Bergdoll.

PIGEON HOLE. Written and directed by Meny Beriro. August 26, 1998. With Jonathan Panczyk, Kelly Miller, Michael Driscoll, Jessica Chandlee Smith.

THE BLACK MARBLE SHOESHINE STAND. Written and directed by Louis LaRusso II. September 9, 1998. With Bob Harbaum, Michael Pare, George Pollock, Joseph Ragno.

HEMINGWAYS. By Ralph Hunt. September 17, 1998. Director, Christopher Bellis. With Beth Deitz, Anna Kelley, Christopher Benson Reed, Michael Thurston.

GUN HILL ROAD. Written and directed by Philip Cioffari. September 23, 1998. With Julia Guidi, Maureen Hayes.

GONE TO COLORADO. Written and directed by James Jennings. September 30, 1998. With Antoinette Gallo, Susan Kerner, Nick Rose, Edward Stein.

LUNCH BREAK written and directed by Michael Kalmar; NEXT OF KIN by Lois Shapley, directed by Barry Kaplan (one-act plays). October 28, 1998. With Christopher Benson Reed, Phasaan Orange, Colleen Rafferty, Jason Luciano, Mark Ehrlich.

MAD by Greg Kalleres, directed by Mike Kellehes; PUNCHLINE by Jonathan Heaps, directed by Richard Cagan (one-act plays). November 4, 1998. With Robbie Taylor, Sean Patterson, Wanda O'Connell, Sam Levassar, Matt Sarter.

YOUNG AND DEADLY. Written and directed by David Gaard. November 11, 1998. With Philip Alberti, Patrick Blindauer.

HIDDEN AGENDA. By Mel Cook. November 18, 1998. Director, Marc Anthony Thomas. With Melanie Bean, Michael Colombo, Ken Coughlin, Todd Fredericks, Joe Leone, Nick Rose.

WISHBONES AND FALLING STARS. Written and directed by James Jennings. December 16, 1998. With Lyndi Prettyman, Jacquelin Bowman, Bill McHugh, Ben Linder. Reopened March 18, 1999.

CHRISTMAS AT SANDY'S. By Vincent A. Apollo. January 6, 1999. Director, John Borras. With Wanda O'Connell, Alex Keomurjian, Michael Pace, Michael McClelland, Rich Odell, Al Choy, Samantha Ryan.

MR. REBBETZIN. By Steve Feffer. January 6, 1999. Director, Elysabeth Kleinhans. With Dina Drew, Jim Fromewick, Simona Berman, Neil Levine, Dana McLeod, Charles Walters.

THE SUBSTITUTE by Ralph Hunt, directed by Heidi Shurak; LOLLY by Donald Dewey, directed by Ryan Janis (one-act plays). January 13, 1999. With Jim Hazard, Thea Henry, Naomi Kale, Scott Parker, Ben Davis, Tanya Oesterling.

STILLS by Jim Beggarly, directed by Stephen Weitz; THE NIGHT REMEMBERS by Donally Miller, directed by Blake Lawrence (one act plays). January 27, 1999. With Michael McClelland, Alisha Snider, Will Buchanan, Stephen De Cordova, Pete Barker, Erica Kreutz.

HANK MANQUE by Tom Lavagnino, directed by David Vining; CONVERSATIONS WITH A KLEAGLE by Rudy Gray, directed by Kayla Solomon (one-act plays). February 3, 1999. With Ben Linder, Courtney Munch, Gregory O'Connor, Ken Coughlin, Robbie Taylor, Victor Trevino.

RAT LAB. By Ralph Hunt. February 10, 1999. Director, C.C. Banks. With Melanie Bean, Bertrand Buchin.

WORDS by Sally Domet, directed by David Lane; PARADOX OF AUTHORSHIP by Norman Rhodes, directed by Colleen Davie (one-act plays). February 24, 1999. With Dina Drew, Joseph Somma, Michael Deeg, Todd Fredericks, Leah Owen.

TENNIS, ANYONE by Wendy Aron, directed by Andrea Andresakis; TRUST ME by Anise Mouette Stevens, directed by Karen Millard (one-act plays). March 3, 1999. With Kenneth Garson, Donna Lee Michaels, Randi Jean Sobel, Ken Coughlin, Christina Parker.

MANHATTAN SPECIAL. By Ian Chambers. April 7, 1999. Director, Ryan Janis. With Allison Shigo, Daniel Paquin.

GRASSHOPPERS. By Burton Swartz. April 14, 1999. Director, Rich Cook. With Robert Atkins, Pete Barker, Todd Fredericks, Leah Owen, Julie Zimmermann.

THE REMEMBRANCE OF THINGS PRESENT. By John Bowers. April 21, 1999. Director, Craig David Rosen. With Eve Austin, Marty Bischoff.

SOMEONE'S COMIN' HUNGRY. By Neil Selden and McCrea Imbrie. May 19, 1999. Director, Ajala King. With Randy Frazier, Barbara Fears, Anselm Richardson.

THE OTHER SIDE OF LIFE. By Joe Iacona. May 26, 1999. Director, Tom Bruce. With Tom Bruno, Jan Gelberman, Joe Iacona, Joseph Leone, Constance Parisi.

ATLANTIC THEATER COMPANY—Josh Hamilton and Jillian Armenante in *The Cider House Rules, Part 1: Here in St. Cloud's,* Peter Parnell's stage adaptation of material from the novel by John Irving

Atlantic Theater Company. Produces new plays or reinterpretations of classics that speak to audiences in a contemporary voice on issues reflecting today's society. Neil Pepe artistic director, Hilary Hinckle managing director.

WOLF LULLABY (27). By Hilary Bell. October 29, 1998. Director, Neil Pepe; scenery, Walt Spangler; lighting, Howard Werner; costumes, Linda Cho; music and sound, Donald DiNicola. With Kate Blumberg, Mary McCann, Jordan Lage, Larry Bryggman.

THE HOTHOUSE (31). By Harold Pinter. February 25, 1999. Director, Karen Kohlhaas; scenery, Walt Spangler; lighting, Robert Perry; costumes, Rick Gradone; sound, Raymond D. Schilke. With Larry Bryggman, Jordan Lage, Liam Christopher O'Brien, Kate Blumberg, Patrick Breen, Stephen Mendillo.

THE CIDER HOUSE RULES, PART I: HERE IN ST. CLOUD'S (32). Adapted by Peter Parnell from the novel by John Irving, conceived and directed by Tom Hulce and Jane Jones. May 6, 1999. Scenery, John Arnone; lighting, Adam Silverman; costumes, David Zinn; music, Dan Wheetman. With Jillian Armenante, Eboni Booth, Lucy Avery Brooke, James Chesnutt, Cynthia Darlow, Aunjanue Ellis, Ross Gibby, Margo Grib, Josh Hamilton, Leslie Hendrix, Marceline Hugot, Katie MacNichol, Colm Meaney, Bill Moor, Martin Moran, Peggy Roeder, Louis Tucci, Todd Weeks, David-Paul Wichert.

Blue Light Theater Company. Produces a wide range of plays and strives to give young working actors the opportunity to grow by working with established theater artists. Greg Naughton actor-manager, William S. Doble general manager.

OEDIPUS (30). Written and directed by Dare Clubb. October 11, 1998. Scenery, Narelle Sissons; lighting, Christopher J. Landy; costumes, Christianne Myers; sound, Obadiah Eaves. With Frances McDormand, Billy Crudup, Johanna Day, Jeffrey Donovan, Lawrence Nathanson, Jon De Vries, Camilia Sanes, Kevin Geer, Alan Tudyk, Alex Draper, Jonathan Fried, Carolyn McCormick.

THE PITCHFORK DISNEY (36). By Philip Ridley. April 8, 1999. Director, Rob Bundy; scenery, George Xenos; lights, Greg MacPherson; costumes, Theresa Squire; music and sound, Obadiah Eaves. With Alex Draper, Lynn Hawley, Brandt Johnson, Alex Kilgore.

Brooklyn Academy of Music Next Wave Festival. Since 1981, this annual three-month festival has presented over 200 events, including more than 50 world premieres. Featuring leading international artists, it is one of the world's largest festivals of contemporary performing arts. Harvey Lichtenstein president and executive producer.

Schedule included:

ECLIPSE (41). Conceived, directed and designed by Bartabas. September 9, 1998. With Zingaro Equestrian Theater.

THE WORLD MYSTERIES: THE MYSTERIES OF ELEUSIS (5). Conceived, written and directed by Vasilios Calitsis; co-written by Tasos Roussos. October 14, 1998. Choreography, Apostolia Papadamaki; scenery, Merope Vachlioti; lighting, Matthew Frey; costumes, Mary McFadden; sound, Bruce Odland and Mark McCoin; music, Vasilios Calitsis and Yorgos Boudouvis. With Irene Worth, Vasilios Calitsis, Paolo Proletti, Rene Schubert, Carmen Dell'Orefice, Lola Greco, Apostolia Papadamaki, Muriel Louveau, Antonis Frangakis, Gregory Stamoulis, Irene Tsotra, Manos Pantelides, Timos Supprian-Katsoulis.

MONSTERS OF GRACE (opera) (13). Music, Philip Glass; lyrics, Jalaluddin Rumi, translated and adapted by Coleman Barks. December 9, 1998. Design and visual concept, Robert Wilson; sound, Kurt Munkacsi; musical direction, Michael Riesman. With Philip Glass and the Philip Glass Ensemble.

Classic Stage Company. Reinventing and revitalizing the classics for contemporary audiences. Barry Edelstein artistic director, Beth Emelson producing director.

WAITING FOR GODOT (43). By Samuel Beckett. November 18, 1998. Director, Andrei Belgrader; scenery, Andrei Both; lighting, Michael Chybowski; costumes, Elizabeth Hope Clancy. With John Turturro, Tony Shalhoub, Christopher Lloyd, Richard Spore.

THE MISANTHROPE (33). By Moliere, adapted by Martin Crimp. February 14, 1999. Director, Barry Edelstein; scenery, Narelle Sissons; lighting, Stephen Strawbridge; costumes, Martin Pakledinaz; sound, Darron L. West; music, Michael Torke. With Roger Rees, Uma Thurman, Michael Emerson, Nick Wyman, Adina Porter, John Gould Rubin, Seth Gilliam, Mary Lou Rosato, Brian Keane.

A SIMPLE HEART (dance-theater) (28). April 8, 1999. Direction, Annie-B Parson and Paul Lazar; scenery, Joanne Howard; lighting, David Moodey; costumes, Claudia Stephens; sound, Jane Shaw. With Tymberly Canale, Stacy Dawson, Molly Hickok, Cynthia Hopkins, David Neumann.

Drama Dept. A collective of actors, directors, designers, stage managers, writers and producers who collaborate to create new works and revive neglected classics. Douglas Carter Beane artistic director, Michael S. Rosenberg managing director.

AS THOUSANDS CHEER (44). Sketches, Moss Hart; music and lyrics, Irving Berlin. June 14, 1998. Director, Christopher Ashley; choreography, Kathleen Marshall; scenery, Allen Moyer; lighting, Kirk Bookman; costumes, Jonathan Bixby and Gregory A. Gale. With Kevin Chamberlin, Judy Kuhn, Howard McGillin, Paula Newsome, Mary Beth Peil, B.D. Wong.

'HOPE' IS THE THING WITH FEATHERS (16). By Frank Pugliese. December 9, 1998. Director, Randolph Curtis Rand; scenery and projections, Wendall K. Harrington; costumes, Jonathan Bixby and Gregory A. Gale; sound, Jerry Yager. With Cynthia Nixon, Maria Tucci, Keith Nobbs, Paula Garces, Avery Glymph, Robert Hogan.

THE AUTHOR'S VOICE by Richard Greenberg and IMAGINING BRAD by Peter Hedges (one-act plays) (16). May 20, 1999. Director, Evan Yionoulis; scenery, Allen Moyer; lighting, Kenneth Posner; costumes, Linda Cho; sound, Robert Murphy; music, Ray Leslee. With Polly Draper, Philip Seymour Hoffman, Christopher Orr, Amy Ryan, Paige Turco.

En Garde Arts. Dedicated to developing the concept of "site-specific theater" in the streets, parks and buildings of the city. Anne Hamburger founder and producer.

THE SECRET HISTORY OF THE LOWER EAST SIDE: THE PATRON SAINT OF THE NAMELESS DEAD by Carlos Murillo, NEW CULTURE FOR A COUNTRY by Alice Tuan, HESTER STREET HIDEAWAY: A LOWER EAST SIDE LOVE STORY by Peter Ullian (24). September 13, 1998. Director, Matthew Wilder; scenery, Richard Dennis; lighting, Christien Methot and Andris Kaspaorovics; costumes, Mary Myers; sound, David A. Schnirman. With Rafael Baez, Elaina Erika Davis, Saul Stein, Alice Tuan.

Ensemble Studio Theater. Membership organization of playwrights, actors, directors and designers dedicated to supporting individual theater artists and developing new works for the stage. Over 200 projects each season, ranging from readings to fully-mounted productions. Curt Dempster artistic director.

OCTOBERFEST 1998. Festival of over 80 new works by members. October 2-November 2, 1998.

STEP IN AND STAND CLEAR: A CITY SLAM (14). Conceived and performed by the Lexington Group, with additional material by Henry Haggerty and Jonathan Tipton Myers. November 15, 1998. Director, India Cooper. With Karine Andresen, Geneva Carr, India Cooper, Tristan Fitch, Holli Harms, Tom Paitson Kelly, David Reidy, Sean Sutherland.

GRETTY GOOD TIME (15). By John Belluso. January 24, 1999. Director, Susann Brinkley; scenery, Dan Kuchar; lighting, Greg MacPherson; costumes, Amela Baksic; sound, Jeremy M. Posner. With Fiona Gallagher; Richard Joseph Paul, Anna Li, Ted Neustadt, Sally Loeb, Baxter Harris.

GOING TO THE RIVER (festival of plays by African-American women): FAST BLOOD by Judy Tate; ONLY IN AMERICA by Aishah Rahman; MAIDEN LANE by Cassandra Medley; RE/MEMBERING AUNT JEMIMA: A MENSTRUAL SHOW by Breena Clarke and Glenda Dickerson; BLACK COMEDY: THE WACKY SIDE OF RACISM by Nancy Giles; SHAKIN' THE MESS OUTTA MISERY by Shay Youngblood; FLYIN' WEST by Pearl Cleage. February 9–21, 1999. Lighting, Greg MacPherson.

CLARENCE DARROW TONIGHT (15). Written, directed and performed by Laurence Luckinbill. March 7, 1999.

TESLA'S LETTERS (18). By Jeffrey Stanley. April 7, 1999. Director, Curt Dempster; scenery, Paula Sjoblom; lighting, Jeff Croiter; costumes, Julie Doyle; sound, Robert Gould. With Kiera Naughton,

Victor Slezak, Irma St. Paule, Grant James Varjas. (Part of the First Light Festival of new dramatic works exploring the worlds of science and technology.)

MARATHON '99 (festival of new one-act plays). ALL ABOUT AL by Cherie Vogelstein, directed by Jamie Richards; MAIDEN LANE by Cassandra Medley, directed by Irving Vincent; DEAF DAY written and directed by Leslie Ayvazian; GOODBYE OSCAR by Romulus Linney, directed by Peter Maloney; THE GOLF BALL by Frank D. Gilroy, directed by Chris Smith; DREAMTIME FOR ALICE by Susan Kim, directed by Richard Lichte; IN THE WESTERN GARDEN by Stuart Spencer, directed by Judy Minor; THE 'I' WORD: INTERN by Michael Louis Wells, directed by Jamie Richards; UP, DOWN, STRANGE, CHARMED, BEAUTY AND TRUTH by Edward Allan Baker, directed by Ron Stetson; WAR by Bill Bozzone, directed by Christine Farrell; THE ONCE ATTRACTIVE WOMAN by Christine Farrell, directed by Eliza Beckwith; ROMAN FEVER by Jamie Richards and Kevin Harris, adapted from Edith Wharton's short story, directed by Eileen Myers. May 5-June 13, 1999.

INTAR. Mission is to identify, develop and present the talents of gifted Hispanic American theater artists and multicultural visual artists. Max Ferra artistic director.

100 YEARS OF GARCIA LORCA (three plays by Federico Garcia Lorca): THE HOUSE OF BERNARDA ALBA, translated by Michael Dewell and Carmen Zapata, directed by Max Ferra; AS FIVE YEARS PASS, translated by Caridad Svich, directed by Michael John Garces; THE SHOEMAKER'S PRODIGIOUS WIFE, translated by Michael Dewell and Carmen Zapata, directed by Max Ferra. October 27-November 29, 1998. Scenery, Van Santvoord; lighting, Robert Williams; costumes, Katherine Roth; sound, Johnna Doty; puppets and masks, Ralph Lee. With Denise Casano, Miriam Cruz, Oscar de la Fe Colon, Doris DiFarnecio, Yetta Gottesman, Mercedes Herrero, Sol Miranda, Alba Oms, Carlos Orizondo, Carlos Rafart, Virginia Rambal, Bill Torres, Marilyn Torres.

NewWorks Lab Series '99. 3 performances each
Schedule included:

1, 2, 3. MUERTE, MUERTE, MORTE: PRESSED. By Paulo Nunes-Ueno; ODISEO, COULD YOU STOP AND PICK UP SOME EGGS AND MILK ON THE WAY HOME? By Jorge Ignacio Cortinas; FLYIN' HIGH by Henry Guzman (one-act plays). April 30, 1999. Director, Paulo Nunes-Ueno.

ARRIVALS AND DEPARTURES. Written and directed by Rogelio Martinez. May 7, 1999. Scenery, Lucy Thurber; lighting, Veronica Diaz Rodriguez; sound, Erin Hill. With Vanessa Aspillaga, Tony Gillan, Carlos Orizondo.

TRAVERSING JACOB. By Ignacio Lopez. May 14, 1999. Director, Alexandra Lopez.

Irish Repertory Theater. Aims to bring works by Irish and Irish American masters and contemporary playwrights to a wider audience and to develop new works focusing on a wide range of cultural experiences. Charlotte Moore artistic director, Ciaran O'Reilly producing director.

THE IRISH ... AND HOW THEY GOT THAT WAY. By Frank McCourt. Reopened June 10, 1998 for 32 performances.

THE SHAUGHRAUN (THE VAGABOND) (96). By Dion Boucicault. November 12, 1998. Director, Charlotte Moore; scenery, Klara Zieglerova; lighting, Ken Davis; costumes, Linda Fisher. With Jimmy Cunningham, Terry Donnelly, Lucinda Faraldo, Patrick Fitzgerald, Daniel Gerroll, Jason Killalee, Paul McGrane, Marion Thomas Griffin, Ciaran O'Reilly, Amy Redmond, Peter Rogan, Geddeth Smith, Fiona Walsh.

KRAPP'S LAST TAPE (28). By Samuel Beckett. November 5, 1998. Director, Vincent O'Neill. With Jerry Finnegan.

OH, COWARD! (42). Based on the life and works of Noel Coward, devised by Roderick Cook. February 16, 1999. Director, Augustine Towey; choreography, Lynn Kirziel-Formato; scenery, Charlotte Moore; lighting, Jason Cina; costumes, Geraldine Dusk. With William B. Hubert 2d, Brendan Powers, Maggie Runfola, Stephen Vasta.

THE SHADOW OF A GUNMAN (55). By Sean O'Casey. April 15, 1999. Director, Charlotte Moore; scenery, Akira Yoshimura and N. Joseph De Tullio; costumes, David Toser. With Declan Mooney, Ciaran O'Reilly, Sean Power, Denis O'Neill, Aedin Maloney, John Keating, Rosemary Fine, Michael Judd, Terry Donnelly, Peter Rogan.

Jewish Repertory Theater. Presents plays in English relating to the Jewish experience. Ran Avni artistic director, Michael Lichtenstein managing director.

THE FISHKIN TOUCH (24). Book, David Javerbaum; music, Greg Armbruster; lyrics, Lenore Skenazy. June 14, 1998. Director, Alan Fox; scenery, Craig Clipper; lighting, Robert Williams; costumes, Gail Cooper-Hecht; sound, Joshua Bender-Dubiel. With Mike Burstyn, Joan Copeland, Carolann Page, Jordan Leeds, Beth Thompson.

KUNI-LEML (31). Book, Nahma Sandrow, based on Avrom Goldfadn's play; music, Raphael Crystal; lyrics, Richard Engquist. November 1, 1998. Director, Ran Avni; scenery, Elizabeth Chaney; lighting, Deborah Constantine; sound, Joshua Bender-Dubiel; musical direction, David Wolfson. With Danny Gurwin, Jay Brian Winnick, Joel Newsome, David Brummel, Jennifer Rosin, Paul Harman, Jonathan Hadley, Farah Alvin.

A MAJORITY OF ONE (31). By Leonard Spigelgass. January 24, 1999. Director, Richard Sabellico; scenery, Todd Edward Ivins; lighting, Richard Latta; costumes, Gail Baldoni. With Elaine Grollman, Phyllis Newman, Julia Dion, Danny Gurwin, Randall Duk Kim, Mio Takada, Konrad Aderer, Ako.

NEVER ON FRIDAY (one-man show) (31). Conceived and performed by Dudu Fisher, written by Larry Amoros. April 25, 1999. Director, Ran Avni; scenery, Paul S. Morrill; lighting, Richard Latta; costumes, Shai Shalom; musical direction, Gil Nagel.

THE GATHERING. By Arje Shaw. June 10, 1999. Director, Rebecca Taylor; scenery, Joel Schwartz; lighting, Scott Clyve; costumes, Susan L. Soetaert; sound, Jeremy M. Posner; music, Andy Stein. With Theodore Bikel, Robert Fass, Susan Warrick Hasho, Peter Hermann.

The Joseph Papp Public Theater/New York Shakespeare Festival. Schedule of special projects, in addition to its regular off-Broadway productions. George C. Wolfe producer, Rosemarie Tichler artistic producer, Mark Litvin managing director, Michael Hurst general manager, Margaret M. Lioi senior director of external affairs.

Joe's Pub. Schedule included:

WAY BACK TO PARADISE (songs). By Jason Robert Brown, Jenny Giering, Ricky Ian Gordon, Adam Guettel, Michael John LaChiusa. October 19, 1998. Musical direction, Ted Sperling. With Audra McDonald.

INSIDE THE CREOLE MAFIA. By and with Roger Guenveur Smith and Mark Broyard. November 13, 1998.

WHAT THE LIVING DO (songs). By Ricky Ian Gordon, based on Marie Howe's poems. November 23, 1998. With Terry McCarthy.

THE LORCA FESTIVAL (readings, poetry, puppet works, theater pieces by Federico Garcia Lorca). November 27–December 5, 1998.

AN INTIMATE PARTY WITH BETTY & ADOLPH. By and with Betty Comden and Adolph Green. February 1, 1999.

SLANT (Wayland Quintero, Rick Ebihara, Perry Yung). April 13, 1999.

DREAM EXPRESS. By Len Jenkins. May 1, 1999. With Deirdre O'Connell, Stephen Mellor.

NEW WORK NOW! (festival of staged readings): CAROLINE, OR CHANGE by Tony Kushner; TOPDOG/UNDERDOG by Suzan-Lori Parks; –14: AN AMERICAN MAUL by Robert O'Hara; MYOPIA (one-man show) by and with David Greenspan; OFFSPRING OF THE COLD WAR by Carlos Murillo, directed by Liz Diamond; REFERENCES TO SALVADOR DALI MAKE ME HOT by Jose Rivera, directed by Jo Bonney; AJAX (POR NOBODY) by Alice Tuan; KING OF COONS by Michael Henry Brown, directed by Marion McClinton; BRINGING THE FISHERMEN HOME by Deb Margolin; THE GLORY OF LIVING by Rebecca Gilman; BLUR by Melanie

Marnich; STARGAZERS by Chiori Miyagawa; FALL by Bridget Carpenter; ILLUMINATING VERONICA by Rogelio Martinez; KIT MARLOWE by David Grimm. April 19-May 3, 1999.

FIRST STAGES (works-in-progress): CIVIL SEX written and directed by Brian Freeman. May 19, 1999. Lighting, D.M. Wood; costumes, Anita Yavich; sound, Guy Sherman. With LaTonya Borsay, Duane Boutte, Brian Freeman, Michael Stebbins, John Patrick Walker.

La Mama (a.k.a. LaMama) Experimental Theater Club (ETC). A busy workshop for experimental theater of all kinds. Ellen Stewart founder and director.

Schedule included:

HARRY AND THE CANNIBALS. Written and directed by Susan Mosakowski. June 4, 1998. Scenery, Paula Longendyke; lighting, Howard Thies; costumes, Julia Van Vliet; sound, Joe Gallant.

With Malcolm Adams, Frank Deal, Louise Favier, David Giambusso, Lars Hanson, Eva Patton, Greig Sargeant, Raphael Nash Thompson, Sean Weil.

A CANON FOR THE BLUE MOON. By the North American Cultural Lab. June 4, 1998. Direction, Brad Krumholz and Tannis Kowalchuk.

HAMATSA. By Nate Harvey. June 18, 1998. Direction, Jean Taylor and Shelley Wyant.

CONVERTIBLE. Book and lyrics, Elizabeth West Versalie; music, Peter Dizozza. June 18, 1998. Direction and choreography, Tyr Throne; lighting, Herrick Goldman. With Michael A. Ballos, Lisa Dery, Peter Dizozza, Kate Lunsford, Pamela Lehman, Case Murphy, J.R. Robinson, Cody Smolik, Cezar Williams.

ALL TALK. By the Todd Theater Troupe. June 18, 1998. Director, Mervyn Willis.

THE BALD SOPRANO and THE LESSON. By Eugene Ionesco, translated by Donald M. Allen. September 24, 1998. Direction, Nicholas and Ulla Wolcz.

LEIR REX (multimedia work). Conceived and adapted by Ernest Abuba, Shigeko Suga and Richard Scanlon from William Shakespeare's *King Lear.* September 24, 1998. CRAZY ME, CRAZY YOU + DIGNITY. By and with Poppo and the GoGo Boys. October 2, 1998.

THE DIS-ADVENTURES OF PETER PAN VS. CAPTAIN MALEDETTO. Adapted from J. M. Barrie's novel and directed by Dario D'Ambrosi. October 8, 1998.

LE MENAGE. By Aida M. Croal. October 15, 1998. Director, Robert Allen.

THE TAMING OF THE SHREW. By William Shakespeare. October 27, 1998. Director, Andrei Serban; scenery, Jun Maeda; lighting, Howard Thies; costumes, Leslie Scott; sound, Tim Schellenbaum.

GOD, THE CRACKHOUSE AND THE DEVIL. By Levy Lee Simon Jr. October 29, 1998. Director, Mary Beth Easley.

GEEK CIRCUS, THE TWISTED SHOCKFEST. By and with Scott Baker. October 29, 1998.

TO BE A TURK. By Huseyin Katircioglu. November 5, 1998.

CIVIL DISOBEDIENCE; MORNING IS WHEN I AM AWAKE AND THERE IS AN AURORA IN ME. Adapted from Henry David Thoreau's writings, directed and performed by Denise Stoklos. November 19, 1998. Scenery, Gringo Cardia; lighting, Maneco Quindere; costumes, Rebecca Nassauer.

JEWS AND JESUS. Book, Oren Safdie; music and lyrics, Ronnie Cohen. December 2, 1998. Director, Anthony Patellis. With Sean Power, Hope Salas, Dee Ann Newkirk, Kevin Merritt, Mary Ann Conk, Teddy Coluca.

PASSIONATE WOMEN. By Mario Fratti. December 3, 1998. Director, Joumana Rizk; scenery, Jonathan Marvel; lighting, Howard Thies; costumes, Quina Fonseca; sound, Han Young. With Tony Torn, Maria Cellario, Holly Cate, Rebecca Nelson, Bruce Katzman, Susan Wands, Jeanne Langston, Charmaine Lord.

THE CAT AND THE MOON. By William Butler Yeats. December 4, 1999. Director, Huseyin Katircioglu.

WET SPOT. By and with Slant (Richard Ebihara, Wayland Quintero, Perry Yung). January 2, 1999.

COYOTE, TAKE ME THERE! By Sophia Murashkovsky. January 2, 1999. Director, Leslie Lee.

RUSALKA, THE LITTLE RIVERMAID. Adapted from a Czech folk tale and directed by Vit Horejs. January 7, 1999. Music, William Parker. With the Czechoslovak-American Marionette Theater.

THE BANQUET OF THE BEHEADED. By Nicola L. January 14, 1999. Director, Michael Warren Powell,; scenery, Kevin Joseph Roach,; costumes, Gohnny Power. With Michael Warren Powell, Alice King, Roger Michaelson, Jannie Wolff, Stuart Rudin, Maureen Campbell, Kurt Williams, Nadia Steinitz, Maria Bunina, James Lurie, Edith Meeks, Robert Jiminez, Tom Bozell, Susan Cella.

VAUDEVILLE 2000 (revue). By Laraine Goodman. January 21, 1999.

TILT. Written and composed by Ellen Maddow. January 24, 1999. Director, Will Pomerantz; scenery, Christine Jones; lighting, Carol Mullins; costumes, Mattie Ullrich; sound, Miles Green. With the Talking Band (Ellen Maddow, Joe Roseto, Tina Shepard, Paul Zimet, Zakia Babb, Isaac Maddow-Zimet).

BLOODLETTING. By Michael DiAntonio. January 21, 1999. Director, George Ferencz.

ROMAN RUINS. By Philippe Minyana. February 25, 1999.

THE LONE RUNNER. Written and directed by Jane Catherine Shaw. March 4, 1999.

FLIGHT OF THE WHITE BIRD. By Yara Arts Group and Buryat National Theater. March 5, 1999. Director, Virlana Tkacz; scenery, Watoku Ueno; costumes, Luba Kierkosz; music, Genji Ito and Erzhena Zhanbalov.

WAR, SEX AND DREAMS (one-man show). By and with Jean-Claude Van Itallie. March 20, 1999. Director, Joel Gluck; lighting, Larry Lawlor.

TOPSY ON THE BOARDWALK. Written and directed by Edward Kinchley Evans. March 25, 1999. With Glenn Z. Gless, Adrienne Wehr.

FRAGMENTS OF A GREEK TRILOGY (MEDEA, ELECTRA and THE TROJAN WOMEN). Conceived by Andrei Serban and the Great Jones Repertory Company; music, Elizabeth Swados. March 26, 1999. Director, Andrei Serban; scenery, Jun Maeda; lighting, David Adams; costumes, Sandra Muir and Gabriel Berry; musical direction, Bill Ruyle. With Neal Harris, Karen Kandel, George Drance Jr., Onni Johnson Valois, Mia Yoo, Perry Yung, Maura Nguyen Donohue, Charley Hayward, Brian Nishii, Kim Ima, Julia Martin, Charlotte Brathwaite, Carlo Wertenbaker.

BODY OF CRIME, PART II: A HISTORY OF WOMEN IN PRISON. Created, designed and directed by Theodora Skipitares; music and lyrics, Barry Greenhut. April 15, 1999. Lighting, Pat Dignan; additional design, Holly Laws and Jane Catherine Shaw. With Preston Foerder, Michael Moran, Sarah Provost, Tom Ross, Felice Rosser, Shaheen Chamarbagwala, Charlotte Braithwaite.

ASPHYXIA AND OTHER PROMISES. By Henry Israel. April 15, 1999. Director, Brad Krumholz.

SPRING AWAKENING. By Frank Wedekind, adapted by Andrea Paciotto and Donna Linderman. May 6, 1999.

THE BRIDE AND THE BUTTERFLY HUNTER. By Nissim Aloni, translated by Valerie Amon. May 12, 1999. Direction, Victor Attar and Geula Jeffet. With Victor Attar, Liat Ron.

HENRY V. By William Shakespeare. May 27, 1999. Director, Alexander Harrington; music, John Allman. With the Eleventh Hour Theater Company.

FIRST KILL. By Frank Damico. Director, Harold Dean James. May 27, 1999.

Lincoln Center Festival. An annual international summer arts festival offering classic and contemporary works. For Lincoln Center for the Performing Arts, Beverly Sills chairman, Nathan Leventhal president, Nigel Redden festival director.

Schedule included:

VILLAGE. By Joshua Sobol. July 7, 1998. With the Gesher Theater.

ADAM RESURRECTED. By Alexander Chervinsky, based on Yoram Kaniuk's novel. July 14, 1998. Director, Yevgeny Arye; choreography, Valentine Menuhin; scenery and costumes, Elena Stepanova; lighting, Niv Sade; music, Avi Benjamin. With Igor Mirkurbanov, Yevgenya Dodina, Maria Gamburg, Israel Demidov, Vladimir Halemsky, Nelly Gosheva, Natalia Voltulevich-Manor (Gesher Theater).

TWELFTH NIGHT, OR, WHAT YOU WILL. By William Shakespeare. See Plays Produced on Broadway section of this volume.

THE STREET OF CROCODILES. Devised by Théâtre de Complicité, based on Bruno Schulz's stories; adapted by Simon McBurney and Mark Wheatley. July 6, 1998. Director, Simon McBurney; scenery, Rae Smith; lighting, Paule Constable; sound, Chris Shutt. With Cesar Sarachu, Matthew Scurfield, Annabel Arden, Clive Mendus, Charlotte Medcalf, Antonio Gil Martinez, Bronagh Gallagher, Asta Sighvats, Eric Mallet, Stefan Metz.

F@UST: VERSION 3.0 (5). Conceived by Pablo Ley, Alex Olle, Carlos Padrissa and Magda Puyo, based on Parts 1 and 2 of Goethe's play. July 22, 1998. Direction, Alex Olle and Carlos Padrissa. With La Fura dels Baus.

Mabou Mines. Theater collective whose work is a synthesis of motivational acting, narrative acting and mixed-media performance. Collective artistic leadership. Frederick Neumann, Terry O'Reilly, Ruth Maleczech, Lee Breuer artistic directors.

LAS HORAS DE BELEN – A BOOK OF HOURS (13). Poems and lyrics by Catherine Sasanov, translated by Luz Aurora Pimentel and Alberto Blanco. May 15, 1999. Director, Ruth Maleczech; choreography, Jesusa Rodriguez; scenery, lighting and projections, Julie Archer; sound, Miles Green; music, Liliana Felipe. With Jesusa Rodriguez, Monica Dionne, Liliana Felipe, Julie Archer, Joe Stackell, Lute Ramblin.

RESIDENT ARTIST SERIES. Schedule included YI SANG COUNTS TO THIRTEEN by Sung Rno; CHERRY VANILLA by Martha Elliot; THE EVA HESSE PROJECT conceived and directed by Michele Coleman; MURDER, MADNESS AND LADY MACBETH by Rebecca Ortese and Michele Minnick; FROM THIRD WORLD TO THIRD WARD: A BLACK GIRL'S SONG by Toya Ane Lillard; THE OLDEST PROFESSION by Erin B. Mee; BIRD by Sarah Cathcart and Anjel Van Slyke; I LOVE DICK adapted by Leslie Mohn from Chris Kraus's novel; SELF DEFENSE, OR DEATH OF SOME SALESMAN by Carson Kreitzer; CAVERNS created by Christine Sang, text by Ruth Margraff. June 1–27, 1999.

MCC Theater. Dedicated to the promotion of emerging writers, actors, directors and theatrical designers. Robert LuPone and Bernard Telsey artistic directors.

WIT (93). By Margaret Edson. September 17, 1998. Director, Derek Anson Jones; scenery, Myung Hee Cho; lighting, Michael Chybowski; costumes, Ilona Somogyi; music and sound, David Van Tieghem. With Kathleen Chalfant, Walter Charles, Alec Phoenix, Paula Pizzi, Helen Stenborg, Brian J. Carter, Daniel Sarnelli, Alli Steinberg, Lisa Tharps. Transferred to off Broadway; see its entry in the Plays Produced Off Broadway section of this volume.

THE ENGLISH TEACHERS (11). By Edward Napier. April 21, 1999. Director, Robert LuPone; scenery, Rob Odorisio; lighting, Jon Luton; costumes, Juliet Polcsa; music and sound, Bruce Ellman. With Pat Nesbit, Amy Whitehouse, Michael Hall, Alma Cuervo, Ruthie Davis, Ruth Williamson, Sally Parrish.

ANGELIQUE (11). By Lorena Gale. June 17, 1999. Director, Derek Anson Jones; scenery, Myung Hee Cho; lighting, Michael Chybowski; costumes, Marion Williams. With Lisa Gay Hamilton, Earl Baker, Jr., Angel Desai, Jonathan Fried, Pamela Nyberg, Jonathan Walker, Jason Weinberg.

Music-Theater Group. Pioneering in the development of new music-theater. Lyn Austin producing director, Diane Wondisford general director.

RUNNING MAN (28). Text by Cornelius Eady; story and music, Diedre Murray. February 24, 1999. Director, Diane Paulus; scenery, Myung Hee Cho; lighting, John Lasiter; costumes, Christianne Myers; sound, Richard Jansen. With Ronnell Bey, Roberta Gumbel, Darius de Haas, Robert Jason Jackson, Kimberly Jajuan, Chris Rustin. (Produced in association with HERE.)

New Dramatists. An organization devoted to playwrights; member writers may use the facilities for anything from private cold readings of their material to public script-in-hand readings. Todd London artistic director, Jana Jevnikar director of administration and finance, Paul A. Slee executive director.

Readings:

DREAMLANDIA by Octavio Solis, directed by Loretta Greco; LAST TRAIN TO NIBROC by Arlene Hutton, directed by Michael Montel; DOWN TOWN by Luis Alfaro; PHOTOGRAPHS FROM S-21 by Catherine Filloux, directed by Ron Nakahara; BLACK MILK book, lyrics and direction by Paul Zimet, music by Ellen Maddow; September 14, 1998.

A BEAUTIFUL WHITE ROOM. By Barry Jay Kaplan. September 16, 1998. Director, Richard Caliban.

AY, CARMELA! By Jose Sanchis Sinisterra, translated and adapted by Nilo Cruz and Catalina Botello. September 17, 1998. Director, Karin Coonrod.

NIGHT VISION. Book and lyrics, Ruth Margraff; concept, music and musical direction, Fred Ho. September 18, 1998.

INTRIGUE WITH FAYE. By Kate Robin. September 21, 1998. Director, Richard Caliban.

THE SINGING. Book, Lenora Champagne; music, Daniel Levy; lyrics, Lenora Champagne and Daniel Levy. October 1, 1998. Director, Eleanor Holdridge; musical direction, Douglas Coates.

THE HOTEL CARTER. By Stephanie Fleischmann. October 6, 1998. Director, Alison Summers.

TWO-HEADED. By Julie Jensen. October 13, 1998. Director, Wendy Liscow.

LEAVING QUEENS. Book and lyrics, Kate Moira Ryan; music Kim D. Sherman. October 15, 1998. Director, Joan Vail Thorne.

MARY AND MYRA. By Catherine Filloux. October 19, 1998.

FIVE FROZEN EMBRYOS. Written and directed by David Greenspan. October 20, 1998.

LES TROIS DUMAS. By Charles Smith. October 26, 1998. Director, Thomas Caruso.

THE WORGELT STUDY. By Kate Moira Ryan. October 27, 1998. Director, Marya Cohn.

NINE SCENES ABOUT LOVE. Written and directed by Peter Mattei. October 28, 1998.

SHINER. Written and directed by Erik Ehn. October 29, 1998.

SISTER WEEK. By Heather McCutchen. October 30, 1998. Director, Kate Loewald.

TO MANDELA. By Herman Daniel Farrell III. November 4, 1998. Director, Michael Sexton.

A FLAW IN THE FLEW. By Mark Dundas Wood. November 12, 1998. Director, Michael Sexton.

BURNERS. By Kenneth Urban. November 18, 1998. Director, Michael Sexton.

THE SUN ALWAYS ROSE. By Catherine Filloux. November 21, 1998. Director, Eva Saks.

TAKING IN OPEN-LIGHT. By Jennifer Johung. December 8, 1998. Director, Rhea Gaisner.

PASCHAL FULL MOON. By Andrew Irons. December 14, 1998. Director, Alison Summers.

THE SECRET MACHINE. Written and directed by Gordon Dahlquist. December 17, 1998.

ROCK AND ROY. Book and lyrics, Barry Jay Kaplan; music, Stephen Weinstock. January 14, 1999. Director, Jean Randich.

FIGHTING WORDS by Sunil Kuruvilla, directed by Richard Caliban; REGENERATION (EX?) by Barbara Labinger, directed by Alison Summers; GOD'S ACRE by Cahir O'Doherty, directed by Jerry Manning. January 15, 1999.

WHAT CORBETT KNEW. Written and directed by Jeffrey Hatcher. February 8, 1999.

THE WOMEN OF LOCKERBIE. By Deborah Baley Brevoort. February 10, 1999. Director, Lou Jacob.

RAW DEALS AND SOME SATISFACTION. By Silvia Gonzalez S. February 17, 1999. Director, Eleanor Holdridge.

DEATH OF A SOCIAL SECURITY BENEFIT. By Silvia Gonzalez S. February 19, 1999.

UNTITLED LIFE. By Jollina Walker. February 22, 1999. Director, Lou Jacob.

ILLUMINATING VERONICA. By Rogelio Martinez. March 1, 1999. Director, Michael Garces.

THE BIG BLUE NAIL. By Carlyle Brown. March 8, 1999. Director, Loy Arcenas.

COATICOOK. By Lenora Champagne. March 10, 1999. Director, Eleanor Holdridge.

THE REST IS EASY. By Chay Yew. March 12, 1999. Director, David Mowers.

BLESSED ARE: SCENES FROM SHAKER LIFE. Written and directed by Beth-Arlene. March 13, 1999.

HARSH MEDICINES. By Gordon Dahlquist. March 27, 1999.

SICK AGAIN. By Gordon Dahlquist. April 5, 1999.

COMRADES AND WORMS. By Rogelio Martinez. April 14, 1999. Director, Lou Jacob.

MOTHER'S DAY. By Herman Daniel Farrell III. April 22, 1999. Director, Nancy Jones.

THE WIG LADY. By Leslie Lee. April 22, 1999.

SIGNATURE THEATER COMPANY—*Above,* Adam Grupper as Young
Andrew and Kate Burton as Young Agnes; and, *below,* Betty Miller and Ralph
Waite as those same characters at a later age, in the world premiere production
of John Guare's *Lake Hollywood,* the climax of a season of Guare plays presented by this company under James Houghton's artistic directorship

THE END OF JAZZ. By Herman Daniel Farrell III. April 26, 1999. Director, Nancy Jones.

SQUEEZED AVOCADOES. By Silvia Gonzalez S. May 15, 1999. Director, Ian Morgan.

THE MYSTERY SCHOOL. By Victor Lodato. May 19, 1999.

A BOOK OF HARSH GEOMETRY. By Victor Lodato. May 26, 1999.

THE PRICE YOU PAY. By Arlene Hutton. June 2, 1999. Director, Judith Royer.

THE EARTH SINGS FA-MI. By Paul Zimet and Ellen Maddow. June 3, 1999.

ACAPULCO. Written and directed by Jacquelyn Reingold. June 4, 1999.

CLARK IN SARAJEVO. By Catherine Zimdahl. June 8, 1999.

BODY LANGUAGE. By Louis C. Adelman. June 10, 1999.

CORPORATE LAW. By Herman Daniel Farrell III. June 28, 1999.

PORCHES. By Herman Daniel Farrell III. June 29, 1999.

New Federal Theater. Dedicated to integrating minorities and women into the mainstream of American theater by training artists and by presenting plays by minorities and women to integrated, multicultural audiences. Woodie King Jr. producing director.

VALENTINE'S DAY (one-man show) (12). By and with Val Coleman. June 16, 1998. Director, Ann Bowen; lighting, Antoinette Tynes; sound, Tim Schellenbaum.

THE TRIAL OF ONE SHORT-SIGHTED BLACK VS. MAMMY LOUISE AND SAFREETA MAE (40). By Marcia L. Leslie. October 21, 1998. Director, Paul Carter Harrison; scenery, Felix E. Cochren; lighting, Kathy Perkins; costumes, Helen L. Simmons; sound and video, David Wright. With Ebony Jo-Ann, Carla Brothers, JoAnna Rhinehart, Brenda Denmark, Petronia Paley, Reg Flowers, Barbara Montgomery.

ROSE McCLENDON: HARLEM'S GIFT TO BROADWAY (one-woman show) (24). By and with Vinie Burrows. April 14, 1999. Director, Douglas Turner Ward; choreography, Louis Johnson; scenery, Kent Hoffman; lighting, Antoinette Tynes; costumes, Anita Ellis; sound, Tim Schellenbaum.

IN DAHOMEY (30). Written and directed by Shauneille Perry. June 17, 1999. Choreography, Chequita Ross Glover; scenery, Robert Joel Schwartz; lighting, Shirley Prendergast; costumes, Evelyn Nelson; musical direction, Julius P. Williams. With Shirley Verrett, Tanya Alexander, Cedric D. Cannon, Brian Chandler, LaTrice Verrett, Lucio P. Fernandez, Keith Lee Grant, Jim Jacobson, Trina Parks, Charles Reese, Kim Sullivan.

The New Group. Provides an artistic home for artists by launching fresh acting, writing and design talent. Committed to cultivating a young and diverse theatergoing audience by providing accessible ticket prices. Scott Elliott artistic director, Claudia Catania executive producer.

SOME VOICES (48). By Joe Penhall. January 7, 1999. Director, Frank Pugliese; scenery, Kevin Price; lighting, James Vermeulen; costumes, Mattie Ullrich; music, Tom Kochan. With Jamie Harris, Mitchell McGuire, Max Baker, David Thornton, Ana Reeder.

HALFWAY HOME (27). By Diane Bank. March 3, 1999. Director, Steven Williford; scenery, Kevin Price; lighting, James Vermeulen; costumes, Daryl Stone; sound, Bob Murphy. With Jill Bowman, Christina Chang, Judy Frank, Kate Levy, Lori Mahl, Christina Rouner, Nick Sandow, Welker White.

EAST IS EAST. By Ayub Khan-Din. May 3, 1999. Co-produced by Manhattan Theater Club; see its entry in the Plays Produced Off Broadway section of this volume.

The New Victory Theater. Purpose is to introduce young people and families, reflective of New York City's diverse communities, to live performances. Cora Cahan president.

Schedule included:

WAKE BABY (9). By and with Reckless Moments; text, Gillian Rubenstein. October 17, 1998. Director, Nigel Jamieson; scenery, Richard Jeziorny; lighting, Philip Lethlean; music, Jeff Evans. With Paul O'Keeffe, Naomi Audette.

METAMURPHOSIS MINOR (one-man show) (9). By and with Tom Murphy. November 6, 1998.

GRIMM TALES (49). Adapted by Carol Ann Duffy; music, Adrian Lee. November 20, 1998. Director, Tom Supple; scenery, costumes and choreography, Melly Still; lighting, Paule Constable; sound, Paul Bull; musical direction, Sylvia Hallett. With The Young Vic Theater Company (Sarah C. Cameron, Flaminia Cinque, Thusitha Jayasundera, Paul M. Meston, Dan Milne, Christopher Saul, Godfrey Walters, Andy Williams.)

MYTHOLOJAZZ (11). Conceived, written and performed by David Gonzalez; music, D.D. Jackson. February 12, 1999. Director, Leonard Petit; scenery, Bryan Johnson; lighting, David J. Lander.

THE ANGELS' CRADLE (10). By Elizabeth Wiseman and John Flax. March 4, 1999. Direction, Elizabeth Wiseman, John Flax and Diane Schenker; lighting, Ian Rosenkranz. With Fred Nelson, Aman Geroy, Elizabeth Wiseman, John Flax, Erica Jett.

THE STAR KEEPER (10). Storyboard by Richard Lacroix, Andre Laliberte and Richard Morin; conceived by Guy Coderre, Jean Cummings, Richard Lacroix, Andre Laliberte and Richard Morin. April 16, 1999. Director, Richard Laliberte; scenery, Richard Lacroix; lighting, Luc Desilets; puppets, Richard Morin; music, Libert Subirana. With Jean Cummings, Olivier Perrier, Sylvain Racine, Graham Soul.

THE NEW SHANGHAI CIRCUS (23). April 29, 1999. Director, Zhao Lizhi; lighting, Jeff Davis. With Yo Bojun, Xu Jun, Zhang Yun, Jiang Yi, Zhang Bihuan, Ye Haojie, Song Dezhon, Chen Zhengjie, Pan Lianhua, Wang Yingying Wang, Xu Ying, Yu Wentong, Xiao Lin, Wang Qi, Hong Yijia Hong, Zhu Jing, Yang Luni, Xu Yan, Wang Xinyi, Yu Haizhu, Gao Shengsheng.

Ontological-Hysteric Theater. Avant garde productions written, directed and designed by Richard Foreman. Richard Foreman artistic director, Damon Kiely producing director.

Schedule included:

BLACK MASK (12). By Damon Kiely and Frank Bradley. August 29, 1998. Director, Damon Kiely; scenery, Vicki Davis; lighting, Michael Gottlieb; costumes, Carol Bailey. With Lillith Beitchman, Rob Donaldson, Jason Howard, Johanna McKeon, Bryan Webster, Seana Wyman, Lia Yang.

THE FOUL STENCH OF DEATH (6). By Jonas Oppenheim. September 3, 1998. Director, Padraic Lillis. With Patrick Burch, Jeff Burchfield, Jamie Campos, Kevin Cristaldi, Melinda Kuhn, Dennis McNitt, Jordan Meadows.

SONATA DA CAMERA OBSCURA (9). Devised, directed and designed By Ken Nintzel. September 18, 1998. With Chuck Blasius, Kenneth Bonavitacola, Christopher M. Crowthers, Tracy Christian, Billy Gallo, Jessie Hawley, Ken Nintzel, Robin Punsalan, Dan Thaler, Susan Tierney, Curt Wagner.

PARADISE HOTEL (70). Written, directed, designed and composed by Richard Foreman. January 13, 1999. Lighting, Scott Zelinski; costumes, Carol Bailey. With Juliana Francis, Tom Pearl, Jay Smith, Tony Torn, Gary Wilmes.

Pan Asian Repertory Theater. Celebrates and provides opportunities for Asian American artists to perform under the highest professional standards and to create and promote plays by and about Asians and Asian Americans. Tisa Chang artistic/producing director.

THE 18 MIGHTY MOUNTAIN WARRIORS (comedy group) (5). October 21, 1998. With Harold S. Byun, Linda Chuan, Rhoda Gravador, Rania Ho, Michael Chih Ming Hornbuckle, Todd Nakagawa, Michael Premsrirat, Peter J. Wong.

CARRY THE TIGER TO THE MOUNTAIN (35). By Cherylene Lee. November 12, 1998. Director, Ron Nakahara; choreograpy, Jamie H.J. Guan; scenery, Cornell H. Riggs; lighting, Novella Smith; costumes, Juliet Ouyoung; sound, Peter Griggs. With Andrew Pang, Peter Von Berg, Alison Lenox, Tom Matsusaka, Emily Hsu, Wai Ching Ho, Jennifer Kato, David Newer, Jens Rasmussen, Michael Dufault, Timothy Jenkins.

THE JOY LUCK CLUB (35 +). By Susan Kim, based on Amy Tan's novel. April 22, 1999. Direction and choreography, Tisa Chang; scenery, Catherine Chung; lighting, Victor En Yu Tan; costumes, Terry Leong; sound, Peter Griggs. With Jo Yang, Ruth Zhang, Kati Kuroda, Tina Chen, Scarlett

Lam, Ann Hu, Donna Leichenko, Fay Ann Lee, Ben Lin, Scott Wakefield, Les J.N. Mau, Tom Matsusaka, Carol A. Honda, Jodi Lin, Tran T. Thuc Hanh.

Performance Space 122. Exists to give artists of a wide range of experience a chance to develop their work and find an audience. Mark Russell executive/artistic director.

Schedule included:

HERSTORY OF PORN: REEL TO REAL (15). By and with Annie Sprinkle. October 14, 1998. Director, Emilio Cubeiro.

TOTAL FICTIONAL LIE. By and with Elevator Repair Service. October 22, 1998.

MORNING, NOON AND NIGHT (work-in-progress) (8). By and with Spalding Gray. November 2, 1998.

HOUSE (16+). Written, directed and composed by Richard Maxwell. November 19, 1998. Scenery, Jane Cox. With Gary Wilmes, Laurena Allan, John Becker, Yehuda Duenyas.

BABY REDBOOTS' REVENGE (120). By Philip-Dimitri Galas. December 3, 1998. Director, Lynne Griffin. With Sean Sullivan.

BEN FRANKLIN: UNPLUGGED (16). By Josh Kornbluth and David Dower. January 7, 1999. With Josh Kornbluth.

JAYWALKER (one-woman show) (13). By and with Marga Gomez. January 10, 1999.

OEDIPUSSY by and with Jonathan Ames; SPRAY by and with Mike Albo. (In repertory January 28-February 21, 1999.)

ICHABOD REVEALED. By and with The Elementals. March 4, 1999.

BAD REPUTATION. By and with Penny Arcade. March 4, 1999.

THE FINAL EPISODE (12). By and with Linda Simpson. April 1, 1999. Director, Robert Molossi; scenery Steven Hammel.

Primary Stages. Dedicated to new American plays by new American playwrights. Casey Childs artistic director, Margaret Chandler general manager, Janet Reed associate artistic director.

THE OLD SETTLER (95). By John Henry Redwood. October 28, 1998. Director, Harold Scott; scenery, Bob Phillips; lighting, Frances Aronson; costumes, Debra Stein; sound, Jim van Bergen. With Leslie Uggams, Lynda Gravatt, Godfrey L. Simmons Jr., Rosalyn Coleman.

HIGH LIFE (34). By Lee MacDougall. January 27, 1999. Director, Casey Childs; scenery, Walt Spangler; lighting, Deborah Constantine; costumes, Debra Stein; music and sound, Fabian Obispo. With David Greenspan, John Bedford Lloyd, Matthew Mabe, Isiah Whitlock.

THE TURN OF THE SCREW (34). Adapted by Jeffrey Hatcher, from Henry James's novel. March 24, 1999. Director, Melia Bensussen; scenery, Christine Jones; lighting, Dan Kotlowitz; costumes, Claudia Stephens; music and sound, David Van Tieghem. With Rocco Sisto, Enid Graham.

LIPS (34). By Constance Congdon. April 28, 1999. Director, Greg Leaming; scenery, Rob Odorisio; lighting, Jeff Croiter; costumes, Mary Myers; music and sound, Fabian Obispo. With Lizbeth Mackay, Robin Morse, Stephen Barker Turner.

THIS LIME TREE BOWER (34+). By Conor McPherson. May 19, 1999. Director, Harris Yulin; scenery, Walt Spangler; lighting, Deborah Constantine; costumes, Debra Stein. With T.R. Knight, Drew McVety, Thomas Lyons.

Puerto Rican Traveling Theater. Professional company presenting bilingual productions of Puerto Rican and Hispanic playwrights, emphasizing subjects of relevance today. Miriam Colon founder and producer.

Schedule included:

BITTER LEMON. By Jaime Salom, translated by Patricia W. O'Connor. April 1, 1999. Director,

Max Ferra; scenery, Richard Dennis; lighting, Robert Williams; costumes, Isabel Rubio; sound, Johnna Doty. With Edouard De Soto, Doris De Farnecio, Mateo Gomez, Yetta Gottesman, Sol Miranda.

JULIA DE BURGOS, CHILD OF THE WATER. By Carmen Rivera, translated by Raul Davis. May 12, 1999. Director, Manuel Martin; scenery, Salvatore Tagliarino; lighting, Alan Baron; costumes, Harry Nadal. With Sol Miranda, Mateo Gomez, Lourdes Martin, Ricardo Puente, Tony Chiroldes, Puli Toro.

Signature Theater Company. Dedicated to the exploration of a playwright's body of work. James Houghton founding artistic director, Bruce E. Whitacre managing director.

MARCO POLO SINGS A SOLO (43). By John Guare. September 27, 1998. Director, Mel Shapiro; scenery, E. David Cosier; lighting, Brian Aldous; costumes, Teresa Snider-Stein; sound, Red Ramona. With Bruce Norris, Judith Hawking, Jack Koenig, Opal Alladin, Beeson Carroll, Polly Holliday, Robert Morgan, Chuck Cooper.

BOSOMS AND NEGLECT (13). By John Guare. December 13, 1998. Director, Nicholas Martin; scenery, James Noone; lighting, Frances Aronson; costumes, Gail Brassard; sound, Red Ramona. With Mary Louise Wilson, David Aaron Baker, Katie Finneran.

LAKE HOLLYWOOD (54). By John Guare. April 29, 1999. Director, Doug Hughes and Itamar Kubovy; scenery, E. David Cosier; lighting, Michael Chybowski and Joe Saint; costumes, Teresa Snider-Stein; sound, Red Ramona. With Kate Burton, Adam Grupper, Amy Wright, Joshua Harto, Pamela Nyberg, Alan North, Betty Miller, Nathalie Paulding, Ralph Waite, Mason Adams, Doc Dougherty.

Residency II Pilot Program:

WALKING OFF THE ROOF (20). By Anthony Clarvoe. February 2, 1999. Director, Darrell Larson; scenery, Michael Brown; lighting, Jan Kroeze; costumes, Jonathan Green; sound, Red Ramona. With Wendy Hoopes, Erin O'Brien, Chris Payne Gilbert, Paul Michael Valley.

Soho Rep. Dedicated to new and avant-garde American playwrights. Daniel Aukin artistic director, Alexandra Conley executive director.

SUMMER CAMP 4: Schedule included DOES THINKING TAKE PLACE OUT LOUD? written and directed by David Barker; 100 VARIATIONS ON A FAMILY THEME by Aaron Petrovich, directed by Hilary Adams; STRAIGHT AS A LINE by Luis Alfaro, directed by John Lawler; QUIET STORMS by Mark Green, directed by Simon Hammerstein. July 8-August 1, 1998.

20 performances each

COWBOYS AND INDIANS. By Richard Maxwell and Jim Strahs. March 11, 1999. Director, Richard Maxwell; scenery, lighting and costumes, Jane Cox. With Aaron Landsman, Peter Simpson, Paul Lazar, Julia Jarcho, Johanna S. Meyer, Ford Wright, David Cote, Eric Dean Scott, Sally Eberhardt, Lakpa T. Bhutia, Okwuchukwu Okpokwasili.

THE ESCAPIST. Conceived and performed by The Flying Machine (Richard Crawford, Colin Gee, Jessica Green, Gonzalo Munoz). May 4, 1999. Director, Josh Carlebach.

ALICE'S EVIDENCE. Conceived and directed by Ellen Beckman. May 5, 1999. With Josh Conklin, Aya Ogawa, Kurt Williams, Robert Saietta, Corey Tazmania Stieb. Co-produced by Sweet Jane Productions.

Theater for the New City. Developmental theater and new American experimental works. Crystal Field executive director.

Schedule included:

TAXI! TAXI! OR THE EQUALITY OF LIFE (13). Music, Christopher Cherney, Darby Dizard and Joel Diamond; lyrics and direction, Crystal Field. August 8, 1998. Scenery, Walter Gurbo; costumes, Mimi Jourdan; sound, Paul Garrity. With Stephen De Lorenzo, Crystal Field, Michael David Gordan, Jerry Jaffe, Terry Lee King, Mark Marcante, Craig Meade.

30 YEARS IN THE LIFE OF CLEOPATRA JACKSON. By and with Carmen Mathis. September 10, 1998. Director, Rich Crooks.

CO-OP. By Barbara Kahn. September 15, 1998. Director, Lisa Marjorie Barnes; music, Marianne Speiser. With Jackie S. Freeman, Barbara Kahn, Marina Lisa Pulido.

MORE THAN MURDER. By Bina Sharif. September 24, 1998. With Jerry Jaffe, Kevin Mitchell Martin, Bina Sharif, Crystal Field.

VIDEO VIAGRA. By Larry Myers. November 12, 1998. Directed and designed by Rich Crooks.

STONE. By Philip Courtney. November 12, 1998. Director, Eduardo Machado; scenery, A.J. Weissbard; costumes, Katherine Beatrice Roth; music, Joel Diamond. With Vanessa Aspillaga, Philip Courtney, Kristin Linklater, Tatyana Yassukovich.

DEGENERATE ART (revised version). By and with the Irondale Ensemble Project. November 25, 1998. Director, Jim Niesen; scenery, Kennon Rothchild III; lighting, Herrick Goldman; costumes, Christianne Meyers; music, Walter Thompson.

WISE GUISE III: GETTING IT UP!. Written, directed and performed by Craig Meade, T. Scott Lilly, Juan Villegas and Daniel Wilkes Kelly. December 3, 1998. Lighting, Ian L. Gordon.

BREAD AND PUPPET THEATER: THE PROLETARIANS and BREAD AND PUPPET CIRCUS. December 9–20, 1998.

TIME IT IS. Written and directed by Lissa Moira. January 14, 1999. Scenery, lighting and sound, Israel Cruz. With Richard O'Brien, Lissa Moira, Martina Lotun, George Roberson, Billy Cobb, Dennis Horvitz, Rey Howard, Valdet Bajraktari, JillAnne Smith.

SHANGHAI MOON. By Charles Busch. January 20, 1999. Director, Carl Andress; scenery, B.T. Whitehill; lighting, Michael Lincoln; costumes, Michael Bottari and Ron Case; sound, Jason M. Scott. With Marcy McGuigan, Sekiya Billman, Becky London, Jodie Lynne McClintock, James Saito, Charles Busch.

BEANIE BABY ADDICTION. By Larry Myers. January 28, 1999. Director, Charles Day; scenery, Mark Marcante and Tony Angel; lighting, Kyle KasaKaitas.

GINT. Written and directed by Romulus Linney, adapted from Henrik Ibsen's *Peer Gynt*. February 12, 1999. Scenery, Mark Marcante; lighting, Jon D. Andreadakis; costumes, Jonathan Green. With David Van Pelt, Christine Parks, Christopher Roberts, Rebecca Harris, Christopher Cappiello, Heather Melton, Scott Sowers, T. Cat Ford, Anthony Pick, Adrienne Thompson.

WILD DOG CASINO. Written and directed by E. Macer-Story. February 18, 1999. Lighting and sound, Sarah Keating. With Sharon Becker, Ralph Carideo, Matthew J. Hamm, Andrea J. Johnson, Tony Mennuto, Muriel Maida, Andrea Szucs, Peter Whalen, Caterina Xiroyanni.

HEAVEN AND EARTH. Written and directed by Barbara Kahn. February 18, 1999. Scenery and lighting, Todd M. Reemtsma; costumes, Andy Wallach. With Andi Hogan, Jolie Dechev, Jackie S. Freeman, Lacie Katrina Pulido.

JUST ANOTHER GENOCIDE SHOW, THE HUMAN RACE and ADJUNCT. By Walter Corwin. February 25, 1999. Direction, Ian L. Gordon and Jason LaRosa; lighting, Kyle KasaKaitas; sound, Yuji Takematsu. With Stephen DeLorenzo, Rookie Twari, Frank Marzullo, David Aronson, Danielle Fink, Rachel Mabey.

OPEN THE GATE. Book based on Isaac Bashevis Singer's *The Manor*; lyrics, David Willinger; music, Arthur Abrams. March 1, 1999. Musical direction, Mimi Stern-Wolfe. With Jeremy Black, Mark Enis, Annette Hunt, Eric Kuttner, Mitch Poulos (concert performance)

CHILDREN OF THE HOUSE AFIRE. Book and lyrics, D.H. Melhem; music and musical direction, Grenoldo Frazier; additional music, D.H. Melhem. March 1, 1999. Director, Lissa Moira; choreography, Larl Becham; scenery, Donald L. Brooks; lighting, Jon D. Andreadakis. With Monica Callan, Israel Cruz, Dennis Horvitz, Reginald James, Yolanda Karr.

WPA THEATER—Patricia Kilgarriff, Joe Quintero *(in rear)* and
Brian Murray in a scene from *Spread Eagle* by Jim Luigs

GIRLS TOWN. Adapted from the film *Girls Town* and choreography by Robin Carrigan. March 11, 1999. Director, Mark Hammond; scenery and lighting, David Obele and Steve Ovenden; costumes, Max Darling; sound, Robin Carrigan and C.P. Roth. With Billie Madley, Anney Giobbe, Jack Crosley, Susan O'Connor.

BENNY'S BARBERSHOP. Written and directed by T. Scott Lilly and Mark Marcante; music, Joel Diamond and T. Scott Lilly. March 18, 1999. Choreography, Craig Meade and Crystal Field; scenery, Kyle KasaKaitas; lighting, Jon D. Andreadakis; costumes, David Obele; sound, Yuji Takematsu. With Mark Marcante, Crystal Field, Craig Meade, Frank Biancamano, Cheryl Gadsden, Michael Vasquez, Jerry Jaffe, Liana Rosario.

AMERICAN TIEN. By Rafael M. Burga. April 15, 1999. Director, Alexis Rehrmann; scenery, Tom Lenz; lighting, Marc Schmittroth; music, Giancarlo Vulcano. With Ngo Thanh Nhan, Josephine Wan, Eric Dong, Isabel Lin, Bernadette Ellorin, Yuichi Tamano.

CROCODILE EYES. Written and directed by Eduardo Machado. April 22, 1999. Scenery, Mark Marcante; lighting, Jon D. Andreadakis; costumes, David Obele. With Ed Vassallo, Victor Argo, Tom Soper, Ron Riley, Jerry Jaffe, Rolando Morales, Joe Quintero, Crystal Field, Heather Hill, Tatyana Yassukovich.

Ubu Repertory Theater. Committed to acquainting American audiences with new works by contemporary French-speaking playwrights from around the world in English translations, as well as modern classics in the original French. Francoise Kourilsky artistic director.

THE BALD SOPRANO (5). By Eugene Ionesco. March 4, 1999. Director, Francoise Kourilsky; scenery, Watoku Ueno; lighting, Greg MacPherson; costumes, Carol Ann Pelletier; sound, Genji Ito.

With Isabelle Cyr, Marc Forget, Simon Fortin, Louise-Marie Mennier; Michel Moinot, Genevieve Schartner.

Staged Reading

THE QUEENS by Normand Chaurette. June 15, 1999.

The Vineyard Theater. Multi-art chamber theater dedicated to the development of new plays and musicals, music-theater collaborations and innovative revivals. Douglas Aibel artistic director, Barbara Zinn Krieger executive director, Jeffrey Solis managing director.

MERCY (37). By Laura Cahill. December 15, 1998. Director, Loretta Greco; scenery, William Barclay; lighting, Kevin Adams; costumes, Elizabeth Hope Clancy; music and sound, David Van Tieghem. With Amelia Campbell, Marianne Hagan, Matt Keeslar, Adam Trese.

THE EROS TRILOGY (37). By Nicky Silver. February 8, 1999. Director, David Warren; scenery, Neil Patel; lighting, Jeff Croiter; costumes, David C. Woolard; music and sound, Donald DiNicola. With Betty Buckley, Zak Orth, T. Scott Cunningham.

DREAM TRUE: MY LIFE WITH VERNON DEXTER (43). Book, Tina Landau, inspired by George du Maurier's novel *Peter Ibbetson;* music, Ricky Ian Gordon; lyrics, Tina Landau with additional lyrics by Ricky Ian Gordon. April 17, 1999. Director, Tina Landau; scenery and costumes, G.W. Mercier; lighting, Scott Zielinski; sound, David Moses Schrier. With Jeff McCarthy, Judy Kuhn, Alex Bowen, Jase Blankfort, Jessica Molaskey, Amy Hohn, Stephen Skybell, Francis Jue, Bryan T. Donovan, Michael Cole, Daniel Jenkins.

The Women's Project and Productions. Nurtures, develops and produces plays written and directed by women. Julia Miles artistic director, Patricia Taylor managing director.

THE KNEE DESIRES THE DIRT (27). By Julie Hebert. November 4, 1998. Director, Susana Tubert; scenery, Peter Harrison; lighting, David Higham; costumes, Tracy Dorman; music and sound, Fabian Obispo. With Barbara Gulan, Al Espinosa, Sarah Rose, Lynn Cohen, Reed Birney.

THE CHEMISTRY OF CHANGE (27). By Marlane Meyer. February 21, 1999. Director, Lisa Peterson; scenery, Zhanna Gurvich and Christopher Barreca; lighting, Kevin Adams; costumes, Katherine Roth; sound, Laura Grace Brown. With Carlin Glynn, Larry Pine, Jodi Thelen, Brenda Wehle, Hamish Linklater, Barry Del Sherman, Christopher Innvar. Co-produced by Playwrights Horizons.

THE EXACT CENTER OF THE UNIVERSE (35). By Joan Vail Thorne. April 7, 1999. Director, John Tillinger; scenery, Michael Brown; lighting, Philip Widmer; costumes, Carrie Robbins; sound, Laura Grace Brown. With Frances Sternhagen, Tracy Thorne, Reed Birney, Bethel Leslie, Marge Redmond.

WPA Theater. Produces new American plays and neglected American classics in the realistic idiom. Kyle Renick artistic director, Lori Sherman managing director.

STUPID KIDS (28). By John C. Russell. June 13, 1998. Director, Michael Mayer; choreography, Ken Roberson; scenery, David Gallo; lighting, Kevin Adams; costumes, Michael Krass; sound, Laura Grace Brown. With James Carpinello, Shannon Burkett, Mandy Siegfried, Keith Nobbs. Transferred to off Broadway; see also its entry in the Plays Produced Off Broadway section of this volume.

'TIL THE RAPTURE COMES (35). By Edward Napier. October 6, 1998. Director, Pamela Berlin; scenery, Vicki Davis; lighting, Chris Dallos; costumes, Amela Baksic; sound, Bruce Ellman. With Pamela Payton-Wright, Jase Blankfort, Cynthia Darlow, Richard Poe, Zack Schaffer.

SPREAD EAGLE (39). By Jim Luigs. December 15, 1998. Director, Constance Grappo; scenery, Debra Booth; lighting, Jack Mehler; costumes, Ilona Somogyi; sound, Robert Murphy. With Brian Murray, Anne James, Graeme Malcolm, Patricia Kilgarriff, William Meisle, Steve Mones, Matthew Saldivar, Joe Quintero, Mark H. Dold.

THE JOB. Written and directed by Shem Bitterman. June 15, 1999. Scenery, J. Gregor Veneklase; lighting, Ryan Schmidt; costumes, Candice Cain; sound, Timothy Joy. With Robert Cicchini, Barry Cullison, Deborah Offner, Ron Orbach, Jack Stehlin.

York Theater Company. In addition to the regular off-Broadway productions, staged concert versions of underappreciated musicals from Broadway's past are performed. James Morgan artistic director, Joseph V. De Michele managing director.

Musicals in Mufti; 3 performances each

DARLING OF THE DAY. Book, Nunnally Johnson, based on Arnold Bennett's novel; music, Jule Styne; lyrics, E.Y. Harburg. September 11, 1998. Director, Michael Montel.

KELLY. Book and lyrics, Eddie Lawrence; music, Moose Charlap. September 18, 1998. Director, Donna Kaz.

BILLION DOLLAR BABY. Book and lyrics, Betty Comden and Adolph Green; music, Morton Gould. September 25, 1998. Director, B.T. McNicholl. With Debbie Gravitte, Richard B. Schull, Marc Kudisch, Michael McCormick, Kristin Chenoweth, Lesley Blumenthal, James Darrah, Susan Owen, Charles Pistone, Darcie Roberts, Casey Nickolaw, Kay Walbye.

Miscellaneous

In the additional listing of 1998–99 off-off-Broadway productions below, the names of the producing groups or theaters appear in CAPITAL LETTERS and the titles of the works in *italics*. This list consists largely of new or reconstituted works. It includes a few productions staged by groups which rented space from the more established organizations listed previously.

ADOBE THEATER COMPANY. *Larry and the Werewolf* by Jeff Goode. August 1, 1998. Directed by Jeremy Dobrish; with Arthur Halpern, Erin Quinn Purcell, Arthur Aulisi, Michael Garin, Janice O'Rourke, Stacey Leigh Ivey, Jim McCauley. *Duet! A Romantic Fable* by Gregory Jackson and Erin Quinn Purcell. October 6, 1998. Directed by Gregory Jackson, Erin Quinn Purcell and Jeremy Dobrish; with Erin Quinn Purcell, Derin Basden, Gregory Jackson, Noam Pearlstein, Frank Ensenberger. *Meanwhile on the Other Side of Mount Vesuvius* by Jay Reiss. April 1, 1999. Directed by Damon Kiely; with Daniel Pearce, Arthur Aulisi, Gregory Jackson, Henry Caplan, Erin Quinn Purcell, Janice O'Rourke, Maggie Siff.

ALICE TULLY HALL. *The Flying Karamazov Brothers: Sharps, Flats and Accidentals* written, directed and performed by the Flying Karamazov Brothers (Paul Magid, Howard Jay Patterson, Michael Preston, Tim Furst). December 18, 1998.

ALTERED STAGES. *Let's Play Two* by Anthony Clarvoe. February, 1998. Directed by Miky Wolf; with Elissa Olin, John Sloan. *Wish You Were Here: Acapulco* by Steven Berkoff, directed by Jason Chaet and *Death and the Maiden* by Susan Kim, directed by Delora Whitney (one-act plays). March 4, 1999. With Jonathan Gellert, Christopher Mako, James Shue, Jennifer Carta, Jay Gordon, Sean Sutherland.

AMERICAN THEATER OF ACTORS THEATER. *Sweatshop* written and directed by Louis LaRusso II. November 6, 1998. With Janet Sarno, Dan Grimaldi, George Pollock, Andrea DeVaynes. *Tokyo Can Can 2* written and directed by Yutaka Okada; music by Saburo Iwakawa. March 7, 1999. With Travis Leung, Jennifer Little, Cynthia Solis, Michael Leonard James, Hiromi Dames.

ANGEL ORENSANZ FOUNDATION CENTER FOR THE ARTS. *Binlids* by Christine Poland, Brenda Murphy, Danny Morrisson and Jake MacSiacais. October 11, 1998. Directed by Pam Brighton; with AnneMarie Adams, Mairead Ui Adhmaill, Maura Brown, Jim Doran, Niamh Flanagan, Conor Grimes, Neil Kempton, Noel McGee, Bridie McMahon, Brenda Murphy, Mark O'Shea, Sue Ramsey, Tony Nooney, Terence O'Neill, Rachel Fitzgerald.

ARCLIGHT THEATER. *Jodie's Body* (one-woman play) by and with Aviva Jane Carlin. February 18, 1999. Directed by Kenneth Elliott. *A Mom's Life* by and with Kathryn Grody. February 28, 1999. Directed by Jack Hofsiss. *Tennessee Williams Remembered* (excerpts from Tennessee Williams's works). May 16, 1999. Directed by Gene Saks; with Anne Jackson, Eli Wallach.

ASIA SOCIETY. *The Road Home: Stories of Children at War* by James Lecesne, conceived and directed by Lawrence Sacharow. April 13, 1999. With Priya Ayyar, Daniel Carlton, Stephen Douglas, Wendy vanden Heuvel, Yolanda King, Ken Leung.

THE BARROW GROUP. *Spring Fever: Tabletop* by Robert Weston Ackerman, directed by Paul Rice; *Another American: Asking and Telling* by Marc Wolf; *The Fabulous Invalid* by Jon Marans; *The Washington-Sarajevo Talks* by Carla Seaquist, directed by Lee Brock; *Nanna* by David Simpatico, directed by Steven Williford; *The Flying Cloud* by Julia Ryan, directed by Fran Arkus (staged readings). April 10-May 15, 1999. *Thy Kingdom's Coming* by Jeff Daniels. May 27, 1999. Directed by Seth Barrish; with Larry Clarke, Gregory Cook, Reade Kelly, Patrick Kline.

BAT THEATER COMPANY. *The Return of the Chocolate-Smeared Woman* by Karen Finley. June 17, 1998. Directed by Jim Simpson; with Karen Finley and the Furballs (Kathryn Benson, Daniel Gurian, Jun Kim, Nicole Kovacs, Phillipe Leong, Angela Tweed, Nikki Wooster, Sarah Yorra, Pamela Zimmerman.) *They Still Mambo in Havana* by Rogelio Martinez. September 4, 1998. Directed by Eduardo Machado; with Marc Ardito, Vanessa Aspillaga, Philip Courtney, David Zayas. *Bedfellows* by Herman Daniel Farrell III. October 10, 1998. Directed by Jim Simpson; with Gerry Bamman, Brian Clark, Peter Jay Fernandez, Reed Birney, Lazaro Perez, Phyllis Somerville. *Cher Maitre* adapted from the Gustave Flaubert-George Sand correspondence by Peter Eyre, translated by Francis Steegmuller and Barbara Bray. November 21, 1998. With Irene Worth, Peter Eyre. *Cellophane* by Mac Wellman. January 21, 1999. Directed by Jim Simpson. *Benten Kozo* by Kawatake Mokuami, adapted and directed by Jim Simpson. February 11, 1999. *Offending the Audience* by Peter Handke. May 21, 1999. Directed by Simon Hammerstein.

BLUE HERON ARTS CENTER. *Admissions* by Tony Vellela. March 5, 1999. Directed by Austin Pendleton.

CHAIN LIGHTNING THEATER. *The Time of Your Life* by William Saroyan. October, 1998. Directed by Lisa Brailoff; with Brandee Graff, Tony Butler, Monroe M. Bonnell, Spencer Scott Barrows, Karl Herlinger, David Comstock, Edmund Day, Duncan M. Rogers. *A Lovely Sunday for Creve Coeur* by Tennessee Williams. January 28, 1999. Directed by Amy Wright; with Cheryl Horne, Blainie Logan, Ginger Grace, Brandee Graff.

CHELSEA PLAYHOUSE. *The Tramway End* by Dermot Bolger. August 19, 1998. Directed by Jim Jermanok; with Ray Yeates. *1348* written and directed by Tom Dulack. April 8, 1999. With Darby Townsend, Tim Smith, Michael Medeiros, Richard Albershardt, Ilvi Dulack. Craig Rovere, S.M. Girasuolo.

CONNELLY THEATER. *The New York Idea* by Langdon Mitchell. June 7, 1998. Directed by Connie Rotunda; with Ken Bolden, Ed Chemaly, Page Clements, Gregory Couba, Diana Henry, Mark Hirschfield, Angela Parks. *Antigone Through Time* based on a concept by Gloria Madden, adapted from Sophocles's play by the company. August 21, 1998. Directed by Richard S. Bach; with Christina Fanizzi, Michael Fawcett, David Greenwood. *A Midsummer Night's Dream* by William Shakespeare. May 19, 1999. Directed by Gregory Wolfe; with Paula Stevens, Gregory J. Sherman, Kathy Keane, Sasha Eden, Catherine Mueller, James Wolfe, Mark Hammer, Rusty Magee.

CUCARACHA THEATER. *The Moment of Aha* by Leslie Nipkow. December 6, 1998. Directed by Richard Caliban; with Missy Hargraves, Ruth Bauers, Robert O'Gorman, Frank S. Palmer, Kathryn Rossetter, Sean Runnette. *Birth Rite* by and with Elizabeth Hess. February 6, 1999. Directed by Richard Caliban.

CURRICAN THEATER. *The After-Dinner Joke* by Caryl Churchill. October 16, 1998. Directed by Victoria Pero and Marcus Geduld; with Matt Frederick, Lisa Blankenship. *Dirty Day* by Brian McGrail. March 28, 1999. Directed by William Mierzejewski; with Kevin Anton, Jack R. Marks, Brian McGrail, Derek Phillips.

THE DIRECTORS COMPANY. *Avow* by Bill C. Davis. June 22, 1998. Directed by Michael Parva; with Reathel Bean, Richard Cox, Judith Hawking, Robert Petkoff, Peggy Pope, Marge Redmond, Mitchell Riggs.

DOMINION THEATER. *Waiting for the Parade* by John Murrell. February 8, 1999. Directed by Edward Berkeley; with Alice Cannon, Yasmine Delawari, Amy Gaipa, Molly Owen, Angela Redman.

DON'T TELL MAMA. *I Want To Be Happy* (songs of Vincent Youmans). September 27, 1998. Directed by Ted Sperling; with William Youmans, Emily Loesser, Bill Buell.

DOUGLAS FAIRBANKS THEATER. *Star Billing* (one-man show) conceived, directed and performed by Alexander H. Cohen. November 9, 1998.

EMERGING ARTISTS THEATER COMPANY. *The Kitchen of Heaven* by Larry Harris. February 22, 1999. Directed by Michael LaPolla; with Kim Ders, Sally Kemp, Carter Inskeep, Stan Lachow, Michael Warga.

EXCELLENT ART MANUFACTURING. *Playstation Levels 1–4* written and directed by Judy Elkan. July 20, 1998. With Judy Elkan, Jennifer Krasinski, Susan Tierney.

FLEA THEATER. *Language Instruction: Love Family vs. Andy Kaufman* by and with Elevator Repair Service. April 8, 1999.

42ND STREET WORKSHOP. *Angel Wings* by Murray Schisgal. October 29, 1998. Directed by G.W. Reed; with Rhonda Christou, David Cruz, James DeMarse, Andrea Gabriel, Willie Ann Gissendanner, Helen Hanft, Mike Jankowitz, Brendan O'Malley, Jennifer Hodges, Stuart Steinberg, Bill Tatum, Elizabeth Ann Townsend.

4TH STREET THEATER. *Island of Dogs* by Gordon Dahlquist. June 4, 1998. Directed by Will Pomerantz.

FREESTYLE REPERTORY THEATER. (improvisation) *Author! Author!* October 8, 1998. Directed by Michael Rock. *The Sydney Prescott Show.* October 15, 1998. Directed by A.J. Mass. *Off-Book* . October 22, 1998. Directed by Ross Aseron and Laura Livingston. *Theatersports.* March 18, 1999. Directed by Christine Turner. *Spontaneous Broadway.* April 8, 1999. Directed by A.J. Mass and Adam Felber.

FROG AND PEACH THEATER COMPANY. *The Merchant of Venice* by William Shakespeare. April 18, 1999. Directed by Lynnea Benson; with Austin Pendleton, Josephine Gallarello, Jason Kuschner.

GREENWICH STREET THEATER. *The Countess* by Gregory Murphy. March 14, 1999. Directed by Ludovica Villar-Hauser; with Jennifer Woodward, James Riordan, Jy Murphy, Honora Fergusson, Kristin Griffith, Frederick Neumann, John Quilty.

GROVE STREET PLAYHOUSE. *An Evening with Quentin Crisp* (one-man show) by and with Quentin Crisp. June 17, 1998. *Queen of Hearts* book and direction by Stephen Stahl; music and lyrics by Claudia Perry. October 5, 1998. With Kendra Munger, James A. Walsh.

HAROLD CLURMAN THEATER. *Nijinsky Speaks* (one-man show) by and with Leonard Crofoot. August 24, 1998.

HERE. *Caught in the Act* (festival of one-act plays): *The Chinese Icebox* by Carl Laszlo, translated by George E. Wellwarth; *Moment of Truth* by Arthur Schnitzler, translated by Eugene Brogyanyi; *The Aspiring Fox* by Slawomir Mrozek, translated by Jacek Laskowsk; *The Dry Cleaner's Integrity, The World of Statistics* and *Volunteer Firemen* by Geza Paskandi, translated by Eugene Brogyanyi; *Edward and Agrippina* by Rene de Obaldia, translated by Donald Watson; *The Wayfarer* by Valerii Briusov, translated by Daniel C. Gerould; *Hanjo* by Yukio Mishima, translated by Donald Keene; *The Curve* by Tankred Dorst, translated by James L. Rosenberg; *Orison* by Fernando Arrabal, translated by Barbara Wright; *The Little Theater of the Green Goose* (selections) by Konstanty Ildefons Galczynski, translated by Daniel C. Gerould; *A Sunny Morning* by Serafin and Joaquin Alvarez-Quintero, translated by Lucretia Xavier Floyd; *The Mirror* by Emilio Carballido, translated by Margaret Sayers Peden; *The Open Couple* by Dario Fo and Franca Rame, translated by Stuart Hood. *The Liddy Plays* by Brooke Berman. September 10-October 4, 1998. *The Women of Orleans* adapted by Kristin Marting and Celise Kalke from Kate Chopin's novel, *The Awakening.* November 8, 1998. Directed by Kristin Marting; with Kevin Bergen, Andre Canty, Leslie Jones, Gretchen Lee Krich, Mari Newhard, Richard Toth. *The Cry Pitch Carrolls* book by Ruth Margraff; music by Matthew Pierce. November 20, 1998. Directed by Tim Maner; with Christina Campanella, Culver Casson, Kimberly Gambino, Annette Houlihan-Verdolino, Darryl Gibson. *The Invisible Hand* (monologues) by Tom Gilroy. December 1, 1998. *Culturemart* (performance art). Schedule included *Animal Confessions* written, directed and performed by Graham Willoughby;

MA-YI THEATER ENSEMBLE—Nicky Paraiso, Ariel Estrada, Joan Almedilla and Lydia Gaston in *peregriNasyon* (the Tagalog word for "wandering," with the capital N evoking "wandering nations") written and directed by Chris B. Millado

Eye Sling Shots Lions (one-man show) by and with Elliott Peter Earls; *Everything Must Go* by and with David Mills; *Clinging to Roadkill* written and directed by Matt Jenson. January 2–24, 1999. *BJ: The Trail of a Transgender Country Rock Singing Star* (one-man show) by and with Scott Hess. March 1, 1999.

INTAR THEATER. *Chuppah* by Lance Crowfoot-Suede. June 15, 1998. Directed by Frank Pisco; with Matthew Wexler, Wendell Laurent. *Deep Down* by Doug Grissom. August 31, 1998. Directed by John Lawler; with Ruben Santiago-Hudson, Christopher Murney, Catherine Zambri, Bill Sims Jr.

INTERNATIONAL FESTIVAL OF PUPPET THEATER. Schedule included *Slap Head: Demon Barber* by Green Ginger, music by Simon Preston, directed by Kevin Brooking; *Terra Prenyada* by Joan Baixas; *Dieu!: God Mother Radio* by Roman Paska and Massimo Schuster; Toy Theater (*The Iliad* by Homer and *Terror As Usual* by Bertolt Brecht) with Great Small Works; *Colores* conceived, directed and choreographed by Federico Restrepo and Loco 7; *Late Night at P.S. 122* with Dan Hurlin, Chinese Theater Workshop and Great Small Works; *The Golem* adapted by Vit Horejs, music by Frank London, with the Czechoslovak-American Marionette Theater; *Dr. Kronopolis and the Timekeeper Chronicles* by The Cosmic Bicycle Theater; *Short Stories* by Teatro Hugo and Ines (Hugo Suarez and Ines Pasic); *Kwaidan* conceived and directed by Ping Chong, based on Lafcadio Hearn's book; *A Harlot's Progress* by Theodora Skipitares and Barry Greenhut; *Never Been Anywhere* by Sandglass Theater (Eric Bass and Ines Zeller Bass); *Fishing for a Wife/Meiboku Sendi Hagi* by Youki-Za; *Kafka, or the Search Goes On* adapted, directed and performed by Yehuda Almagor and Teatron Theater. *The Firebird* from Igor Stravinsky's *L'Oiseau de Feu,* directed by Fabrizio Montecchi, performed by Teatro Gioco Vita. September 9–27, 1998. Host theaters included the Joseph Papp Public Theater, La Mama ETC, The New Victory Theater and P.S. 122; for additional entries, see also the Plays Produced Off Broadway section of this volume.

IRISH ARTS CENTER. *Moonshine* by Jim Nolan. September 24, 1998. Directed by Don Creedon; with Johnnie McConnell, John Leighton, Jacqueline Kealy, John Keating, Elizabeth Whyte, A. Ryan McGuigan. *Dream City Twosome* by Tony Howarth. February 14, 1999. Directed by Ted Forlow; with John DiGiacomo, Michele Santopietro. *Molloy* by Samuel Beckett. May 6, 1999. Directed by Judy Hegarty; with Conor Lovett.

JEAN COCTEAU REPERTORY. *No Exit* by Jean-Paul Sartre, adapted by Paul Bowles. August 8, 1998. Directed by David Travis; with Charles Parnell, Tim Deak, Elise Stone, Tracey Atkins. *Rhinoceros* by Eugene Ionesco, translated by Derek Prouse. September 27, 1998. Directed by Eve Adamson; with Craig Smith, Harris Berlinsky, Christopher Black, Patrick Hall, Tracey Atkins. *Loot* by Joe Orton. November 22, 1998. Directed by Scott Shattuck; with Harris Berlinsky, Tracey Atkins, Tim Deak, Charles Parnell, Craig Smith, Jason Crowl. *Caesar and Cleopatra* by George Bernard Shaw. January 17, 1999. Directed by Robert Hupp; with Craig Smith, Elise Stone. *Winterset* by Maxwell Anderson. March 14, 1999. Directed by Eve Adamson; with Tim Deak, Elise Stone, Charles Parnell, Patrick Hall, Harris Berlinsky, Christopher Black, Jason Crowl, Craig Smith. *Happy Days* by Samuel Beckett. May 28, 1999. Directed by Jonathan R. Polgar; with Angela Vitale, Duncan Hazard.

JOHN MONTGOMERY THEATER COMPANY. *When I Was a Girl, I Used to Scream and Shout* by Sharman Macdonald. August 8, 1998. Directed by Patricia Minskoff; with Roberta Maxwell, Robin Morse, Juliet Pritner, Fred Koehler.

JUDITH ANDERSON THEATER. *The Winds of God* written and directed by Masayuki Imai. June 23, 1998. With Masahiro Matsumoto, Masayuki Imai, Atsushi Yoshida, Masanobu Yada, Rome Kanda. *Boys' Life* by Howard Korder. August 31, 1998. Directed by Anders Cato; with Victor Lirio, Jason Kaufman, Dan Schachner, Sean Powell, Katy Medders, Illana Zauderer, Tracey Mitchell, Natalie Duckett, Natasha Marco. *Private Battles* by Jan Buttram. September 27, 1998. Directed by Stephen Hollis; with Mikel Sarah Lambert, Edward Tully, Lucy Martin, Daphne Gaines, Martin LaPlatney, Ed Steele. *Moses, My Love* adapted from the Biblical books of Moses, music and lyrics by Paul Dick. October 16, 1998. Directed by Marc Geller; with Walter Willison, David Jordon. *The American Jew* written and directed by Tuvia Tenenbom. January 7, 1999. With Catherine Curtin. *The Appearance of Impropriety* by John Petrick. February 14, 1999. With William Langan, Pamela Paul, Reese Madigan, Mark Shanahan, Luisa Battista, Fred Burrell.

KRAINE THEATER. *American Passenger* by Theron Albis. February 11, 1999. Directed by Stephen Golux; with Rob King, Danny Mastrogiorgio, Kristen Lee Kelly, Jennifer Regan, Evan Dexter Parke, Torquil Campbell, Brent Black.

LARK THEATER COMPANY. *Pera Palas.* By Sinan Unel. June 11, 1998. Directed by Steven Williford; with Betsy Aidem, Maggie Burke, Defne Halman, Tom Lee, Lou Liberatore, Craig Mathers, Annie Meisels, Evan Pappas, Ali Poyrazoglu, Jennifer Dorr White.

LAURIE BEECHMAN THEATER. *Babes in the Woods: 7 Urban Sightings* by Cynthia Babak and Michael Huston. February 4, 1999. Directed by Darleen Jaeger; with Cynthia Babak, Michael Huston, Chris Clavelli. *Take It Like Amanda* (cabaret) by and with Amanda Green. March 6, 1999.

LOVE CREEK PRODUCTIONS. *6 Women's Voices: Monster and Wife* by Eric Wiley; *Affair on the Air* by Susan Hansell; *The White Mimosa* by Sally Dixon Wiener; *Apathy* by Jude Davis; *A Flower or Something* by Jolene Goldenthal; *The Cassandra Complex* by Linda Eisenstein. July 11, 1998. Directed by Elysabeth Kleinhans.

MA-YI THEATER ENSEMBLE. *peregriNasyon* written and directed by Chris B. Millado. August 16, 1998. With Joan Almedilla, Lydia Gaston, Ariel Estrada, Gene Silvers, Nicky Paraiso.

MARTIN R. KAUFMAN THEATER. *W-Wow! Radio: The Blood Money Caper* and *The Man Who Was Death* (radio plays). September 9, 1998. Directed by Andrew Frank; with Jennie Berkson, Elizabeth Block, John DeBenedetto, Mim Granahan, Deborah Hertzberg, Andrew Markowitz, Hector Ricci Jr., Bob Rutan, Steve Viola. *The Story Goes On: The Music of Maltby and Shire* (music of Richard Maltby Jr. and David Shire). November 24, 1998. With Loni Ackerman. *Human Resources* (one-man show) by and with Richard Hoehler. January 21, 1999. Directed by Jarlath Conroy. *Manhunt* by David Latham. March 22, 1999. Directed by Gary Schwartz; with Premium Bob (David Latham and Bob Boocock). *Vicki Sue Robinson . . . Behind the Beat* by Vicki Sue Robinson and Bill Good. May 9, 1999. Directed by Patrick Trettentero; with Vicki Sue Robinson, Julie Sei, Tyrone Davis.

McGINN/CAZALE THEATER. *Murder in America* by Allen Blumberg. February 23, 1999. Directed by David Hutchman; with Laura Beckwith, Tibor Feldman, Nicholas J. Giangiulio, Dan Grimaldi, Angela Hodges, Jeff Jerome, Michael Colby Jones, Steven Marcus, Aleta Mitchell, Kate Norby, Samuel F. Reynolds, Libby Roe, Rocco Rosanio, Michael Santoro, Harum Ulmer, Jr. *Drowning in Euphoria* by Liza Lentini. May 17, 1999. Directed by Sharon Rosen; with Michelle Davis, Amanda Dubois, Mark W. Evans, J. Russell Marcel, Steve O'Keefe, Judith J. K. Polson.

MANHATTAN PLAYHOUSE. *Many a Good Hanging Prevents a Bad Marriage* conceived by Diana Walker, co-conceived and directed by Alex Papoutsis; music by Dan Schamir. February 13, 1999.

MELTING POT THEATER. *Woody Guthrie's American Song* (Woody Guthrie's songs and writings) conceived and directed by Peter Glazer. December 6, 1998. With Ernestine Jackson, David M. Lutken, Sean McCourt, James J. Stein Jr., Lisa Asher. *Oy!* by Rich Orloff. February 14, 1999. Directed by Lori Steinberg; with Matthew Arkin, Elaine Bromka, Heather Goldenhersh, Frank Vlastnik, Lee Wilkof. *Fables in Slang: A Ragtime Revue* by Gene Jones, based on George Ade's writings. April 25, 1999. Directed by Nick Corley; with Nancy Anderson, Elizabeth Arnold, Jeff Edgerton, Gene Jones, Michael Mandell.

METTAWEE RIVER THEATER COMPANY. *The Woman Who Fell From the Sky* adapted from portions of the Iroquois creation story by Ralph Lee and the Company; poems and lyric by Bob Holman; music by Karen Hansen. September 11, 1998. With Bruce Connelly, Anthea Fane, Doris DiFarnecio, Tom Marion.

MINT THEATER. *Winding the Ball* by Alex Finlayson. August 27, 1998. *Loss of D-Natural* by N. Richard Nash. September 8, 1998. Directed by Matt Conley; with Robert Boardman, George Cavey, James Doerr, Michelle Enfield, Eva Lowe, Jennifer Sternberg, Rusty Ross. *August Snow* and *Night Dance* by Reynolds Price. November 12, 1998. Directed by Jonathan Bank; with Lisa Bostnar, Allyn Burrows, Michael William Connors, Donna Davis, Patricia Dunnock, Chris Payne Gilbert, Stephen Payne. *Letter Perfect* (based on the correspondence of famous Americans). April 26, 1999. Directed by Jonathan Bank; with Lisa Bostnar, Don Clark Williams, Gus Kaikkonen.

MIRANDA THEATER COMPANY. *Snapshots* by Erin Sanders. April 14, 1999. Directed by Joel Goldes; with Tom Aulino, Mary Stout, Andrew Elvis Miller, Wendy Martling. *Goldberg Variations* by Marcy Kahan. May 13, 1999. Directed by Alison Summers; with Scotty Bloch, Antoinette La Vecchia, Molly Powell, Amy Resnick, Andre Sogliuzzo, Richard Topol.

MUSICAL THEATER WORKS. *Nothin's Easy and Nobody's Happy* by Colette Hawley and Michael Schiralli. March 12, 1999. Directed by Michael Schiralli; with Colette Hawley.

NAKED ANGELS. *Hesh* by Matthew Weiss. September 27, 1998. Directed by Frank Pugliese; with Matthew Weiss, Ned Eisenberg, Marcus Weiss. *Snakebit* by David Marshall Grant. November 22, 1998. Directed by Jace Alexander; with David Alan Basche, Jodie Markell, Geoffrey Nauffts, Michael Weston.

NATIONAL ASIAN AMERICAN THEATER. *Falsettoland* by William Finn and James Lapine; music and lyrics by William Finn. July 16, 1998. Directed by Alan Muraoka; with Jason Ma, Welly Yang, Ann Harada, Christine Toy Johnson, Kennedy Kanagawa, Merv Maruyama, Mimosa. *He Who Says Yes/He Who Says No* by Bertolt Brecht. March 11, 1999. Directed by Jean Randich; with Lexine Bondoc, Rich Ceraulo, Elizabeth Chiang, Lydia Gaston, Frank Kamai, Peter Kim, Thomas Kouo, Alan Muraoka, Timothy Murphy, Eileen Rivera.

NEW DIRECTIONS THEATER. *Triptych* by Richard Willett. February 15, 1999. Directed by Eliza Beckwith; with Charles Loffredo, Bill Dobbins, Cindy Chesler, Patricia Randell, Joseph Jude Zito, Lynn Laurence.

NEW YORK GILBERT AND SULLIVAN PLAYERS. *H.M.S. Pinafore.* December 30, 1998. With Heather Buck, Stephen O'Brien, Keith Jurosko. *Ruddigore.* January 7, 1999.

NEW YORK INTERNATIONAL FRINGE FESTIVAL. Schedule included *Synchronized Swimming: The Dry Version* by and with Ursus and Nadeschkin; *Penitentiary of Love* by and with Jason Thompson and Christian Laurin, directed by Michael Kennard; *Something, Something Uber Alles* by and with Assurbanipal Babilla, directed by David Cote; *Misshapen Jack, the Nebraska Hunchback* by Mountebanks, with Trav S.D.; *Rum and Vodka* by Conor McPherson, directed by Ed Sahely; *The Interpreter of Horror* by Kelly Stuart, directed by Carolyn Rendell; *The Importance of Being Earnest* by Oscar Wilde, adapted and directed by Hugh Hysell; *Queen Esther: Unemployed Superstar* by and with Queen Esther;

Gizmos, Gadgets, Laughs & Lies by and with Russ Merlin; *The Bald Soprano* by Eugene Ionesco, directed by Madi Distefano; *Last Train to Nibroc* by Arlene Hutton, directed by Michael Montel; *Lizzie Borden's Tempest* written and directed by Brendan Byrnes; *Once Vaudeville* (puppets) by Kevin Augustine. August 19–30, 1998.

NEW YORK PERFORMANCE WORKS. *Needles* by Kate Browne. February 11, 1999.

NEW YORK PUBLIC LIBRARY FOR THE PERFORMING ARTS READING ROOM READINGS. Schedule included *A Girl's Life* by Kathleen Tolan. March 22, 1999. *Aloha, Say the Pretty Girls* by Naomi Iizuka. June 21, 1999.

NUYORICAN POETS CAFÉ. *Mother Hubbard* by Ishmael Reed; music by Ronald L. McIntyre. October 16, 1998. Directed by Rome Neal; with Frances McAlpin Sharp, Theo Polites, Rod Bladel, Frank Swingler, Joy E. Styles, Elliott Williams, Kathryn Chilson, William Williams. *Oshun: The Goddess of Love* by David D. Wright. February 11, 1999. Directed by Rome Neal; with Keisha Monique Booker, Angela Brown, Robert Turner, Spelman M. Beaubrun, Henry Afro-Bradley.

OHIO THEATER. *Rebel Women* by Thomas Babe. January 22, 1999. Directed by Alex Lippard; with Margot Ebling, James Elmore, Nicole Haywood, Harriet Koppel, Sean McArthur, Karla Mason, James Schlag, Mark Shelton. *The Bad Seed* by Maxwell Anderson. May 6, 1999. Directed by John G. Young; with Kathryn Gracey, James Kaliardos, John Kuntz, Alessandro Magania. *Noah's Archives* by Stephen Spoonamore. May 27, 1999. Directed by Darcy Marta; with Tim Moore, Caroline Strong, William Peden.

PEARL THEATER COMPANY. *Candida* by George Bernard Shaw. September 14, 1998. Directed by Claire Davidson; with Joanne Camp, Daniel J. Shore, Dan Daily, Christopher Moore, Kia Christina Heath. *The Miser* by Molière, translated by John Wood. November 9, 1998. Directed by David Schechter; with Robert Hock, Patricia Dalen, Bo Foxworth, Christopher Moore, Lauren Stamile. *The Country Wife* by William Wycherly. January 4, 1999. Directed by Shepard Sobel; with Ray Virta, Patricia Dalen, Dan Daily, Hope Chernov, Christopher Moore. *The Seagull* by Anton Chekhov, translated by Earle Edgerton. March 1, 1999. Directed by Shepard Sobel; with Joanne Camp, Christopher Moore, Margot White, Ray Virta. *Angel Street* by Patrick Hamilton. April 26, 1999. Directed by Rob Urbinati; with Richmond Hoxie, Carol Schultz, Dan Daily.

PHIL BOSAKOWSKI THEATER. *Traveling Companions* by Kathleen Reynolds. November 1, 1998. Directed by David DeBeck; with Christopher Cantwell, Heather Muir, Vivian Nesbitt, Robert Steffen, Michael Stone.

THE PIANO STORE. *Menkharis* by and with Mitch Stripling. February 4, 1999.

PLAYHOUSE AT ST. CLEMENT'S. *Flahooley* book by E.Y. Harburg and Fred Saidy; music by Sammy Fain; lyrics by E.Y. Harburg. September 3, 1998. Directed by Alisa Roost; with April Allen, Christopher Budnich, Natalie Buster, Mark Cortale, Clay Hansen.

PLAYHOUSE 91. *Dante's Inferno* by Dante Alighieri, translated by Robert Pinsky, adapted and directed by Robert Scanlan. September 26, 1998. With Leslie Beatty, Bill Camp, Reg E. Cathey, Jack Willis.

PRODUCERS' CLUB. *Notes: A Love Story@www.com* written and directed by Tony Tanner. August 20, 1998. With Terry Kaye, James Sobol. *What We Don't Confess* by Tony Vellela. October 14, 1998. Directed by Jay Falzone; with Deana Barone, Joe Pioggia, Jason Williams, Douglas Dickerman, Amy Sloane, James Joseph Shlag. *A Question of Loyalty: The Rise and Fall of Edward R. Murrow* written and directed by Michael Hickey. October 21, 1998. With Joseph Lustig, Don Creech, Michael Barry Greer, Robert Mason, Susan Brandner, Kimberly Purnell. *The Private Life of Sir Isaac Newton* by Judd Blaise. May 9, 1999. Directed by Jesse Merz.

PROVINCETOWN PLAYHOUSE. *Bread and Butter* by Eugene O'Neill. August 21, 1998. Directed by Stephen Kennedy Murphy; with Stan Carp, Stacie Lents, Avram Ludwig, Salem Ludwig, Kristoffer Polaha, Paulette O'Dowd, Brent Vimtrup.

PUBLIC DOMAIN. *The Circle Hamlet* adapted from William Shakespeare's play by Derek Lucci. September 17, 1998. Directed by Derek Lucci and John Edwards; with Derek Lucci, Tom Huston, Joe Muzikar, Christopher George, David Saire, M.J. Karmi, Jenni Blong, Louis Vuolo.

PULSE THEATER. *A Brief Excursion* by John Greiner. November 16, 1998. Directed by Matthew Putman; with Robert DiFalco, Sally Kemp, Holly King, Robert Margolis, Elizabeth Brownlee.

RATTLESTICK PRODUCTIONS. *The Weatherbox* by Travis Baker. September 13, 1998. Directed by Kimberly Levin; with Rob Sedgwick, Ivan Martin, Johanna Leister, Geneva Carr. *Starstruck* by and with Eric Bernat. November 15, 1998. Directed by David Drake. *Stuck* by Jessica Goldberg. January 25, 1999. Directed by Abby Epstein.

RAW SPACE. *The End of Civilization* by George F. Walker. January 22, 1999. Directed by Randy White; with Sarah Brockus, Jamie Heinlein, Bryan Johnson, Mick Weber. *Flirting with Rescue: Even Steven, Dotted Line* and *A Wink & a Smile* by Anthony Giunta. March 30, 1999. (Plays in repertory.)

RED ROOM. *Brown and Black and White All Over* by and with Antonio Sacre. November 1, 1998. Directed by Jenny Magnus. *Stavrogin's Confession* by John Regis, based on Dostoyevsky's novel, *Demons*. May 16, 1999. Directed by Peter Dobbins; with Laurence Drozd, Dan Berkey, Frances Vargas.

THE SALON. *The Night of the Tribades* by Per Olov Enquist. September 27, 1998. Directed by Marco Capalbo; with Kevin Baggott, Flo Cabre-Andrews, Bo Corre, Michael Margotta. *Prater Violet* adapted from Christopher Isherwood's novel and directed by Will Pomerantz. November 15, 1998. With Kameron Steele, Dylan Green, Frank Dowd, Laura Kachergus, John McAdams, Ashok Sinha.

SAMUEL BECKETT THEATER. *Hot Air, Boys Will Be Boys, 2B* and *Signature Required* (one-act plays) by Richard Willett. June 16, 1998. Directed by Eliza Beckwith. *Hurlyburly* by David Rabe. July 22, 1998. Directed by Clyde Fitch; with Jim Brown, Annie Connor, Mark Courtien, Mark Love, Mary Anne Schofield, Christina Starbuck, Curt Branom. *The Brothers Booth* written and directed by Roger Kristian Jones. September 16, 1998. With Paul Riopelle, Peter Riopelle, Jay Nickerson, Emma Vogel. *Lyz!* book and lyrics based on Aristophanes's *Lysistrata* by Joe Lauinger; music by Jim Cowdery. January 10, 1999. Directed by John Rue; with Jill Paxton. *The Girl Who Said Yes to the Guy in the Brown Subaru* by Margaret Elman. March 17, 1999. Directed by Laura Josepher; with Marsha Dietlein, Paul Reggio.

SANFORD MEISNER THEATER. *Franny, Isadora and the Angels* by John Preston. October 1, 1998. Directed by William E. Hunt; with Ron Bagden, Judd Jones, Michael Lipton, Mike Rogers, Doug Wirth. *Get to the Part About Me* (one-woman show) by and with Rose Abdoo. January 20, 1999. *The Ball of Roses* by Adrian Bewley. April 12, 1999. Directed by Marcus Geduld. *Slap 'Em Down* by Jefferson D. Arca. April 13, 1999. Directed by Ted Sluberski. *Train Stories: Travelogue* by Ring Lardner, *Drawing Room B* by John O'Hara and *The Man in the Brooks Brothers Shirt* by Mary McCarthy, adapted by Carol Goodheart and Cindy Sandmann. May 6, 1999. Directed by Carol Goodheart; with Mark Zeisler, Leslie Browne.

78TH STREET THEATER LAB. *The Undoing* by William Mastrosimone. June 4, 1998. Directed by Eric Nightengale; with Betty Anne Cohen, Etya Dudko, Judith Granite, Laurie LeFever, Vincent Sagona. *That's My Time* by and with Vanessa Hollingshead. June 8, 1998. Directed by Jeanne Heaton. *Last Train to Nibroc* by Arlene Hutton. February 18, 1999. Directed by Michael Montel; with Alexandra Geis, Benim Foster.

SIX FIGURES THEATER COMPANY. *The Awakening* by Andria Laurie, adapted from Kate Chopin's novel. June 11, 1998. Directed by April-Dawn Gladu; with Chris Campbell, Pia Caro, Dori May Kelly, Michael Latshaw, Shellen Lubin, Jason Madera, Jim McHugh. *Clowning the Bard* conceived by Linda Ames Key. October 20, 1998. Directed by Julie Hamberg, Linda Ames Key, Dick Monday and Tiffany Riley.

STUDIO THEATER. *Kosher Franks* (one-act plays) by Sid Frank. May 24, 1999. Directed by John Morrison; with Barbara Bonilla, Chris Boyd, Michael DeNigris, David Sussman, Leslie Wheeler.

SULLIVAN STREET LOUNGE. *Reno Finds Her Mind* by and with Reno. June 4, 1998. Directed by Linda Mancini.

SYLVIA AND DANNY KAYE PLAYHOUSE. *Gen (Hadashi-no-Gen)* by Keiji Nakazawa, adapted and directed by Kyo Kijima; music by Hajime Hayashi; lyrics by Kyo Kijima. January 16, 1999. With Miyuki Tanaka, Masako Tanaka, Teruhiko Ogimi, Noboru Mitani.

SYNCHRONICITY SPACE. *The Soho Triptych* (one-act plays): *Countrymen* by Alex Ladd, directed by Mark Gorman; *We Beat Whitey Ford* by Kal Wagenheim, directed by Vincent Marano; *The Acting Thing* by Marie Trusits, directed by Nora Brown; *Counting on My Fingers* by Frank Verderame, directed by Connie George; *Hello, I Love You* written and directed by Marc Meyers; *Don't Pick Up* by Susannah Nolan, directed by Ami Rothschild; *Cleaned and Burned* by Victoria Janis, directed by Kim Ferraro;

SAMUEL BECKETT THEATER—Twin brothers Peter Riopelle
(with mustache) as John Wilkes Booth and Paul Riopelle as Edwin
Booth in a scene from *The Brothers Booth* written and directed by
Roger Kristian Jones

Nicetown by Alex Ladd, directed by Lisa Kerekes; *Got Your Number* by Gerry Silver, directed by Loren-
Paul Caplin; *The Love Song of Eleanor Purdy* written and directed by Auguste Netzband; *The Adven-
tures of Power Mommy* by Beth Ann Holden, directed by Deborah Clapp. July 1–19, 1998. *When the
Bough Breaks* by Robert Clyman. September 10, 1998. Directed by James Knopf; with Chris Clavelli,
Tamara Scott, Jane Ross, Jerry Rockwood. *Are We There Yet?* by Garth Wingfield. April 27, 1999.
Directed by James Knopf; with Karin Sibrava, Michael Anderson, Peter J. Crosby, Jane Ross, Kim
Reinle, Nicholas Rohlfing.

TAIPEI THEATER. *Making Tracks* book and lyrics by Brian Yorkey, Matt Eddy and Welly Yang;
music by Woody Pak. February 4, 1999. Directed by Lenny Leibowitz; with Cindy Cheung, Mel Gionson,
Tom Kouo, Aiko Nakasone.

TARGET MARGIN THEATER. *The Seagull* by Anton Chekhov, translated by Erika Warmbrunn.
February 24, 1999. Directed by David Herskovits; with Will Badgett, Beresford Bennett, Nicole Halmos,
Gretchen Krich, Lenore Pemberton, Steven Rattazzi, Greig Sargeant, T. Ryder Smith, Raphael Nash
Thompson, Carolyn Vujcec.

THEATER FOR A NEW AUDIENCE. *The Iphigenia Cycle* by Euripides, translated by Nicholas
Rudall. January 24, 1999. Directed by JoAnne Akalaitis; with Wilson Cain III, Anne Dudek, Ora Jones,
Taylor Price, Jack Willis, Genevra Gallo, Lynn House, Carmen Roman, Genevieve VenJohnson, Nich-
olas Kepros, Sophia Salguero, Anne Louise Zachry. *Macbeth* by William Shakespeare. March 14, 1999.
Directed by Ron Daniels; with Bill Camp, Elizabeth Marvel.

THEATER ROW THEATER. *The Night They Burned Washington* written and directed by Mark R.
Glesser. October 6, 1998. *Inappropriate* conceived by A. Michael DeSisto and Lonnie McNeil; adapted
by Lonnie McNeil; music and lyrics by Michael Sottile. March 10, 1999.

THEATER TEN TEN. *Park Avenue* by George S. Kaufman and Nunnally Johnson; music by Arthur
Schwartz; lyrics by Ira Gershwin. May 7, 1999. Directed by David Fuller.

THEATER 3. *Gogol* by Len Jenkins. July 24, 1998. Directed by Sarah E. Orth; with Bob Izzo, Mark
Nichols, Annie Parisse.

30TH STREET THEATER. *Making Peter Pope* by Edmund De Santis. February 15, 1999. Directed by Derek Todd; with Michael Anderson, Harry Bouvy, Joanne Dorian, Carol Hache, Eric Morace, Alysia Reiner, Fred Velde.

TRIBECA PLAYHOUSE. *Snapshots '98* (one-act plays): *Holy Water* and *A Coupla Bimbos Sittin Around Talkin* by Richard Vetere; *Welcome to the Moon* by John Patrick Shanley; *The Cardinal Detoxes* by Thomas M. Disch; *Imagining Brad* by Peter Hedges; *Landscape and Dream* by Nancy Krusoe. September 27, 1998. Directed by Jeff Cohen. *Eight! Henry VIII, That Is!* book by Steeve Arlen; music and lyrics by Donald Eugster and Steeve Arlen. November 8, 1998. Directed by Jeff Cohen; with Steeve Arlen.

TRILOGY THEATER. *Real* by and with Norman Siopsis. May 6, 1999. Directed by J.D. Wolfe.

29TH STREET REPERTORY THEATER. *Vegetable Love* by Tammy Ryan. September 20, 1998. Directed by Tim Farrell; with Elizabeth Elkins, Paula Ewin, Moira MacDonald, Lois Markle, Kevin Hagen. *The Censor* by Anthony Neilson. April 12, 1999. Directed by Jason McConnell Buzas; with Charles Willey, Paula Ewin, Elizabeth Elkins.

URBAN STAGES. *A Dream of Wealth* by Arthur Giron. September 13, 1998. Directed by Richard Harden; with Magaly Colimon, Gilberto Arribas, Mick Weber, Frank Rodriguez. *Macs (A Macaroni Requiem)* by David Simpatico. March 17, 1999. Directed by Mark Roberts; with David Brummel, Charlotte Colavin, Mary Fogarty, Antoinette LaVecchia, Scott Lucy, Mark Romeo, Roger Serbagi, Gary Wolf.

WESTBETH THEATER CENTER. *Miss Coco Peru's Liquid Universe* by and with Clinton Leupp. June 21, 1998. Directed by Charles Randolph-Wright. *Correct Me If I'm Right* by and with Kate Clinton. January 28, 1999. *Thwak* by and with David Collins and Shane Dundas (the Umbilical Brothers). March 18, 1999. Directed by Philip William McKinley.

WILLOW CABIN THEATER. *The Sirens* by Darrah Cloud. February 11, 1999. Directed by Mark Wade; with Vanessa Aspillaga, Cynthia Besteman, John Billeci, George Causil, Fiona Davis, Ken Forman, Larry Gleason, Robert Harte, Charmaine Lord, Lisa Renee Pitts, Kimberly Poppe, Jed Sexton, Joel Van Liew. *The Ages of Man* (one-act plays) by Thornton Wilder. May 23, 1999. Directed by Edward Berkeley; with John Bolger, Larry Gleason, Sarah Lively, Linda Powell, Jed Sexton.

THE WOOSTER GROUP. *House/Lights* by The Wooster Group, based on Gertrude Stein's *Doctor Faustus Lights the Lights.* January 9, 1999. Directed by Elizabeth LeCompte; with Kate Valk, Suzzy Roche, Roy Faudree, Ari Fliakos,Tanya Selvaratnam, Helen Eve Pickett, Sheena See, John Collins.

THE WORKING THEATER. *Belmont Avenue Social Club* by Bruce Graham. April 22, 1999. Directed by Constance Grappo; with William Wise, David Kener, Malachy Cleary, Ernest Mingione, Michael P. Moran.

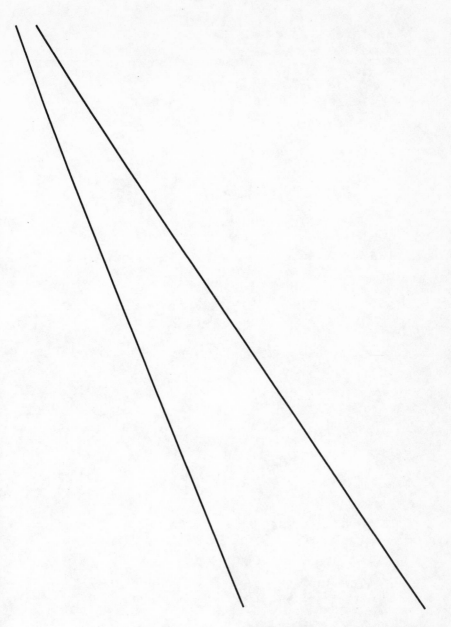

THE SEASON
AROUND
THE UNITED STATES

O
O
O

OUTSTANDING NEW PLAYS
CITED BY
AMERICAN THEATER CRITICS
ASSOCIATION
and
A DIRECTORY OF NEW-PLAY
PRODUCTIONS

O
O
O

THE American Theater Critics Association (ATCA) is the organization of more than 280 leading drama critics in all media in all sections of the United States. One of this group's stated purposes is "To increase public awareness of the theater as a *national* resource" (italics ours). To this end, beginning in 1977 ATCA has annually cited outstanding new plays produced around the U.S., to be represented in our coverage by excerpts from each of their scripts demonstrating literary style and quality. This year, one of these—the drama *Book of Days* by Lanford Wilson, produced by the Purple Rose Theater in Chelsea, Mich.—has been designated ATCA's 23d annual principal citation and its 14th annual New Play Award winner of $1,000.

Two other 1999 ATCA new play citations for plays first produced in the calendar year 1998 went to the comedy-drama *Dinner With Friends* by Donald Margulies, which premiered at the Actors Theater of Louisville in its Humana Festival of New American Plays, and Lisa Loomer's comedy-drama *Expecting Isabel,* produced at Washington, D.C.'s Arena Stage.

ATCA's fifth annual Elizabeth Osborn Award for an emerging playwright was voted to Dan O'Brien for his *Lamarck* at the Perishable Theater in Providence, R.I.

Of the 15 new scripts nominated by ATCA members for the New Play Award, six were selected as finalists by the 1999 awards committee before making their final citations. Arena Stage was the production source of two of these six: the cited Loomer play and *Dimly Perceived Threats to the System* by Jon Klein. Also selected as finalists were *Rocket Man* by Steven Dietz, from the Arizona Theater Company at Tucson and Phoenix, and *Safe as Houses* by Richard Greenberg, from the Mc-Carter Theater in Princeton.

The nine other New Play Award nominees were *The Day Maggie Blew Off Her Head* by Amy Bridges, from Anchorage, Alaska; *Dogeaters* by Jessica Hagedorn, from the La Jolla, Calif. Playhouse; *Taking Leave* by Nagle Jackson, from Denver Center Theater Company; *Black No More*, with book and lyrics by Syl Jones and music by Fabian Obispo, from Arena Stage (its third nominee) and the Guthrie Theater, Minneapolis; *A Joyful Noise* by Tim Slover, from Brigham Young University Theater, Salt Lake City; *Flyovers* by Jeffrey Sweet, from Victory Gardens Theater, Chicago; *The Balkan Women* by Jules Tasca, from Bristol, Pa. Riverside Theater; *The Trestle at Pope Lick Creek* by Naomi Wallace, the Humana Festival's second nominee; and *Hannah Senesh* by John Wooten, from the Forum Theater, Metuchen. N.J.

The process of selection of these outstanding plays is as follows: any ATCA member may nominate the first full professional production of a finished play (not a reading or an airing as a play-in-progress) during the calendar year under consideration. Nominated 1998 scripts were studied and discussed by the 1999 ATCA play-reading committee chaired by Michael Grossberg of the Columbus *Dispatch* and comprising assistant chairman Lawrence Bommer (freelance stringer, Chicago *Tribune* and *Windy City Times*), Marianne Evett (Cleveland *Plain Dealer*), Barbara Gross (freelance critic, Baltimore and Washington, D.C. area), Alec Harvey (Birmingham *News*), Robert Hurwitt (San Francisco *Examiner*), and Herb Simpson (Rochester, N.Y. *City Newspaper*). The committee members made their choices on the basis of script rather than production. If the timing of nominations and openings prevents some works from being considered in any given year, they will be eligible for consideration the following year if they haven't since moved to New York. We offer our sincerest thanks and admiration to the ATCA members and their committee for the valuable insights into the 1998 theater year around the United States which their selections provide for this *Best Plays* record, in the form of excerpts from the outstanding scripts, and most particularly in the introductory reviews by Lawrence DeVine *(Book of Days)*, Michael Grossberg *(Dinner With Friends)* and Marianne Evett *(Expecting Isabel)*.

1998 ATCA New Play Award

○○○
○○○
○○○
○○○
○○○
○○○

BOOK OF DAYS

A Play in Two Acts

BY LANFORD WILSON

Cast and credits appear on pages 405–406

LANFORD WILSON, one of the most important and effective playwrights of the 20th century, was born in Lebanon, Mo. April 13, 1937 and was raised in Ozark, Mo. He was educated at San Diego State College and the University of Chicago, where he started writing plays and has never since stopped. Arriving in New York in 1963, he gravitated to the Caffe Cino, one of the first of the off-off-Broadway situations. He made his New York playwriting debut there with So Long at the Fair, *followed by* Home Free *and* The Madness of Lady Bright, *the latter for 250 performances. In 1965 his first full length play,* Balm in Gilead, *was produced at Cafe La Mama and directed by Marshall W. Mason, who has figured importantly in Wilson's career. That same year the prolific author's* Ludlow Fair *and* This Is the Rill Speaking *were presented at Caffe Cino.*

Wilson's off-Broadway debut took place with the appearance of Home Free *on a New Playwrights Series program for 23 performances at the Cherry Lane Theater in February 1965.* Ludlow Fair *and* The Madness of Lady Bright *appeared off Broadway and in London in 1966.* The Rimers of Eldritch (*a development of* This Is the Rill Speaking) *won its author a Vernon Rice Award off Broadway in 1967. In 1968 his* Wandering *was part of the off-Broadway program* Collision Course, *and he tried out an untitled work with Al Carmines at Judson Poets' Theater.*

On April 23, 1969 Wilson moved to Broadway for the first time with the short-lived (5 performances) but favorably-remembered The Gingham Dog, *following its production the previous season at the Washington, D.C. Theater Club. Also short-lived on Broadway (opened May 17, 1970, ran 17 performances) but even more favorably received was his* Lemon Sky. *The following year he wrote the libretto for Lee Hoiby's opera version of Tennessee Williams's* Summer and Smoke, *which premiered in St. Paul, Minn. and was presented by New York City Opera in 1972. He also collaborated with Williams on the film script* The Migrants, *which was produced by CBS and won an Emmy nomination and a Christopher Award.*

Wilson was a founding member of Marshall W. Mason's Circle Theater (later Circle Repertory Company) and was one of its 21 playwrights-in-residence. Wilson scripts which immediately emerged at this home base were Sextet (Yes) *in 1971 and* The Great Nebula in Orion, The Family Continues *and* Ikke, Ikke, Nye, Nye, Nye *during the 1972 season. All were directed by Mason, as was* The Hot l Baltimore, *which premiered as an OOB production at the Circle January 27, 1973, moved to an off-Broadway theater March 22, 1973 where it ran for 1,166 performances (a new record for an American straight play), was named a Best Play of its season, won the Critics (best American play), Obie and Outer Circle Awards and was adapted into a TV series.*

In 1975 Wilson's The Mound Builders *was produced at the Circle under Mason's direction, won an Obie and was filmed for the Theater in America series on WNET-TV. In the season of 1975–76 the well-established Circle group moved up from OOB to off-Broadway status; and Wilson's* Serenading Louie *was produced May 2, 1976 for 33 performances, becoming its author's second Best Play. It had been written between* Lemon Sky *and* The Hot l Baltimore *and was rewritten for this production.*

In 1977–78 the Circle produced Wilson's one-acter Brontosaurus *as well as his third Best Play, the full-length* The 5th of July, *which opened its 159-performance run April 27, 1978. The second play in Wilson's Missouri trilogy,* Talley's Folly, *opened at the Circle under Mason's direction May 1, 1979 and played 44 performances. It moved uptown to Broadway February 20, 1980 for 277 more performances, winning Wilson's fourth Best Play citation plus the Pulitzer Prize and the Critics Award for best-of-bests.*

The first play of this trilogy was then remounted for Broadway November 5, 1980 as Fifth of July, *playing 239 performances and earning both Wilson and Mason Tony nominations. The third,* A Tale Told, *appeared at the Circle June 11, 1981 for 30 performances. On October 7, 1982 Wilson returned to matters other than the Talley family with his fifth Best Play,* Angels Fall, *under Mason's direction, for 65 performances at the Circle and 64 on Broadway beginning January 22, 1983. In 1987 Wilson's* Burn This *played a special series of 21 subscription performances at Circle Rep before moving to Broadway October 14 for 437 performances.*

The record of Wilson's playwriting achievements goes on and on through the 1990s from Eukiah *(1992 at the Actors Theater of Louisville's Humana Festival) to* Redwood Curtain *(March 30, 1993 on Broadway for 40 performances) to* Moonshot and Cosmos *(a pair of monologues at Circle Rep May 3, 1994 for 32 performances) to* Day *(a one-acter on the Manhattan Theater Club program* By the Sea by the Sea by the Beautiful Sea *May 30, 1996 for 38 performances) to* Sympathetic Magic *(off Broadway at Second Stage April 16, 1997 for 38 performances). And now his* Book of Days *is this year's ATCA New Play Award winner for its 1998 premiere at the Purple Rose Theater in Chelsea, Mich.*

Wilson has been the recipient of the Brandeis University Creative Arts Award, the Institute of Arts and Letters Award, plus Rockefeller, Guggenheim and ABC Yale fellowships. For the past two seasons he has served on the Tony nominating committee. He is a bachelor and lives in Sag Harbor, N.Y.

INTRODUCTION: Commercially and spiritually, playwright Lanford Wilson never has forgotten the Missouri hill towns of his beginnings. The good stories came early to him around the one-stoplight towns of his boyhood, like Lebanon and Ozark in the south-central part of the state, 25 miles above the Arkansas line. Like many a Wilson play before it, his new and extraordinary *Book of Days* is set in that rolling region of farms and Pentecostal churches—there is a county named "Christian" not far from Wilson's hometown of Lebanon, Missouri, but his latest work already has been seen as a departure in style and scope for him and as a milestone in his long career.

Book of Days was a year late in showing up at the one hundred-seat Purple Rose Theater on elm-shaded Park Street in the hamlet of Chelsea, Michigan (population 4,000), which is 70 miles due west of Detroit and sits amid a bunch of dots on the map with names like Unadilla, Munith and Fitchburg, which sound as if they might come from Lanford Wilson plays.

As Wilson comes from Lebanon, Missouri, his longtime friend and Circle Repertory Theater colleague, Jeff Daniels, comes from Chelsea, Michigan. Daniels's father owns the lumberyard there. Daniels began the Purple Rose Theater to present new plays there.

Once invited—or begged—by Daniels to accept a commission for a new play, Wilson promised something for the 1996–1997 season. Purple Rose was on tenterhooks: an original work by a Pulitzer Prize-winning author (for 1980's *Talley's Folly*)! But Wilson, pleading sloth and writer's block, put them off for a year. What finally showed up in the spring of 1998 was this two-act drama about a life-changing event in an apparently easy going place in rural mid-America, especially suitable for the theater where it premiered. It's small-town contemporary, set in "a community not unlike Chelsea," said its gifted Michigan director Guy Sanville, around the time of the play's premiere in April 1998.

Sketched out, Wilson's play may sound like an unlikely combination of people and institutions. A cheese factory? A suspicious death? Ruth the factory bookkeeper playing George Bernard Shaw's Joan of Arc both onstage and off? The Missouri that Wilson returns to is a creative landscape, drawn by him, of good folks, hoodwinked victims, boondocks wheeler-dealers and not a few religious bullies. It is an intense play, packed with events, side roads, philosophical musings (including some unlikely, articulate thoughts from Ruth's husband, Len, the plant manager, about provolone and cheddar) and kaleidoscopic characters. As such, *Book of Days* resists easy excerpting and/or condensation. What's presented here, one hopes, is a wafting of Wilson prose coming at you from across the Pentecostal baptizing pools and the courthouse lawn of fictional Dublin, Mo. In this scene are Ruth, Len, the dead Walt's wife, Sharon, the *Saint Joan* director, Boyd, and the slippery employee, Earl. Imagine a play that is about frightened people: townspeople afraid to stand up and be counted, some with secrets, some cowed by old-time religion, some just numb. Wilson's Missouri village comes to look universal in lively storytelling by one of our best playwrights.

—LAWRENCE DEVINE

Excerpt from *Book of Days*

LEN: Oh, good lord.

RUTH: What?

LEN: Sheriff says Walt got killed last night, out in the storm.

RUTH: Oh, no. Oh, God.

LEN: How?

SHERIFF: Some kind of hunting accident. Facts are pretty sketchy. Just a monster mother of a tornado come through down by the lake last night. I thought maybe you'd drive with me over to tell Sharon.

> *Sharon strides on, followed by Boyd, Ginger and Earl. Sharon is refusing to do the scene.*

SHARON *(ad lib)*: No, no, no! I didn't say any of those words. That didn't happen. I don't say words like that! *(Etc.)* Well, I'm not about to do it. I'm sorry, no!

BOYD *(to Earl)*: Something funny? Ladies and gentlemen, when an actor is unable to perform a scene, it is customary for the stage manager to step in. Ginger, would you please step in and do Sharon Bates's breakdown for—

SHARON: I didn't have any breakdown and I don't say words like that.

BOYD: Ginger, would you please step in and do Sharon Bates's breakdown for us?

GINGER: Sure.

> *Boyd gestures to Len. Len begins scene.*

LEN: Sharon.

> *Ginger, playing Sharon, screams. Len, the Sheriff, Earl, LouAnn, and Ruth run to join her. The real Sharon stands at one side, deeply moved, but barely tolerant.*

GINGER *(as Sharon, truly livid. A harridan, total reversal of character; beating on Earl)*: What the hell were you doing setting out for a duck blind in the middle of the night? Ducks don't fucking fly at that goddamned hour.

SHARON: I don't say—

BOYD: Sshh!

GINGER *(continued; hitting Earl everywhere)*: It's your goddamned fault, you piece of shit. Son of a bitch! How in hell could you let that happen?! What did you do? You answer me, you bastard. Don't you have any sense at all?

EARL *(over the above, as she hits him)*: I'm sorry, Sharon, I'm sorry, I'm sorry.

GINGER: I want to see him!

SHERIFF: Sharon, you don't want to see what that shotgun did to Walt; you don't want to—

GINGER: —Goddamnit, you're going to fucking take me there now. LouAnn, where's that asshole, worthless son of mine?

LOUANN *(strong):* I don't know, Sharon.

GINGER: Well, then you drive me down to the morgue to see the body of my husband.

Everyone leaves except Earl, Len, Ruth and Sharon.

SHARON: I didn't say any of those words. And if I had, I would have been perfectly justified. *(She looks around.)* Oh, my God. How can I live without that man? I know you all cared for him. But I want the sisters from my church with me now.

She leaves.

EARL: I swear to God, it looked like the storm was letting up. We'd been planning this for over a month. I come up to the back door; I thought, he's not going to be up; he'll have chickened out and gone back to bed with this rain. I was already gettin' pissed he hadn't called me, save me from coming over. I knocked real light on the back door—hell, he was up and dressed, had a thermos of coffee made, rarin' to go. I swear it looked like the storm had passed; we thought it was over. It was starting to get light out. Then by the time we got out to see the lake, it started getting darker and darker; we got out of the truck, walked to the blind with Walt's flashlight, it started raining like I don't remember ever seeing rain before; you couldn't see your hand in front of your face. And the wind, goddamn, I never been in a wind like that. And then she comes. Goddamn. Barreling down like a freight train. Oh, Jesus. We couldn't see a goddamn thing, but Walt and me both knew what it was. Walt had his mouth right in my ear, yellin', "Lay down flat and hang on to something." My ears were poppin', chest about to explode from the change in pressure. You never hear about that; no one had ever told me about that. I took the Sheriff out to see the place. The track it left was, the Sheriff said, almost a quarter of a mile wide, twelve miles long. It had taken every tree, every bit of underbrush, every blade of grass right down to the mud. You could see how the actual twister missed us by about thirty feet. But it had downed a lot of trees around where Walt and me was. Walt must have been pushed or twisted around, disoriented. Goddamn, was he strong. You could see where he had crawled maybe ten feet. He had his shotgun there, under him, and he was down under the branches of this oak; you couldn't tell if the tree got him first or his gun did. Sheriff said it looked like the tree pushed him, got him off balance, caused him to twist the gun around. God, Len, his chest, part of his face, is just gone. Sharon can no way have an open casket.

LEN: I didn't hear a thing but the rain and thunder.

RUTH: I didn't even hear that; I slept right through it.

LEN: I have to go down to see him.

RUTH: I'll come with you.

LEN: Maybe you hadn't better . . .

RUTH: Oh, hush, Len. You're the one that'll faint, not me.

FIRST CHORUS *:* If you listen very carefully. Silence. Silence. Then a distant gun-shot.

SECOND CHORUS: June twelfth.

SHARON *(sitting, talking to Martha):* When you're so close to someone, when everything you do is for him, all you've known is him, your life is just him—and then he's taken away—it's like there's more of you gone than there is left. He was a hard man to know. Even on simple things. I'd say, "What do you feel like having for supper?" And he'd say, "Oh, anything's fine." You don't want to hear "any-thing's fine." Most of the time I was wondering what I should say, how I should say I'd like to go hear the Christmas carols at the school. Or, if I was thinking of some-thing nice, maybe someplace we'd been that I'd enjoy talking about—how I should say it. And trying not to let my face show that I was wondering how to talk to the man I shared my life with.

   Pause.

I was the prettiest girl in my class. When we started going out, it was just so logical. I was eight years younger than him, but even that was right. He had graduated from high school, started the cheese plant, worked down there building it up, and hadn't gone out with a girl once in all that time. Said he didn't have time for it. I was so thankful that I was pretty for him because he deserved that. Someone who'd keep herself up and keep things running smoothly. We wanted a daughter, too, but that wasn't in the cards. I think I made a good, steady life for him. I know I tried. I hope that's what he wanted.

MARTHA: You need to get a life, Sharon.

SHARON: I'm never going to get used to the way you talk. I was looking in the mirror this morning. I was thinking, I'm fifty-two. I don't know if that's young or old. I could say I was middle-aged, but how many people do you know who are a hundred and four?

MARTHA: You're a woman with her life ahead of her.

SHARON: James is going to need me now.

MARTHA: That's a big hole you don't want to fall into. It's your life. Live it for yourself.

SHARON: No, my life has been buried out in that graveyard with a big vulgar stone getting ready to be put on top of it.

MARTHA: You can choose any stone you want if you don't like it.

SHARON: No, that's probably the last thing I can do for him. The monument people called up; I said, just the biggest, most vulgar one you've got. I'm worried about James. He hasn't said a word since Walt died. Not one word. And that's not James.

   James and LouAnn. James has a hard, silent expression, which is our focus.

FIRST CHORUS: June thirteenth.

LOUANN: It was a beautiful service. I think everyone in town was there. Farmers from all over, and their families. I'll bet every dairy farmer within a hundred-mile radius. He was the most respected man in this part of the state. Would you like something to drink? I made a pot of coffee. There's sodas in the fridge. Iced tea? *(Pause, no change of tone.)* I've never been so humiliated in my life. Sheriff comes to the door with Ruth and Len, six in the morning, asking for you. Wanted you to go with him to help him tell your mom. I didn't even lie. I said I don't know where James is. He didn't come home last night. He sometimes doesn't come home till nine or ten in the morning. Sometimes he just goes right to the courthouse without coming home first. Always with a clean shirt and a clean shave, and a clean change of clothes. He's a very clean young man. Innocent Len Hoch, naïve as a child. Said, "Where does he go to, LouAnn?" And I said I don't give a good goddamn, Len. *Where* he goes. Or what he does there.

      Ruth and Boyd are at the theater.
FIRST CHORUS: June fourteenth.
RUTH: It's just difficult to concentrate. All this . . .
BOYD: What are you feeling?
RUTH: Boyd, I'm so screwed up with what I'm feeling, I can't get in touch with myself at all. I'm feeling—I've never had a death in my family, someone close, someone I really knew or worked with. Worked for.
BOYD: Both your folks are still living?
RUTH: Yeah, they're in Arizona; Dad has emphysema. I never knew any of my grandparents. I'm feeling what? Shocked, ashamed. Just the other day I was upset because our stupid cat had killed a bird. Now, that seems almost sacrilegious to— and—*(indicating the script)* this! Is just so insignificant and pointless and petty. We're going to "put on a show." You just want to laugh at the inappropriate, self-serving smallness of it.
BOYD: Seems like that sometimes, doesn't it.
RUTH: And I keep thinking, I don't know what, but something's not right. Walt was the most careful son of a bitch with firearms I'd ever—I don't see how he could—It's just not—well, something's not right.
BOYD: It's always hard to accept that someone's really gone, especially in an accident, something sudden.
RUTH: It's not just that. And I mean, I know nothing will bring him back, but just to be working on something so—
BOYD: No, Ruth, nothing you can do will bring Walt back.
RUTH: I'm hip.
BOYD: But you can bring back George Bernard Shaw. And you can bring back Joan of Arc.
RUTH: That's not what I meant.
BOYD: I know it's just two days after the funeral—
RUTH: Boyd, something's not right.
BOYD: Okay, something's not right, but we have to keep to schedule or tech will be a nightmare.

      Ruth comes from the theater. She is preoccupied and deeply disturbed.
FIRST CHORUS: June sixteenth.

BOOK OF DAYS—The 12-member ensemble of the Purple Rose Theater Company performing the ATCA New Play Award-winning play by Lanford Wilson

LEN: Took the Chevy into the shop. Thought I'd hitch a ride with you. How'd it go today?

RUTH *(not hearing):* What go?

LEN: Rehearsal.

RUTH: Len, don't ask every damn day how it's—Who knows? We're into the trial scene. The bastards forced Joan to recant. She thought after that they'd let her go home. Then she finds out, even after she'd recanted, they intended to hold her in a dungeon for the rest of her life.

LEN: Who did?

RUTH: The Inquisitor, the Chaplain, The *Church,* Len. I thought you read the damn play.

> *She breaks off. She's thinking over these quotes, not performing.*

She says, "I can live on bread and clean water, when have I asked for more? But to shut me from the light of the sky." *(Pause.)* You know, she says how can you shut me away from all the simple things of life like—the fields, trees, sunshine. And: "Without these things I cannot live; and by your wanting to take them away from me, or from any human creature, I know that your counsel is of the devil, and that mine is of God." (*Pause.*) She actually said that. Joan of Arc actually said that. She called The Church the counsel of the devil.

>   *Beat.*

That sure cooked her goose.

LEN: I'd guess it would.

RUTH: But the thing is, it hasn't changed in six hundred years. They were just hiding behind dogma and power. Refusing to hear or see anything other than their blind . . . What's different?

>   *She falls into thinking. A pause.*

LEN: You want to drive? You want me to drive?

RUTH: What?

LEN: Where's your mind, honey? What do you feel like having for—

RUTH (*overlapping him*): —Len, damnit, don't ask me what I want for dinner. I don't give a damn what I eat. Go home, I'll walk, forget it.

LEN: It's more than two miles—

RUTH: I know the goddamn distance, damnit. Go on!

>   *LouAnn storms into James and Earl's conversation.*

LOUANN (*angrily*): Hiding out in your office? This must be special; I haven't seen you in here in three months.

JAMES: LouAnn, you know d—a—m—n well not to come in here when I'm with someone.

LOUANN: You'll enjoy this one, this is rich.

JAMES: We're talking business here. There's going to be some swift changes made around here, sweetheart; you'd better hold onto your panties.

LOUANN: Honey, you have no idea. I paid a visit to your girl friend in Springfield this morning. You know her, Earl? Cheap as shit—

JAMES: What the hell are you talking about?

LOUANN: —but I'll bet she gives great head. You know her, Earl?

EARL: I don't know what you're talking about, LouAnn.

JAMES (*over*): You just get out of here with that talk.

LOUANN: Well, you should see her. You'd get a big kick out of it. 'Cause she happens to be five months pregnant with James's kid.

JAMES: LouAnn, I'll hit you, I swear to God I will.

LOUANN: You will not 'cause I will sue you for every cent you've got. Yeah, she was real proud, bragging about it. What you have to know, Earl, if you boys don't talk about these things and you don't already know it, is that James and me have not once had sex without a condom since the day—

JAMES: —Shut your filthy mouth—

LOUANN: —we were married four years ago, because James doesn't want children yet. Not by me. Not ones he'd have to take responsibility for.

JAMES: Get out. Just get on out of here with that crap.

LOUANN: You think there's going to be some swift changes? Honey, you ain't got no idea of the swift changes there's gonna be around here.

She storms out.

JAMES *(overlapping her):* And you can stay gone for all I care!

The Sheriff enters with Walt's gun as Ruth, Len, Boyd and Sharon enter. James and Earl stay on watching, not in the scene.

RUTH: Would you look at that gorgeous piece of hardware.

SHERIFF: I knew James would want to have Walt's gun.

SHARON: I don't want that stinking thing in my sight ever again.

RUTH *(smelling the gun, holding it):* Boy, that smell takes me back. Hopping Number Nine Powder Solvent. Nothing else in the world smells like that.

LEN: Don't put that up to your face, Ruth, scare me to death.

RUTH: It's not loaded, Len. Come on.

LEN: It still gives me the willies. Just put it down. *(Beat.)* Honey?

RUTH: Conroy, have you done anything to this gun?

SHERIFF: What do you mean?

RUTH: You didn't clean it or anything like that?

SHERIFF: No, ma'am. Didn't want to handle it any more than I had to, if you want to know.

RUTH: Smell the end of the barrel. Does that smell like a stinking gun to you?

The Sheriff holds the gun to his nose, gingerly; smells.

SHERIFF: *What?*

RUTH *(exasperated):* That gun has not been shot . . .

Book of Days *was originally produced by the Purple Rose Theater Company in Chelsea, Michigan, April 10, 1998 under the direction of Guy Sanville; Jeff Daniels executive director; Guy Sanville artistic director; Alan Ribant managing director.*

ATCA New Play Citation

OOO OOO
OOO
OOO
OOO
OOO
OOO

DINNER WITH FRIENDS

A Play in Two Acts

BY DONALD MARGULIES

Cast and credits appear on page 369 of *The Best Plays of 1997–98*

DONALD MARGULIES was born in Brooklyn September 2, 1954. His father was a salesman in a store selling wallpaper, and the future playwright showed an early interest, not in writing, but in the visual arts. After attending public school and John Dewey High School, he studied graphic design at Pratt Institute and proceeded to SUNY Purchase where he received his BFA in visual arts in 1977. But at SUNY he began to take an interest in playwriting—for no particular reason he can put his finger on now—and approached Julius Novick, who was teaching the subject there. Novick asked Margulies if he'd ever written a play, and Margulies replied frankly, "No." Novick nevertheless agreed to sponsor the young man in a playwriting tutorial, "a life-changing event," as Margulies looks back on it.

The first Margulies scripts were put on at SUNY, and in New York City he first surfaced off off Broadway with Luna Park, *a one-act adaptation of a Delmore Schwartz short story, commissioned by Jewish Repertory Theater and staged by them February 5, 1982. There followed* Resting Place *OOB at Theater for the New City (1982),* Gifted Children *at JRT (1983) and finally the full-fledged off-Broadway production of* Found a Peanut *at New York Shakespeare Festival June 17, 1984 for 33 performances.*

Later that season, Manhattan Theater Club produced Margulies's What's Wrong With This Picture? *in previews, but this one was withdrawn before opening and wasn't officially presented until 1988 in a revised version at the Back Alley Theater in Los Angeles (and it was produced on Broadway December 8, 1994 for 13 performances). Los Angeles was also the site of Margulies's* The Model Apartment *in 1989. Its author won a New York State arts grant (its New York appearances took place OOB at JRT in 1990 and at Primary Stages in 1995). JRT also staged his* Zimmer *in 1987.*

Margulies's The Loman Family Picnic *ran for only 16 off-Broadway performances when first produced by MTC June 20, 1989, but Jeffrey Sweet enthusiastically designated it a Best Play of its season; and indeed, MTC revived it November 18, 1993 for a 62-performance run. Margulies's second Best Play,* Sight Unseen, *was commissioned by and first produced in 1991 at South Coast Repertory in Costa Mesa, Calif., after which MTC provided its New York debut on January 20, 1992 for 263 performances. It won Margulies an Obie for playwriting and was nominated for many major awards including the New York Drama Critics Circle, Pulitzer, Outer Critics Circle and Drama Desk best-play citations.*

In 1995, Actors Theater of Louisville premiered Margulies's July 4, 1994 in its Humana Festival of New American Plays and did the same for his Dinner With Friends *at the 1998 Humana Festival, winning Margulies a 1998 ATCA citation as one of the cross-country year's best scripts. And on May 20, 1997 Margulies returned to MTC with* Collected Stories *for an 80-performance run. This play opened again off Broadway in a revival production August 13, 1998 for a run of 232 performances.*

Margulies is also the author of Women in Motion, *commissioned by the Lucille Ball Festival, and the recipient of a 1991 National Endowment for the Arts grant in playwriting. He is a member of both New Dramatists and the Dramatists Guild and lives with his wife and son in New Haven, Conn. where he is a visiting lecturer at the Yale School of Drama.*

INTRODUCTION: A mid-career playwright dramatizes mid-life crisis with compassion, humor and middle-aged maturity in *Dinner with Friends,* a poignant portrait of marriage, divorce and friendship. Fortysomething Donald Margulies, commissioned by the Actors Theater of Louisville to write a new work for last season's 22nd annual Humana Festival of New American Plays, examines the responsibilities, reversals and regrets of upper-middle-class, fortysomething adulthood with shrewd insight while avoiding clichés of the domestic genre. Many Margulies plays explore how life's transitions affect relationships, but few do so with such charming, thought-provoking transparency and gently satiric realism. In two acts, four characters and six scenes, with the children always offstage, Margulies explores the unsettling impact on the friendship between two couples when one separates.

Initially, *Dinner* scores as an observant comedy of affluent manners. The opening scene certainly invites easy laughter, as its comfortable characters don't seem to have anything more serious to talk about than gourmet food. *Dinner's* first dinner couldn't sound more delicious: grilled lamb and pumpkin risotto, with lemon-almond polenta for dessert. Gabe, a food writer, and Karen, his wife and collaborator, talk about their latest pomodoro-obsessed pilgrimage to Italy while sharing a home-cooked meal with Beth, while her husband Tom is away and the kids are watching a Disney movie in the basement. Suddenly, Beth begins sobbing and blurts out that Tom is leaving her for another woman. Gabe and Karen's loyalties are torn after hearing Beth out and, later, Tom's quite different story. Gradually, both couples are forced to reevaluate their fondest assumptions about themselves and each other.

Wistful perspective, sharpened by hindsight, comes in the second act's opening 12-year flashback to the carefree Martha's Vineyard weekend when Gabe and Karen introduced Tom and Beth. As the foursome mince garlic, spin the salad or sauté shrimp, Tom and Beth reveal conflicting ingredients of personality—he's earthy; she's artsy/spacey—that makes one question Gabe and Karen's matchmaking. Ironically, five months after the divorce, Beth and Tom seem much happier than Gabe and Karen. While the separated couple is eager to start new lives, the married couple is still coping with a sense of loss, betrayal and even guilt while skirting their own marital issues. Even so, Margulies offers hints that Tom and Beth's future may be less fulfilling than Gabe and Karen's now-anxious marriage. As Karen has lunch on her patio with Beth, the men meet for a quick drink in a New York bar. In these powerful overlapping scenes of changing and fading friendships, *Dinner* arrives at the aching heart of Margulies's theme. Tom, 43, describes his new girl friend Nancy as a "very mature" 26—in a gushing burst of naiveté that only reveals his immaturity. Disgusted, Gabe lectures Tom about the virtues of marriage and the importance of following through on one's commitments. Gabe may be Margulies's clearest alter ego, but the playwright gives each character sympathetic life and plausible (if not always forgivable) motivations.

Actors Theater's expert production, directed by Michael Bloom on resident designer Paul Owens's functional kitchens and comfortable bedrooms, fleshed out Margulies's complex, believable characters. Adam Grupper was especially convincing and touching as Gabe opposite Linda Purl's smilingly anxious Karen, David Byron's immature Tom, and Devora Millman's wounded but resilient Beth.

Spiced with amusing dialogue that suggests that the couples' lust for food may be compensation (and relatively small consolation) for a diminishing sex life, *Dinner* embraces the paunchy perspective of middle age with a disarmingly rueful self-awareness. Cooking and sharing meals become pungent metaphors for the mundane intimacies of everyday life and the challenges of blending personalities into a satisfying relationship. However complex a recipe for pumpkin risotto or chicken tikka masala, preparing a gourmet feast is easy compared to keeping a marriage cooking. With more understanding and ambivalence than many younger playwrights, and perhaps with more urgent immediacy than an older playwright, Margulies confronts the ambiguities of middle-aged happiness in an unstable world and examines the qualities of character required to sustain relationships.

Initially one of Margulies's funniest plays, *Dinner* ultimately becomes one of his wisest works, sobering in its recognition that even the happiest marriage requires courage, commitment and compromise. As Margulies wrote in a program note for the second production at South Coast Rep in Costa Mesa, California, directed by Daniel Sullivan, even couples who work hard at building and maintaining good marriages are not "exempt from the abyss." In an era when so much popular culture encourages adults to act childishly, Margulies offers an uncompromised affirmation of adulthood.

—MICHAEL GROSSBERG

Excerpt From *Dinner With Friends*

In the second scene of the second act, Beth and Karen meet on the patio of Karen's house for lunch, while Gabe (Karen's husband) and Tom (Beth's separated husband) meet for drinks in a bar.

KAREN: Try being alone for a while. That's what *I* would do . . .

BETH *(over "That's what I would do . . . ")*: What's so great about being alone? Huh? What's so great about it?

KAREN *(continuous)*: I would indulge myself; get to know myself better . . .

BETH: That's easy for *you* to say: you have *Gabe,* you have this *life* . . .

KAREN: Beth . . .

BETH: You know what *I* think? I think you *love* it when I'm a mess.

KAREN: What?!

BETH: You do. You love it when I'm all-over-the-place, flailing about. I finally find someone who's like a, like an *anchor* and you don't want to hear about it!

KAREN: That is not true.

BETH: As long as I'm artsy and incompetent, everything is fine. The minute I show any signs of being on an equal footing with you, forget it; you can't deal with it, you have to knock me over!

KAREN: How can you say that?

BETH: Come on, you *need* to think of me as a mess; you're *invested* in it. Every Karen needs a Beth. Any doubts about your life, just take a look at *mine* . . .

KAREN: That really isn't fair.

BETH: We all play the parts we're handed. I was The Mess, The Ditz, The Comic Relief. You got to be Miss Perfect: everything just right. Just the right wine, just the right spice, just the right husband, just the right kids. How was I supposed to compete with *that?*

KAREN: Nobody was asking you to compete with anything.

BETH: You're right, there was no contest; I couldn't possibly reciprocate . . . The hostess gifts you would give me! I could never tell if you were being remedial or just plain hostile. Either way, I always found them slightly condescending.

KAREN: I had no idea you felt this way . . .

BETH: We can't all *be* like you, Karen. God knows I've tried. No matter how much I stir, the soup still sticks to the pot, you know?

   Pause.

KAREN: We loved nothing more than having you in our home and cooking you meals.

BETH: We did, too.

KAREN: You're my family. I spent my first twenty years doing whatever the hell I could to get *away* from my family and my second twenty years doing everything I could to cobble together a family of my own. I thought if I could *choose* my family this time, if I could make my friends my family . . .

BETH: Congratulations. The family you've chosen is just as fucked up and fallible as the one you were born into.

Lights up on the men. The women eat in silence.

TOM *(leaning forward):* The things she's got me *doing,* Gabe ... !

GABE: Lucky you.

TOM: Nancy has more imagination, more daring, more *wisdom* at twenty-six than I'll ever have as long as I live. I mean, it just goes to show you how age is totally irrelevant. I'm a boy-toy at forty-three! She is so at home in her own body. See, I've never known what that was like. A lover teaches you that; it's something you learn together. Beth and I *never* had that; she was *never* comfortable in her own body ...

GABE: Really? Gee, I ...

TOM *(continuous):* So how could I expect her to be comfortable with mine?

BETH: Well, I really should, uh ...

Beth puts down her napkin, goes.

KAREN: Beth, wait ...

She follows Beth out.

TOM: Nancy and I'll be strolling along and she'll put her hand on my ass or something, just like that, without even thinking about it. It's this energy that exists between us that we celebrate every chance we get.

GABE: A whole lotta celebratin' goin' on, huh?

TOM: With *Beth,* sex was always up to me. It was never about her *want*ing me, it was never about *desire,* it was all about obligation. And then once the kids came ... Well, *you* know how *that* is.

GABE: Uh, huh.

TOM: Sex became one more thing on my list of things to do. You know? Nancy and I, we are *totally* in sync. She just has to stroke my *fing*ers and I get hard, or give me a look, or laugh a certain way.

GABE: Do you two ever ... *talk?*

TOM: Oh, yeah. Are you kidding? We talk all the time. All my old stories are new again. It's great! Remember what that's like when you're starting a relationship? All that talk, all that sex, all that laughter? Nancy really hears me. She *hears* me.

GABE: Uh huh.

TOM: She saved my life, Gabe. She really did; she breathed life back into me.

GABE *(nods, then):* Good. That's great. I'm glad.

(Gabe sips his drink. Tom looks at him.)

What.

TOM: What are you thinking?

GABE: What do you mean?

TOM: Come on, Gabe, I *know* you, I know that *look* ...

GABE: I'm just listening. You don't want me to say anything, right?

TOM *(over "right?"):* Oh, Christ ...

GABE: No, isn't that what you told me?

TOM: I said that to you ... when I was still very raw ...

GABE: Oh. And you're not so raw anymore? Well, what are the rules, then? You've gotta fill me in here, pal. I've gotta know the rules so I don't step out of bounds.

TOM: Gabe . . .

GABE: Okay, you want to know what I'm thinking? I'm thinking: I hear you *talk*ing, Tom, I hear these *words* coming out, and you sound like a fucking *Moonie* to me, Tom, you really do . . .

TOM *(over "you really do . . . "):* I'm trying to tell you . . . I was dying, Gabe! You don't understand that, do you? I was losing all the will to live; isn't that dying? The life I was leading had no relationship to who I was or what I wanted. The constant logistics of "You pick up Sam and take him to lollipop tennis, I'll take Laurie to hockey practice . . . "

GABE: But, Tom, that's . . .

TOM *(continuous):* This is what we'd talk about! No, really. This would pass for conversation in our house.

GABE: I know.

TOM: The dog finished me off. Oh, man, that dog. Sarge. It wasn't enough that we had two cats and fish and a guinea pig; no, Beth felt the kids *had* to have a dog because *she* had a dog. I'd spent my entire adult life cleaning up one form of shit or another; now I was on to *dog* shit. I should've gone into waste management. How do you keep love alive when you're shoveling shit all day long?

GABE: We've all made sacrifices to our kids. It's the price you pay for having a family.

TOM: Yeah, but you have to really *want* that. You and Karen: you really *wanted* it. That's what I realized: I never really did.

GABE: What are you talking about?

TOM: I don't know what I was thinking. It was completely against my nature. Just one more thing I did because it was expected of me, not because I had any real passion for it. Like law: I just kind of got on a certain track that made my father happy, and that was that. I always felt, I don't know, *inauthentic* living this life.

GABE: What, you were a party boy trapped in the body of a family man? Tommy, I could swear I actually saw you *enjoy*ing yourself on a number of occasions in the last decade or so.

TOM: Well, sure. But, honestly, most of the time I was just being a good sport.

GABE: A good sport?!

TOM: You know what I mean . . .

GABE *(continuous):* Wait a minute. You were faking it?! You mean to tell me that all those years—all those *years,* Tom!—the four of us together, raising our *kids* together, the dinners, the vacations, the hours of videotape, you were just being a good sport?

TOM: No . . .

GABE: Then what, Tom, I don't get it. I was there, as well as you. This *misery* you describe, the agony. Gee, I thought we were all just living our lives, you know?

Sharing our humdrum little existences. I *thought* you were there, wholeheartedly there. And now, you're saying you had an eye on the clock and a foot out the door?!

TOM: You've got to stop taking this so personally.

GABE: How would *you* take it? You say you were wasting your life, that's what you've said.

TOM (*over " . . . that's what you've said."*): I don't mean you and Karen. I don't mean *you*, I'd never mean *you;* you're my best friend, I've got to be able to say this stuff to you. I'm talking about my marriage.

GABE: But it's not that simple, Tom. We were there. Karen and Danny and Isaac and I, we were all there; we were all a big part of that terrible life you had to get the hell away from. Isaac's totally freaked out by this, by the way. So, when you repudiate your entire adult life . . .

TOM: That's not what I've done . . .

GABE: That's essentially what you've done. And I can understand how you might find it necessary to do that: it must be strangely *exhilarating* blowing everything to bits.

TOM: Gabe . . .

GABE: I mean it. You spend all of your adult life building something that's precarious in even the best of circumstances, and you succeed, or at least you make it *look* like you've succeeded, your *friends* think you have, you had *us* fooled, and then, one day, you blow it all up! It's like, I watch Danny and Isaac sometimes, dump all their toys on the floor—Legos and blocks and train tracks—and build these elaborate cities together. They'll spend hours at it, they'll plan and collaborate, and squabble and negotiate, but they'll do it. And then what do they do? They wreck it! No pause to revel in what they accomplished, no sigh of satisfaction; no, they just launch into a full-throttle attack, bombs bursting, and tear the whole damn thing apart.

> *Pause.*

TOM (*quietly*): Well . . .

GABE: It all goes by so fast, Tom, I know. The hair goes, and the waist. And the stamina; the capacity for staying up late, to read or watch a movie, never mind sex. Want to hear a shocker? Karen is pre-menopausal. That's right: my sweetheart, my lover, that sweet girl with whom I lolled around on endless Sundays, is getting hot flashes. It doesn't seem possible. (*A beat.*) We spend our youth unconscious, feeling immortal, then we marry and have kids and awaken with a shock to mortality—theirs, ours—that's all we see; we worry about them, *their* safety, our *own,* air bags, plane crashes, pederasts, and spend our middle years wanting back the dreamy, carefree part—the part we fucked and pissed away. Now we want that back, 'cause now we know how fleeting it all is; now we know, and it just doesn't seem fair that so much is gone when there's really so little left. So, some of us try to regain unconsciousness. Some of us blow up our homes . . . And others of us . . . take up piano; I'm taking piano.

> *Pause.*

DINNER WITH FRIENDS—Devora Millman as Beth and Linda Purl as Karen
in the Actors Theater of Louisville production of Donald Margulies's play

TOM: I just want you to be my friend. That's all. I want you to be happy for me.
Happy I turned my life around.

GABE: Sure, Tom. I'm happy for you.

TOM *(quietly):* No you're not.

GABE: I'm not even sure it's happiness you want. Contentment suggests to me a
kind of calm. And that, apparently, is the *last* thing you want. You want your freedom. You want to boogie. What happens when your girl friend decides she wants
to have kids? You walk out and reinvent yourself all over again?

TOM: She won't.

GABE: How do you know?

TOM: Because I know she doesn't; we've talked about it.

GABE: But she's very young—twenty-six, right?

TOM: That's not that young.

GABE: Tom, twenty-six is very young.

TOM: But I told you: she's incredibly mature for her age.

GABE: Still, there's plenty of time for her to change her mind.

TOM: She's not going to. Believe me, she's the first to admit, she likes kids well
enough, but she has very little interest in *having* them . . .

GABE: How can you be so sure?

TOM: Because I know her. And she knows herself.

GABE: Who knows themself at twenty-six?

TOM: *She* does.

GABE: Uh huh. *(Backing off.)* Okay.

TOM: You know, you can be so fucking smug sometimes.

GABE: What?

TOM: You're not immune to all this, you know. Even you and Karen—*(Stops himself.)*

GABE: What.

TOM: Never mind.

GABE: *What.*

TOM: Come on, Gabe, I've heard you complain.

GABE: Well, sure, we all *complain,* Tom. That's what married friends do: we joke about sex and bellyache about our wives and kids, but that doesn't mean we're about to *leave* them. Marriages all go through a kind of baseline wretchedness from time to time, but we do what we can to ride those patches out.

TOM: Don't you ever just want to chuck it all? Don't you, Gabe?

GABE: Yeah. Sure. Of course I do.

TOM *(a victory):* Okay.

GABE: But the feeling passes. The key to civilization, I think, is *fighting* the impulse to chuck it all. Where would we be with everybody's ids running rampant?

TOM: Boy, Karen really has you well-trained, doesn't she?

GABE: That's what *I* believe; Karen has nothing to do with it. I cling to Karen; I cling to her. Imagining a life without her doesn't excite me; it just makes me anxious.

TOM: Look, all I'm saying is, don't do what *I* did. Don't shut your eyes. I was so steeped in denial and resignation. I know the signs, believe me. I'd hate for you to wake up at fifty and . . .

GABE: Why are you doing this? Huh? Why?

TOM: I'm your friend.

> *Gabe nods. Pause.*

GABE: We had a vow, too, you know, not a marriage but something like it.

TOM: Yeah?

GABE *(nods, then):* We were supposed to get old and fat together, the four of us, and watch each other's kids grow up, and cry together at their weddings . . .

TOM: It's not like I'm *dead,* you know . . .

GABE *(looks at him; a beat):* I guess I mean, I thought we were in this together. You know? For life.

TOM: Isn't that just another way of saying misery loves company?

> *Gabe still looks at him. A beat.*

I'm kidding.

> *Gabe's expression doesn't change.*

Hey, I'll still be there. But it won't be with Beth.

> *Gabe nods, but he doesn't agree that Tom will be there. Silence.*

How *is* she?

GABE: Fine, I think. We actually haven't seen that much of her lately. Karen was supposed to have lunch with her today.

TOM: You meet David yet?

GABE: David?

TOM: *You* know: the guy she's seeing.

This is news to Gabe, but he tries not to show his surprise.

GABE: Oh, yeah, no, we, uh . . .

TOM: He's actually a very nice guy; I don't hold anything against him. You've got to hand it to him: hanging in there all these years, finally getting what he wanted . . .

GABE: Uh huh. How do you mean?

TOM: He really *fell* for Beth, you know, he was really in love with her. I'm sure she's told you all about it.

GABE *(lying):* Uh huh.

TOM: That's what's so weird about this: we could've broken up back then, when they had their thing, but we stuck it out. Ten years and two kids later, they're back together!

Shakes his head, finishes his drink, looks at the time.

I'd better go; I told Nancy I'd meet her at Saks. She loves taking me shopping. She hates my ties; she gave me this one for Christmas.

GABE: Nice.

TOM: Listen, I'll call you. Hey, how about, I'm seeing the kids next weekend, what if I . . .

GABE: Actually, we're gonna be away next weekend.

TOM: Oh.

GABE: My sister's in New Hampshire. We said we'd . . .

TOM: Uh huh. *(Pause.)* Well, next time, then.

GABE: Sure.

TOM: I can't wait for you to meet Nancy. I'm telling you, you're gonna love her. She knows a lot about food.

GABE: Oh, yeah?

TOM: She wants to be a nutritionist.

GABE: Really. I thought she was a travel agent.

TOM: She is. I mean, she doesn't want to do that forever; she wants to go back to school and get a degree, *you* know.

GABE: Uh huh.

TOM: We'll all go out to dinner, the four of us. How's that?

Gabe nods. Tom takes out his wallet.

GABE: No, no, this is on me.

TOM: You sure? Thanks. I'll get the next one.

GABE: That's right, the next one.

TOM: When's your train? I'll walk out with you.

GABE: No, I thought I'd stay for a minute. You know, gird myself for the ride home.

TOM *(nods, then):* Well . . .

> *Tom opens his arms to his friend. Gabe hugs him for the last time.*

GABE: Goodbye, Tom.

TOM: I feel so badly; we didn't get a chance to talk about *you.*

GABE: That's okay; nothing much to report. Same old. *You* know. So, take care.

TOM: You, too. I'll call you.

> *Gabe nods. Tom starts to go.*

Say hi to Karen if you think she'd be glad to hear from me. And send my love to the boys. Tell Isaac everything's gonna be okay.

GABE *(nods, then):* Bye.

> *Tom waves and goes. Gabe's smile fades as he watches him walk away. He smiles and waves again. Tom has looked back one last time. Gabe stands there until he can no longer see him. Lights fade.*

Dinner with Friends *was first produced at the Actors Theater of Louisville, March 5, 1998 during the 22d annual Humana Festival of New American Plays under the direction of Michael Bloom.*

MIRANDA: Yeah?

NICK: You want the good news or the bad?

MIRANDA: Gimme the bad news first.

NICK: He gave me the name of an infertility specialist.

MIRANDA: And the good news?

NICK *(smiles; shrugs):* Sperm's fine . . .

MIRANDA: So, if I'm fine and you're fine, why—?

NICK: That's what we're going to the infertility specialist to find out.

Nick and Miranda consult a fertility specialist, Dr. Wilde, who decides to inseminate Miranda with Nick's sperm, to "eliminate any slow swimmers," and to start her on clomid, a fertility drug that will help her produce a number of eggs. He adds that it has a few side effects—"bloating, hot flashes, mood swings, migraine . . . But I'm sure you'll do just fine."

MIRANDA: And, on the day of my first insemination, I woke up at six with a migraine and set about getting a sperm sample from my husband who, like me, is not a morning person, which has always been a source of compatibility in our marriage.
   Nick is looking for names.
Nick wanted me to dress up a little and help him out . . .
   Nick looks up as she strips.
So I put on a bustier and some black stockings over my bloated body . . .
   A Sanitation Worker passes by upstage, interested.
And, unfortunately, the sanitation worker passed by the window of our ground floor apartment at the key moment, distracting Nick—whose sperm missed the sterile cup provided by the clinic . . . and went shooting across the room.
   The Sanitation Worker follows the arc of the sperm with his eyes.
Being my mother's daughter, I managed to salvage a smidgen of our posterity, and I wrapped it in a sock and stuck it in my bustier to keep it warm.
   She dresses fast.
Then I headed out to the clinic because the stuff's only good for an hour and a half. *(Pause.)* By now it was snowing, and this being New York, I couldn't get a cab. So I stood there in the snow, had a couple of hot flashes, and finally got a gypsy cab.
   A Russian cabbie with a thick accent comes on with two chairs. Miranda takes one and they drive off.
Lousy weather, huh?

CABBIE: This is what you call lousy? Maybe you never worked outside digging ditches all day in a labor camp in the gulag.

MIRANDA: No . . .

CABBIE *(pounds his chest):* Fourteen years.

MIRANDA: I'm sorry. Look, do you think we should try Ninth? Because the traffic's not moving—

CABBIE *(paranoid):* So—you are saying I don't know way around city? Listen. After I escaped from prison, I walked across Soviet Union barefoot, with head filled with experimental psychiatric drugs. I think I can find way across town.

>*Beat.*

You know what is like to lose your entire family?

MIRANDA: Just my father.

CABBIE: Hmmmph. You have children?

MIRANDA: No. *(Beat. Touches cup.)* I don't think so—

CABBIE: Good. It's a terrible world.

MIRANDA: I know.

CABBIE: You ever live in one-room apartment with twelve people next door to nuclear weapons plant?

MIRANDA: I live in a pre-war building on the Upper West Side.

CABBIE *(smirks):* "Pre-war building"—in country that's never been invaded.

>*Re: Traffic.*

Look at this. What are they honking horns for? Where are they going? Nowhere. Everybody wants to be the first shmuck there.

MIRANDA: Look, I better get out. Here's a twenty.

CABBIE: Please. Do not insult me. *(Looks towards sidewalk.)* Look at that. Picking up after poodle with little shovel and Ziplock bag. And children in my country are waiting in orphanages, three in one bed—

MIRANDA: You know, I think I better walk.

CABBIE: Relax. Read newspaper.

>*Hands her one.*

You see article about teenager who gave birth in bathroom during senior prom?

MIRANDA: I haven't read the paper yet this morning.

CABBIE: She put baby in trash, washed hands, and went back to dance with boyfriend. What kind of world is this?

MIRANDA: Look. TAKE THE TWENTY AND LET ME OUT OF THIS FUCKING CAB!

>*She gets out. He picks up his chair and leaves.*

CABBIE *(dryly):* Sure. You have nice day, too.

>*Honking horns, traffic sounds. Miranda turns around and rails at the cars.*
>*A bedraggled Streetperson comes on and observes.*

MIRANDA: Move! Goddam car-driving New Yorkers, what's wrong with you? This is a city! Take the goddam train! Cocksuckers!

>*Turns to audience.*

That was my first month on clomid. And while I was waving my arms at the traffic, the little cup was dislodged from my cleavage—

>*The Streetperson picks it up from the gutter.*

STREETPERSON: Here you go—

>*Hands it back to her and leaves.*

MIRANDA: Thanks—

>*To audience.*

EXPECTING ISABEL—Ellen Karas as Miranda and Nick
Olcott as the Cabbie in a scene from the play by Lisa Loomer
at Arena Stage, Washington, D.C.

And I stuck it in my purse and ran down into the subway . . .
A Junkie runs by and grabs her bag.
Where some junkie stole my purse—*(To Junkie)* HEY!
  JUNKIE: Fuck you.
  MIRANDA: And my sperm.

    After continual failure, both Nick and Miranda are frustrated and exhausted.
Nick is ready to give up, but by now Miranda has become absolutely determined to
have a baby, whatever the cost. At the end of the act, they angrily separate.
    In Act II, however, they realize how much they love each other and reunite,
deciding to discontinue infertility treatments and adopt a child instead. This decision,
however, launches them on another wild ride, with a whole new team of specialists
and a new support group. Eventually, they meet some prospective birth mothers,
pregnant women whose circumstances compel them to give up their babies. The first

two—a high school Valley Girl and a hardened punk—do not work out. Then they meet Lupe.

> *Miranda gets up slowly and nods. Lupe Santiago enters, startling them. She's in her 30s, nine months pregnant, straightforward, proud. She has a bunch of kids' toys that she sets on the floor, as sounds of kids are heard in the next room. There's a soberness to this meeting, unlike the others.*

LUPE: Hi, I'm Lupe; come in.

> *She rearranges the stage furniture, straightening her apartment.*

Sorry I couldn't meet you at the Burger King like we said. One of my kids fell down 'cause the stairs was broke again, and I had to take him over to Mount Sinai to make sure he was okay. Why don't you sit down?

MIRANDA: Thank you.

> *They all sit.*

NICK: How many kids do you have, Lupe?

LUPE: You mean with me?

> *They nod, surprised at the question.*

Two. And I got another one with my mother in Puerto Rico. Look—I'm just gonna tell you like it is because the first couple I picked, after we had lunch and all, they changed their mind. *(Pained.)* And I could be having this baby any day now, so . . .

NICK: That's not going to happen here, Lupe. We want this child.

> *Miranda nods. Lupe nods.*

LUPE *(presses on):* So I already filled out the medical forms . . . I don't take no drugs, and one of my kids was taken away for a little while, and it's on my record, but I'm just gonna tell you straight out, it was his father called the child welfare on me because he wanted Michael to go live with *him*—but I'm telling you, he's the one that's unfit. One time I caught him watching TV with my son, and he was like— nibbling on his ear. I told my worker about it; she didn't do a damn thing.

> *Nick nods. Miranda is too shocked to get the nod together.*

NICK: How do your kids feel about the adoption?

LUPE: Oh, they don't know. They're inside watching the TV. I don't let them out of the apartment unless I'm with them, because there's some bad people around here. *(Pause; with difficulty.)* I haven't told them I can't keep the baby . . . They're real sensitive kids, and their feelings get broke easy.

> *Nick and Miranda nod.*

You're Christian, right?

NICK: Catholic.

> *Miranda starts to say something—but doesn't.*

LUPE: Yeah, me too. Only now I go to this other church with the Pentecostals, and they come to my house and tell me it's a sin to give up my baby, and if I take Jesus into my heart, the baby will be okay. I told them I already have Jesus in my heart, and could they lend me the money for diapers and formula, and they told me to pray . . .

A DIRECTORY
OF NEW-PLAY PRODUCTIONS

Professional productions June 1, 1998–May 31, 1999 (plus a very few that opened too late in the spring of 1998 to be included in last year's *Best Plays* volume) of new plays by leading resident companies around the United States, who supplied information on casts and credits at Camille Dee's request, are listed here in alphabetical order of the locations of more than 60 producing organizations. Date given is opening date. Most League of Resident Theaters (LORT) and other regularly-producing Equity groups were queried for this comprehensive Directory. Active cross-country theater companies not included in this list either did not offer new or newly-revised scripts during the year under review or had not responded to our query by press time. Most productions listed below are world premieres; a few are American premieres, new revisions, noteworthy second looks or scripts not previously reported in *Best Plays*.

Abingdon, Va.: Barter Theater

(Richard Rose artistic director)

FRANKENSTEIN. Adapted by Richard Rose from the novel by Mary Shelley. October 8, 1998. Director, Richard Rose; The Creature designed and created by Dean Gates; scenery, Charlie Morgan; costumes and dance choreography, Amanda Aldridge; lighting, Wendy Luedtke; sound, Bobby Beck.

ACT I

Scene 1: 1810, a ship lost in the Arctic Sea
Capt Robert Walton .... Will Hines
Boatswain .... Chris Pomeroy
Sailor #1 .... Thaddeus Stephenson
Sailor #2 .... Pamela Chermansky
Sailor #3 .... Doug Presley
Sailor #4 .... Quinn Hawkesworth
Victor Frankenstein .... John Hardy

Scene 2: 1797, the drawing room of the Frankenstein home, Geneva, Switzerland
Alphonse Frankenstein .... Tom Celli
Caroline Beaufort Frankenstein .. Rebecca Rich
Young Victor .... Davis Sweatt
Justine Moritz .... Quinn Hawkesworth
Young Elizabeth .... Stephanie Demaree
Young Henry .... Harrison Cook

Scene 3: 1800, A tree in the mountains outside of Geneva, three years later
Adolescent Victor .... Conrad Koski,
Caleb Wilson
Adolescent Elizabeth ...... Elizabeth Mansfield,
Mindy Miller

Adolescent Henry .... Andrew McElroy,
Ben Price

Scene 4: A room and attached chamber in the Frankenstein home
Midwife .... Pamela Chermansky

Scene 5: Fall of 1807, outside the ballroom of the Frankenstein home
William Frankenstein .... Davis Sweatt
Dancing Couple .... Pamela Chermansky,
Thaddeus Stephenson
Elisabeth Lavenza .... Tricia Ann Kelly
Henry Clerval .... Nicholas Piper

Scene 6: 1807 to 1808, the University at Ingolstadt, Germany
Prof. M. Waldman .... Tom Celli
Prof M. Krempe .... Will Hines
Prof. M. Schiller .... Rebecca Rich

Scene 7: 1808 to 1809, the laboratory at Ingolstadt
The Creature .... Eugene Wolf

Scene 8: A street in Ingolstadt
Young Woman .... Pamela Chermansky
Her Daughter .... Elizabeth Mansfield,
Mindy Miller
Two Gentlemen .... Thaddeus Stephenson,
Chris Pomeroy
Beggar Woman .... Rebecca Rich
Boy .... Harrison Cook
Hessian Guard .... Will Hines

400

Scene 9: 1809, a cabin in the mountains
of Switzerland
DeLacey .... Tom Celli
Agatha .... Pamela Chermansky
Felix .... Chris Pomeroy
Evi .... Stephanie Demaree
Philippe .... Andrew McElroy, Ben Price
Scene 9: A river in a forest in the mountains
of Switzerland
Scene 10: A cliff in the mountains
near Geneva

ACT II

Scene 1: The forest surrounding
the Frankenstein home
Search Party .... Company
Scene 2: A sitting room
in the Frankenstein home
Scene 3: 1809, a public square, Geneva
French Magistrate .... Will Hines
French Clerk .... Doug Presley
Guard .... Thaddeus Stephenson
Servant .... Chris Pomeroy
Market Woman .... Rebecca Rich
Boy .... Conrad Koski, Caleb Wilson
People at the Trial .... Company
Scene 4: The Frankenstein home
and the Magistrate's quarters
Scene 5: A jail cell
Priest .... Chris Pomeroy
Scene 6: A public square set up
for the hanging of Justine
Crowd at Hanging .... Company
Scene 8: A street in Geneva
and the Frankenstein home
Scene 9: Victor's laboratory
in the mountains near Geneva
Scene 10: Courtyard of
the Frankenstein home

Priest .... Chris Pomeroy
Wedding Guests; Servants .... Company
Scene 11: The wedding chamber
Scene 12: The forest surrounding Geneva
Scene 13: The ship
Scene 14: The Arctic tundra

THE HONKY TONK ANGELS. By Ted Swindley. February 10, 1999. Director, Ted Swindley; musical direction and arrangements, August Eriksmoen; scenery, Linda Thistle; costumes, Amanda Aldridge; lighting, Kevin Shaw; sound, Bobby Beck.
Angela .... Becky Barta
Darlene .... Jessica Welch
Sue Ellen .... Teresa Williams
    MUSICAL NUMBERS, ACT I: "Honky Tonk Angels," "He Thinks He'll Keep Her," "One of These Days," "Stand By Your Man," "Coal Miner's Daughter," "9 to 5," "Paradise Road," "Ode to Billy Joe," "Don't Come Home a Drinkin'"/"The Pill" (medley), "Mr. Walker, It's All Over," "Take This Job and Shove It," "Amazing Grace," "Let Her Fly," "I Will Always Love You," "Paradise Road" (Reprise), "Delta Dawn," "Calling All Angels," "It's Time for Me to Fly," "I'll Fly Away."
    ACT II: "Honky Tonk Attitude;" Bad Girl Medley—"Your Good Girl's Gonna Go Bad," "Silver Threads, Golden Needle," "Night Life;" Honky Tonk Hall of Fame—"Cleopatra Queen of Denial," "Harper Valley PTA," "Fancy;" Good Girl Medley—"You're Looking at Country," "Barroom Habits," "Cowboy's Sweetheart," "Cornell Crawford," "Almost Persuaded," "Sittin' on the Front Porch Swing;" Finale—"Honky Tonk Heaven" (a.k.a. "I Dreamed of Hillbilly Heaven"), "On the Wings of a Dove," "Amazing Grace," "Will the Circle Be Unbroken."

Arlington, Va.: Signature Theater

(Eric D. Schaeffer artistic director; Paul Gamble managing director)

OVER & OVER. Musical based on *The Skin of Our Teeth* by Thornton Wilder; book by Joseph Stein; music by John Kander; lyrics by Fred Ebb. January 6, 1999. Director, Eric D. Schaeffer; choreography, Bob Avian; musical direction, Patrick Vaccariello; scenery, Lou Stancari; costumes, Anne Kennedy; lighting, Howell Binkley; sound, David Maddox; orchestrations, Michael Gibson; dance arrangements, Jim Laev.
Sabina .... Sherie Scott
Bob Corleone; Telegram Boy;
    Announcer .... Mario Cantone
Maggie Antrobus .... Linda Emond

Gladys Antrobus .... Megan Lawrence
Henry Antrobus .... Jim Newman
George Antrobus .... David Garrison
Socrates .... Lawrence Redmond
Homer .... Hugh Nees
Moses .... Thomas Adrian Simpson
Jesus .... Bruce Nelson
B.V.M.; Elsa Fitt;
    Lulu Shriner .... Dorothy Loudon
Fortune Teller .... Sharon Watkins
Dancing Gauchos .... Karl Christian, Marc Oka
    Ensemble—Erika Lynn Rupli, Jennifer Swiderski, Johanna Gerry, Karl Christian, Kenneth J.

Ewing Jr., Daniel Felton, Jason Gilbert, Marc Oka, Richard Pelzman, R. Scott Thompson.

MUSICAL NUMBERS, ACT I: Prologue, "Eat the Ice Cream," "Sabina!", "He Always Comes Home to Me," "Telegram #1," "We're Home," "The Wheel," "Someday, Pasadena," "A Whole Lot of Lovin'," "Abou Ben Adhem," "Numbers," "The Library," Finale.

ACT II. "Rain," "As You Are," "Beauty Contest," "This Life," "You Owe It to Yourself," "Nice People," "The Promise," "The Promise" (Reprise), "Military Man," "Lullaby," "Telegram #2," "Home," "Nice People" (Reprise), "The Skin of Our Teeth," "Antrobus Waltz," "At the Rialto."

Ashland, Ore.: Oregon Shakespeare Festival

(Libby Appel artistic director; Paul E. Nicholson executive director)

THE GOOD PERSON OF SZECHUAN. By Bertolt Brecht; newly translated by Douglas Langworthy. February 27, 1999. Director, Penny Metropulos; scenery, Riccardo Hernandez; costumes, Smaranda Branescu; lighting, Ann G. Wrightson; composer, Larry Delinger.

Wong	Michael J. Hume
Shen Te/Shui Ta	BW Gonzalez
Mrs. Shin	Demetra Pittman
Husband; Carpet Dealer	Barry Kraft
Wife; Carpet Dealer's Wife	Linda Halaska
Nephew	David Kelly
Sister-in-Law	Melany Bell
Brother; Yang Sun	Michael Elich
Boy; Waiter	Anthony James
Niece	Suzanne Irving
Grandfather	Robert Vincent Frank
Unemployed Man	Armando Durán
Lin To	J.P. Phillips
Mrs. Mi Tzu	Robynn Rodriguez
Policeman; Priest	Charlie Bachmann
Old Prostitute; Mrs. Yang	Dee Maaske
Shu Fu	Mark Murphey

Musicians: Daniel Flick, Jennifer Perry

Three Gods: Robert Vincent Frank, Suzanne Irving, David Kelly.

Place: The province of Szechuan, which stands for all places where man is exploited by man. One intermission.

Atlanta: Alliance Theater Company

(Kenny Leon artistic director; Paul A. Stuhlreyer III managing director)

ELABORATE LIVES: THE LEGEND OF AIDA. Musical suggested by the opera; book by Linda Woolverton; music by Elton John; lyrics by Tim Rice. September 17, 1998. Director, Robert Jess Roth; musical direction and vocal arrangements, Paul Bogaev; choreography, Matt West; scenery, Stanley A. Meyer; costumes, Ann Hould-Ward; lighting, Natasha Katz; sound, Steve C. Kennedy; fight direction, Rick Sordelet; music arrangements, Guy Babylon, Paul Bogaev; orchestrations, Steve Margoshes, Guy Babylon, Paul Bogaev; dance arrangements, Bob Gustafson; presented by special arrangement with Walt Disney Theatrical Productions.

Pharoah	Neal Benari
Nehebka	Mary Bentley-LaMar
Nenu	Future Davis
Shu	Pamela Gold
Aida	Heather Headley
Zoser	Rich Hebert
Hefnut	Jenny Hill
Nekhen	Scott Irby-Ranniar
Amonasro	Roger Robinson
Amneris	Sherie Scott
Radames	Hank Stratton

Ensemble: Neal Benari, Mary Bentley-LaMar, Kevin M. Burrows, Eric L. Christian, Imani Cogen, Zack Dobbins, Pamela Gold, Jenny Hill, Regi Jennings, Kyra Little, Christia Leigh Mantzke, Kenya Unique Massey, Don Mayo, Andie Mellom, Phineas Newborn, Raymond Rodriguez, Brittani Warrick. Swings: Gino Berti, Catrice Joseph, Marc Oka, Roger Robinson, Amber Stone.

One intermission.

MUSICAL NUMBERS: "Every Story Is a Love Story," "Our Nation Holds Sway," "The Past Is Another Land," "Another Pyramid," "How I Know You," "My Strongest Suit," "Night of Nights," "Enchantment Passing Through," "The Dance of the Robe," "Elaborate Lives," "A Step Too Far," "Easy as Life," "Like Father Like Son," "The Gods Love Nubia," "Written in the Stars," "I Know the Truth," "The Judgment," "The Messenger."

ASHLAND—Michael J. Hume *(foreground)*, Robert Vincent Frank, Suzanne Irving and David Kelly in a scene from Douglas Langworthy's translation of Bertolt Brecht's *The Good Person of Szechuan* at Oregon Shakespeare Festival

Baltimore: Center Stage

(Irene Lewis artistic director; Peter W. Culman managing director)

GUM. By Karen Hartman. March 7, 1999. Director, Tim Vasen; scenery, Myung Hee Cho; costumes, Anita Yavich; lighting, Matthew Frey; music, Kim D. Sherman; sound, Sten Severson.

Lina	Millie Chow
Rahmi	Miriam A. Laube
Inayat	Joseph Kamal
Auntie	Dale Soules
Young Man	Danyon Davis

Time: The present. Place: A walled garden adjoining a grand house in a fictitious faraway country. No intermission.

Theater for a New Generation
Staged Readings

A QUESTION OF WATER. By Steve Schutzman. February 8, 1999.

THE OTHER SIDE OF ALICE. By Judlyne Lilly; music by Woody Cunningham. February 22, 1999.

TODD UNDER MITLEIDGEN. By John Morogiello. March 1, 1999.

Berkeley, Calif: Berkeley Repertory Theater

(Tony Taccone artistic director; Susan Medak managing director)

HYDRIOTAPHIA, OR THE DEATH OF DR. BROWNE. By Tony Kushner. September 16, 1998. Director, Ethan McSweeny; scenery and projections, Jeff Cowie; costumes, David C. Woolard; lighting, Peter Maradudin; composer, Mel Marvin; sound, Matthew Spiro; production supervised by Michael Wilson; produced in association with the Alley Theater, Houston, Gregory Boyd artistic director.

Sir Thomas Browne	Jonathan Hadary
His Soul	Anika Noni Rose
Dame Dorothy Browne	Shelley Williams
Babbo	Sloane Shelton
Maccabbee	Rod Gnapp
Dr. Emil Schadenfreude	Charles Dean
Dr. Leviticus Dogwater	J.R. Horne
Leonard Pumpkin	Hamish Linklater
Abbess of X	Sharon Lockwood
Doña Estrelita	Wilma Bonet
Sarah	Delia MacDougall
Mary	Moya Furlow
Ruth	Louise Chegwidden
Death	Paul Hope

Time: April 3, 1667 (more or less). Place: The sickroom of Sir Thomas Browne, Norfolk, England (more or less). Two intermissions.

RAVENSHEAD. Solo musical performance by Rinde Eckert; libretto by Rinde Eckert; music by Steve Mackey. March 10, 1999. Director, Tony Taccone; scenery and lighting, Alexander V. Nichols.

With the Paul Dresher Ensemble Electro-Acoustic Band.

THE FIRST 100 YEARS. By Geoff Hoyle; developed by Geoff Hoyle and Tony Taccone. May 14, 1999. Director, Tony Taccone; scenery, Christopher Barreca; costumes, Peggy Snider; lighting, Peter Maradudin; sound, Matthew Spiro.

Jack Proust	Geoff Hoyle
The Kid	Kailey Hoyle

Time: The present. Place: Liberty Theater. No intermission.

1999 School Touring Prodution

THE QUEEN OF THE SEA. By Anne Galjour. January 25, 1999. Director, Cliff Mayotte; scenery, Kate Edmunds; costumes, Keiko Shimosato; composer, Paul Goodwin.

With Anne Galjour, Harry Waters Jr., Paul Santiago, Keiko Shimosato.

Boca Raton, Fla.: Caldwell Theater Company

(Michael Hall artistic and managing director)

COMEDY OF EROS. By Paul Firestone. December 31, 1998. Director, Michael Hall; scenery, Tim Bennett; costumes, Penny Koleos Williams; original music and sound, Steve Shapiro.

Lee-lla La Belle	Tamara Guffey
Joanna Cohen	Erin Neill
Mrs. Lulubeth La Belle	Nicole Orth-Pallavicini
William Jefferson Davis Powers	Robert Stoeckle
William Powers Jr.	Christopher Baker
Fefferkookenman	Steve Wilson

Time: The present. Place: Thebes, Alabama. One intermission.

THE KING'S MARE. By Oscar E. Moore; adapted from Jean Canolle's *La Jument du Roi.* April 16, 1999. Director, Michael Hall; scenery, Tim Bennett; costumes, Penny Koleos Williams; lighting, Thomas Salzman; original music and sound, Steve Shapiro.

Master Holbein .... Dan Leonard

Anne of Cleves	Elizabeth Dimon
Lady Osenbruk	Joy Johnson
King Henry VIII	Michael O. Smith
Prime Minister Cromwell	John Fitzgibbon
Archbishop Cranmer	George Kapetan
Duke of Norfolk	John Fionte
Sir Thomas Wriothsley	John Felix
Kathryn Howard	Colleen McDermott

Act I: A guarantee of peace. Act II: The wedding night. Act III: Reverberations.

Playsearch Staged Readings

SECOND SUMMER. By Gary Richards. November 30, 1998.

SPRING KILLING. By Julie Gilbert. January 18, 1999.

DON'T TELL THE TSAR. By Michael McKeever. March 8, 1999.

NUREMBERG. By Eric Ferguson. April 26, 1999.

Cambridge, Mass.: American Repertory Theater

(Robert Brustein artistic director)

PHAEDRA. By Jean Racine; translated and adapted by Paul Schmidt. November 27, 1998. Director, Liz Diamond; scenery, Riccardo Hernandez; costumes, Catherine Zuber; lighting, Michael Chybowski; original music and sound, Christopher Walker.

Theseus	Jonathan Epstein
Phaedra	Randy Danson
Hippolytus	Benjamin Evett
Aricia	Caroline Hall
Enone	Karen MacDonald
Theramenes	Stephen Rowe
Ismene	Kelly Mizell
Panope	Emily Vail

No intermission.

VALPARAISO. By Don DeLillo. January 29, 1999; Director, David Wheeler; scenery, Karl Eigsti; costumes, Catherine Zuber; lighting, John Ambrosone; sound, Christopher Walker.

Michael Majeski	Will Patton
Livia Majeski	Caroline Hall
Male Interviewers	Stephen Rowe
Female Interviewers	Karen MacDonald
Delfina Treadwell	Randy Danson
Teddy Hodell	Thomas Derrah

Camera Crew; Chorus—Remo Airaldi, Dina Comolli, Sophia Fox-Long, Jonathan Hova.
One intermission.

THE MASTER BUILDER. By Henrik Ibsen; adapted by Robert Brustein. February 12, 1999. Directed by Kate Whoriskey; scenery, Christine Jones; costumes, Catherine Zuber; lighting, Michael Chybowski; sound, Christopher Walker.

Halvard Solness	Christopher McCann
Aline Solness	Sharon Scruggs
Dr. Herdal	Will LeBow
Knut Brovik	Jeremy Geidt
Ragnar Brovik	Benjamin Evett
Kaja Fosli	Aysan Celik
Hilde Wangel	Kristin Flanders

One intermission.

CHARLIE IN THE HOUSE OF RUE. Adapted from Robert Coover's novella. April 6, 1999. Director, Bob McGrath; scenery, Laurie Olinder, Fred Tietz; costumes, Catherine Zuber; lighting, John Ambrosone; sound, Christopher Walker; projections, Laurie Olinder; film, Bill Morrison.

Charlie	Thomas Derrah
Lady	Caroline Hall
Bald Man	Remo Airaldi
Maid	Karen MacDonald
Old Man	Alvin Epstein
Policeman	Benjamin Evett

No intermission.

Cedar City, Utah: Utah Shakespearean Festival

(Davey Marlin-Jones supervising director)

New Plays-in-Progress Readings

A GRIEF OF MIND. By Carl O'Neal Rich. August 6, 1998. Director, Davey Marlin-Jones.

SIMPLY THE THING SHE IS. By Kate Hawley. August 13, 1998. Director, Ann Tully.

MARCH TALE. By Tim Slover. August 20, 1998. Director, Sylvie Drake.

SWEET MAGGIE BLUES. By Kay Kellam Cook. Director, Davey Marlin-Jones.

Chelsea, Mich.: Purple Rose Theater Company

(Jeff Daniels executive director; Guy Sanville artistic director; Alan Ribant managing director)

BOOK OF DAYS. By Lanford Wilson. April 10, 1998 (not reported in last year's listing). Directed by Guy Sanville; scenery, Bartley H. Bauer; costumes, Mary K. Copenhagen; sound, Daniel C. Walker.

Ruth Hoch	Suzi Regan
Len Hoch	Wayne David Parker
Ginger Reed	Carey Crim
Boyd Middleton	Dennis E. North
Martha Hoch	Sandra Birch
Walt Bates	Jim Porterfield
James Bates	John Lepard
Earl	Joseph Albright
LouAnn Bates	Lisa Sodman
Sharon Bates	Michelle Mountain
Rev. Bobby Groves	John Hawkinson
Sheriff Conroy Atkins	Randall Godwin

Time: A recent summer. Place: Dublin, Missouri, county seat of Chosen County. One intermission.
Winner of the 1998 ATCA New Play Award; see introduction to this section.

BOOM TOWN. By Jeff Daniels. October 16, 1998. Director, Jeff Daniels; scenery, Bartley H. Bauer; costumes, Colleen Ryan-Peters; lighting, Dana White; sound, Vince Mountain.

Stu .... Guy Sanville
Angela .... Sandra Birch
Frank .... John Lepard
Time: Last summer. Place: Somewhere in the Midwest. One intermission.

Chicago: Goodman Theater

(Robert Falls artistic director; Roche Edward Schulfer executive director)

OO–BLA–DEE. By Regina Taylor. March 15, 1999. Directors, Regina Taylor, Susan V. Booth; scenery, Donald Eastman; costumes, Mara Blumenfeld; lighting, T.J. Gerckens; music and musical direction, Coleridge-Taylor Perkinson; sound, Michael Bodeen.

Gin Del Sol .... Caroline Clay
Stage Manager; Mother; Bette Davis; Luna C;
    Lady Day; Blue Black Shining Woman;
    White Woman .... Sabrina Le Beauf
Soldiers; Arthur; Carnival Barker;
    Paul Henreid; Announcers .... Jimi Antoine
Lulu .... Margo Moorer
Ruby .... Cheryl Lynn Bruce
Shorty .... Ernest Perry Jr.
Evelyn .... Jacqueline Williams
Other Voices .... Ensemble
    Movement One: Backstage, St. Louis. Movement Two: On the Road. Movement Three: Chicago. Two intermissions.

1998–99 Studio Series

STRAIGHT AS A LINE. By Luis Alfaro. September 22, 1998. Director, Henry Godinez; scenery and projection design, John Boesche; costumes, Nan Zabriskie; lighting, David Gipson; music, Kamys; sound, Robert Neuhaus.

Paulie .... Guy Adkins
Mum .... Linda Kimbrough
    Time: The present. Place: Scene 1, Vacation. Scene 2, Las Vegas. Scene 3, Telecommunications. Scene 4, Tea time. Scene 5, Motherhood. Scene 6, Transition. Scene 7, Baptism. Scene 8, Redemption. Scene 9, Reckoning. Scene 10, Fencing. Scene 11, Reversal. Scene 12, Dementia. Scene 13, (-------). Scene 14, Love for sale. No intermission.

JACOB MARLEY'S CHRISTMAS CAROL. Solo performance by Tom Mula; written by Tom Mula. December 4, 1998. Director, Steve Scott; scenery and lighting, John Culbert; original music, Larry Schanker; sound, Robert Neuhaus.
    One intermission.

Chicago: Steppenwolf Theater Company

(Martha Lavey artistic director; Michael Gennaro executive director)

THE BERLIN CIRCLE. By Charles L. Mee. October 4, 1998. Director, Tina Landau; scenery, James Schuette; costumes, Mara Blumenfeld; lighting, Scott Zielinski; sound and musical composition, Rob Milburn, Michael Bodeen.

Mr. Market; Werner .... Ian Barford
Translator; Cook's Assistant;
    Ursula .... Alexandra Billings
Ping; Warren; Rokstar; Masseur .... Tim Grimm
Title Man; Costume Designer, Concierge;
    Clown .... Voki Kalfayan
Christa .... Elizabeth Laidlaw
Dulle Griet .... Mariann Mayberry
Pamela Dalrymple .... Amy Morton
Erich Honecker; Hermann ..... Yasen Payankov
Egan Krenz; Cook; Gunter ...... Daniel Ruben
Heiner Muller .... Matthew Sussman
Hans Modrow; Helmut .... Troy West
    Actors, Crowd, Wedding Guests, Beggars, etc.—Lucinda Bingham, Elizabeth Birkrant, Cassandra Bissell, Stephanie Childers, Catherine Cooper, Brad Johnson, Chloe Johnston, Walker Lambert, Saket Soni, Eddie Shin, Julian Stetkevych, David Stern.
    Time: 1989. Place: East Berlin and other locales across Germany.

Chicago: Victory Gardens Theater

(Dennis Zacek artistic director; Marcelle McVay managing director)

AMONG FRIENDS. By Kristine Thatcher. March 19, 1999. Director, Dennis Zacek; scenery, Mary Griswold; costumes, Judith Lundberg; lighting, Joel Moritz; sound, Andre Pluess, Ben Sussman.

Will .... Dev Kennedy
Matt .... Peter Burns
Dan .... David Darlow
    Time: The present. Place: Chicago. Scene 1: Will's study, just prior to Labor Day. Scene 2: Dan's study, on or about Columbus Day. Scene 3: Matt's living room, just before Halloween. Scene 4: Matt's living room, Veteran's Day. Scene 5:

Will's den, Thanksgiving Day. Scene 6: Will's den, just before Christmas. One intermission.

THE HISTORY OF BOWLING. By Mike Ervin. April 15, 1999. Director, Susan Nussbaum; scenery, Mary Griswold; costumes, Frances Maggio; lighting, Charles Jolls; sound, Andre Pluess, Ben Sussman.

Cornelius .... James William Joseph
Chuck .... Robert Ness
Barnes .... Jeff Rogers
Lou .... Doran Schranz
    Time: The present. Place: On an American college campus. One intermission.

Cincinnati: Cincinnati Playhouse in the Park

(Edward Stern artistic director)

RED CORNERS. By Cecilia Fannon. January 8, 1999. Director, Edward Stern; scenery, Karen TenEyck; costumes, Gordon DeVinney; lighting, Dan Kotlowitz.
Waiter .... Alex Shaklin

Mitchell .... David Rosenbaum
Beth .... Deirdre Madigan
Claude .... Tony Carlin
Irina .... Libby Christophersen
    One intermission.

Cleveland: The Cleveland Play House

(Peter Hackett artistic director; Dean R. Gladden managing director)

THE INVISIBLE MAN. By Ken Hill; based on the novel by H.G. Wells; music by Brendan Healy. December 8, 1998 (American premiere). Director, Frank Dunlop; associate director, Jim Dale; musical direction, Mike Petrone; scenery, James Youmans; costumes, Dona Granata; lighting, Brian MacDevitt; sound, Robin Heath; illusions, Jim Steinmeyer.
MC .... John Hines
Freda .... Vicki Stuart
Thomas Marvel .... Jim Dale
The Terrible Tale of the Awful Events That Cropped Up in the Village of Iping
    Fearenside; Wadgers;
    Col. Adye .... Charles Antalosky
    Griffin .... J. Paul Boehmer
    Miss Statchell .... Judith Hawking
    Dr. Cuss;
    Rev. Bunting .... Michael Hayward-Jones
    Squire Burdock;
    Police Constable .... John Hines
    Millie .... Tina Jones
    Teddy Henfrey;
    Police Constable .... Steve Ramshur
    Jeffers; Dr. Kemp .... Ian Stuart

Mrs. Hall .... Vicki Stuart
Wicksteed; Police
    Constable .... John Leonard Thompson
    Follies: Charles Antalosky, Judith Hawking, Michael Hayward-Jones, Tina Jones, Steve Ramshur, Ian Stuart, John Leonard Thompson.
    Time: 1904. Place: On the stage of the Empire Music Hall, Bromley.
    MUSICAL NUMBERS, ACT I: "1904," "Freda and the Follies." ACT II: "Who's There," "Freda and the Follies," "1904" (Reprise).

THE SMELL OF THE KILL. By Michele Lowe. January 12, 1999. Director, Scott Kanoff; scenery, Linda Buchanan; costumes, Claudia Stephens; lighting, Richard Winkler; sound, Robin Heath.
Nicky .... Henny Russell
Molly .... Linda Marie Larson
Debra .... Babo Harrison
Jay .... Greg Sanders
Danny .... Joe Hickey
Marty .... David A. Tyson
    Time: The present, the end of October. Place: Nicky's kitchen in Wilmette, Ill., about 30 miles from Chicago. No intermission.

COSTA MESA—Greg Stuhr and Richard Doyle in *But Not for Me* by Keith Reddin at South Coast Repertory

Costa Mesa, Calif.: South Coast Repertory

(David Emmes producing artistic director; Martin Benson artistic director; Paula Tomei managing director)

BUT NOT FOR ME. By Keith Reddin. November 6, 1998. Director, David Emmes; scenery, Thomas Buderwitz; costumes, Alex Jaeger; lighting, Doc Ballard.

Roy .... Richard Doyle
Dick .... Greg Stuhr
Stan .... David Denman
Helen .... Linda Gehringer
Melvyn .... Dan Kern
Act I: A room in the Beverly Hills Hotel. Act II: A different room in the hotel, one week later.

ON THE JUMP. By John Glore; from a story by Amy Dunkleberger. May 21, 1999. Director, Mark Rucker; scenery, Neil Patel; costumes, Walter Hicklin; lighting, Scott Zielinski; composer, Dennis McCarthy; sound, Justus Matthews.

Colleen Ferguson .... Kellie Waymire
Billy; Bartender; Derelict; Cop;
  Colleen's Father; Fred Feathers ... John Fleck
Albert III .... Joseph Fuqua
Forrester .... Richard Doyle
Arabella Wheatcroft .... Patricia Fraser
Dorie .... Julyana Soelistyo
Albert Wheatcroft .... Alan Oppenheimer
Ellen O'Connell; Waitress .... Melanie Chartoff
Place: An American city. One intermission.

Pacific Playwrights Festival
June 18–28, 1998

Workshop Productions

WALKING OFF THE ROOF. By Anthony Clarvoe. June 18, 1998. Bill Rauch, director.

Kelly .... Amy Brenneman
Daniel .... Jesus Mendoza
Lydia .... Katherine Heasley
Brett .... J.C. MacKenzie
  Time: The present. Place: Bedrooms and terraces in an American City. No intermission.

LANDLOCKED. By Cusi Cram. June 19, 1998. Director, Juliette Carrillo.

Anna .... Svetlana Efremova
Camilla; Reporter .... L. Scott Caldwell
Linda; Constanza .... Kadina Halliday
Pierre-Luigi .... Richard Coca
Aldo .... Mikael Salazar
Dr. Bob .... Jeff Allin
  Time: The present. Place: Zurich, Rome and Greece. One intermission.

Staged Readings

THE HOLLOW LANDS. By Howard Korder. June 19, 1998. Director, David Chambers.

THE SINS OF SOR JUANA. By Karen Zacarías. June 25, 1998. Director, Lisa Portes.

THE MECHANICS. By Chris Van Grogingen. June 26, 1998. Director, Andrew J. Robinson.

ON THE JUMP. By John Glore; from a story by Amy Dunkleberger. June 26, 1998. Director, Lee Shallat-Chemel.

DOGEATERS. By Jessica Hagedorn. June 27, 1998. Director, Michael Greif.

Festival director: Jerry Patch. Designers: Nephelie Andonyadis, Doc Ballard, Mitchell Greenhill, John Iacovelli.

Dallas: Dallas Theater Center

(Richard Hamburger artistic director; Edith H. Love managing director)

ALICE: TALES OF A CURIOUS GIRL. Adapted from Lewis Carroll by Karen Hartman. March 2, 1999. Director, Jonathan Moscone; scenery, Riccardo Hernandez; costumes, Katherine B. Roth; lighting, Christopher Akerlind; music, Gina Leishman.

Alice	Sarah "Squid" Lord
Man 1	Khary Payton
Man 2	Raphael Parry
Man 3	Bruce DuBose
Woman	Lisa Lee Schmidt

One intermission.

Denver: The Changing Scene

(Donovan Marley artistic director)

TRACES OF THE WESTERN SLOPES. By Jeremy Cole. August 20, 1998. Director, Pavlina Emily Morris; scenery, Raymond Fernandez; costumes and sound, Pavlina Emily Morris; lighting, William Malle.

Bill	Augie Truhn
Lily	Louniece San Filippo
Kate	Anna Hadzi
Alan	Darren Schroader
Geoff	Karl deMarrais
Ed	Ken Witt
Alice	Ruth Crowley

Time: During a blizzard. Place: The common room of a bed and breakfast in the Sierra Madres. Act I : Day one. Act II: Day two.

IN THE BALANCE. By A. David Redish. November 19, 1998. Director, Trace Oakley; design, Matthew Schultz.

Cass	Megan Wallace
Matt	Robert Quarles
Kostya	Rudy Gomez
Alicia	Christy Naplin

JACQUES ET SON MAITRE. By Milan Kundera. May 6, 1999. Director, Dan Hiester; scenery and lighting, Denis Bontems; costumes, Laura Cuetara; presented in the L'Alliance & Co. production, Frieda Sanidas producer, in the French language with English surtitles.

Celui Qui Est La-Haut	Dan Hiester
Le Maitre	Christian Roche

Le Chevalier de Saint-Ouen	Alain Ranwez
Le Fils Bigre; Le Commissaire	Mark Herzog
Le Pere Bigre; Le Marquis;	
Le Bailli	Antoine Valot
Justine; La Mere	Dominique Shortridge
Agathe; La Fille	Chantal Bancilhon

Summerplay XII, July 16–Aug. 2, 1998
Festival of New Works

DANCE OF LIFE. By Melissa Wells. Director, Sara Wright.

Jasmine	Donna Wheaton
Margo	Elena Lawrence
Jake	Chris Berliner
Tony	Nick Webb
Starmark	Daniel Horsey

GETTING ON TOP. By Sam Deleo. Director, Terrence Shaw.

Dan Helix	Daniel Horsey
Kamalon Kumar	Augie Truhn
Kelsey Powers	Michelle Bruckner

THE CUSTOMER IS ALWAYS RIGHT. By Thomas Owen Meinen. Director, Dwayne Carrington; co-director, Trace Oakley.

Christy	Louniece San Filippo
Randall	Ken Witt
Karl	Chris Berliner
Keely	Megan Wallace
Stephen Arthur Landrew III	Walter Newton

Denver: Denver Center Theater Company

(Donovan Marley artistic director)

A CHRISTMAS CAROL. Adapted from Charles Dickens by Laird Williamson and Dennis Powers; with music by Lee Hoiby; lyrics by Laird Williamson. November 27, 1998. Director, Laird Williamson; musical direction, Lee Stametz; choreography, Ann McCauley; scenery, Robert Blackman; costumes, Andrew V. Yelusich; lighting, Don Darnutzer; sound, David R. White.

Boy Caroler; Boy Scrooge;
  Boy in the Street .... Luke Eberl
Charles Dickens; Ghost of
  Christmas Past .... Robert Westenberg
Ebenezer Scrooge .... Richard Risso
Bob Cratchit .... Anthony Powell
Charitable Gentleman; Topper ... Randy Moore
Charitable Woman; Mrs. Fezziwig;
  Miner's Wife .... Kathleen M. Brady
Fred .... Mark Rubald
Child in Christmas Walk;
  Shepherd Girl .... Stephanie Ault
Child in Christmas Walk;
  Miner's Son .... Scott Merchant
Carol Seller; Toy Cat; Want .... Lauren Bulloch
Delivery Boy; Toy Pig;
  Ignorance .... Myron Andrew Sanders
Toy Seller; Son of Christmas Past;
  Toy Clown .... Shantell Simmons
Woodcarrier; Miner; Old Joe .... Keith L. Hatten
Woman in the Street;
  Shepherd's Daughter .... Leslie Henson
Daughter of the Woman; Daughter of Christmas
  Past; Toy Ballerina .... Sara C. Smith
Beggar Girl; Little Fan;
  Sally Cratchit .... Aaryn Smith
Beggar Girl;
  Belinda Cratchit ... Hannah Rae Montgomery
Ghost of Jacob Marley .... John Hutton
Wife of Christmas Past;
  Miner's Daughter .... Mercedes Perez
Young Scrooge .... Ted Bettridge
Belle Cousins; Miner's Daughter ... Ingrid Shea
Fezziwig .... Harvy Blanks
Dick Wilkins;
  Ghost of Christmas Future .... Paul Cosentino
Toy Bear; Miner's Son .... Matt Waysdorf
Ghost of Christmas Present ...... William Denis
Mrs. Cratchit .... Gabriella Cavallero
Peter Cratchit .... Ben Dignan
Ned Cratchit .... Daniel E. James
Martha Cratchit .... Christine Jugueta
Tiny Tim Cratchit .... Winston Anton Sanks
Mary; Mrs. Dilber .... Carol Halstead
Jack; Dark Angel .... Mark Evans
Ted; Dark Angel .... Lee Eskey

Beth .... Laurie Strickland
Meg; Mrs. Filcher .... Leslie O'Carroll
Shepherd Son;
  Undertaker's Boy .... Martin Marion
Shepherd Boy .... Sam Stookesberry

The Sled Boys—Ben Dignan, Daniel E. James, Winston Anton Sanks, Sam Stookesberry, Matt Waysdorf. The Christmas Eve Walkers—Ted Bettridge, Harvy Blanks, Gabriella Cavallero, Paul Consentino, William Denis, Lee Eskey, Mark Evans, Carol Halstead, Christine Jugueta, Martin Marion, Leslie O'Carroll, Mercedes Perez, Ingrid Shea, Laurie Strickland, Eric Tieze. The Horse Boys—Ben Dignan, Daniel E. James, Winston Anton Sanks, Sam Stookesberry. Fezziwig Party Guests—Lee Eskey, Mark Evans, Carol Halstead, Leslie Henson, Martin Marion, Leslie O'Carroll, Laurie Strickland, Eric Tieze. Men With Gifts—Harvy Blanks, John Hutton, Robert Westenberg. Businessmen—Harvy Blanks, John Hutton, Randy Moore, Mark Rubald, Robert Westenberg.

With the Colorado Symphony Orchestra Chorus and the Colorado Children's chorale.

No intermission.

KINGDOM. By Richard Hellesen. April 29, 1999. Director, Israel Hicks; choreography, Carolyn Dyer; music composed and arranged by Lee Stametz; music and lyrics for "The Castle Kids," Richard Hellesen; scenery and costumes, Andrew V. Yelusich; lighting, Charles R. MacLeod; sound, Christopher A. Ruggeri.

Ron Smaiks .... Robert Westenberg
Rick Blair .... Brian Keeler
Bonnie .... Susan Spencer
Cubby Van Sant .... William Denis
Don Covell .... Eric Tieze
The Castle Kids:
  Jimmy; Lars .... Ashton Byrum
  Tommy; Gus the Goose ..... Michael McGurk
  Karen; Angelina .... Jacqueline Maloney
Bob McTaggart .... Randy Moore
Teri Montoya .... Vanessa Quijas
Marisa .... Rocio Valenzuela

Ensemble: Lauren Berst, T. Ramon Campbell, Mayhill Fowler, Shannon Koob, Rodney Lizcano, Jeffrey Roark, Gregory Sanders, Brian Shea.

Time: The present. Place: The West Coast. One intermission.

THE ELEVATION OF THIEVES. By Nagle Jackson. May 6, 1999. Director, Nagle Jackson; scenery and lighting, Paul Dobrusky; costumes, Kevin Copenhaver; sound, David R. White.

THE SEASON AROUND THE UNITED STATES 411

Johnny .... Douglas Harmsen
Tulip .... Sarah Flanagan
Arthur St. George .... Jamie Horton
Niki Dunn .... Patricia Dalen
Youssef Omir .... Steven Memran
Meg .... Corliss Preston
Bishop .... Tony Church
Albert Farr .... Anthony De Fonte
Miss Ketzel .... Kathleen M. Brady
Emory .... Anthony Powell
Mr. Farleigh .... John Hutton
    Time: The present. Place: A town in Western
Europe. One intermission.

1999 U S West Theaterfest
Staged Readings, May 31–June 5, 1999

BYRD'S BOY. By Bruce J. Robinson.

A HOTEL ON MARVIN GARDENS. By Nagle Jackson.

FALL. By Bridget Carpenter.

AMERICA MALL. By Peter Sagal.

BLUR. By Melanie Marnich.

WAITING TO BE INVITED. By S.M. Shephard-Massat.

INNA BEGINNING. By Gary Leon Hill; conceived by Gary Leon Hill, Jamie Horton and Lee Stametz.

1933. Adapted by Randal Myler and Brockman Seawell from the novel *1933 Was a Bad Year* by John Fante.

East Farmingdale, N.Y.: Arena Players Repertory Company of Long Island

(Frederic DeFeis producer/director)

LOSING WEIGHT. By Carl Gonzalez. February 11, 1999. Director, Frederic DeFeis; design, Fred Sprauer; costumes, Lois Lockwood; lighting, Al Davis.
Brandon .... John F. Anderson

Owen .... Craig Mitchell
Sharon .... Anita Garland
    Time and place: Act I, A one-family house in the heights section of Jersey City. Act II, Later that evening. One intermission.

East Haddam and Chester, Conn.: Goodspeed Opera House

(Michael P. Price executive director)

MIRETTE. Musical based on *Mirette on the High Wire* by Emily Arnold McCully; book by Elizabeth Diggs; music by Harvey Schmidt; lyrics by Tom Jones. July 1, 1998. Director, Andre Ernotte; musical direction, Michael O'Flaherty; choreography, Janet Watson; scenery, Neil Patel; costumes, Suzy Benzinger; lighting, Timothy Hunter; orchestrations, Larry Moore; vocal arrangements, Gary Adler; produced for the Goodspeed Opera House by Michael P. Price.
Tabac .... Jason Wooten
Mme. Rouspenskaya .... Marsha Bagwell
Clouk .... Paul Blankenship
Claire .... Leslie Ann Hendricks
Gaby .... Amanda Watkins
Camembert .... Steve Pudenz
Mirette .... Cassandra Kubinski
Mme. Gateau .... Anne Allgood

Bellini .... James J. Mellon
Max .... Michael Hayward-Jones
    Others: September Bigelow, Bob Freschi, Timothy Charles Johnson, Carrie Wilshusen.
    Time: The 1890s. Place: Mme. Gateau's hotel in Paris. One intermission.
    MUSICAL NUMBERS, ACT I: "Sitting on the Edge," "Madame Gateau's Colorful Hotel," "Maybe," "Someone in the Mirror," "Irkutsk," "Practicing," "Learning Who You Are," "Juggling," "The Show Goes On," "Feet Upon the Ground," "Learning Who You Are" (Reprise), "Clouk & Claire," "If You Choose to Walk Upon the Wire," "She Isn't You."
    ACT II: "The Great God Pan," "The Great Bellini," "Sometimes You Just Need Someone," "Madame Gateau's Desolate Hotel," "All of a Sudden," Finale.

Goodspeed-at-Chester Production

(Michael P. Price executive director; Sue Frost associate producer; Warren Pincus casting director; Michael O'Flaherty resident musical director)

JUST SO. Musical adapted from the *Just So* stories by Rudyard Kipling; book and lyrics by Anthony Drewe; music by George Stiles; story by Anthony Drewe and George Stiles. November 5, 1998 (American premiere). Director, Lou Jacob; musical direction, Michael O'Flaherty; choreography, Jennifer Paulson Lee; scenery, David Gallo; costumes, Anita Yavich; lighting, Tom Hase; sound, Tony Meola; orchestrations, Christopher Jahnke, John Clancy; produced in association with Cameron Mackintosh.

Eldest Magician	Tom Nelis
Elephant's Child	Cory Shafer
Kolokolo Bird	Sheri C. Sanders
Parsee Man	Gabriel Barre
Cooking Stove; Kangaroo	Timothy Gulan
Rhino	Ben Lipitz
Zebra	Katy Grenfell
Giraffe	Amy Bodnar
Leopard	Stephen Bienskie
Jaguar	Curtiss I. Cook
Dingo	Julia Haubner

Elephants, Cake Ingredients, Others—Company.

MUSICAL NUMBERS, ACT I: "A World of Possibilities," "Just So," "Another Tempest," "There's No Harm in Asking," "The Limpopo River," "Living on This Island," Thick Skin," "The Parsee Cake Walk," "The Crime," "Pick Up Your Hooves and Trot," "We Want to Take the Ladies Out," "Jungle Light," "Putting on Appearances," "The Limpopo River" (Reprise).

ACT II: Entr'acte/"Just So" (Reprise), "The Argument," "Roll Up, Roll Up," "Leaps and Bounds," "Wait a Bit," "Take Your Time," "Putting on Appearances" (Reprise), "Please Don't Touch My Stove," "Little One Come Hither," "Does the Moment Ever Come," "If the Crab," "Finale."

Evanston, Ill.: The Next Theater Company

(Kate Buckley artistic director; Peter Rybolt managing director)

SCIENTIFIC ROMANCES: H.G. WELLS'S *THE WAR OF THE WORLDS* AND *THE INVISIBLE MAN*. By Steve Pickering and Charley Sherman. October 10, 1998. Director, Steve Pickering; scenery, Angela Weber-Miller; costumes, Kristine Knanishu; lighting, Agnieszka Kunska; sound, Barry G. Funderburg, Teff Uchima; fight choreography, Peter Rybolt; Martian conceptual designs, Charlie Athanas.

Millie; Newsboy; Ensemble	Genna Brocone
Wife; Ensemble	Kipleigh Brown
Mrs. Hall; Ensemble	Amanda Clower
Griffin	Michael Grant
Ogilvy; Marvel; Ensemble	Michael Hagedom
The Man	Derek Hasenstab
Mr. Hall; Ensemble	Raymond Kester
Millicent; Fearenside; Curate; Ensemble	Michele Messmer
Henderson; Kemp; Ensemble	David Silvis
Henfrey; Artilleryman; Ensemble	Luke Wilkins

BETWEEN EAST & WEST. By Richard Nelson. January 15, 1999. Director, Doug Finlayson; scenery, Geoffrey M. Curley; costumes, Linda Roethke; lighting, Charles W. Jolls; sound, Teff Uchima.

Ema	Peggy Dunne
Gregor	Peter Rybolt

THE ADVENTURES OF HERCULINA. By Kira Obolensky. March 12, 1999. Director, Sarah Tucker; scenery, Scott Cooper; costumes, Kristine Knanishu; lighting, Sharon McKinney; sound, Joe Cerqua.

CAST: The Abbess, Edwina Hawsey, Sarah Bernhardt, Enith, Francesca the Bearded Lady—Alexandra Billings; Sara—Bridget Crawford; Jean-Claude, Clarence, Leopold, Sailor, Edgar—Ian Christopher; The Monsieur, Alphonse Daumier, Jacques, Louis the Lion Tamer—Kurt Ehrmann; Herculina—Louise Lamson; Adelaide, Gerald, Boyd the Stone-Eating Boy—Katherine Martinez Ripley; Doctor, Hawker—Daniel Ruben.

Time: The late 19th century. Place: Various places in France, England and the United States. One intermission.

HARTFORD—Novella Nelson and Ray Anthony Thomas in a scene from *Digging Eleven* by Kia Corthron at Hartford Stage

Gloucester, Mass.: Gloucester Stage Company

(Israel Horovitz artistic director)

STATIONS OF THE CROSS. One-act play by Israel Horovitz. August 23, 1998. Directors, Paul Dervis, Israel Horovitz; scenery and costumes, Lisa Pegnato; lighting, Jeff Benish, Ian McColl; sound, Anne Bunting; choreography, Adrienne Minez; presented on a program with *Free Gift* by Israel Horovitz.

David Saltz .... Israel Horovitz

Young Lila .... Hannah Horovitz
Adult Lila .... Adrienne Minez
Older Lila .... Sarah deLima
Marjorie .... Lisa Simmons
Nigel Quint; Haggis; Others ...... David Jones
Ticket Collector, David's Mother,
    Others .... Judy Holmes

Hartford, Conn.: Hartford Stage Company

(Michael Wilson artistic director)

DIGGING ELEVEN. By Kia Corthron. January 14, 1999. Director, Reggie Montgomery; scenery, Jim Youmans; costumes, Felix E. Cochren; lighting, Rui Rita; sound, David Budries.

Gram	Novella Nelson
Uncle Lee	Helmar Augustus Cooper
Ness	Rori Godsey
Io	Chad L. Coleman
Carter	Ray Anthony Thomas
Ray	Sharon Washington

Time: The present. Place: A small factory town. One intermission.

THE CLEARING. By Helen Edmundson. April 15, 1999. Director, Tracy Brigden; scenery, Jeff Cowie; costumes, Susan Hilferty; lighting, Howell Binkley; original music and sound, John Gromada.

Killaine Farrell	Patricia Dunnock
Pierce Kinsellagh	Simon Brooking
Solomon Winter	Joseph Costa
Susaneh Winter	Sandra Shipley
Robert Preston	Stevie Ray Dallimore
Madeleine Preston	Alyssa Bresnahan
Sir Charles Sturman	Sam Catlin
Soldier; Commissioner of Transplantation; Sailor; Appeal Judge	Steve Juergens

Acts I and II: Autumn 1652. Act III: Christmas 1653. Act IV: Summer 1654. Act V: Autumn 1655. One intermission between Acts II and III.

Houston: Alley Theater

(Gregory Boyd artistic director, Paul R. Tetreault managing director)

NOT ABOUT NIGHTINGALES. By Tennessee Williams. June 5, 1998 (American premiere). Director, Trevor Nunn; associate director, Stephen Rayne; scenery, Richard Hoover; costumes, Karyl Newman; lighting, Chris Parry; music arrangements, Steven Edis; sound, Christopher Shutt; fights, Malcolm Ranson; the Royal National Theater and Moving Theater co-production, presented in association with the Alley Theater.

Voice of the Lorelei	Mark Heenehan
Mrs. Bristol; Goldie	Sandra Dickinson
Eva Crane	Sherri Parker Lee
Jim Allison	Finbar Lynch
Boss Whalen	Corin Redgrave
Jack Bristol	Richard Leaf
Schultz	Richard Ziman
Butch O'Fallon	James Black
The Queen	Jude Akuwudike
Joe	Alex Giannini
McBurney	Craig Pinder
Oliver Armsted	Dion Graham
Shapiro	Joel Leffert
Jeremy Trout	Mark Dexter
Mex	Chico Andrade
Kraus	Daniel Stewart
Alberts; Rev. Hooker	Noble Shropshire
Tom; Chaplain	Tom Hodgkins

Guards, Convicts, Troopers—Mark Heenahan, Richard Leaf, Daniel Stewart, Noble Shropshire.

Time: August 1938. Place: A large American prison. One intermission.

THE CIVIL WAR. Musical by Frank Wildhorn, Gregory Boyd and Jack Murphy; music by Frank Wildhorn. September 8, 1998. Director, Nick Corley; musical staging, George Faison; production supervised by Gregory Boyd; musical direction, Jeff Lams; scenery, Douglas W. Schmidt; costumes, Mark Wendland; lighting, Howell Binkley; sound, Karl Richardson; projections, Wendall K. Harrington; orchestrations, Kim Scharnberg; musical supervision, Jason Howland; vocal direction, Dave Clemmons.

The Civilians:

Sarah McEwen	Irene Molloy
Hannah Ropes	Linda Eder
Mrs. Lydia Bixby; Violet	Beth Leavel
Autolycus Fell	Jesse Lenat
Mabel	Hope Harris
Young Girl	Armani Greer, Deandrea Yowman

The Enslaved:

Clayton Toler	Michel Bell
Benjamin Reynolds	Lawrence Clayton
Frederick Douglass	Keith Byron Kirk
Exter Thomas	Wayne Pretlow
Bessie Toler	Cheryl Freeman
Hope Jackson	Capathia Jenkins
Liza Hughes	Cassandra White

Of the Union Army:

Emmet Lochran	Michael Lanning
William McEwen	Gilles Chiasson
Nathaniel Taylor	Matt Bogart
Horatio Taylor	Ron Sharpe
Charles Spencer	Bart Shatto
Byron Richardson	Royal Reed
Bartholomew Patrick Anderson	David Bryant

Of the Confederate Army:

Billy Pierce	Gene Miller
Henry Stewart	David Lutken
Darius Barksdale	Kim Strauss
Virgil Franklin	Dave Clemmons
Cyrus Stevens	Jim Price
Sam Welles	John Sawyer
John Beauregard	Timothy Browning

Pit Singers: David Michael Felty, Hope Harris, Christopher Roberts.

MUSICAL NUMBERS, ACT I: A House Divided—"Brother, My Brother," "By the Sword"/"Sons of Dixie," "Angel's Lullaby," "Tell My Father." Fourth of July—"Freedom's Child," "Missing You (My Bill)." The Peculiar Institution—"The Peculiar Institution," "If Prayin' Were Horses," "Virginia." A Villainous Greasy Side—"Greenback," "Judgment Day." River Jordan—

"I Never Knew His Name," "Father, How Long?", "River Jordan."

ACT II: A Year in the Life of Two Armies—"I'll Never Pass This Way Again," "How Many Devils," "Candle in the Window," "Oh! Be Joyful," "The Day the Sun Stood Still," "Five Boys." Emancipation—"Someday," "Sarah," "The Honor of Your Name," "North Bound Train." Gettysburg—"Last Waltz for Dixie," "The Glory."

HYDRIOTAPHIA, OR THE DEATH OF DR. BROWNE. By Tony Kushner. September 16, 1998. Director, Ethan McSweeny; co-produced with the Berkeley, Calif. Repertory Theater, Tony Taccone artistic director; see its entry in the Berkeley section of this listing.

Key West, Fla.: Key West Theater Festival

(Joan McGillis artistic director; Charles A. Munroe executive producer)

7th Annual Key West Theater Festival
Oct. 15–18, 1998

BIRTHDAY PIE. By Arthur Wooten. Director, Joan McGillis; scenery and lighting, Seat-of-Our-Pants Productions; costumes, Connie Graham.

Trudy Lee Martindale	Chris Stone
Bert Martindale	Jed Sloe
Roscoe Martindale	Mark Hayes
Lex Martindale	Danny Weathers
Mona Lee Martindale	Sally O'Boyle
Junior Martindale	Richard Grusin
Clairese Martindale	Mary Falconer
Mattie Lee Martindale	Erin Elkins
Anastasia Battles	Ellen Davis

SKY WATCHING. By John Lordan. Director, Barry Steinman; design, Seat-of-Our-Pants Productions.

Brian Carnahan	Michael McKeever
Margaret Carnahan	Elizabeth Dimon
Michael Carnahan	Steve Wise

JUMPING FOR JOY. By Jack Heifner. Director, Tom Caruso; scenery and lighting, Seat-of-Our-Pants Productions.

CAST: Clara—Susan Greenhill. Woman #1 (Marilyn, Helen, Telephone Operator, Clara's Mother)—Marge Redmond. Woman #2 (Screener at Radio Station, Clara's Sister, Daria)—Tasha Lawrence. Man # 1 (Policeman, Clara's Father, Hospital Orderly, Clara's Husband, Carl)—D. Michael Berkowitz. Man #2 (Car Thief, Doctor, Gary, Clara's Brother, Bobby)—Mark Lynch.

Time: The present. Place: Los Angeles.

Play Readings

ERDEMOVIC. By Kitty Felde. October 15, 1998.

COMMA, A SINGLE WOMAN. By Mariann M. O'Connor. October 16, 1998.

DUEL PARDONING. By Brenda Edwards. October 17, 1998.

La Jolla, Calif.: La Jolla Playhouse

(Michael Greif artistic director; Terrence Dwyer managing director)

DOGEATERS. By Jessica Hagedorn. September 8, 1998. Director, Michael Greif; scenery, Loy Arcenas; costumes, Brandin Barón; lighting, Kenneth Posner; sound, Mark Bennett; projection design, Woo Art International.
1959:

Rio Gonzaga	Sandra Oh
Dolores	Emily Kuroda
Freddie	Ricardo Chavira
Lola Narcisa	Ching Valdes-Aran
Pucha	Natalie Griffith
Lorenza	Lori Yeghiayan
Barbara Villanueva	Melody Butiu
Nestor Noralez	Bernard White

1980s:

Lolita Luna	Natalie Griffith
Trinidad Gamboa	Emily Kuroda

Romeo Rosales; Andres Alacran, a.k.a
Perlita; Steve Jacobs .... Alec Mapa

Cora Camacho .... Lori Yeghiayan
Sen. Domingo Avila;
   "Uncle" .... Alberto Isaac
Pedro; Gen. Nicasio Ledesma; Tito
   Alvarez; Waiter .... Jojo Gonzalez
Joey Sands .... Seth Gilliam
Rainer Fassbinder; Bob Stone;
   Tourist .... Christopher Donahue
First Lady; Leonor
   Lendesma .... Ching Valdes-Aran
Daisy Avila .... Tess Lina
Lt. Pepe Carreon .... Ricardo Chavira
Severo "Chuchi" Alacran ...... Bernard White
Chiquiting Moreno ... John-Andrew Morrison
Clarita Avila .... Melody Butiu

Time: 1959, 1981, 1982. Place: Manila, capital of the Philippines. One intermission.

PlayLabs Readings
Nov. 9–21, 1998

BAREFOOT BOY WITH SHOES ON. By Edwin Sanchez.

SONNETS FOR AN OLD CENTURY. By Jose Rivera.

THE FLIMFLAM MAN. By Melanie Marnich.

CAVEDWELLER. By Kate Moira Ryan.

WITH ALLISON'S EYES. By Adele Shank

BIG NIGHT. By Dawn Powell.

Lansing, Mich: BoarsHead Theater

(John L. Peakes founding artistic director; Judith Peakes managing director)

BOOMERS. Musical with book and lyrics by Dick Hill; music by Jeff English. May 20, 1999. Director, John Peakes; additional staging, Dick Hill; musical directors, Jeff English, Stephanie Gewirtz; scenery, John Peakes; costumes, Holly Speers; lighting, Rob Berry; voice overs, Michael Hays.
   With Susie Breck, Jeff English, Ann Harvey, Dick Hill.
   One intermission.
   MUSICAL NUMBERS, ACT I: "Behold a

Nation," "Boomer Generation," "First Love," "Separate Bedrolls," "Grandmother's Platter," "Go Tell It on the Modem," "Macho Samba," "Man Was Born to Hunt," "What Do I Do?", "I'll Be There."
   ACT II: "Wrinkling," "Charlie Hustle," "You Are Not Other," "Mama," "Spiritual Soft Shoe," "Hey Jack," "What I Miss Most," "John Holmes Farm," "Life Is a Dance," "Share the Load."

Little Rock: Arkansas Repertory Theater

(Cliff Fannin Baker producing artistic director)

Educational Touring Production

MYTH. Conceived by Brad Mooy. February 1, 1999. Director, Brad Mooy; fight choreographer, Lance Brannon.
   With Paula Isbell, Daryl Minefee, Christopher Zorker.

The Myths: Creation (Ovid's *Metamorphoses*), Jason & Medea (Euripides's *Medea*), Venus & Adonis (Shakespeare), The Trojan War, The 12 Labors of Hercules (Homer, Apollodorus, Pisander, Euripides), Phaethon (Ovid's *Metamorphoses*).

Los Angeles: Center Theater Group/Mark Taper Forum

(Gordon Davidson artistic director; Charles Dillingham managing director; Robert Egan producing director)

PUTTING IT TOGETHER. Musical revue based on an idea by Stephen Sondheim and Julia McKenzie; music and lyrics by Stephen Sondheim. October 8, 1998. Director, Eric D. Schaeffer; musical staging, Bob Avian; musical direction, Jon Kalbfleisch; scenery, Bob Crowley; costumes, Bob Mackie; lighting, Howard Harrison; sound, Jon Gottlieb; projections, Wendall K. Harrington; orchestrations, Jonathan Tunick; presented in association with Cameron McIntosh.

Amy .... Carol Burnett
Charles .... John McCook
Barry .... John Barrowman
Julie .... Susan Egan
The Observer .... Bronson Pinchot
   Time: Now. Place: An apartment in New York City. One intermission.

MUSICAL NUMBERS, Act I: "Invocation and Instructions to the Audience," "Putting It Together," "Rich and Happy," "Do I Hear a Waltz?", "Merrily We Roll Along," "Hello, Little Girl," "My Husband the Pig," "Every Day a Little Death," "Come Play Wiz Me," "Have I Got a Girl for You," "Pretty Women," "Sooner or Later," "Bang!", "Country House," "Unworthy of Your Love," "Could I Leave You."

Act II: Entr'acte, "Back in Business," "It's Hot Up Here," "The Ladies Who Lunch," "The Road You Didn't Take," "Live Alone and Like It," "More," "There's Always a Woman," "Buddy's Blues," "Good Thing Going," "Marry Me a Little," "Not Getting Married Today," "Being Alive," "Like It Was," "Old Friends."

ENIGMA VARIATIONS. By Eric-Emmanuel Schmitt; translated by Roeg Jacob. May 5, 1999 (American premiere). Director, Daniel Roussel; scenery, Ming Cho Lee; costumes, Candice Cain; lighting, Robert Wierzel; music, Edward Elgar, adapted by Karl Fredrik Lundeberg; sound, Jon Gottlieb.

Abel Znorko .... Donald Sutherland
Erik Larsen .... Jamey Sheridan
No intermission.

THE FIRST PICTURE SHOW. Musical with book and lyrics by Ain Gordon and David Gordon; music by Jeanine Tesori. May 12, 1999. Director and choreographer, David Gordon; co-produced with American Conservatory Theater, Carey Perloff artistic director; see its entry in the San Francisco listing in this section.

Los Angeles: Geffen Playhouse

(Gilbert Cates producing director; Lou Moore managing director)

HEDDA GABLER. By Henrik Ibsen; adapted by Jon Robin Baitz from a literal translation by Anne-Charlotte Hanes Harvey. March 24, 1999. Director, Daniel Sullivan; scenery, Riccardo Hernandez; costumes, Dunya Ramicova; lighting, Pat Collins; sound, Jon Gottlieb.

Aunt Julia Tesman .... Rosemary Murphy
Berta .... Marjorie Lovett
George Tesman .... Byron Jennings
Hedda Gabler .... Annette Bening
Judge Brack .... Paul Guilfoyle
Thea Elvsted .... Carolyn McCormick
Eilert Lovborg .... Patrick O'Connor
One intermisson.

Louisville, Ky.: Actors Theater of Louisville

(Jon Jory producing director; Alexander Speer executive director)

23d Annual Humana Festival
Of New American Plays
February 23–March 28, 1999

ALOHA, SAY THE PRETTY GIRLS. By Naomi Iizuka. February 23, 1999. Directed by Jon Jory; scenery, Paul Owen; costumes, Jack Taggart; lighting, Pip Gordon; sound, Malcolm Nicholls.

Will; Derek .... Bruce McKenzie
Vivian .... Carla Harting
Joy; Lee .... Peter Pamela Rose
Myrna; Richard .... Nick Garrison
Jed; Efran .... Todd Cerveris
Wendy .... Caitlin Miller
Jason .... Derek Cecil
Time: The not-too-distant past and the not-too-distant future. Place: New York City and many other exotic locales. One intermission.

Y2K. By Arthur Kopit. February 27, 1999. Director, Bob Balaban; scenery, Paul Owen; costumes, Nanzi J. Adzima; lighting, Pip Gordon; sound, Malcolm Nicholls.

Costa Astrakhan Caka BCuzICan;
ISeeU; FlowBear .... Dallas Roberts
Joseph Elliot .... Graeme Malcolm
Orin Slake .... Fred Major
Dennis McAlvane .... Thomas Lyons
Joanne Summerhays Elliot ..... Lucinda Faraldo
Time: The present. No intermission.

GOD'S MAN IN TEXAS. By David Rambo. March 3, 1999. Director, John Dillon; scenery, Paul Owen; costumes, Michael Oberle; lighting, Mimi Jordan Sherin; sound, Jeremy Lee.

Dr. Jeremiah "Jerry"
    Mears .... V Craig Heidenreich
Hugo Taney .... Bob Burrus
Dr. Philip Gottschall .... William McNulty
Time: The present. Place: The pulpit, minister's rooms and various other locations on the campus of Rock Baptist Church, Houston. One intermission.

THE COCKFIGHTER. By Frank Manley; adapted by Vincent Murphy. March 7, 1999. Director, Vincent Murphy; scenery, Paul Owen; cos-

Above, Trip Hope and Ginna Hoben in the "car play" by Richard Dresser, *What Are You Afraid Of?; right,* Bruce McKenzie and Carla Harting in a ten-minute play, *The Blue Room* by Courtney Baron; *below,* the cast of *Cabin Pressure* in a scene from a full-length conceived by Anne Bogart and created by the SITI Company

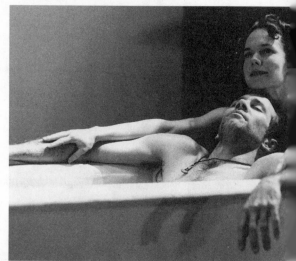

tumes, Nanzi J. Adzima; lighting, Pip Gordon; sound, Malcolm Nicholls.

Father .... Phillip Clark
Mother; Uncle .... Ellen McQueen
The Boy .... Danny Seckel
    Time: The present. Place: Rural America. No intermission.

CABIN PRESSURE. Conceived by Anne Bogart; created by the SITI Company. March 18, 1999. Director, Anne Bogart; scenery, Paul Owen; costumes, Walt Spangler; lighting, Mimi Jordan Sherin; sound, Darron L. West.
    With Will Bond, Ellen Lauren, Kelly Maurer, Barney O'Hanlon, Stephen Webber.
    Time: Now. Place: In a theater. No intermission.

*Life Under 30: A Bill
Of Ten-Minute Plays, March 12–27, 1999*

SLOP–CULTURE. By Robb Badlam. Director, Maria Mileaf.
Brian .... Bryan Richards
Dylan .... Derek Cecil
Danielle .... Monica Koskey
Cindy .... Carolyn Baeumler
    Time: The present. Place: New York.

MPLS., ST. PAUL. By Julia Jordan. Director, Abby Epstein.
Mel .... Erica Blumfield
Billy .... C. Andrew Bauer
    Time: 1985. Place: A rooftop in Minneapolis or St. Paul.

DRIVE ANGRY. By Matt Pelfrey. Director, Abby Epstein.
Chemo Boy .... Bryan Richards
Rex the Mex .... Derek Cecil
    Time: Night: Place: A Los Angeles freeway.

JUST BE FRANK. By Caroline Williams. Director, Maria Mileaf.
Diane .... Carolyn Baeumler
Charlene .... Monica Koskey
Jan .... Caitlin Miller
Secretary .... Erica Blumfield
Boss .... Todd Cerveris
    Time: The present. Place: A busy office.

DANCING WITH A DEVIL. By Brooke Berman. Director, Abby Epstein.
Woman .... Carolyn Baeumler
Younger Woman .... Monica Koskey
Devil .... C. Andrew Bauer
    Time: Now. Place: Here.

FORTY MINUTE FINISH. By Jerome Hairston. Director, Maria Mileaf.
Ike .... Derek Cecil

Terry .... Nick Garrison
    Time: The present. Place: A grocery store.

THE BLUE ROOM. By Courtney Baron. Director, Maria Mileaf.
Woman .... Carla Harting
Sailor .... Bruce McKenzie
    Place: The middle of the South Pacific.

LABOR DAY. By Sheri Wilner. Director, Abby Epstein.
One .... Nick Garrison
Two .... Erica Blumfield
Three .... C. Andrew Bauer
Four .... Monica Koskey
Five .... Bryan Richards
Six .... Carolyn Baeumler
    Time: Ten minutes before Labor Day. Place: A living room.

    Designers: Scenery, Paul Owen; costumes, Michael Oberle; lighting, Mimi Jordan Sherin; sound, Darron L. West.

A Car Play, February 24–March 28

WHAT ARE YOU AFRAID OF? By Richard Dresser. Costumes, Kevin McLeod; sound, Malcolm Nicholls.
Directed by Stuart Carden:
    Man .... Tudor Sherrard
    Woman .... Jessica Jory
Directed by Frazier W. Marsh:
    Man .... Trip Hope
    Woman .... Ginna Hoben

*Phone Plays, February 22–March 28
Directed by Jon Jory*

WILL YOU ACCEPT THE CHARGES? By Neal Bell.
Bobby .... Bruce McKenzie
Nan .... Laurie Williams

SPEECH THERAPY. By Rebecca Gilman.
Peter .... Matt Meyer
Lisa .... Andrea Clark

THEM. By David Greenspan
Voice 1 .... Preston Dyches
Voice 2 .... V Craig Heidenreich
Voice 3 .... Joanna Buckner

VISTATION. By Rebecca Reynolds.
Arlene .... Adale O'Brien
Teddy .... David Weynand
Marylizbeth .... Laurie Williams

HAPPY BIRTHDAY JACK. By Diana Son.
Brian .... Jon Brent Curry
Jack .... V Craig Heidenreich

Designers: Scenery, Paul Owen; sound, Jeremy Lee.

T(ext) Shirt Plays
Printed on T Shirts

MERCHANDISING. By David Henry Hwang.
AND THE TORSO EVEN MORE SO. By Tony Kushner.

STUFFED SHIRTS. By Jane Martin.
MANIFESTO. By Naomi Wallace.
TO T OR NOT TO T. By Wendy Wasserstein.
THE FEZ. By Mac Wellman.

Madison, N.J.: Playwrights Theater of New Jersey

(Producing artistic director, John Pietrowski; artistic director, Joseph Megel)

Workshop production

THE QUARREL.By David Brandes and Joseph Telushkin; based on the screen play by David Brandes from the short story *My Quarrel With Hersh Rasseyner* by Chaim Grade. February 18, 1999. Director, Susan Fenichell; scenery, Ron Kadri; costumes, Meganne George; lighting, Christopher Gorzelnik.

Chaim Kovler .... Sam Guncler
Hersh Rasseyner .... Reuven Russell
Joshua .... Philip Alberti
    Time: Early fall, 1948. Place: Mount Royal Park, Montreal.

Concert Readings

EDEN. By Jennifer Maisel. September 25, 1998.

THE BOUNDARY. By Tammy Ryan. October 23, 1998.

FOREIGN EXCHANGE. By Peter Hays. November 13, 1998.

SOUTHERN CHRISTMAS. By Guillermo Reyes. December 18, 1998.

LINDSTROM AND MOTAMBI. By Dan Owens. March 12, 1999.

TRAVERSE DES SIOUX. By Buzz McLaughlin. March 26, 1999.

Millburn, N.J.: Paper Mill Playhouse

(Angelo Del Rossi executive producer; Robert Johanson artistic director)

DR. JEKYLL AND MR. HYDE. Musical based on the novella by Robert Louis Stevenson; book and lyrics by David Levy and Leslie Eberhard; music by Phil Hall. November 4, 1998. Director and choreographer, Philip Wm. McKinley; musical direction, Jim Coleman; scenery, Michael Anania; costumes, Scott A. Lane; lighting, Kirk Bookman; sound, Craig Cassidy.

Dr. Jekyll .... Richard White
Mr. Hyde .... Marc Kudisch
Richard Enfield .... Christopher Yates
Mr. Utterson .... Peter Cormican
Dr. Gerald Lanyon .... Bob Dorian
Amanda Lanyon .... Glory Crampton
Mrs. Utterson .... Regina O'Malley
Rev. Carew .... Bill Kocis
Constable .... Kevin Kraft
Inspector .... William Ryall
Poole .... Charles Goff
Bubble .... Constance Barron
Lily .... Judy McLane
Peg .... Valerie Fagan
Viv .... Mary Rotella
Puck .... Christopher Eid
Mrs. Root .... Gwendolyn Jones
Mavis .... Beth Manning
Nurse Bingham .... Ingrid Ladendorf
Dying Man .... Chris Weikel

Town Crier .... Christopher Vettel
    Ensemble: Kurt Bardele, Constance Barron, Peter Cormican, Christopher Eid, Will Erat, Valerie Fagan, Charles Goff, Gwendolyn Jones, Bill Kocis, Kevin Kraft, Ingrid Ladendorf, Beth Manning, Regina O'Malley, Aaron Ramey, Mary Rotella, William Ryall, Amanda Satchell, Valerie Sneade, Laurie Sondermeyer, Christopher Vettel, Chris Weikel, Christopher Yates.
    Time: 1893. Place: The streets of London. One intermission.
    SCENES AND MUSICAL NUMBERS, ACT I—Prologue: The streets of London ("Two Sides of London"). Scene 1: The Lanyon drawing room ("Under the Skin," "Rest Now, My Friend," "In Your Eyes"). Scene 2: Jekyll's laboratory/The front door of Jekyll's home/Lanyon's study ("Pushing Back the Sky"). Scene 3: The exterior/interior of Squire's Music Hall ("Hot House Rose," "Stranger"). Scene 4: Amanda's boudoir ("Speak My Heart"). Scene 5: The exterior of Squire's Music Hall/The streets of London/Jekyll's laboratory ("Another Man"). Scene 6: The Blind Beggar Tavern ("Life at the Bottom of the Glass"). Scene 7: Lily's bedroom ("I Am the Night"). Scene 8: St. Paul's Hospital—corridor and examination room ("Love Treats Us All the Same," "Jekyll's Discovery"). Scene 9: Outside St. Paul's Hospital/Jekyll's laboratory (Finale, Act I).

ACT II—Scene l: Amanda's party in the Lanyon home/Jekyll's bedchamber ("The Waltz Montage"). Scene 2: The streets of London/Lily's bedroom ("Once More"). Scene 3: Squire's Music Hall ("Take What You Can Get"). Scene 4: Jekyll's front door. Scene 5: The Lanyon solarium ("A Father's Song," "Tell Me It's Not True"). Scene 6: The streets of London ("Jekyll's Soliloquy," "Voices Rushing Through My Head"). Scene 7: Jekyll's home/Jekyll's laboratory ("Lily's Ditty"). Scene 8: The streets of London ("Two Sides of London" Reprise, Finale).

UP, UP AND AWAY. Musical revue with the songs of Jimmy Webb; conceived by Robert Johanson. January 6, 1999. Director, Robert Johanson; choreography, Rob Ashford; musical direction, Lon Hoyt; scenery, Michael Anania; costumes, Angelina Avallone; lighting, Jack Mehler; sound, Craig Cassidy; musical arrangements, Albert Evans; orchestrations, Edmund Cionek, Albert Evans.

With Darius de Haas, Robert Johanson, Judy McLane, Kelly Rabke.

Backup Singers: Emma Lampert, J. Robert Spencer.

MUSICAL NUMBERS, ACT I: The Early Years—"Our Movie," "Song Seller," "Up, Up and Away," "Paper Cup," "Where's the Playground, Susie?", "Carpet Man," "Angel Heart," "The Girls Song," "Wichita Lineman," "Everybody Gets to Go to the Moon," "Lightning in a Bottle." Lost Generation Medley: "That's the Way It Was," "And the Yard Went on Forever," "Little Tin Soldier," "Lost Generation," "When Eddie Comes Home," "Galveston," "Saturday Night," "The Worst That Could Happen," "I Keep It Hid," "By the Time I Get to Phoenix," "MacArthur Park."

ACT II: The Later Years—"The Highwayman," "Pocketful of Keys," "The Moon's a Harsh Mistress," "Friends to Burn," "I Don't Know How to Love You Anymore," "Adios," "All I Know,"

"Nobody Likes to Hear a Rich Boy Sing the Blues," "What Does a Woman See in a Man," "It Won't Bring Him Back," "Almost Alright Again," "Sandy Cove"/"Still Within the Sound of My Voice." Finale: "If These Walls Could Speak," "Time Enough for Love," "Up, Up and Away" (Reprise), "Didn't We."

WUTHERING HEIGHTS. Adapted by Robert Johanson from the novel by Emily Brontë. February 24, 1999. Director, Robert Johanson; scenery, Michael Anania; costumes, Gregg Barnes; lighting, Jack Mehler; sound, Craig Cassidy; music, Albert Evans; fight direction, Rick Sordelet.
At Wuthering Heights,
The Earnshaw Family:
  Mr. Earnshaw;
    Hindley Earnshaw .... David Weynand
    Catherine Earnshaw .... Libby Christophersen
    Young Catherine .... Jennifer Reynolds
    Young Hindley .... Ricky Franco
  Heathcliff .... David Ledingham
  Young Heathcliff;
    Young Hareton .... Noah D. Peyser
  Frances Earnshaw .... Amy Tribbey
  Hareton Earnshaw .... Jeb Brown
  Linton Heathcliff .... Chris Stafford
Servants:
  Ellen (Nelly) Dean .. Jodie Lynne McClintock
  Joseph .... Christopher Wynkoop
  Zillah (offstage voice) .... Ruth Moore
At Thrushcross Grange,
The Linton Family:
  Edgar Linton .... Mark H. Dold
  Isabella Linton .... Elizabeth Roby
  Cathy Linton .... Libby Christophersen
  Fanny .... Fanny
  Mr. Lockwood .... Ezra Barnes
  Time: Back and forth from 1775 to 1802. Place: Wuthering Heights, Thrushcross Grange and Penistone Crag on the Yorkshire moors, England. One intermission.

Milwaukee: Milwaukee Repertory Theater

(Joseph Hanreddy artistic director; Timothy J. Shields managing director)

FORCE OF NATURE. By Steven Dietz; based on Goethe's Elective Affinities. April 9, 1999. Director, Joseph Hanreddy; scenery and lighting, Kent Dorsey; costumes, Laura Crow; sound, Michael Bodeen, Rob Milburn.
Ed; Edward .... Andrew May
Charlotte .... Laura Gordon
Cap; The Captain .... James Pickering
Ottilie .... Kirsten Potter
Curt; The Count .... Peter Silbert
Sharon; The Baroness .... Rose Pickering

Nick; Nicolas .... Brian Vaughn
Lucy; Lucianne .... Deborah Staples
Mittler .... Lee E. Ernst
Young Woman .... Melissa Cannaday
Husband .... Jeremy Woods
  Ensemble: Damon Dunay, Sharon Golinski, Kate McDermott, Samantha Montgomery, Thomas Rosenthal, Aaron Simms.
  Time and place: The present, a park. 1809, an estate in the German countryside. One intermission.

Minneapolis: Guthrie Theater

(Joe Dowling artistic director; David Hawkanson managing director)

THE VENETIAN TWINS. By Carlo Goldoni; new adaptation by Michael Bogdanov; additional material by Kevin Kling. October 2, 1998. Director, Michael Bogdanov; scenery and costumes, Kendra Ullyart; lighting, Marcus Dilliard; fight direction, Malcolm Ranson; composer and arranger, Terry Mortimer; sound, Scott Edwards; choreography, Marcela K. Lorca.

Dr. Balanzoni	Stephen Yoakum
Brighella	Richard Ooms
Rosaura	Kirsten Frantzich
Columbina	Starla Benford
Lelio	Rainn Wilson
Pancrazio	Peter Schmitz
Zanetto; Tonino	Christopher Evan Welch
Arlecchino	Ed Kershen
Beatrice	Hope Chernov
Florindo	Jim Iorio
Tiburzio	Emil Herrera
Bargello	Ralph Remington

Ensemble: Jennifer Blagen, Edna D. Duncan, Catherine Eaton, Laura Esping, Nathaniel Fuller, Jim Lichtscheidl, Kris Nelson, Omari Shakir.

Time: In the course of a single day. Place: Verona. One intermission.

Montgomery, Ala.: Alabama Shakespeare Festival

(Kent Thompson artistic director; Kevin Maifeld managing director)

VERNON EARLY. By Horton Foote. May 26, 1998. Director, Charles Towers; scenery, Doug Huszti; costumes, Kristine Kearney; lighting, Liz Lee; music, Jim Conely; sound, Cynthia L Kehr.

Mildred Early	Jill Tanner
Vernon Early	Philip Pleasants
Velma	Sonja Lanzener
Miss Ethel	Mary Fogarty
Erma	Elizabeth Omilami
Lou Ann	Lanier Walker, Blaine Wise
Douglas	Danno Allgrove, Cameron Doucette
Jackie	Yvette Jones-Smedley
Gertrude Mayfield	Fiona Macleod
Harry Reavis	Bary Boys
Reenie Reavis	Monica Bell
Grant	Virgil Wilson
Elreese	Jeff Obafemi Carr
Sheriff	Reese Phillip Purser

Time, Fall 1950. Place. Harrison, Tex. Friday, Scene 1: The Early bedroom, 3 a.m. Scene 2: The Dennis home, 3:30 a.m. Scene 3: The Early bedroom, 10 a.m. Scene 4: The Reavis apartment, Houston, 7 p.m. Scene 5: Vernon Early's car, 9:30 p.m. Scene 6: The Early bedroom, 11 p.m. Monday, Scene 7: The Dennis home, 8 p.m. Thursday, Scene 8: The Early bedroom, 5 p.m. Scene 9: The Early bedroom, 7:30 p.m. No intermission.

FAIR AND TENDER LADIES. Adapted from Lee Smith's novel by Eric Schmiedl; music and lyrics by Tommy Goldsmith, Tom House and Karren Pell. November 13, 1998. Director, Susan Willis; musical direction, Thom Jenkins; scenery, Michael Smith; costumes, Sandra Knapp; lighting, Terry Cermak; sound, Scott Robertson.

CAST: Ivy Rowe—Greta Lambert. Silvaney. Miss Torrington, Joli—Debra Funkhouser. Maudy, Beulah, Geneva—Kim Ders. Singer/Musician, Mama—Teresa Williams. Granny, Mrs. Bostick, Singer/Musician, Curtis—Samuel D. Cohen. Franklin, Oakley, Singer/Musician, Mr. Canaway—Woody Jenkins.

Time: 1970s, remembering as far back as 1912. Place: The mountains of western Virginia.

LURLEEN. By Barbara Lebow. March 26, 1999. Director, Frank Wittow; scenery, Robert N. Schmidt; costumes, Susan Mickey; lighting, Liz Lee; sound, Bethany Tucker; fight direction, Colleen Kelly; assistant director, Jennifer Hebblethwaite.

CAST: Lurleen—Monica Bell. Dee, Chorus, Estelle, Ensemble—Stephanie Cozart. Lu Ann, Chorus, Ensemble—Regan Thompson. Jeannie, Chorus, Moselle, Ensemble—Heather Robison. Martha, Chorus, Ensemble—Rochelle Hogue. George—Conan McCarty. Gerald, Teen Boy, Crony, Voices—Chris Mixon. Henry, Teen Boy, Photographer, Voices—Philip Pleasants.

Time: 1942–1968. Place: Various locations mostly in the state of Alabama.

New Brunswick, N.J.: Crossroads Theater Company

(Ricardo Khan artistic director)

LOST CREEK TOWNSHIP. By Charlotte A. Gibson. April 8, 1999. Director, Reggie Montgomery; scenery, Donald Eastman; costumes, Felix E. Cochren; lighting, Frances Aronson; sound, JR

NYACK—Alix Korey, Ian Kahn, Doris Belack *(foreground)* and To-vah Feldshuh in a scene from *Danny and Faye* by Benjamin Feldman at the Helen Hayes Performing Arts Center

Conklin; produced in association with AT&T: *OnStage.*

Rev. Missus	Gena Bardwell
Silas	Brian J. Coffee
Crystal	Magaly Colimon
Rev. Helmer	Augustus Cooper
Zachery Mark	Gerald Douglass
Noah	Joseph Edward
Belinda	Wiyatta Fahnbulleh
Bradley	Avery Glymph
Sister Woman	Sheyvonne Wright
Little Girl	Vanity Jenkins
Samuel Perry; Cambridge	Cedric Turner
Dorothy	Elizabeth Van Dyke
Rupert	David Wolos-Fonteno

One intermission.

New Brunswick, N.J.: George Street Playhouse

(David Saint artistic director; Tom Werder managing director)

DARLENE and THE GUEST LECTURER. Program of two one-act plays by A.R. Gurney. October 24, 1998. Director, John Rando; scenery, Rob Odorisio; costumes, David Murin; lighting, Dan Kotlowitz; music, Tom Cabaniss.

Darlene
Angela .... Nancy Opel
Jim .... Robert Stanton

The Guest Lecturer
Pat .... Mary Ehlinger
Mona .... Nancy Opel
Fred .... Rex Robbins
Hartley .... Robert Stanton
No intermission.

JOLSON SINGS AGAIN. By Arthur Laurents; revised version. February 27, 1999. Director, David Saint; scenery, James Youmans; costumes,

Theoni V. Aldredge; lighting, Howell Binkley; music, David Van Tieghem.
Julian .... Robert Petkoff
Robbie .... Betsy Aidem
Sidney .... Jonathan Hadary
Andreas .... Armand Schultz
    Time and Place—Act I, Afterword, Part 1: The stage of the Shubert Theater in New Haven, fall 1962. Scene 1: Robbie and Sidney's, Hollywood, spring 1947. Scene 2: Julian's, fall 1947. Scene 3: Robbie's office, fall 1947. Scene 4: The studio commissary, fall 1949. Scene 5: Robbie's office, spring 1950. Scene 6: Robbie and Sidney's, spring 1951. Scene 7: Julian's, the next day.
    Act II, Scene 1: Robbie's office, fall 1951. Scene 2: Robbie and Sidney's, fall 1951. Scene 3: Robbie's office, spring 1952. Scene 4: Julian's, two days later. Afterword, Part 2: The stage of the Shubert Theater in New Haven, fall 1962.

New Haven, Conn.: Long Wharf Theater

(Doug Hughes artistic director)

ABSTRACT EXPRESSION. By Theresa Rebeck. November 18, 1998. Director, Greg Leaming; scenery, Neil Patel; costumes, David Zinn; lighting, Dan Kotlowitz; original music, Fabian Obispo; sound, Matthew Mezick.
Charlie .... David Wolos-Fonteno
Sylvia .... Beth Dixon
Lillian .... Kristine Nielsen
Eugene .... Bray Poor
Lucas; Ray .... Larry Gilliard Jr.
Philip; Jordy; Policeman .... Glenn Fleshler
Jenny .... Angie Phillips
Kidman; Detective .... Jack Willis
Willie .... Mark Nelson
One intermission.

WORKING. Revised version by Stephen Schwartz and Nina Faso of the musical based on the book by Studs Terkel; songs by Craig Carnelia, Micki Grant, Mary Rodgers and Susan Birkenhead, Stephen Schwartz and James Taylor. March 10, 1999. Director, Christopher Ashley; musical direction, Danny Kosarin; musical staging, Dawn

DiPasquale; dance music, Michele Brourman; scenery, Neil Patel; costumes, David C. Woolard; lighting, Christopher Akerlind; sound, T. Richard Fitzgerald; projections, Jan Hartley.
    With Gavin DeGraw, Ann Harada, John Herrera, Pamela Isaacs, Alix Korey, Ken Prymus, Rex Robbins, Matthew Saldivar, Emily Skinner.
    No intermission.
    MUSICAL NUMBERS: "All the Livelong Day," "Traffic Jam," "Lovin' Al," "If I Could've Been," "Nobody Tells Me How," "Checkers," "Un Mejor Dia Vendra," "Just a Housewife," "Millwork," "The Mason," "Brother Trucker," "It's an Art," "Joe," "Cleanin' Women," "Fathers and Sons," "Something to Point To."

Stage II

THE GIMMICK. Solo performance by Dael Orlandersmith; written by Dael Orlandersmith; originally conceived and directed by Peter Askin. November 4, 1998. Director, Jaye Austin-Williams; scenery, Thomas Lynch; costumes, Anita Yavich; lighting, Allen Lee Hughes; sound, Mio Morales.

Norfolk, Va.: Virginia Stage Company

(Charlie Hensley artistic director; Steven Martin managing director)

NOBODY LONESOME FOR ME. By Lanie Robertson. October 25, 1998. Director, Charlie

Hensley; scenery, Rob Odorisio; costumes, Patricia Darden; lighting, Brian Nason; sound, Joe

Payne; musical direction, Shane Isenberg.

Hank Williams .... Troy Allan Burgess

Musician .... Shane Isenberg
No intermission.

Nyack, N.Y.: Helen Hayes Performing Arts Center

(Tony Stimac executive producer; Rod Kaats artistic director; Joel Warren managing director; Marilyn Stimac associate producer)

DANNY AND FAYE. By Benjamin Feldman. June 20, 1998. Director, Gordon Greenberg; scenery, Narelle Sissons; costumes, Gail Cooper-Hecht; lighting, Jeff Croiter; sound, Aural Fixation.

Danny .... Ian Kahn
Faye .... Tovah Feldshuh
Esther .... Doris Belack
Edith .... Alix Korey
Rudolf .... Michael Malone
Abigail; Dee Dee .... Jessica Stone
One intermission.

BIG ROSEMARY. By Blake Edwards. February 20, 1999. Director, Blake Edwards; choreography, Arte Phillips; scenery, Derek McLane; costumes, Gail Cooper-Hecht; lighting, John Tees III; sound, Matt Berman; musical supervision and dance arrangements, Joseph Thalken.

Barney .... James Murtaugh
Soldier #1; Detective #2 ...... John DiBenedetto
Max Mazetti .... Joe Siravo
Soldier #2; Police Captain ... Michael Goldfinger
Hit Man; Rob Lupo; Drunk; Detective #1;
Stubby Carl .... Lara Teeter
Fandangoette;
Molly Rafferty .... Elizabeth Mozer

Fandangoette; Duty Nurse Holden;
Stripper .... Nancy Lemenager
Fandangoette; Sweet Loraine ..... Caitlin Carter
Big Al Fusary .... Sam Coppola
Vince Vasco .... Mark Lotito
Emcee; Two Gun; Detective #3;
Primo .... Tom Sardinia
Rosemary Lebeau .... Cady Huffman
Jimmy O'Malley .... Jack Mulcahy
Waiter; George Eagle; Priest ...... Victor Truro
Newsboy .... Tom Richards
Dr. Leonard Horowitz; Ziggy;
Dominic Roderigo .... George De La Pena
One intermission.

MISSING FOOTAGE. By Gen LeRoy. April 10, 1999. Director, Tony Walton; scenery, Klara Zieglerova; costumes, Willa Kim; lighting, Brian Nason; sound, Peter Fitzgerald.

Julianna Ricci .... Tanya Gingerich
Marcia Etthridge .... Tracy Shayne
Lynn Drew .... Anne Rogers
Anton Mate .... Rob Sedgwick
Jack Benneton; Caryl Ezyzske ..... Jack Ryland
Time: The present. Place: Devon and London, England. One intermission.

Pasadena: Pasadena Playhouse

(Sheldon Epps artistic director; Lars Hansen executive director)

IF MEMORY SERVES. By Jonathan Tolins. September 11, 1998. Director, Leonard Foglia; scenery, Michael McGarty; costumes, Chrisi Karvonides-Dushenko; lighting, Russell H. Champa; sound, Jon Gottlieb; music, Peter Matz.

Linda Simmons; Helen Menken ... Marilyn Sokol
Diane Barrow .... Brooke Adams
Pam Goldman; Michelle .. Pamela Segall Adlon
Russell Burke; Adam Burke .... Michael Landes
Paul Michael .... Bill Brochtrup
Taylor McDonald; Tim .... Steven Culp
Dr. Margaret Thurm;
Mrs Kennedy .... Paula Kelly
Stan Burke; Mr. Wilcox .... David Groh
Time: 1955. Place: New York and Los Angeles. One intermission.

ONLY A KINGDOM. Musical with book, music and lyrics by Judith Shubow Steir. November 6,

1998. Director Scott Schwartz; musical direction and additional vocal arrangements, James Vukovich; choreography, Daniel Stewart; scenery, James Joy; lighting, Michael Gilliam; costumes, Diana Eden; sound, Jon Gottlieb, Philip G. Allen; music supervision, arrangements and orchestrations, Peter Mansfield.

Edward, Prince of Wales .... Stan Chandler
Wallis Simpson .... Kaitlin Hopkins
Elsa Maxwell .... Mary Pat Gleason
Ensemble:
King George V;
News Dealer .... Jack Ritschel
Queen Mary .... Eileen Barnett
George, Duke of York .... Kevin Burns
Elizabeth, Duchess of York;
Night Club Singer .... Jennifer Gordon
George, Lord Bellimore .... Hap Lawrence
Dr. Cosmo Lang .... David Parker

Welsh Miner;
Winston Churchill .... John Connolly
Welsh Miner's Wife .... Michelle Scarpa
Stanley Baldwin .... Tom Knickerbocker
Baldwin's Secretary;
Sailor .... Mark Allen Reugg
Lady Thelma Furness .... Leslie Stevens
Ernest Simpson .... Peter Schmidt
Bessie Merryman .... Christopher Callen
Simon Palmsy .... Chad Borden
Time and place: 1953, Elsa Maxwell's House,
The Mews at Dilly Dally; 1931–36, Britain and the
Continent.
MUSICAL NUMBERS, ACT I: "All They
Want Is a Wave," "I Shall Serve," "What Would
You Give for Love?", "Off to Fort Belvedere,"
"The Moment," "What Does He See in Her,"
"Uh-Uh," "All Is Love," "I Shall Serve" (Reprise), "Hold Back the Night," "In Wonderland,"
"Unfit to Rule," "What Is Forever?".

ACT II: "He Could Have Married," "What Is
Forever?" (Reprise), "The King's Party," "Except
Good-Bye," "Just Enjoy Today," "Rally at Downing Street," "David's Meditation," "The Moment"/"All Is Love" (Reprise). Epilogue: "Home
Is Where the Duchess Is."

THE PRESENTMENT. By D. Paul Thomas.
March 21, 1999. Director, Richard Seyd; scenery,
John Iacovelli; costumes, Maggie Morgan; lighting, Michael Gilliam; sound, Anthony Carr.
Jonathan Malone .... Jeff Allin
Michael Jennings .... Daniel Nathan Spector
Rebecca Jennings .... Maura Vincent
Samuel Jennings .... Jerry Hardin
Eleanor Jennings .... K Callan
David Thompson .... John Demita
Time: The present. Act I: The apartment of
Rebecca and Michael Jennings, New York City, a
late afternoon in March. Act II: The apartment,
early that evening.

Philadelphia: Philadelphia Theater Company

(Sara Garonzik producing artistic director; Ada Coppock general manager)

LIVES OF THE SAINTS. By David Ives. January
22, 1999. Director, John Rando; scenery, Russell
Metheny; costumes, Kaye Voyce; lighting, Robert
Wierzel; sound, Jim Van Bergen.

Babel's in Arms
Gorph .... Danton Stone
Cannapflit .... Arnie Burton
Businesswoman .... Nancy Opel
Priestess .... Anne O'Sullivan
Cheerleader .... Bradford Cover
Time: Circa 1000 B.C. Place: The desert.

Enigma Variations
Bill 1 .... Arnie Burton
Bebe .... Nancy Opel
Bill 2 .... Bradford Cover
Bebe 2 .... Anne O'Sullivan
Fifi .... Danton Stone
Place: A doctor's office.

The School of Natural Philosophy
Mr. Smith; Man's Voice .... Bradford Cover
"Ms. Jones" .... Nancy Opel
Mr. Brrrowwwn .... Arnie Burton
Woman's Voice;
Mousy Young Woman .... Anne O'Sullivan
Place: An office.

Lives of the Saints or Polish Joke
Edna .... Nancy Opel
Flo .... Anne O'Sullivan
Stagehands—Arnie Burton, Bradford Cover,
Danton Stone
Place: A kitchen in a church basement.

Soap Opera
Maitre D'; Official .... Arnie Burton
Repairman .... Danton Stone
Mother; Mabel .... Anne O'Sullivan
Washing Machine .... Nancy Opel
Friend .... Bradford Cover
Place: Cafe Paradis and other locations.

Saint Francis Talks to the Birds
Mike .... Arnie Burton
Angela .... Anne O'Sullivan
St. Francis .... Bradford Cover
Fish .... Danton Stone
Grandmother .... Nancy Opel
Place: The desert.
One intermission following *The School of Natural Philosophy*.

Philadelphia: Walnut Street Theater

(Bernard Havard producing artistic director)

HOTEL SUITE. By Neil Simon. January 12, 1999.
Director, Charles Abbott; scenery, Gregory Hill;
costumes, Gail Cooper-Hecht; lighting, Jeffrey S.
Koger; sound, Scott Smith.

ACT I: Early 1980s

Diana and Sidney, Part I

Diana .... Marina Sirtis
Sidney .... Reed Birney
    Place: Suites 203–204 in the Beverly Hills Hotel.

Visitor From Philadelphia

Marvin .... Robert Ari
Millie .... Evalyn Baron
Bunny .... Megan Bellwoar
Bellhop .... Marc O'Donnell
    Place: Suites 203–204 in the Beverly Hills Hotel.

ACT II: 16 years later

Diana and Sidney, Part II

Grace .... Megan Bellwoar
Diana .... Marina Sirtis
Sidney .... Reed Birney
    Place: Suites 402–404 in an old but very fashionable London hotel.

Visitors From Forest Hills

Norma Hubley .... Evalyn Baron
Roy Hubley .... Robert Ari
Borden Eisler .... Marc O'Donnell
Mimsey Hubley .... Megan Bellwoar
    Place: Suite 1219, the Plaza Hotel, New York City.

    Hotel Staff—Marc O'Donnell, Don Allen, Christie Ricapito, Juliet Lincoln.

OSCAR WILDE'S LOVER. By Will Stutts. March 30, 1999. Director, Will Stutts; scenery, Conrad Maust; costumes, Colleen McMillan; lighting, Joe Levy; sound, Scott Smith.

Actor One .... Dan Olmstead
Actor Two .... Paul Soileau
    Time: Early spring 1945 and various other periods of time from 1892–1945. Place: A small hotel in Worthing, near the sea, in the English countryside and various other places.

Portland, Me: Portland Stage Company

(Anita Stewart artistic director; Ted Strickland managing director)

MANIFEST. By Brian Silberman. February 19, 1999. Director, Christopher Grabowski; scenery and lighting, Anita Stewart; costumes, April Soroko.

    CAST: Israel Gutman, Director, 8-Year-Old Boy at Lodz, Janek, Guard—Ron Botting. Flute, Strings—Carl Dimow. Bass, Strings, Vocals—Julie Goell. Roza Robota, Alice Treiber, 5-Year-Old Girl at Lodz—Mercedes Herrero. Shoshana Robota, Esther Wajsblum, Raya Fleichmann, Agent, Old Woman, Miriam—Susan Knight. Mala Zimetbaum, Ragina Safin, Mishka Treiber, Eva—Jennifer Mattern. Clarinet—Danny Mills. Dada, Noah Zabladowicz, Master of Ceremonies—Thomas Pasley. Drums, Percussion—Hayes Porterfield. Adek Galinski, Levi Stein, Moishe Kulka, Simon—Benjamin Rosen. Anna Treiber, Ella Gardner, Sylvie Fleichmann, Rachel, Small Child—Bess Welden. Additional Roles—Company.
    One intermission.

TALES OF WASHINGTON IRVING, OR THE OLD DUTCH BOWLING LEAGUE. Adapted by Bartlett Sher with Peter John Still. March 19, 1999. Director, Bartlett Sher; scenery, Anita Stewart; costumes, Caitlin Ward; lighting, Christopher Akerlind; music and sound, Peter John Still; puppets, Jeremy Woodward.

Diedrich Knickerbocker;
    Rip Van Winkle .... Aled Davies
Wolfert Webber; The Devil ...... Allen Gilmore
Tom Walker .... Darrell James
Fiddler .... Edward Kiniry-Ostro
Dame Van Winkle; Katrina
    Von Tassel .... Susan Riley Stevens
    Ensemble: Ed Bauer, Alex Brinkman-Young, Alexandra Heller, Jocelyn Gammon, Noah Shibley.
    One intermission.

Little Festival of the Unexpected
Staged Readings, April 28–May 8, 1999

THE PAVILION. By Craig Wright. Director, Aaron Posner.

LOOKING FOR LOVE. By Terrance Vorwald. Director, Matthew Arbour.

A GIRL'S GUIDE TO THE DIVINE COMEDY. By Shelley Berc. Director, Christopher Grabowski.

FIRST LADY. By Erica Christ. Director, Jonathan Moscone.

CAPTAIN 11. By Joseph Goodrich. Director, Nick Faust.

QUASI UN FANTASIA and TERMINAL EXIT. By Joseph Goodrich. Director, Nick Faust.

Princeton, N.J.: McCarter Theater

(Emily Mann artistic director; Jeffrey Woodward managing director)

ELECTRA. By Sophocles; newly adapted by Frank McGuinness. September 15, 1998 (American premiere). Director, David Leveaux; scenery and costumes, Johan Engels; lighting, Paul Pyant; sound, Fergus O'Hare; movement direction, Jonathan Butterell; produced in association with the Donmar Warehouse Theater and Duncan C. Weldon.

Servant to Orestes .... Stephen Spinella
Orestes .... Michael Cumpsty
Pylades .... Ivan Stamenov
Electra .... Zoë Wanamaker
Chorus .... Mirjana Jokovic
Chorus of Mycenae .... Pat Carroll
Chorus .... Myra Lucretia Taylor
Chrysothemis .... Marin Hinkle
Clytemnestra .... Claire Bloom
Aegisthus .... Daniel Oreskes

MESHUGAH. By Emily Mann; adapted from the story by Isaac Bashevis Singer. October 20, 1998. Director, Emily Mann; scenery, Thomas Lynch; costumes, Jennifer von Mayrhauser; lighting, Neil Peter Jampolis; composer, Mel Marvin; sound, David Budries.

Aaron Greidinger .... David Chandler
Max .... Michael Constantine
Waiter; Stanley .... Jason Kolotouros
Priva; The Woman Who Tells .... Rita Zohar
Tzlova; Stefa .... Gordana Rashovich
Miriam .... Elizabeth Marvel
Chaim Joel; Leon; Morris; Rabbi .... Allen Swift
   Time: 1952. Place: New York and Israel.

TWO SISTERS AND A PIANO. By Nilo Cruz. February 16, 1999. Director, Brian Kulick; scenery, Mark Wendland; costumes, Anita Yavich; lighting, Mimi Jordan Sherin; composer, Mark Bennett; sound, JR Conklin.

Militia Guard; Victor Manuel .... Gary Perez
Lt. Portuondo .... Bobby Cannavale
Maria Celia .... Ivonne Coll
Sofia .... Marissa Chibas
   Time: 1991. Place: Cuba.

Providence, R.I.: Trinity Repertory Company

(Oskar Eustis artistic director; William P. Wingate managing director)

A PREFACE TO THE ALIEN GARDEN. By Robert Alexander. March 3, 1999. Director, Edris Cooper-Anifowoshe; design, Eugene Lee, William Lane, Yael Lubetzky, Peter Hurowitz; fight choreography, Normand Beauregard.

Lisa Body .... Nehassaiu deGannes
G Roc .... Keskhemnu
Slick Rick .... John Douglas Thompson
Crazy Mike .... Donn Swaby
Sheila .... Tanganyika
Candi .... Sandy York
Ice Pick .... Jay Walker
B Dog .... Anthony Burton
   One intermission.

New Play Readings

THE RULES OF CHARITY. By John Belluso. March 8, 1999. Director, Oskar Eustis.

SLAUGHTERHOUSE FIVE. Adapted by Eric Simonson from the novel by Kurt Vonnegut. March 15, 1999. Director, Eric Simonson.

LOOK WHAT A WONDER. By Walter Robinson. March 22, 1999. Director, Walter Robinson.

UNTITLED play. By Leslie Ayvazian. March 29, 1999.

FALL. By Bridget Carpenter. April 5, 1999. Director, Neal Baron.

Rochester, N.Y.: Geva Theater

(Mark Cuddy artistic director)

FAMOUS ORPHEUS. Musical with book by OyamO (Charles Gordon); music and lyrics by Charles Bevel; additional music by Carlos Valdez and Gregg Coffin; additional lyrics by OyamO and Gregg Coffin. Opened May 26, 1998. Director, Mark Cuddy; choreography, Garth Fagan; musical direction, Carlos Valdez; scenery, Debra Booth; costumes, Loyce Arthur; lighting, Brian Aldous; sound, Dan Roach; vocal arrangements, Gregg Coffin; presented in collaboration with Garth Fagan Dance.

Sweet Mout' Virgil; Uncle Herman;
   Poseidon .... Bob Devin Jones
Orpheus .... Evan Dexter Parke
Euridice .... Eisa Davis
Stranger .... Steve Humphrey

PRINCETON—David Chandler and Elizabeth Marvel in *Meshugah*,
adapted from the story by Isaac Bashevis Singer and directed by Emily
Mann, at the McCarter Theater

Apollo; Charon; Sisyphus .... Ron Bobb-Semple
Mariella; Persephone .... Adrienne Hurd
Dion; Pluto .... Alvin Crawford
Myra .... Nicolette Depass
Toogie .... Valentina Alexander
Mama Cli'pe; Hecate .... Harriett D. Foy
Suki .... Porshia Johnson
Ping .... Joseph Solomon
Cerebus .... Vishal Shetty
Rocks .... Bill Ferguson, Lutin Tanner
Tityus .... Chris Morrison
  Mama Cli'pe Spirits—Natalie Rogers, Nor-
wood Pennewell, Lutin Tanner, Joel Valentin.

Sexy Sirens—Natalie Rogers, Sharon Skepple,
Micha Willis. Dock Workers, Carnival Revelers,
Spirits—Company.
  Garth Fagan Dance: Norwood Pennewell,
Steve Humphrey, Valentina Alexander, Natalie
Rogers, Chris Morrison, Sharon Skepple, Micha
Willis, Bill Ferguson, Joel Valentin, Nicolette De-
pass, Lutin Tanner, Vishal Shetty, Steve St. Juste
(understudy).
  Singers: Nadine Carey, Clara Davis, Kenita
Miller.
  Time: The days of Carnival that precede Ash
Wednesday. Place: Talingo Island. Act I: From

sunrise on Sunday to 2 a.m. Monday morning, the start of Jouvet. Act II: Monday and Tuesday of Carnival and the day after, Ash Wednesday .

MUSICAL NUMBERS, ACT I (by Charles Bevel with exceptions noted): "Orpheus Man" (lyrics by OyamO), "Homage to the Sea" (music by Carlos Valdez and Gregg Coffin, lyrics by OyamO and Gregg Coffin), "Do It!", "Eurydice," "Dreams," "Dreamsong" (music by Gregg Coffin, lyrics by OyamO), "Caribbean Lullabye."

ACT II: "Land of Ethiope," "Stinky Styx" (music by Charles Bevel and Carlos Valdez) "Man Only Want Woman for Sex," "If I Reach Out,"

"Orpheus Man" (Reprise), "Homage to the Sea" (Reprise).

THE ONE-EYED MAN IS KING. By Carter W. Lewis. September 1, 1998. Director, Andrew J. Traister; scenery, Rosario Provenza; costumes, Clare Henkel; lighting, F. Mitchell Dana; sound, Dan Roach; composer, Gregg Coffin.

Lise .... Julie Eccles
Bendalli .... Steve Memran
Elliot .... Careena Melia
Ludviccio .... Jim Mohr
    Time: Autumn. Place: An elegant home in upstate New York. One intermission.

Sag Harbor, N.Y.: Bay Street Theater

(Sybil Christopher, Emma Walton artistic directors; Stephen Hamilton executive director; Murphy Davis producer; Norman Kline general manager)

HOUSE. By Jon Robin Baitz and Terrence McNally. August 12, 1998. Director, Joe Mantello; scenery, Tony Walton; costumes, Jess Goldstein; lighting, Brian MacDevitt; sound, Randall Fried.

Honor Caldwell .... Rue McClanahan
Edith Stone .... Marsha Mason

Lilly Kerr .... Debra Monk
Michael Stone .... Richard Dreyfuss
Ben Kerr .... Daniel Stern
    Time: late summer, the present. Place: Noyac, N.Y. One intermission.

St. Paul: Ordway Music Theater

(Kevin McCollum president & CEO)

TRIBE. Musical conceived by Matt Zemon; story by Raoul Trujillo, Matt Zemon, M. Derek Cromer and Doron Krinetz; music and lyrics by Brulé; colyricist, Barnes. June 25, 1998. Director, Raoul Trujillo; musical direction, Brulé; choreography, Alejandro Ronceria; scenery, Michael E. Downs; costumes, MJ Helmer; lighting, David Neville; sound, T. Richard Fitzgerald; presented by arrangement with Red Sky Productions.

With George Stonefish Bearskin, Benito Concha, Jonathan Fisher, Nicholas Foote, Happy Frejo, Ray Hernandez, Annie Humphrey, Julia Jamieson, Audrey Redman Langer, Star Nayea, Brandon Oakes, Christine Friday O'Leary, Wayashti Perkins, Kalani Queypo, Petur Redbird, Darice Sampson, Nicole Summers, Rulan Tangen, Tonemah.

San Diego: Old Globe Theater

(Jack O'Brien artistic director; Thomas Hall managing director; Craig Noel executive director)

GETTING AND SPENDING. By Michael J. Chepiga. July 26, 1998. Director, John Tillinger; scenery, James F. Noone; costumes, Michael Krass; lighting, Kevin Adams; sound, Jeff Ladman.

Brother Thaddeus;
    Judge Keefe .... MacIntyre Dixon
Brother Alfred .... Derek Smith
Richard O'Neill .... James Morrison
Elizabeth Panelli .... Kali Rocha
Victoria Phillips .... Linda Purl
Charles Humboldt .... David Lansbury

Mary Phillips .... Debra Mooney
    Time: The present. Place: Various places in Kentucky and New York City.

PARAMOUR. Musical based on Jean Anouilh's play *The Waltz of the Toreadors;* book and lyrics by Joe Masteroff; music by Howard Marren. September 20, 1998. Director, Joseph Hardy; musical direction and vocal and music arrangements, Joel Fram; choreography, Melinda Buckley; scenery, Ralph Funicello; costumes, Lewis Brown; lighting, David F. Segal; sound, Jeff Ladman; orchestrations, Douglas Besterman.

Gen. St. Pé .... Len Cariou
Mme. St. Pé .... Melissa Hart
Angelique St. Denis .... Amanda Naughton
Gaston .... Joel Carlton
Estelle .... Danielle Ferland
Sidonia .... Stacey Lynn Brass
Paulette; Pamela .... Catherine Brunell
Dr. Bonfant .... David Pursley
Father Ambrose .... John Seidman
She .... Jo Ann Cunningham
He .... Lee Lobenhofer
Her .... Marguerite Shannon
Him .... Peter Flynn

MUSICAL NUMBERS, Act I, Scene 1: Orchestral Prelude, " At the Garrison Ball," "Liar!", "Pale Blue Letters," "We've Nothing to Wear," "I Wonder What My Life Will Be," "The Enchantment of the Dance," "Dear Faithful Diary," "Make Me Live." Scene 2: "Little Girls Grow Up," "You Should Be Ashamed," "Paramour," "The Confrontation."

Act II: Orchestral Entr'acte, "These Four and I," "I Am His," "Act Four," "And Yet," "Montauban Marie," "Bugles at Sunset," "Closing My Eyes."

ALBEE'S PEOPLE. Repertory of two programs of selections from *The Zoo Story, A Delicate Balance, Who's Afraid of Virginia Woolf?, Seascape, Three Tall Women, The Marriage Play* and other works of Edward Albee chosen by Glyn O'Malley. ALBEE'S WOMEN February 13, 1999; ALBEE'S MEN February 14, 1999. Director, Glyn O'Malley; scenery, Robin Sanford Roberts; costumes, Austin Sanderson; sound, Jeff Ladman.

CAST: Albee's Women—Carol Mayo Jenkins, Lois Markle, Jennifer Roberts; Albee's Men—Richard Easton, Brian Hutchison, Allen Williams.

San Francisco: American Conservatory Theater

(Carey Perloff artistic director; Heather Kitchen managing director)

INDIAN INK. By Tom Stoppard. February 24, 1999 (American premiere). Director, Carey Perloff; scenery, Loy Arcenas; costumes, Walter Hicklin; lighting, Frances Aronson; original music and sound score, Michael Roth; sound, Garth Hemphill.

Flora Crewe .... Susan Gibney
Coomaraswami .... Steven Anthony Jones
Nazrul; Questioner .... Dileep Rao
Eleanor Swan .... Jean Stapleton
Eldon Pike .... Ken Grantham
Nirad Das .... Art Malik
Anish Das .... Firdous Bamji
David Durance .... David Conrad
Dilip; Rajah's Servant .... Anil Kumar
Englishman .... Brian Keith Russell
Englishwoman .... Kathryn Crosby
Resident .... Tom Blair
Club Servant .... Amir Talai
Rajah; Politiciam .... Shelly Desai
Nell .... Roxanne Raja
Eric .... Christopher Rydman

Ensemble: Tom Blair, Kathryn Crosby, Roxanne Raja, Brian Keith Russell, Christopher Rydman, Adriana Sevan, Adam Suleman, Amir Talai.

Time and place: 1930 in India and the mid-1980s in England and in India. One intermission

THE FIRST PICTURE SHOW. Musical with book and lyrics by Ain Gordon and David Gordon; music by Jeanine Tesori. May 12, 1999. Director and choreographer, David Gordon; musical direction, Peter Maleitzke; scenery, Robert Brill; costumes, Judith Anne Dolan; lighting, Jennifer Tipton; sound, Garth Hemphill; projection design, Jan Hartley; associate director, Ain Gordon; co-produced with Center Theater Group/Mark Taper Forum, Gordon Davidson artistic director, in association with AT&T: *OnStage* and the Pick Up Performance Company.

CAST: Henry Hooks, Carl Laemmle, Chairman Howe, Cleo Madison, Mac—John Apicella. Ann First (age 99)—Anne Gee Bird. Camerawoman, Attendant—Cindy Cheung. Thelma March, Lois Weber—Kathleen Conry. Connie Gardner, Gene Gauntier, May Furstmann, W. Steven Bush—Norma Fire. Billy's Assistant, Attendant, Nell Shipman—Karen Graham. Anne First (ages 15–38)—Ellen Greene. Jane Furstmann—Dinah Lenney. Billy Friend, Storage Man, Justice McKenna, Ida May Park, Dudley M. Hughes—Ken Marks. Louis Furstmann, Margery Wilson, Secretary Slicklen, Monty Latour, Mass—Evan Pappas. Nurse Tina, Cindy Su, Marion E. Wong, T.V. Newscaster—Jeanne Sakata. Rev. Wilbur F. Crafts, Alice Guy Blache, Mrs. Klinkman, Movie Assistant, Awards Host—Valda Setterfield. Attendant, Customs Official, Newsman—Michael Gene Sullivan. Doctor, Percy Waters, Ben Tyler—Harry Waters Jr.

Time: 1895–1995. Place: The United States. One intermission.

San Francisco: Magic Theater

(Larry Eilenberg artistic director)

A COMMON VISION. By Neena Beber. January 13, 1999. Director, Mary Coleman; scenery, Mikiko Uesugi; costumes, Callie Floor; lighting, York Kennedy; sound, Gregory Kuhn.

Dolores .... Anne Darragh
Richard .... John Flanagan

Jim .... Eric Siegel
Mona .... Amy Resnick
Elliot .... Warren D. Keith
Janine .... Sally Dana
    Time: The present. Place: A city with tall buildings. One intermission.

San Jose, Calif.: San Jose Repertory Theater

(Timothy Near artistic director; Benjamin Moore managing director)

SISTERS MATSUMOTO. By Philip Kan Gotanda. January 4, 1999. Produced in association with Seattle Repertory Theater, Sharon Ott artistic directer; see its entry in the Seattle Repertory Theater section of this listing.

LEGACY. Musical inspired by Studs Terkel's *Coming of Age;* book by Jon Marans and Ronnie Gilbert; music by Jeff Langley and Henry Mollicone; lyrics by Ronnie Gilbert. February 20, 1999. Director, Timothy Near; musical direction, Henry Mollicone; dance direction, Bick Goss; scenery, Ralph Funicello; costumes, B. Modern; lighting, Derek Duarte; sound, Jeff Mockus.
    CAST: Esther Thompson, Jacob Lawrence, Guadalupe Reyes, Juanita Nelson, Uta Hagen, Ensemble—Yolande Bavan, Eldred, Paul Miller, Milt Hinton, Wallace Nelson, Aki Kurose, Ensemble—Carleton Carpenter, Katherine Kuh, Ruth, Genora Johnson, Estelle Strongin, Ensemble—Ronnie Gilbert, Emily, Bessie Doenges, Hazel Wolf, Kit Tremain, Ensemble—Joan Roberts. Harry Hay, Bresci Thompson, M. Jacoby, Ensemble—David Rogers.
    MUSICAL NUMBERS: "I Don't Want No Rocking Chair," "When You're Old," "The Portrait of a Soul," "Time Flies," "A Community of Caring," "Invisible," "Strip Down to the Bare Essentials," "Little Too Old for Me," "Legacy Waltz."

*New America Playwrights Festival
Staged Readings*

KRISIT. By Y York. October 17, 1998. Director, Melia Bensussen.

Krisit .... Scotty Bloch
Lulu .... Nancy Carlin
Peter .... J. Michael Flynn

THE BIG BLUE NAIL. By Carlyle Brown. October 18, 1998. Director, Loy Arcenas.

Peary .... J. Michael Flynn
Henson .... Mujahid Abdul Rashid
Tupi .... Del Padagat
The Future .... Cassondra Campbell
    Inuits—Robert Hampton, Jack Kohler, Sean San Jose, Phil Begin-Young.

BEATBOX: A RAPARETTA. By Dan Wolf and Tommy Shepherd. October 18, 1998. Director, John McCluggage.

Mickey Finch .... Tommy Shepherd
Tet .... Carlos Aguirre
Malloy .... Dan Wolf
Scat .... Gendell Hernandez
Jazz .... Keith Pinto
Zac .... Taymour Ghazi
Parry .... Nicole Antelo
000 .... Karen Altree Piemme

Seattle: A Contemporary Theater

(Gordon Edelstein artistic director; Susan Baird Trapnell managing director; Gregory A. Falls founding director)

SCENT OF THE ROSES. By Lisette Lecat Ross. July 17, 1998. Director, Gordon Edelstein; scenery, Thomas Lynch; costumes, Martin Pakledinaz; lighting, Peter Kaczorowski; music and sound, John Gromada.

Annalise Morant .... Julie Harris
Imogen Ellis .... Jeanne Paulsen
Nigel Morant .... Jay Patterson

Kate Morant .... Kate Forbes
Young Annalise .... Jessalyn Gilsig
Maraai .... Kirsten Williamson
Julius Van George .... Ntare Mwine
Alistair Leyton-Clark .... William Biff McGuire
Tshipi .... Bobby Bermea
    One Intermission.

THE SUMMER MOON. By John Olive. August 28, 1998. Director, Les Waters; scenery and costumes, Annie Smart; lighting, David Lee Cuthbert; music and sound, Michael Roth.

Naotake Fukushima .... Greg Watanabe
Rosie Yoshida .... Tamlyn Tomita
Arnie Stengel .... Robert Knepper
Woman .... Mary Kae Irvin
Time: Circa 1958; the final scene in 1974. Place: Various locales in Southern California. One intermission.

Seattle: Intiman Theater

(Warner Shook artistic director)

RED. By Chay Yew. September 2, 1998. Director, Lisa Peterson; scenery, Rachel Hauck; costumes, Michael Olich; lighting, Mary Louise Geiger; sound, Nathan Wang; choreography, Jamie H.J. Guan.

Lin .... Michi Barall
Sonja .... Jeanne Sakata
Hua .... Sab Shimono
One intermission.

Seattle: Seattle Repertory Theater

(Sharon Ott artistic director; Benjamin Moore managing director)

SISTERS MATSUMOTO. By Philip Kan Gotanda. January 4, 1999. Director, Sharon Ott; scenery, Kate Edmunds; costumes, Lydia Tanji; lighting, Nancy Schertler; composer, Dan Kuramoto; sound, Stephen LeGrand; produced in association with San Jose Repertory Theater, Timothy Near artistic director; developed in association with Asian American Theater Company, Pamela A. Wu producing director.

Grace .... Kim Miyori
Rose .... Michi Barall
Chiz .... Lisa Li
Bola .... Stan Egi
Hideo .... Nelson Mashita
Henry Sakai .... Ryun Yu
Mr. Hersham .... Will Marchetti
Time: 1945. Place: The Matsumoto farm outside Stockton, California. One intermission.

Stockbridge, Mass.: Berkshire Theater Festival

(Kate Maguire producing director; Larry Carpenter, John Rando artistic associates)

TRANSIT OF VENUS. By Maureen Hunter. July 7, 1998 (American premiere). Director, John Rando; scenery, Rob Odorisio, based on an original concept by Alexander Okun; costumes, Murell Horton; lighting, Dan Kotlowitz; composer, Scott Killian; sound, Richard Jansen.

Le Gentil .... Michel R. Gill
Demarais .... Jason Butler Harner
Celeste .... Marin Hinkle
Mme. Sylvie .... Pamela Payton-Wright
Margot .... Maryann Urbano
Place: A country home in France. Act I: March 1760. Act II: July 1766. Act III: November 1771.

AN EMPTY PLATE IN THE CAFE DU GRAND BOEUF. By Michael Hollinger. August 18, 1998. Director, John Rando; scenery, Rob

Odorisio; costumes, David Murin; lighting, Brian Nason; projection, Elaine J. McCarthy; sound, Jim van Bergen; presented by special arrangement with Roy Gabay.

Antoine .... Bradford Cover
Claude .... Jonathan Freeman
Mimi .... Lynn Hawley
Victor .... Don Lee Sparks
Miss Berger .... Nance Williamson
Gaston .... Brian Reddy
Time: July 1961. Place: Paris, the Café du Grand Boeuf.

New Musical Theater Series
Staged Reading

THE PEOPLE VS. MONA. Musical by Jim Wann. May 28, 1999. Artistic director, Stephen Schwarz.

WATERBURY—A scene from Mary Hanes's *In Service* at Seven Angels Theater

Storrs, Conn.: *Connecticut Repertory Theater*

(Gary M. English artistic director; Robert Wildman managing director)

EASTVILLE. By Ellen M. Lewis. July 17, 1998. Director, Susan V. Booth; scenery, Gary M. English; costumes, Laura Crow; lighting, Michael Philippi; sound, Darren Reid Sussman.

Christine Cuffee .... Starla Benford
Harriet Tubman .... Ora Jones
Jake Morell .... Thomas Vincent Kelly

Time: After the passing of the fugitive slave laws. Place: The home of Christine and Isaiah Cuffee in Eastville, Long Island. No intermission.

Teaneck, N.J.: *American Stage Company*

(James M. Vagias artistic director; Matthew L. Parent managing director)

LIZZIE BORDEN. Musical with book and lyrics by Christopher McGovern and Amy Powers; music by Christopher McGovern. October 31, 1998. Director and choreographer, Bill Castellino; musical direction, Rick Church; scenery, Michael Anania; costumes, Dale DiBernardo; lighting, Ted Mather.

The Girl .... Madeline Blue
Mrs. Durfee .... Bethanne Collins
Adelaide Churchill .... Brenda Cummings

Mrs. Brayton .... Marian Steiner
Lutton; Phillip .... Steven L. Hudson
Detective Fleet .... Jamey McGaugh
The State; Robert Flaherty ...... Michael Babin
Bridget Sullivan .... Rose McGuire
Abby Borden .... Eleanor Glockner
Emma Borden .... Joan Barber
The Judge; Andrew Borden .... Rex Hays
Lizzie Borden .... Alison Fraser
    One intermission.
    MUSICAL NUMBERS: "Even for August,"
"Quiet Little Town," "Before the Tea Party,"
"The House on the Hill," "First Tea Party,"
"Every Time I Look at You," "Buttons," "Fly
Away," "Second Tea Party," "The Maggie Work,"
"Another Dinner," "Hot," "The Trial of Lizzie

Borden Unwinds," "Oh How Awful! Oh How
Sad!", "Ever Since August," "Bridget Unwinds,"
"So Easily," "I Cry Alone," "Third Tea Party,"
"Story of the Year."

THE ART OF MURDER. By Joe DiPietro.
March 3, 1999. Director, John Rando; scenery,
Loren Sherman; costumes, Barbara Forbes; lighting, Greg Guarnaccia; fight direction and special
effects, Rick Sordelet.
Jack Brooks .... Gregory Salata
Annie Brooks .... Erika Rolfsrud
Vincent Cummings .... John Tillotson
Kate .... Kate Stoutenborough
    Time: The present. Place: The living room of
Jack and Annie's country home. One intermission.

Washington, D.C.: Arena Stage

(Molly Smith artistic director; Stephen Richard executive director)

EXPECTING ISABEL. By Lisa Loomer. October 7, 1998. Director, Douglas C. Wager; scenery,
Thomas Lynch; costumes, David C. Woolard;
lighting, Allen Lee Hughes; original music, Joe
Romano; sound, Timothy M. Thompson.
    CAST: Miranda—Ellen Karas. Nick—John
Ottavino. Dominic, Gary, Bob, Eugene, Neil—
Marc Odets. Yolanda, Nurse Paula—Rondi Reed.
Lila, Therapist, Group Leader, Judy—Brigid

Cleary. Sal, Richard, John, Cabbie, Val, Harvey—
Nick Olcott. Pat, Adele, Social Worker, Lupe—
Eileen Galindo. Tina, Taylor, Jennifer, Lisa, Isabel—Mary Fortuna. Clerks, Fans, Nurses, Pedestrians, Waiters, Others—Company.
    Bass Player: Jeffrey Koczela.
    One intermission.
    Winner of a 1998 ATCA New Play Citation;
see introduction to this section.

Waterbury, Conn.: Seven Angels Theater

(Semina De Laurentis artistic director).

IN SERVICE. By Mary Hanes. March 6, 1999. Director, Don Amendolia; scenery, Richard Meyer;
costumes, Jennifer Emerson; lighting, David
O'Connor; sound, Asa Wember.
George O'Reilly .... Scott Christian
Emma Tuckwell .... Susanna Frazer
Lionel Gibbons .... David Haugen
Mrs. Sheridan .... Celia Howard
Mabel Sander .... Caroline Kiely
Lou Passero .... Kristofer Soul
Rebecca Tuckwell .... Brooke Tansley
Detective Morris .... Vince Viverito
    ACT I, Scene 1: Servants' downstairs dining
room, Dec. 10, 1927, 3 p.m. Scene 2: Downstairs
dining room, Dec. 2, evening. Scene 3: Upstairs
drawing room/foyer, later. Scene 4: The same,
Dec. 5, early evening. Scene 5: The same, later.
Scene 6: Servants' downstairs dining room, Dec. 8,

morning. Scene 7: Upstairs drawing room/foyer,
late afternoon. Scene 8: The same, early evening.
    ACT II, Scene 1: Upstairs drawing room/foyer,
moments later. Scene 2: Servants' downstairs dining room, evening. Scene 3: Upstairs drawing
room/foyer, late evening. Scene 4: Servants'
downstairs dining room, Dec. 9, morning. Scene 5:
Upstairs drawing room/foyer, afternoon. Scene 6:
Servants' downstairs dining room, Dec. 10, morning. Scene 7: The same, late afternoon.

Readings

MEXICAN STANDOFF AT FAT SQUAW
SPRINGS. By Matthew Cowles. January 29, 1999.
IMPRESARIO! THE ZIEGFELD GIRLS. Musical with book by Jonathan Diamond; music and
lyrics by Leonard Diamond. April 9, 1999. Director, David O'Connor.

Waterford, Conn.: Eugene O'Neill Theater Center

(George C. White founder and chairman of the board; Wendy D. Hodge general manager; Kathy Agolio director of operations; Lloyd Richards artistic director, National Playwrights Conference; Paulette Haupt artistic director, National Music Theater Conference)

National Playwrights Conference
July 5–Aug. 1, 1998
Staged Readings

MANHATTAN CASANOVA. By Jenny Lyn Bader.

FIVE ROOMS OF FURNITURE. By Dhana-Marie Branton.

HOW I BECAME AN INTERESTING PERSON. By Will Dunne.

THE LAST COMMUNIST TRIO. By Dmitry Gelfand.

THE WHITE BLACK MAN (MUNDELE NDOMBE). By Charles (OyamO) Gordon.

EXTENUATING CIRCUMSTANCES. By Dan Gurskis.

FUDDY MEERS. By David Lindsay-Abaire.

THE DEAD BOY. By Joe Pintauro.

BAREFOOT BOY WITH SHOES ON. By Edwin Sanchez.

THE KITCHEN. By Charlie Schulman.

ORNITHOLOGY. By Aleksandr Stroganov.

FOLK MACHINE. By Alexandra Tolk.

Directors: Casey Childs, Richard Hamburger, Israel Hicks, Karen Nersisyan, William Partlan, Amy Saltz.

National Music Theater Conference
Aug. 3–15, 1998
Staged Concert Readings

THE BUBBLY BLACK GIRL SHEDS HER CHAMELEON SKIN. Musical-in-progress with book, music and lyrics by Kirsten Childs.

LOLA. Musical-in progress with book by Chris Safan and Kirby Tepper; music by Chris Safan; lyrics by Kirby Tepper.

RADIANT BABY. Musical-in-progress with book by Stuart Ross; music by Debra Barsha. Director and choreographer, Joey McKneely.

Music directors: Fred Carl, Albin Konopka. Directors: BT McNicholl, Wilfredo Medina.

Westport, Conn.: Westport Country Playhouse

(James B. McKenzie executive producer; Eric Friedheim associate producer)

LAWYERS. By Henry G. Miller. June 15, 1998. Director, John Berry; scenery, Richard Ellis; costumes, Ingrid Maurer; lighting, Susan Roth; sound, Margaret Pine; presented by special arrangement with Arthur Cantor.
Alex Sterling .... Kevin Conway
Thomas Hudson .... Henry G. Miller
Grant Bradford .... Sam Freed
Loretta Del Gaudio .... Lauree Dash
Richard Kilmer .... Ford Austin
"Red" Calhoun .... Tom Ligon
   Time: The present, over a period of time. Place: A law firm in New York City. One intermission.

WENDELL & BEN. By W.M. Whitehead and Warren Press. June 29, 1998. Director, Richard Zavaglia; scenery, Richard Ellis; costumes, Franne Lee; lighting, Susan Roth; sound, Bruce Ellman.
T. Wendell Clark .... Dan Lauria
Benjamin Mueller .... Fred Savage
   Act I, Scene 1: The den of Wendell Clark's suburban home. Scene 2: Same location, four months later. Scene 3: Wendell's den, six months later. Act II, Scene 1: Wendell's den, two years later. Scene 2: Same location, six monbths later.

Williamstown, Mass: Williamstown Theater Festival

(Michael Ritchie producer; Deborah Fehr general manager)

THE MOST FABULOUS STORY EVER TOLD. By Paul Rudnick. July 1, 1998. Director, Christopher Ashley; scenery, Michael Brown; costumes, Marion Williams; lighting, Rui Rita; sound, Kurt B. Kellenberger.

Stage Manager .... Dara Fisher
Adam .... Alan Tudyk
Steve .... Bobby Cannavale
Matinee Lady; Whiskers; Mom #1; Ftatateeta;
   Rabbi Sharon Kloper .... Maggie Moore

Priest; Bugs; Rhino; Dad #2; Brad;
Kevin Markham .... Michael Wiggins
Latecomer; Peter; Zizi; Dad #1; Pharoah;
Trey Pomfret .... Peter Bartlett
Cheryl Mindle; Mittens; Fifi; Mom #2;
Peggy .... Michi Barall
Jane .... Becky Ann Baker
Mabel .... Jessica Hecht
One intermission.

FAR EAST. By A.R. Gurney. July 15, 1998. Director, Daniel Sullivan; scenery, Michael Brown; costumes, Daniel Castronovo; lighting, Rui Rita; sound, Jerry Yager.
Reader .... Tohoru Masamune
Sparky Watts .... Scott Wolf
James Anderson .... Bill Smitrovich
Julia .... Linda Emond
Bob Munger .... Paul Fitzgerald
Percussionist: Pun Boonyarata-Pun. Stage Assistants: David Mason, Jose Sanchez, Lisa Schmon, Olevia White.
One intermission.

EVOLUTION. By Jonathan Marc Sherman. July 29, 1998. Director, Nicholas Martin; scenery, Alexander Dodge; costumes, Marisa Timperman; lighting, Stephen Brady; sound, Jerry Yager; video, Vanessa Mizzone.
Storyteller .... Dylan Baker
Henry Tollman .... Matt McGrath
Hope Braverman .... Marin Hinkle
Gina Bello .... Anna Belknap
Ernie Braverman .... Justin Kirk
Rex .... Sam Breslin Wright
Prof. Tollman .... Christopher Wigle
One intermission.

CORNERS. By David Rabe. August 12, 1998. Director, Scott Ellis; scenery, Allen Moyer; costumes, Constance Hoffman; lighting, Brian Nason; sound, Eileen Tague; fight direction, David S. Leong.
Ronnie .... Joe Pacheco
Ray .... Robert Pastorelli
Joey .... Christopher Meloni
Uncle Malvolio .... Victor Argo
Muscular Man .... Ty Burrell
Teresa .... Kathryn Hahn
Time: The present, over a period of several hours. Place: In and around Lower Manhattan.

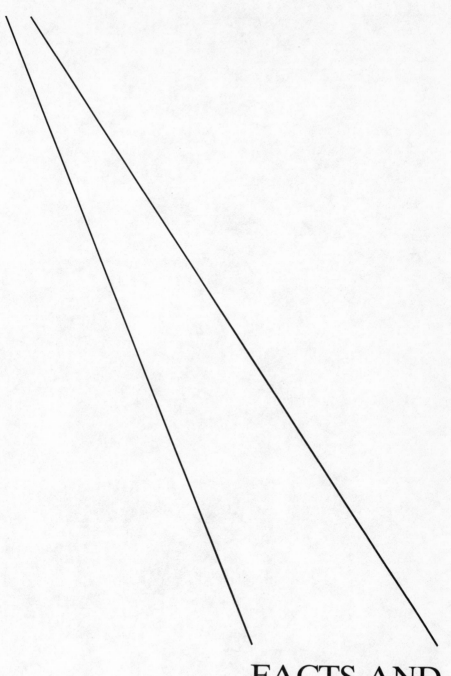

FACTS AND
FIGURES

LONG RUNS ON BROADWAY

The following shows have run 500 or more continuous performances in a single production, usually the first, not including previews or extra non-profit performances, allowing for vacation layoffs and special one-booking engagements, but not including return engagements after a show has gone on tour. In all cases, the numbers were obtained directly from the show's production offices. Where there are title similarities, the production is identified as follows: (p) straight play version, (m) musical version, (r) revival, (tr) transfer.

THROUGH MAY 31, 1999

(PLAYS MARKED WITH ASTERISK WERE STILL PLAYING JUNE 1, 1999)

Plays	Number Performances	Plays	Number Performances
*Cats	6,950	Evita	1,567
A Chorus Line	6,137	The Voice of the Turtle	1,557
Oh! Calcutta! (r)	5,959	Barefoot in the Park	1,530
*Les Misérables	5,031	Brighton Beach Memoirs	1,530
*The Phantom of the Opera	4,762	Dreamgirls	1,522
42nd Street	3,486	Mame (m)	1,508
Grease	3,388	Grease (r)	1,503
*Miss Saigon	3,373	Same Time, Next Year	1,453
Fiddler on the Roof	3,242	Arsenic and Old Lace	1,444
Life With Father	3,224	The Sound of Music	1,443
Tobacco Road	3,182	Me and My Girl	1,420
Hello, Dolly!	2,844	How to Succeed in Business Without	
My Fair Lady	2,717	Really Trying	1,417
Annie	2,377	Hellzapoppin	1,404
Man of La Mancha	2,328	The Music Man	1,375
Abie's Irish Rose	2,327	Funny Girl	1,348
Oklahoma!	2,212	Mummenschanz	1,326
*Beauty and the Beast	2,138	Angel Street	1,295
Pippin	1,944	Lightnin'	1,291
South Pacific	1,925	*Rent	1,289
The Magic Show	1,920	Promises, Promises	1,281
Deathtrap	1,793	The King and I	1,246
Gemini	1,788	Cactus Flower	1,234
Harvey	1,775	Sleuth	1,222
Dancin'	1,774	Torch Song Trilogy	1,222
*Smokey Joe's Cafe	1,772	1776	1,217
La Cage aux Folles	1,761	Equus	1,209
Hair	1,750	Sugar Babies	1,208
The Wiz	1,672	Guys and Dolls	1,200
Born Yesterday	1,642	Amadeus	1,181
The Best Little Whorehouse in		Cabaret	1,165
Texas	1,639	Mister Roberts	1,157
Crazy for You	1,622	Annie Get Your Gun	1,147
Ain't Misbehavin'	1,604	Guys and Dolls (r)	1,144
Mary, Mary	1,572	The Seven Year Itch	1,141

Plays	Number Performances	Plays	Number Performances
*Bring in 'da Noise Bring in 'da Funk	1,130	Song of Norway	860
Butterflies Are Free	1,128	Chapter Two	857
Pins and Needles	1,108	A Streetcar Named Desire	855
Plaza Suite	1,097	Barnum	854
They're Playing Our Song	1,082	Comedy in Music	849
Grand Hotel (m)	1,077	Raisin	847
Kiss Me, Kate	1,070	Blood Brothers	839
Don't Bother Me, I Can't Cope	1,065	You Can't Take It With You	837
The Pajama Game	1,063	La Plume de Ma Tante	835
*Chicago (m, r)	1,059	Three Men on a Horse	835
Shenandoah	1,050	The Subject Was Roses	832
The Teahouse of the August Moon	1,027	Black and Blue	824
Damn Yankees	1,019	The King and I (r)	807
Never Too Late	1,007	Inherit the Wind	806
Big River	1,005	Anything Goes (r)	804
The Will Rogers Follies	983	Titanic	804
Any Wednesday	982	No Time for Sergeants	796
Sunset Boulevard	977	Fiorello!	795
A Funny Thing Happened on the Way to the Forum	964	Where's Charley?	792
The Odd Couple	964	The Ladder	789
Anna Lucasta	957	Forty Carats	780
Kiss and Tell	956	Lost in Yonkers	780
Show Boat (r)	949	The Prisoner of Second Avenue	780
Dracula (r)	925	M. Butterfly	777
Bells Are Ringing	924	Oliver!	774
The Moon Is Blue	924	The Pirates of Penzance (1980 r)	772
Beatlemania	920	Woman of the Year	770
The Elephant Man	916	My One and Only	767
Kiss of the Spider Woman	906	Sophisticated Ladies	767
Luv	901	Bubbling Brown Sugar	766
The Who's Tommy	900	Into the Woods	765
Chicago (m)	898	State of the Union	765
Applause	896	Starlight Express	761
Can-Can	892	The First Year	760
Carousel	890	Broadway Bound	756
I'm Not Rappaport	890	You Know I Can't Hear You When the Water's Running	755
Hats Off to Ice	889	Two for the Seesaw	750
Fanny	888	Joseph and the Amazing Technicolor Dreamcoat (r)	747
Children of a Lesser God	887	Death of a Salesman	742
Follow the Girls	882	For Colored Girls, etc.	742
City of Angels	878	Sons o' Fun	742
Camelot	873	Candide (m, r)	740
I Love My Wife	872	Gentlemen Prefer Blondes	740
*Jekyll & Hyde	872	The Man Who Came to Dinner	739
The Bat	867	Nine	739
My Sister Eileen	864	Call Me Mister	734
No, No, Nanette (r)	861	Victor/Victoria	734
		West Side Story	732

Plays	*Number Performances*	*Plays*	*Number Performances*
High Button Shoes	727	Auntie Mame (p)	639
Finian's Rainbow	725	A Man for All Seasons	637
Claudia	722	Jerome Robbins' Broadway	634
The Gold Diggers	720	The Fourposter	632
Jesus Christ Superstar	720	The Music Master	627
Carnival	719	Two Gentlemen of Verona (m)	627
The Diary of Anne Frank	717	The Tenth Man	623
A Funny Thing Happened on the Way to the Forum (r)	715	The Heidi Chronicles	621
I Remember Mama	714	Is Zat So?	618
Tea and Sympathy	712	Anniversary Waltz	615
Junior Miss	710	The Happy Time (p)	614
Last of the Red Hot Lovers	706	Separate Rooms	613
The Secret Garden	706	Affairs of State	610
Company	705	Oh! Calcutta! (tr)	610
Seventh Heaven	704	Star and Garter	609
Gypsy (m)	702	The Mystery of Edwin Drood	608
The Miracle Worker	700	The Student Prince	608
That Championship Season	700	Sweet Charity	608
Da	697	Bye Bye Birdie	607
Cat on a Hot Tin Roof	694	Irene (r)	604
Li'l Abner	693	Sunday in the Park With George	604
The Children's Hour	691	Adonis	603
Purlie	688	Broadway	603
Dead End	687	Peg o' My Heart	603
The Lion and the Mouse	686	Master Class	601
White Cargo	686	Street Scene (p)	601
Dear Ruth	683	Flower Drum Song	600
East Is West	680	Kiki	600
Come Blow Your Horn	677	A Little Night Music	600
The Most Happy Fella	676	Agnes of God	599
Defending the Caveman	671	Don't Drink the Water	598
The Doughgirls	671	Wish You Were Here	598
The Impossible Years	670	Sarafina!	597
Irene	670	A Society Circus	596
Boy Meets Girl	669	Absurd Person Singular	592
The Tap Dance Kid	669	A Day in Hollywood/A Night in the Ukraine	588
Beyond the Fringe	667	The Me Nobody Knows	586
Who's Afraid of Virginia Woolf?	664	The Two Mrs. Carrolls	585
Blithe Spirit	657	Kismet (m)	583
A Trip to Chinatown	657	Gypsy (m, r)	582
The Women	657	Brigadoon	581
Bloomer Girl	654	Detective Story	581
The Fifth Season	654	No Strings	580
*The Lion King	649	Brother Rat	577
Rain	648	Blossom Time	576
Witness for the Prosecution	645	Pump Boys and Dinettes	573
Call Me Madam	644	Show Boat	572
Janie	642	The Show-Off	571
The Green Pastures	640	Sally	570

Plays	Number Performances	Plays	Number Performances
*Ragtime	570	Damn Yankees (r)	533
Jelly's Last Jam	569	The Unsinkable Molly Brown	532
Golden Boy (m)	568	The Red Mill (r)	531
One Touch of Venus	567	Rumors	531
The Real Thing	566	A Raisin in the Sun	530
Happy Birthday	564	Godspell (tr)	527
Look Homeward, Angel	564	Fences	526
Morning's at Seven (r)	564	The Solid Gold Cadillac	526
The Glass Menagerie	561	Biloxi Blues	524
I Do! I Do!	560	Irma La Douce	524
Wonderful Town	559	The Boomerang	522
The Last Night of Ballyhoo	557	Follies	521
Rose Marie	557	Rosalinda	521
Strictly Dishonorable	557	*Art	521
Sweeney Todd, the Demon Barber of		The Best Man	520
Fleet Street	557	Chauve-Souris	520
The Great White Hope	556	Blackbirds of 1928	518
A Majority of One	556	The Gin Game	517
The Sisters Rosensweig	556	Sunny	517
Sunrise at Campobello	556	Victoria Regina	517
Toys in the Attic	556	Fifth of July	511
Jamaica	555	Half a Sixpence	511
Stop the World—I Want to Get Off	555	The Vagabond King	511
Florodora	553	The New Moon	509
Noises Off	553	*The Sound of Music (r)	509
Ziegfeld Follies (1943)	553	The World of Suzie Wong	508
Dial "M" for Murder	552	The Rothschilds	507
Good News	551	On Your Toes (r)	505
Peter Pan (r)	551	Sugar	505
How to Succeed in Business Without		Shuffle Along	504
Really Trying (r)	548	Up in Central Park	504
Let's Face It	547	Carmen Jones	503
Milk and Honey	543	The Member of the Wedding	501
Within the Law	541	Panama Hattie	501
Pal Joey (r)	540	Personal Appearance	501
What Makes Sammy Run?	540	Bird in Hand	500
The Sunshine Boys	538	Room Service	500
What a Life	538	Sailor, Beware!	500
Crimes of the Heart	535	Tomorrow the World	500

LONG RUNS OFF BROADWAY

Plays	Number Performances	Plays	Number Performances
*The Fantasticks	16,188	Nunsense	3,672
*Perfect Crime	5,002	*Tubes	3,556
*Tony 'n' Tina's Wedding	3,857	The Threepenny Opera	2,611

Plays	Number Performances	Plays	Number Performances
Forbidden Broadway 1982–87	2,332	True West	762
*Stomp	2,210	Isn't It Romantic	733
Little Shop of Horrors	2,209	Dime a Dozen	728
Godspell	2,124	The Pocket Watch	725
Vampire Lesbians of Sodom	2,024	The Connection	722
Jacques Brel	1,847	The Passion of Dracula	714
Forever Plaid	1,811	Adaptation & Next	707
Vanities	1,785	Oh! Calcutta!	704
You're a Good Man Charlie Brown	1,597	Scuba Duba	692
The Blacks	1,408	The Foreigner	686
One Mo' Time	1,372	The Knack	685
Grandma Sylvia's Funeral	1,360	The Club	674
Let My People Come	1,327	The Balcony	672
Driving Miss Daisy	1,195	Penn & Teller	666
*I Love You, You're Perfect, Now Change	1,179	*Secrets Every Smart Traveler Should Know	649
The Hot l Baltimore	1,166	America Hurrah	634
I'm Getting My Act Together and Taking It on the Road	1,165	Oil City Symphony	626
Little Mary Sunshine	1,143	Hogan's Goat	607
Steel Magnolias	1,126	Beehive	600
El Grande de Coca-Cola	1,114	The Trojan Women	600
The Proposition	1,109	The Dining Room	583
Beau Jest	1,069	Krapp's Last Tape & The Zoo Story	582
Tamara	1,036	Three Tall Women	582
One Flew Over the Cuckoo's Nest (r)	1,025	The Dumbwaiter & The Collection	578
The Boys in the Band	1,000	Forbidden Broadway 1990	576
Fool for Love	1,000	Dames at Sea	575
Other People's Money	990	The Crucible (r)	571
Cloud 9	971	The Iceman Cometh (r)	565
Sister Mary Ignatius Explains It All for You & The Actor's Nightmare	947	The Hostage (r)	545
Your Own Thing	933	What's a Nice Country Like You Doing in a State Like This?	543
Curley McDimple	931	Forbidden Broadway 1988	534
Leave It to Jane (r)	928	Gross Indecency: The Three Trials of Oscar Wilde	534
Forbidden Broadway Strikes Back	850	Frankie and Johnny in the Clair de Lune	533
*Late Night Catechism	841	Six Characters in Search of an Author (r)	529
When Pigs Fly	840	All in the Timing	526
The Mad Show	871	Oleanna	513
Scrambled Feet	831	Making Porn	511
The Effect of Gamma Rays on Man-in-the-Moon Marigolds	819	The Dirtiest Show in Town	509
A View From the Bridge (r)	780	Happy Ending & Day of Absence	504
The Boy Friend (r)	763	Greater Tuna	501
		A Shayna Maidel	501
		The Boys From Syracuse (r)	500

NEW YORK DRAMA CRITICS CIRCLE AWARDS, 1935-36 TO 1998-99

Listed below are the New York Drama Critics Circle Awards from 1935-36 through 1998-99 classified as follows: (1) Best American Play, (2) Best Foreign Play, (3) Best Musical, (4) Best, Regardless of Category (this category was established by new voting rules in 1962-63 and did not exist prior to that year).

1935-36—(1) Winterset
1936-37—(1) High Tor
1937-38—(1) Of Mice and Men, (2) Shadow and Substance
1938-39—(1) No award, (2) The White Steed
1939-40—(1) The Time of Your Life
1940-41—(1) Watch on the Rhine, (2) The Corn Is Green
1941-42—(1) No award, (2) Blithe Spirit
1942-43—(1) The Patriots
1943-44—(2) Jacobowsky and the Colonel
1944-45—(1) The Glass Menagerie
1945-46—(3) Carousel
1946-47—(1) All My Sons, (2) No Exit, (3) Brigadoon
1947-48—(1) A Streetcar Named Desire, (2) The Winslow Boy
1948-49—(1) Death of a Salesman, (2) The Madwoman of Chaillot, (3) South Pacific
1949-50—(1) The Member of the Wedding, (2) The Cocktail Party, (3) The Consul
1950-51—(1) Darkness at Noon, (2) The Lady's Not for Burning, (3) Guys and Dolls
1951-52—(1) I Am a Camera, (2) Venus Observed, (3) Pal Joey (Special citation to Don Juan in Hell)
1952-53—(1) Picnic, (2) The Love of Four Colonels, (3) Wonderful Town
1953-54—(1) The Teahouse of the August Moon, (2) Ondine, (3) The Golden Apple
1954-55—(1) Cat on a Hot Tin Roof, (2) Witness for the Prosecution, (3) The Saint of Bleecker Street
1955-56—(1) The Diary of Anne Frank, (2) Tiger at the Gates, (3) My Fair Lady
1956-57—(1) Long Day's Journey Into Night, (2) The Waltz of the Toreadors, (3) The Most Happy Fella
1957-58—(1) Look Homeward, Angel, (2) Look Back in Anger, (3) The Music Man
1958-59—(1) A Raisin in the Sun, (2) The Visit, (3) La Plume de Ma Tante
1959-60—(1) Toys in the Attic, (2) Five Finger Exercise, (3) Fiorello!
1960-61—(1) All the Way Home, (2) A Taste of Honey, (3) Carnival

1961-62—(1) The Night of the Iguana, (2) A Man for All Seasons, (3) How to Succeed in Business Without Really Trying
1962-63—(4) Who's Afraid of Virginia Woolf? (Special citation to Beyond the Fringe)
1963-64—(4) Luther, (3) Hello, Dolly! (Special citation to The Trojan Women)
1964-65—(4) The Subject Was Roses, (3) Fiddler on the Roof
1965-66—(4) The Persecution and Assassination of Marat as Performed by the Inmates of the Asylum of Charenton Under the Direction of the Marquis de Sade, (3) Man of La Mancha
1966-67—(4) The Homecoming, (3) Cabaret
1967-68—(4) Rosencrantz and Guildenstern Are Dead, (3) Your Own Thing
1968-69—(4) The Great White Hope, (3) 1776
1969-70—(4) Borstal Boy, (1) The Effect of Gamma Rays on Man-in-the-Moon Marigolds, (3) Company
1970-71—(4) Home, (1) The House of Blue Leaves, (3) Follies
1971-72—(4) That Championship Season, (2) The Screens (3) Two Gentlemen of Verona (Special citations to Sticks and Bones and Old Times)
1972-73—(4) The Changing Room, (1) The Hot l Baltimore, (3) A Little Night Music
1973-74—(4) The Contractor, (1) Short Eyes, (3) Candide
1974-75—(4) Equus (1) The Taking of Miss Janie, (3) A Chorus Line
1975-76—(4) Travesties, (1) Streamers, (3) Pacific Overtures
1976-77—(4) Otherwise Engaged, (1) American Buffalo, (3) Annie
1977-78—(4) Da, (3) Ain't Misbehavin'
1978-79—(4) The Elephant Man, (3) Sweeney Todd, the Demon Barber of Fleet Street
1979-80—(4) Talley's Folly, (2) Betrayal, (3) Evita (Special citation to Peter Brook's Le Centre International de Créations Théâtrales for its repertory)
1980-81—(4) A Lesson From Aloes, (1) Crimes of the Heart (Special citations to Lena

446

Horne: The Lady and Her Music and the New York Shakespeare Festival production of The Pirates of Penzance)

1981–82—(4) The Life & Adventures of Nicholas Nickleby, (1) A Soldier's Play

1982–83—(4) Brighton Beach Memoirs, (2) Plenty, (3) Little Shop of Horrors (Special citation to Young Playwrights Festival)

1983–84—(4) The Real Thing, (1) Glengarry Glen Ross, (3) Sunday in the Park With George (Special citation to Samuel Beckett for the body of his work)

1984–85—(4) Ma Rainey's Black Bottom

1985–86—(4) A Lie of the Mind, (2) Benefactors (Special citation to The Search for Signs of Intelligent Life in the Universe)

1986–87—(4) Fences, (2) Les Liaisons Dangereuses, (3) Les Misérables

1987–88—(4) Joe Turner's Come and Gone, (2) The Road to Mecca, (3) Into the Woods

1988–89—(4) The Heidi Chronicles, (2) Aristocrats (Special citation to Bill Irwin for Largely New York)

1989–90—(4) The Piano Lesson, (2) Privates on Parade, (3) City of Angels

1990–91—(4) Six Degrees of Separation, (2) Our Country's Good, (3) The Will Rogers Follies (Special citation to Eileen Atkins for her portrayal of Virginia Woolf in A Room of One's Own)

1991–92—(4) Dancing at Lughnasa, (1) Two Trains Running

1992–93—(4) Angels in America: Millennium Approaches, (2) Someone Who'll Watch Over Me, (3) Kiss of the Spider Woman

1993–94—(4) Three Tall Women (Special citation to Anna Deavere Smith for her unique contribution to theatrical form)

1994–95—(4) Arcadia, (1) Love! Valour! Compassion! (Special citation to Signature Theater Company for outstanding artistic achievement)

1995–96—(4) Seven Guitars, (2) Molly Sweeney, (3) Rent

1996–97—(4) How I Learned to Drive, (2) Skylight, (3) Violet (Special citation to Chicago)

1997–98—(4) Art, (1) Pride's Crossing, (3) The Lion King (Special citation to the revival production of Cabaret)

1998–99—(4) Wit, (3) Parade, (2) Closer. (Special citation to David Hare for his contributions to the 1998–99 theater season: Amy's View, Via Dolorosa and The Blue Room)

NEW YORK DRAMA CRITICS CIRCLE VOTING 1998–99

At their May 4, 1999 session of voting for the bests of the New York theater season, the members of the New York Drama Critics Circle found themselves, if not in agreement, at least in immediate consensus. All three of their contests were decided on the first ballot, as they named Margaret Edson's drama *Wit* the year's best of bests, *Parade* (with book by Alfred Uhry, music and lyrics by Jason Robert Brown, co-conceived by Harold Prince) the best musical and the British play *Closer* by Patrick Marber the best foreign play.

In addition, the Critics voted a special citation to the British playwright David Hare "for his contributions to the 1998–99 theater season," which consisted of three new plays on Broadway within the same season: *Amy's View, Via Dolorosa* (a solo show performed as well as written by Hare himself) and *The Blue Room.*

Twenty-four of the Circle's 25 members were present and voting (two—Ben Brantley and John Heilpern—by proxy, with Jack Kroll absent). *Wit* received the 12 votes required for an immediate first-ballot victory from Clive Barnes, *Post;* Mary Campbell, AP; Alexis Greene, *InTheater;* Aileen Jacobson, *Newsday;* Michael Kuchwara, AP; Jacques le Sourd, Gannett Newspapers; Peter Marks, *Times;* Frank Scheck, *Monitor;* John Simon, *New York*; Michael Sommers, Newhouse Group; Sam Whitehead, *Time Out,* and Linda Winer, *Newsday.* The remaining 12 votes were scattered among five contenders, as follows: *Closer* 4 (John Heilpern, *Observer;* Charles Isherwood, *Variety;* David Kaufman, *Daily News;* Ken Mandelbaum, *In-Theater), Betty's Summer Vacation* 3 (Michael Feingold, *Village Voice;* David Sheward, *Backstage;* David Patrick Stearns, *USA Today), Side Man* 2 (Robert Feldberg, Bergen *Record;* Donald Lyons, *Post), The Lonesome West* 2 (Fintan O'Toole, *Daily News;* Richard Zoglin, *Time)* and 1 vote for *Not About Nightingales* (Ben Brantley, *Times).*

Having selected an American play best of bests, the Critics proceeded to the selection of a best foreign play. *Closer,* which had already been a contender, ran away with 17 of the Critics' votes in this category (Barnes, Feingold, Greene, Heilpern, Isherwood, Kaufman, Kuchwara, le Sourd, Mandelbaum, Marks, Scheck, Sheward, Simon, Sommers, Stearns, Whitehead, Winer) against 3 for *The Lonesome West* (Lyons, O'Toole, Zoglin), 3 for *The Weir* (Brantley, Campbell, Feldberg) and 1 for *Blue Heart* (Jacobson).

A sizeable minority of 9 Critics (Feldberg, Greene, Heilpern, Isherwood, le Sourd, Lyons, O'Toole, Scheck, Zoglin) voted to abstain in the best-musical category. *Parade* was named the best musical of the season, with a majority of 10 of the remaining votes (Barnes, Campbell, Kaufman, Kuchwara, Mandelbaum, Simon, Somers, Stearns, Whitehead, Winer) against 3 for *A New Brain* (Campbell, Jacobson, Sheward) and 2 for *Running Man* (Brantley, Marks).

CHOICES OF SOME OTHER CRITICS

Critic	Best Play	Best Musical
Sherry Eaker
Backstage	Wit	Parade
Martin Gottfried
N.Y. *Law Journal*	Wit	Parade
Ralph Howard
WINS Radio	Wit	Parade
Alvin Klein
N.Y. *Times* Suburban	Wit	Abstain
Roma Torre
NY1 News	Wit	Parade

PULITZER PRIZE WINNERS 1916–17 TO 1998–99

1916–17—No award

1917–18—Why Marry?, by Jesse Lynch Williams

1918–19—No award

1919–20—Beyond the Horizon, by Eugene O'Neill

1920–21—Miss Lulu Bett, by Zona Gale

1921–22—Anna Christie, by Eugene O'Neill

1922–23—Icebound, by Owen Davis

1923–24—Hell-Bent fer Heaven, by Hatcher Hughes

1924–25—They Knew What They Wanted, by Sidney Howard

1925–26—Craig's Wife, by George Kelly

1926–27—In Abraham's Bosom, by Paul Green

1927-28—Strange Interlude, by Eugene O'Neill

1928-29—Street Scene, by Elmer Rice

1929-30—The Green Pastures, by Marc Connelly

1930-31—Alison's House, by Susan Glaspell

1931-32—Of Thee I Sing, by George S. Kaufman, Morrie Ryskind, Ira and George Gershwin

1932-33—Both Your Houses, by Maxwell Anderson

1933-34—Men in White, by Sidney Kingsley

1934-35—The Old Maid, by Zoe Akins

1935-36—Idiot's Delight, by Robert E. Sherwood

1936-37—You Can't Take It With You, by Moss Hart and George S. Kaufman

1937-38—Our Town, by Thornton Wilder

1938-39—Abe Lincoln in Illinois, by Robert E. Sherwood

1939-40—The Time of Your Life, by William Saroyan

1940-41—There Shall Be No Night, by Robert E. Sherwood

1941-42—No award

1942-43—The Skin of Our Teeth, by Thornton Wilder

1943-44—No award

1944-45—Harvey, by Mary Chase

1945-46—State of the Union, by Howard Lindsay and Russel Crouse

1946-47—No award

1947-48—A Streetcar Named Desire, by Tennessee Williams

1948-49—Death of a Salesman, by Arthur Miller

1949-50—South Pacific, by Richard Rodgers, Oscar Hammerstein II and Joshua Logan

1950-51—No award

1951-52—The Shrike, by Joseph Kramm

1952-53—Picnic, by William Inge

1953-54—The Teahouse of the August Moon, by John Patrick

1954-55—Cat on a Hot Tin Roof, by Tennessee Williams

1955-56—The Diary of Anne Frank, by Frances Goodrich and Albert Hackett

1956-57—Long Day's Journey Into Night, by Eugene O'Neill

1957-58—Look Homeward, Angel, by Ketti Frings

1958-59—J.B., by Archibald MacLeish

1959-60—Fiorello!, by Jerome Weidman, George Abbott, Sheldon Harnick and Jerry Bock

1960-61—All the Way Home, by Tad Mosel

1961-62—How to Succeed in Business Without Really Trying, by Abe Burrows, Willie Gilbert, Jack Weinstock and Frank Loesser

1962-63—No award

1963-64—No award

1964-65—The Subject Was Roses, by Frank D. Gilroy

1965-66—No award

1966-67—A Delicate Balance, by Edward Albee

1967-68—No award

1968-69—The Great White Hope, by Howard Sackler

1969-70—No Place To Be Somebody, by Charles Gordone

1970-71—The Effect of Gamma Rays on Man-in-the-Moon Marigolds, by Paul Zindel

1971-72—No award

1972-73—That Championship Season, by Jason Miller

1973-74—No award

1974-75—Seascape, by Edward Albee

1975-76—A Chorus Line, by Michael Bennett, James Kirkwood, Nicholas Dante, Marvin Hamlisch and Edward Kleban

1976-77—The Shadow Box, by Michael Cristofer

1977-78—The Gin Game, by D.L. Coburn

1978-79—Buried Child, by Sam Shepard

1979-80—Talley's Folly, by Lanford Wilson

1980-81—Crimes of the Heart, by Beth Henley

1981-82—A Soldier's Play, by Charles Fuller

1982-83—'night, Mother, by Marsha Norman

1983-84—Glengarry Glen Ross, by David Mamet

1984-85—Sunday in the Park With George, by James Lapine and Stephen Sondheim

1985-86—No award

1986-87—Fences, by August Wilson

1987-88—Driving Miss Daisy, by Alfred Uhry

1988-89—The Heidi Chronicles, by Wendy Wasserstein

1989-90—The Piano Lesson, by August Wilson

1990-91—Lost in Yonkers, by Neil Simon

1991-92—The Kentucky Cycle, by Robert Schenkkan

1992-93—Angels in America: Millennium Approaches, by Tony Kushner

1993-94—Three Tall Women, by Edward Albee

1994-95—The Young Man From Atlanta, by Horton Foote

1995-96—Rent, by Jonathan Larson

1996-97—No award

1997-98—How I Learned to Drive, by Paula Vogel

1998-99—Wit, by Margaret Edson

TONY AWARDS

The American Theater Wing's 53d annual Tony (Antoinette Perry) Awards are presented in recognition of distinguished achievement in the Broadway Theater. The League of American Theaters and Producers and the American Theater Wing present these awards, founded by the Wing in 1947. Legitimate theater productions opening in 37 eligible Broadway theaters during the present Tony season—April 30, 1998 to April 28, 1999—were considered by the Tony Awards Nominating Committee (appointed by the Tony Awards Administration Committee) for the awards in 21 regular and several special categories. The 1998–99 Nominating Committee comprised Billie Allen, actress and director; Maureen Anderman, actress; Lisa Aronson, scenic designer; Price Berkley, publisher; Donald Brooks, costume designer; Kate Burton, actress; Marge Champion, choreographer; Betty L. Corwin, theater archivist; Gretchen Cryer, composer; Merle Debuskey, publicist; Mallory Factor, entrepreneur; Jack Goldstein, administrator; A.R. Gurney, playwright; Jay Harnick, artistic director; Allen Lee Hughes, lighting designer; Betty Jacobs, script consultant; Robert Kamlot, general manager; Jack Lee, musical director; Stuart Little, writer and editor; Thomas Meehan, librettist; Joanna Merlin, actress and casting director; Jon Nakagawa, administrator; Estelle Parsons, actress; Polly Pen, author and composer; Shirley Rich, casting director; David Richards, writer; Frances Sternhagen, actress, and Franklin E. Weissberg, judge.

The Tony Awards are voted from the list of nominees, usually four in each category, by members of the theater and journalism professions: the governing boards of the five theater artists' organizations—Actors' Equity Association, the Dramatists Guild, the Society of Stage Directors and Choreographers, the United Scenic Artists and the Casting Society of America—the members of the designated first night theater press, the board of directors of the American Theater Wing and the membership of the League of American Theaters and Producers. Because of fluctuation in these groups, the size of the Tony electorate varies from year to year. For the 1998–99 season there were 812 qualified Tony voters.

The list of 1997–98 nominees follows, with winners in each category listed in **bold face type**.

BEST PLAY (award goes to both author and producer). *Closer* by Patrick Marber, produced by Robert Fox, Scott Rudin, Roger Berlind, Carole Shorenstein Hays, ABC Inc., The Shubert Organization and The Royal National Theater. *The Lonesome West* by Martin McDonagh, produced by Randall L. Wreghitt, Steven M. Levy, Norma Langworthy, Gayle Francis, Dani Davis & Jason Howland, Joan Stein & Susie Dietz, Everett King and The Druid Theater Company/Royal Court Theater. *Not About Nightingales* by Tennessee Williams, produced by Carole Shorenstein Hays, Stuart Thompson, Marsha Garces Williams, Kelly Gonda, The Royal National Theater, Alley Theater and Moving Theater. *Side Man* by **Warren Leight**, produced by **Jay Jarrus, Peter Manning, Roundabout Theater Company, Todd Haimes, Ellen Richard, Ron Kastner, James Cushing** and **Joan Stein.**

BEST MUSICAL (award goes to the producer). *The Civil War* produced by Pierre

Cossette, PACE Theatrical Group/SFX Entertainment, Bomurwil Productions, Kathleen Raitt and Jujamcyn Theaters. *Fosse* produced by **Livent (U.S.) Inc.** *It Ain't Nothin' But the Blues* produced by Eric Krebs, Jonathan Reinis, Lawrence Horowitz, Anita Waxman, Elizabeth Williams, CTM Productions, Anne Squadron, Lincoln Center Theater, Crossroads Theater Company, San Diego Repertory Theater and Alabama Shakespeare Festival. *Parade* produced by Lincoln Center Theater, Andre Bishop, Bernard Gersten and Livent (U.S.) Inc.

BEST BOOK OF A MUSICAL. *Footloose* by Dean Pitchford and Walter Bobbie. *It Ain't Nothin' But the Blues* by Charles Bevel, Lita Gaithers, Randal Myler, Ron Taylor and Dan Wheetman. *Marlene* by Pam Gems. *Parade* by **Alfred Uhry.**

BEST ORIGINAL SCORE (music & lyrics) WRITTEN FOR THE THEATER. *Footloose* music and lyrics by Tom Snow, Dean Pitchford, Eric Carmen, Sammy Hagar, Kenny Loggins and Jim Steinman. *Parade* music and lyrics by **Jason Robert Brown.** *The Civil War* music by Frank Wildhorn, lyrics by Jack Murphy. *Twelfth Night* music by Jeanine Tesori.

BEST REVIVAL OF A PLAY (award goes to the producer). *Death of a Salesman* produced by **David Richenthal, Jujamcyn Theaters, Allan S. Gordon, Fox Theatricals, Jerry Frankel** and **The Goodman Theater.** *Electra* produced by Eric Krebs, Randall L. Wreghitt, Anita Waxman, Elizabeth Williams, Lawrence Horowitz, McCarter Theater/Donmar Warehouse and Duncan C. Weldon. *The Iceman Cometh* produced by Allan S. Gordon, Bill Haber, Ira Pittelman, Elan McAllister, Trigger Street Productions and Emanuel Azenberg. *Twelfth Night* produced by Lincoln Center Theater, Andre Bishop and Bernard Gersten.

BEST REVIVAL OF A MUSICAL (award goes to the producer). *Annie Get Your Gun* produced by **Barry** & **Fran Weissler, Kardana, Michael Watt, Irving Welzer** and **Hal Luftig.** *Little Me* produced by Roundabout Theater Company, Todd Haimes, Ellen Rich-

ard and Julia C. Levy. *Peter Pan* produced by McCoy Rigby Entertainment, The Nederlander Organization, La Mirada Theater for the Performing Arts, Albert Nocciolino, Larry Payton and J. Lynn Singleton. *You're a Good Man, Charlie Brown* produced by Michael Leavitt, Fox Theatricals, Jerry Frankel, Arthur Whitelaw, Gene Persson.

BEST PERFORMANCE BY A LEADING ACTOR IN A PLAY. **Brian Dennehy** in *Death of a Salesman.* Brian F. O'Byrne in *The Lonesome West.* Corin Redgrave in *Not About Nightingales.* Kevin Spacey in *The Iceman Cometh.*

BEST PERFORMANCE BY A LEADING ACTRESS IN A PLAY. Stockard Channing in *The Lion in Winter.* **Judi Dench** in *Amy's View.* Marian Seldes in *Ring Round the Moon.* Zoë Wanamaker in *Electra.*

BEST PERFORMANCE BY A LEADING ACTOR IN A MUSICAL. Brent Carver in *Parade.* Adam Cooper in *Swan Lake.* **Martin Short** in *Little Me.* Tom Wopat in *Annie Get Your Gun.*

BEST PERFORMANCE BY A LEADING ACTRESS IN A MUSICAL. Carolee Carmello in *Parade.* Dee Hoty in *Footloose.* **Bernadette Peters** in *Annie Get Your Gun.* Siân Phillips in *Marlene.*

BEST PERFORMANCE BY A FEATURED ACTOR IN A PLAY. Kevin Anderson in *Death of a Salesman.* Finbar Lynch in *Not About Nightingales.* Howard Witt in *Death of a Salesman.* **Frank Wood** in *Side Man.*

BEST PERFORMANCE BY A FEATURED ACTRESS IN A PLAY. Claire Bloom in *Electra.* Samantha Bond in *Amy's View.* Dawn Bradfield in *The Lonesome West.* **Elizabeth Franz** in *Death of a Salesman.*

BEST PERFORMANCE BY A FEATURED ACTOR IN A MUSICAL. **Roger Bart** in *You're a Good Man, Charlie Brown.* Desmond Richardson in *Fosse.* Ron Taylor in *It Ain't Nothin' But the Blues.* Scott Wise in *Fosse.*

BEST PERFORMANCE BY A FEATURED ACTRESS IN A MUSICAL. Gretha Boston in *It Ain't Nothin' But the Blues*. **Kristin Chenoweth** in *You're a Good Man, Charlie Brown*. Valarie Pettiford in *Fosse*. Mary Testa in *On the Town*.

BEST DIRECTION OF A PLAY. Howard Davies for *The Iceman Cometh*. **Robert Falls** for *Death of a Salesman*. Garry Hynes for *The Lonesome West*. Trevor Nunn for *Not About Nightingales*.

BEST DIRECTION OF A MUSICAL. **Matthew Bourne** for *Swan Lake*. Richard Maltby Jr. and Ann Reinking for *Fosse*. Michael Mayer for *You're a Good Man, Charlie Brown*. Harold Prince for *Parade*.

BEST SCENIC DESIGN. Bob Crowley for *The Iceman Cometh* and *Twelfth Night*. Riccardo Hernandez for *Parade*. **Richard Hoover** for *Not About Nightingales*.

BEST COSTUME DESIGN. **Lez Brotherston** for *Swan Lake*. Santo Loquasto for *Fosse*. John David Ridge for *Ring Round the Moon*. Catherine Zuber for *Twelfth Night*.

BEST LIGHTING DESIGN. **Andrew Bridge** for *Fosse*. Mark Henderson for *The Iceman Cometh*. Natasha Katz for *Twelfth Night*. Chris Parry for *Not About Nightingales*.

BEST CHOREOGRAPHY. Patricia Birch for *Parade*. **Matthew Bourne** for *Swan Lake*. A.C. Ciulla for *Footloose*. Rob Marshall for *Little Me*.

BEST ORCHESTRATIONS. **Ralph Burns** and **Douglas Besterman** for *Fosse*. David Cullen for *Swan Lake*. Don Sebesky for *Parade*. Harold Wheeler for *Little Me*.

SPECIAL TONY AWARDS. To a regional theater company that has displayed a continuous level of artistic achievement contributing to the growth of the theater nationally, recommended by the American Theater Critics Association—**Crossroads Theater Company** of New Brunswick, N.J. For lifetime achievement in the theater—**Uta Hagen**, actress; **Arthur Miller**, playwright; **Isabelle Stevenson**, president of the American Theater Wing. For a live theater event—**Fool Moon.**

TONY AWARD WINNERS, 1947–1999

Listed below are the Antoinette Perry (Tony) Award winners in the catgories of Best Play and Best Musical from the time these awards were established until the present.

1947—No play or musical award
1948—Mister Roberts; no musical award
1949—Death of a Salesman; Kiss Me, Kate
1950—The Cocktail Party; South Pacific
1951—The Rose Tattoo; Guys and Dolls
1952—The Fourposter; The King and I
1953—The Crucible; Wonderful Town
1954—The Teahouse of the August Moon; Kismet
1955—The Desperate Hours; The Pajama Game
1956—The Diary of Anne Frank; Damn Yankees
1957—Long Day's Journey Into Night; My Fair Lady
1958—Sunrise at Campobello; The Music Man
1959—J.B.; Redhead
1960—The Miracle Worker; Fiorello! and The Sound of Music (tie)

1961—Becket; Bye Bye Birdie
1962—A Man for All Seasons; How to Succeed in Business Without Really Trying
1963—Who's Afraid of Virginia Woolf?; A Funny Thing Happened on the Way to the Forum
1964—Luther; Hello, Dolly!
1965—The Subject Was Roses; Fiddler on the Roof
1966—The Persecution and Assassination of Marat as Performed by the Inmates of the Asylum of Charenton Under the Direction of the Marquis de Sade; Man of La Mancha
1967—The Homecoming; Cabaret
1968—Rosencrantz and Guildenstern Are Dead; Hallelujah, Baby!
1969—The Great White Hope; 1776
1970—Borstal Boy; Applause

1971—Sleuth; Company
1972—Sticks and Bones; Two Gentlemen of Verona
1973—That Championship Season; A Little Night Music
1974—The River Niger; Raisin
1975—Equus; The Wiz
1976—Travesties; A Chorus Line
1977—The Shadow Box; Annie
1978—Da; Ain't Misbehavin'
1979—The Elephant Man; Sweeney Todd, the Demon Barber of Fleet Street
1980—Children of a Lesser God; Evita
1981—Amadeus; 42nd Street
1982—The Life & Adventures of Nicholas Nickleby; Nine
1983—Torch Song Trilogy; Cats
1984—The Real Thing; La Cage aux Folles
1985—Biloxi Blues; Big River

1986—I'm Not Rappaport; The Mystery of Edwin Drood
1987—Fences; Les Misérables
1988—M. Butterfly; The Phantom of the Opera
1989—The Heidi Chronicles; Jerome Robbins' Broadway
1990—The Grapes of Wrath; City of Angels
1991—Lost in Yonkers; The Will Rogers Follies
1992—Dancing at Lughnasa; Crazy for You
1993—Angels in America, Part I: Millennium Approaches; Kiss of the Spider Woman
1994—Angels in America, Part II: Perestroika; Passion
1995—Love! Valour! Compassion!; Sunset Boulevard
1996—Master Class; Rent
1997—The Last Night of Ballyhoo; Titanic
1998—Art; The Lion King
1999—Side Man; Fosse

LUCILLE LORTEL AWARDS

The Lucille Lortel Awards for outstanding off-Broadway achievement were established in 1985 by a resolution of the League of Off-Broadway Theaters and Producers, which administers them and has presented them annually since 1986. Eligible for the 14th annual awards in 1999 were all off-Broadway productions which opened between March 1, 1998 and March 31, 1999 except any which moved from an off-Broadway to a Broadway theater. The 1998–99 selection committee comprised Clive Barnes, Sherry Eaker, Peter Filichia, John Heilpern, Charles Isherwood, Alvin Klein, Michael Kuchwara, Ken Mandelbaum, Emily Nunn, John Simon, Sam Whitehead, John Willis and Linda Winer.

PLAY. *Wit* by Margaret Edson.

REVIVAL. *The Mystery of Irma Vep* produced by Steve Asher, Richard Frankel, Thomas Viertel, Steven Baruch and Marc Routh.

ACTOR. **Mark Ruffalo** in *This Is Our Youth.*

ACTRESS: **Kathleen Chalfant** in *Wit.*

DIRECTION. **Derek Anson Jones** for *Wit.*

SCENERY. **Robert Brill** with **Scott Pask** for *The Mineola Twins.*

COSTUMES. **Jess Goldstein** for *The Mineola Twins.*

LIGHTING. **Kevin Adams** for *The Mineola Twins;* **Michael Chybowski** for *Wit* (tie).

BODY OF WORK. **CSC** (Classic Stage Company).

SPECIAL ACHIEVEMENT. **BAM** (Brooklyn Academy of Music).

LIFETIME ACHIEVEMENT. **Harold Pinter**.

EDITH OLIVER AWARD FOR SUSTAINED EXCELLENCE IN ACTING. **Jerry Orbach**.

LORTEL AWARD WINNERS, 1986–1999

Listed below are the Lucille Lortel Award winners in the categories of Outstanding Play and Outstanding Musical from the time these awards were established until the present.

1986—Woza Africa!; no musical award
1987—The Common Pursuit; no musical award
1988—No play or musical award
1989—The Cocktail Hour; no musical award
1990—No play or musical award
1991—Aristocrats; Falsettoland
1992—Lips Together, Teeth Apart; And the World Goes 'Round

1993—The Destiny of Me; Forbidden Broadway
1994—Three Tall Women; Wings
1995—Camping With Henry & Tom; Jelly Roll!
1996—Molly Sweeney; Floyd Collins
1997—How I Learned to Drive; Violet
1998—Gross Indecency, and The Beauty Queen of Leenane (tie); no musical award
1999—Wit; no musical award

ATCA PRINCIPAL CITATIONS AND NEW PLAY AWARD WINNERS, 1976–1998

Beginning with the season of 1976–77, the American Theater Critics Association (ATCA) has cited one or more outstanding new plays in cross-country theater; the principal ones, listed below, to be presented in script excerpts in *Best Plays* and—since 1985—to receive the ATCA New Play Award (see the complete 1998 ATCA citations in The Season Around the United States section of this volume).

1976—And the Soul Shall Dance, by Wakako Yamauchi
1977—Getting Out, by Marsha Norman
1978—Loose Ends, by Michael Weller
1979—Custer, by Robert E. Ingham
1980—Chekhov in Yalta, by John Driver and Jeffrey Haddow
1981—Talking With, by Jane Martin
1982—Closely Related, by Bruce MacDonald
1983—Wasted, by Fred Gamel
1984—Scheherazade, by Marisha Chamberlain
1985—Fences, by August Wilson
1986—A Walk in the Woods, by Lee Blessing
1987—Heathen Valley, by Romulus Linney
1988—The Piano Lesson, by August Wilson

1989—2, by Romulus Linney
1990—Two Trains Running, by August Wilson
1991—Could I Have This Dance?, by Doug Haverty
1992—Children of Paradise: Shooting a Dream, by Steven Epp, Felicity Jones, Dominique Serrand and Paul Walsh
1993—Keely and Du, by Jane Martin
1994—The Nanjing Race, by Reggie Cheong-Leen
1995—Amazing Grace, by Michael Cristofer
1996—Jack and Jill, by Jane Martin
1997—The Cider House Rules, Part II, by Peter Parnell
1998—Book of Days, by Lanford Wilson.

ADDITIONAL PRIZES AND AWARDS, 1998–99

The following is a list of major prizes and awards for achievement in the theater this season. In all cases the names of winners appear in **bold face type**.

18th ANNUAL WILLIAM INGE FESTIVAL AWARD. For distinguished achievement in American theater. **John Guare.** New voice: **David Hirson.**

21st ANNUAL KENNEDY CENTER HONORS. For distinguished achievement by individuals who have made significant contributions to American culture through the arts. **Shirley Temple Black, Bill Cosby, Fred Ebb, John Kander, Willie Nelson, Andre Previn.**

1999 HENRY HEWES DESIGN AWARDS (formerly American Theater Wing Design Awards). For design originating in the U.S., selected by a committee comprising Tish Dace (chairman), Mario Fratti, Mel Gussow, Henry Hewes, Jeffrey Eric Jenkins and Joan Ungaro. Scenic design: **Robert Brill** with **Scott Pask** for *The Mineola Twins.* Costume design: **Jess Goldstein** for *The Mineola Twins.* Lighting design: **Michael Chybowski** for *Cymbeline* and *Wit.* Noteworthy unusual effect: **Theodora Skipitares** for *A Harlot's Progress.*

21st ANNUAL SUSAN SMITH BLACKBURN PRIZES. For women who deserve recognition for having written works of outstanding quality for the English-speaking theater. First prize: **Jessica Goldberg** for *Refuge.* Second prize: **Julie Hebert** for *The Knee Desires the Dirt.*

1998 ELIZABETH HULL–KATE WARRINER AWARD. To the playwright whose work dealt with controversial subjects involving the fields of political, religious or social mores of the time, selected by the Dramatists Guild Council. **Margaret Edson** for *Wit.*

14th ANNUAL STAGE DIRECTORS AND CHOREOGRAPHERS FOUNDATION AWARDS. Mr. Abbott Award for outstanding achievement by a director/choreographer: **Graciela Daniele.** President's Awards for outstanding contribution to the theater: **Betty Comden, Adolph Green, RCA Victor/BMG Classics.** Joe A. Callaway Award for excellence in the craft of direction and choreography: **Frank Galati** and **Graciela Daniele** for *Ragtime.*

1998 NATIONAL MEDALS OF THE ARTS. For individuals and organizations who have made outstanding contributions to the excellence, growth, support and availability of the arts in the United States, selected by the President from nominees presented by the National Endowment for the Arts. **Jacques D'Amboise, Gregory Peck, Roberta Peters, Steppenwolf Theater Company, Gwen Verdon.**

1998 RICHARD RODGERS AWARDS. For production or staged readings, administered by the American Academy of Arts and Letters and selected by a jury of its musical theater members comprising Stephen Sondheim (chairman), Lynn Ahrens, Jack Beeson, Sheldon Harnick, R.W.B. Lewis, Richard Maltby Jr., Francis Thorne and Robert Ward. *Bat Boy* by Brian Flemming and Laurence O'Keefe; *Blood on the Dining Room Floor* by Jonathan Sheffer; *The Bubbly Black Girl Sheds Her Chameleon Skin* by Kirsten Childs; *Dream True: My Life With Vernon Dexter* by Ricky Ian Gordon and Tina Landau; *The Singing* by Lenora Champagne and Daniel Levy.

18th ANNUAL ASTAIRE AWARDS. For excellence in dance and choreography, administered by the Theater Development Fund. Choreography: **Patricia Birch** for *Parade.* Performance: **Adam Cooper** in *Swan Lake.* Special Award: **Matthew Bourne** for the conception and direction of *Swan Lake.*

64th ANNUAL DRAMA LEAGUE AWARDS. For distinguished achievement in the American theater. Play: *Wit.* Musical: *Fosse.* Revival of a play or musical: *Death of a Salesman.*

GEORGE AND ELISABETH MARTON AWARD. To an American playwright, selected by a committee of Young Playwrights, Inc. **Warren Leight** for *Side Man.*

54th ANNUAL CLARENCE DERWENT AWARDS. For the most promising male and female actors on the metropolitan scene during the 1998–99 season. **Robert Sella** in *Side Man;* **Kristin Chenoweth** in *You're a Good Man, Charlie Brown.*

GEORGE JEAN NATHAN AWARD. For dramatic criticism, administered by the Cornell University English Department. **Alisa Solomon.**

1998 JUJAMCYN THEATERS AWARD. For a resident theater that has made an outstanding contribution to the development of creative talent for the theater. **Atlantic Theater Company.**

O'NEILL SOCIETY MEDAL. For contribution to the work of the playwright Eugene O'Neill. **Theodore Mann.**

AMERICAN THEATER WING ANNUAL HONORS. For distinguished achievement in the theater. "Men for All Seasons"—**Ossie Davis, Kevin Kline, Jason Robards, Patrick Stewart, Sam Waterston.**

1998 GEORGE OPPENHEIMER AWARD. To the best new American playwright, presented by *Newsday.* **Warren Leight** for *Side Man.*

10th ANNUAL OSCAR HAMMERSTEIN AWARD. For lifetime achievement in musical theater. **David Merrick.**

1999 *THEATER WORLD* AWARDS. For outstanding debut performers on Broadway or off Broadway during the 1998–99 season. **Jillian Armenante** in *The Cider House Rules,* **James Black** in *Not About Nightingales,* **Brendan Coyle** in *The Weir,* **Anna Friel, Rupert Graves** and **Ciaran Hinds** in *Closer,* **Lynda Gravatt** in *The Old Settler,* **Nicole Kidman** in *The Blue Room,* **Ute Lemper** in *Chicago,* **Sandra Oh** in *Stop Kiss,* **Clarke Peters** in *The Iceman Cometh,* **Toby Stephens** in *Ring Round the Moon.*

Special Award: **Jerry Herman** for his Broadway debut and lifetime achievement.

49th ANNUAL OUTER CRITICS CIRCLE AWARDS. For outstanding achievement in the 1998–99 season, voted by critics on out-of-town periodicals and media. Broadway play: *Not About Nightingales.* Off-Broadway play: *Wit.* Revival of a play: *The Iceman Cometh.* Actor in a play: **Kevin Spacey** in *The Iceman Cometh.* Actress in a play: **Kathleen Chalfant** in *Wit.* Featured actor in a play: **Kevin Anderson** in *Death of a Salesman.* Featured actress in a play: **Claire Bloom** in *Electra.* Director of a play: **Howard Davies** for *The Iceman Cometh.* Broadway musical: *Fosse.* Off-Broadway musical: *A New Brain.* Revival of a musical: *Annie Get Your Gun.* Actor in a musical: **Martin Short** in *Little Me.* Actress in a musical: **Bernadette Peters** in *Annie Get Your Gun.* Featured actor in a musical: **Michel Bell** in *The Civil War.* Featured actress in a musical: **Kristin Chenoweth** in *You're a Good Man, Charlie Brown.* Director of a musical: **Matthew Bourne** for *Swan Lake.* Choreography: **Matthew Bourne** for *Swan Lake.* Scenic design: **Richard Hoover** for *Not About Nightingales.* Costume design: **Lez Brotherston** for *Swan Lake.* Lighting design: **Paul Gallo** for *The Civil War.* Solo performance: **David Hare** in *Via Dolorosa.*

John Gassner Playwriting Award: **Margaret Edson** for *Wit.* Special Achievement Award: **The cast of *Closer***—**Natasha Richardson, Rupert Graves, Anna Friel** and **Ciaran Hinds**—for ensemble performance.

44th ANNUAL DRAMA DESK AWARDS. For outstanding achievement in the 1998–99 season, voted by an association of New York drama reporters, editors and critics from nominations made by a committee. New play: *Wit.* New Musical: *Parade.* Musical revue: *Fosse.* Revival of a play: *Death of a Salesman* and *The Iceman Cometh*

(tie). Revival of a musical: *You're a Good Man, Charlie Brown.* Book of a musical: *Parade* by **Alfred Uhry.** Music: *Parade* by **Jason Robert Brown.** Lyrics: *Forbidden Broadway Cleans Up Its Act* by **Gerard Alessandrini.** Actor in a play: **Brian Dennehy** in *Death of a Salesman.* Actress in a play: **Kathleen Chalfant** in *Wit.* Featured actor in a play: **Kevin Anderson** in *Death of a Salesman.* Featured actress in a play: **Anna Friel** in *Closer.* Actor in a musical: **Brent Carver** in *Parade.* Actress in a musical: **Carolee Carmello** in *Parade* and **Bernadette Peters** in *Annie Get Your Gun* (tie). Featured actor in a musical: **Roger Bart** in *You're a Good Man, Charlie Brown.* Featured actress in a musical: **Kristin Chenoweth** in *You're a Good Man, Charlie Brown.* Director of a play: **Trevor Nunn** for *Not About Nightingales.* Director of a musical: **Matthew Bourne** for *Swan Lake.* Choreography: **Matthew Bourne** for *Swan Lake.* Orchestrations: **Don Sebesky** for *Parade.* Set design of a play: **Richard Hoover** for *Not About Nightingales.* Set design of a musical: **Lez Brotherston** for *Swan Lake.* Costume design: **Lez Brotherston** for *Swan Lake.* Lighting: **Chris Parry** for *Not About Nightingales.* Sound design: **Christopher Shutt** for *Not About Nightingales.* Music in a play: **Jeanine Tesori** for *Twelfth Night.* Solo performance: **David Hare** in *Via Dolorosa.* Unique theatrical experience: *Swan Lake.*

44th ANNUAL *VILLAGE VOICE* OBIE AWARDS. For outstanding achievement in off- and off-off-Broadway theater, selected by a committee comprising Brian Parks (chairman), Una Chudhuri, Liz Diamond, Michael Feingold, Dael Orlandersmith, Mark Russell and Alisa Solomon. Playwriting: **W. David Hancock** for *The Race of the Ark Tattoo,* **Dare Clubb** for *Oedipus,* **Christopher Durang** for *Betty's Summer Vacation.* Performance: **Liev Schreiber** in *Cymbeline,* **Kathleen Chalfant** in *Wit,* **Matthew Maher** in *The Race of the Ark Tattoo,* **Darius de Haas** in *Running Man,* **Viola Davis** in *Everybody's Ruby,* **Kristine Nielsen** in *Betty's Summer Vacation,* **Swoosie Kurtz** in *The Mineola Twins;* **Daniel Gerroll, Randall Duk Kim, Mina Bern** for sustained excellence of performance. Direction: **Jim Simpson** for *Benten Kozo,* **Melia Bensussen** for *The Turn of the Screw,* **Nicholas Martin** for *Betty's Summer Vacation,* **Declan Donnellan** for *Le Cid.* Design: **Thomas Lynch** for sustained excellence of set design, **Michael Chybowski** for sustained excellence of lighting design, **Martin Pakledinaz** costumes for *The Misanthrope,* **Diedre Murray Score** design for *Running Man.* Production: **The Wooster Group** for *House/ Lights.* Sustained achievement: **Wynn Handman.**

Special citations: **Peggy Shaw** for *Menopausal Gentlemen,* **Richard Maxwell** for *House,* **Carmelita Tropicana, David Cale** for *Lillian,* **Kim**

Hughes and **Aasaf Mandvi** for *Sakina's Restaurant,* **Ronnie Burkett** for *Tinka's New Dress,* **Lisa Kron** for *2.5 Minute Ride,* **Basil Twist** for *Symphonie Fantastique.*

9th ANNUAL CONNECTICUT CRITICS CIRCLE AWARDS. For outstanding achievement in Connecticut theater during the 1998–99 season. Production of a play: **Hartford Stage** for *The Clearing.* Production of a musical: **Goodspeed Opera House** for *On the Twentieth Century.* Actress in a play: **Alyssa Bresnahan** in *The Clearing.* Actor in a play: **Edward Hibbert** in *The Importance of Being Earnest.* Actress in a musical: **Karen Kandel** in *Peter and Wendy.* Actor in a musical: **Mark Jacoby** in *On the Twentieth Century* and **Ron Wisniski** in *Damn Yankees.* Direction of a play: **Tracy Brigden** for *The Clearing* and **Doug Hughes** for *The Playboy of the Western World.* Direction of a musical: **Lee Breuer** for *Peter and Wendy.* Choreography: **Peggy Hickey** for *On the Twentieth Century.* Set design: **Warren Karp** for *A Rosen by Any Other Name* and *The Grandmama Tree.* Lighting design: **Howell Binkley** for *The Clearing.* Costume design: **Jane Greenwood** for *Hay Fever.* Sound design: **David Van Tieghem** for *The Grey Zone.* Ensemble performance: **Todd Anthony-Jackson, David Barrus, Stan W. Bayley, Joe Beaudin, Heather Britton-Schrager, Beth Carusillo, Rob Gil, Stephen Graybill** and **Bobby Moynihan Jr.** in *The Boys Next Door.* Roadshow: **Shubert Performing Arts Center** for *Barrymore.*

Lucille Lortel Debut Award: **Kelli O'Hara** in *Phantom.* Lifetime Achievement Award: **Al Pia** of Staples High School and Sterling Barn Theater. Tom Killen Memorial Award: **Semina De Laurentis** of Seven Angels Theater.

17th ANNUAL ELLIOT NORTON AWARDS. For outstanding contribution to the theater in Boston, voted by a Boston Theater Critics Association Selections Committee comprising Skip Ascheim, Terry Byrne, Carolyn Clay, Iris Fanger, Arthur Friedman, Joyce Kulhawik, Jon Lehman, Bill Marx, Ed Siegel and Caldwell Titcomb. Productions—Visiting company: *Ragtime.* Musical revival: *Hair* by North Shore Music Theater. Large resident company: *Jitney* by Huntington Theater Company. Small resident company: *Dealer's Choice* by Gloucester Stage Company. Local fringe company: *Sing Me to Sleep* by Coyote Theater. New script: *Valparaiso* by **Don DeLillo.** Solo performance: **Melinda Lopez** in *God Smells Like a Roast Pig.* Actor—Large company: **Jonathan Epstein** in *Phaedra* and *The Merchant of Venice.* Small company: **Ronald Hunter** in *Dealer's Choice.* Actress—Large Company: **Ellen McLaughlin** in *The Threepenny Opera.* Small company: **Sheila Ferrini** in *Lost in Yonkers.* Director—

Large company: **Michael Bloom** for *Gross Indecency.* Small company: **Spiro Veloudos** for *Lost in Yonkers, Assassins* and *Never the Sinner.* Designer—Large company: **Catherine Zuber** (costumes) for *The Imaginary Invalid, Phaedra* and *The Merchant of Venice.* Small company: **J. Hagenbuckle** (sound) for *Marisol, The Santaland Diaries, The Swan* and *Sing Me to Sleep.*

Achievement in playwriting: **Paula Vogel,** who courageously explores the dark, the difficult and the daring through the charming, the crotchety and the comical. Norton Prize for Sustained Excellence: **Andrei Serban,** a visionary director whose resonant images stir the mind and stick in the memory. Special citation: **Theater Offensive,** a venue for gay and lesbian theater featuring challenging homegrown productions and cutting-edge imports.

14th ANNUAL HELEN HAYES AWARDS. In recognition of excellence in Washington, D.C. theater, presented by the Washington Theater Awards Society. Resident productions—Play: *Nijinsky's Last Dance* by **The Signature Theater.** Musical: *Thunder Knocking on the Door* by **Arena Stage.** Lead actress, musical: **Marva Hicks** in *Thunder Knocking on the Door.* Lead actor, musical: **Stephen Bienskie** in *The Fix.* Lead actress, play: **S. Epatha Merkerson** in *The Old Settler.* Lead actor, play: **Ted van Griethuysen** in *The Steward of Christendom.* Supporting performer, musical: **Sal Mistretta** in *The Fix.* Supporting actress, play: **Rena Cherry Brown** in *A Delicate Balance.* Supporting actor, play: **J. Fred Shiffman** in *Lovers and Executioners.* Set design, play or musical: **Tony Cisek** for *Much Ado About Nothing.* Costume design, play or musical: **Paul Tazewell** for *Peer Gynt.* Lighting design, play or musical: **Daniel MacLean Wagner** for *Nijinsky's Last Dance.* Sound design, play or musical: **David Maddox** for *Nijinsky's Last Dance.* Director, musical: **Jesse Berger** for *Marat/Sade.* Director, play: **Joe Calarco** for *Nijinsky's Last Dance.* Musical direction, play or musical: **Anderson Edwards** for *Thunder Knocking on the Door.* Choreography: **Debbie Allen** for *Brothers of the Night.*

Non-resident productions—Production: *Ragtime.* Lead actress: **Jane Lapotaire** in *All Is True, or The Famous History of the Life of King Henry VIII.* Lead actor: **Alex Jennings** in *Hamlet.* Supporting performer: **Guy Henry** in *Cymbeline.*

Charles MacArthur Award for outstanding new play: *Lovers and Executioners* by **John Strand.** American Express Tribute: **John Kander** and **Fred Ebb.** KMPG Award for distinguished service to the Washington theater community: **The Chevy Chase Bank** for including theater space for Round House Theater in its corporate headquarters.

30th ANNUAL JOSEPH JEFFERSON AWARDS. For achievement in Chicago theater during the 1997–98 season, selected by a 45-member Jefferson Awards Committee from 113 Equity productions offered by 45 producing organizations. Special Lifetime Achievement Award: **Nathan Davis** for his decades of contribution to Chicago Theater, both as a performer and as an activist in Actors' Equity.

Resident productions—New work: *A Mislaid Heaven* by **Carson Grace Becker**, *The Angels of Lemnos* by **Jim Henry**, *Flyovers* by **Jeffrey Sweet**. New Adaptation: *The Idiot* by **David Catlin**, *The Iphigenia Cycle* by **Nicholas Rudall**. Production of a play: **The Journeymen's** *Angels in America, Parts I & II*. Production of a musical: **Goodman Theater's** *Play On!* Production of a revue: **Court Theater's** *Putting It Together*. Director of a play: **David Cromer** and **The Company** for *Angels in America, Parts I & II*. Director of a musical: **Sheldon Epps** for *Play On!* Director of a revue: **Gary Griffin** for *Putting It Together*. Actor in a principal role, play: **Chaney Kley** in *The Angels of Lemnos*. Actress in a principal role, play: **Kate Buddeke** in *David's Mother*, **Jennifer Friedmann** in *The Glass Menagerie*, **Kirsten Sahs** in *Beautiful Thing*. Actor in a supporting role, play: **Roderick Peoples** in *Dealer's Choice*. Actress in a supporting role, play: **Annabel Armour** in *Angels in America, Parts I & II*. Actress in a cameo role: **Annabel Armour** in *After-Play*, **Kate Buddeke** in *Gypsy*. Actor in principal role, musical: **Brian Stepanek** in *Me and My Girl*. Actress in a principal role, musical: **Angela Iannone** in *Guys and Dolls*, **Cindy Marchionda** in *Kiss of the Spider Woman*. Actor in a supporting role, musical: **Andre De Shields** in *Play On!*. Actress in a supporting role, musical: **Mary Robin Roth** in *Follies*. Actor in a revue: **John Steven Crowley** in *Ain't Misbehavin'*. Actress in a supporting role, revue: **Rachel Dratch** in *Promise Keepers, Losers Weepers*, **Queen Roy** in *Wang Dang Doodle*, **Paula Scrofano** in *Putting It Together*. Ensemble: *Angels in America, Parts I & II, Let Me Live*. Scenic design: **Dex Edwards** for *The Comedy of Errors*. Costume design: **Linda Roethke** for *An Ideal Husband*. Lighting design, **Scott Zielinski** for *Space*. Sound design: **N.A. Gibson** and **David Zerlin** for *Angels in America, Parts I & II*. Choreography: **Maria Lamper** for *Kiss of the Spider Woman*. Original music: **John Kamys** for *El Paso Blue*, **Henry Marsh** for *The Comedy of Errors*, **Malachi Thompson** for *The Sutherland*. Musical direction: **Tom Murray** for *Putting It Together*, **J. Leonard Oxley** for *Play On!*, **Joe Payne** for *Buddy: The Buddy Holly Story*.

Non-resident productions—Production: **Walt Disney Productions'** *Beauty and the Beast*. Actor in a principal role: **Charles Durning** in *The Gin Game*. Actress in a principal role: **Julie Harris** in *The Gin Game*. Actor in a supporting role: **Shaun Earl** in *Rent*, **Dirk Lumbard** in *The Wizard of Oz*, **Patrick Page** in *Beauty and the Beast*.

26th ANNUAL JOSEPH JEFFERSON CITATIONS WING AWARDS. For achievement in professional productions during the 1998–99 season of Chicago area theaters not operating under union contracts. Productions: *Dream Boy* by **About Face Theater**, *The Freedom of the City* by **Mary-Arrchie Theater Company**. Ensembles: *The Freedom of the City*, *Hurlyburly*. Directors: **Richard Cotovsky** for *The Freedom of the City*, **Eric Rosen** for *Dream Boy*. Actresses in principal roles: **Marguerite Hammersley** in *The Waiting Room*, **Donna Smother** in *The Freedom of the City*. Actors in principal roles: **Michael Dobbs** in *Hurlyburly*, **Michael Nowak** in *The Turn of the Screw*. Actresses in a supporting roles: **Rebecca Jordan** in *Frozen Assets*, **Stephanie Manglaras** in *Hurlyburly*, **Seema Sueka** in *The Waiting Room*. Actors in supporting roles: **Daniel Fine** in *Belmont Avenue Social Club*, **Bart Petty** in *Hurlyburly*. Scenic design: **José Luis de la Fuente** for *The Art of Dining*, **David Krajecki** and **Patrick Uphues** for *Lips Together, Teeth Apart*, **Joey Wade** for *A Month in the Country*. Costume design: **Nicole Evangelista** for *Chéri*. Lighting design: **Joel Moritz** for *Dream Boy*. Sound design: **Andre Pluess** and **Ben Sussman** for *Dream Boy*, **Michael Weber** and **Brian Johnson** for *Warhawks & Lindberghs*. Musical direction: **Michael Duff** for *Female Problems*. Original music: **Alex Ferrill** and **Jonathan Watkins** for *Edward II*, **Andre Pluess** and **Ben Sussman** for *Hamlet*. New work: **Jim McDermott** for *Warhawks & Lindberghs*, **Robert Myers** for *The Lynching of Leo Frank*. New adaptation: **Kyle Hall** for *A Home at the End of the World*.

Special citation: **Richard Shavzin** of Strawdog Theater for creating the Unified Non-Equity General Auditions in 1994.

1997–98 LOS ANGELES OVATIONS. Year's best, peer-judged by Theater LA, an association of more than 130 theater companies and producers. All theaters—Writing of a world premiere play or musical: **Pamela Forrest** for *Valsetz*. New translation/adaptation: **Milena Albert** for *The Seagull*. Lead actor in a musical: **Deven May** in *Bat Boy*. Lead actor in a play: **Tony Abatemarco** in *The Mystery of Irma Vep*. Lead actress in a musical: **Charlotte d'Amboise** in *Chicago—The Musical*. Lead actress in a play: **Patricia Place** in *Valsetz*. Featured actor in a musical: **Wilson Cruz** in *Rent*. Featured actor in a play: **Tom Beyer** in *The Cider House Rules*. Featured actress in a musical: **Jennifer Leigh Warren** in *Hello Again*. Featured actress in a play: **Stephanie Faracy** in *Two Rooms*. Ensemble performance: Cast of *Forever Plaid*.

Director of a musical: **Tim Dang** for *Pacific Overtures*. Director of a play: **Andrew J. Robinson** for *Yield of the Long Bond*. Choreography: **Derick K. Grant** for *Bring in 'da Noise Bring in 'da Funk*.

In a larger theater—Musical: *Chicago—The Musical* at the Ahmanson Theater. Play: *The Cider House Rules* at the Mark Taper Forum. Scenery: **John Napier** for *An Enemy of the Poeple*. Costumes: **Naomi Yoshida Rodriguez** for *Pacific Overtures*. Lighting: **Peggy Eisenhauer** and **Jules Fisher** for *Bring in 'da Noise Bring in 'da Funk*. Sound: **Red Ramona** for *Old Wicked Songs*.

In a smaller theater—Musical: *On the Twentieth Century* at the Colony Studio Theater. Play: *Great Men of Science Nos. 21 & 22* at the Circle X Theater Company. Scenery: **Gary Smoot** for *Great Men of Science Nos. 21 & 22*. Costumes: **M.E. Dunn** for *Great Men of Science Nos. 21 & 22*. Lighting: **Deena Lynn Mullen** for *Request Concert*. Sound: **Bob Blackburn** for *Request Concert*.

THE THEATER HALL OF FAME

The Theater Hall of Fame was created in 1971 to honor those who have made outstanding contributions to the American theater in a career spanning at least 25 years, with at least five major credits. Members are elected annually by the nation's drama critics and editors (names of those so elected in 1998 and inducted February 1, 1999 appear in **bold face italics**).

GEORGE ABBOTT
MAUDE ADAMS
VIOLA ADAMS
STELLA ADLER
EDWARD ALBEE
THEONI V. ALDREDGE
IRA ALDRIDGE
JANE ALEXANDER
WINTHROP AMES
JUDITH ANDERSON
MAXWELL ANDERSON
ROBERT ANDERSON
JULIE ANDREWS
MARGARET ANGLIN
JEAN ANOUILH
HAROLD ARLEN
GEORGE ARLISS
BORIS ARONSON
ADELE ASTAIRE
FRED ASTAIRE
EILEEN ATKINS
BROOKS ATKINSON
LAUREN BACALL
PEARL BAILEY
GEORGE BALANCHINE
WILLIAM BALL
ANNE BANCROFT
TALLULAH BANKHEAD
RICHARD BARR
PHILIP BARRY
ETHEL BARRYMORE
JOHN BARRYMORE
LIONEL BARRYMORE
NORA BAYES
BRIAN BEDFORD
S.N. BEHRMAN
NORMAN BEL GEDDES
DAVID BELASCO
MICHAEL BENNETT
RICHARD BENNETT
ROBERT RUSSELL BENNETT
ERIC BENTLEY
IRVING BERLIN

SARAH BERNHARDT
LEONARD BERNSTEIN
EARL BLACKWELL
KERMIT BLOOMGARDEN
JERRY BOCK
RAY BOLGER
EDWIN BOOTH
JUNIUS BRUTUS BOOTH
SHIRLEY BOOTH
PHILIP BOSCO
ALICE BRADY
BERTOLT BRECHT
FANNIE BRICE
PETER BROOK
JOHN MASON BROWN
BILLIE BURKE
ABE BURROWS
RICHARD BURTON
MRS. PATRICK CAMPBELL
ZOE CALDWELL
EDDIE CANTOR
MORRIS CARNOVSKY
MRS. LESLIE CARTER
GOWER CHAMPION
FRANK CHANFRAU
CAROL CHANNING
RUTH CHATTERTON
PADDY CHAYEFSKY
ANTON CHEKHOV
INA CLAIRE
BOBBY CLARK
HAROLD CLURMAN
LEE J. COBB
RICHARD L. COE
GEORGE M. COHAN
ALEXANDER H. COHEN
JACK COLE
CY COLEMAN
CONSTANCE COLLIER
BETTY COMDEN
MARC CONNELLY
BARBARA COOK
KATHARINE CORNELL

NOEL COWARD
JANE COWL
LOTTA CRABTREE
CHERYL CRAWFORD
HUME CRONYN
RUSSEL CROUSE
CHARLOTTE CUSHMAN
JEAN DALRYMPLE
AUGUSTIN DALY
E.L. DAVENPORT
OSSIE DAVIS
RUBY DEE
ALFRED DE LIAGRE JR.
AGNES DeMILLE
COLLEEN DEWHURST
HOWARD DIETZ
DUDLEY DIGGES
MELVYN DOUGLAS
EDDIE DOWLING
ALFRED DRAKE
MARIE DRESSLER
JOHN DREW
MRS. JOHN DREW
WILLIAM DUNLAP
MILDRED DUNNOCK
CHARLES DURNING
ELEANORA DUSE
JEANNE EAGELS
FRED EBB
FLORENCE ELDRIDGE
LEHMAN ENGEL
MAURICE EVANS
ABE FEDER
JOSE FERRER
CY FEUER
ZELDA FICHANDLER
DOROTHY FIELDS
HERBERT FIELDS
LEWIS FIELDS
W.C. FIELDS
JULES FISHER
MINNIE MADDERN FISKE
CLYDE FITCH

GERALDINE FITZGERALD
HENRY FONDA
LYNN FONTANNE
HORTON FOOTE
EDWIN FORREST
BOB FOSSE
RUDOLF FRIML
CHARLES FROHMAN
GRACE GEORGE
GEORGE GERSHWIN
IRA GERSHWIN
JOHN GIELGUD
W.S. GILBERT
JACK GILFORD
WILLIAM GILLETTE
CHARLES GILPIN
LILLIAN GISH
JOHN GOLDEN
MAX GORDON
RUTH GORDON
ADOLPH GREEN
PAUL GREEN
CHARLOTTE GREENWOOD
JOEL GREY
JOHN GUARE
TYRONE GUTHRIE
UTA HAGEN
LEWIS HALLAM
OSCAR HAMMERSTEIN II
WALTER HAMPDEN
OTTO HARBACH
E.Y. HARBURG
SHELDON HARNICK
EDWARD HARRIGAN
JED HARRIS
JULIE HARRIS
ROSEMARY HARRIS
SAM H. HARRIS
REX HARRISON
LORENZ HART
MOSS HART
TONY HART
HELEN HAYES
LELAND HAYWARD
BEN HECHT
EILEEN HECKART
THERESA HELBURN
LILLIAN HELLMAN
KATHARINE HEPBURN
VICTOR HERBERT
JERRY HERMAN
JAMES A. HERNE
AL HIRSCHFELD

RAYMOND HITCHCOCK
CELESTE HOLM
HANYA HOLM
ARTHUR HOPKINS
DE WOLF HOPPER
JOHN HOUSEMAN
EUGENE HOWARD
LESLIE HOWARD
SIDNEY HOWARD
WILLIE HOWARD
BARNARD HUGHES
HENRY HULL
JOSEPHINE HULL
WALTER HUSTON
EARLE HYMAN
HENRIK IBSEN
WILLIAM INGE
BERNARD B. JACOBS
ELSIE JANIS
JOSEPH JEFFERSON
AL JOLSON
JAMES EARL JONES
MARGO JONES
ROBERT EDMOND JONES
TOM JONES
RAUL JULIA
JOHN KANDER
GARSON KANIN
GEORGE S. KAUFMAN
DANNY KAYE
ELIA KAZAN
GENE KELLY
GEORGE KELLY
FANNY KEMBLE
JEROME KERN
WALTER KERR
MICHAEL KIDD
RICHARD KILEY
SIDNEY KINGSLEY
FLORENCE KLOTZ
JOSEPH WOOD KRUTCH
BERT LAHR
BURTON LANE
LAWRENCE LANGNER
LILLIE LANGTRY
ANGELA LANSBURY
CHARLES LAUGHTON
ARTHUR LAURENTS
GERTRUDE LAWRENCE
JEROME LAWRENCE
EVA LE GALLIENNE
MING CHO LEE
ROBERT E. LEE

LOTTE LENYA
ALAN JAY LERNER
SAM LEVENE
ROBERT LEWIS
BEATRICE LILLIE
HOWARD LINDSAY
FRANK LOESSER
FREDERICK LOEWE
JOSHUA LOGAN
PAULINE LORD
LUCILLE LORTEL
ALFRED LUNT
CHARLES MACARTHUR
STEELE MACKAYE
ROUBEN MAMOULIAN
RICHARD MANSFIELD
ROBERT B. MANTELL
FREDRIC MARCH
JULIA MARLOWE
ERNEST H. MARTIN
MARY MARTIN
RAYMOND MASSEY
SIOBHAN MCKENNA
TERRENCE MCNALLY
HELEN MENKEN
BURGESS MEREDITH
ETHEL MERMAN
DAVID MERRICK
JO MIELZINER
ARTHUR MILLER
MARILYN MILLER
HELENA MODJESKA
FERENC MOLNAR
LOLA MONTEZ
VICTOR MOORE
ZERO MOSTEL
ANNA CORA MOWATT
PAUL MUNI
THARON MUSSER
GEORGE JEAN NATHAN
MILDRED NATWICK
NAZIMOVA
JAMES M. NEDERLANDER
MIKE NICHOLS
ELLIOT NORTON
SEAN O'CASEY
CLIFFORD ODETS
DONALD OENSLAGER
LAURENCE OLIVIER
EUGENE O'NEILL
GERALDINE PAGE
JOSEPH PAPP
OSGOOD PERKINS

BERNADETTE PETERS
MOLLY PICON
HAROLD PINTER
CHRISTOPHER PLUMMER
COLE PORTER
ROBERT PRESTON
HAROLD PRINCE
JOSE QUINTERO
ELLIS RABB
JOHN RAITT
TONY RANDALL
MICHAEL REDGRAVE
ADA REHAN
ELMER RICE
LLOYD RICHARDS
RALPH RICHARDSON
CHITA RIVERA
JASON ROBARDS
JEROME ROBBINS
PAUL ROBESON
RICHARD RODGERS
WILL ROGERS
SIGMUND ROMBERG
HAROLD ROME
LILLIAN RUSSELL
DONALD SADDLER
GENE SAKS
WILLIAM SAROYAN
JOSEPH SCHILDKRAUT
HARVEY SCHMIDT
ALAN SCHNEIDER
GERALD SCHOENFELD

ARTHUR SCHWARTZ
GEORGE C. SCOTT
MARIAN SELDES
IRENE SHARAFF
GEORGE BERNARD SHAW
SAM SHEPARD
ROBERT E. SHERWOOD
J.J. SHUBERT
LEE SHUBERT
HERMAN SHUMLIN
NEIL SIMON
LEE SIMONSON
EDMUND SIMPSON
OTIS SKINNER
MAGGIE SMITH
OLIVER SMITH
STEPHEN SONDHEIM
E.H. SOTHERN
KIM STANLEY
MAUREEN STAPLETON
ROGER L. STEVENS
ELLEN STEWART
DOROTHY STICKNEY
FRED STONE
LEE STRASBERG
AUGUST STRINDBERG
ELAINE STRITCH
JULE STYNE
MARGARET SULLAVAN
ARTHUR SULLIVAN
JESSICA TANDY
LAURETTE TAYLOR

ELLEN TERRY
TOMMY TUNE
GWEN VERDON
ROBIN WAGNER
NANCY WALKER
ELI WALLACH
JAMES WALLACK
LESTER WALLACK
TONY WALTON
DOUGLAS TURNER WARD
DAVID WARFIELD
ETHEL WATERS
CLIFTON WEBB
JOSEPH WEBER
MARGARET WEBSTER
KURT WEILL
ORSON WELLES
MAE WEST
ROBERT WHITEHEAD
THORNTON WILDER
BERT WILLIAMS
TENNESSEE WILLIAMS
LANFORD WILSON
P.G. WODEHOUSE
PEGGY WOOD
ALEXANDER WOOLLCOTT
IRENE WORTH
ED WYNN
VINCENT YOUMANS
STARK YOUNG
FLORENZ ZIEGFELD
PATRICIA ZIPPRODT

THE THEATER HALL OF FAME
FOUNDERS AWARD

Established in 1993 in honor of Earl Blackwell, James M. Nederlander, Gerard Oestreicher and Arnold Weissberger, The Theater Hall of Fame Founders Award is voted annually by the Hall's board of directors to an individual for his or her outstanding contribution to the theater.

1993   JAMES M. NEDERLANDER
1994   KITTY CARLISLE HART
1995   HARVEY SABINSON

1996   HENRY HEWES
1997   OTIS L. GUERNSEY JR.
1998   EDWARD COLTON

MARGO JONES
CITIZEN OF THE THEATER
MEDAL

Presented annually to a citizen of the theater who has made a lifetime commitment to the encouragement of the living theater in the United States and has demonstrated an understanding and affirmation of the craft of playwriting.

1961 LUCILLE LORTEL	1968 DAVEY MARLIN-JONES
1962 MICHAEL ELLIS	ELLEN STEWART
1963 JUDITH RUTHERFORD	(Workshop Award)
MARECHAL	1969 ADRIAN HALL
GEORGE SAVAGE	EDWARD PARONE &
(University Award)	GORDON DAVIDSON
1964 RICHARD BARR,	(Workshop Award)
EDWARD ALBEE &	1970 JOSEPH PAPP
CLINTON WILDER	1971 ZELDA FICHANDLER
RICHARD A. DUPREY	1972 JULES IRVING
(University Award)	1973 DOUGLAS TURNER
1965 WYNN HANDMAN	WARD
MARSTON BALCH	1974 PAUL WEIDNER
(University Award)	1975 ROBERT KALFIN
1966 JON JORY	1976 GORDON DAVIDSON
ARTHUR BALLET	1977 MARSHALL W. MASON
(University Award)	1978 JON JORY
1967 PAUL BAKER	1979 ELLEN STEWART
GEORGE C. WHITE	1980 JOHN CLARK DONAHUE
(Workshop Award)	1981 LYNNE MEADOW

1982 ANDRE BISHOP
1983 BILL BUSHNELL
1984 GREGORY MOSHER
1985 JOHN LION
1986 LLOYD RICHARDS
1987 GERALD CHAPMAN
1988 NO AWARD
1989 MARGARET GOHEEN
1990 RICHARD COE
1991 OTIS L. GUERNSEY JR.
1992 ABBOT VAN NOSTRAND
1993 HENRY HEWES
1994 JANE ALEXANDER
1995 ROBERT WHITEHEAD
1996 AL HIRSCHFELD
1997 GEORGE C. WHITE
1998 JAMES HOUGHTON

1998–99 PUBLICATION
OF RECENTLY-PRODUCED NEW PLAYS
AND NEW TRANSLATIONS/ADAPTATIONS

American Beauty. Cliff Fannin Baker et al. Dramatic Publishing (libretto, acting edition).
As Bees in Honey Drown. Douglas Carter Beane. Dramatists Play Service (acting edition).
Baby Anger. Peter Hedges. Dramatists Play Service (acting edition).
Beauty Queen of Leenane, The, and Other Plays. Martin McDonagh. Random House.
Blue Heart. Caryl Churchill. TCG (paperback).
Blue Room, The. David Hare. Grove (paperback).
Cakewalk. Peter Feibleman. Dramatists Play Service (acting edition).
Corpus Christi. Terrence McNally. Grove (paperback), (acting edition, Dramatists Play Service).
Cripple of Inishmaan, The. Random House (paperback), (acting edition, Dramatists Play Service).
Crunch Time, The. Mark Medoff and Phil Treon. Dramatists Play Service (acting edition).
Dimly Perceived Threats to the System. Jon Klein. Dramatists Play Service (acting edition).
For the Pleasure of Seeing Her Again. Michel Tremblay, translated by Linda Gaboriau. Talon (paperback)
Golden Child. David Henry Hwang. TCG. (paperback).
Gun-Shy. Richard Dresser. Dramatists Play Service (acting edition).
Herbal Bed, The. Peter Whelan. International Musical Publishing (paperback), (acting edition, Dramatists Play Service).
Home Fires. Jack Heifner. Dramatic Publishing (acting edition).
How I Learned to Drive. Paula Vogel. Dramatists Play Service (acting edition).
I Ain't Yo' Uncle. Robert Alexander. Dramatists Play Service (acting edition).
Humanafestival '98, The Complete Plays. Edited by Michael Bigelow and Amy Wegener. Smith & Kraus (paperback).
Insurrection: Holding History. Robert O'Hara. TCG (paperback).
Joy of Going Somewhere Definite, The. Quincy Long. Dramatists Play Service (acting edition).
Labor Day. A. R. Gurney. Dramatists Play Service (acting edition).
Lonesome West, The. Martin McDonagh. Methuen (paperback), (acting edition, Dramatists Play Service).
Marlene. Pam Gems. Oberon (paperback).
Men on the Verge of a His-panic Breakdown. Guillermo Reyes. Dramatic Publishing (acting edition).
Mr. Bundy. Jane Martin. Samuel French (acting edition).
Mr. Peters' Connections. Arthur Miller. Dramatists Play Service (acting edition).
Mud, River, Stone. Lynn Nottage. Dramatists Play Service (acting edition).
Mizlansky/Zilinsky or "Schmucks." Jon Robin Baitz. TCG (paperback), (acting edition, Dramatists Play Service).
New York Stories. Jason Milligan. Samuel French (acting edition).
Old Settler, The John Henry Redwood. Dramatists Play Service. (acting edition).
One-Act Plays edited by Marisa Smith. Ensemble Studio Theater Marathon 1996. Smith & Kraus (paperback).
One-Act Plays edited by Marisa Smith. Ensemble Studio Theater Marathon 1997. Smith & Kraus (paperback).
Phèdre. Racine, translated by Ted Hughes. Farrar Straus.
Plunge. Christopher Kyle. Dramatists Play Service. (acting edition).
Pride's Crossing. Tina Howe. TCG (paperback).
Question of Mercy, A. David Rabe. Grove (paperback).
Side Man. Warren Leight. Grove (paperback).
Skull in Connemara, A. Martin McDonagh. Methuen (paperback).
Steward of Christendom, The. Sebastian Barry. Methuen USA (paperback).
Sympathetic Magic. Lanford Wilson. Dramatists Play Service (acting edition).
Three Days of Rain. Richard Greenberg. Dramatists Play Service (acting edition).
Unexpected Man, The. Yasmina Reza. Faber & Faber (paperback).

Valparaiso. Don DeLillo. Scribners.
Vernon Early. Horton Foote. Dramatists Play Service (acting edition).
Via Dolorosa & When Shall We Live? David Hare. Faber & Faber (paperback).
Visiting Mr. Green. Jeff Baron. Dramatists Play Service (acting edition).
Water Children, The. Wendy MacLeod. Dramatists Play Service (acting edition).
Weir, The. Conor McPherson. Nick Hern (paperback).
Wit. Margaret Edson. Faber & Faber (paperback).

A SELECTED LIST OF OTHER PLAYS PUBLISHED IN 1998–99

After Darwin. Timberlake Wertenbaker. Faber & Faber (paperback).
Black South African Women: An Anthology of Plays, edited by Kathy Perkins. Routledge (paperback).
Blues for an Alabama Sky. Pearl Cleage. Dramatists Play Service (acting edition).
Cabaret: The Illustrated Book & Lyrics. Joe Masteroff, John Kander and Fred Ebb. Newmarket.
Collected Works: Volume II 1970–1983. Lanford Wilson. Smith & Kraus (paperback).
Collected Short Plays by Thornton Wilder—Volume II, The. TCG (paperback).
Contemporary African Plays, edited by Martin Banham and Jane Plastow. Methuen (paperback).
Death of a Saleman: 50th Anniversary Edition. Arthur Miller. Penguin and DBS (also paperback).
Four Jacobean Sex Tragedies, edited by Martin Wiggins. Oxford (paperback).
From the Other Side of the Century II: A New American Drama 1960–1995, edited by Douglas Messerli and Mac Wellman. Sun & Moon Press (paperback).
God, Man and Devil: Yiddish Plays in Translation, translated by Nahma and Sandrow. (paperback).
Haroun and the Sea of Stories. Salman Rushdie, adapted by Tim Supple and David Tushingham. Faber & Faber (paperback).
Leo Tolstoy: Plays—Volume Three, 1894–1910, translated by Marvin Kantor and Tanya Tulchinksy. Northwestern University Press (paperback).
Marat/Sade, The Investigation, The Shadow of the Body of the Coachman. Peter Weiss, edited and introduced by Robert Cohen. Continuum (paperback).
Marsha Norman: Collected Works—Volume One. Smith & Kraus (paperback).
My Night With Reg. Kevin Elyot. Nick Hern (paperback).
New Plays: Joyce Carol Oates. Braziller (cloth and paperback).
Operas & Plays. Gertrude Stein. Barrytown (paperback).
Peter Pan. J. M. Barrie, adapted by Caird and Nunn. Methuen (paperback).
Plays by Richard Nelson: Volume One. Richard Nelson. Broadway Play Publishing (paperback).
Plays by Richard Nelson: Volume Two. Richard Nelson. Broadway Play Publishing (paperback).
Plays 3—David Storey. David Storey. Methuen (paperback).
Queen Amarantha: A Romantic Adventure. Charles Busch. Samuel French (acting edition).
Russian Mirror—Three Plays by Russian Women, edited by Melissa Smith (paperback).
Sanctuary. David Williamson. Currency Press (paperback).
Scotland Plays: New Scottish Drama, introduced by Philip Howard. Nick Hern (paperback).
Sean O'Casey: Plays 1. Sean O'Casey. Faber & Faber (paperback).
Sean O'Casey: Plays 2. Sean O'Casey. Faber & Faber (paperback).
7 Short Farces. Anton Chekhov, translated by Paul Schmidt. Dramatists Play Service (paperback).
Tartuffe and The Bourgeois Gentleman. Molière. Dover (paperback).
Two Comedies by Catherine the Great. Catherine the Great, translated and edited by Lurana Donnels O'Malley. Harwood (paperback).
Two Trilogies. Israel Horovitz. Smith & Kraus (paperback).
Wake, The. Steve Allen. Dramatic Publishing (acting edition).
Weir and Other Plays, The. Conor McPherson. TCG (paperback).

NECROLOGY
MAY 1998–MAY 1999

PERFORMERS

Allen, Robert (92)—October 9, 1998
Alyn, Kirk (88)—March 15, 1999
Ballantine, Bill (88)—May 14, 1999
Barnes, Binnie (95)—July 27, 1998
Bartok, Eva (69)—August 1, 1998
Bates, Clayton (91)—December 6, 1998
Bentley, Muriel (82)—March 8, 1999
Beriosova, Svetlana (66)—November 10, 1998
Blau, Gina (92)—October 23, 1998
Bowman, Patricia (mid-90s)—March 18, 1999
Brooks, David (83)—March 31, 1999
Brown, Charles (76)—January 21, 1999
Brown, Vanessa (71)—May 21, 1999
Bykov, Rolan (68)—October 6, 1998
Caccialanza, Gisella (83)—July 16, 1998
Calhoun, Rory (76)—April 28, 1999
Cameron, Hope (78)—November 20, 1998
Carelli, Gabor (83)—January 22, 1999
Carter, Helen (70)—June 2, 1998
Cass, Peggy (74)—March 8, 1999
Chambers, Madelaine (72)—April 30, 1999
Clark, Dana (85)—September 11, 1998
Clark, Lon (86)—October 1998
Cody, Iron Eyes (80s)—December 30, 1998
Corby, Ellen (87)—April 14, 1999
Corio, Ann (80s)—March 1, 1999
Cornelius, Ruth (98)—November 30, 1998
D'Andrea, Tom (88)—May 14, 1998
Dayton, Danny (75)—February 6, 1999
Dempsey, Jerome (69)—August 27, 1998
Denison, Michael (82)—July 22, 1998
Denning, Richard (85)—October 11, 1998
Douglas, Robert (89)—January 11, 1999
Edwards, Penny (70)—August 25, 1998
Feuillere, Edwige (91)—November 13, 1998
Field, Sylvia (97)—July 31, 1998
Fowley, Douglas V. (86)—May 21, 1998
Frann, Mary (55)—September 23, 1998
Gerson, Betty Lou (84)—January 12, 1999
Gilbert, Edmund (67)—May 8, 1999
Gomez, Thomas (77)—October 29, 1998
Goring, Marius (86)—September 30, 1998
Grillo, Joann (59)—February 1, 1999
Hall, Huntz (78)—January 20, 1999
Hatfield, Hurd (80)—December 25, 1998
Hervey, Irene (89)—December 20, 1998
Hickson, Joan (92)—October 17, 1998
Hobson, Valerie (81)—November 13, 1998
Hutchinson, Josephine (94)—June 4, 1998
Jones, Henry (87)—May 17, 1999

Khambatta, Persis (49)—August 18, 1998
Kiley, Richard (76)—March 5, 1999
King, Brett (79)—January 14, 1999
Kinskey, Leonid (95)—September 9, 1998
Korvin, Charles (90)—June 18, 1998
Layburn, Shirley Dinsdale (72)—May 9, 1999
Leeds, Phil (82)—August 16, 1998
Lewis, Bobo (72)—November 6, 1998
Lewis, Shari (65)—August 2, 1998
Maher, Joseph (64)—July 17, 1998
Manners, David (97)—December 23, 1998
Marais, Jean (84)—November 8, 1998
Marshall, E. G. (88)—August 24, 1998
Martinez, Enrique (72)—November 17, 1998
Mason, Margaret (58)—March 26, 1999
McAllister, Bob (63)—July 21, 1998
McDowall, Roddy (70)—October 3, 1998
Menken, Shepard (77)—January 2, 1999
Merrell, Richard (75)—September 13, 1998
Merritt, Theresa (75)—June 12, 1998
Micale, Paul J. (83)—January 16, 1999
Miller, Buzz (75)—February 23, 1999
Morton, Gary (74)—March 30, 1999
Nijinsky, Kyra (84)—September 1, 1998
Nitch, Dorothy Tuttle (80)—August 12, 1998
Nolan, Jeanette (89)—June 5, 1998
Olvis, William Edward (70)—November 27, 1998
O'Neill, Dick (70)—November 17, 1998
O'Sullivan, Maureen (87)—June 22, 1998
Paris, Jonni (66)—January 26, 1999
Parla, Alicia (84)—October 10, 1998
Pearlman, Stephen (63)—September 30, 1998
Peck, Bob (53)—April 4, 1999
Peterson, Norma (83)—September 24, 1998
Pierce, Charles (72)—May 25, 1999
Popwell, Albert (72)—April 9, 1999
Preston, William (77)—July 10, 1998
Ralov, Kirsten (77)—May 31, 1999
Ray, Leah (82)—May 27, 1999
Reed, Oliver (61)—May 2, 1999
Reilly, Hugh (82)—July 17, 1998
Remsen, Bert (74)—April 22, 1999
Rogers, Charles "Buddy" (94)—April 21, 1999
Rogers, Helen Priest (85)—March 2, 1999
Rolle, Esther (78)—November 17, 1998
Rossington, Norman (70)—May 21, 1999
Sabin, Evelyn (90)—October 27, 1998
Santacroce, Mary Nell—February 17, 1999
Schmidt, Paul (65)—February 19, 1999
Schnabel, Stefan (87)—March 13, 1999
Shirley, Mercedes (71)—January 29, 1999
Squires, Dorothy (83)—April 14, 1998
St. Cyr, Lili (80)—January 29, 1999

Sterling, Philip (76)—November 30, 1998
Stern, Joan Engel (78)—January 18, 1999
Stickney, Dorothy (101)—June 2, 1998
Stoler, Shirley (70)—February 17, 1999
Strasberg, Susan (60)—January 21, 1999
Strickland, David (29)—March 22, 1999
Taylor, Don (78)—December 29, 1998
Terrell, St. John (81)—October 9, 1998
Thomas, Michelle (29)—December 22, 1998
Thompson, Kay (95)—July 2, 1998
Thornton, Barbara (48)—November 8, 1998
Trow, Bob (72)—November 3, 1998
Truex, Sylvia Field (97)—July 31, 1998
Vander Pyl, Jean (79)—April 10, 1999
Verrill, Virginia (82)—January 18, 1999
Vore, Lucille (82)—April 8, 1999
Wallace, Billye Ree (73)—March 3, 1999
Wedemeyer, Herman (74)—January 25, 1999
Wences, Senor (103)—April 20, 1999
Wendt, William Charles (64)—December 11, 1998
Whitehead, O. Z. (87)—July 29, 1998
Wilson, Flip (64)—November 25, 1998
Wilson, Orlandus (81)—December 30, 1998
Young, Gayle (63)—January 8, 1999
Young, Robert (91)—July 21, 1998
Zaslow, Michael (54)—December 6, 1998
Zucco, Stella (90)—April 5, 1999

PLAYWRIGHTS

Alfred, William (76)—May 22, 1999
Aloni, Nissim (72)—June 13, 1998
Apstein, Theodore (80)—July 26, 1998
Auerbach, Arnold M. (86)—October 19, 1998
Carter, Randolph (90)—October 12, 1998
Delgado, Louis A. Jr. (55)—December 1, 1998
Ernotte, Andre Gilbert (55)—March 8, 1999
Farris, Jack (77)—November 26, 1998
Goldman, James (71)—October 28, 1998
Green, Julian (97)—August 13, 1998
Hopkins, John R. (67)—July 23, 1998
Kane, Sarah (28)—February 20, 1999
Kanin, Garson (86)—March 13, 1999
Lardner, Rex (80)—July 27, 1998
Locke, Sam (81)—September 18, 1998
Marasco, Robert (62)—December 6, 1998
Miller, Sigmund (87)—August 5, 1998
Newley, Anthony (67)—April 14, 1999
Spies, Adrian (78)—October 2, 1998
Stone, Jesse (97)—April 1, 1999
Turney, Catherine (92)—September 9, 1998
Weidman, Jerome (85)—October 6, 1998
Wright, Damon (48)—December 29, 1998

COMPOSERS, LYRICISTS SONGWRITERS

Albright, William (53)—September 17, 1998
Barer, Marshall (75)—August 25, 1998
Bart, Lionel (68)—April 3, 1999
Boatwright, Howard (80)—February 20, 1999
Collis, John Leon (92)—January 12, 1999
Driftwood, Jimmy (91)—July 12, 1998
Eliscu, Edward (96)—June 18, 1998
Foxx, Charlie (64)—September 18, 1998
Gold, Ernest (77)—March 17, 1999
Gold, Wally (70)—June 7, 1998
Higgins, Dick (60)—October 25, 1998
Holmes, James (59)—January 7, 1999
Kallen, Lucille (76)—January 18, 1999
Kim, Earl (78)—November 19, 1998
McRae, Theodore (91)—March 4, 1999
Meyerowitz, Jan (85)—December 15, 1998
Misraki, Paul (90)—October 26, 1998
Moss, Jeffrey (56)—September 24, 1998
Page, Gene (58)—August 24, 1998
Schnittke, Alfred (63)—August 3, 1998
Spence, Alexander (52)—April 16, 1999
Sur, Donald (64)—May 26, 1999
Wells, Robert (76)—September 23, 1998

PRODUCERS, DIRECTORS CHOREOGRAPHERS

Allyn, William (71)—January 3, 1999
Arron, Judith (56)—December 18, 1998
Berger, Richard H. (94)—October 8, 1998
Box, Betty Evelyn (78)—January 15, 1999
Bull, Richard (67)—July 4, 1998
Burge, Gregg (40)—July 4, 1998
Butler, Henry (79)—August 1, 1998
Cates, Joseph (74)—October 19, 1998
Coleman, Shepard (74)—May 12, 1998
Cratty, Bill (47)—September 9, 1998
Dalrymple, Jean (96)—November 15, 1998
Farber, Viola (67)—December 24, 1998
Garth, Midi (83)—January 28, 1999
Golovine, Serge (73)—July 31, 1998
Grade, Lew (91)—December 13, 1998
Grotowski, Jerzy (65)—January 14, 1999
Gunsberg, Sheldon (78)—June 18, 1998
Hammerstein, James (57)—January 7, 1999
Kormendi, Joan M. (81)—May 18, 1998
Kubrick, Stanley—March 7, 1999
Kulik, Buzz (76)—January 13, 1999
Kurosawa, Akira (88)—September 6, 1998
Levenson, Emanuel (81)—June 9, 1998
Lortel, Lucille (98)—April 4, 1999
Manuel, Michael (70)—April 5, 1999

McEwen, Terence A. (69)—September 14, 1998
Pakula, Alan J. (70)—November 19, 1998
Penn, Leo (77)—September 5, 1998
Price, Lorin E. (77)—December 28, 1998
Quintero, Jose (74)—February 27, 1999
Robbins, Jerome (79)—July 29, 1998
Sher, Louis K. (84)—November 25, 1998
Turner, Lily (92)—December 28, 1998
Valaire, Rosemary (68)—May 7, 1999
Wright, Garland (52)—July 24, 1998

DESIGNERS

Brecht, Mary (65)—June 3, 1998
DeVerna, Francis P. (70)—May 27, 1998
Edwards, Ben (82)—February 12, 1999
Lisz, Gary (44)—August 11, 1998
Moore, Gene (88)—November 23, 1998
Roberts, Don (64)—January 10, 1999
Sabbatini, Enrico (66)—November 25, 1998

MUSICIANS

Abram, Jacques (83)—October 5, 1998
Alexay, Alexander (97)—April 20, 1999
Blades, James (97)—May 19, 1999
Byard, Jaki (76)—February 11, 1999
Crowson, Lamar (73)—August 25, 1998
Deems, Barrett (83)—September 15, 1998
Dixon, Joe (81)—May 28, 1998
Dunbar, Ted (61)—May 29, 1998
Haufrecht, Herbert (88)—June 23, 1998
Hirt, Al (76)—April 26, 1999
Kaplan, Max (87)—August 4, 1998
Liston, Melba (73)—April 23, 1999
McCreary, Lewis Melvin (71)—January 20, 1999
Menuhin, Yehudi (82)—March 12, 1999
Norvo, Red (91)—April 6, 1999
Parker, Errol (72)—July 2, 1998
Petrucciani, Michel (36)—January 6, 1999
Ryan, Thomas F. (97)—July 26, 1998
Shamblin, Eldon (82)—August 5, 1998
Sweet, Darrell (51)—April 30, 1999
Tapscott, Horace (64)—February 28, 1999
Troup, Bobby (80)—February 7, 1999
Van Eps, George (85)—November 29, 1998
Wann, Lois (87)—February 23, 1999
Waters, Benny (96)—August 11, 1998
Wright, George (77)—May 10, 1998

CONDUCTORS

Addison, John (78)—December 7, 1998
de Paur, Leonard (83)—November 7, 1998
Irwin, William C.K. (91)—October 23, 1998
MacLean, Bryan (52)—December 25, 1998
Sacher, Paul (93)—May 21, 1999
Wechter, Julius (63)—February 1, 1999
Whallon, Evan (74)—June 14, 1998

CRITICS

Carmody, John (74)—March 1, 1999
Coe, Donna (46)—June 13, 1998
Dance, Stanley (88)—February 23, 1999
Kaplan, Mike (80)—August 23, 1998
Manners, Dorothy (95)—August 25, 1998
Overbey, David (62)—December 16, 1998
Siskel, Gene (53)—February 20, 1999
Strongin, Theodore (79)—November 24, 1998
Williamson, Bruce (71)—October 6, 1998

OTHERS

Adams, David (85)—December 27, 1998
    Chairman, NBC
Aiken, Elaine (71)—July 12, 1998
    Acting teacher
Althoff, Adolf (85)—October 14, 1998
    German circus executive
Ambler, Eric (85)—October 22, 1998
    Novelist
Autry, Gene (91)—October 2, 1998
    Cowboy star
Baer, Nancy Van Norman (55)—September 29, 1998
    Curator of dance, theater
Berle, Phil (97)—January 2, 1999
    Brother of Milton
Cobb, Sally (83)—September 22, 1998
    Top fashion model
Currie, Steve (52)—October 2, 1998
    CBS TV executive
de Rothschild, Batsheva (84)—April 20, 1999
    Patron of Martha Graham
Delany, Sarah (109)—January 25, 1999
    Subject of play
Dickler, Gerald (86)—February 13, 1999
    Attorney
Dokoudovsky, Vladimir (79)—December 2, 1998
    Founder, Ballet Theater

Elias, Eddie (69)—November 15, 1998
Attorney
Faine, Hyman R. (88)—April 8, 1999
American Guild of Musical Artists
Ferguson, Magdalene (91)—January 24, 1999
Publicist
Forest, Jean-Claude (68)—December 30, 1998
Created *Barbarella*
Frank, Gerold (91)—September 17, 1998
Author
Gallagher, William P. (77)—November 14, 1998
Entertainment executive
Githens, William (92)—November 10, 1998
Newsreel pioneer
Godden, Rumer (90)—November 8, 1998
Author
Godowsky, Frances Gershwin (92)—January 18, 1999
Sister of George and Ira
Golden, Fred (83)—July 3, 1998
Advertising executive
Groman, Arthur (84)—December 1, 1998
Attorney
Harrington, Sybil (89)—September 17, 1998
Philanthopist
Horowitz, Wanda Toscanini (90)—August 21, 1998
Widow of Vladimir
Hudes, Albert B. (75)—February 8, 1999
City Opera
Johnson, Deane F. (80)—February 28, 1999
Attorney
Joseph, Peter T. (47)—June 25, 1998
American Ballet Theater
Joyner, Florence Griffith (38)—September 21, 1998
Track star
Kane, Bob (83)—November 3, 1998
Created *Batman*
Keaton, Eleanor Norris (80)—October 19, 1998
Widow of Buster
Keysar, Franklin (60)—January 25, 1999
Stage manager
Lee, Francis (85)—May 29, 1998
D-Day cameraman
Lyons, John T. (54)—July 16, 1998
ABC News Radio
Machlis, Joseph (92)—October 17, 1998
Opera translator

Margolis, Ben (88)—January 27, 1999
Attorney
Mitosky, Morton (91)—February 5, 1999
Attorney
Mossman, Stuart (56)—March 2, 1999
Guitar maker
Murrow, Janet (88)—December 18, 1998
Widow of Edward R.
Norel, Lillias (88)—January 23, 1999
Wardrobe mistress
O'Connor, Kendall (90)—May 27, 1998
Disney layout artist
Peters, Alton E. (64)—May 31, 1999
Metropolitan Opera Guild
Prokofiev, Oleg (69)—August 20, 1998
Son of composer
Rabinovitch, Reuben (94)—July 12, 1998
Publicist
Roberts, Flora (77)—December 12, 1998
Agent
Rogers, Roy (86)—July 6, 1998
Cowboy star
Roventini, Johnny (86)—November 30, 1998
"Call for Philip Morris" voice
Samuel, Harold E. (75)—April 20, 1999
Music librarian
Schwerner, Armand (71)—February 4, 1999
Poet
Searchinger, Marian (81)—March 16, 1999
Agent
Shaw, Sam (87)—April 5, 1999
Photojournalist
Shipstad, Eddie (91)—August 20, 1998
Ice Follies
Sloane, Irving (73)—June 21, 1998
Guitar maker
Smith, Claire M. (64)—August 15, 1998
Agent
Stewart, Rudolph (74)—April 28, 1999
Carnegie Hall
Torchia, Emily (91)—October 7, 1998
Publicist
Treyz, Oliver E. (80)—June 14, 1998
ABC Television
Ward, Peter (61)—March 18, 1999
Variety
Weaver, Richard B. (88)—May 17, 1998
Publicist
Wells, Davina (58)—June 24, 1998
Agent

THE BEST PLAYS, 1894–1996;
THE MAJOR PRIZEWINNERS, 1997–1998

Listed in alphabetical order below are all those works selected as Best Plays in previous volumes of the *Best Plays* series through 1995–96, and the major prize-winners and special *Best Plays* citation in 1996–98. Opposite each title is given the volume in which the play appears, its opening date and its total number of performances. Two separate opening-date and performance-number entries signify two separate engagements off Broadway and on Broadway when the original production was transferred from one area to the other, usually in an off-to-on direction. Those plays marked with an asterisk (*) were still playing on June 1, 1999 and their number of performances was figured through May 31, 1999. Adaptors and translators are indicated by (ad) and (tr), the symbols (b), (m) and (l) stand for the author of the book, music and lyrics in the case of musicals and (c) signifies the credit for the show's conception, (i) for its inspiration. Entries identified as 94–99 and 99–09 are 19th century plays from one of the retrospective volumes. 94–95, 95–96, 96–97 and 97–98 are late 20th century plays.

PLAY	VOLUME	OPENED	PERFS
ABE LINCOLN IN ILLINOIS—Robert E. Sherwood	38–39	Oct. 15, 1938	472
ABRAHAM LINCOLN—John Drinkwater	19–20	Dec. 15, 1919	193
ACCENT ON YOUTH—Samson Raphaelson	34–35	Dec. 25, 1934	229
ADAM AND EVA—Guy Bolton, George Middleton	19–20	Sept. 13, 1919	312
ADAPTATION—Elaine May; and NEXT—Terrence McNally	68–69	Feb. 10, 1969	707
AFFAIRS OF STATE—Louis Verneuil	50–51	Sept. 25, 1950	610
AFTER THE FALL—Arthur Miller	63–64	Jan. 23, 1964	208
AFTER THE RAIN—John Bowen	67–68	Oct. 9, 1967	64
AFTER-PLAY—Anne Meara	94–95	Jan. 31, 1995	400
AGNES OF GOD—John Pielmeier	81–82	Mar. 30, 1982	599
AH, WILDERNESS!—Eugene O'Neill	33–34	Oct. 2, 1933	289
AIN'T SUPPOSED TO DIE A NATURAL DEATH—(b, m, l) Melvin Van Peebles	71–72	Oct. 20, 1971	325
ALIEN CORN—Sidney Howard	32–33	Feb. 20, 1933	98
ALISON'S HOUSE—Susan Glaspell	30–31	Dec. 1, 1930	41
ALL MY SONS—Arthur Miller	46–47	Jan. 29, 1947	328
ALL IN THE TIMING—David Ives	93–94	Feb. 17, 1994	526
ALL OVER TOWN—Murray Schisgal	74–75	Dec. 29, 1974	233
ALL THE WAY HOME—Tad Mosel, based on James Agee's novel *A Death in the Family*	60–61	Nov. 30, 1960	333
ALLEGRO—(b, l) Oscar Hammerstein II, (m) Richard Rodgers	47–48	Oct. 10, 1947	315
AMADEUS—Peter Shaffer	80–81	Dec. 17, 1980	1,181
AMBUSH—Arthur Richman	21–22	Oct. 10, 1921	98
AMERICA HURRAH—Jean-Claude van Itallie	66–67	Nov. 6, 1966	634
AMERICAN BUFFALO—David Mamet	76–77	Feb. 16, 1977	135
AMERICAN ENTERPRISE—Jeffrey Sweet (special citation)	93–94	Apr. 13, 1994	15
AMERICAN PLAN, THE—Richard Greenberg	90–91	Dec. 16, 1990	37

PLAY	VOLUME	OPENED	PERFS
AMERICAN WAY, THE—George S. Kaufman, Moss Hart.......	38–39 ..	Jan. 21, 1939 ..	164
AMPHITRYON 38—Jean Giraudoux, (ad) S.N. Behrman........	37–38 ..	Nov. 1, 1937 ..	153
AND A NIGHTINGALE SANG—C.P. Taylor.......................	83–84 ..	Nov. 27, 1983 ..	177
ANDERSONVILLE TRIAL, THE—Saul Levitt......................	59–60 ..	Dec. 29, 1959 ..	179
ANDORRA—Max Frisch, (ad) George Tabori	62–63 ..	Feb. 9, 1963 ..	9
ANGEL STREET—Patrick Hamilton.............................	41–42 ..	Dec. 5, 1941 ..	1,295
ANGELS FALL—Lanford Wilson	82–83 ..	Oct. 17, 1982 ..	65
	82–83 ..	Jan. 22, 1983 ..	64
ANGELS IN AMERICA, PART I: MILLENNIUM APPROACHES— Tony Kushner...	92–93 ..	May 4, 1993 ..	367
ANGELS IN AMERICA, PART II: PERESTROIKA—Tony Kushner...	93–94 ..	Nov. 23, 1994 ..	216
ANIMAL KINGDOM, THE—Philip Barry	31–32 ..	Jan. 12, 1932 ..	183
ANNA CHRISTIE—Eugene O'Neill................................	21–22 ..	Nov. 2, 1921 ..	177
ANNA LUCASTA—Philip Yordan.................................	44–45 ..	Aug. 30, 1944 ..	957
ANNE OF THE THOUSAND DAYS—Maxwell Anderson..........	48–49 ..	Dec. 8, 1948 ..	286
ANNIE—(b) Thomas Meehan, (m) Charles Strouse, (l) Martin Charnin, based on Harold Gray's comic strip *Little Orphan Annie*..........	76–77 ..	Apr. 21, 1977 ..	2,377
ANOTHER LANGUAGE—Rose Franken	31–32 ..	Apr. 25, 1932 ..	344
ANOTHER PART OF THE FOREST—Lillian Hellman	46–47 ..	Nov. 20, 1946 ..	182
ANTIGONE—Jean Anouilh, (ad) Lewis Galantiere	45–46 ..	Feb. 18, 1946 ..	64
APPLAUSE—(b) Betty Comden and Adolph Green, (m) Charles Strouse, (l) Lee Adams, based on the film *All About Eve* and the original story by Mary Orr......................	69–70 ..	Mar. 30, 1970 ..	896
APPLE TREE, THE—(b, l) Sheldon Harnick, (b, m) Jerry Bock, (add'l b) Jerome Coopersmith, based on stories by Mark Twain, Frank R. Stockton and Jules Feiffer	66–67 ..	Oct. 18, 1966 ..	463
ARCADIA—Tom Stoppard...	94–95 ..	Mar. 30, 1995 ..	173
ARISTOCRATS—Brian Friel......................................	88–89 ..	Apr. 25, 1989 ..	186
ARSENIC AND OLD LACE—Joseph Kesselring	40–41 ..	Jan. 10, 1941 ..	1,444
*ART—Yasmina Reza..	97–98 ..	Mar. 1, 1998 ..	521
AS HUSBANDS GO—Rachel Crothers	30–31 ..	Mar. 5, 1931 ..	148
AS IS—William M. Hoffman......................................	84–85 ..	Mar. 10, 1985 ..	49
	84–85 ..	May 1, 1985 ..	285
ASHES—David Rudkin...	76–77 ..	Jan. 25, 1977 ..	167
AUNT DAN AND LEMON—Wallace Shawn.......................	85–86 ..	Oct. 1, 1985 ..	191
AUTUMN GARDEN, THE—Lillian Hellman	50–51 ..	Mar. 7, 1951 ..	101
AWAKE AND SING—Clifford Odets...............................	34–35 ..	Feb. 19, 1935 ..	209
BAD MAN, THE—Porter Emerson Browne	20–21 ..	Aug. 30, 1920 ..	350
BAD HABITS—Terrence McNally.................................	73–74 ..	Feb. 4, 1974 ..	273
BAD SEED—Maxwell Anderson, based on William March's novel	54–55 ..	Dec. 8, 1954 ..	332
BARBARA FRIETCHIE—Clyde Fitch	99–09 ..	Oct. 23, 1899 ..	83
BAREFOOT IN ATHENS—Maxwell Anderson	51–52 ..	Oct. 31, 1951 ..	30
BAREFOOT IN THE PARK—Neil Simon...........................	63–64 ..	Oct. 23, 1963 ..	1,530
BARRETTS OF WIMPOLE STREET, THE—Rudolf Besier	30–31 ..	Feb. 9, 1931 ..	370
BEAUTY QUEEN OF LEENANE, THE—Martin McDonagh	97–98 ..	Feb. 26, 1998 ..	46
	97–98 ..	Apr. 23, 1998 ..	372
BECKET—Jean Anouilh, (tr) Lucienne Hill......................	60–61 ..	Oct. 5, 1960 ..	193

PLAY	VOLUME	OPENED	PERFS
BEDROOM FARCE—Alan Ayckbourn	78–79 ..	Mar. 29, 1979 ..	278
BEGGAR ON HORSEBACK—George S. Kaufman, Marc Connelly	23–24 ..	Feb. 12, 1924 ..	224
BEHOLD THE BRIDEGROOM—George Kelly	27–28 ..	Dec. 26, 1927 ..	88
BELL, BOOK AND CANDLE—John van Druten	50–51 ..	Nov. 14, 1950 ..	233
BELL FOR ADANO, A—Paul Osborn, based on John Hersey's novel	44–45 ..	Dec. 6, 1944 ..	304
BENEFACTORS—Michael Frayn	85–86 ..	Dec. 22, 1985 ..	217
BENT—Martin Sherman	79–80 ..	Dec. 2, 1979 ..	240
BERKELEY SQUARE—John L. Balderston	29–30 ..	Nov. 4, 1929 ..	229
BERNARDINE—Mary Chase	52–53 ..	Oct. 16, 1952 ..	157
BEST LITTLE WHOREHOUSE IN TEXAS, THE—(b) Larry L. King, Peter Masterson, (m, l) Carol Hall	77–78 ..	Apr. 17, 1978 ..	64
	78–79 ..	June 19, 1978 ..	1,639
BEST MAN, THE—Gore Vidal	59–60 ..	Mar. 31, 1960 ..	520
BETRAYAL—Harold Pinter	79–80 ..	Jan. 5, 1980 ..	170
BEYOND THE HORIZON—Eugene O'Neill	19–20 ..	Feb. 2, 1920 ..	160
BIG FISH, LITTLE FISH—Hugh Wheeler	60–61 ..	Mar. 15, 1961 ..	101
BILL OF DIVORCEMENT, A—Clemence Dane	21–22 ..	Oct. 10, 1921 ..	173
BILLY BUDD—Louis O. Coxe, Robert Chapman, based on Herman Melville's novel	50–51 ..	Feb. 10, 1951 ..	105
BILOXI BLUES—Neil Simon	84–85 ..	Mar. 28, 1985 ..	524
BIOGRAPHY—S.N. Behrman	32–33 ..	Dec. 12, 1932 ..	267
BLACK COMEDY—Peter Shaffer	66–67 ..	Feb. 12, 1967 ..	337
BLITHE SPIRIT—Noel Coward	41–42 ..	Nov. 5, 1941 ..	657
BOESMAN AND LENA—Athol Fugard	70–71 ..	June 22, 1970 ..	205
BORN IN THE R.S.A.—Barney Simon in collaboration with the cast	86–87 ..	Oct. 1, 1986 ..	8
BORN YESTERDAY—Garson Kanin	45–46 ..	Feb. 4, 1946 ..	1,642
BOTH YOUR HOUSES—Maxwell Anderson	32–33 ..	Mar. 6, 1933 ..	72
BOY MEETS GIRL—Bella and Samuel Spewack	35–36 ..	Nov. 27, 1935 ..	669
BOY FRIEND, THE—(b, m, l) Sandy Wilson	54–55 ..	Sept. 30, 1954 ..	485
BOYS IN THE BAND, THE—Mart Crowley	67–68 ..	Apr. 15, 1968 ..	1,000
BRIDE OF THE LAMB, THE—William Hurlbut	25–26 ..	Mar. 30, 1926 ..	109
BRIEF MOMENT—S.N. Behrman	31–32 ..	Nov. 9, 1931 ..	129
BRIGADOON—(b, l) Alan Jay Lerner, (m) Frederick Loewe	46–47 ..	Mar. 13, 1947 ..	581
BROADWAY—Philip Dunning, George Abbott	26–27 ..	Sept. 16, 1926 ..	603
BROADWAY BOUND—Neil Simon	86–87 ..	Dec. 4, 1986 ..	756
BURLESQUE—George Manker Watters, Arthur Hopkins	27–28 ..	Sept. 1, 1927 ..	372
BUS STOP—William Inge	54–55 ..	Mar. 2, 1955 ..	478
BUTLEY—Simon Gray	72–73 ..	Oct. 31, 1972 ..	135
BUTTER AND EGG MAN, THE—George S. Kaufman	25–26 ..	Sept. 23, 1925 ..	243
BUTTERFLIES ARE FREE—Leonard Gershe	69–70 ..	Oct. 21, 1969 ..	1,128
CABARET—(b) Joe Masteroff, (m) John Kander, (l) Fred Ebb, based on John van Druten's play *I Am a Camera* and stories by Christopher Isherwood	66–67 ..	Nov. 20, 1966 ..	1,165
CACTUS FLOWER—Abe Burrows, based on a play by Pierre Barillet and Jean-Pierre Gredy	65–66 ..	Dec. 8, 1965 ..	1,234

PLAY	VOLUME	OPENED	PERFS
CAGE AUX FOLLES, LA—(see *La Cage aux Folles*)			
CAINE MUTINY COURT-MARTIAL, THE—Herman Wouk, based on his novel	53–54	Jan. 20, 1954	415
CALIFORNIA SUITE—Neil Simon	76–77	June 10, 1976	445
CALIGULA—Albert Camus, (ad) Justin O'Brien	59–60	Feb. 16, 1960	38
CALL IT A DAY—Dodie Smith	35–36	Jan. 28, 1936	194
CAMPING WITH HENRY & TOM—Mark St. Germain	94–95	Feb. 20, 1995	88
CANDIDE—(b) Lillian Hellman, based on Voltaire's satire (l) Richard Wilbur, John Latouche, Dorothy Parker, (m) Leonard Bernstein	56–57	Dec. 1, 1956	73
CANDLE IN THE WIND—Maxwell Anderson	41–42	Oct. 22, 1941	95
CARETAKER, THE—Harold Pinter	61–62	Oct. 4, 1961	165
CASE OF REBELLIOUS SUSAN, THE—Henry Arthur Jones	94–99	Dec. 20, 1894	80
CAT ON A HOT TIN ROOF—Tennessee Williams	54–55	Mar. 24, 1955	694
*CATS—(m) Andrew Lloyd Webber, based on T.S. Eliot's *Old Possum's Book of Practical Cats,* (add'l l) Trevor Nunn, Richard Stilgoe	82–83	Oct. 7, 1982	6,950
CELEBRATION—(b, l) Tom Jones, (m) Harvey Schmidt	68–69	Jan. 22, 1969	109
CHALK GARDEN, THE—Enid Bagnold	55–56	Oct. 26, 1955	182
CHANGELINGS, THE—Lee Wilson Dodd	23–24	Sept. 17, 1923	128
CHANGING ROOM, THE—David Storey	72–73	Mar. 6, 1973	192
CHAPTER TWO—Neil Simon	77–78	Dec. 4, 1977	857
CHICAGO—Maurine Dallas Watkins	26–27	Dec. 30, 1926	172
CHICAGO—(b) Fred Ebb, Bob Fosse, (m) John Kander, (l) Fred Ebb, based on the play by Maurine Dallas Watkins	75–76	June 3, 1975	898
CHICKEN FEED—Guy Bolton	23–24	Sept. 24, 1923	144
CHILDREN OF A LESSER GOD—Mark Medoff	79–80	Mar. 30, 1980	887
CHILDREN'S HOUR, THE—Lillian Hellman	34–35	Nov. 20, 1934	691
CHILD'S PLAY—Robert Marasco	69–70	Feb. 17, 1970	342
CHIPS WITH EVERYTHING—Arnold Wesker	63–64	Oct. 1, 1963	149
CHORUS LINE, A—(c) Michael Bennett, (b) James Kirkwood, Nicholas Dante, (m) Marvin Hamlisch, (l) Edward Kleban	74–75	Apr. 15, 1975	101
	75–76	July 25, 1975	6,137
CHRISTOPHER BLAKE—Moss Hart	46–47	Nov. 30, 1946	114
CIRCLE, THE—W. Somerset Maugham	21–22	Sept. 12, 1921	175
CITY OF ANGELS—(b) Larry Gelbart, (m) Cy Coleman, (l) David Zippel	89–90	Dec. 11, 1989	878
CLARENCE—Booth Tarkington	19–20	Sept. 20, 1919	306
CLAUDIA—Rose Franken	40–41	Feb. 12, 1941	722
CLEARING IN THE WOODS, A—Arthur Laurents	56–57	Jan. 10, 1957	36
CLIMATE OF EDEN, THE—Moss Hart, based on Edgar Mittleholzer's novel *Shadows Move Among Them*	52–53	Nov. 13, 1952	20
CLIMBERS, THE—Clyde Fitch	99–09	Jan. 21, 1901	163
CLOUD 9—Caryl Churchill	80–81	May 18, 1981	971
CLUTTERBUCK—Benn W. Levy	49–50	Dec. 3, 1949	218
COCKTAIL HOUR, THE—A.R. Gurney	88–89	Oct. 20, 1988	351
COCKTAIL PARTY, THE—T.S. Eliot	49–50	Jan. 21, 1950	409
COLD WIND AND THE WARM, THE—S.N. Behrman	58–59	Dec. 8, 1958	120
COLLECTION, THE—Harold Pinter	62–63	Nov. 26, 1962	578
COME BACK, LITTLE SHEBA—William Inge	49–50	Feb. 15, 1950	191

PLAY	VOLUME	OPENED	PERFS
COMEDIANS—Trevor Griffiths	76–77	Nov. 28, 1976	145
COMMAND DECISION—William Wister Haines	47–48	Oct. 1, 1947	408
COMPANY—(b) George Furth, (m, l) Stephen Sondheim	69–70	Apr. 26, 1970	705
COMPLAISANT LOVER, THE—Graham Greene	61–62	Nov. 1, 1961	101
CONDUCT UNBECOMING—Barry England	70–71	Oct. 12, 1970	144
CONFIDENTIAL CLERK, THE—T.S. Eliot	53–54	Feb. 11, 1954	117
CONNECTION, THE—Jack Gelber (supplement)	60–61	Feb. 22, 1961	722
CONSTANT WIFE, THE—W. Somerset Maugham	26–27	Nov. 29, 1926	295
CONTRACTOR, THE—David Storey	73–74	Oct. 17, 1973	72
CONVERSATIONS WITH MY FATHER—Herb Gardner	91–92	Mar. 29, 1992	402
COQUETTE—George Abbott, Ann Preston Bridgers	27–28	Nov. 8, 1927	366
CORN IS GREEN, THE—Emlyn Williams	40–41	Nov. 26, 1940	477
COUNTRY GIRL, THE—Clifford Odets	50–51	Nov. 10, 1950	235
COUNTY CHAIRMAN, THE—George Ade	99–09	Nov. 24, 1903	222
CRADLE SONG, THE—Gregorio & Maria Martinez Sierra, (tr) John Garrett Underhill	26–27	Jan. 24, 1927	57
CRAIG'S WIFE—George Kelly	25–26	Oct. 12, 1925	360
CRAZY FOR YOU—(b) Ken Ludwig, (m) George Gershwin, (l) Ira Gershwin, (c) Ken Ludwig, Mike Ockrent, (i) Guy Bolton, John McGowan	91–92	Feb. 19, 1992	1,622
CREATION OF THE WORLD AND OTHER BUSINESS, THE—Arthur Miller	72–73	Nov. 30, 1972	20
CREEPS—David E. Freeman	73–74	Dec. 4, 1973	15
CRIMES OF THE HEART—Beth Henley	80–81	Dec. 9, 1980	35
	81–82	Nov. 4, 1981	535
CRIMINAL CODE, THE—Martin Flavin	29–30	Oct. 2, 1929	173
CRUCIBLE, THE—Arthur Miller	52–53	Jan. 22, 1953	197
CRYPTOGRAM, THE—David Mamet	94–95	Apr. 13, 1995	62
CURTAINS—Stephen Bill	95–96	May 21, 1996	64
CYNARA—H.M. Harwood, R.F. Gore-Browne	31–32	Nov. 2, 1931	210
DA—Hugh Leonard	77–78	May 1, 1978	697
DAISY MAYME—George Kelly	26–27	Oct. 25, 1926	112
DAMASK CHEEK, THE—John van Druten, Lloyd Morris	42–43	Oct 22, 1942	93
DANCE AND THE RAILROAD, THE—David Henry Hwang	81–82	July 16, 1981	181
DANCING AT LUGHNASA—Brian Friel	91–92	Oct. 24, 1991	421
DANCING MOTHERS—Edgar Selwyn, Edmund Goulding	24–25	Aug. 11, 1924	312
DARK AT THE TOP OF THE STAIRS, THE—William Inge	57–58	Dec. 5, 1957	468
DARK IS LIGHT ENOUGH, THE—Christopher Fry	54–55	Feb. 23, 1955	69
DARKNESS AT NOON—Sidney Kingsley, based on Arthur Koestler's novel	50–51	Jan. 13, 1951	186
DARLING OF THE GODS, THE—David Belasco, John Luther Long	99–09	Dec. 3, 1902	182
DAUGHTERS OF ATREUS—Robert Turney	36–37	Oct. 14, 1936	13
DAY IN THE DEATH OF JOE EGG, A—Peter Nichols	67–68	Feb. 1, 1968	154
DEAD END—Sidney Kingsley	35–36	Oct. 28, 1935	687
DEADLY GAME, THE—James Yaffe, based on Friedrich Duerrenmatt's novel	59–60	Feb. 2, 1960	39
DEAR RUTH—Norman Krasna	44–45	Dec. 13, 1944	683

PLAY	VOLUME	OPENED	PERFS
DEATH OF A SALESMAN—Arthur Miller	48–49	Feb. 10, 1949	742
DEATH TAKES A HOLIDAY—Alberto Casella, (ad) Walter Ferris	29–30	Dec. 26, 1929	180
DEATHTRAP—Ira Levin	77–78	Feb. 26, 1978	1,793
DEBURAU—Sacha Guitry, (ad) Harley Granville Barker	20–21	Dec. 23, 1920	189
DECISION—Edward Chodorov	43–44	Feb. 2, 1944	160
DECLASSEE—Zoë Akins	19–20	Oct. 6, 1919	257
DEEP ARE THE ROOTS—Arnaud d'Usseau, James Gow	45–46	Sept. 26, 1945	477
DELICATE BALANCE, A—Edward Albee	66–67	Sept. 22, 1966	132
DEPUTY, THE—Rolf Hochhuth, (ad) Jerome Rothenberg	63–64	Feb. 26, 1964	109
DESIGN FOR LIVING—Noel Coward	32–33	Jan. 24, 1933	135
DESIRE UNDER THE ELMS—Eugene O'Neill	24–25	Nov. 11, 1924	208
DESPERATE HOURS, THE—Joseph Hayes, based on his novel	54–55	Feb. 10, 1955	212
DESTINY OF ME, THE—Larry Kramer	92–93	Oct. 20, 1992	175
DETECTIVE STORY—Sidney Kingsley	8–49	Mar. 23, 1949	581
DEVIL PASSES, THE—Benn W. Levy	31–32	Jan. 4, 1932	96
DEVIL'S ADVOCATE, THE—Dore Schary, based on Morris L. West's novel	60–61	Mar. 9, 1961	116
DIAL "M" FOR MURDER—Frederick Knott	52–53	Oct. 29, 1952	552
DIARY OF ANNE FRANK, THE—Frances Goodrich, Albert Hackett, based on Anne Frank's *The Diary of a Young Girl*	55–56	Oct. 5, 1955	717
DINING ROOM, THE—A.R. Gurney	81–82	Feb. 24, 1982	583
DINNER AT EIGHT—George S. Kaufman, Edna Ferber	32–33	Oct. 22, 1932	232
DISENCHANTED, THE—Budd Schulberg, Harvey Breit, based on Mr. Schulberg's novel	58–59	Dec. 3, 1958	189
DISRAELI—Louis N. Parker	09–19	Sept. 18, 1911	280
DISTAFF SIDE, THE—John van Druten	34–35	Sept. 25, 1934	177
DODSWORTH—Sidney Howard, based on Sinclair Lewis's novel	33–34	Feb. 24, 1934	315
DOUBLES—David Wiltse	84–85	May 8, 1985	277
DOUGHGIRLS, THE—Joseph Fields	42–43	Dec. 30, 1942	671
DOVER ROAD, THE—A.A. Milne	21–22	Dec. 23, 1921	324
DREAM GIRL—Elmer Rice	45–46	Dec. 14, 1945	348
DRESSER, THE—Ronald Harwood	81–82	Nov. 9, 1981	200
DRINKING IN AMERICA—Eric Bogosian	85–86	Jan. 19, 1986	94
DRIVING MISS DAISY—Alfred Uhry	86–87	Apr. 15, 1987	1,195
DROOD—(see *The Mystery of Edwin Drood*)			
DUEL OF ANGELS—Jean Giraudoux's *Pour Lucrèce*, (ad) Christopher Fry	59–60	Apr. 19, 1960	51
DULCY—George S. Kaufman, Marc Connelly	21–22	Aug. 13, 1921	246
DYBBUK, THE—S. Ansky, (ad) Henry G. Alsberg	25–26	Dec. 15, 1925	120
DYLAN—Sidney Michaels	63–64	Jan. 18, 1964	153
EASIEST WAY, THE—Eugene Walter	09–19	Jan. 19, 1909	157
EASTERN STANDARD—Richard Greenberg	88–89	Oct. 27, 1988	46
	88–89	Mar. 25, 1989	92
EASTWARD IN EDEN—Dorothy Gardner	47–48	Nov. 18, 1947	15

PLAY	VOLUME	OPENED	PERFS
EDWARD, MY SON—Robert Morley, Noel Langley	48–49 ..	Sept. 30, 1948 ..	260
EFFECT OF GAMMA RAYS ON MAN-IN-THE-MOON MARIGOLDS, THE—Paul Zindel	69–70 ..	Apr. 7, 1970 ..	819
EGG, THE—Felicien Marceau, (ad) Robert Schlitt	61–62 ..	Jan. 8, 1962 ..	8
ELEPHANT MAN, THE—Bernard Pomerance	78–79 ..	Jan. 14, 1979 ..	73
	78–79 ..	Apr. 19, 1979 ..	916
ELIZABETH THE QUEEN—Maxwell Anderson	30–31 ..	Nov. 3, 1930 ..	147
EMERALD CITY—David Williamson	88–89 ..	Nov. 30, 1988 ..	17
EMPEROR JONES, THE—Eugene O'Neill	20–21 ..	Nov. 1, 1920 ..	204
EMPEROR'S CLOTHES, THE—George Tabori	52–53 ..	Feb. 9, 1953 ..	16
ENCHANTED, THE—Maurice Valency, based on Jean Giraudoux's play *Intermezzo*	49–50 ..	Jan. 18, 1950 ..	45
END OF SUMMER—S.N. Behrman	35–36 ..	Feb. 17, 1936 ..	153
ENEMY, THE—Channing Pollock	25–26 ..	Oct. 20, 1925 ..	203
ENOUGH, FOOTFALLS AND ROCKABY—Samuel Beckett	83–84 ..	Feb. 16, 1984 ..	78
ENTER MADAME—Gilda Varesi, Dolly Byrne	20–21 ..	Aug. 16, 1920 ..	350
ENTERTAINER, THE—John Osborne	57–58 ..	Feb. 12, 1958 ..	97
EPITAPH FOR GEORGE DILLON—John Osborne, Anthony Creighton	58–59 ..	Nov. 4, 1958 ..	23
EQUUS—Peter Shaffer	74–75 ..	Oct. 24, 1974 ..	1,209
ESCAPE—John Galsworthy	27–28 ..	Oct. 26, 1927 ..	173
ETHAN FROME—Owen and Donald Davis, based on Edith Wharton's novel	35–36 ..	Jan. 21, 1936 ..	120
EVE OF ST. MARK, THE—Maxwell Anderson	42–43 ..	Oct. 7, 1942 ..	307
EXCURSION—Victor Wolfson	36–37 ..	Apr. 9, 1937 ..	116
EXECUTION OF JUSTICE—Emily Mann	85–86 ..	Mar. 13, 1986 ..	12
EXTRA MAN, THE—Richard Greenberg	91–92 ..	May 19, 1992 ..	39
EXTREMITIES—William Mastrosimone	82–83 ..	Dec. 22, 1982 ..	325
FAIR COUNTRY, A—Jon Robin Baitz	95–96 ..	Oct. 29, 1995 ..	153
FALL GUY, THE—James Gleason, George Abbott	24–25 ..	Mar. 10, 1925 ..	176
FALSETTOLAND—William Finn, James Lapine	90–91 ..	June 28, 1990 ..	215
FAMILY BUSINESS—Dick Goldberg	77–78 ..	Apr. 12, 1978 ..	438
FAMILY PORTRAIT—Lenore Coffee, William Joyce Cowen	38–39 ..	May 8, 1939 ..	111
FAMOUS MRS. FAIR, THE—James Forbes	19–20 ..	Dec. 22, 1919 ..	344
FAR COUNTRY, A—Henry Denker	60–61 ..	Apr. 4, 1961 ..	271
FARMER TAKES A WIFE, THE—Frank B. Elser, Marc Connelly, based on Walter D. Edmonds's novel *Rome Haul*	34–35 ..	Oct. 30, 1934 ..	104
FATAL WEAKNESS, THE—George Kelly	46–47 ..	Nov. 19, 1946 ..	119
FENCES—August Wilson	86–87 ..	Mar. 26, 1987 ..	526
FIDDLER ON THE ROOF—(b) Joseph Stein, (l) Sheldon Harnick, (m) Jerry Bock, based on Sholom Aleichem's stories	64–65 ..	Sept. 22, 1964 ..	3,242
5TH OF JULY, THE—Lanford Wilson (also called *Fifth of July*)	77–78 ..	Apr. 27, 1978 ..	159
FIND YOUR WAY HOME—John Hopkins	73–74 ..	Jan. 2, 1974 ..	135
FINISHING TOUCHES—Jean Kerr	72–73 ..	Feb. 8, 1973 ..	164
FIORELLO!—(b) Jerome Weidman, George Abbott, (l) Sheldon Harnick, (m) Jerry Bock	59–60 ..	Nov. 23, 1959 ..	795
FIREBRAND, THE—Edwin Justus Mayer	24–25 ..	Oct. 15, 1924 ..	269

PLAY	VOLUME	OPENED	PERFS
FIRES IN THE MIRROR—Anna Deavere Smith	91–92	May 12, 1992	109
FIRST LADY—Katherine Dayton, George S. Kaufman	35–36	Nov. 26, 1935	246
FIRST MONDAY IN OCTOBER—Jerome Lawrence, Robert E. Lee	78–79	Oct. 3, 1978	79
FIRST MRS. FRASER, THE—St. John Ervine	29–30	Dec. 28, 1929	352
FIRST YEAR, THE—Frank Craven	20–21	Oct. 20, 1920	760
FIVE FINGER EXERCISE—Peter Shaffer	59–60	Dec. 2, 1959	337
FIVE-STAR FINAL—Louis Weitzenkorn	30–31	Dec. 30, 1930	175
FLIGHT TO THE WEST—Elmer Rice	40–41	Dec. 30, 1940	136
FLOATING LIGHT BULB, THE—Woody Allen	80–81	Apr. 27, 1981	65
FLOWERING PEACH, THE—Clifford Odets	54–55	Dec. 28, 1954	135
FOLLIES—(b) James Goldman, (m, l) Stephen Sondheim	70–71	Apr. 4, 1971	521
FOOL, THE—Channing Pollock	22–23	Oct. 23, 1922	373
FOOL FOR LOVE—Sam Shepard	83–84	May 26, 1983	1,000
FOOLISH NOTION—Philip Barry	44–45	Mar. 3, 1945	104
FOREIGNER, THE—Larry Shue	84–85	Nov. 1, 1984	686
FORTY CARATS—Pierre Barillet, Jean-Pierre Gredy, (ad) Jay Allen	68–69	Dec. 26, 1968	780
FOXFIRE—Susan Cooper, Hume Cronyn, (m) Jonathan Holtzman; based on materials from the *Foxfire* books	82–83	Nov. 11, 1982	213
42ND STREET—(b) Michael Stewart, Mark Bramble, (m, l) Harry Warren, Al Dubin, (add'l l) Johnny Mercer, Mort Dixon, based on the novel by Bradford Ropes	80–81	Aug. 25, 1980	3,486
FOURPOSTER, THE—Jan de Hartog	51–52	Oct. 24, 1951	632
FRONT PAGE, THE—Ben Hecht, Charles MacArthur	28–29	Aug. 14, 1928	276
GENERATION—William Goodhart	65–66	Oct. 6, 1965	299
GEORGE WASHINGTON SLEPT HERE—George S. Kaufman, Moss Hart	40–41	Oct. 18, 1940	173
GETTING OUT—Marsha Norman	78–79	Oct. 19, 1978	259
GIDEON—Paddy Chayefsky	61–62	Nov. 9, 1961	236
GIGI—Anita Loos, based on Colette's novel	51–52	Nov. 24, 1951	219
GIMME SHELTER—Barrie Keefe (*Gem, Gotcha* and *Getaway*)	78–79	Dec. 10, 1978	17
GIN GAME, THE—D.L. Coburn	77–78	Oct. 6, 1977	517
GINGERBREAD LADY, THE—Neil Simon	70–71	Dec. 13, 1970	193
GIRL ON THE VIA FLAMINIA, THE—Alfred Hayes, based on his novel	53–54	Feb. 9, 1954	111
GLASS MENAGERIE, THE—Tennessee Williams	44–45	Mar. 31, 1945	561
GLENGARRY GLEN ROSS—David Mamet	83–84	Mar. 25, 1984	378
GOBLIN MARKET—(ad) Peggy Harmon, Polly Pen from the poem by Christina Rosetti, (m) Polly Pen (special citation)	85–86	Apr. 13, 1986	89
GOLDEN APPLE, THE—(b, l), John Latouche, (m) Jerome Moross	53–54	Apr. 20, 1954	125
GOLDEN BOY—Clifford Odets	37–38	Nov. 4, 1937	250
GOOD—C.P. Taylor	82–83	Oct. 13, 1982	125
GOOD DOCTOR, THE—(ad) Neil Simon and suggested by stories by Anton Chekhov	73–74	Nov. 27, 1973	208
GOOD GRACIOUS ANNABELLE—Clare Kummer	09–19	Oct. 31, 1916	111
GOOD TIMES ARE KILLING ME, THE—Lynda Barry	90–91	May 21, 1991	207
GOODBYE, MY FANCY—Fay Kanin	48–49	Nov. 17, 1948	446

PLAY	VOLUME	OPENED	PERFS
GOOSE HANGS HIGH, THE—Lewis Beach	23–24	Jan. 29, 1924	183
GRAND HOTEL—Vicki Baum, (ad) W. A. Drake	30–31	Nov. 13, 1930	459
GRAND HOTEL: THE MUSICAL—(b) Luther Davis, (m, l) Robert Wright, George Forrest, (add'l m, l) Maury Yeston, based on Vicki Baum's *Grand Hotel*	89–90	Nov. 12, 1989	1,077
GRAPES OF WRATH, THE—(ad) Frank Galati from the novel by John Steinbeck	89–90	Mar. 22, 1990	188
GREAT DIVIDE, THE—William Vaughn Moody	99–09	Oct. 3, 1906	238
GREAT GOD BROWN, THE—Eugene O'Neill	25–26	Jan. 23, 1926	271
GREAT WHITE HOPE, THE—Howard Sackler	68–69	Oct. 3, 1968	556
GREEN BAY TREE, THE—Mordaunt Shairp	33–34	Oct. 20, 1933	166
GREEN GODDESS, THE—William Archer	20–21	Jan. 18, 1921	440
GREEN GROW THE LILACS—Lynn Riggs	30–31	Jan. 26, 1931	64
GREEN HAT, THE—Michael Arlen	25–26	Sept. 15, 1925	231
GREEN JULIA—Paul Abelman	72–73	Nov. 16, 1972	147
GREEN PASTURES, THE—Marc Connelly, based on Roark Bradford's *Ol' Man Adam and His Chillun*	29–30	Feb. 26, 1930	640
GROSS INDECENCY: THE THREE TRIALS OF OSCAR WILDE—Moisés Kaufman	97–98	June 5, 1997	534
GUS AND AL—Albert Innaurato	88–89	Feb. 27, 1989	25
GUYS AND DOLLS—(b) Jo Swerling, Abe Burrows, based on a story and characters by Damon Runyon, (m, l) Frank Loesser	50–51	Nov. 24, 1950	1,200
GYPSY—Maxwell Anderson	28–29	Jan. 14, 1929	64
HADRIAN VII—Peter Luke, based on works by Fr. Rolfe	68–69	Jan. 8, 1969	359
HAMP—John Wilson, based on an episode from a novel by J.L. Hodson	66–67	Mar. 9, 1967	101
HAPGOOD—Tom Stoppard	94–95	Dec. 4, 1994	129
HAPPY TIME, THE—Samuel Taylor, based on Robert Fontaine's book	49–50	Jan. 24, 1950	614
HARRIET—Florence Ryerson, Colin Clements	42–43	Mar. 3, 1943	377
HARVEY—Mary Chase	44–45	Nov. 1, 1944	1,775
HASTY HEART, THE—John Patrick	44–45	Jan. 3, 1945	207
HE WHO GETS SLAPPED—Leonid Andreyev, (ad) Gregory Zilboorg	21–22	Jan. 9, 1922	308
HEART OF MARYLAND, THE—David Belasco	94–99	Oct. 22, 1895	240
HEIDI CHRONICLES, THE—Wendy Wasserstein	88–89	Dec. 11, 1988	81
	88–89	Mar. 9, 1989	621
HEIRESS, THE—Ruth and Augustus Goetz, suggested by Henry James's novel *Washington Square*	47–48	Sept. 29, 1947	410
HELL-BENT FER HEAVEN—Hatcher Hughes	23–24	Jan. 4, 1924	122
HELLO, DOLLY!—(b) Michael Stewart, (m, l) Jerry Herman, based on Thornton Wilder's *The Matchmaker*	63–64	Jan. 16, 1964	2,844
HER MASTER'S VOICE—Clare Kummer	33–34	Oct. 23, 1933	224
HERE COME THE CLOWNS—Philip Barry	38–39	Dec. 7, 1938	88
HERO, THE—Gilbert Emery	21–22	Sept. 5, 1921	80
HIGH TOR—Maxwell Anderson	36–37	Jan. 9, 1937	171
HOGAN'S GOAT—William Alfred	65–66	Nov. 11, 1965	607

PLAY	VOLUME	OPENED	PERFS
HOLIDAY—Philip Barry	28–29	Nov. 26, 1928	229
HOME—David Storey	70–71	Nov. 17, 1970	110
HOME—Samm-Art Williams	79–80	Dec. 14, 1979	82
	79–80	May 7, 1980	279
HOMECOMING, THE—Harold Pinter	66–67	Jan. 5, 1967	324
HOME OF THE BRAVE—Arthur Laurents	45–46	Dec. 27, 1945	69
HOPE FOR A HARVEST—Sophie Treadwell	41–42	Nov. 26, 1941	38
HOSTAGE, THE—Brendan Behan	60–61	Sept. 20, 1960	127
HOT L BALTIMORE, THE—Lanford Wilson	72–73	Mar. 22, 1973	1,166
HOUSE OF BLUE LEAVES, THE—John Guare	70–71	Feb. 10, 1971	337
HOUSE OF CONNELLY, THE—Paul Green	31–32	Sept. 28, 1931	91
HOW I LEARNED TO DRIVE—Paula Vogel	96–97	May 4, 1997	400
HOW TO SUCCEED IN BUSINESS WITHOUT REALLY TRYING—(b) Abe Burrows, Jack Weinstock, Willie Gilbert, based on Shepherd Mead's novel, (m, l) Frank Loesser	61–62	Oct. 14, 1961	1,417
HURLYBURLY—David Rabe	84–85	June 21, 1984	45
	84–85	Aug. 7, 1984	343
I AM A CAMERA—John van Druten, based on Christopher Isherwood's Berlin stories	51–52	Nov. 28, 1951	214
I KNOW MY LOVE—S.N. Behrman, based on Marcel Achard's *Auprès de Ma Blonde*	49–50	Nov. 2, 1949	246
I NEVER SANG FOR MY FATHER—Robert Anderson	67–68	Jan. 25, 1968	124
I OUGHT TO BE IN PICTURES—Neil Simon	79–80	Apr. 3, 1980	324
I REMEMBER MAMA—John van Druten, based on Kathryn Forbes's book *Mama's Bank Account*	44–45	Oct. 19, 1944	714
ICEBOUND—Owen Davis	22–23	Feb. 10, 1923	171
ICEMAN COMETH, THE—Eugene O'Neill	46–47	Oct. 9, 1946	136
IDIOT'S DELIGHT—Robert E. Sherwood	35–36	Mar. 24, 1936	300
IF I WERE KING—Justin Huntly McCarthy	99–09	Oct. 14, 1901	56
I'M NOT RAPPAPORT—Herb Gardner	85–86	June 6, 1985	181
	85–86	Nov. 18, 1985	890
IMMORALIST, THE—Ruth and Augustus Goetz, based on André Gide's novel	53–54	Feb. 8, 1954	96
IN ABRAHAM'S BOSOM—Paul Green	26–27	Dec. 30, 1926	116
IN THE MATTER OF J. ROBERT OPPENHEIMER—Heinar Kipphardt, (tr) Ruth Speirs	68–69	Mar. 6, 1969	64
IN THE SUMMER HOUSE—Jane Bowles	53–54	Dec. 29, 1953	55
IN TIME TO COME—Howard Koch, John Huston	41–42	Dec. 28, 1941	40
INADMISSABLE EVIDENCE—John Osborne	65–66	Nov. 30, 1965	166
INCIDENT AT VICHY—Arthur Miller	64–65	Dec. 3, 1964	99
INDIANS—Arthur L. Kopit	69–70	Oct. 13, 1969	96
INHERIT THE WIND—Jerome Lawrence, Robert E. Lee	54–55	Apr. 21, 1955	806
INNOCENTS, THE—William Archibald, based on Henry James's *The Turn of the Screw*	49–50	Feb. 1, 1950	141
INNOCENT VOYAGE, THE—Paul Osborn, based on Richard Hughes's novel *A High Wind in Jamaica*	43–44	Nov. 15, 1943	40
INSPECTOR CALLS, AN—J.B. Priestley	47–48	Oct. 21, 1947	95
INTO THE WOODS—(b) James Lapine, (m, l) Stephen Sondheim	87–88	Nov. 5, 1987	765

PLAY	VOLUME	OPENED	PERFS
ISLAND, THE—Athol Fugard, John Kani, Winston Ntshona	74–75	Nov. 24, 1974	52
"IT'S A BIRD IT'S A PLANE IT'S SUPERMAN"—(b) David Newman and Robert Benton, (l) Lee Adams, (m) Charles Strouse, based on the comic strip "Superman"	65–66	Mar. 29, 1966	129
IT'S ONLY A PLAY—Terrence McNally	85–86	Jan. 12, 1986	17
J.B.—Archibald MacLeish	58–59	Dec. 11, 1958	364
JACOBOWSKY AND THE COLONEL—S.N. Behrman, based on Franz Werfel's play	43–44	Mar. 14, 1944	417
JANE—S.N. Behrman, suggested by W. Somerset Maugham's story	51–52	Feb. 1, 1952	100
JANE CLEGG—St. John Ervine	19–20	Feb. 23, 1920	158
JEFFREY—Paul Rudnick	92–93	Mar. 6, 1993	365
JASON—Samson Raphaelson	41–42	Jan. 21, 1942	125
JEROME ROBBINS' BROADWAY—(c) Jerome Robbins (special citation)	88–89	Feb. 26, 1989	634
JESSE AND THE BANDIT QUEEN—David Freeman	75–76	Oct. 17, 1975	155
JEST, THE—Sem Benelli, (ad) Edward Sheldon	19–20	Sept. 19, 1919	197
JOAN OF LORRAINE—Maxwell Anderson	46–47	Nov. 18, 1946	199
JOE EGG—(see *A Day in the Death of Joe Egg*)			
JOE TURNER'S COME AND GONE—August Wilson	87–88	Mar. 27, 1988	105
JOHN FERGUSON—St. John Ervine	09–19	May 13, 1919	177
JOHN LOVES MARY—Norman Krasna	46–47	Feb. 4, 1947	423
JOHNNY JOHNSON—(b, l) Paul Green, (m) Kurt Weill	36–37	Nov. 19, 1936	68
JOINED AT THE HEAD—Catherine Butterfield	92–93	Nov. 15, 1992	41
JOURNEY'S END—R.C. Sherriff	28–29	Mar. 22, 1929	485
JUMPERS—Tom Stoppard	73–74	Apr. 22, 1974	48
JUNE MOON—Ring W. Lardner, George S. Kaufman	29–30	Oct. 9, 1929	273
JUNIOR MISS—Jerome Chodorov, Joseph Fields	41–42	Nov. 18, 1941	710
K2—Patrick Meyers	82–83	Mar. 30, 1983	85
KATAKI—Shimon Wincelberg	58–59	Apr. 9, 1959	20
KENTUCKY CYCLE, THE—Robert Schenkkan	93–94	Nov. 14, 1993	34
KEY LARGO—Maxwell Anderson	39–40	Nov. 27, 1939	105
KILLING OF SISTER GEORGE, THE—Frank Marcus	66–67	Oct. 5, 1966	205
KINGDOM OF GOD, THE—G. Martinez Sierra, (ad) Helen and Harley Granville Barker	28–29	Dec. 20, 1928	92
KISS AND TELL—F. Hugh Herbert	42–43	Mar. 17, 1943	956
KISS OF THE SPIDER WOMAN—(b) Terrence McNally, (m) John Kander, (l) Fred Ebb, based on the novel by Manuel Puig	92–93	May 3, 1993	906
KISS THE BOYS GOODBYE—Clare Boothe	38–39	Sept. 28, 1938	286
KNOCK KNOCK—Jules Feiffer	75–76	Jan. 18, 1976	41
	75–76	Feb. 24, 1976	152
KVETCH—Steven Berkoff	86–87	Feb. 18, 1987	31
LA BETE—David Hirson (special citation)	90–91	Feb. 10, 1991	25
LA CAGE AUX FOLLES—(b) Harvey Fierstein, (m, l) Jerry Herman, based on the play by Jean Poiret	83–84	Aug. 21, 1983	1,761

PLAY	VOLUME	OPENED	PERFS
LA TRAGEDIE DE CARMEN—(ad) Peter Brook, Jean-Claude Carrière, Marius Constant from Georges Bizet's opera *Carmen* (special citation)	83–84	Nov. 17, 1983	187
LADY FROM DUBUQUE, THE—Edward Albee	79–80	Jan. 31, 1980	12
LADY IN THE DARK—(b) Moss Hart, (l) Ira Gershwin, (m) Kurt Weill	40–41	Jan. 23, 1941	162
LARGO DESOLATO—Vaclav Havel, (tr) Marie Winn	85–86	Mar. 25, 1986	40
LARK, THE—Jean Anouilh, (ad) Lillian Hellman	55–56	Nov. 17, 1955	229
LAST MEETING OF THE KNIGHTS OF THE WHITE MAGNOLIA, THE—Preston Jones	76–77	Sept. 22, 1976	22
LAST MILE, THE—John Wexley	29–30	Feb. 13, 1930	289
LAST NIGHT OF BALLYHOO, THE—Alfred Uhry	96–97	Feb. 27, 1997	557
LAST OF MRS. CHEYNEY, THE—Frederick Lonsdale	25–26	Nov. 9, 1925	385
LAST OF THE RED HOT LOVERS—Neil Simon	69–70	Dec. 28, 1969	706
LATE CHRISTOPHER BEAN, THE—(ad) Sidney Howard from the French of Rene Fauchois	32–33	Oct. 31, 1932	224
LATE GEORGE APLEY, THE—John P. Marquand, George S. Kaufman, based on John P. Marquand's novel	44–45	Nov. 23, 1944	385
LATER LIFE—A.R. Gurney	92–93	May 23, 1993	126
LAUGHTER ON THE 23RD FLOOR—Neil Simon	93–94	Nov. 22, 1993	320
LEAH KLESCHNA—C.M.S. McLellan	99–09	Dec. 12, 1904	131
LEFT BANK, THE—Elmer Rice	31–32	Oct. 5, 1931	242
LEND ME A TENOR—Ken Ludwig	88–89	Mar. 2, 1989	481
LES LIAISONS DANGEREUSES—Christopher Hampton, based on Choderlos de Laclos's novel	86–87	Apr. 30, 1987	148
*LES MISERABLES—(b) Alain Boublil, Claude-Michel Schönberg, (m) Claude-Michel Schönberg, (l) Herbert Kretzmer, add'l material James Fenton, based on Victor Hugo's novel	86–87	Mar. 12, 1987	5,031
LESSON FROM ALOES, A—Athol Fugard	80–81	Nov. 17, 1980	96
LET US BE GAY—Rachel Crothers	28–29	Feb. 19, 1929	353
LETTERS TO LUCERNE—Fritz Rotter, Allen Vincent	41–42	Dec. 23, 1941	23
LIFE, A—Hugh Leonard	80–81	Nov. 2, 1980	72
LIFE & ADVENTURES OF NICHOLAS NICKLEBY, THE—(ad) David Edgar from Charles Dickens's novel	81–82	Oct. 4, 1981	49
LIFE IN THE THEATER, A—David Mamet	77–78	Oct. 20, 1977	288
LIFE WITH FATHER—Howard Lindsay, Russel Crouse, based on Clarence Day's book	39–40	Nov. 8, 1939	3,224
LIFE WITH MOTHER—Howard Lindsay, Russel Crouse, based on Clarence Day's book	48–49	Oct. 20, 1948	265
LIGHT UP THE SKY—Moss Hart	48–49	Nov. 18, 1948	216
LILIOM—Ferenc Molnar, (ad) Benjamin Glazer	20–21	Apr. 20, 1921	300
LION IN WINTER, THE—James Goldman	65–66	Mar. 3, 1966	92
*LION KING, THE—(b) Roger Allers, Irene Mecchi, (m, l) Elton John, Tim Rice, (add'l m, l) Lebo M, Mark Mancina, Jay Rifkin, Julie Taymore, Hans Zimmer	97–98	Nov. 13, 1997	649
LIPS TOGETHER, TEETH APART—Terrence McNally	91–92	June 25, 1991	406
LITTLE ACCIDENT—Floyd Dell, Thomas Mitchell	28–29	Oct. 9, 1928	303
LITTLE FOXES, THE—Lillian Hellman	38–39	Feb. 15, 1939	410
LITTLE MINISTER, THE—James M. Barrie	94–99	Sept. 27, 1897	300

PLAY	VOLUME	OPENED	PERFS
LITTLE NIGHT MUSIC, A—(b) Hugh Wheeler, (m, l) Stephen Sondheim, suggested by Ingmar Bergman's film *Smiles of a Summer Night*	72–73	Feb. 25, 1973	600
LIVING ROOM, THE—Graham Greene	54–55	Nov. 17, 1954	22
LIVING TOGETHER—Alan Ayckbourn	75–76	Dec. 7, 1975	76
LOMAN FAMILY PICNIC, THE—Donald Margulies	89–90	June 20, 1989	16
LONG DAY'S JOURNEY INTO NIGHT—Eugene O'Neill	56–57	Nov. 7, 1956	390
LOOK BACK IN ANGER—John Osborne	57–58	Oct. 1, 1957	407
LOOK HOMEWARD, ANGEL—Ketti Frings, based on Thomas Wolfe's novel	57–58	Nov. 28, 1957	564
LOOSE ENDS—Michael Weller	79–80	June 6, 1979	284
LOST HORIZONS—Harry Segall, revised by John Hayden	34–35	Oct. 15, 1934	56
LOST IN THE STARS—(b, l) Maxwell Anderson, based on Alan Paton's novel *Cry, the Beloved Country,* (m) Kurt Weill	49–50	Oct. 30, 1949	273
LOST IN YONKERS—Neil Simon	90–91	Feb. 21, 1991	780
LOVE LETTERS—A.R. Gurney	89–90	Aug. 22, 1989	64
	89–90	Oct. 31, 1989	96
LOVE OF FOUR COLONELS, THE—Peter Ustinov	52–53	Jan. 15, 1953	141
LOVE! VALOUR! COMPASSION!—Terrence McNally	94–95	Nov. 1, 1994	72
	94–95	Feb. 14, 1995	249
LOVERS—Brian Friel	68–69	July 25, 1968	148
LOYALTIES—John Galsworthy	22–23	Sept. 27, 1922	220
LUNCH HOUR—Jean Kerr	80–81	Nov. 12, 1980	262
LUTE SONG—(b) Sidney Howard, Will Irwin from the Chinese classic *Pi-Pa-Ki,* (l) Bernard Hanighen, (m) Raymond Scott	45–46	Feb. 6, 1946	385
LUTHER—John Osborne	63–64	Sept. 25, 1963	211
LUV—Murray Schisgal	64–65	Nov. 11, 1964	901
M. BUTTERFLY—David Henry Hwang	87–88	Mar. 20, 1988	777
MA RAINEY'S BLACK BOTTOM—August Wilson	84–85	Oct. 11, 1984	275
MACHINAL—Sophie Treadwell	28–29	Sept. 7, 1928	91
MAD FOREST—Caryl Churchill	91–92	Dec. 4, 1991	54
MADNESS OF GEORGE III, THE—Alan Bennett	93–94	Sept. 28, 1993	17
MADWOMAN OF CHAILLOT, THE—Jean Giraudoux, (ad) Maurice Valency	48–49	Dec. 27, 1948	368
MAGIC AND THE LOSS, THE—Julian Funt	53–54	Apr. 9, 1954	27
MAGNIFICENT YANKEE, THE—Emmet Lavery	45–46	Jan. 22, 1946	160
MAHABHARATA, THE—Jean-Claude Carrière, (ad) Peter Brook	87–88	Oct. 13, 1987	25
MALE ANIMAL, THE—James Thurber, Elliott Nugent	39–40	Jan. 9, 1940	243
MAMMA'S AFFAIR—Rachel Barton Butler	19–20	Jan. 29, 1920	98
MAN FOR ALL SEASONS, A—Robert Bolt	61–62	Nov. 22, 1961	637
MAN FROM HOME, THE—Booth Tarkington, Harry Leon Wilson	99–09	Aug. 17, 1908	406
MAN IN THE GLASS BOOTH, THE—Robert Shaw	68–69	Sept. 26, 1968	268
MAN OF LA MANCHA—(b) Dale Wasserman, suggested by the life and works of Miguel de Cervantes y Saavedra, (l) Joe Darion, (m) Mitch Leigh	65–66	Nov. 22, 1965	2,328
MAN WHO CAME TO DINNER, THE—George S. Kaufman, Moss Hart	39–40	Oct. 16, 1939	739

PLAY	VOLUME	OPENED	PERFS
MARAT/SADE—(see *The Persecution and Assassination of Marat,* etc.)			
MARGIN FOR ERROR—Clare Boothe	39–40	Nov. 3, 1939	264
MARRIAGE OF BETTE AND BOO, THE—Christopher Durang	84–85	May 16, 1985	86
MARVIN'S ROOM—Scott McPherson	91–92	Dec. 5, 1991	214
MARY, MARY—Jean Kerr	60–61	Mar. 8, 1961	1,572
MARY OF SCOTLAND—Maxwell Anderson	33–34	Nov. 27, 1933	248
MARY ROSE—James M. Barrie	20–21	Dec. 22, 1920	127
MARY THE 3RD—Rachel Crothers	22–23	Feb. 5, 1923	162
MASS APPEAL—Bill C. Davis	81–82	Nov. 12, 1981	214
MASTER CLASS—Terrence McNally	95–96	Nov. 5, 1995	601
MASTER HAROLD . . . AND THE BOYS—Athol Fugard	81–82	May 4, 1982	344
MATCHMAKER, THE—Thornton Wilder, based on Johann Nestroy's *Einen Jux Will Er Sich Machen,* based on John Oxenford's *A Day Well Spent*	55–56	Dec. 5, 1955	486
ME AND MOLLY—Gertrude Berg	47–48	Feb. 26, 1948	156
MEMBER OF THE WEDDING, THE—(ad) Carson McCullers, from her novel	49–50	Jan. 5, 1950	501
MEN IN WHITE—Sidney Kingsley	33–34	Sept. 26, 1933	351
MERRILY WE ROLL ALONG—George S. Kaufman, Moss Hart	34–35	Sept. 29, 1934	155
MERTON OF THE MOVIES—George S. Kaufman, Marc Connelly, based on Harry Leon Wilson's novel	22–23	Nov. 13, 1922	381
MICHAEL AND MARY—A.A. Milne	29–30	Dec. 13, 1929	246
MILK TRAIN DOESN'T STOP HERE ANYMORE, THE—Tennessee Williams	62–63	Jan. 16, 1963	69
MINICK—George S. Kaufman, Edna Ferber	24–25	Sept. 24, 1924	141
MISERABLES, LES—(see *Les Misérables*)			
MISS FIRECRACKER CONTEST, THE—Beth Henley	83–84	May 1, 1984	131
*MISS SAIGON—(b) Alain Boublil, Claude-Michel Schönberg (m) Claude-Michel Schönberg, (l) Richard Maltby Jr., Alain Boublil, (add'l material) Richard Maltby Jr.	90–91	Apr. 11, 1991	3,373
MISTER ROBERTS—Thomas Heggen, Joshua Logan, based on Thomas Heggen's novel	47–48	Feb. 18, 1948	1,157
MOLLY SWEENEY—Brian Friel	95–96	Jan. 7, 1996	145
MOON FOR THE MISBEGOTTEN, A—Eugene O'Neill	56–57	May 2, 1957	68
MOON IS DOWN, THE—John Steinbeck	41–42	Apr. 7, 1942	71
MOONCHILDREN—Michael Weller	71–72	Feb. 21, 1972	16
MORNING'S AT SEVEN—Paul Osborn	39–40	Nov. 30, 1939	44
MOTHER COURAGE AND HER CHILDREN—Bertolt Brecht, (ad) Eric Bentley	62–63	Mar. 28, 1963	52
MOURNING BECOMES ELECTRA—Eugene O'Neill	31–32	Oct. 26, 1931	150
MR. AND MRS. NORTH—Owen Davis, based on Frances and Richard Lockridge's stories	40–41	Jan. 12, 1941	163
MRS. BUMSTEAD-LEIGH—Harry James Smith	09–19	Apr. 3, 1911	64
MRS. KLEIN—Nicholas Wright	95–96	Oct. 24, 1995	280
MRS. MCTHING—Mary Chase	51–52	Feb. 20, 1952	350
MRS. PARTRIDGE PRESENTS—Mary Kennedy, Ruth Hawthorne	24–25	Jan. 5, 1925	144
MY CHILDREN! MY AFRICA!—Athol Fugard	89–90	Dec. 18, 1989	28
MY FAIR LADY—(b, l) Alan Jay Lerner, based on George Bernard Shaw's *Pygmalion,* (m) Frederick Loewe	55–56	Mar. 15, 1956	2,717

PLAY	VOLUME	OPENED	PERFS
MY ONE AND ONLY—(b) Peter Stone, Timothy S. Mayer, (m) George Gershwin from *Funny Face* and other shows, (l) Ira Gershwin	82–83	May 1, 1983	767
MY SISTER EILEEN—Joseph Fields, Jerome Chodorov, based on Ruth McKenney's stories	40–41	Dec. 26, 1940	864
MY 3 ANGELS—Samuel and Bella Spewack, based on Albert Husson's play *La Cuisine des Anges*	52–53	Mar. 11, 1953	344
MYSTERY OF EDWIN DROOD, THE—(b, m, l) Rupert Holmes (also called *Drood*)	85–86	Aug. 4, 1985	24
	85–86	Dec. 12, 1985	608
NATIONAL HEALTH, THE—Peter Nichols	74–75	Oct. 10, 1974	53
NATIVE SON—Paul Green, Richard Wright, based on Mr. Wright's novel	40–41	Mar. 24, 1941	114
NEST, THE—(ad) Grace George, from Paul Geraldy's *Les Noces d'Argent*	21–22	Jan. 28, 1922	152
NEVIS MOUNTAIN DEW—Steve Carter	78–79	Dec. 7, 1978	61
NEW ENGLAND—Richard Nelson	95–96	Nov. 7, 1995	54
NEXT (see *Adaptation*)			
NEXT TIME I'LL SING TO YOU—James Saunders	63–64	Nov. 27, 1963	23
NICE PEOPLE—Rachel Crothers	20–21	Mar. 2, 1921	247
NICHOLAS NICKLEBY—(see *The Life & Adventures of Nicholas Nickleby*)			
NIGHT AND HER STARS—Richard Greenberg	94–95	Apr. 26, 1995	39
NIGHT OF THE IGUANA, THE—Tennessee Williams	61–62	Dec. 28, 1961	316
'NIGHT, MOTHER—Marsha Norman	82–83	Mar. 31, 1983	380
	83–84	Apr. 14, 1984	54
NINE—(b) Arthur L. Kopit, (m, l) Maury Yeston, (ad) Mario Fratti from the Italian	81–82	May 9, 1982	739
NO MORE LADIES—A.E. Thomas	33–34	Jan. 23, 1934	162
NO PLACE TO BE SOMEBODY—Charles Gordone	68–69	May 4, 1969	250
NO TIME FOR COMEDY—S.N. Behrman	38–39	Apr. 17, 1939	185
NO TIME FOR SERGEANTS—Ira Levin, based on Mac Hyman's novel	55–56	Oct. 20, 1955	796
NOEL COWARD IN TWO KEYS—Noel Coward (*Come Into the Garden Maud* and *A Song at Twilight*)	73–74	Feb. 28, 1974	140
NOISES OFF—Michael Frayn	83–84	Dec. 11, 1983	553
NORMAN CONQUESTS, THE—(see *Living Together, Round and Round the Garden* and *Table Manners*)			
NUTS—Tom Topor	79–80	Apr. 28, 1980	96
O MISTRESS MINE—Terence Rattigan	45–46	Jan. 23, 1946	452
ODD COUPLE, THE—Neil Simon	64–65	Mar. 10, 1965	964
OF MICE AND MEN—John Steinbeck	37–38	Nov. 23, 1937	207
OF THEE I SING—(b) George S. Kaufman, (m) George Gershwin, Morrie Ryskind, (l) Ira Gershwin	31–32	Dec. 26, 1931	441
OH DAD, POOR DAD, MAMA'S HUNG YOU IN THE CLOSET AND I'M FEELIN' SO SAD—Arthur L. Kopit	61–62	Feb. 26, 1962	454
OHIO IMPROMPTU, CATASTROPHE AND WHAT WHERE— Samuel Beckett	83–84	June 15, 1983	350
OKLAHOMA!—(b, l) Oscar Hammerstein II, based on Lynn Riggs's play *Green Grow the Lilacs,* (m) Richard Rodgers	42–43	Mar. 31, 1943	2,212

PLAY	VOLUME	OPENED	PERFS

OLD MAID, THE—Zoe Akins, based on Edith Wharton's
  novel .... 34–35 .. Jan. 7,   1935 .. 305
OLD SOAK, THE—Don Marquis .... 22–23 .. Aug. 22, 1922 .. 423
OLD TIMES—Harold Pinter .... 71–72 .. Nov. 16, 1971 .. 119
OLD WICKED SONGS—Jon Marans .... 96–97 .. Sept. 5, 1996 .. 210
OLDEST LIVING GRADUATE, THE—Preston Jones .... 76–77 .. Sept. 23, 1976 .. 20
OLEANNA—David Mamet .... 92–93 .. Oct. 25, 1992 .. 513
ON BORROWED TIME—Paul Osborn, based on Lawrence
  Edward Watkin's novel .... 37–38 .. Feb. 3,   1938 .. 321
ON GOLDEN POND—Ernest Thompson .... 78–79 .. Sept. 13, 1978 .. 30
                                       78–79 .. Feb. 28, 1979 .. 126
ON TRIAL—Elmer Rice .... 09–19 .. Aug. 19, 1914 .. 365
ONCE IN A LIFETIME—Moss Hart, George S. Kaufman .... 30–31 .. Sept. 24, 1930 .. 406
ONCE ON THIS ISLAND—(b, l) Lynn Ahrens, (m) Stephen
  Flaherty, based on the novel *My Love My Love* by Rosa
  Guy .... 89–90 .. May 6,   1990 .. 24
                                       90–91 .. Oct. 18, 1990 .. 469
ONE SUNDAY AFTERNOON—James Hagan .... 32–33 .. Feb. 15, 1933 .. 322
ORPHEUS DESCENDING—Tennessee Williams .... 56–57 .. Mar. 21, 1957 .. 68
OTHER PEOPLE'S MONEY—Jerry Sterner .... 88–89 .. Feb. 16, 1989 .. 990
OTHERWISE ENGAGED—Simon Gray .... 76–77 .. Feb. 2,   1977 .. 309
OUR COUNTRY'S GOOD—Timberlake Wertenbaker .... 90–91 .. Apr. 29, 1991 .. 48
OUTRAGEOUS FORTUNE—Rose Franken .... 43–44 .. Nov. 3,   1943 .. 77
OUR TOWN—Thornton Wilder .... 37–38 .. Feb. 4,   1938 .. 336
OUTWARD BOUND—Sutton Vane .... 23–24 .. Jan. 7,   1924 .. 144
OVER 21—Ruth Gordon .... 43–44 .. Jan. 3,   1944 .. 221
OVERTURE—William Bolitho .... 30–31 .. Dec. 5,   1930 .. 41

P.S. 193—David Rayfiel .... 62–63 .. Oct. 30, 1962 .. 48
PACIFIC OVERTURES—(b) John Weidman, (m, l) Stephen
  Sondheim, (add'l material) Hugh Wheeler .... 75–76 .. Jan. 11, 1976 .. 193
PACK OF LIES—Hugh Whitemore .... 84–85 .. Feb. 11, 1985 .. 120
PAINTING CHURCHES—Tina Howe .... 83–84 .. Nov. 22, 1983 .. 206
PARIS BOUND—Philip Barry .... 27–28 .. Dec. 27, 1927 .. 234
PASSION—(b) James Lapine, (m) Stephen Sondheim, based on
  the film *Passione D'Amore* .... 93–94 .. May 9,   1994 .. 280
PASSION OF JOSEPH D., THE—Paddy Chayevsky .... 63–64 .. Feb. 11, 1964 .. 15
PATRIOTS, THE—Sidney Kingsley .... 42–43 .. Jan. 29, 1943 .. 173
PERFECT GANESH, A—Terrence McNally .... 93–94 .. June 27, 1993 .. 124
PERFECT PARTY, THE—A.R. Gurney .... 85–86 .. Apr. 2,   1986 .. 238
PERIOD OF ADJUSTMENT—Tennessee Williams .... 60–61 .. Nov. 10, 1960 .. 132
PERSECUTION AND ASSASSINATION OF MARAT AS
  PERFORMED BY THE INMATES OF THE ASYLUM OF
  CHARENTON UNDER THE DIRECTION OF THE MARQUIS DE
  SADE, THE—Peter Weiss, English version by Geoffrey
  Skelton, verse (ad) Adrian Mitchell .... 65–66 .. Dec. 27, 1965 .. 144
PETRIFIED FOREST, THE—Robert E. Sherwood .... 34–35 .. Jan. 7,   1935 .. 197
*PHANTOM OF THE OPERA, THE—(b) Richard Stilgoe,
  Andrew Lloyd Webber, (m) Andrew Lloyd Webber, (l)
  Charles Hart, (add'l l) Richard Stilgoe, adapted from the
  novel by Gaston Leroux (special citation) .... 87–88 .. Jan. 26, 1988 .. 4,762
PHILADELPHIA, HERE I COME!—Brian Friel .... 65–66 .. Feb. 16, 1966 .. 326

PLAY	VOLUME	OPENED	PERFS
PHILADELPHIA STORY, THE—Philip Barry	38–39	Mar. 28, 1939	417
PHILANTHROPIST, THE—Christopher Hampton	70–71	Mar. 15, 1971	72
PHYSICISTS, THE—Friedrich Duerrenmatt, (ad) James Kirkup	64–65	Oct. 13, 1964	55
PIANO LESSON, THE—August Wilson	89–90	Apr. 16, 1990	329
PICK UP GIRL—Elsa Shelley	43–44	May 3, 1944	198
PICNIC—William Inge	52–53	Feb. 19, 1953	477
PLAY'S THE THING, THE—Ferenc Molnar, (ad) P.G. Wodehouse	26–27	Nov. 3, 1926	260
PLAZA SUITE—Neil Simon	67–68	Feb. 14, 1968	1,097
PIGEONS AND PEOPLE—George M. Cohan	32–33	Jan. 16, 1933	70
PLEASURE OF HIS COMPANY, THE—Samuel Taylor, Cornelia Otis Skinner	58–59	Oct. 22, 1958	474
PLENTY—David Hare	82–83	Oct. 21, 1982	45
	82–83	Jan. 6, 1983	92
PLOUGH AND THE STARS, THE—Sean O'Casey	27–28	Nov. 28, 1927	32
POINT OF NO RETURN—Paul Osborn, based on John P. Marquand's novel	51–52	Dec. 13, 1951	364
PONDER HEART, THE—Joseph Fields, Jerome Chodorov, based on Eudora Welty's story	55–56	Feb. 16, 1956	149
POOR BITOS—Jean Anouilh, (tr) Lucienne Hill	64–65	Nov. 14, 1964	17
PORGY—Dorothy and DuBose Heyward	27–28	Oct. 10, 1927	367
POTTING SHED, THE—Graham Greene	56–57	Jan. 29, 1957	143
PRAYER FOR MY DAUGHTER, A—Thomas Babe	77–78	Dec. 27, 1977	127
PRELUDE TO A KISS—Craig Lucas	89–90	Mar. 14, 1990	33
	89–90	May 1, 1990	440
PRICE, THE—Arthur Miller	67–68	Feb. 7, 1968	429
PRIDE AND PREJUDICE—Helen Jerome, based on Jane Austen's novel	35–36	Nov. 5, 1935	219
PRIDE'S CROSSING—Tina Howe	97–98	Dec. 7, 1997	137
PRISONER OF SECOND AVENUE, THE—Neil Simon	71–72	Nov. 11, 1971	780
PROLOGUE TO GLORY—E.P. Conkle	37–38	Mar. 17, 1938	70
QUARTERMAINE'S TERMS—Simon Gray	82–83	Feb. 24, 1983	375
R.U.R.—Karel Capek	22–23	Oct. 9, 1922	184
RACKET, THE—Bartlett Cormack	27–28	Nov. 22, 1927	119
*RAGTIME—(b) Terrence McNally, (m) Stephen Flaherty, (l) Lynn Ahrens, based on E.L. Doctorow's novel	97–98	Jan. 18, 1998	570
RAIN—John Colton, Clemence Randolph, based on the story by W. Somerset Maugham	22–23	Nov. 7, 1922	648
RAISIN IN THE SUN, A—Lorraine Hansberry	58–59	Mar. 11, 1959	530
RATTLE OF A SIMPLE MAN—Charles Dyer	62–63	Apr. 17, 1963	94
REAL ESTATE—Louise Page	87–88	Dec. 1, 1987	55
REAL THING, THE—Tom Stoppard	83–84	Jan. 5, 1984	566
REBEL WOMEN—Thomas Babe	75–76	May 6, 1976	40
REBOUND—Donald Ogden Stewart	29–30	Feb. 3, 1930	114
RED DIAPER BABY—Josh Kornbluth	92–93	June 12, 1992	59
REHEARSAL, THE—Jean Anouilh, (ad) Pamela Hansford Johnson, Kitty Black	63–64	Sept. 23, 1963	110

PLAY	VOLUME	OPENED	PERFS
REMAINS TO BE SEEN—Howard Lindsay, Russel Crouse	51–52 ..	Oct. 3, 1951 ..	199
*RENT—(b,m,l) Jonathan Larson	95–96 ..	Feb. 13, 1996 ..	56
	95–96 ..	Apr. 29, 1996 ..	1289
REQUIEM FOR A NUN—Ruth Ford, William Faulkner, adapted from William Faulkner's novel	58–59 ..	Jan. 30, 1959 ..	43
REUNION IN VIENNA—Robert E. Sherwood.....................	31–32 ..	Nov. 16, 1931 ..	264
RHINOCEROS—Eugene Ionesco, (tr) Derek Prouse.............	60–61 ..	Jan. 9, 1961 ..	240
RITZ, THE—Terrence McNally....................................	74–75 ..	Jan. 20, 1975 ..	400
RIVER NIGER, THE—Joseph A. Walker.........................	72–73 ..	Dec. 5, 1972 ..	120
	72–73 ..	Mar. 27, 1973 ..	280
ROAD—Jim Cartwright..............................	88–89 ..	July 28, 1988 ..	62
ROAD TO MECCA, THE—Athol Fugard	87–88 ..	Apr. 12, 1988 ..	172
ROAD TO ROME, THE—Robert E. Sherwood	26–27 ..	Jan. 31, 1927 ..	392
ROCKABY—(see *Enough, Footfalls* and *Rockaby*)			
ROCKET TO THE MOON—Clifford Odets........................	38–39 ..	Nov. 24, 1938 ..	131
ROMANCE—Edward Sheldon.......................................	09–19 ..	Feb. 10, 1913 ..	160
ROPE DANCERS, THE—Morton Wishengrad	57–58 ..	Nov. 20, 1957 ..	189
ROSE TATTOO, THE—Tennessee Williams........................	50–51 ..	Feb. 3, 1951 ..	306
ROSENCRANTZ AND GUILDENSTERN ARE DEAD—Tom Stoppard	67–68 ..	Oct. 16, 1967 ..	420
ROUND AND ROUND THE GARDEN—Alan Ayckbourn	75–76 ..	Dec. 7, 1975 ..	76
ROYAL FAMILY, THE—George S. Kaufman, Edna Ferber......	27–28 ..	Dec. 28, 1927 ..	345
ROYAL HUNT OF THE SUN—Peter Shaffer	65–66 ..	Oct. 26, 1965 ..	261
RUGGED PATH, THE—Robert E. Sherwood.....................	45–46 ..	Nov. 10, 1945 ..	81
RUNNER STUMBLES, THE—Milan Stitt	75–76 ..	May 18, 1976 ..	191
ST. HELENA—R.C. Sheriff, Jeanne de Casalis....................	36–37 ..	Oct. 6, 1936 ..	63
SAME TIME, NEXT YEAR—Bernard Slade	74–75 ..	Mar. 13, 1975 ..	1,453
SATURDAY'S CHILDREN—Maxwell Anderson....................	26–27 ..	Jan. 26, 1927 ..	310
SCREENS, THE—Jean Genet, (tr) Minos Volanakis	71–72 ..	Nov. 30, 1971 ..	28
SCUBA DUBA—Bruce Jay Friedman.............................	67–68 ..	Oct. 10, 1967 ..	692
SEA HORSE, THE—Edward J. Moore (James Irwin)............	73–74 ..	Apr. 15, 1974 ..	128
SEARCHING WIND, THE—Lillian Hellman.......................	43–44 ..	Apr. 12, 1944 ..	318
SEASCAPE—Edward Albee	74–75 ..	Jan. 26, 1975 ..	65
SEASON IN THE SUN—Wolcott Gibbs............................	50–51 ..	Sept. 28, 1950 ..	367
SEASON'S GREETINGS—Alan Ayckbourn........................	85–86 ..	July 11, 1985 ..	20
SECOND THRESHOLD—Philip Barry, revisions by Robert E. Sherwood	50–51 ..	Jan. 2, 1951 ..	126
SECRET SERVICE—William Gillette..............................	94–99 ..	Oct. 5, 1896 ..	176
SEPARATE TABLES—Terence Rattigan............................	56–57 ..	Oct. 25, 1956 ..	332
SERENADING LOUIE—Lanford Wilson	75–76 ..	May 2, 1976 ..	33
SERPENT: A CEREMONY, THE—Jean-Claude van Itallie	69–70 ..	May 29, 1973 ..	3
SEVEN GUITARS—August Wilson.................................	95–96 ..	Mar. 28, 1996 ..	187
SEVEN KEYS TO BALDPATE—(ad) George M. Cohan, from the novel by Earl Derr Biggers....................	09–19 ..	Sept. 22, 1913 ..	320
1776—(b) Peter Stone, (m, l) Sherman Edwards, based on a conception by Sherman Edwards...................	68–69 ..	Mar. 16, 1969 ..	1,217
SEX, DRUGS, ROCK & ROLL—Eric Bogosian	89–90 ..	Feb. 8, 1990 ..	103
SHADOW AND SUBSTANCE—Paul Vincent Carroll..............	37–38 ..	Jan. 26, 1938 ..	274
SHADOW BOX, THE—Michael Cristofer.........................	76–77 ..	Mar. 31, 1977 ..	315
SHADOW OF HEROES—(see *Stone and Star*)			

PLAY	VOLUME	OPENED	PERFS
SHADOWLANDS—William Nicholson	90–91	Nov. 11, 1990	169
SHE LOVES ME—(b) Joe Masteroff, based on Miklos Laszlo's play *Parfumerie*, (l) Sheldon Harnick, (m) Jerry Bock	62–63	Apr. 23, 1963	301
SHINING HOUR, THE—Keith Winter	33–34	Feb. 13, 1934	121
SHIRLEY VALENTINE—Willy Russell	88–89	Feb. 16, 1989	324
SHORT EYES—Miguel Piñero	73–74	Feb. 28, 1974	54
	73–74	May 23, 1974	102
SHOW-OFF, THE—George Kelly	23–24	Feb. 5, 1924	571
SHRIKE, THE—Joseph Kramm	51–52	Jan. 15, 1952	161
SIGHT UNSEEN—Donald Margulies	91–92	Jan. 20, 1992	263
SILVER CORD, THE—Sidney Howard	26–27	Dec. 20, 1926	112
SILVER WHISTLE, THE—Robert E. McEnroe	48–49	Nov. 24, 1948	219
SISTERS ROSENSWEIG, THE—Wendy Wasserstein	92–93	Oct. 22, 1992	149
	92–93	Mar. 18, 1993	556
SIX CYLINDER LOVE—William Anthony McGuire	21–22	Aug. 25, 1921	430
SIX DEGREES OF SEPARATION—John Guare	90–91	June 14, 1990	155
	90–91	Nov. 8, 1990	485
6 RMS RIV VU—Bob Randall	72–73	Oct. 17, 1972	247
SKIN GAME, THE—John Galsworthy	20–21	Oct. 20, 1920	176
SKIN OF OUR TEETH, THE—Thornton Wilder	42–43	Nov. 18, 1942	359
SKIPPER NEXT TO GOD—Jan de Hartog	47–48	Jan. 4, 1948	93
SKRIKER, THE—Caryl Churchill	95–96	May 12, 1996	17
SKYLARK—Samson Raphaelson	39–40	Oct. 11, 1939	256
SKYLIGHT—David Hare	96–97	Sept. 19, 1996	116
SLEUTH—Anthony Shaffer	70–71	Nov. 12, 1970	1,222
SLOW DANCE ON THE KILLING GROUND—William Hanley	64–65	Nov. 30, 1964	88
SLY FOX—Larry Gelbart, based on *Volpone* by Ben Jonson	76–77	Dec. 14, 1976	495
SMALL CRAFT WARNINGS—Tennessee Williams	71–72	Apr. 2, 1972	192
SOLDIER'S PLAY, A—Charles Fuller	81–82	Nov. 20, 1981	468
SOLDIER'S WIFE—Rose Franken	44–45	Oct. 4, 1944	253
SPEED-THE-PLOW—David Mamet	87–88	May 3, 1988	278
SPIC-O-RAMA—John Leguizamo	92–93	Oct. 27, 1992	86
SPLIT SECOND—Dennis McIntyre	84–85	June 7, 1984	147
SQUAW MAN, THE—Edward Milton Royle	99–09	Oct. 23, 1905	222
STAGE DOOR—George S. Kaufman, Edna Ferber	36–37	Oct. 22, 1936	169
STAIRCASE—Charles Dyer	67–68	Jan. 10, 1968	61
STAR-WAGON, THE—Maxwell Anderson	37–38	Sept. 29, 1937	223
STATE OF THE UNION—Howard Lindsay, Russel Crouse	45–46	Nov. 14, 1945	765
STEAMBATH—Bruce Jay Friedman	70–71	June 30, 1970	128
STEEL MAGNOLIAS—Robert Harling	87–88	June 19, 1987	1,126
STICKS AND BONES—David Rabe	71–72	Nov. 7, 1971	121
	71–72	Mar. 1, 1972	245
STONE AND STAR—Robert Ardrey (also called *Shadow of Heroes*)	61–62	Dec. 5, 1961	20
STOP THE WORLD—I WANT TO GET OFF—(b, m, l) Leslie Bricusse, Anthony Newley	62–63	Oct. 3, 1962	555
STORM OPERATION—Maxwell Anderson	43–44	Jan. 11, 1944	23
STORY OF MARY SURRATT, THE—John Patrick	46–47	Feb. 8, 1947	11
STRANGE INTERLUDE—Eugene O'Neill	27–28	Jan. 30, 1928	426
STREAMERS—David Rabe	75–76	Apr. 21, 1976	478
STREET SCENE—Elmer Rice	28–29	Jan. 10, 1929	601

PLAY   VOLUME   OPENED   PERFS

STREETCAR NAMED DESIRE, A—Tennessee Williams .... 47–48 .. Dec. 3, 1947 .. 855
STRICTLY DISHONORABLE—Preston Sturges .... 29–30 .. Sept. 18, 1929 .. 557
SUBJECT WAS ROSES, THE—Frank D. Gilroy .... 64–65 .. May 25, 1964 .. 832
SUBSTANCE OF FIRE, THE—Jon Robin Baitz .... 90–91 .. Mar. 17, 1991 .. 120
SUBURBIA—Eric Bogosian .... 93–94 .. May 22, 1994 .. 113
SUGAR BABIES—(ad) Ralph G. Allen from traditional
  material (special citation) .... 79–80 .. Oct. 8, 1979 .. 1,208
SUM OF US, THE—David Stevens .... 90–91 .. Oct. 16, 1990 .. 335
SUMMER OF THE 17TH DOLL—Ray Lawler .... 57–58 .. Jan. 22, 1958 .. 29
SUNDAY IN THE PARK WITH GEORGE—(b) James Lapine,
  (m, l) Stephen Sondheim .... 83–84 .. May 2, 1984 .. 604
SUNRISE AT CAMPOBELLO—Dore Schary .... 57–58 .. Jan. 30, 1958 .. 556
SUNSET BOULEVARD—(b, l) Don Black, Christopher
  Hampton, (m) Andrew Lloyd Webber, based on the film by
  Billy Wilder .... 94–95 .. Nov. 17, 1994 .. 977
SUNSHINE BOYS, THE—Neil Simon .... 72–73 .. Dec. 20, 1972 .. 538
SUN-UP—Lula Vollmer .... 22–23 .. May 25, 1923 .. 356
SUSAN AND GOD—Rachel Crothers .... 37–38 .. Oct. 7, 1937 .. 288
SWAN, THE—Ferenc Molnar, (tr) Melville Baker .... 23–24 .. Oct. 23, 1923 .. 255
SWEENEY TODD, THE DEMON BARBER OF FLEET STREET—
  (b) Hugh Wheeler, (m, l) Stephen Sondheim, based on a
  version of Sweeney Todd by Christopher Bond .... 78–79 .. Mar. 1, 1979 .. 557
SWEET BIRD OF YOUTH—Tennessee Williams .... 58–59 .. Mar. 10, 1959 .. 375

TABLE MANNERS—Alan Ayckbourn .... 75–76 .. Dec. 7, 1975 .. 76
TABLE SETTINGS—James Lapine .... 79–80 .. Jan. 14, 1980 .. 264
TAKE A GIANT STEP—Louis Peterson .... 53–54 .. Sept. 24, 1953 .. 76
TAKING OF MISS JANIE, THE—Ed Bullins .... 74–75 .. May 4, 1975 .. 42
TALLEY'S FOLLEY—Lanford Wilson .... 78–79 .. May 1, 1979 .. 44
                                                                    79–80 .. Feb. 20, 1980 .. 277
TARNISH—Gilbert Emery .... 23–24 .. Oct. 1, 1923 .. 248
TASTE OF HONEY, A—Shelagh Delaney .... 60–61 .. Oct. 4, 1960 .. 376
TCHIN-TCHIN—Sidney Michaels, based on François
  Billetdoux's play .... 62–63 .. Oct. 25, 1962 .. 222
TEA AND SYMPATHY—Robert Anderson .... 53–54 .. Sept. 30, 1953 .. 712
TEAHOUSE OF THE AUGUST MOON, THE—John Patrick,
  based on Vern Sneider's novel .... 53–54 .. Oct. 15, 1953 .. 1,027
TENTH MAN, THE—Paddy Chayefsky .... 59–60 .. Nov. 5, 1959 .. 623
THAT CHAMPIONSHIP SEASON—Jason Miller .... 71–72 .. May 2, 1972 .. 144
                                                                    72–73 .. Sept. 14, 1972 .. 700
THERE SHALL BE NO NIGHT—Robert E. Sherwood .... 39–40 .. Apr. 29, 1940 .. 181
THEY KNEW WHAT THEY WANTED—Sidney Howard .... 24–25 .. Nov. 24, 1924 .. 414
THEY SHALL NOT DIE—John Wexley .... 33–34 .. Feb. 21, 1934 .. 62
THOUSAND CLOWNS, A—Herb Gardner .... 61–62 .. Apr. 5, 1962 .. 428
THREE POSTCARDS—(b) Craig Lucas, (m, l) Craig Carnelia ... 86–87 .. May 14, 1987 .. 22
THREE TALL WOMEN—Edward Albee .... 93–94 .. Apr. 5, 1994 .. 582
THREEPENNY OPERA—(b, l) Bertolt Brecht, (m) Kurt Weill,
  (tr) Ralph Manheim, John Willett .... 75–76 .. Mar. 1, 1976 .. 307
THURBER CARNIVAL, A—James Thurber .... 59–60 .. Feb. 26, 1960 .. 127
TIGER AT THE GATES—Jean Giraudoux's La Guerre de Troie
  n'Aura Pas Lieu, (tr) Christopher Fry .... 55–56 .. Oct. 3, 1955 .. 217

PLAY	VOLUME	OPENED	PERFS
TIME OF THE CUCKOO, THE—Arthur Laurents	52–53	Oct. 15, 1952	263
TIME OF YOUR LIFE, THE—William Saroyan	39–40	Oct. 25, 1939	185
TIME REMEMBERED—Jean Anouilh's *Léocadia,* (ad) Patricia Moyes	57–58	Nov. 12, 1957	248
TINY ALICE—Edward Albee	64–65	Dec. 29, 1964	167
TITANIC—(b) Peter Stone, (m, 1) Maury Yeston	96–97	Apr. 23, 1997	804
TOILET, THE—LeRoi Jones (a.k.a. Amiri Baraka)	64–65	Dec. 16, 1964	151
TOMORROW AND TOMORROW—Philip Barry	30–31	Jan. 13, 1931	206
TOMORROW THE WORLD—James Gow, Arnaud d'Usseau	42–43	Apr. 14, 1943	500
TORCH SONG TRILOGY—Harvey Fierstein (*The International Stud, Fugue in a Nursery, Widows and Children First*)	81–82	Jan. 15, 1982	117
	82–83	June 10, 1982	1,222
TOUCH OF THE POET, A—Eugene O'Neill	58–59	Oct. 2, 1958	284
TOVARICH—Jacques Deval, (tr) Robert E. Sherwood	36–37	Oct. 15, 1936	356
TOYS IN THE ATTIC—Lillian Hellman	59–60	Feb. 25, 1960	556
TRACERS—John DiFusco (c); Vincent Caristi, Richard Chaves, John DiFusco, Eric E. Emerson, Rick Gallavan, Merlin Marston, Harry Stephens with Sheldon Lettich	84–85	Jan. 21, 1985	186
TRAGEDIE DE CARMEN, LA—(see *La Tragédie de Carmen*)			
TRANSLATIONS—Brian Friel	80–81	Apr. 7, 1981	48
TRAVESTIES—Tom Stoppard	75–76	Oct. 30, 1975	155
TRELAWNY OF THE WELLS—Arthur Wing Pinero	94–99	Nov. 22, 1898	131
TRIAL OF THE CATONSVILLE NINE, THE—Daniel Berrigan, Saul Levitt	70–71	Feb. 7, 1971	159
TRIBUTE—Bernard Slade	77–78	June 1, 1978	212
TUNA CHRISTMAS, A—Jaston Williams, Joe Sears, Ed Howard	94–95	Dec. 15, 1994	20
TWILIGHT: LOS ANGELES, 1992—Anna Deavere Smith	93–94	Mar. 23, 1994	13
	93–94	Apr. 17, 1994	72
TWO BLIND MICE—Samuel Spewack	48–49	Mar. 2, 1949	157
TWO TRAINS RUNNING—August Wilson	91–92	Apr. 13, 1992	160
UNCHASTENED WOMAN, THE—Louis Kaufman Anspacher	09–19	Oct. 9, 1915	193
UNCLE HARRY—Thomas Job	41–42	May 20, 1942	430
UNDER MILK WOOD—Dylan Thomas	57–58	Oct. 15, 1957	39
VALLEY FORGE—Maxwell Anderson	34–35	Dec. 10, 1934	58
VALLEY SONG—Athol Fugard	95–96	Dec. 12, 1995	96
VENUS OBSERVED—Christopher Fry	51–52	Feb. 13, 1952	86
VERY SPECIAL BABY, A—Robert Alan Aurthur	56–57	Nov. 14, 1956	5
VICTORIA REGINA—Laurence Housman	35–36	Dec. 26, 1935	517
VIEW FROM THE BRIDGE, A—Arthur Miller	55–56	Sept. 29, 1955	149
VIOLET—(b,1) Brian Crawley, (m) Jeanine Tesori, based on *The Ugliest Pilgrim* by Doris Betts	96–97	Mar. 11, 1997	32
VISIT, THE—Friedrich Duerrenmatt, (ad) Maurice Valency	57–58	May 5, 1958	189
VISIT TO A SMALL PLANET—Gore Vidal	56–57	Feb. 7, 1957	388
VIVAT! VIVAT REGINA!—Robert Bolt	71–72	Jan. 20, 1972	116
VOICE OF THE TURTLE, THE—John van Druten	43–44	Dec. 8, 1943	1,557
WAGER, THE—Mark Medoff	74–75	Oct. 21, 1974	104
WAITING FOR GODOT—Samuel Beckett	55–56	Apr. 19, 1956	59

PLAY	VOLUME	OPENED	PERFS
WALK IN THE WOODS, A—Lee Blessing	87–88	Feb. 28, 1988	136
WALTZ OF THE TOREADORS, THE—Jean Anouilh, (tr) Lucienne Hill	56–57	Jan. 17, 1957	132
WATCH ON THE RHINE—Lillian Hellman	40–41	Apr. 1, 1941	378
WE, THE PEOPLE—Elmer Rice	32–33	Jan. 21, 1933	49
WEDDING BELLS—Salisbury Field	19–20	Nov. 12, 1919	168
WEDNESDAY'S CHILD—Leopold Atlas	33–34	Jan. 16, 1934	56
WENCESLAS SQUARE—Larry Shue	87–88	Mar. 2, 1988	55
WHAT A LIFE—Clifford Goldsmith	37–38	Apr. 13, 1938	538
WHAT PRICE GLORY?—Maxwell Anderson, Laurence Stallings	24–25	Sept. 3, 1924	433
WHAT THE BUTLER SAW—Joe Orton	69–70	May 4, 1970	224
WHEN LADIES MEET—Rachel Crothers	32–33	Oct. 6, 1932	191
WHEN YOU COMIN' BACK, RED RYDER?—Mark Medoff	73–74	Dec. 6, 1973	302
WHERE HAS TOMMY FLOWERS GONE?—Terrence McNally	71–72	Oct. 7, 1971	78
WHITE HOUSE MURDER CASE, THE—Jules Feiffer	69–70	Feb. 18, 1970	119
WHITE STEED, THE—Paul Vincent Carroll	38–39	Jan. 10, 1939	136
WHO'S AFRAID OF VIRGINIA WOOLF?—Edward Albee	62–63	Oct. 13, 1962	664
WHO'S TOMMY, THE—(b) Pete Townshend, Des McAnuff, (m, l) Pete Townshend, (add'l m, l) John Entwistle, Keith Moon (special citation)	92–93	Apr. 22, 1993	900
WHOSE LIFE IS IT ANYWAY?—Brian Clark	78–79	Apr. 17, 1979	223
WHY MARRY?—Jesse Lynch Williams	09–19	Dec. 25, 1917	120
WHY NOT?—Jesse Lynch Williams	22–23	Dec. 25, 1922	120
WIDOW CLAIRE, THE—Horton Foote	86–87	Dec. 17, 1986	150
WILD BIRDS—Dan Totheroh	24–25	Apr. 9, 1925	44
WILD HONEY—Michael Frayn, from an untitled play by Anton Chekhov	86–87	Dec. 18, 1986	28
WINGED VICTORY—Moss Hart, (m) David Rose	43–44	Nov. 20, 1943	212
WINGS—Arthur L. Kopit	78–79	June 21, 1978	15
	78–79	Jan. 28, 1979	113
WINGS—(b, l) Arthur Perlman, (m) Jeffrey Lunden, based on the play by Arthur L. Kopit	92–93	Mar. 9, 1993	47
WINGS OVER EUROPE—Robert Nichols, Maurice Browne	28–29	Dec. 10, 1928	90
WINSLOW BOY, THE—Terence Rattigan	47–48	Oct. 29, 1947	215
WINTER SOLDIERS—Daniel Lewis James	42–43	Nov. 29, 1942	25
WINTERSET—Maxwell Anderson	35–36	Sept. 25, 1935	195
WISDOM TOOTH, THE—Marc Connelly	25–26	Feb. 15, 1926	160
WISTERIA TREES, THE—Joshua Logan, based on Anton Chekhov's The Cherry Orchard	49–50	Mar. 29, 1950	165
WITCHING HOUR, THE—Augustus Thomas	99–09	Nov. 18, 1907	212
WITNESS FOR THE PROSECUTION—Agatha Christie	54–55	Dec. 16, 1954	645
WOMEN, THE—Clare Boothe	36–37	Dec. 26, 1936	657
WONDERFUL TOWN—(b) Joseph Fields, Jerome Chodorov, based on their play My Sister Eileen and Ruth McKenney's stories, (l) Betty Comden, Adolph Green, (m) Leonard Bernstein	52–53	Feb. 25, 1953	559
WORLD WE MAKE, THE—Sidney Kingsley, based on Millen Brand's novel The Outward Room	39–40	Nov. 20, 1939	80
YEARS AGO—Ruth Gordon	46–47	Dec. 3, 1946	206
YES, MY DARLING DAUGHTER—Mark Reed	36–37	Feb. 9, 1937	405

PLAY	VOLUME	OPENED	PERFS
You and I—Philip Barry	22–23	Feb. 19, 1923	178
You Can't Take It With You—Moss Hart, George S. Kaufman	36–37	Dec. 14, 1936	837
You Know I Can't Hear You When the Water's Running—Robert Anderson	66–67	Mar. 13, 1967	755
Young Man From Atlanta, The—Horton Foote	94–95	Jan. 27, 1995	24
Young Woodley—John van Druten	25–26	Nov. 2, 1925	260
Youngest, The—Philip Barry	24–25	Dec. 22, 1924	104
Your Own Thing—(b) Donald Driver, (m, l) Hal Hester and Danny Apolinar, suggested by William Shakespeare's *Twelfth Night*	67–68	Jan. 13, 1968	933
You're a Good Man Charlie Brown—(b, m, l) Clark Gesner, based on the comic strip *Peanuts* by Charles M. Schulz	66–67	Mar. 7, 1967	1,597
Zooman and the Sign—Charles Fuller	80–81	Dec. 7, 1980	33

INDEX

Play titles appear in **bold face**. *Bold face italic* page numbers refer to those pages where cast and credit listings may be found.

Abad, Ramon, 276
Abatemarco, Tony, 458
Abbott, Charles, 426
ABC Inc., 243, 254, 256, 275, 450
Abdoo, Rose, 361
Abernathy, Lee Roy, 270
Abhann Productions, 228
About Face Theater, 458
Abrams, Arthur, 351
Abrams, Judith Ann, 251, 265
Abstract Expression, *424*
Abuba, Ernest, 342
Acapulco, *347*
Ackerman, Loni, 358
Ackerman, Meyer, 297, 303
Ackerman, Peter, 40, 305
Ackerman, Robert Weston, 355
Acting Company, The, 36, 224, 270, 305
Acting Thing, The, *361*
Actors' Equity Association, 450
Actors Theater of Louisville, 367, 417
Adam Resurrected, *343*
Adams, AnneMarie, 354
Adams, Brooke, 425
Adams, Candi, 280
Adams, Chadwick T., 311
Adams, David, 343
Adams, Hilary, 350
Adams, J.B., 243
Adams, Kenneth G., 237
Adams, Kevin, 232, 275, 281, 288, 353, 430, 453
Adams, Malcolm, 342
Adams, Mason, 350

Adams, Richard Todd, 316
Adams, Sarah, 229
Adamson, Eve, 358
Addison, Larry, 260, 304
Ade, George, 359
Adelman, Louis C., 347
Aderer, Konrad, 340
Adhmaill, Mairead Ui, 354
Adilifu, Kamau, 237, 298, 299, 301
Adilman, Victoria, 292, 293
Adkins, Guy, 406
Adler, Gary, 411
Adler, Jay, 288
Adler, Joanna P., 277
Adler, Richard, 247
Adlon, Pamela Segall, 425
Admissions, *355*
Adobe Theater Company, 282, 354
Adventures in Motion Pictures, 23, 229
Adventures of Herculina, The, *412*
Adventures of Power Mommy, The, *362*
Adzima, Nanzi J., 417, 419
Aeschylus, vii
Affair on the Air, *358*
Afro-Bradley, Henry, 360
After-Dinner Joke, The, *355*
After-Play, 458
After the Fair, 265
Agee, Martin, 298, 299, 301
Ager/Yellen, 252
Ages of Man, The, *363*
Agin, Susan, 273
Agolio, Kathy, 436

Aguirre, Carlos, 432
Agustin, Julio, 245, 246
Ahern, Kieran, 255
Ahrens, Lynn, 24, 222, 240, 455
Aibel, Douglas, 279, 353
Aidem, Betsy, 358, 424
Ain't Misbehavin', 458
Airaldi, Remo, 405
Ajax (Por Nobody), *340*
Akaaboune, Soumaya, 234
Akalaitis, JoAnne, 362
Akerlind, Christopher, 279, 281, 409, 424, 427
Akiko Aizawa, 277
Ako, 340
Akuwudike, Jude, 249, 414
Alabama Shakespeare Festival, 243, 259, 303, 422, 451
Alassia, Cecilia, 269
Albee, Edward, 327, 329, 431
Albee's Men, *431*
Albee's People, *431*
Albee's Women, *431*
Albershardt, Richard, 355
Albert, Milena, 458
Alberti, Philip, 335, 420
Albertie, Dante, 290
Albis, Theron, 358
Albo, Mike, 349
Albrecht, Lisa, 229
Albright, Joseph, 405
Alda, Alan, 307
Aldous, Brian, 350, 428
Aldredge, Theoni V., 424
Aldridge, Amanda, 400, 401
Alessandrini, Gerard, 46, 264, 294, 456
Alexander, Adinah, 243, 244

493

Alexander, Detlev, 229
Alexander, Jace, viii, 37, 303, 327, 359
Alexander, Khandi, 312
Alexander, Lori, 240
Alexander, Robert, 428
Alexander, Stephan, 319
Alexander, Tanya, 347
Alexander, Valentina, 429
Alfaro, Luis, 344, 350, 406
Alice: Tales of a Curious Girl, 409
Alice Tully Hall, 354
Alice's Evidence, 350
Alighieri, Dante, 360
Alit, I Dewa Ketut, 276
All About Al, 339
All Is True, or The Famous History of the Life of King Henry VIII, 457
All Talk, 342
All That Jazz, 247, 248
All Under Heaven, 36, **294**
Alladin, Opal, 350
Allan, Laurena, 349
Allan, Lewis, 260, 304
Allen, April, 360
Allen, Billie, 450
Allen, Debbie, 457
Allen, Don, 427
Allen, Donald M., 342
Allen, Jennifer, 236
Allen, Melanie, 234
Allen, Philip G., 425
Allers, Roger, 222
Alley Theater, 249, 250, 257, 404, 414, 450
Allgood, Anne, 411
Allgrove, Danno, 422
Alliance Theater Company, 402
Allin, Jeff, 408, 426
Allman, John, 343
Almagor, Yehuda, 357
Almedilla, Joan, 315, 316, 358
Almeida Theater Company, 256, 290
Almquist, Leasen Beth, 251
Aloha, Say the Pretty Girls, 360, 417
Aloni, Nissim, 343
Alonso, Rodrigo, 303
Alonso, Valeria, 269
Altered Stages, 354
Altman, Chelsea, 249, 321
Alvarez-Quintero, Joaquin, 356
Alvarez-Quintero, Serafin, 356
Alvin, Farah, 340
AMAS Musical Theater, 253, 296, 333

Amazing Grace, 454
Ambler, Jim, 230
Ambler, Scott, 229
Ambrosone, John, 405
Amendolia, Don, 435
America Mall, 411
American Academy of Arts and Letters, 455
American Conservatory Theater, 417, 431
American Daughter, An, 9
American Express, 240
American Express Tribute, 457
American Jew, The, 358
American Music Theater Festival, 252
American Passenger, 358
American Place Theater, The, 272, 289, 334
American Renegade Theater, The, 275
American Repertory Theater, 405
American Stage Company, 281, 434
American Theater Critics Association (ATCA), viii, 367, 368, 452, 454
American Theater Critics Association New Play Award, 330, 406, 454
American Theater of Actors, 334
American Theater of Actors Theater, 354
American Theater Wing, 450, 452
American Theater Wing Annual Honors, 455
American Tien, 352
Ames, Jonathan, 349
Amirante, Robert, 311
Amon, Valerie, 343
Among Friends, 407
Amoros, Larry, 340
Amos, Kevin, 256
Amy's View, 4, 9, 10, 11, **256**, 447, 451
Amyot, Shaun, 251
An, So Youn, 225
Anania, Michael, 261, 420, 421, 434
Anbri, Christiana, 320
And the Soul Shall Dance, 454
And the Torso Even More So, 420
And the World Goes 'Round, 454
Anderman, Maureen, 450
Anderson, Brad, 245, 246

Anderson, Christian, 318
Anderson, Dennis, 237, 258, 301
Anderson, Elman, 235
Anderson, Jacqueline, 229
Anderson, John F., 411
Anderson, Kevin, 15, 249, 451, 456
Anderson, Lawrence, 316
Anderson, Maxwell, 358, 360
Anderson, Melissa Rain, 298
Anderson, Michael, 362, 363
Anderson, Nancy, 359
Anderson, Stephen Lee, 27, 230, 313
Andonyadis, Nephelie, 409
Andos, Randall T., 237, 259
Andrade, Chico, 249, 250, 414
Andreadakis, Jon D., 351, 352
Andreas, Christine, 319
Andres, Barbara, 310
Andresakis, Andrea, 335
Andresen, Karine, 338
Andress, Carl, 351
Andrews, Dwight, 284
Andrews, Simeon, 290
Andros, Andrea, 235
Andujar, Elena, 303
Angel Orensanz Foundation Center for the Arts, 21, 354
Angel Street, 360
Angel, Tony, 351
Angel Wings, 356
Angeline, Barbara, 234
Angelique, 344
Angell, Billy, 230
Angels in America, 37, 327
Angels in America, Parts I & II, 458
Angels of Lemnos, The, 458
Angels' Cradle, The, 348
Animal Confessions, 356
Anna Karenina, 36, **290**
Annie, 322
Annie Get Your Gun, 3, 4, 27, 28, 33, **250, 251**, 451, 456
Another American: Asking and Telling, 355
Anouilh, Jean, 18, 243
Antaky, Matthew, 276
Antalosky, Charles, 407
Antelo, Nicole, 432
Anthony, Cartier, 298
Anthony, Philip, 250
Anthony-Jackson, Todd, 457
Antigone Through Time, 355
Antoine, Jimi, 406
Anton, Kevin, 355
Apathy, 358
Apicella, John, 431

Apollo, Vincent A., 335
Aposkitis, Aristotellis, 279
Apostolou, Evgenia, 280
Appearance of Impropriety, The, *358*
Appel, Libby, 402
Applegate, Fred, 320
Araca Group, The, 297
Araiza, J. Ed, 277
Aranha, Ray, 243
Arauz, Abby, 234
Arbeiter, Jean, 311
Arbour, Matthew, 427
Arca, Jefferson D., 361
Arcade, Penny, 349
Arcenas, Loy, 281, 286, 345, 415, 431, 432
Archer, Julie, 344
Archer, Nicholas, 251
ArcLight Theater Company, The, 21, 303, 354
Ard, Kenneth, 311, 320
Arden, Annabel, 343
Ardito, Marc, 355
Arditti, Paul, 245, 255, 260, 292
Are We There Yet?, *362*
Arena Players Repertory Company of Long Island, 411
Arena Stage, 367, 368, 435, 457
Argo, Victor, 352, 437
Ari, Robert, 427
Aristocrats, *454*
Aristophanes, 361
Arizona Theater Company, 368
Arkansas Repertory Theater, 416
Arkin, Alan, 264, 317
Arkin, Matthew, 359
Arkin, Michael, 280
Arkus, Fran, 355
Arlen, Harold, 260
Arlen, Steeve, 363
Armbruster, Greg, 340
Armenante, Jillian, 337, 456
Armitage, Robert, 234
Armour, Annabel, 458
Armstrong, Karen, 238, 245
Arnett, Kim, 239
Arnold, Elizabeth, 359
Arnold, Jacqueline, 278
Arnold, Michael, 236
Arnold, Robert S., 270
Arnone, John, 256, 284, 337
Aron, Wendy, 335
Aronson, David, 351
Aronson, Frances, 270, 349, 350, 422, 431
Aronson, Henry, 235, 244
Aronson, Lisa, 450

Aronstein, Martin, 239
Arrabal, Fernando, 356
Arribas, Gilberto, 363
Arrington, Joseph, Jr., 247
Arrivals and Departures, *339*
Art, 3, 18, 223, 447, 453
Art of Dining, The, 458
Art of Murder, The, *435*
Arthur, Loyce, 428
Artificial Intelligence, 264
Arts at St. Ann's, 252
Arts Communications (A-Com), 225
Arye, Yevgeny, 343
Arzberger, Kenneth, 235
As Five Years Pass, *339*
As Thousands Cheer, *338*
Asbury, Donna Marie, 312
Ascenzo, Paul J., 258, 259
Asch, Leslee, 276
Ascheim, Skip, 457
Ascoe, Karen, 290
Ascott, Mavis, 228
Aseron, Ross, 356
Ash, Jeffrey, 239, 252
Asher, Lisa, 359
Asher, Steve, 280, 453
Ashes to Ashes, 3, 36, 40, 41, *287*, *288*
Ashford, Robert, 244, 298, 421
Ashley, Christopher, 275, 277, 338, 424, 436
Ashley, Mary Ellen, 256
Ashman, Howard, 221
Ashmanskas, Brooks, 236
Ashmore, Catherine, viii
Ashton, Craig, 323
Ashworth, Jody, 286, 334
Asia Society, 355
Asian American Theater Company, 433
Askin, Peter, 279, 424
Aspel, Brad, 237, 300
Asphyxia and Other Promises, *343*
Aspillaga, Vanessa, 339, 351, 355, 363
Aspiring Fox, The, *356*
Assael, Deborah, 239
Assassins, 457
Astaire Awards, 455
AT&T: *On Stage*, 423, 431
ATCA (see American Theater Critics Association)
Athanas, Charlie, 412
Atkins, Robert, 335
Atkins, Tracey, 358
Atkinson, Barry, 229
Atlantic Theater Company, 41, 330, 331, 336, 455

Attar, Victor, 343
Attard, Sandrine, 292
Auberjonois, Tessa, 294
Audette, Naomi, 347
August Snow, *359*
Augustine, Kevin, 360
Aukin, Daniel, 350
Auld, Robert, 274
Aulino, Tom, 237, 359
Aulisi, Arthur, 354
Ault, Stephanie, 410
Aural Fixation, 245, 253, 286, 294, 425
Austin, Eve, 335
Austin, Ford, 436
Austin, Lyn, 330, 344
Austin-Williams, Jaye, 424
Author! Author!, *356*
Author's Voice, The, *338*
Avallone, Angelina, 421
Avery, Val, 281
Avian, Bob, 401, 416
Avni, Ran, 340
Avow, *355*
Awakening, The, 356, *361*
Awon, Kim, 224
Ax, Mark, 306
Axelrod, Wendy, 275
Axtell, Barry, 272
Ay, Carmela, *345*
Ayckbourn, Alan, 39, 40, 274
Aycock, Janet, 241
Ayvazian, Leslie, 331, 339, 428
Ayyar, Priya, 355
Azenberg, Emanuel, 255, 451
Azenberg, Karen, 334
Aznavour, Charles, 3, 20, 230
Aznavour on Broadway, 4, *230*
Azzolina, Jay, 297

Babak, Cynthia, 358
Babatunde, Obba, 313
Babb, Zakia, 343
Babcock, Karen, 261
Babe, Thomas, 360
Babel's in Arms, *426*
Babes in Arms, 36, 42, *297*, *298*
Babes in the Woods: 7 Urban Sightings, *358*
Babiar, Steven, 234, 261
Babilla, Assurbanipal, 359
Babin, Michael, 435
Baby Redboots' Revenge, *349*
Babylon, Guy, 402
Bach, Del-Bourree, 240
Bach, Richard, 334, 355
Bachmann, Charlie, 402
Bad Reputation, *349*
Bad Seed, The, *360*

Bader, Jenny Lyn, 436
Badgett, Will, 362
Badlam, Robb, 419
Baeumler, Carolyn, 419
Baez, Rafael, 338
Bagden, Ron, 241, 361
Baggott, Kevin, 361
Bagwell, Marsha, 411
Bailey, Adrian, 320
Bailey, Alan, 269, 270
Bailey, Carol, 348
Bailey, Kevin, 251
Bailey, Victoria, 285
Baitz, Jon Robin, 417, 430
Baixas, Joan, 357
Bajraktari, Valdet, 351
Baker, Becky Ann, 277, 437
Baker, Christopher, 404
Baker, Cliff Fannin, 416
Baker, Darrin, 265
Baker, David Aaron, 350
Baker, Dylan, 290, 437
Baker, Earl, Jr., 344
Baker, Edward Allan, 339
Baker, Joseph, 230, 231
Baker, Matthew, 240
Baker, Max, 347
Baker, Ray, 290
Baker, Scott, 342
Baker, Simon, 255
Baker, Taft, 229
Baker, Travis, 331, 361
Baksic, Amela, 338, 353
Balaban, Bob, 417
Bald Soprano, The, *342, 352*,
  360
Baldassari, Mike, 305
Baldauff, Julie, 239, 270
Baldini, Gabriella, 269
Baldinu, Pichon, 269
Baldoni, Gail, 340
Baldwin, Kate, 298
Balgord, Linda, 311
Balkan Women, The, 368
Balkwill, Dean, 318
Ball of Roses, The, *361*
Ballagh, Robert, 228, 280
Ballantyne, Scott D., 286
Ballard, Doc, 408, 409
Ballard, Kay, 281
Ballinger, Matthew, 298, 320
Ballos, Michael A., 342
Balsam, Mark, 230
Baltimore Waltz, The, 38
BAM (see Brooklyn Academy
  of Music)
Bamji, Firdous, 431
Bamman, Gerry, 355
Bancilhon, Chantal, 409

Band in Berlin, 3, 4, 9, 21, *252*
Banham, Teresa, 290
Bank, Diane, 347
Bank, Jonathan, 359
Banks, C.C., 335
Banquet of the Beheaded, The,
  342
Barón, Brandin, 415
Barak, Ehud, 10
Barall, Michi, 433, 437
Barata, I Dewa, 276
Barber, Joan, 435
Barberio, Gabriela, 269
Barbour, James, 307
Barbousi, Vasso, 280
Barclay, William, 353
Bardele, Kurt, 420
Bardwell, Gena, 423
Barefoot Boy With Shoes On,
  416, 436
Barefoot in the Park, 40
Barford, Ian, 406
Barker, David, 350
Barker, Gary, 314
Barker, Katharine, 290
Barker, Pete, 335
Barker, Tim, 305, 306
Barks, Coleman, 337
Barlow, John, 243, 255, 256
Barlow, Leslie, 234
Barlow, Roxane, 236
Barna, Craig, 239
Barnard, Tod, 239
Barnes, 430
Barnes, Bruce, 239
Barnes, Clive, 447, 453
Barnes, Ezra, 421
Barnes, Gregg, 235, 261, 299,
  421
Barnes, Lisa Marjorie, 351
Barnett, Eileen, 425
Barnett, Ken, 240
Barnett, Ron, 294
Baron, Alan, 350
Baron, Courtney, 419
Baron, Evalyn, 427
Baron, Jeff, 264
Baron, Neal, 428
Barone, Deana, 360
Barone, Richard, 278
Barre, Gabriel, 412
Barreca, Christopher, 353, 404
Barrett, Brent, 313
Barrett, Joe, 334
Barrie, J.M., 239, 342
Barrish, Seth, 355
Barron, Constance, 270, 420
Barron, Sarah, 229
Barrow Group, The, 355

Barrowman, John, 416
Barrows, Spencer Scott, 355
Barruch, Adam, 240, 241
Barrus, David, 457
Barry, B.H., 275
Barry, Brian, 311
Barry, Philip, 223
Barry, Sarah, 228
Barry, Tara, 228
Barrymore, 22, 457
Barsha, Debra, 436
Bart, Roger, 29, 248, 451, 456
Barta, Becky, 401
Bartabas, 337
Barter Theater, 400
Barth, Frank, 334
Bartlett, Peter, 277, 309, 437
Bartlett, Rob, 7, 230
Bartley, Robert, 266
Bartner, Robert G., 282
Barton, Steve, 316
Bartosik, Steve, 239
Baruch, Steven, 255, 280, 453
Barzee, Anastasia, 314
Basche, David Alan, 37, 303,
  327, 359
Basden, Derin, 282, 354
Bass, Eric, 357
Bass, Ines Zeller, 357
Bassett, Rick, 224
Bast, Stephanie, 232
Bastine, Ronald Cadet, 240
Bat Boy, 455, 458
Bat Theater Company, 329,
  355
Bates, Anne, 305, 306
Bates, Dearbhail, 228
Batista, Wilson A., 229
Batt, Bryan, 46, 294
Battista, Luisa, 358
Battle, Hinton, 313
Bauduc, Ray, 247
Bauer, Bartley H., 405, 406
Bauer, C. Andrew, 419
Bauer, Ed, 427
Bauer, Irvin S., 253, 296
Bauer, Martin, 269
Bauer-Espinosa, Cynthia, 253
Bauers, Ruth, 355
Baum, L. Frank, 260
Baumann, Michel, 292
Bavan, Yolande, 432
Baxter, Robin, 230
Bay Street Theater, 430
Bayer, Jennifer, 234
Bayley, Stan W., 457
Bayuga, Pierre, 319
Beach, Albert Askew, 256
Beach, Gary, 309

Beal, Harrison, 309
Beal, John, 298, 299, 301
Beal, Melody, 333
Bean, Melanie, 335
Bean, R., 313
Bean, Reathel, 355
Beane, Douglas Carter, 338
Beanie Baby Addiction, *351*
Bearskin, George Stonefish, 430
Beatbox: A Raparetta, *432*
Beatty, John Lee, 47, 231, 245, 280, 297, 298, 299, 301
Beatty, Leslie, 360
Beaubrun, Spelman M., 360
Beaudin, Joe, 457
Beauregard, Normand, 428
Beausoleil-Baldwin, Linda, 234
Beautiful Thing, 36, 40, *302*, 458
Beautiful White Room, A, *345*
Beauty and the Beast, 221, 307, 458
Beauty Queen of Leenane, The, 3, 12, 223, 454
Beber, Neena, 432
Becham, Larl, 351
Beck, Bobby, 400, 401
Becker, Bonnie L., 233
Becker, Carson Grace, 458
Becker, John, 349
Becker, Peter, 252
Becker, Sharon, 351
Beckett, Samuel, 337, 339, 358
Beckett, Tom, 274
Beckler, Steven, 231
Beckman, Claire, 303
Beckman, Ellen, 350
Beckwith, Eliza, 339, 359, 361
Beckwith, Laura, 359
Bedella, David, 321
Bedfellows, *355*
Bedford, Brian, 292
Bedi, Purva, 287
Beditz, David, 321
Beeks, James, 320
Beeson, Jack, 455
Befeler, Roger, 307
Beggarly, Jim, 335
Begin-Young, Phil, 432
Behind the Counter Productions, 290
Behind the Counter With Mussolini, 36, *290*
Behnke, Corey, 285
Beitchman, Lillith, 348
Belack, Doris, 425
Belgrader, Andrei, 331, 337
Belknap, Anna, 437

Bell, Hilary, 336
Bell, Melany, 402
Bell, Melissa, 321
Bell, Michel, 26, 257, 323, 414, 456
Bell, Monica, 422
Bell, Neal, 419
Bellis, Christopher, 334
Belluso, John, 338, 428
Bellwoar, Megan, 427
Belmont Avenue Social Club, *363*, 458
Ben Franklin: Unplugged, *349*
Benanti, Laura, 320
Benari, Neal, 402
Benator, Andrew, 305
Bender-Dubiel, Joshua, 340
Bendul, Kristine, 237
Benesch, Vivienne, 284
Benford, Starla, 422, 434
Benham, Craig A., 311
Bening, Annette, 417
Benish, Jeff, 413
Benjamin, Adria, 241
Benjamin, Avi, 343
Benjamin, P.J., 312
Benko, Tina, 249
Bennett, Alan, 234, 310
Bennett, Arnold, 354
Bennett, Beresford, 362
Bennett, Keith, 315
Bennett, Kiki, 234
Bennett, Mark, 237, 270, 284, 415, 428
Bennett, Matthew, 321
Bennett, Robert Russell, 299
Bennett, Susan, 302
Bennett, Tim, 404
Benny's Barbershop, *352*
Benson, Kathryn, 355
Benson, Lynnea, 356
Benson, Martin, 408
Benson, Peter, 236
Bensussen, Melia, 349, 432, 456
Benten Kozo, 329, *355*, 456
Benthal, John, 230
Bentley-LaMar, Mary, 402
Benzinger, Suzy, 411
Berata, I Dewa, 277
Berata, I Dewa Putu, 276
Berc, Shelley, 427
Berdy, Kimberly Ann, 303
Bergdoll, Brian, 334
Bergen, Kevin, 356
Berger, Jesse, 457
Berger, Stephanie, viii
Berger, Stephen, 269
Bergeron, Charles, 241

Bergeron, Francois, 239
Bergl, Emily, 237
Bergman, Hayes, 240
Beringer, Kim, 292
Berinstein, Dori, 239
Beriro, Meny, 334
Berkeley, Edward, 356, 363
Berkeley Repertory Theater, 404, 415
Berkey, Dan, 361
Berkley, Price, 450
Berkoff, Steven, 354
Berkowitz, D. Michael, 415
Berkowitz, Michael, 241, 301
Berkshire Theater Festival, 281, 433
Berkson, Jennie, 358
Berlin Circle, The, *406*
Berlin, Irving, 230, 247, 250, 338
Berlin, Pamela, 353
Berlind, Roger, 243, 254, 256, 275, 450
Berliner, Chris, 409
Berlinsky, Harris, 358
Berlioz, Hector, 265
Berloni, William, 261
Berman, Ariana, 334
Berman, Brooke, 331, 419
Berman, Mark, 259
Berman, Matt, 295, 425
Berman, Robert, 236
Berman, Simona, 335
Bermea, Bobby, 432
Bern, Mina, 456
Bernat, Eric, 361
Bernhard, Sandra, 3, 20, 234
Bernstein, Anne L., 256
Bernstein, Betsy D., 251
Bernstein, Douglas, 264
Bernstein, Jonathan, 255
Bernstein, Leonard, 29, 229, 237
Bero, Veronica, 334
Berresse, Michael, 258, 259, 313
Berry, Anita, 323
Berry, Bill, 275
Berry, Gabriel, 343
Berry, John, 436
Berry, Michael, 324
Berry, Rob, 416
Berry, Sarah Uriarte, 324
Berson, Misha, viii
Berst, Lauren, 410
Berti, Gino, 402
Berti, Michelle, 239
Bertish, Suzanne, 286
Bertles, Steve, 311

Besteman, Cynthia, 363
Besterman, Douglas, 235, 241, 246, 430, 452
Beth-Arlene, 345
Bettridge, Ted, 410
Betty's Summer Vacation, 36, 38, *280*, 456
Between East & West, *412*
Between the Ages, *334*
Bevel, Charles, 243, 259, 260, 303, 304, 428, 430, 451
Bewley, Adrian, 361
Bey, Ronnell, 344
Beyer, Tom, 458
Bhutia, Lakpa T., 350
Biancamano, Frank, 352
Bianco, Carla, 278, 319
Bienskie, Stephen, 311, 412, 457
Big, 26
Big Blue Nail, The, *345, 432*
Big Deal, 33, 246, 247
Big Night, 416
Big Rosemary, *425*
Bigelow, September, 411
Bigelow, Susan, 230
Biggs, Natalie, 228
Bihari, Jules, 254, 297
Bihuan, Zhang, 348
Bikel, Theodore, 331, 340
Bill Evans & Associates, 281
Billeci, John, 363
Billings, Alexandra, 406, 412
Billington, Ken, 224, 231, 235, 301
Billman, Sekiya, 351
Billmann, Nancy, 229
Billotti, David, 275
Binder, David, 269
Binder, Jay, 230, 248, 255, 298, 299, 305
Binder, Jeff, 223
Bingham, Lucinda, 406
Binghamon, Vincent, 310
Binkley, Howell, 244, 401, 414, 424, 457
Binkley, James, 293
Binlids, *354*
Birch, Patricia, 21, 25, 244, 252, 266, 452, 455
Birch, Sandra, 405, 406
Bird, *344*
Bird, Anne Gee, 431
Birkenhead, Susan, 223, 424
Birkrant, Elizabeth, 406
Birney, Reed, 353, 355, 427
Birth Rite, *355*

Birthday Party, The, 330
Birthday Pie, *415*
Bischoff, Marty, 335
Bishoff, Joel, 281
Bishop, Andre, 224, 243, 269, 294, 451
Bishop, Karen-Angela, 323
Bissell, Cassandra, 406
Bittenbender, Sarah, 282
Bitter Lemon, *350*
Bitter Sauce, *270, 271*
Bitterman, Shem, 354
Bixby, Jonathan, 252, 338
Björnson, Maria, 292
BJ: The Trail of a Transgender Country Rock Star, *357*
Black, Brent, 358
Black, Christopher, 358
Black Comedy: The Wacky Side of Racism, *338*
Black, James, 7, 249, 414, 456
Black, Jeremy, 351
Black Marble Shoeshine Stand, The, *334*
Black Mask, *348*
Black Milk, *344*
Black No More, 368
Black, Rachel, 240
Black, Shirley Temple, 455
Blackall, Nora, 320
Blackburn, Bob, 459
Blackman, Robert, 410
Blackwell, Karen Byers, 322
Bladel, Rod, 360
Blagen, Jennifer, 422
Blair, Tom, 431
Blaise, Judd, 360
Blake, Richard H., 314, 318
Blanchard, Lisa, 234
Blanchard, Steve, 307, 309
Blancher, Philippe, 292
Blanco, Alberto, 344
Blankenbuehler, Andy, 245, 246
Blankenship, Lisa, 355
Blankenship, Paul, 411
Blankfort, Jase, 353
Blanks, Harvy, 410
Blasius, Chuck, 348
Blasquez, Pedro, 303
Bleeke, Mark, 252
Blendick, James, 292
Blessed Are: Scenes From Shaker Life, *345*
Blessing, Lee, 454
Blindauer, Patrick, 335
Blinn, David, 299

Bloch, Scotty, 359, 432
Block, Alan, 260, 304
Block, Elizabeth, 358
Blong, Jenni, 360
Blood Money Caper, The, *358*
Blood on the Dining Room Floor, 455
Bloodletting, *343*
Bloom, Claire, 19, 242, 428, 451, 456
Bloom, Mark, 275
Bloom, Michael, 457
Bloomfield, Allen, 275
Blount, William, 237
Blue Heart, 36, *290, 292*, 331, 448
Blue Heron Arts Center, 355
Blue Kettle, *290, 292*
Blue Light Theater Company, 332, 337
Blue, Madeline, 434
Blue Man Group, 264
Blue Room, The, 3, 4, 9, 11, 18, *243, 419*, 447, 456
Bluestone, Alan, 265
Blumberg, Allen, 359
Blumberg, Kate, 336, 337
Blumenfeld, Mara, 406
Blumenthal, Francesca, 264
Blumfield, Erica, 419
Blumsack, Amy Lord, 264
Blunt, Gabrielle, 292
Blur, *340*, 411
BMG Classics, 455
Boardman, Robert, 359
BoarsHead Theater, 416
Bobb-Semple, Ron, 429
Bobbie, Walter, 230, 231, 451
Bobbitt, Wendy, 232, 266
Bobby, Anne, 40, 275
Bochman/Lenow, 252
Bodeen, Michael, 287, 406, 421
Bodnar, Amy, 412
Body of Crime, Part II: A History of Women in Prison, *343*
Boehmer, J. Paul, 407
Boesche, John, 406
Bogaev, Paul, 286, 402
Bogardus, Stephen, 323
Bogart, Anne, 277, 419
Bogart, Matt, 257, 316, 414
Bogdanov, Michael, 422
Bogosian, Eric, 270
Bohanek, James, 232
Bojarski, Stanley, 299, 300
Bojun, Yo, 348

Bolden, Ken, 355
Bolger, Dermot, 355
Bolger, John, 363
Boll, Patrick, 303
Bommer, Lawrence, 368
Bomurwil Productions, 256, 451
Bonadio, Renee, 311
Bonanni, John, 235
Bonard, Mayra, 269
Bonavitacola, Kenneth, 348
Bond, Clint, Jr., 232
Bond, Samantha, 10, 256, 451
Bond, Will, 419
Bondoc, Lexine, 359
Bonds, Rufus, Jr., 25, 243
Boneau/Bryan-Brown, 223, 229, 231, 233, 236, 239, 255, 256, 259, 260, 270, 280, 282, 285, 288, 297, 305
Boneau, Chris, 239, 259, 260, 297
Bonet, Wilma, 404
Bonilla, Barbara, 361
Bonnell, Monroe M., 355
Bonney, Jo, 37, 284, 340
Bontems, Denis, 409
Bontrager, Laura, 257, 269
Boocock, Bob, 358
Book of Days, 367, 368, 369–378, *405*, 454
Book of Harsh Geometry, A, *347*
Booker, Keisha Monique, 360
Bookman, Kirk, 252, 266, 338, 420
Boom Town, *406*
Boomers, *416*
Boonyarata-Pun, Pun, 437
Booth, Debra, 353, 428
Booth, Eboni, 337
Booth, Susan V., 406, 434
Bootz/Karlick, 252
Borden, Chad, 322, 426
Borle, Christian, 314
Borowski, Michael S., 234, 275
Borras, John, 335
Borsay, LaTonya, 341
Bosco, Philip, 18, 19, 224
Bosley, Tom, 309, 323
Bosoms and Neglect, 329, *350*
Bostnar, Lisa, 359
Boston, Gretha, 31, 259, 304, 323, 452
Boston Theater Critics Association, 457
Botello, Catalina, 345

Both, Andrei, 337
Bottari, Michael, 351
Boublil, Alain, 221
Boucicault, Dion, 331, 339
Boudouvis, Yorgos, 337
Boundary, The, *420*
Bourne, Matthew, 23, 24, 229, 452, 455, 456
Boutsikaris, Dennis, 290
Boutté, Duane, 244, 341
Bouvy, Harry, 363
Bowen, Alex, 234, 353
Bowen, Ann, 347
Bowen, Graham, 229
Bowen, Melissa, 256
Bowen, Paul James, 334
Bowen, Steven D., 299
Bowers, Bill, 315
Bowers, John, 335
Bowie, David, 275
Bowles, Paul, 358
Bowman, Jacqueline, 335
Bowman, Jill, 347
Boyd, Chris, 361
Boyd, Gregory, 249, 256, 257, 404, 414
Boyd, Guy, 281
Boyer, Katherine Lee, 282
Boyington, Kathryn, 270
Boys, Bary, 422
Boys Next Door, The, *457*
Boys' Life, *358*
Boys Will Be Boys, *361*
Bozell, Tom, 342
Bozzone, Bill, 339
Bracchitta, Jim, 281
Brackett, Anthony, 229
Bradfield, Dawn, 260, 451
Bradley, Brad, 251
Bradley, David, 291
Bradley, Frank, 348
Bradley, Lorna, 228
Brady, Kathleen M., 410, 411
Brady, Patrick S., 246, 247
Brady, Stephen, 437
Brailoff, Lisa, 355
Braithwaite, Charlotte, 343
Brancato, Joe, 305
Brand, Gibby, 309
Brandes, David, 420
Brandner, Susan, 360
Brandt, Alan, 305
Branescu, Smaranda, 402
Brannon, Lance, 416
Branom, Curt, 361
Brantley, Ben, 447, 448
Branton, Allen, 234

Branton, Dhana-Marie, 436
Brass, Stacey Lynn, 431
Brassard, Gail, 350
Brassea, Bill, 261
Brathwaite, Charlotte, 343
Bravo, Luis, 222
Braxton, Brenda, 320
Braxton, Toni, 309
Bray, Barbara, 355
Brazington, Wendy, 292
Bread and Butter, *360*
Bread and Puppet Circus, *351*
Bread and Puppet Theater, 351
Brecht, Bertolt, 357, 359, 402
Breck, Susie, 416
Breedlove, Gina, 315
Breen, Patrick, 337
Breese, Timothy, 299, 300
Breitbart, Howard, 273
Brennan, Martin, 228
Brenneman, Amy, 408
Bresnahan, Alyssa, 414, 457
Breuer, Lee, 344, 457
Brevoort, Deborah Baley, 345
Brice, Richard, 229, 286, 299
Bricusse, Leslie, 222
Bride and the Butterfly Hunter, The, *343*
Bridge, Andrew, 246, 452
Bridges, Amy, 368
Bridges, Campbell, 334
Bridges, Marina, 273
Bridges, Scott, 239
Brief Excursion, A, *360*
Brigden, Tracy, 414, 457
Briggs, Kelly, 310
Brigham Young University Theater, 368
Bright Lights Big City, 36, 44, *277*, *278*, 327
Brightman, Sarah, 316
Brighton, Pam, 280, 354
Brill, Robert, viii, 38, 268, 288, 431, 453, 455
Brimmer, J. David, 289
Bring in 'da Noise Bring in 'da Funk, 44, 222, 309, 459
Bringing the Fishermen Home, *340*
Brinkley, Susann, 338
Brinkman-Young, Alex, 427
Brisa, Nuria, 228, 229
Bristol, Pa. Riverside Theater, 368
Britannicus, 36, *290*, *291*, *292*, 331
Brito, Betty, 334

Britton-Schrager, Heather, 457
Briusov, Valerii, 356
Broadhurst, Kent, 288
Brochtrup, Bill, 425
Brock, Lee, 355
Brocker, Kurt, 302
Brockman, Jane, 241
Brockus, Sarah, 361
Brocone, Genna, 412
Broderick, Kate, 275
Broderick, Matthew, 15, 17, 252
Broecker, Tom, 223, 305
Brogyanyi, Eugene, 356
Brokaw, Mark, 285, 290
Bromka, Elaine, 359
Brontë, Emily, 421
Brooke, Lucy Avery, 337
Brooking, Kevin, 357
Brooking, Simon, 414
Brooklyn Academy of Music (BAM), 36, 290, 293, 331, 453
Brooklyn Academy of Music Next Wave Festival, 337
Brooks, Donald, 351, 450
Brooks, Gwendolyn, 253, 296
Brooks, Jeff, 309
Brothers Booth, The, *361*
Brothers, Carla, 347
Brothers of the Night, 457
Brotherston, Lez, 229, 452, 456
Brourman, Michele, 424
Brown, Adam, 234
Brown, Alvin, 261
Brown and Black and White All Over, *361*
Brown, Angela, 360
Brown, Ann, 234
Brown, Blair, 310
Brown, C.C., 318
Brown, Carlyle, 345, 432
Brown, Deborah, 253
Brown, Jason Robert, 23, 24, 25, 46, 243, 269, 271, 340, 447, 451, 456
Brown, Jeb, 421
Brown, Jim, 361
Brown, Kipleigh, 412
Brown, Larry W., 253, 296, 333
Brown, Laura Grace, 275, 353
Brown, Lew, 246
Brown, Lewis, 430
Brown, Maura, 354
Brown, Michael, 264, 277, 350, 353, 436, 437
Brown, Michael Henry, 340

Brown, Nora, 361
Brown, Rena Cherry, 457
Brown, Rosalind, 230, 313
Brown, Sonnie, 294
Browne, Kate, 360
Browne, Leslie, 361
Browning, Timothy, 415
Brownlee, Elizabeth, 360
Brownstone, Diana, 244
Broyard, Mark, 340
Bruce, Cheryl Lynn, 406
Bruce, Tom, 335
Bruckner, Michelle, 409
Brulé, 430
Brumley, Albert E., 270
Brummel, David, 340, 363
Brunell, Catherine, 431
Brunner, Michael, 250, 294
Bruno, Abraham, 229
Bruno, Louis, 286
Bruno, Tom, 335
Brustein, Robert, 405
Bryan-Brown, Adrian, 223, 231, 233, 236, 243, 255, 256, 259, 288, 305
Bryant, Andrew, 288
Bryant, Brienin, 267
Bryant, David, 315, 414
Bryant, Mary, 246
Brydon, Angela, 230
Bryggman, Larry, 330, 336, 337
Bubbly Beds, *276*
Bubbly Black Girl Sheds Her Chameleon Skin, The, 436, 455
Buchanan, Linda, 407
Buchanan, Will, 335
Buchin, Bertrand, 335
Buck, Heather, 359
Buck, Pearl S., 294
Buck, Peter, 275
Buckhannan, Jack, 229
Buckley, Betty, 311, 353
Buckley, Candy, 245, 274
Buckley, Erick, 286
Buckley, Kate, 412
Buckley, Melinda, 430
Buckner, Joanna, 419
Buddeke, Kate, 249, 458
Buddy: The Buddy Holly Story, 458
Buderwitz, Thomas, 408
Budnich, Christopher, 360
Budries, David, 414, 428
Buell, Bill, 321, 356
Buliung, Evan, 293
Bull, Paul, 348

Bulloch, Lauren, 410
Bullock, Donna, 318
Bundonis, Al, 225
Bundy, Rob, 337
Bunina, Maria, 342
Bunn, David Alan, 253, 254, 296, 297, 333
Bunting, Anne, 413
Buntrock, Stephen R., 315, 321
Burba, Blake, 278
Burch, Patrick, 348
Burchfield, Jeff, 348
Burga, Rafael M., 352
Burgess, Troy Allan, 425
Burke, Edward, 280
Burke, Liam, 240
Burke, Maggie, 358
Burkett, Ronnie, 276, 457
Burkett, Shannon, 275, 353
Burks, Charles Anthony, 268
Burmester, Leo, 257
Burners, *345*
Burnett, Carol, 416
Burns, Bill, 245, 246
Burns, Kevin, 425
Burns, Peter, 407
Burns, Ralph, 246, 452
Burrell, Fred, 358
Burrell, Pamela, 232
Burrell, Ty, 437
Burridge, Bud, 259
Burridge, Hollis, 235
Burroughs, Don, 334
Burrows, Allyn, 289, 359
Burrows, Kevin M., 402
Burrows, Vinie, 347
Burrus, Bob, 417
Burstein, Danny, 314, 321
Burstyn, Mike, 340
Burton, Anthony, 428
Burton, Arnie, 426
Burton, Kate, 309, 350, 450
Burward-Hoy, Kenneth, 299
Buryat National Theater, 343
Busackino, Barbara, 265
Busch, Charles, 351
Bush, Michael, 285
Bush Theater, 329
Buss, Tesha, 311
Buster, Natalie, 360
Bustle, Jonathan, 275
But Not for Me, *408*
Buterbaugh, Keith, 316, 323
Butiu, Melody, 415, 416
Butler, Jean, 228
Butler, Kerry, 308, 315
Butler, Terence, 303

Butler, Tony, 355
Butt, Billy, 235
Butterbeans and Suzie, 254, 297
Butterell, Jonathan, 242, 428
Buttram, Jan, 358
Butz, Norbert Leo, 310, 318
Buzas, Jason McConnell, 363
Byk, Jim, 248, 249, 303
Byrd, Debra, 310
Byrd's Boy, 411
Byrne, Derek, 228
Byrne, Rachel, 228
Byrne, Terry, 457
Byrnes, Brendan, 360
Byrum, Ashton, 410
Byun, Harold S., 348

Cabaniss, Tom, 424
Cabaret, 3, 31, 46, 222, 246, 247, 447
Cabin Pressure, *419*
Cabre-Andrews, Flo, 361
Cacciotti, Tony, 294
Caesar and Cleopatra, *358*
Caesar, Sid, 30
Cagan, Richard, 335
Cahan, Cora, 303, 347
Cahill, Laura, 353
Cahn, Danny, 236, 259
Cahn, Larry, 318
Cahoon, Kevin, 298, 315
Cain, Candice, 285, 354, 417
Cain, Wilson III, 362
Caissie, Zeph, 228
Calamia, Marc, 245, 246
Calarco, Joe, 264, 457
Calaway, Belle, 312
Calder, John W. III, 272
Caldwell, L. Scott, 408
Caldwell Theater Company, 404
Cale, David, 268, 456
Calhoun, Jeff, 27, 28, 251
Caliban, Richard, 345, 355
Calitsis, Vasilios, 337
Callan, K, 426
Callan, Monica, 351
Callen, Christopher, 426
Calleri, James, 280, 281
Callner, Marty, 234
Calvert, Carter, 259, 304
Cameron, Ben, 231
Cameron, Bruce, 301
Cameron, Sarah C., 348
Camino Real, 332
Camp, Bill, 360, 362

Camp, Joanne, 360
Campanella, Christina, 356
Campanella, Stephen, 237, 238, 299
Campbell, Amelia, 353
Campbell, Cassondra, 432
Campbell, Catherine, 230, 313
Campbell, Chris, 361
Campbell, David, 298
Campbell, Mary, 447
Campbell, Maureen, 342
Campbell, Shawn, 293
Campbell, T. Ramon, 410
Campbell, Torquil, 284, 358
Camping With Henry & Tom, 454
Campion, David, 293
Campo, John, 251, 301
Campos, Jamie, 348
Canale, Tymberly, 338
Canby, Vincent, 29
Candida, *360*
Cannaday, Melissa, 421
Cannavale, Bobby, 428, 436
Cannold, Sammi Rose, 239
Cannon, Alice, 356
Cannon, Cedric D., 347
Canolle, Jean, 404
Canon for the Blue Moon, A, *342*
Cantone, Mario, 401
Cantor, Arthur, 436
Cantor, Geoffrey P., 223
Cantwell, Christopher, 360
Canty, Andre, 356
Canvin, Rue E., viii
Capalbo, Marco, 361
Capitol Steps, 46, 273
Caplan, Henry, 282, 354
Caplin, Loren-Paul, 362
Capone, Steven, 282
Capone, Tony, 299, 300
Cappiello, Christopher, 351
Capps, Lisa, 324
Captain 11, 427
Captain's Tiger: A Memoir for the Stage, The, 35, 36, *285, 286*
Captains Courageous, the Musical, 36, 44, *285, 286*
Carballido, Emilio, 356
Carbonneau, Peg, 294
Carden, Stuart, 419
Carden, William, 274
Cardia, Gringo, 342
Cardinal Detoxes, The, *363*
Cardona, Debra, 240

Cardwell, Jay, 271
Carey, Helen, 270
Carey, Nadine, 429
Carideo, Ralph, 351
Cariou, Len, 323, 431
Carl, Christopher, 316
Carl, Fred, 436
Carlebach, Josh, 350
Carley, Christopher Murphy, 309
Carlile, Rupert, 292
Carlin, Aviva Jane, 42, 303, 332, 354
Carlin, Nancy, 432
Carlin, Tony, 407
Carlson, Jeffrey, 268, 284
Carlton, Daniel, 355
Carlton, Joel, 431
Carlyle, Scott, 310
Carmello, Carolee, 25, 26, 243, 319, 451, 456
Carmen, Eric, 231, 451
Carmichael, Clark Scott, 306
Carnahan, Jim, 223, 236, 237, 270, 275, 288, 290
Carnelia, Craig, 424
Caro, Pia, 361
Caroline, or Change, *340*
Carollo, Scott, 318
Caron, Meredith, 293
Carp, Stan, 360
Carpenter, Barnaby, 294
Carpenter, Bridget, 341, 411, 428
Carpenter, Carleton, 432
Carpenter, Larry, 433
Carpinello, James, 275, 353
Carr, Anthony, 426
Carr, Geneva, 281, 331, 338, 361
Carr, Jeff Obafemi, 422
Carrière, Berthold, 293
Carrière, Jean-Claude, 285
Carrigan, Robin, 352
Carrillo, Juliette, 408
Carrington, Dwayne, 409
Carroll, Barbara, 250, 294
Carroll, Beeson, 350
Carroll, Bryant, 230
Carroll, Diahann, 321
Carroll, Kevin, 284
Carroll, Lewis, 409
Carroll, Pat, 19, 242, 428
Carroll, Ronn, 251
Carruthers, Mike, 273
Carry the Tiger to the Mountain, *348*

Carta, Jennifer, 354
Carter, Brian J., 282, 344
Carter, Caitlin, 425
Carter, Nell, 322
Carter, Sarah, 235, 244
Carusillo, Beth, 457
Caruso, Thomas, 345, 415
Carusone, Leo P., 272
Carvell, Jason Alan, 271
Carver, Brent, 25, 26, 243, 451, 456
Casale, Glenn, 239
Casano, Denise, 339
Case, Ron, 351
Casel, Ayodele, 305
Casella, Carlos, 269
Casella, Max, 315
Casey, Peter, 225
Cassandra Complex, The, *358*
Cassidy, Craig, 420, 421
Cassidy, Joe, 240
Casson, Culver, 356
Castay, Leslie, 300, 301, 309
Castellón, Roberto, 303
Castellino, Bill, 434
Casting Society of America, 450
Castree, Paul, 230
Castronovo, Daniel, 437
Cat and the Moon, The, *342*
Catania, Claudia, 285, 347
Cate, Holly, 342
Cates, Gilbert, 417
Cathcart, Sarah, 344
Cathey, Reg E., 360
Catlin, David, 458
Catlin, Sam, 268, 414
Cato, Anders, 358
Catra, I Nyoman, 276, 277
Cats, 221, 310
Catti, Christine, 294
Caught in the Act, 356
Causil, George, 363
Cavallero, Gabriella, 410
Cavanagh, Barry, 239, 241, 322
Cavari, Jack, 244
Cavari, Perry, 246, 248
Cavarra, Nick, 232
Cavedweller, 416
Caverns, *344*
Cavey, George, 359
Cea, Kim, 322
Cearcy, Darlesia, 318
Ceballos, Rene, 311
Cecil, Derek, 417, 419
Celik, Aysan, 405
Cell, Steve, 249
Cella, Susan, 342
Cellario, Maria, 342

Celli, Tom, 400, 401
Cellophane, *355*
Censor, The, *363*
Center Stage, 403
Center Theater Group, 416, 431
Ceraulo, Rich, 359
Cermak, Terry, 422
Cerqua, Joe, 412
Cerullo, Jonathan, 252, 266
Cerutti, David, 229
Cerveris, Michael, 321
Cerveris, Todd, 417, 419
Cesarano, Anthony, 235
Chéri, 458
Chadwick, Fiona, 229
Chaet, Jason, 354
Chaim's Love Song, 36, *275*
Chain Lightning Theater, 355
Chairs, The, 223
Chait, Marcus, 321
Chalfant, Kathleen, 34, 282, 344, 453, 456
Chamarbagwala, Shaheen, 343
Chamberlain, Andrea, 236
Chamberlain, Marisha, 454
Chamberlain, Richard, 29, 320
Chamberlin, Kevin, 299, 300, 338
Chambers, David, 408
Chambers, Ian, 335
Chambers, Jennifer Paige, 311
Champa, Russell H., 425
Champagne, Lenora, 345, 455
Champion, Marge, 450
Champlain, Donna Lynne, 334
Chandler, Brian, 347
Chandler, David, 428
Chandler, Margaret, 349
Chandler, Nat, 232, 299, 300
Chandler, Stan, 425
Chaney, Elizabeth, 340
Chang, Christina, 347
Chang, Tisa, 348
Changing Scene, The, 409
Channing, Stockard, 18, 237, 451
Chapin, Schuyler, 267
Chapman, David Peter, 310
Chapman, Tracy Nicole, 315
Charlap, Moose, 239, 354
Charles MacArthur Award, 457
Charles, Walter, 282, 344
Charlie in the House of Rue, *405*
Charlston, Erik, 299, 301
Charney-Sprei, Elizabeth, 234
Charters, Lanene, 311

Chartoff, Melanie, 408
Chase, Anthony, 252
Chase, David, 232, 235, 236
Chase, Michelle, 234
Chase, Will, 316
Chaskes, Peter, 334
Chastain, Don, 243
Chaurette, Normand, 353
Chavira, Ricardo, 415, 416
Chechile, Dana, 240, 241
Chegwidden, Louise, 404
Chekhov, Anton, 360, 362
Chekhov in Yalta, 454
Chelsea Playhouse, 355
Chemaly, Ed, 355
Chemistry of Change, The, *353*
Chen, Tina, 348
Cheng, Diane, 293
Chenoweth, Kristin, 29, 248, 269, 452, 455, 456
Cheong-Leen, Reggie, 454
Chepiga, Michael J., 7, 232, 430
Chepulis, Kyle, 330
Cher Maitre, 329, *355*
Chermansky, Pamela, 400, 401
Cherney, Christopher, 350
Chernoff, Marvin, 275
Chernov, Hope, 360, 422
Cherpakov, Howie, 251
Cherry Vanilla, *344*
Chervinsky, Alexander, 343
Chesler, Cindy, 359
Chesnutt, James, 337
Chester, Phil, 239
Cheung, Cindy, 362, 431
Chiang, Elizabeth, 359
Chiasson, Christophe, 293
Chiasson, Gilles, 257, 414
Chibas, Marissa, 428
Chicago, 25, 222, 246, 247, 312, 447, 456
Chicago—The Musical, 458, 459
Chichester Festival, 19, 243
Chicoine, Susan, 223, 253, 271, 272, 289, 306
Chila, Doreen, 239
Child, Christine, 287
Childers, Stephanie, 406
Children of Paradise: Shooting a Dream, 454
Children of the House Afire, *351*
Childs, Casey, 329, 349, 436
Childs, Kirsten, 436, 455
Chilson, Kathryn, 360
Chinese Icebox, The, *356*
Chinese Theater Workshop, 357

Chiroldes, Tony, 350
Cho, Linda, 336, 338
Cho, Margaret, 332
Cho, Myung Hee, 282, 330, 344, 403
Choi, Hyung O, 225
Choi, Ji Soo, 225
Choi, So Young, 225
Choi, Young Jae, 225
Chong, Ping, 357
Chopek, Claudia, 278
Chopin, Kate, 356, 361
Chorus Line, A, 25
Chow, Millie, 403
Choy, Al, 335
Christ, Erica, 427
Christensen, Tom, 239
Christian, Eric L., 402
Christian, Karl, 401
Christian, Scott, 435
Christian, Tracy, 348
Christianson, Mike, 232, 261
Christmas at Sandy's, *335*
Christmas Carol, A, 4, *240*, *241*, *410*
Christopher, Amy, 288
Christopher, Dennis, 289
Christopher, Ian, 412
Christopher, Kenn, 324
Christopher, Sybil, 430
Christophersen, Libby, 407, 421
Christou, Rhonda, 356
Chuan, Linda, 348
Chudhuri, Una, 456
Chung, Catherine, 348
Chuppah, *357*
Church, Joseph, 259
Church, Rick, 434
Church, Tony, 411
Churchill, Caryl, 290, 331, 355
Churchill/Morley, 252
Chybowski, Michael, 268, 282, 337, 344, 350, 405, 453, 455, 456
Cicchini, Robert, 354
Cider House Rules, Part I: Here in St. Cloud's, The, *337*
Cider House Rules, Part II, The, 330, 454
Cider House Rules, The, 330, 456, 458, 459
Cina, Jason, 339
Cincinnati Playhouse in the Park, 407
Cinque, Flaminia, 348
Cioffari, Philip, 334, 335
Cionek, Edmund, 421
Cionnaith, Paula Nic, 228
Cippola, John M., 235

Circle Hamlet, The, *360*
Circle in the Square, 6, 270, 293
Circle X Theater Company, 459
Cisek, Tony, 457
City Center, 298
City of Angels, 297
City Theater, 277
Ciulla, A.C., 231, 452
Civil Disobedience; Morning Is When I Am Awake and There Is an Aurora in Me, *342*
Civil Sex, *341*
Civil War, The, 4, 24, 26, *256*, *414*, 450, 451, 456
Clancy, Elizabeth Hope, 284, 337, 353
Clancy, John, 412
Clapp, Deborah, 362
Clarence Darrow Tonight, *338*
Clarence Derwent Awards, 5, 455
Clark, Abe, 322
Clark, Andrea, 419
Clark, Brian, 355
Clark, Dwayne, 318
Clark, G. Thomas, 251
Clark in Sarajevo, *347*
Clark, Petula, 324
Clark, Phillip, 419
Clark, Richard, 251
Clark, Tom, 288
Clark, Victoria, 310, 321
Clark, Winston, 265
Clarke, Breena, 338
Clarke, Denise, 276
Clarke, Judith Lightfoot, 275
Clarke, Kerri, 323
Clarke, Larry, 355
Clarke, Richard, 245
Clarvoe, Anthony, 350, 354, 408
Classic Stage Company (CSC), 5, 268, 331, 337, 453
Clausell, Eric, 234
Clausen, Paul, 311
Clavelli, Chris, 358, 362
Clay, Caroline, 406, 457
Clay, Paul, 278
Clayton, Lawrence, 257, 414
Cleale, Lewis, 324
Cleaned and Burned, *361*
Clearing, The, *414*, 457
Cleary, Brigid, 435
Cleary, Malachy, 363
Cleevely, Gretchen, 288
Clemence, Andy, 273

Clemente, Rene, 311
Clements, Page, 355
Clemmons, Dave, 257, 414, 415
Cleveland, 330
Cleveland Play House, The, 407
Cline, Perry, 236
Clinging to Roadkill, *357*
Clinkard, Theo, 229
Clinton, Kate, 363
Clipper, Craig, 340
Clippinger, Jennifer, 234
Clonts, John, 323
Closely Related, 454
Closer, 4, 9, 11, 12, 18, 47, 192–217, *254*, 447, 448, 450, 456
Cloud, Darrah, 363
Clower, Amanda, 412
Clowers, Michael, 234, 235
Clowning the Bard, *361*
Clubb, Dare, 337, 456
Clyman, Robert, 362
Clyve, Scott, 340
Coates, Douglas, 345
Coates, Wendy, 260, 261
Coates, William Alan, 239
Coaticook, *345*
Cobb, Billy, 351
Coca, Richard, 408
Cochrane, Steve, 261
Cochren, Felix E., 347, 414, 422
Cockfighter, The, *417*
Cocktail Hour, The, 454
Coconut Grove Playhouse, 224
Coderre, Guy, 348
Cody, Jennifer, 311
Coffee, Brian J., 423
Coffin, Gregg, 428, 430
Cogen, Imani, 402
Cohen, Alexander H., 20, 356
Cohen, Betty Anne, 361
Cohen, Buzz, 268, 284
Cohen, Jason, 266, 290
Cohen, Jeff, 363
Cohen, Lynn, 353
Cohen, Lynne, 261
Cohen, Robert L., 243
Cohen, Ronnie, 342
Cohen, Samuel D., 422
Cohenour, Patti, 320
Cohn, Marya, 345
Coid, Marshall, 224
Cointepas, Odile, 292
Colavin, Charlotte, 363
Colby, Michael, 334
Cole, Darren Lee, 288
Cole, Dennis, 324
Cole, Jeremy, 409
Cole, Kelly, 234

Cole, Michael, 353
Cole, Nora, 237
Cole, Stephen, 265
Coleman, Chad L., 414
Coleman, Chris, 279
Coleman, Cy, 30, 32, 45, 222, 236, 246, 247, 265, 266
Coleman, Jim, 420
Coleman, Lee, 245
Coleman, Mary, 432
Coleman, Michele, 344
Coleman, Rosalyn, 349
Coleman, Val, 347
Colgan, Casey, 260
Colimon, Magaly, 363, 423
Colin Quinn—An Irish Wake, 4, *228*
Coll, Ivonne, 428
Collected Stories, 36, 41, *273, 274*
Collins, Bethanne, 434
Collins, David, 363
Collins, Derek, 228
Collins, Jacqueline, 234
Collins, John, 363
Collins, Pat, 417
Collins, Renee, 234
Colombo, Michael, 335
Colombo, Patti, 239
Colon, Lillian, 234
Colon, Miriam, 349
Colony Studio Theater, 459
Colores, *357*
Colt, Alvin, 294
Coluca, Teddy, 342
Columbia Artists, 258, 294
Comédie Française, 292
Comden, Betty, 29, 237, 239, 297, 340, 455
Comedian Harmonists, 21, 252
Comedy of Eros, *404*
Comedy of Errors, The, 458
Coming of Age, 432
Comma, a Single Woman, 415
Common Pursuit, The, 454
Common Vision, A, *432*
Communicating Doors, 36, 39, 40, *274*
Comolli, Dina, 405
Company, The, 458
Comrades and Worms, *345*
Comstock, David, 355
Concha, Benito, 430
Conely, Jim, 422
Conery, Edward, 321
Congdon, Constance, 349
Conk, Mary Ann, 342
Conklin, Helen, 234
Conklin, John, 268

Conklin, Josh, 350
Conklin, JR, 280, 284, 422, 428
Conley, Alexandra, 350
Conley, Matt, 359
Conn, Didi, 293
Connecticut Critics Circle Awards, 457
Connecticut Repertory Theater, 434
Connelly, Bruce, 359
Connelly Theater, 355
Connolly, John, 426
Connolly, Patrick, 228
Connor, Annie, 361
Connors, Michael William, 359
Conrad, David, 431
Conroy, Frances, 41, 42, 245, 267, 284
Conroy, Jarlath, 255, 358
Conry, Kathleen, 431
Consentino, Paul, 410
Constable, Paule, 255, 343, 348
Constantine, Deborah, 334, 340, 349
Constantine, Michael, 428
Contemporary Prods, A, 225
Contemporary Productions, 234
Contemporary Theater, A, 432
Conversations With a Kleagle, *335*
Converse, Tony, 281
Convertible, *342*
Convery, Melissa, 228
Conway, Dan, 295
Conway, Kevin, 436
Cook, Candy, 240
Cook, Curtiss I., 412
Cook, Gregory, 355
Cook, Harrison, 400
Cook, Kay Kellam, 405
Cook, Mel, 335
Cook, Patrick, 285
Cook, Rich, 335
Cook, Roderick, 339
Cook, Susan, viii
Cook, Terrence, 251
Cook, Victor Trent, 320
Cook, Virginia, 270
Cooley, Eddie, 260, 304
Coonrod, Karin, 345
Co-op, *351*
Cooper, Adam, 229, 451, 455
Cooper, Augustus, 423
Cooper, Brian, 273
Cooper, Catherine, 406
Cooper, Chuck, 350
Cooper, David, viii
Cooper, Helmar Augustus, 414

Cooper, India, 331, 338
Cooper, Kevin, 259, 304
Cooper, Marilyn, 300, 301
Cooper, Scott, 412
Cooper, Terrence, 253, 296
Cooper-Anifowoshe, Edris, 428
Cooper-Hecht, Gail, 340, 425, 426
Coover, Robert, 405
Copeland, Carolyn Rossi, 270
Copeland, Joan, 281, 340
Copenhagen, Mary K., 405
Copenhaver, Kevin, 410
Coppock, Ada, 426
Coppola, Sam, 425
Corbett, Andrew, 229
Cordell, Christopher, 320
Cordon, Susie, 256
Corduner, Allan, 321
Corley, Nick, 359, 414
Cormican, Peter, 420
Corneille, Pierre, 290, 331
Cornell, Rayme, 305
Cornell University English Department, 455
Corners, *437*
Cornwell, Eric, 21, 229
Corp, Katherine, 234
Corp, Kimberly, 234
Corporate Law, *347*
Corporation, Marie B., 270
Corpus Christi, 34, 35, 36, *285*
Corre, Bo, 361
Correct Me If I'm Right, *363*
Correia, Don, 298
Cortale, Mark, 360
Corthron, Kia, 414
Corti, Jim, 318
Cortinas, Jorge Ignacio, 339
Corwin, Betty L., 450
Corwin, Walter, 351
Cosby, Bill, 455
Cosentino, Paul, 410
Cosier, E. David, 350
Cosla, Edward, 259, 304
Cosmic Bicycle Theater, The, 357
Cossette, Pierre, 232, 256, 450
Costa, Joseph, 414
Costabile, David, 321
Cote, David, 350, 359
Cotovsky, Richard, 458
Cottrell, Richard, 280
Couba, Gregory, 355
Coughlin, Bruce, 238, 251
Coughlin, Ken, 335
Could I Have This Dance?, 454
Councill, Christopher, 251
Countess, The, *356*

Counting on My Fingers, *361*
Country Wife, The, *360*
Countryman, Michael, 252
Countrymen, *361*
Coupla Bimbos Sittin Around Talkin, A, *363*
Couple of Blaguards, A, 36, *295*
Court Theater, 458
Courtien, Mark, 361
Courtney, Philip, 351, 355
Cover, Bradford, 426, 433
Cowan, Grant, 309
Coward, Noel, 339
Cowboys and Indians, *350*
Cowdery, Jim, 361
Cowie, Jeff, 404, 414
Cowles, Matthew, 435
Cowley, Graham, 290
Cox, Brian, 307, 329
Cox, Catherine, 230, 313
Cox, David A., 275
Cox, Elizabeth, 275
Cox, Jane, 349, 350
Cox, Richard, 355
Cox, Veanne, 280
Coyle, Bill, 238, 251, 267, 282
Coyle, Brendan, 255, 456
Coyne, Randy, 234
Coyote, Take Me There, *342*
Coyote Theater, 457
Cozart, Stephanie, 422
Cozzarelli, Ralph, 334
Crabtree, D. Matt, 273
Crabtree, Howard, 264
Craig, Caral, 273, 274, 305
Craig, Kyle, 273
Cram, Cusi, 408
Crampton, Glory, 420
Crandall, Dean, 235
Craven, Kim, 237, 238
Craver, Mike, 270
Crawford, Alvin, 429
Crawford, Bridget, 412
Crawford, Jared, 310
Crawford, Michael, 316
Crawford, Richard, 350
Crazy Me, Crazy You + Dignity, *342*
Creech, Don, 360
Creedon, Don, 358
Creek, Luther, 318
Cresswell, Luke, 264
Creyton, Barry, 264
Crim, Carey, 405
Crimp, Martin, 223, 331, 337
Crisp, Quentin, 356
Cristaldi, Kevin, 348
Cristofer, Michael, 454

Croal, Aida M., 342
Crochet, Laurie, 234
Crocodile Eyes, *352*
Crofoot, Leonard, 356
Croft, Paddy, 253
Croiter, Jeff, 338, 349, 353, 425
Crom, Rick, 230, 231
Cromarty, Alice, 230
Cromarty & Co., 224, 276
Cromarty, Peter, 224, 230, 276
Cromer, David, 458
Cromer, M. Derek, 430
Cromwell, David, 232
Crooks, Rich, 351
Crosby, B.J., 320
Crosby, Bob, 247
Crosby, Kathryn, 431
Crosby, Peter J., 362
Crosley, Jack, 352
Crosse, Margaret, 228
Crossroads Theater Company, 243, 259, 303, 422, 451, 452
Croteau, Jeff, 237
Crough, Ethan, 260, 261
Crouse, Russel, 223
Crow, Laura, 421, 434
Crowder, Bill, 271
Crowfoot-Suede, Lance, 357
Crowl, Jason, 358
Crowley, Bob, 19, 224, 255, 256, 416, 452
Crowley, Dermot, 255
Crowley, John Steven, 458
Crowley, Ruth, 409
Crowthers, Christopher M., 348
Crudup, Billy, 337
Cruikshank, Holly, 245, 246
Cruz, David, 356
Cruz, Israel, 351
Cruz, Miriam, 339
Cruz, Nilo, 345, 428
Cruz, Wilson, 319, 458
Cry Pitch Carrolls, The, *356*
Cryer, Gretchen, 450
Crystal, Raphael, 340
CSC (see Classic Stage Company)
CTM Productions, 239, 259, 451
Cubeiro, Emilio, 349
Cucaracha Theater, 355
Cuccioli, Robert, 314
Cudahy, Michael, 275
Cuddy, Mark, 428
Cuden, Steve, 222
Cuervo, Alma, 321, 344
Cuetara, Laura, 409
Cuillo, Bob, 230
Culbert, John, 406

Cullen, David, 229, 452
Cullison, Barry, 354
Culliver, Karen, 316
Cullman, Joan, 256
Culman, Peter W., 403
Culp, Steven, 425
Culpepper, Daniel, 235
Culture of Desire, 36, *277*
Culturemart, 356
Cumming, Alan, 46, 310
Cummings, Brenda, 434
Cummings, Jean, 348
Cummings, Krysten, 319
Cummins, Stephanie, 230
Cumpsty, Michael, 19, 242, 428
Cunneen, Paddy, 243, 255, 260
Cunningham, Jimmy, 339
Cunningham, Jo Ann, 431
Cunningham, John, 320
Cunningham, T. Scott, 353
Cunningham, Woody, 403
Curley, Andrea, 228
Curley, Geoffrey M., 412
Curnock, Richard, 293
Curran, Jennifer, 228
Currican Theater, 355
Currin, Brenda, 288
Curry, Jon Brent, 419
Curtin, Catherine, 358
Curtin, Saranne, 229
Curtis, Ann, 293
Curtis, June, 243
Curve, The, *356*
Cushing, James, 223, 450
Cuskern, Dominic, 324
Custer, 454
Customer Is Always Right, The, *409*
Cuthbert, David Lee, 433
Cutlip, Cheryl Hebert, 234
Cwikowski, Bill, 294
Cymbeline, 36, 42, *267*, *268*, 455, 456, 457
Cyr, Isabelle, 353
Czechoslovak-American Marionette Theater, 342, 357

da Silva, Dan, 260
D'Ambrosi, Dario, 342
d'Amboise, Charlotte, 312, 458
D'Amboise, Jacques, 455
D'Ambrosio, Frank, 316
D'Ambrosio, Tom, 259, 275, 280
D'Angeles, Evan, 319
D'Aquila, Fabio, 269
D'Avanzo, Sylvia, 239
D'Beck, Patti, 251

D'Monroe, 318
Dace, Tish, viii, 455
Daggett, Larry, 318
Dahlquist, Gordon, 345, 356
Daily, Dan, 360
Dalby, Matthew, 229
Daldry, Stephen, 245
Dale, Jim, 407
Dalen, Patricia, 360, 411
Dallas Theater Center, 409
Dallimore, Stevie Ray, 309, 414
Dallman, Marilyn, 293
Dallos, Chris, 274, 353
Daltrey, Roger, 240
Dalzell, Oliver, 265
Damane, David Aron, 240
Dames, Hiromi, 354
Damico, Frank, 343
Damn Yankees, 246, 247, 457
Dana, F. Mitchell, 430
Dana, Sally, 432
Dance of Life, *409*
Dance Theater Workshop, 276
Dancin', 33, 34, 246, 247, 248
Dancing With a Devil, *419*
Dang, Tim, 459
Daniel, Lenny, 260, 261
Daniel, Michal, viii
Daniele, Graciela, 27, 251, 269, 455
Danielle, Marlene, 311
Daniels, Jeff, 355, 405, 406
Daniels, Kevin, 224
Daniels, Monique, 319
Daniels, Ron, 362
Danielson, Ake, 277
Danilow, Basia, 229
Daniluk, Lauren, 304
Danner, Blythe, 41
Dannheisser, Adam, 224
Danny and Faye, *425*
Danson, Randy, 405
Dante's Inferno, *360*
Danvers, Marie, 316
Danza, Tony, 14, 255, 321
Darden, Patricia, 424
Darlene, *424*
Darling, Max, 352
Darling of the Day, *354*
Darlow, Cynthia, 337, 353
Darlow, David, 407
Darnell, Rick, 260, 304
Darnutzer, Don, 259, 304, 410
DaRosa, Stephen, 271
Darragh, Anne, 432
Dartley, David, 252
Dash, Lauree, 436
Dashiell, Anita, 253
Davenport, John, 260, 304
Davey, Chris, 291

David Rothenberg Associates, 270, 275, 294
David's Mother, 458
Davidson, Claire, 360
Davidson, Gordon, 282, 416, 431
Davidson, Jack, 224
Davidson, Richard M., 305
Davie, Colleen, 335
Davies, Aled, 427
Davies, Fred, 235
Davies, Howard, 14, 255, 452, 456
Davies, Jason, 234
Davis, Al, 411
Davis, Ben, 335
Davis, Bill C., 355
Davis, Billy, Jr., 322
Davis, Christopher F., 237
Davis, Clara, 429
Davis, Dani, 260, 450
Davis, Danyon, 403
Davis, Donna, 359
Davis, Eisa, 428
Davis, Elaina Erika, 338
Davis, Ellen, 415
Davis, Fiona, 363
Davis, Future, 402
Davis, Helene, 255, 280
Davis, Jeff, 348
Davis, Jimmy, 270
Davis, Jude, 358
Davis, Ken, 339
Davis, Marshall L., Jr., 310
Davis, Michelle, 359
Davis, Mindy Paige, 309
Davis, Murphy, 430
Davis, Nathan, 458
Davis, Ossie, 455
Davis, Randy, 239
Davis, Raul, 350
Davis, Regi, 286
Davis, Ruthie, 344
Davis, Thulani, 282
Davis, Tyrone, 358
Davis, Vicki, 348, 353
Davis, Viola, 284, 456
Davison, Lesley, 264
Davoren, Tony, 228
Dawson, Craig, 273
Dawson, Lori A., 276
Dawson, Stacy, 338
Day, Charles, 351
Day, David, 265
Day, Edmund, 355
Day, Johanna, 337
Day Maggie Blew Off Her Head, The, 368
Daykin, Judith E., 292, 298
De Carlo, Ken, 229

De Cordova, Stephen, 335
De Farnecio, Doris, 350
De Fonte, Anthony, 411
de Ganon, Clint, 230
De Gioia, Eric, 235, 298
de Haas, Darius, 32, 258, 259, 330, 344, 421, 456
de Jong, Holly, 291
de la Fe Colon, Oscar, 339
de la Fuente, José Luis, 458
De La Guarda, 36, 43, 44, *269*
De La Pena, George, 425
De Laurentis, Semina, 435, 457
De Lorenzo, Stephen, 351
De Michele, Joseph V., 265, 354
de Obaldia, Rene, 356
De Santis, Edmund, 363
De Shields, Andre, 458
De Soto, Edouard, 350
De Tullio, N. Joseph, 340
de Voragine, Jacobus, 271
De Vries, Jon, 337
Deacon, Simon, 273
Dead Boy, The, 436
Deaf Day, 331, *339*
Deak, Tim, 358
Deakin, Ian, 293
Deal, Frank, 342
Dealer's Choice, 12, 457, 458
Dean, Charles, 404
Deans, Jonathan, 244, 246
Dear World, 225
Death and the Maiden, *354*
Death of a Salesman, 3, 4, 14, 15, 41, *249*, 451, 452, 455, 456
Death of a Social Security Benefit, *345*
Death of Papa, The, 17
deBeauvais, Leslie, 275
DeBeck, David, 360
DeBenedetto, John, 358
Debuskey, Merle, 450
Decareau, Dick, 286
DeChant, Alice C., 311
Dechev, Jolie, 351
DeCiutiis, Mario, 235
DeCoudreaux, Debbie, 323
Dee, Camille, viii, 400
Deeg, Michael, 335
Deep Down, *357*
DeFeis, Frederic, 411
deGannes, Nehassaiu, 428
Degenerate Art, *351*
DeGraw, Gavin, 424
Deitch, Kathy, 230, 313
Deitz, Beth, 334
Dejean, Gilbert, 232
Del Priore, Cathy, 241, 261
Del Rossi, Angelo, 261, 420

DeLaria, Lea, 29, 30, 237, 312
Delawari, Yasmine, 356
DeLeo, Carmen, 235
Deleo, Sam, 409
Delicate Balance, A, 431, 457
DeLillo, Don, 405, 457
deLima, Sarah, 413
Delinger, Larry, 402
Delivering Dad, *334*
Dell'Orefice, Carmen, 337
DeLorenzo, Stephen, 351
Delphi or Bust, *334*
Delsener Slater, 228, 230
Demaree, Stephanie, 400, 401
deMarrais, Karl, 409
DeMarse, James, 356
Demidov, Israel, 343
Demita, John, 426
Demons, 361
Demou, Vasiliki, 280
Dempster, Curt, 331, 338
Dench, Judi, 10, 256, 451
DeNigris, Michael, 361
Denis, William, 410
Denman, David, 408
Denmark, Brenda, 347
Dennehy, Brian, 14, 15, 34, 47, 249, 451, 456
Dennin, Anne, 276
Dennis, Katie, 261
Dennis, Patrick, 236
Dennis, Richard, 338, 350
Dent, Kelly, 232, 261
'Dentity Crisis, 38
Dentone, Julieta, 269
Denver Center Theater Company, 30, 368, 410
Depass, Nicolette, 429
Derenne, Josephine, 292
DeRosa, Stephen, 47, 271, 280, 300, 301
Derrah, Thomas, 405
Ders, Kim, 356, 422
Dervis, Paul, 413
Dery, Lisa, 342
Desai, Angel, 344
Desai, Shelly, 431
Desilets, Luc, 348
DeSisto, A. Michael, 362
Desponds, Laurent, 292
Destiny of Me, The, 454
DeVaynes, Andrea, 354
DeVine, Lawrence, viii, 368
DeVinney, Gordon, 407
DeVries, David, 309
DeVries, Jon, 281
DeVries, Michael, 286
Dewell, Michael, 339
Dewey, Donald, 335
DeWolf, Nat, 281

Dexter, Mark, 249, 414
Deyle, John, 230
Dezhon, Song, 348
Diamond, Joel, 350, 351, 352
Diamond, Jonathan, 435
Diamond, Leonard, 435
Diamond, Liz, 340, 405, 456
Diamond, Neil, 246
Diana and Sidney, Part I, *427*
Diana and Sidney, Part II, *427*
DiAntonio, Michael, 343
Diary of Anne Frank, The, 222
Dias, Laura, 319
Diaz, Natascia, 278
DiBenedetto, John, 425
DiBernardo, Dale, 434
Dick, Paul, 358
Dickens, Charles, 240, 410
Dickerman, Douglas, 360
Dickerson, Glenda, 338
Dickinson, Sandra, 249, 414
Dietlein, Marsha, 281, 361
Dietrich, John, 234, 235
Dietrich, Marlene, 22, 23, 256
Dietz, Howard, 247
Dietz, Steven, 368, 421
Dietz, Susie, 260, 450
Dieu!: God Mother Radio, *357*
DiFalco, Robert, 360
DiFarnecio, Doris, 339, 359
Digging Eleven, *414*
Diggs, Elizabeth, 411
Diggs, Taye, 318
DiGiacomo, John, 358
Dignan, Ben, 410
Dignan, Pat, 343
Dillan, Jessica, 311
Dilley, Carol, 311
Dilliard, Marcus, 422
Dillingham, Charles, 416
Dillon, John, 417
Dillon, Paul, 289
Dilly, Erin, 298, 305, 308
DiMaggio, Lou, 228
Dime Savings Bank, 260
Dimly Perceived Threats to the System, 368
Dimon, Elizabeth, 404, 415
Dimow, Carl, 427
Dinah Was, 24, 264
DiNicola, Donald, 336, 353
Dinner With Friends, 367, 368, 379
Dion, Julia, 340
Dionne, Monica, 344
DiPasquale, Dawn, 424
DiPietro, Joe, 40, 264, 281, 435
Directors Company, The, 355
Dirocco, Henry, viii
Dirty Day, *355*

Dis-Adventures of Peter Pan vs. Captain Maledetto, The, *342*
Disbennett, Bill, 234
Disch, Thomas M., 363
Distefano, Madi, 360
Diveny, Mary, 22, 256
Dixon, Beth, 424
Dixon, Ed, 255
Dixon, Jerry, 278
Dixon, MacIntyre, 232, 309, 430
Dixon, Willie, 260, 304
Dizard, Darby, 350
Dizozza, Peter, 342
DLT Entertainment, 252
Do Gooder Productions, 305
Do Re Mi, 36, 42, *297*, *300*, *301*
Dobbins, Bill, 359
Dobbins, Peter, 361
Dobbins, Zack, 402
Dobbs, Michael, 458
Dobie, Paul, 324
Doble, William S., 337
Dobrish, Jeremy, 282, 354
Dobrusky, Paul, 410
Dockery, Leslie, 253, 296
Doctorow, E.L., 222
Dodd, Jonathan, vii
Dodd, Lisa, 334
Dodge, Alexander, 437
Dodger Endemol Theatricals, 229, 230, 241
Dodger Management, 231
Dodger Theatricals, 304
Dodina, Yevgenya, 343
Doerr, James, 359
Does Thinking Take Place Out Loud?, *350*
Dogeaters, 368, 409, *415*
Doh, Jeong Ju, 225
Doherty, Caroline, 234
Doherty, Moya, 228, 229
Dokuchitz, Jonathan, 321
Dolan, Judith, 244, 431
Dolan, Rick, 244, 261
Dold, Mark H., 353, 421
Doll, Lauren, 242
Domet, Sally, 335
Dominczyk, Dagmara, 255
Dominion Theater, 356
Don Miller Orchestra, 225
Don't Pick Up, *361*
Don't Tell Mama, 356
Don't Tell the Tsar, 404
Donahue, Christopher, 416
Donaldson, Martha, 278, 279
Donaldson, Randy, 251
Donaldson, Rob, 348

Dondlinger, Mary Jo, 265, 270
Dong, Eric, 352
Donmanian, Jean, 305
Donmar Warehouse, 19, 242, 243, 428, 451
Donne, John, 34
Donnellan, Declan, 292, 331, 456
Donnelly, Candice, 268, 271, 281, 289
Donnelly, Terry, 339, 340
Donohue, Maura Nguyen, 343
Donovan, Bryan T., 353
Donovan, Jeffrey, 281, 305, 337
Donovan, Maripat, 264
Donovan, Peter, 237, 256
Donovan, Tate, 10, 256
Dooley, Sean, 270
Doré, Katharine, 229
Doran, Jim, 354
Dorgan, Theo, 228
Dorian, Bob, 420
Dorian/Horda, 252
Dorian, Joanne, 363
Doris, Susanne, 234
Dorman, Tracy, 353
Doron, Abraham, 228
Dorsey, Kent, 421
Dorst, Tankred, 356
Dossett, John, 318
Dostoyevsky, 361
Dotted Line, *361*
Doty, Johnna, 281, 305, 339, 350
Doucette, Cameron, 422
Dougherty, Doc, 350
Douglas Fairbanks Theater, 356
Douglas, Stephen, 355
Douglass, Gerald, 423
Dove, Dennis J., 310
Dove, Jonathan, 292
Dowd, Frank, 361
Dowds, Marty, 228
Dower, David, 349
Dowling, Joe, 422
Down Town, *344*
Downs, Don, 246
Downs, Michael E., 430
Doyle, Gerard, 255
Doyle, Julie, 338
Doyle, Lori M., 290
Doyle, Richard, 408
Dr. Jekyll and Mr. Hyde, *420*
Dr. Kronopolis and the Timekeeper Chronicles, *357*
Draghici, Marina, 268
Drake, David, 361
Drake, Donna, 238, 261

Drake, Sylvie, 405
Drama Dept., 338
Drama Desk, 9, 14
Drama Desk Awards, 456
Drama League Awards, 455
Dramatists Guild, 450
Dramatists Guild Council, 455
Drance, George, Jr., 268, 343
Draper, Alex, 337
Draper, Polly, 338
Dratch, Rachel, 458
Drawing Room *B*, *361*
Dream Boy, 458
Dream City Twosome, *358*
Dream Express, *340*
Dream of Wealth, A, *363*
Dream True: My Life With Vernon Dexter, 330, *353*, 455
Dreaming in Cuban: Rhythm, Rum, Café Con Leche and Nuestros Abuelos, *334*
Dreamlandia, *344*
Dreamtime for Alice, *339*
Dresser, Richard, 419
Drew, Dina, 335
Drewe, Anthony, 412
Drewes, Glenn, 236, 246, 248, 299
Dreyer, Dave, 247
Dreyfuss, Richard, 430
Driscoll, Michael, 334
Drive Angry, *419*
Driver, John, 454
Driver, Kip, 311
Driving Miss Daisy, 25
Drowning in Euphoria, *359*
Drozd, Laurence, 361
Druid Theater Company, 260, 450
Drummond, Joseph, 249
Dry Cleaner's Integrity, The, *356*
du Maurier, George, 353
Duarte, Derek, 432
Duarte, Myrna E., 290
Duboff, Jill, 273
Dubois, Amanda, 359
DuBose, Bruce, 409
Dubrow, Marsha, 252
Duckett, Natalie, 358
Ducron, Nicolas, 292
Dudek, Anne, 362
Dudko, Etya, 361
Duel Pardoning, 415
Duenyas, Yehuda, 349
Duet!, 36, *282*
Duet! a Romantic Fable, *354*
Dufault, Michael, 348

Duff, Michael, 458
Duffin, Shay, 295
Dugan, Duff, 275
Dugan, Sean, 285
Duggan, Annmarie, 304
Duke, Vernon, 297
Dulack, Ilvi, 355
Dulack, Tom, 355
duMaine, Wayne, 257
Dumakude, Thuli, 315
Dunay, Damon, 421
Duncan C. Weldon Production, 242
Duncan, Edna D., 422
Duncan, Lindsay, 40, 288
Duncan-Gibbs, Mamie, 312
Dundas, Shane, 363
Dunham, Christine, 240
Dunkleberger, Amy, 408, 409
Dunlop, Frank, 407
Dunn, Colleen, 322
Dunn, Erin, 223, 236, 282, 288
Dunn, M.E., 459
Dunn, Ryan, 224
Dunne, Colin, 228
Dunne, Peggy, 412
Dunne, Will, 436
Dunne, William Patrick, 310
Dunnock, Patricia, 359, 414
Dupé, Benjamin, 292
DuPre, Lynette G., 310
Duquesnay, Ann, 222, 310
Durán, Armando, 402
Durang, Christopher, 9, 38, 280, 456
Durell, R.J., 237, 238
Durning, Charles, 458
Dusk, Geraldine, 339
Dvorak/Langsfelder, 252
Dwyer, Terrence, 415
Dwyer, Tom, 271, 272
Dybas, James, 232
DyBisz, Ken, 241, 251
Dyches, Preston, 419
Dye, Melissa, 318
Dyer, Carolyn, 410
Dying Gaul, The, 11, 34, 36, 37, *279*
Dzindzihashvili, Dan, 290

Eady, Cornelius, 344
Eaker, Sherry, 453
Eakes, Jenny, 234
Earl, Shaun, 319, 458
Earle, Dottie, 237, 299
Earley, Kevin, 315
Earls, Elliott Peter, 357
Earth Sings Fa-Mi, The, *347*

Easley, Bill, 246
Easley, Byron, 235
Easley, Mary Beth, 342
East Is East, 36, *285*, *287*, *347*
Easterlin, John, 252
Eastman, Donald, 406, 422
Easton, Richard, 431
Eastville, *434*
Eastwood International
  Children's Choir, 241
Eaton, Catherine, 422
Eaton, Lothair, 271
Eaton, Trevor McQueen, 251
Eaves, Dashiell, 320
Eaves, Obadiah, 337
Ebb, Fred, 30, 222, 247, 401,
  455, 457
Eberhard, Leslie, 420
Eberhardt, Sally, 350
Eberl, Luke, 410
Ebersole, Christine, 299, 300
Ebihara, Richard, 340, 342
Ebling, Margot, 360
Eccles, Julie, 430
Echo New York, 257
Eckert, Rinde, 404
Eclipse, *337*
eda-Young, Barbara, 249
Eddy, Matt, 362
Edelman, Gregg, 319
Edelstein, Barry, 337
Edelstein, Gordon, 432
Eden, 420
Eden, Diana, 425
Eden, Sasha, 355
Eder, Linda, 314, 414
Edge, Kenneth, 228
Edgecomb, Chris, 257
Edgerton, Earle, 360
Edgerton, Jeff, 243, 244, 359
Edington, Pamela, 255, 274
Edis, Steven, 250, 414
Edith Oliver Award, 453
Edlund, Eric, 252
Edmead, Wendy, 311
Edmund Gaynes, 275
Edmunds, Kate, 404, 433
Edmundson, Helen, 290, 414
Edson, Margaret, ix, 34, 282,
  327, 344, 447, 449, 455, 456
Edward and Agrippina, *356*
Edward II, 458
Edward, Joseph, 289, 423
Edwards, Anderson, 457
Edwards, Blake, 425
Edwards, Brenda, 415
Edwards, Dex, 458
Edwards, John, 360
Edwards, Omar, 305, 310

Edwards, Scott, 422
Edwards, Sherman, 222
Efremova, Svetlana, 408
Egan, Eilis, 228
Egan, Jered, 224
Egan, John Treacy, 311
Egan, Robert, 416
Egan, Susan, 308, 416
Egi, Stan, 433
Egolf, Gretchen, 18, 245
Ehinger, Jim, 259, 304
Ehlert, Madeleine, 251
Ehlinger, Mary, 424
Ehn, Erik, 345
Ehrlich, Mark, 335
Ehrmann, Kurt, 412
Eichenberger, Rebecca, 318
Eid, Christopher, 420
Eidem, Bruce, 241, 301
Eight! Henry VIII, That Is!,
  363
**18 Mighty Mountain Warriors,
  The**, *348*
Eigsti, Karl, 405
Eilenberg, Larry, 432
Eilers, Carin, 277
Eisenberg, Ned, 359
Eisenhauer, Peggy, 241, 259,
  269, 459
Eisenstein, Linda, 358
El Paso Blue, 458
**Elaborate Lives: The Legend
  of Aida**, *402*
Eldred, Mike, 257
Eldridge, Lynn, 234
Electra, 4, 19, *242*, *428*, 451,
  456
Electric Factory Concerts, 259
Elective Affinities, 421
Elementals, The, 349
Elevation of Thieves, The, *410*
Elevator Repair Service, 349,
  356
Eleventh Hour Theater
  Company, 343
Elg, Taina, 321
Elgar, Avril, 291
Elgar, Edward, 417
Elich, Michael, 402
Elinder, Kristoffer, 234
Eliot, T.S., 221
Elizabeth Hull–Kate Warriner
  Award, 455
Elizabeth Osborn Award, 368
Elkan, Judy, 356
Elkins, Elizabeth, 363
Elkins, Erin, 415
Ellet, Trey, 318
Ellington, Duke, 252, 254, 296

Elliot, Martha, 344
Elliot Norton Awards, viii, 457
Elliott, Kate, 229
Elliott, Kenneth, 303, 354
Elliott, Scott, 285, 287, 347
Ellis, Anita, 347
Ellis, Aunjanue, 337
Ellis, Darren, 229
Ellis, Richard, 436
Ellis, Scott, 237, 288, 290, 437
Ellison, William, 251
Ellman, Bruce, 344, 353, 436
Ellorin, Bernadette, 352
Ellstein, Abraham, 230
Elman, Margaret, 361
Elmore, James, 360
Elsass, Jeffrey, 239
Emelson, Beth, 337
Emerging Artists Theater
  Company, 356
Emerson, Jennifer, 435
Emerson, Michael, 14, 255, 337
Emery, Kenneth, 235
Emery, Lisa, 37, 294
Emily, Pavlina, 409
Emmes, David, 408
Emmons, Beverly, 251, 268
Emond, Linda, 279, 319, 401,
  437
**Empty Plate in the Cafe Du
  Grand Boeuf, An**, *433*
En Garde Arts, 338
En Yu Tan, Victor, 348
Encores! Great American
  Musicals in Concert, 36, 297
End of Civilization, The, *361*
End of Jazz, The, *347*
Enemy of the Poeple, An, 459
Enfield, Michelle, 359
Engel/Berger/Rotter, 252
Engels, Johan, 19, 242, 428
English, Drake, 239, 323
English, Gary M., 434
English, Jeff, 416
English Teachers, The, *344*
Engquist, Richard, 340
Enigma Variations, *417*, *426*
Enis, Mark, 351
Enquist, Per Olov, 290, 361
Ensemble Studio Theater, 331,
  338
Ensenberger, Frank, 282, 354
Epp, Steven, 454
Epps, Sheldon, 425, 458
Epstein, Abby, 361, 419
Epstein, Alvin, 405
Epstein, Jonathan, 405, 457
Equity Library Theater, 245,
  253

Erat, Will, 420
Erdemovic, 415
Erdy, Brent, 334
Erickson, T. Charles, viii
Eriksmoen, August, 401
Ernotte, Andre, 411
Ernst, Lee E., 421
Eros Trilogy, The, *353*
Erskine, Julian, 228
Ervin, Mike, 407
Esbjornson, David, 284
Escapist, The, *350*
Eskey, Lee, 410
Espada, Marisol, 251
Esping, Laura, 422
Espinosa, Al, 353
Espinoza, Brandon, 286
Estrada, Ariel, 294, 358
Etzwiler, Michael, 311
Eugene O'Neill Theater
    Center, 436
Eugster, Donald, 363
Eureka, 47
Euripides, 19, 279, 334, 362,
    416
Eustis, Oskar, 428
Eva Hesse Project, The, *344*
Evan, Robert, 314
Evangelista, Nicole, 458
Evans, Albert, 421
Evans, Bill, 281
Evans, Edward Kinchley, 343
Evans, Harvey, 232
Evans, Jeff, 347
Evans, Mark, 359, 410
Evans, Timothy Leigh, 252
Evans, Vicky, 229
Evans, William Thomas, 232
Even Steven, *361*
**Evening With Jerry Herman,
    An**, 4, 33, *224*
**Evening with Quentin Crisp,
    An**, *356*
Everett, Sonny, 273
Everybody's Ruby, 36, *282*,
    284, *285*, 456
Everything Must Go, *357*
Evett, Benjamin, 405
Evett, Marianne, 368
Evil That Men Do, The, *334*
Evolution, *437*
Ewin, Paula, 363
Ewing, Kenneth J., Jr., 401
**Exact Center of the Universe,
    The**, 332, *353*
Exactly Like You, 36, 45, *265*,
    266
Excellent Art Manufacturing,
    356

Exit, Eric Y., viii
Expecting Isabel, 367, 368,
    390–399, *435*
Extenuating Circumstances,
    436
Eye Sling Shots Lions, *357*
Eyewash, Inc., 299
Eyre, Peter, 329, 355
Eyre, Richard, 256

F@ust: Version 3.0, 332, *344*
**Fables in Slang: A Ragtime
    Revue**, *359*
Fabulous Invalid, The, *355*
Facer, Susan, 316
Factor, Mallory, 450
Fadale, Christina, 319
Fagan, Garth, 428
Fagan, Valerie, 420
Fahnbulleh, Wiyatta, 423
Fain, Sammy, 360
Fair and Tender Ladies, *422*
Fairfoul, John, 291
Fairley, Michelle, 13, 255
Faison, George, 414
Faith, Percy, 235
Falco, Edie, 5, 223
Falconer, Mary, 415
Falk, Willy, 316
Fall, *341*, 411, 428
Falls, Gregory A., 432
Falls, Robert, 14, 15, 249, 406,
    452
Falsettoland, *359*, 454
Falsettos, 44
Falzone, Jay, 360
Family Secrets, 43
Famous Door Theater
    Company, The, 302
Famous Orpheus, *428*
Fane, Anthea, 359
Fanger, Iris, 457
Fanizzi, Christina, 355
Fannon, Cecilia, 407
Fanny, 421
Fantasticks, The, 264, 313
Fante, John, 411
Far East, 36, 37, 38, *294*, *437*
Faracy, Stephanie, 458
Faraldo, Lucinda, 339, 417
Farber, Seth, 246
Farina, Carissa, 240, 241
Farley, Timothy, 235
Farmer, James, 271
Farrar, Thursday, 244
Farrell, Christine, 339
Farrell, Herman Daniel III,
    345, 347, 355

Farrell, Kevin, 239
Farrell, Lawrence, 237
Farrell, Tim, 363
Farwell, Bradford, 293
Fascinating Rhythm, 32
Faso, Nina, 424
Fass, Robert, 340
Fast Blood, *338*
Faudree, Roy, 363
Faulty Optic, 276
Fauss, M. Michael, 239
Faust, Nick, 427
Favier, Louise, 342
Favolora, Joseph, 311
Fawcett, Michael, 355
Fay, Tom, 245
Fay, Vince, 230
Fears, Barbara, 335
Feffer, Steve, 335
Fehr, Deborah, 436
Feingold, Barnett, 266
Feingold, Michael, 448, 456
Feist, Gene, 223, 236, 288
Felber, Adam, 356
Feldberg, Robert, 448
Felde, Kitty, 415
Feldman, Benjamin, 425
Feldman, Erika, 270
Feldman, Lawrence, 299
Feldman, Susan, 22, 252
Feldman, Tibor, 359
Feldshuh, Tovah, 300, 301, 425
Felipe, Liliana, 344
Felix, John, 404
Felton, Daniel, 402
Felty, David Michael, 257, 415
Female Problems, 458
Fences, 454
Fender, Jeff, 306
Fenichell, Susan, 420
Fennell, Bob, 229, 234, 275, 294
Fenton, James, 221
Feore, Rory, 293
Ferencz, George, 343
Ferguson, Bill, 429
Ferguson, Eric, 404
Ferguson, Jesse Tyler, 30, 237
Fergusson, Honora, 356
Ferland, Danielle, 431
Fernandez, Lucio P., 347
Fernandez, Margarita, 234
Fernandez, Peter Jay, 355
Fernandez, Raymond, 409
Ferra, Max, 339, 350
Ferraro, Kim, 361
Ferrill, Alex, 458
Ferrini, Sheila, 457
Ferro, Rafael, 269
Ferver, Jack, 281

Festival d'Avignon, 290
Fez, The, 420
Fieger, Addy, 264
Field, Crystal, 350, 351, 352
Fielder, Michael H., 267, 268
Fielder, Sean C., 309
Fields, Dorothy, 27, 246, 250
Fields, Herbert, 27, 250
Fife, Ashlee, 234
Fighting Words, *345*
Filderman, Alan, 269
Filichia, Peter, 453
Filloux, Catherine, 344, 345
Final Episode, The, *349*
Fine, Daniel, 458
Fine, Rosemary, 340
Fineman, Carol R., 238, 267, 282
Finesilver, Mike, 280
Fink, Danielle, 351
Finlayson, Alex, 359
Finlayson, Doug, 412
Finley, Karen, 355
Finn, Jeffrey, viii, 307
Finn, William, 29, 44, 46, 269, 270, 271, 359
Finnegan, Jerry, 339
Finnell, Jan, 334
Finneran, Katie, 255, 270, 350
Fionte, John, 404
Fire, Norma, 431
Firebird, The, *357*
Firestone, Paul, 404
First 100 Years, The, *404*
First Kill, *343*
First Lady, 427
First Light Festival, 339
First Picture Show, The, *417*, *431*
First Stages, 341
Fischer, Juliet, 240
Fishburne, Laurence, 18, 237
Fisher, Dara, 436
Fisher, Dudu, 340
Fisher, Jonathan, 430
Fisher, Jules, 241, 459
Fisher, Linda, 339
Fisher, Rick, 229, 245
Fisher, Rob, 298, 299
Fishing for a Wife/Meiboku Sendi Hagi, *357*
Fishkin Touch, The, *340*
Fishman, Carol, 289
Fitch, Clyde, 361
Fitch, Tristan, 338
Fitzgerald, Allen, 324
Fitzgerald, Christopher, 285, 298
Fitzgerald, David, 245

Fitzgerald, Ed, 286
Fitzgerald, Patrick, 339
Fitzgerald, Paul, 280, 437
Fitzgerald, Peter J., 224, 230, 256, 305, 425
Fitzgerald, Rachel, 354
Fitzgerald, T. Richard, 424, 430
Fitzgibbon, John, 404
Fitzpatrick, Colleen, 300, 301
FitzSimmons, James, 286, 288
Fitzsimmons, Tom, 232
Five Frozen Embryos, *345*
Five Lesbian Brothers, 42
Five Rooms of Furniture, 436
Fix, The, 457
Flaherty, Stephen, 24, 222
Flahooley, *360*
Flamenco Vivo, 303
Flanagan, John, 432
Flanagan, Niamh, 354
Flanagan, Sarah, 411
Flanders, Kristin, 405
Flatley, Michael, 228
Flaubert, Gustave, 329, 355
Flaw in the Flew, A, *345*
Flax, John, 348
Flea Theater, 329, 330, 356
Fleck, John, 408
Fleischmann, Stephanie, 345
Fleming, Eugene, 245, 246
Flemming, Brian, 455
Fleshler, Glenn, 424
Fliakos, Ari, 363
Flick, Daniel, 402
Flight of the White Bird, *343*
Flimflam Man, The, *416*
Flirting With Rescue, *361*
Floor, Callie, 432
Flores, Julia, 239
Flower or Something, A, *358*
Flowers, Ramon, 229
Flowers, Reg, 347
Floyd Collins, 454
Floyd, Lucretia Xavier, 356
Flyin' High, *339*
Flyin' West, *338*
Flying Cloud, The, *355*
Flying Karamazov Brothers: Sharps, Flats and Accidentals, The, *354*
Flying Machine, The, 350
Flynn, J. Lee, 286
Flynn, J. Michael, 432
Flynn, Peter, 431
Flyovers, 368, 458
Fo, Dario, 356
Foard, Merwin, 319
Foerder, Preston, 343
Fogarty, Mary, 363, 422

Foglia, Leonard, 425
Foley, Ellen, 288
Foley, John, 270
Foley, Vanessa, 234
Folk Machine, 436
Follies, 458
Fonseca, Quina, 342
Fool Moon, 3, 4, 24, *239*, 452
Foose, Thomas T., vii, viii, 19
Foote, Horton, 17, 329, 422
Foote, Nicholas, 430
Footloose, 3, 4, 24, 26, 27, *230*, 451, 452
Forbes, Barbara, 435
Forbes, Kate, 432
Forbidden Broadway, 454
Forbidden Broadway Cleans Up Its Act!, 36, 46, *294*, 456
Forbidden Broadway Strikes Back, 264
Force of Nature, *421*
Ford, Paul, 229
Ford, T. Cat, 351
Foreign Exchange, 420
Foreman, Richard, 331, 348
Forever Plaid, 458
Forever Tango, 222
Forget, Marc, 353
Forlow, Ted, 358
Forman, Ken, 363
Formenti, Valentina, 229
Formosa, Roger, 273
Fornara, Ann, 229
Foronda, Joseph Anthony, 316
Forrest, Mort, 334
Forrest, Pamela, 458
Forstmann, Ted, 232
Forsyth, Jo Ellen, 228
Fortin, Simon, 353
Fortner, Keith, 240
Fortuna, Mary, 435
Forty Minute Finish, *419*
Forum Theater, 368
Fosse, 3, 4, 24, 33, 34, 154–163, *245*, 451, 452, 453, 455, 456
Fosse, Bob, 33, 222, 245, 246, 247
Foster, Benim, 361
Foster, Herb, 256, 267, 268
Foster, Hunter, 230, 231
Foster, Janet, 279
Foster, Sutton, 315
Foster, Tobi, 315
Foul Stench of Death, The, *348*
Fountain, Eli, 305
Fouquet, Paul, 232
Fourfront, 228
–14: An American Maul, *340*

4th Street Theater, 356
42nd Street Workshop, 356
Fowler, Beth, 309
Fowler, Julia, 251
Fowler, Mayhill, 410
Fowler, Wally, 270
Fox Hunt, 225
Fox, Alan, 295, 340
Fox, Bret, 241
Fox, Crystal, 284
Fox, Robert, 243, 254, 256, 275, 450
Fox Theatricals, 248, 249, 451
Fox, Tony, 235
Fox-Long, Sophia, 405
Foxworth, Bo, 360
Foy, 239, 241, 261
Foy, Harriett D., 334, 429
Foy, Kenneth, 224
Fraboni, Angelo, 299
Fracé, Jeffrey, 268
Fraelich, Kristine, 257
Fragments of a Greek Trilogy (Medea, Electra and The Trojan Women), *343*
Fram, Joel, 265, 266, 430
Frame, David, 229
France, Wesley, 276
Francis, Black, 275
Francis, Gayle, 252, 260, 450
Francis, Juliana, 348
Francis, Stacy, 230
Franco, Ricky, 421
Frangakis, Antonis, 337
Frank, Andrew, 358
Frank, Annie,, 251
Frank, Helen, 311
Frank, Judy, 347
Frank, Leo, 24, 25, 244
Frank, Robert Vincent, 402
Frank, Sid, 361
Frankel, Jennifer, 237, 238, 299, 300
Frankel, Jerry, 248, 249, 259, 451
Frankel, Richard, 255, 280, 453
Frankenstein, *400*
Franklin, Nancy, 30
Franny, Isadora and the Angels, *361*
Frantzich, Kirsten, 422
Franz, Elizabeth, 14, 15, 47, 249, 451
Franzgrote, Christoph, 298, 299, 301
Frasconi, Miguel, 276, 277
Fraser, Alexander, 289
Fraser, Alison, 435
Fraser, Denise, 234

Fraser, Patricia, 408
Fratti, Mario, 342, 455
Frazer, Susanna, 435
Frazier, Darren Lee, 334
Frazier, Grenoldo, 351
Frazier, Jordan, 229
Frazier, Randy, 335
Freak, 223
Frederick, Matt, 355
Fredericks, Todd, 335
Free Gift, 413
Freed, Amy, 280
Freed, Sam, 436
Freed, Zachary, 324
Freedman, David, 297, 300
Freedman, Glenna, 232, 239, 251, 272, 294
Freedom of the City, The, 458
Freedomland, 36, *280*
Freedson, John, 294
Freeman, Brian, 341
Freeman, Cheryl, 26, 257, 414
Freeman, Chico, 271
Freeman, Christopher, 229
Freeman, Jackie S., 351
Freeman, Jonathan, 237, 433
Freeman, Stan, 264
Freeman, Yvette, 313
Freestyle Repertory Theater, 356
Freeze, Jeffrey Lane, 229
Frejo, Happy, 430
Frenchman Productions, Inc., 253, 296
Frenkel, Ana, 269
Frensly, Mike, 334
Freschi, Bob, 411
Frey, Matthew, 279, 306, 337, 403
Freydberg, James B., 239
Freyer, Frederick, 285
Fried, Jonathan, 337, 344
Fried, Randall, 430
Friedheim, Eric, 436
Friedman, Arthur, 457
Friedman, Daniel Eli, 310
Friedman, Michael, 268
Friedman, Peter, 318
Friedmann, Aloysia, 241
Friedmann, Jennifer, 458
Friedson, Adam, 259
Friedson, David, 259
Friel, Anna, 12, 254, 456
Frimark, Merle, 228
Frog and Peach Theater Company, 356
From Third World to Third Ward: A Black Girl's Song, *344*

Fromewick, Jim, 335
Frosk, John, 298, 299, 301
Frost, Sue, 412
Frozen Assets, 458
Fry, Christopher, 243
Fryberg/von Donop/Kirsten, 252
Fuddy Meers, 436
Fugard, Athol, 35, 285, 286
Fuller, David, 362
Fuller, Nathaniel, 422
Fuller, Penny, 44, 269
Funderburg, Barry G., 412
Funicello, Ralph, 430, 432
Funkhouser, Debra, 422
Fuqua, Joseph, 408
Furballs, 355
Furlow, Moya, 404
Furman, Roy, 245
Furs, Edward, 293
Furst, Tim, 354

Gaard, David, 335
Gabay, Roy, 302, 303, 433
Gabriel, Andrea, 356
Gadsden, Cheryl, 352
Gaffin, Arthur, 256
Gaffney, Mo, 288
Gaines, Boyd, 310
Gaines, Daphne, 358
Gaines, Davis, 316
Gaines, Reg E., 222, 305
Gaipa, Amy, 356
Gaisner, Rhea, 345
Gaithers, Lita, 243, 259, 260, 303, 304, 451
Gajda, Lisa, 245, 246
Galas, Philip-Dimitri, 349
Galati, Frank, 455
Galczynski, Konstanty Ildefons, 356
Galde, Anthony, 257
Gale, Gregory, 252, 338
Gale, Jack, 298, 299, 301
Gale, Lorena, 344
Galindo, Eileen, 334, 435
Galjour, Anne, 404
Gallagher, Bernard, 292
Gallagher, Bronagh, 343
Gallagher, Dick, 264
Gallagher, Fiona, 338
Gallagher, Paul, 234
Gallant, Joe, 341
Gallardo, Edgard, 237
Gallarello, Josephine, 356
Gallo, Antoinette, 335
Gallo, Billy, 348

Gallo, David, 29, 230, 236, 237, 248, 269, 275, 353, 412
Gallo, Genevra, 362
Gallo, Paul, 238, 257, 280, 298, 456
Gambatese, Jennifer, 322
Gambino, Kimberly, 356
Gamble, Julian, 255, 270
Gamble, Paul, 401
Gamburg, Maria, 343
Gamel, Fred, 454
Gammon, James, 290
Gammon, Jocelyn, 427
Gandara, Javier, 229
Gandy, Irene, 273, 274
Ganly, David, 260
Garber, Victor, 307
Garces, Michael, 345
Garces, Michael John, 334, 339
Garces, Paula, 338
Garcia, Alejandro, 269
Garcia, Cristina, 334
Garcia, Tania, 303
Gardner, Dionne McGuire, 270
Gardner, Jeff, 232
Gardner, Rita, 313
Garin, Michael, 282, 354
Garland, Anita, 411
Garman, Andrew, 268
Garner, Kenneth, 293
Garonzik, Sara, 426
Garrett, Becky, 237
Garrett, Russell, 232
Garrison, David, 401
Garrison, Dyke, 294
Garrison, Nick, 417, 419
Garrity, Paul, 351
Garson, Kenneth, 335
Garth Fagan Dance, 428, 429
Gartshore, Will, 244, 299, 300
Gasman, Ira, 222
Gass, Kristen, 305, 306
Gaston, Lydia, 358, 359
Gates, Dean, 400
Gathering, The, 331, *340*
Gattelli, Christopher, 311
Gaudette, Michelle, 234
Geary, Steve, 311
Gebirtig, Mordecai, 230
Geddes, Jill, 334
Geduld, Marcus, 355, 361
Gee, Colin, 350
Geek Circus, the Twisted Shockfest, *342*
Geer, Justin, 298
Geer, Kevin, 6, 223, 337
Geffen Playhouse, 417
Gehrig, Fred, 229
Gehringer, Linda, 408

Geidt, Jeremy, 405
Geiger, Mary Louise, 285, 433
Geis, Alexandra, 361
Gekker, Chris, 232
Gelbart, Larry, 297
Gelberman, Jan, 335
Gelder, Ian, 291
Gelfand, Dmitry, 436
Geller, Marc, 358
Gellert, Jonathan, 354
Gemignani, Paul, 241, 301
Gemini, 289, 329
Gems, Pam, 22, 23, 256, 451
Gen (Hadashi-no-Gen), *361*
General of Hot Desire, The, *270, 271*
Gennaro, Michael, 406
Gentry, Celia, 265
Georgakopoulos, Lazaros, 279
George and Elisabeth Marton Award, 455
George, Christopher, 360
George, Connie, 361
George Jean Nathan Award, 455
George, Lovette, 269
George, Meganne, 420
George Oppenheimer Award, 456
George, Phillip, 294
George, Robert C., viii
George Street Playhouse, 424
Georgiadis, Meletis, 279
Geraci, Drew, 232
Geralis, Antony, 286
Gerard, Monica, 241
Gerber, James J., 334
Gerckens, T.J., 406
Gerould, Daniel C., 356
Geroy, Aman, 348
Gerroll, Daniel, 331, 339, 456
Gerry, Johanna, 401
Gershwin, George, 30, 32, 258
Gershwin, Ira, 258, 297, 300, 362
Gershwins' Fascinating Rhythm, The, 3, 4, 24, 31, *258*
Gersten, Bernard, 224, 243, 269, 294, 451
Gersten, David J., 270, 294
Gesher Theater, 343
Gesner, Clark, 29, 248, 265
Get to the Part About Me, *361*
Gets, Malcolm, 44, 269
Getting and Spending, 3, 4, 7, 8, 9, *232, 430*
Getting on Top, *409*
Getting Out, 454

Geva Theater, 428
Gewirtz, Stephanie, 416
Geyer, Murphy, 270
Ghazi, Taymour, 432
Ghelfi, Chris, 258, 259
Giamatti, Paul, 14, 255
Giambusso, David, 342
Giangiulio, Nicholas J., 359
Gianino, Jack, 233
Giannini, Alex, 249, 414
Giannini, Maura, 239, 298, 299, 301
Gibbons, June, 256
Gibbs, Nancy Nagel, 270
Gibbs, Ron, 261
Gibby, Ross, 337
Gibney, Susan, 431
Gibson, Charlotte A., 422
Gibson, Darren, 237
Gibson, Darryl, 356
Gibson, Deborah, 308
Gibson, Don, 260, 304
Gibson, Harry, 294
Gibson, Meg, 284
Gibson, Michael, 235, 248, 401
Gibson, N.A., 458
Giering, Jenny, 340
Gigl, Aloysius, 318
Gil, Rob, 457
Gilbert, Chris Payne, 350, 359
Gilbert, Jason, 402
Gilbert, John, 293
Gilbert, John Michael, 224
Gilbert, Julie, 404
Gilbert, Ronnie, 432
Giles, Nancy, 338
Gilford/Freeley, 252
Gilkyson, Terry, 256
Gill, Michel R., 433
Gillan, Tony, 339
Gillentine, Meg, 311
Gillette, Michael, 235
Gilliam, Michael, 425, 426
Gilliam, Seth, 337, 416
Gilliard, Larry, Jr., 424
Gillis, Terri, 276
Gilman, Rebecca, 340, 419
Gilmore, Allen, 427
Gilmour, Susan, 315
Gilpin, Jack, 232, 331
Gilroy, Frank D., 339
Gilroy, Tom, 356
Gilsig, Jessalyn, 432
Gimmick, The, 36, 42, *277, 279*, 327, *424*
Gin Game, The, 458
Ginger, Green, 357
Gingerich, Tanya, 425
Ginnety, Susan, 228

Gint, *351*
Giobbe, Anney, 352
Gionson, Mel, 287, 362
Gipson, David, 406
Girasuolo, S.M., 355
Girl Who Said Yes to the Guy in the Brown Subaru, The, *361*
Girl's Guide to the Divine Comedy, A, 427
Girl's Life, A, *360*
Girls Town, *352*
Giron, Arthur, 363
Giroux, Michelle, 292, 293
Girouy, Laurent, 322
Gissendanner, Willie Ann, 356
Giuliani, Rudolph W., 267
Giunta, Anthony, 361
Gizmos, Gadgets, Laughs & Lies, *360*
Gladden, Dean R., 407
Gladu, April-Dawn, 361
Glaser, Sherry, 43
Glass, David, 293
Glass Menagerie, The, 458
Glass, Philip, 331, 337
Glazer, Peter, 359
Gleason, Larry, 363
Gleason, Mary Pat, 425
Glen, Iain, 11, 243
Glendenning, Hugo, viii
Glenn, Scott, 39, 288, 289
Gless, Glenn Z., 343
Glesser, Mark R., 362
Glockner, Eleanor, 435
Glore, John, 408, 409
Glorioso, Bess Marie, 285
Glory of Living, The, *340*
Glotzer, Marci, 224, 289
Gloucester Stage Company, 413, 457
Glover, Abron, 305
Glover, Chequita Ross, 347
Glover, Gavin, 276
Glover, Julian, 291
Glover, Savion, 44, 222, 305, 309
Gluck, Joel, 343
Glymph, Avery, 338, 423
Glynn, Carlin, 353
Gnapp, Rod, 404
Goble, Patty, 311
God's Acre, *345*
God Smells Like a Roast Pig, 457
God, the Crackhouse and the Devil, *342*
God's Heart, 37
God's Man in Texas, *417*

Godfrey, Patrick L., 255
Godfrey, Thomas, vii
Godinez, Henry, 406
Godsey, Rori, 414
Godwin, Randall, 405
Goede, Jay, 284
Goell, Julie, 427
Goell, Kermit, 254, 296
Goerig, Cynthia, 235
Goethe, 344, 421
Goff, Charles, 420
Goggin, Dan, 46, 271, 272
Gogol, *362*
Going to the River, 338
Gold, Daniel Eric, 302
Gold, Pamela, 402
Goldberg, Blair, 251
Goldberg, Jessica, 331, 361, 455
Goldberg, Mark Trent, 299
Goldberg, Naomi, 284
Goldberg, Norbert, 224
Goldberg Variations, *359*
Golden, Annie, 237
Golden Child, 9
Golden Legend, The, 271
Goldenberg, Jon-Erik, 311
Goldenhersh, Heather, 281, 359
Goldenthal, Jolene, 358
Goldes, Joel, 359
Goldfaden, Abraham, 229
Goldfadn, Avrom, 340
Goldfeder, Laurie, 280
Goldfinger, Michael, 425
Goldman, Herrick, 342, 351
Goldman, James, 17, 18, 236
Goldman, Nina, 229
Goldman, Sheilah, 232
Goldoni, Carlo, 422
Goldsmith, Tommy, 422
Goldstein, Jack, 450
Goldstein, Jess, viii, 253, 275, 279, 280, 285, 286, 288, 295, 430, 453, 455
Goldstick, Oliver, 264
Golem, The, *357*
Golf Ball, The, *339*
Golinski, Sharon, 421
Golub, Peter, 280, 281
Golux, Stephen, 358
Gomez, Lino, 298
Gomez, Marga, 349
Gomez, Mateo, 350
Gomez, Rudy, 409
Gonda, Kelly, 249, 450
Gone to Colorado, *335*
Gonzalez, Aldrin, 235, 299, 309
Gonzalez, BW, 402
Gonzalez, Carl, 411

Gonzalez, David, 348
Gonzalez, Jojo, 416
Good, Bill, 358
Good, Casey Miles, 239
Good Friends LLC, 305
Good Person of Szechuan, The, *402*
Goodbye Oscar, 331, *339*
Goode, Jeff, 354
Goodfriend-Koven, Diva, 229
Goodheart, Carol, 361
Goodman, Charles, 270
Goodman, Hazelle, 268
Goodman, Henry, 307
Goodman, John, 42, 267
Goodman, Laraine, 342
Goodman, Paul Scott, 277, 278
Goodman Theater, 249, 406, 451, 458
Goodnight Children Everywhere, 36, *280, 281*
Goodrich, Frances, 222
Goodrich, Joseph, 427
Goodspeed Opera House, 411, 457
Goodwin, Deidre, 312
Goodwin, Paul, 404
Goodwin, Philip, 268, 284
Gordan, Michael David, 351
Gordon, Ain, 417, 431
Gordon, Allan S., 249, 255, 451
Gordon, Charles (OyamO), 428, 430, 436
Gordon, Dan, 43, 280
Gordon, David, 417, 431
Gordon, Ian L., 351
Gordon, Janet Davidson, 273
Gordon, Jay, 354
Gordon, Jennifer, 425
Gordon, Laura, 421
Gordon, Mark, 334
Gordon, Mark Robert, 305
Gordon, Peter J., 286
Gordon, Pip, 417, 419
Gordon, Ricky Ian, 330, 340, 353, 455
Gordon, Susie, 286
Gorman, Mark, 361
Gorski, Kristen Leigh, 230
Gorzelnik, Christopher, 420
Gosheva, Nelly, 343
Goss, Bick, 432
Got Your Number, *362*
Gotanda, Philip Kan, 432, 433
Gottesman, Yetta, 339, 350
Gottfried, Martin, 448
Gottlieb, Jon, 416, 417, 425
Gottlieb, Michael, 348
Gould, Jennifer, 292, 293

Gould, Robert, 338
Goulding, Paula, 228
Gounod, Charles, 254, 297
Grabowski, Christopher, 427
Grace, Ginger, 355
Gracey, Kathryn, 360
Grade, Chaim, 420
Gradone, Rick, 337
Graff, Brandee, 355
Graff, Randy, 42, 300, 301, 315
Graham, Bruce, 363
Graham, Connie, 415
Graham, Dion, 249, 414
Graham, Enid, 349
Graham, Gerrit, 274
Graham, Karen, 431
Grainger, Porter, 254, 297
Granahan, Mim, 358
Granata, Dona, 407
Grand, Murray, 264
Grand Tour, The, 33, 225
Grandma Sylvia's Funeral, 264
Grandmama Tree, The, 457
Graney, John Link, 278
Granite, Judith, 361
Grant, David Marshall, 37, 303, 327, 359
Grant, Derick K., 309, 459
Grant, Gary, 230
Grant, Keith Lee, 347
Grant, Michael, 412
Grant, Micki, 424
Grantham, Ken, 431
Grappo, Constance, 353, 363
Grappone, Ray, 236
Grasshoppers, *335*
Grate, Gail, 284
Gravador, Rhoda, 348
Gravatt, Lynda, 349, 456
Graves, Rupert, 254, 456
Gravis, Frank, 266
Gravitte, Beau, 284
Gray, Charles, 228
Gray, Kevin, 321
Gray, Pamela J., 252
Gray, Rudy, 335
Gray, Sam, 305
Gray, Spalding, 349
Gray-Demmler, Prudence, 234
Graybill, Stephen, 457
Great Jones Repertory Company, 343
Great Men of Science Nos. 21 & 22, 459
Great Small Works, 357
Greaves, Danielle Lee, 319
Greco, Karen, 225
Greco, Lola, 337
Greco, Loretta, 344, 353

Greco, Marco, 290
Green, Adolph, 29, 237, 239, 297, 340, 455
Green, Amanda, 358
Green, Dylan, 361
Green, Eddie, 254, 297
Green, Jackie, 239, 297
Green, Jessica, 350
Green, Jonathan, 350, 351
Green, Mark, 350
Green, Miles, 343, 344
Green, Sinéad, 228
Greenberg, Gordon, 425
Greenberg, Richard, 288, 338, 368
Greene, Alexis, 447
Greene, Brian, 229
Greene, Ellen, 431
Greene, Kim Morgan, 245, 246
Greenfield, Ellen, 265
Greenfield, Tom, 272
Greenhill, Mitchell, 409
Greenhill, Susan, 415
Greenhut, Barry, 343, 357
Greenspan, David, 340, 345, 349, 419
Greenwich Street Theater, 356
Greenwood, David, 355
Greenwood, Jane, 232, 457
Greenwood, Judith, 292
Greer, Adam, 268
Greer, Armani, 414
Greer, Michael Barry, 360
Gregus, Peter, 240, 299, 300
Greif, Michael, 278, 409, 415
Greiner, John, 360
Grenek, Gino, 229
Grenfell, Katy, 412
Gretty Good Time, *338*
Grey, David Berry, 321
Grey, Joel, 312
Grey Zone, The, 457
Grib, Margo, 337
Grice, Brian O., 237
Grief of Mind, A, 405
Griffin, Gary, 302, 458
Griffin, Lynne, 349
Griffin, Marion Thomas, 339
Griffith, Jim, 294
Griffith, John, 270
Griffith, Kristin, 356
Griffith, Natalie, 415
Griffiths, Heidi, 238, 267, 284
Griggs, Peter, 348
Grigsby, Kimberly, 224, 248, 271
Grimaldi, Dan, 354, 359
Grimaldi, John, 253, 296

Grimes, Conor, 354
Grimm, David, 341
Grimm Tales, *348*
Grimm, Tim, 406
Grissom, Doug, 357
Griswold, Mary, 407
Grizzard, George, 323
Grody, Kathryn, 21, 229, 354
Groenendaal, Chris, 318
Groener, Harry, 311
Groenewold, Chris, 303
Grogan, Kyla, 322
Groh, David, 425
Grollman, Elaine, 340
Gromada, John, 271, 275, 414, 432
Gross, Barbara, 368
Gross Indecency: The Three Trials of Oscar Wilde, 14, 264, 454, 457
Gross, Todd, 240
Grossberg, Michael, viii, 368
Grossman, Larry, 235
Grové, Jessica, 260
Grove, Barry, 285
Grove Street Playhouse, 356
Groves, Napiera Daniele, 278
Gruber, Michael, 311, 324
Grupper, Adam, 314, 350
Grusin, Richard, 415
Guan, Jamie H.J., 287, 348
Guarding Erica, 332
Guare, John, 270, 298, 329, 350, 455
Guarnaccia, Greg, 435
Guernsey, Otis L. Jr., ix
Guest Lecturer, The, *424*
Guettel, Adam, 46, 271, 330, 340
Guffey, Tamara, 404
Guidi, Julia, 335
Guilfoyle, Paul, 417
Guirgis, Stephen Adly, 290
Gulan, Barbara, 353
Gulan, Timothy, 412
Gum, *403*
Gumbel, Roberta, 330, 344
Gun Hill Road, *335*
Gunas, Gary, 257
Guncler, Sam, 420
Gunji, Maya, 235
Gunn, Lisa, 322
Gunning, Kim, 276
Gurbo, Walter, 350
Gurian, Daniel, 355
Gurney, A.R., 37, 38, 264, 294, 424, 437, 450
Gurskis, Dan, 436
Gurvich, Zhanna, 353

Gurwin, Danny, 269, 340
Gussow, Mel, viii, 455
Gustafson, Bob, 402
Gustafson, Robert, 232, 286
Gustis, Jamie, 231
Guthrie Theater, 368, 422
Guthrie, Woody, 359
Gutierrez, Gerald, 18, 245, 294
Gutzi, Mary, 311
Guy, Jasmine, 312
Guy, Leslie, 234
Guys and Dolls, 458
Guzman, Henry, 339
Guzzi, Ann, 289
Gyondla, Joey, 311
Gypsy, 458

H.J., Jamie, 433
H.M.S. Pinafore, *359*
Habens, Heather, 229
Haber, Bill, 232, 255, 451
Haberle, Stephanie Roth, 268
Haberman, Linda, 235
Hache, Carol, 363
Hack, Sam, 265
Hackady, Hal, 235, 265
Hackett, Albert, 222
Hackett, Peter, 407
Hadary, Jonathan, 404, 424
Haddow, Jeffrey, 454
Hadley, Jonathan, 334, 340
Hadzi, Anna, 409
Haen, Mark, 273
Haft, Elsa Daspin, 232
Hagan, Marianne, 353
Hagar, Sammy, 231, 451
Hagedom, Michael, 412
Hagedorn, Jessica, 368, 409, 415
Hagen, Kevin, 363
Hagen, Uta, 41, 273, 452
Hagenbuckle, J., 457
Haggart, Bob, 247
Haggerty, Henry, 338
Hahn, Kathryn, 437
Haig, David, 307
Haigh, Colin, 291
Haimes, Todd, 223, 236, 245, 270, 288, 450, 451
Hair, 457
Hairston, Jerome, 419
Haizhu, Yu, 348
Hajj, Edward A., 287
Halaska, Linda, 402
Halemsky, Vladimir, 343
Halfway Home, *347*
Hall, Anthony Blair, 240, 241
Hall, Caroline, 405
Hall, Charles Edward, 234
Hall, Dennis Michael, 240, 241

Hall, Kyle, 458
Hall, La Tanya, 240
Hall, Mary Porter, 246
Hall, Michael, 268, 285, 344, 404
Hall, Mike, 246, 248
Hall, Natalie, 320
Hall, Patrick, 358
Hall, Phil, 420
Hall, Thomas, 430
Hallett, Sylvia, 348
Halliday, Kadina, 408
Halling, Michael, 232
Hallmark Entertainment, 232
Halman, Defne, 358
Halmos, Nicole, 362
Halpern, Arthur, 354
Halstead, Carol, 410
Hamatsa, *342*
Hamberg, Julie, 361
Hamburger, Anne, 338
Hamburger, Richard, 409, 436
Hamel, Amy, 311
Hamilton, Allen, 249
Hamilton, Carrie, 319
Hamilton, Ed, 251
Hamilton, Josh, 330, 337
Hamilton, Lawrence, 318
Hamilton, Lisa Gay, 344
Hamilton, Melinda Page, 245
Hamilton, Patrick, 360
Hamilton, Stephen, 430
Hamlet, 457, 458
Hamlisch, Marvin, 24
Hamm, Matthew J., 351
Hammel, Lori, 294
Hammel, Steven, 349
Hammer, Mark, 355
Hammersley, Marguerite, 458
Hammerstein, James, 40, 281
Hammerstein, Oscar II, vii, 40, 223
Hammerstein, Simon, 350, 355
Hammett, Mary, 289
Hammond, Blake, 237, 300
Hammond, Mark, 352
Hampton, Christopher, 223
Hampton, Kate, 281
Hampton, Robert, 432
Han, Eun Kyoung, 225
Hanan, Stephan, 310
Hance, Michael, 232
Hancock, W. David, 456
Handke, Peter, 355
Handman, Wynn, 272, 289, 334, 456
Handspring Puppet Company, 276
Handy, W.C., 253, 260, 296, 304

Hanes, Mary, 435
Haney, Carol, 246
Haney, Lisa, 278
Hanft, Helen, 356
Hanh, Tran T. Thuc, 349
Hanjo, *356*
Hank Manque, *335*
Hankinson, Jeffrey, 236, 299
Hannah, Ned, 236
Hannah Senesh, 368
Hannett, Juliana, 296
Hanreddy, Joseph, 421
Hansell, Susan, 358
Hansen, Clay, 360
Hansen, Karen, 359
Hansen, Lars, 425
Hansen, Teri, 323
Hanson, Lars, 342
Hanz, Jeff, 259
Haojie, Ye, 348
Happy Birthday Jack, *419*
Happy Days, *358*
Harada, Ann, 359, 424
Harari, Bob, 305
Harbaum, Bob, 334
Harburg, E.Y., 260, 354, 360
Harden, Richard, 363
Hardin, Jerry, 426
Harding, Jan Leslie, 289
Hardwick, Mark, 270
Hardy, John, 400
Hardy, Joseph, 430
Hardy, Mark, 269
Hare, David, 9, 10, 11, 12, 223, 243, 245, 256, 447, 456
Hargraves, Missy, 355
Harker, James, 248
Harkness, Julie, 234
Harley, Ben, 229
Harley, Margot, 270, 305
Harlot's Progress, A, *357,* 455
Harman, Paul, 340
Harmon, Jennifer, 256
Harmon, John J., 286
Harms, Holli, 338
Harmsen, Douglas, 411
Harner, Jason Butler, 433
Harnick, Jay, 450
Harnick, Sheldon, 455
Harold Clurman Theater, 356
Harper, Don, 235
Harper, Ian, 293
Harper, Valerie, 294
Harrell, Gordon Lowry, 246
Harriell, Marcy, 319
Harrington, Alexander, 343
Harrington, Nancy, 239
Harrington, Wendall K., 241, 256, 257, 338, 414, 416
Harris, Arthur, 235

Harris, Artie, 230
Harris, Barnaby, 287
Harris, Baxter, 338
Harris, Daniel, 272
Harris, Dede, 230
Harris, Hope, 257, 414, 415
Harris, Jamie, 235, 347
Harris, Jay, 223
Harris, Jeffrey, 237
Harris, Julie, 432, 458
Harris, Kevin, 339
Harris, Kimberly, 334
Harris, Larry, 356
Harris, Linda, 304
Harris, Neal, 343
Harris, Neil Patrick, 318
Harris, Netousha, 240, 241
Harris, Rebecca, 351
Harris, Roy, 295
Harris, Selena, 235
Harris, Toby, 229
Harrison, Babo, 407
Harrison, Howard, 416
Harrison, Paul Carter, 347
Harrison, Peter, 270, 353
Harry and the Cannibals, *341*
Harsh Medicines, *345*
Hart, Charles, 221
Hart, Lorenz, 297
Hart, Melissa, 431
Hart, Moss, 338
Hart, Timothy Eric, 232
Harte, Robert, 363
Hartenstein, Frank, 245
Hartford Stage, 17, 414, 457
Harting, Carla, 417, 419
Hartley, Jan, 236, 424, 431
Hartley, Richard, 256
Hartman, Karen, 403, 409
Hartman, Michael, 255
Harto, Joshua, 350
Hartung, Billy, 230, 314
Harvey, Alec, 368
Harvey, Ann, 416
Harvey, Anne-Charlotte
    Hanes, 417
Harvey, Dyane, 271
Harvey, Jonathan, 302
Harvey, Katie, 313
Harvey, Nate, 342
Harwell, David, 305
Hase, Tom, 412
Hasenstab, Derek, 412
Hasho, Susan Warrick, 340
Hastings, Tony, 266
Hatcher, Jeffrey, 345, 349
Hatcher, Teri, 310
Hathaway, Donny, 260, 304
Hatten, Keith L., 410
Haubner, Julia, 412

Hauck, Rachel, 285, 433
Haugen, David, 435
Haupt, Paulette, 436
Hausam, Wiley, 238, 267, 282
Havard, Bernard, 426
Haverty, Doug, 454
Hawkanson, David, 422
Hawkes, Colleen, 334
Hawkesworth, Quinn, 400
Hawking, Judith, 350, 355, 407
Hawkins, Jay, 260, 304
Hawkins, Roy, 260, 304
Hawkins, Tim, 231, 232, 241,
    261
Hawkinson, John, 405
Hawley, Colette, 359
Hawley, Jessie, 348
Hawley, Kate, 405
Hawley, Lynn, 337, 433
Hay Fever, 457
Hayashi, Hajime, 361
Hayden, Michael, 37, 294
Hayes, Clancey, 254, 296
Hayes, Jack, 299, 300
Hayes, Mark, 415
Hayes, Maureen, 335
Haynsworth, Brian, 265
Hays, Carole Shorenstein, 249,
    254, 450
Hays, Michael, 416
Hays, Peter, 420
Hays, Rex, 435
Hays, Thomas A., 293
Haythe, Sean, 230, 231
Hayward, Charley, 343
Hayward-Jones, Michael, 407,
    411
Haywood, Nicole, 360
Hazard, Duncan, 358
Hazard, Jim, 335
Hazeldine, James, 14, 255
HB Playwrights Foundation,
    273
HBO, 225
**He Who Says Yes/He Who
    Says No**, *359*
Headley, Heather, 300, 301,
    315, 402
Healy, Brendan, 407
Healy, Gary, 228
Heaps, Jonathan, 335
Hearn, George, 234
Hearn, Lafcadio, 357
Heart, Susan, 234
Heart's Desire, *290*, *292*
Heasley, Katherine, 408
Heath, Kia Christina, 360
Heath, Robin, 407
Heathen Valley, 454
Heaton, Jeanne, 361

Heaven and Earth, *351*
Hebblethwaite, Jennifer, 422
Hebert, Julie, 353, 455
Hebert, Rich, 286, 402
Hecht, Jessica, 35, 284, 437
Heckman, Rick, 244, 299
Hect, Don, 260, 304
Hedda Gabler, *417*
Hedges, Peter, 338, 363
Hedley, Nevin, 239
Hedwig and the Angry Inch,
    264
Heenehan, Mark, 249, 414
Hegarty, Judy, 358
Heggie, Femi S., 253
Heggins, Amy, 237, 299, 300
Heidenreich, V Craig, 417, 419
Heifner, Jack, 415
Heilpern, John, 447, 448, 453
Heimonas, Yorgos, 279
Heinlein, Jamie, 361
Helen Hayes Awards, 457
Helen Hayes Performing Arts
    Center, 425
Helene Davis Publicity, 255
Heller, Alexandra, 427
Heller, Georganne, 280
Hellesen, Richard, 410
Hello Again, 243, 458
Hello, Dolly!, 33, 224
Hello, I Love You, *361*
Helmer, MJ, 430
Hemingways, *334*
Hemphill, Garth, 431
Henderson, Judy, 287
Henderson, Luther, 301
Henderson, Mark, 255, 256,
    292, 452
Henderson, Ray, 246
Hendricks, Floyd, 229
Hendricks, Leslie Ann, 411
Hendrix, Leslie, 337
Hendy, Jessica, 311
Henkel, Clare, 430
Henley, Beth, 287
Henner, Marilu, 312
Henry, Buck, 307
Henry, Diana, 355
Henry, Guy, 457
Henry Hewes Design Awards,
    viii, 455
Henry, Jim, 458
Henry, Martha, 292, 293
Henry, Thea, 335
Henry V, *343*
Henshall, Ruthie, 299, 300, 312
Hensley, Charlie, 424
Hensley, Dale, 300
Henson, Cheryl, 276
Henson, Leslie, 410

Heraty, Noel, 228
Herb Goldsmith Productions, 256
Herber, Pete, 286
Here, 329, 330, 331, 344, 356
Here Arts Center, 265
Heredia, Wilson Jermaine, 319
Herington, John, 257
Herlinger, Karl, 355
Hermalyn, Joy, 240
Herman, Benjamin, 232
Herman, Jerry, 224, 225, 456
Hermann, Peter, 340
Hernandez, Gendell, 432
Hernandez, Juan Carlos, 277
Hernandez, Philip, 315
Hernandez, Ray, 430
Hernandez, Riccardo, 244, 402, 405, 409, 417, 452
Herrera, Emil, 422
Herrera, John, 300, 424
Herrero, Mercedes, 339, 427
Herrick, Alice C., 224
Herskovits, David, 362
Herstory of Porn: Reel to Real, *349*
Hertzberg, Deborah, 358
Herz, Shirley, 265, 279, 289, 302
Herzog, Jonathan C., 271
Herzog, Mark, 409
Hesh, *359*
Hess, Elizabeth, 355
Hess, Nancy, 312
Hess, Scott, 357
Hester, Richard, 251
Hester Street Hideaway: A Lower East Side Love Story, *338*
Hetherington, Leigh, 319
Hewes, Henry, viii, 455
Hewitt, Sarah, 232
Hewitt, Tom, 315
Hibbert, Edward, 256, 457
Hickerson, Vicki, 234
Hickey, Joe, 407
Hickey, John Benjamin, 310
Hickey, Michael, 360
Hickey, Peggy, 457
Hicklin, Walter, 408, 431
Hickok, John, 243
Hickok, Molly, 338
Hicks, D'Atra, 320
Hicks, Israel, 410, 436
Hicks, Marva, 457
Hidalgo, Antonio, 303, 304
Hidden Agenda, *335*
Hiester, Dan, 409
Higgins, Billy, 248
Higgins, Janet, 239

Higgins, Jim, 228
Higgins, Joanna, 228
Higgins, Patience, 305
High Life, *349*
High Society, 223
Higham, David, 353
Hilferty, Susan, 277, 281, 286, 306, 414
Hill/Walter, 252
Hill, Amy, 224
Hill, Andrew, 265
Hill, Dick, 416
Hill, Dulé, 310
Hill, Erin, 339
Hill, Gary Leon, 411
Hill, Gregory, 426
Hill, Heather, 352
Hill, Jenny, 402
Hill, Ken, 407
Hill, Z.Z., 259, 304
Hillner, John, 230
Hinckle, Hilary, 336
Hinds, Ciaran, 11, 12, 254, 456
Hines, John, 407
Hines, Will, 400, 401
Hingle, Pat, 319
Hinkle, Marin, 242, 428, 433, 437
Hirayanagi, Nami, 293
Hired Gun/One Dream, 289
Hirsch, Judd, 307
Hirsch, Stacie, 329
Hirschfeld, Al, vii, 49–77
Hirschfield, Mark, 355
Hirson, David, 455
History of Bowling, The, *407*
Ho, Fred, 345
Ho, Rania, 348
Ho, Wai Ching, 348
Hoben, Ginna, 419
Hoch, Chris, 298, 299
Hoch, Danny, 332
Hochman, Larry, 259
Hock, Robert, 360
Hodge, Richard, 272, 289
Hodge, Wendy D., 436
Hodges, Angela, 359
Hodges, Jennifer, 356
Hodges, Patricia, 40, 237, 274
Hodgkins, Tom, 249, 414
Hoehler, Richard, 358
Hoesl, Joseph, 271
Hoffman, Constance, 437
Hoffman, Dustin, 15, 249
Hoffman, Gary, 294
Hoffman/Goodheart/Nelson/ Ager/Amberg, 252
Hoffman, Kent, 347
Hoffman, Philip, 232, 245, 338

Hofsiss, Jack, 229, 355
Hogan, Andi, 351
Hogan, Kevin, 288
Hogan, Robert, 338
Hogue, Rochelle, 422
Hohn, Amy, 353
Hoiby, Lee, 410
Holcomb, Bill, 257
Holden, Beth Ann, 362
Holder, Donald, 275, 277, 286, 305
Holder, Jimmy, 288
Holder, Laurence, 289
Holdridge, Eleanor, 345
Holgate, Ron, 251, 334
Hollaender, F., 256
Holland, Reece, 316
Hollander/Mehring, 252
Holliday, Polly, 350
Hollinger, Michael, 433
Hollingshead, Vanessa, 361
Hollis, Stephen, 358
Hollow Lands, The, 408
Holman, Bob, 359
Holmes, Judy, 413
Holmes, Lori, 230
Holmes, Rick, 284, 310
Holmes, Violet, 235
Holt, Monique, 267
Holt, Paul, 234
Holton, Alex, 244
Holy Water, *363*
Home at the End of the World, A, 458
Homer, 357
Honda, Carol A., 349
Hong, Hong Yijia, 348
Honky Tonk Angels, The, *401*
Honour, 223
Hood, Stuart, 356
Hooker, John Lee, 260, 304
Hooks, Joey, 333
Hoopes, Wendy, 350
Hoover, Richard, 6, 250, 414, 452, 456
Hoovler, Kathy J., 235
'Hope' Is the Thing With Feathers, *338*
Hope, Paul, 404
Hope, Richard, 291
Hope, Stephen, 232
Hope, Trip, 419
Hopkins, Cynthia, 338
Hopkins, Kaitlin, 425
Hopkins, Ryan, 320
Hopper, Tim, 279
Horejs, Vit, 342, 357
Hornbuckle, Michael Chih Ming, 348
Horne, Ashley, 232, 298

Horne, Cheryl, 355
Horne, J.R., 267, 284, 404
Horne, Marjorie, 281
Horovitz, Hannah, 413
Horovitz, Israel, 293, 413
Horowitz, Lawrence, 242, 259, 451
Horsey, Daniel, 409
Horton, Blaine, 234
Horton, Jamie, 411
Horton, Murell, 433
Horvitz, Dennis, 351
Hoshour, Robert, 311
Hosney, Doug, 259
Hostetter, Curt, 289
Hostetter, Paul, 258
Hot Air, *361*
Hotchner, A.E., 265
Hotel Carter, The, *345*
Hotel on Marvin Gardens, A, 411
Hotel Suite, *426*
Hothouse, The, 41, 330, *337*
Hotopp, Michael, 235
Hoty, Dee, 230, 314, 451
Houghton, James, 350
Hould-Ward, Ann, 230, 236, 402
Houlihan-Verdolino, Annette, 356
Hoult, Jennifer, 241
Hounsell, Ginny, 234
Hourie, Troy, 306
House, *349*, *430*, 456
House/Lights, *363*, 456
House, Lynn, 362
House of Bernarda Alba, The, *339*
House of Horror, The, *276*
House, Tom, 422
Hova, Jonathan, 405
How I Became an Interesting Person, 436
How I Learned to Drive, 38, 327, 447, 449, 454
How to Succeed in Business Without Really Trying, 246
Howar, Tim, 315
Howard, Celia, 435
Howard, Donnacha, 228
Howard, Edward, 260, 304
Howard, Jason, 348
Howard, Joanne, 338
Howard, Kisha, 251
Howard, Peter, 235, 261
Howard, Ralph, 448
Howard, Rey, 351
Howard, Stuart, 275, 280, 294
Howarth, Roger, 237

Howarth, Tony, 358
Howe, Marie, 340
Howe, Sherman M. Jr., viii
Howe, Tina, 328
Howell, Gail Cook, 261
Howland, Jason, 232, 257, 260, 414, 450
Hoxie, Richmond, 360
Hoy, Kim, 316
Hoyle, Geoff, 315, 404
Hoyle, Kailey, 404
Hoyt, Lon, 421
Hsu, Emily, 348
Hu, Ann, 349
Hubbert, Bruce, viii
Huber, Kim, 309
Hubert, William B. 2d., 339
Huddleston, David, 319
Hudson, Steven L., 435
Hudson, Walter, 289
Huff, Neal, 18, 237
Huffman, Cady, 425
Hughes, Allen Lee, 424, 435, 450
Hughes, Amy, 244, 245
Hughes, Doug, 282, 285, 350, 424, 457
Hughes, Julie, 231, 233, 241, 261, 281
Hughes, Jurian, 293
Hughes, Kim, 272, 457
Hughes, Langston, 253, 254, 296, 297, 333
Hughes, Maureen, 260
Hughes, Ted, 290
Hugo, Victor, 221
Hugot, Marceline, 337
Hulce, Tom, 330, 337
Human Resources, *358*
Humana Festival of New American Plays, 367, 417
Hume, Michael J., 402
Humes, Helen, 254, 297
Hummel, Mark, 235
Humphrey, Annie, 430
Humphrey, Steve, 428, 429
Hunt, Alva, 241, 269, 286, 298
Hunt, Annette, 351
Hunt, David, 286
Hunt, Helen, 18, 19, 224
Hunt, Ralph, 334, 335
Hunt, Scott, 318
Hunt, William E., 361
Hunter, Holly, 288
Hunter, Maureen, 433
Hunter, Ronald, 457
Hunter, Tim, 258, 259
Hunter, Timothy, 411
Hunter-Gault, Chuma, 237

Huntington Theater Company, 457
Hupfeld/Rotter/Robinson, 252
Hupp, Robert, 358
Hurd, Adrienne, 251, 429
Hurlin, Dan, 357
Hurlyburly, , *361*, 458
Hurowitz, Peter, 428
Hurrah at Last, 288
Hurst, Michael, 340
Hurwitt, Robert, 368
Huston, Michael, 358
Huston, Tom, 360
Huszti, Doug, 334, 422
Hutcherson, Abbi, 243, 244
Hutchison, Brian, 431
Hutchman, David, 359
Hutt, William, 292, 293
Hutton, Arlene, 344, 347, 360, 361
Hutton, John, 410, 411
Huxhold, Kristin, 240
Hwang, David Henry, 9, 420
Hydraulics Phat Like Mean, *270, 271*
Hydriotaphia, or the Death of Dr. Browne, *404*, *415*
Hylenski, Peter, 266
Hymas, Chris, 265
Hynes, Garry, 260, 452
Hysell, Hugh, 359
Hyslop, David, 235, 243
Hytner, Nicholas, 18, 224

I Love Dick, *344*
I Love You, You're Perfect, Now Change, 264
Theater World Awards, 456
I Want To Be Happy, *356*
'I' Word: Intern, The, *339*
I'm Still Here ... Damn It!, 4, 20, *234*
I'm Telling You for the Last Time, 7
Iacona, Joe, 335
Iacovelli, John, 239, 409, 426
Iacucci, Lisa, 284
Iakoubov, Serguei, 228
Iannone, Angela, 458
Ibsen, Brian, 237
Ibsen, Henrik, 351, 405, 417
Iceman Cometh, The, 3, 4, 13, 14, 15, *255, 256*, 451, 452, 456
Ichabod Revealed, *349*
ICM Artists Ltd., 279
Ideal Husband, An, 458
Idiot, The, 458
If Memory Serves, *425*

Ignite! Entertainment Corp., 272
Iizuka, Naomi, 360, 417
Ikeda, Thomas, 267
Illiad, The, 357
Illuminating Veronica, *341, 345*
Ima, Kim, 343
Image Makers, The, 290
Imaginary Invalid, The, 457
Imagining Brad, *338, 363*
Imai, Masayuki, 358
Imbrie, McCrea, 335
Imbrie, Peggy, 235
Imhoff, Gary, 314
Importance of Being Earnest, The, *359,* 457
Impossible Marriage, 36, *287, 288*
Impresario! the Ziegfeld Girls, 435
Imus, Don, 7
In and Out of the Light, 264
In Dahomey, *347*
In Service, *435*
In the Balance, *409*
In the Western Garden, *339*
Indian Ink, *431*
Ingalls, James F., 281, 287
Ingham, Barrie, 314
Ingham, Robert E., 454
Ingliss, Robert, 298
Ingman, Nick, 228
Ingram, Jason, 239
Ingram, Tad, 243, 244
Inkley, Fred, 307, 314
Inna Beginning, 411
Innaurato, Albert, 289, 329
Innvar, Christopher, 269, 353
Inside the Creole Mafia, *340*
Inskeep, Carter, 356
Intar, 339, 357
International Festival of Puppet Theater, 36, 275, 277, 357
Interpreter of Horror, The, *359*
Intiman Theater, 433
Intimate Party With Betty & Adolph, An, *340*
Intrigue With Faye, *345*
Invisible Hand, The, *356*
Invisible Man, The, *407*
Ion, *334*
Ionesco, Eugene, 223, 342, 352, 358, 360
Iorio, Jim, 422
Iphigenia Cycle, The, *362,* 458
Irby, Michael, 285
Irby-Ranniar, Scott, 298, 402

Irish Arts Center, 358
Irish Arts Theater, 228
Irish ... and How They Got That Way, The, *339*
Irish Repertory Theater, 331, 339
Irish Wake, An, 7, 21
Irons, Andrew, 345
Irvin, Mary Kae, 433
Irving, John, 330, 337
Irving, Suzanne, 402
Irwin, Bill, 24, 30, 239
Isaac, Alberto, 416
Isaacs, Pamela, 424
Isbell, Paula, 416
Isenberg, Shane, 425
Isenegger, Nadine, 322
Isherwood, Charles, 448, 453
Isherwood, Christopher, 222, 361
Island of Dogs, *356*
Islander, J.C., 334
Israel, Henry, 343
Israel, Susannah, 235
It Ain't Nothin' But the Blues, 4, 18, 24, 30, 31, 36, *243, 259, 303, 304,* 451, 452
Itallie, Jean-Claude Van, 343
Ito, Genji, 343, 352
Ivanov, Felix, 306
Ivers, Eileen, 228, 229
Ives, David, 301, 426
Ivey, Dana, 280
Ivey, Stacey Leigh, 354
Ivins, Todd Edward, 340
Iwakawa, Saburo, 354
Izzo, Bob, 362

Jack and Jill, 454
Jackness, Andrew, 232
Jacksina Company, The, 253, 296
Jacksina, Judy, 253, 296
Jackson, Anne, 332, 355
Jackson, D.D., 348
Jackson, Ernestine, 359
Jackson, Gregory, 282, 354
Jackson, Mark Leroy, 318
Jackson, Nagle, 368, 410, 411
Jackson, R. Wade, 255
Jackson, Reuben, 237
Jackson, Robert Jason, 344
Jacob, Abe, 259
Jacob, Lou, 345, 412
Jacob Marley's Christmas Carol, *406*
Jacob, Roeg, 417
Jacobs, Amy, 259, 305

Jacobs, Betty, 450
Jacobs, Jacob, 229, 230
Jacobs, Sally J., 243
Jacobson, Aileen, 447
Jacobson, Eric, 265
Jacobson, Jim, 347
Jacoby, Mark, 316, 318, 457
Jacques et Son Maitre, *409*
Jadbro Productions, 289
Jaeger, Alex, 408
Jaeger, Darleen, 358
Jaffe, Jerry, 351, 352
Jaffe, Jill, 248, 299
Jahan, Marine, 232
Jahi, Meena T., 315
Jahnke, Christopher, 412
Jajuan, Kimberly, 344
James, Anne, 353
James, Anthony, 402
James, Augustina, 269
James, Brian d'Arcy, 321
James C. Nicola, 277
James, Daniel E., 410
James, Darrell, 427
James, Diqui, 269
James, Harold Dean, 343
James, Henry, 349
James LL Morrison & Associates, 243, 252, 256, 259, 268, 275, 280
James, Michael Leonard, 354
James Naughton: Street of Dreams, *297*
James, Reginald, 351
James, Tomas, 269
James, Tommy, 305
James, Toni-Leslie, 231, 269, 298
Jamieson, Julia, 430
Jamieson, Nigel, 347
Jampolis, Neil Peter, 281, 428
Jani, Robert F., 234
Janis, Ryan, 335
Janis, Victoria, 361
Jankowitz, Mike, 356
Janney, Allison, 321
Janowitz, Marc, 294
Jansen, Richard, 344, 433
Jar the Floor, 289
Jarcho, Julia, 350
Jarrus, Jay, 450
Jaudes, Christian, 237, 251
Javerbaum, David, 340
Jayasundera, Thusitha, 348
Jaynes, Carl, 272, 289, 334
Jayson, 36, *272*
Jaywalker, *349*
Jbara, Gregory, 313
Jean, Christopher, 268, 305

Jean Cocteau Repertory, 358
Jefferson, Tavia Riveé, 240, 241
Jeffet, Geula, 343
Jefford, Barbara, 291
Jeffrey Finn Productions, viii, 307
Jeffrey Richards Associates, 273, 274, 282, 303, 305
Jekyll & Hyde, 26, 222
Jellison, John, 237, 238, 269
Jello Is Always Red, The, 29, 36, *265*
Jelly Roll!, 454
Jenkins, Capathia, 257, 414
Jenkins, Carol Mayo, 431
Jenkins, Daniel, 353
Jenkins, Jeffrey Eric, 455
Jenkins, Len, 362
Jenkins, Thom, 422
Jenkins, Timothy, 348
Jenkins, Vanity, 423
Jenkins, Woody, 422
Jennings, Alex, 457
Jennings, Byron, 417
Jennings, James, 334, 335
Jennings, Ken, 240
Jennings, Lesley, 235
Jennings, Regi, 402
Jensen, Erik, 285
Jensen, Julie, 345
Jenson, Matt, 357
Jeong, Young Joo, 225
Jermanok, Jim, 355
Jerome, Jeff, 359
Jerome Robbins' Broadway, 33
Jerome, Tim, 309
Jerry Seinfeld: I'm Telling You for the Last Time, 4, *225*
Jett, Erica, 348
Jevnikar, Jana, 344
Jew of Bleecker Street, The, *334*
Jewish Repertory Theater, 331, 340
Jews and Jesus, *342*
Jeziorny, Richard, 347
Jiménez, Marta, 228
Jim Henson Foundation, The, 275
Jiminez, Robert, 342
Jiminez, Tai, 237
Jing, Zhu, 348
Jitney, 457
Jo-Ann, Ebony, 347
Job, The, *354*
Jodie's Body, 36, 42, *303, 354*
Joe A. Callaway Award, 455

Joffe, Edward, 232, 246
Johann, Susan, viii
Johansen, Mark, 235
Johanson, Robert, 260, 261, 420, 421
John, Elton, 222, 402
John F. Kennedy Center for the Performing Arts, The, 231
John, Joseph, 276
John Montgomery Theater Company, 358
Johnes, Alexandra, 275
Johnson, Andrea J., 351
Johnson, Birch, 257
Johnson, Brad, 406
Johnson, Brandt, 337
Johnson, Brian, 458
Johnson, Bryan, 348, 361
Johnson, Christine Toy, 359
Johnson, Clifford Lee III, 285
Johnson, Craig, 246
Johnson, Jerry, 293
Johnson, Joy, 404
Johnson, Kristen, 42, 267
Johnson, Louis, 347
Johnson, Nunnally, 354, 362
Johnson, Porshia, 429
Johnson, Rebekah, 298, 299, 301
Johnson, Robert L., 260, 304
Johnson, Timothy Charles, 411
Johnson, Tina, 267, 268, 313
Johnson, Todd Alan, 315
Johnson-Liff Associates, 252
Johnston, Chloe, 406
Johung, Jennifer, 345
Jokovic, Mirjana, 242, 428
Jolie-Archer, Danielle, 234
Jolles, Annette, 265
Jolls, Charles, 407, 412
Jolson, Al, 247
Jolson Sings Again, *424*
Jonathan, Mark, 256
Jones, Basil, 276
Jones, Bob Devin, 428
Jones, Charity, 306
Jones, Cherry, 285
Jones, Christine, 343, 349, 405
Jones, David, 413
Jones, Dean, 323
Jones, Denis, 236
Jones, Derek Anson, 282, 344, 453
Jones, Felicity, 286, 454
Jones, Gene, 359
Jones, Gregory, 305
Jones, Gwendolyn, 420
Jones, Jane, 330, 337

Jones, John Christopher, 309
Jones, Judd, 361
Jones, Julia P., 280
Jones, Leslie, 356
Jones, Lindsay, 302
Jones, Margaret, 239
Jones, Marie, 280
Jones, Michael Colby, 359
Jones, Nancy, 345, 347
Jones, Ora, 362, 434
Jones, Pattie Darcy, 320
Jones, Reed, 311
Jones, Richard, 254, 297
Jones, Roger Kristian, 361
Jones, Ron Cephas, 284
Jones, Simon, 245, 270
Jones, Steven Anthony, 431
Jones, Syl, 368
Jones, Tina, 407
Jones, Tom, 264, 411
Jones-Smedley, Yvette, 422
Jordan, Julia, 419
Jordan, Louis, 253, 296
Jordan, Pamela, 234, 298, 299
Jordan, Rebecca, 458
Jordan, S. Marc, 321
Jordon, David, 358
Jory, Jessica, 419
Jory, Jon, 417
Joseph, Catrice, 402
Joseph, James William, 407
Joseph Jefferson Awards, 458
Joseph Jefferson Citations Wing Awards, 458
Joseph Papp Public Theater, The, 21, 36, 42, 237, 238, 267, 276, 282, 284, 285, 340, 357
Joseph, Sandra, 316
Josepher, Laura, 361
Joslyn, Betsy, 309
Jourdan, Mimi, 351
Jovovich, Scott, 245, 246
Joy, James, 425
Joy Luck Club, The, *348*
Joy, Timothy, 354
Joyful Noise, A, 368
Judas Kiss, The, 9, 223
Judd, Michael, 340
Judith Anderson Theater, 358
Judy, James, 232
Jue, Francis, 284, 353
Juergens, Steve, 414
Jugueta, Christine, 410
Jujamcyn Theaters, 249, 255, 256, 451
Jujamcyn Theaters Award, 455
Julia De Burgos, Child of the Water, *350*
Julian, Ivan, 278

Jullien, Claire, 292, 293
Jumping for Joy, 415
Jun, Jun Taek, 225
Jun, Xu, 348
Jung, Ha Yun, 225
Jung, Jin Wook, 225
Jung, Mi Kyung, 225
Jurado, Arantxa, 228, 229
Jurmann/Rotter, 252
Jurosko, Keith, 359
Jury, Brendan, 276
**Just Another Genocide Show,
    the Human Race and
    Adjunct**, *351*
Just Be Frank, *419*
Just, Sloan, 237, 238
Just So, *412*

Kaats, Rod, 425
Kabalan, Svjetlana, 261
Kachel, Roger, 311
Kachergus, Laura, 361
Kaczorowski, Peter, 280, 288,
    294, 298, 299, 432
Kadleck, Tony, 261
Kadri, Ron, 420
**Kafka, or The Search Goes
    On**, *357*
Kahan, Marcy, 359
Kahan, Sharon, 293
Kahn, Barbara, 351
Kahn, Ian, 275, 305, 425
Kahn, Ricardo, 243, 259, 303
Kahrs, Lee, 229
Kaikkonen, Gus, 359
Kakuk, Naomi, 311
Kalbfleisch, Jon, 416
Kale, Naomi, 335
Kalfayan, Voki, 406
Kalfin, Robert Mark, 230, 252
Kaliardos, James, 360
Kalke, Celise, 356
Kalleres, Greg, 335
Kalmar, Bert, 248
Kalmar, Michael, 335
Kamai, Frank, 359
Kamal, Joseph, 403
Kambouri, Viki, 280
Kamlot, Robert, 450
Kamys, , 406
Kamys, John, 458
Kanagawa, Kennedy, 240, 241,
    359
Kanda, Rome, 358
Kandel, Karen, 343, 457
Kandel, Paul, 240
Kander, John, 30, 222, 247, 401,
    455, 457

Kane, Temple, 234
Kanin, Garson, 297
Kaniuk, Yoram, 343
Kanoff, Scott, 407
Kantrowitz, Jason, 235
Kapetan, George, 404
Kaplan, Barry, 335, 345
Kaplan, Mitchell, 234
Kaplin, Stephen, 252
Kapral, Donna, 234
Karabeti, Karyofyllia, 279
Karas, Ellen, 435
Karaty, Daniel, 230
Karayan, Kristin, 334
Karbasnikoff, Sarah, 292
Kardana, 250, 451
Karenjune Sanchez, 277
Karmi, M.J., 360
Karp, Warren, 457
Karr, Yolanda, 351
Karvonides-Dushenko, Chrisi,
    425
KasaKaitas, Kyle, 351, 352
Kashani, Dariush, 287
Kaspaorovics, Andris, 338
Kassen, Mark, 305
Kassoff, Russell, 230
Kastner, Ron, 293, 302, 450
Katircioglu, Huseyin, 342
Kato, Jennifer, 348
Katsaros, Doug, 230, 231, 266
Katsiadaki, Maria, 279
Katz, Natasha, 224, 232, 245,
    402, 452
Katz, Sharon, 334
Katz, Sherri Jean, 276
Katzman, Bruce, 342
Kaufelt, Stanley, 282
Kaufman, Dale, 231
Kaufman, David, 448
Kaufman, George S., 362
Kaufman, Jason, 358
Kaufman, Moisés, 264
Kavanagh, John, 228
Kavner, Julie, 288
Kawahara, Karl, 241
Kaye, Bradley, 294
Kaye, Judy, 318
Kaye, Terry, 360
Kaz, Donna, 354
Kealy, Jacqueline, 358
Keane, Brian, 337
Keane, Kathy, 355
Keaney, Erin, 319
Kearney, Kristine, 422
Keating, Ashlee, 320
Keating, Charles, 270
Keating, John, 340, 358
Keating, Sarah, 351

Keefe, Anne, 253
Keegan, Ted, 316
Keeler, Brian, 410
Keely and Du, 454
Keene, Donald, 356
Keeslar, Matt, 353
Kehr, Cynthia L, 422
Keith, Larry, 321
Keith Sherman & Associates,
    265, 266
Keith, Warren D., 432
Kellard, Bill, 239
Kellehes, Mike, 335
Kellenberger, Kurt B., 279,
    281, 290, 436
Keller, Greg, 270
Keller, Michael, 259
Keller, Sean, 318
Kelley, Anna, 334
Kelley, Dominique, 310
Kelliher, Sean, 228
Kellman, Nina, 261
Kellner, Catherine, 255, 270
Kellogg, Marjorie Bradley, 284
Kellogg, Robert, 249
Kelly, *354*
Kelly, Colleen, 422
Kelly, Daniel Wilkes, 351
Kelly, Daren, 313
Kelly, David, 402
Kelly, David Patrick, 224
Kelly, Donna, 266
Kelly, Dori May, 361
Kelly, Glen, 241, 264
Kelly, Jen, 228
Kelly, John-Charles, 324
Kelly, Kristen Lee, 319, 358
Kelly, Lawrence, 295
Kelly, Mickey, 295
Kelly, Paula, 425
Kelly, Reade, 355
Kelly, Tari, 323
Kelly, Thomas Vincent, 434
Kelly, Tom Paitson, 338
Kelly, Tricia Ann, 400
Kemp, Sally, 356, 360
Kemp, Will, 229
Kempton, Neil, 354
Kendall, Trent Armand, 260,
    261
Kendrick, Louisa, 234
Kener, David, 363
Kennard, Michael, 359
Kenneally, Carrie, 240, 311
Kennedy, Anne, 401
Kennedy Center African
    Odyssey Program, The, 276
Kennedy Center Honors, 455
Kennedy, Dev, 407

Kennedy, Steve C., 402
Kennedy, York, 432
Kenney, Kaitlyn, 331
Kent, Jonathan, 290, 292
Kentridge, William, 276
Keomurjian, Alex, 335
Kepros, Nicholas, 270, 305, 362
Kerekes, Lisa, 362
Kern, Dan, 408
Kerner, Susan, 335
Kerpel, Gabriel, 269
Kershaw, Whitney, 311
Kershen, Ed, 422
Keskhemnu, , 428
Kesselman, Wendy, 222
Kester, Raymond, 412
Key, Benny, 253, 296
Key, Linda Ames, 361
Key West Theater Festival, 415
Khan, Ricardo, 422
Khan-Din, Ayub, 285, 347
Khanna, Rahul, 287
Kianuma, Morris, 251
Kidman, Nicole, 11, 243, 456
Kielar, Paul, 267
Kiely, Caroline, 435
Kiely, Damon, 348, 354
Kierkosz, Luba, 343
Kieronsky, Elizabeth, 286
Kiesewetter, Erica, 229
Kijima, Kyo, 361
Kilgarriff, Patricia, 252, 353
Kilgore, Alex, 337
Killalee, Jason, 339
Killer Joe, 36, 39
Killian, Scott, 433
Kim, Bong Soo, 225
Kim, Chungsun, 244, 261
Kim, Do Hoon, 225
Kim, Do Hyeong, 225
Kim, Hak Muk, 225
Kim, Hee Gab, 225
Kim, Ho Jin, 225
Kim, Hyun Dong, 225
Kim, Hyun Sook, 225
Kim, Jae Wean, 225
Kim, Jun, 355
Kim, Ki Young, 225
Kim, Kwang Lim, 225
Kim, Min Soo, 225
Kim, Peter, 359
Kim, Randall Duk, 268, 331, 340, 456
Kim, Sang Jin, 225
Kim, So Yeoun, 225
Kim, So Young, 225
Kim, Sun Mi, 225
Kim, Sung Ki, 225
Kim, Susan, 339, 348, 354

Kim, Taewon Yi, 225
Kim, Tai Hyun, 225
Kim, Willa, 425
Kim, Wonjung, 225
Kim, Young Hwan, 225
Kim, Young Ju, 225
Kimbrough, Linda, 406
King, Ajala, 335
King, Alice, 342
King, Donna, 311
King, Everett, 260, 450
King, Holly, 360
King Lear, 342
King, Natalie, 234
King of Coons, *340*
King, Raymond, 310
King, Rob, 358
King, Terry Lee, 351
King, Woodie, Jr., 289, 347
King, Yolanda, 355
King's Mare, The, *404*
Kingdom, *410*
Kingwill, Marilyn, viii
Kiniry-Ostro, Edward, 427
Kinsherf, John, 306
Kipling, Rudyard, 285, 412
Kirby, Christopher R., 245, 246
Kirk, Justin, 437
Kirk, Keith Byron, 44, 257, 269, 414
Kirkland, Dale, 251
Kirkpatrick, Bruce, 249, 250
Kirkpatrick, Kelley, 232, 281
Kirsch, Michael, 239
Kirsche, Damon, 299
Kirziel-Formato, Lynn, 339
Kiss Me, Kate, 246
Kiss of the Spider Woman, 25, 458
Kissinger, Brittny, 322
Kit Marlowe, *341*
Kitchen, Heather, 431
Kitchen, The, 436
Kitchen of Heaven, The, *356*
Kittay, Leo, 288
Kittredge, Ann, 241, 300, 301
Kivnick, Eric, 237
Kladitis, Manny, 224, 253, 258
Klebba, Martin, 234, 260, 261
Klein, Alvin, 448, 453
Klein, Emily, 243, 244
Klein, Jon, 368
Kleinbort, Barry, 264
Kleinhans, Elysabeth, 335, 358
Kleps, Dale, 246
Kley, Chaney, 458
Klimkoski, Chris, 282
Kline, Kevin, 455
Kline, Norman, 430

Kline, Patrick, 355
Klineman, Kent, 249
Kling, Kevin, 422
Klinger, Pam, 309
Klohe, Hans-Werner, 229
Kmeck, George, 286
KMPG Award, 457
Knanishu, Kristine, 412
Knapp, Sandra, 422
Knapp, Sarah, 232
Knee Desires the Dirt, The, *353*, 455
Knepper, Robert, 433
Knickerbocker, Tom, 426
Kniffen, Chase, 239, 322
Knight, Susan, 427
Knight, T.R., 349
Knight, Wayne, 307
Knighton, Nan, 222, 232
Knopf, James, 362
Knott, Frederick, 223
Knowlton, Sarah, 30, 237
Knox, Leila, 286, 287
Knudson, Kurt, 309
Koch, Ted, 15, 249
Kochan, Tom, 347
Kocis, Bill, 420
Koczela, Jeffrey, 435
Koehler, Fred, 358
Koenig, Jack, 350
Koessel, Wolfram, 229
Kofoed, Seana, 252, 253, 286
Koger, Jeffrey, 294, 426
Kohler, Adrian, 276
Kohler/Arlen, 252
Kohler, Jack, 432
Kohlhaas, Karen, 330, 337
Kole, Debby, 234
Kolins, Howard, 234
Kolinski, Joseph, 321
Kolotouros, Jason, 428
Komer, Chris, 232
Konopka, Albin, 436
Kontouri, Niketa, 280
Koob, Shannon, 410
Koolhaas, Rem, 328
Koop, Kris, 311
Kopit, Arthur, 223, 417
Koppel, Harriet, 360
Korahai, Pari, 280
Korb, Amy, 334
Korba, John, 257
Korder, Howard, 358, 408
Korey, Alix, 224, 424, 425
Kornberg, Richard, 248, 249, 269, 277, 290, 303
Kornbluth, Josh, 349
Kortman, Cynthia, 258, 259
Kosarin, Danny, 424

Kosek, Kenny, 230
Kosher Franks, *361*
Kosis, Tom, 232, 235
Koskey, Monica, 419
Koski, Conrad, 400, 401
Kossoroukova, Svetlana, 228
Kotlowitz, Dan, 349, 407, 424, 433
Kouo, Thomas, 359, 362
Kourilsky, Francoise, 352
Kourkoulos, Nikos, 279
Koutsavlaki, Eleftheria, 280
Kovacs, Nicole, 355
Kowalchuk, Tannis, 342
Kraft, Barry, 402
Kraft, Kevin, 420
Kraine Theater, 358
Krajecki, David, 458
Kral, Ivan, 275
Krane, David, 236
Krapp's Last Tape, *339*
Krasinski, Jennifer, 356
Krass, Michael, 232, 237, 248, 270, 275, 281, 290, 353, 430
Kraus, Chris, 344
Kravat, Jerry, 294
Krawcek, Amy, 234
Krebs, Eric, 242, 259, 273, 451
Kreisler/Marischka, 252
Kreitzer, Carson, 344
Krell, Jeff, 272
Kretzmer, Herbert, 221
Kreuder, Peter, 256
Kreutz, Erica, 335
Krich, Gretchen, 356, 362
Kriefall, Hans, 310
Krieger, Barbara Zinn, 279, 353
Krieger, Henry, 235
Krinetz, Doron, 430
Kristien, Dale, 316
Kristofferson, Brett, 273, 274, 305
Kritas Productions Inc., 279
Kriz, Zdenek, 290
Kroeze, Jan, 350
Krogstad, Bob, 235
Kroll, Jack, 447
Kron, Lisa, 42, 277, 282, 285, 457
Krones, Fred H., 230
Kronson, Jeff, 275
Krumholz, Brad, 342, 343
Krummenacher, Victor, 275
Krusoe, Nancy, 363
Krutsenko, Olena, 228
Ku, Ed, 253, 296
Ku, Shawn, 235
Kubinski, Cassandra, 411

Kubovy, Itamar, 350
Kubrick, Stanley, 11
Kuchar, Dan, 338
Kuchwara, Michael, viii, 447, 453
Kudisch, Marc, 309, 420
Kuhn, Gregory, 432
Kuhn, Judy, 315, 338, 353
Kuhn, Melinda, 348
Kukoff, Bernie, 281
Kulhawik, Joyce, 457
Kulick, Brian, 267, 282, 284, 428
Kumar, Anil, 431
Kundera, Milan, 409
Kuney, Scott, 257
Kuni-Leml, *340*
Kunska, Agnieszka, 412
Kuntz, John, 360
Kuo, Conway, 229
Kuramoto, Dan, 433
Kuroda, Emily, 415
Kuroda, Kati, 348
Kurtz, Swoosie, 38, 47, 288, 456
Kuruvilla, Sunil, 345
Kuschner, Jason, 356
Kushner, Tony, 270, 327, 340, 404, 415, 420
Kushnier, Jeremy, 27, 230, 314
Kusner, Jon, 253, 296
Kussack, Elaine, 281
Kuttner, Eric, 351
Kwaidan, *357*
Kwak, Yu Lim, 225
Kwon, Hyuk Soon, 225
Kynl, Ivan, viii
Kyrieleison, Jack, 334

L, Nicola, 342
L'Alliance & Co., 409
La Cage aux Folles, 225
La Fura dels Baus, 332, 344
La Jolla Playhouse, 368, 415
La Jument du Roi, 404
La Mama (a.k.a. LaMama) Experimental Theater Club (ETC), 341, 357
La Mirada Theater for the Performing Arts, 239, 451
La Ronde, 11, 243
La Terrasse, 285
La Vecchia, Antoinette, 359
LaBarre, Dede, 245, 246
Labin, Ann, 241
Labinger, Barbara, 345
Labor Day, 264, *419*
Lacey, Florence, 33, 224, 225
LaChanze, 318

LaChiusa, Michael John, 340
Lachow, Stan, 356
Lackey, Herndon, 243
Lacroix, Richard, 348
Ladd, Alex, 362
Ladden, Cassidy, 251
Ladendorf, Ingrid, 420
Ladman, Jeff, 232, 430, 431
Laev, Jim, 401
Lage, Jordan, 330, 336, 337
Laidlaw, Elizabeth, 406
Laing, Eric, 275
Laird, Marvin, 235, 251
Lake Hollywood, 329, *350*
Laliberte, Andre, 348
Laliberte, Richard, 348
Lam, Scarlett, 348
LaManna, Janine, 312, 318
Lamarck, 368
Lamb, Mary Ann, 245, 246
Lambert, Greta, 422
Lambert, Mikel Sarah, 358
Lambert, Walker, 406
Lamberts, Heath, 309
Lambs Theater Company, 270
Lamm, Teri, 255
Lamont, Robert, 334
LaMontagne, Susan, 245, 246
Lamos, Mark, 32, 258, 259, 271
Lamper, Maria, 458
Lampert, Emma, 421
Lampley, Oni Faida, 41, 284
Lams, Jeff, 257, 414
Lamson, Louise, 412
Lance, Herb J., 260, 304
Land, Ken, 232
Landau, Tina, 330, 353, 406, 455
Lander, David J., 348
Landes, Michael, 425
Landey, Nina, 249
Landis, Lynn, 280
Landlocked, *408*
Landscape and Dream, *363*
Landsman, Aaron, 350
Landy, Christopher J., 289, 337
Lane, David, 335
Lane, Donya, 266
Lane, Nathan, 42, 300, 301
Lane, Scott A., 420
Lane, William, 428
Lang, Maire, 228
Lang, Phillip J., 235
Lang, Robert E., 260
Lang, William H., 290
Langan, William, 358
Langel, Jodie, 311
Langer, Audrey Redman, 430
Langley, Jeff, 432

Langman, Donna, 276
Langner, Christine, 311
Langston, Jeanne, 342
Language, Body, 347
Language Instruction: Love Family vs. Andy Kaufman, *356*
Langwell, Kathryn, 282
Langworthy, Douglas, 402
Langworthy, Norma, 232, 260, 450
Lanier, Allen, 275
Lanier, Jane, 245, 246
Lanning, Michael, 256, 414
Lansbury, David, 430
Lanyon, Mark, 298
Lanzener, Sonja, 422
LaPaglia, Anthony, 321
Lapine, James, 269, 359
Lapira, Liza, 278
LaPlatney, Martin, 358
LaPolla, Michael, 356
Lapotaire, Jane, 457
LaPrise, Roland, 229
Lardner, Ring, 361
Largess, Bill, 286
Lark Theater Company, 358
LaRosa, Jason, 351
Larry and the Werewolf, *354*
Larsen, Liz, 265, 269
Larson, Darrell, 350
Larson, Jonathan, 222
Larson, Linda Marie, 407
LaRusso, Louis II, 334, 354
Las Horas De Belen – A Book of Hours, *344*
LaSala, Jeanne, 334
LaSalle, Denise, 260, 304
Lasiter, John, 344
Laskowsk, Jacek, 356
Laspina, Steve, 297
Last Communist Trio, The, 436
Last Empress, The, 4, *225*
Last Night of Ballyhoo, The, 25, 222, 453
Last Train to Nibroc, *344*, *360*, *361*
Laszlo, Carl, 356
Late Night at P.S. 122, *357*
Late Nite Catechism, 264
Latessa, Dick, 281, 310
Latham, David, 358
Lathan, John, 232
Latshaw, Michael, 361
Latta, Richard, 272, 340
Latus, James, 268
Laube, Miriam A., 284, 403
Laufer, Jack, 289
Lauinger, Joe, 361

Lauren, Ellen, 277, 419
Laurence, Lynn, 359
Laurent, Wendell, 357
Laurentis, Semina De, 456
Laurents, Arthur, 424
Lauria, Dan, 436
Laurie, Andria, 361
Laurie Beechman Theater, 358
Laurin, Christian, 359
Lavagnino, Tom, 335
LaVecchia, Antoinette, 363
Lavey, Martha, 406
LaVolpe, Michael, 322
Law, Richard, 252
Lawing, Lee Richard, 334
Lawler, John, 350, 357
Lawless, Carey, 235
Lawlor, Larry, 343
Lawlor, Lee, viii
Lawrence, Blake, 335
Lawrence, Eddie, 354
Lawrence, Elena, 409
Lawrence, Hap, 425
Lawrence, Megan, 315, 401
Lawrence, Robert, 286, 301
Lawrence, Sharon, 285
Lawrence, Tasha, 415
Laws, Debra, 259, 304
Laws, Eloise, 259, 304
Laws, Holly, 343
Lawson, Tony, 309
Lawyers, *436*
Lazar, Paul, 338, 350
Le Beauf, Sabrina, 406
Le Cid, 36, *290*, *292*, 331, 456
Le Menage, *342*
le Sourd, Jacques, 447
León, Alia, 319
Leachman, Cloris, 323
Leaf, Richard, 414
League of American Theaters and Producers, 3, 450
League of Off-Broadway Theaters and Producers, 453
League of Resident Theaters (LORT), 400
Leal, Sharon, 319
Leaming, Greg, 349, 424
Leamy, Deborah, 245, 246
Lean, Ernest, 334
Leavel, Beth, 257, 414
Leaving Queens, *345*
Leavitt, Michael, 248, 451
Lebhar, Dione H., 304
LeBlanc, Jeanne, 298
Lebow, Barbara, 422
LeBow, Will, 405
Lebowsky, Stanley R., 247
Lecesne, James, 355

LeCompte, Elizabeth, 363
Ledbetter, Huddie, 260, 304
Ledingham, David, 421
Lee, Adrian, 348
Lee, Cherylene, 348
Lee, Darren, 237, 238
Lee, Eugene, 228, 428
Lee, Fay Ann, 349
Lee, Franne, 436
Lee, Heather, 309
Lee, Hee Hwan, 225
Lee, Hee Jung, 225
Lee, Jack, 450
Lee, Jae Gu, 225
Lee, Jennifer, 256
Lee, Jennifer Paulson, 412
Lee, Jeremy, 417, 419
Lee, Ji Eun, 225
Lee, Ji Youn, 225
Lee, Keri, 251
Lee, Kyoung Woo, 225
Lee, Leslie, 342, 345
Lee, Liz, 422
Lee, Ming Cho, 417
Lee, Ralph, 339, 359
Lee, Sang Ryul, 225
Lee, Sherri Parker, 7, 249, 414
Lee, Soo Hyoung, 225
Lee, Su Mun, 225
Lee, Sung Ho, 225
Lee, Sung Hoon, 225
Lee, Tom, 358
Lee, Tuck, 239
Lee, Woo Jong, 225
Leeds, Jordan, 314, 321, 340
LeFever, Laurie, 361
LeFevre, Adam, 230, 314
Leffert, Joel, 249, 250, 414
Lefkowitch, Henry, 229
Lefkowitz, David, viii, 3
LeGrand, Stephen, 433
Leguizamo, John, 43, 223
Lehman, Jeanne, 320
Lehman, Jon, 457
Lehman, Pamela, 342
Lehrer, Scott, 298, 299
Leiber, Jerry, 221
Leibowitz, Lenny, 362
Leichenko, Donna, 349
Leigh, Carolyn, 30, 236, 239
Leigh, Jennifer Jason, 46, 310
Leight, Warren, 5, 7, 223, 327, 450, 455, 456
Leighton, John, 358
Leir Rex, *342*
Leishman, Gina, 285, 409
Leister, Johanna, 361
LeLoka, Tsidii, 315
Lemac, Linda, 235

Lemenager, Nancy, 300, 425
Lemper, Ute, 312, 456
Lenat, Jesse, 414
Lenney, Dinah, 431
LeNoire, Rosetta, 253, 296, 333
Lenox, Adriane, 258, 259
Lenox, Alison, 348
Lentini, Liza, 359
Lents, Stacie, 360
Lenz, Tom, 352
Leo, Melissa, 285
Leon, Kenny, 284, 402
Leonard, Dan, 404
Leonard, John A., 255, 292
Leonard, Katharine, 230
Leonard, Nicola, 228
Leonard, Robert Sean, 255, 270
Leone, Joseph, 335
Leone, Vivien, 303
Leong, David, 257, 290
Leong, Phillipe, 355
Leong, Terry, 348
Leonhart, Jay, 264
Lepard, John, 405, 406
Lerner, S., 256
Leroux, Gaston, 221
LeRoy, Gen, 425
Les Misérables, 221, 314
Les Romanesques, 264
Les Trois Dumas, *345*
Leslee, Ray, 338
Leslie, Bethel, 353
Leslie, Marcia L., 347
Lesson, The, *342*
LeStrange, Philip, 249
Let Me Live, 458
Let's Play Two, *354*
Lethlean, Philip, 347
Letter Perfect, *359*
Letts, Tracy, 39, 288
Leung, Ken, 285, 355
Leung, Travis, 354
Leupp, Clinton, 363
Levassar, Sam, 335
Leve, Harriet Newman, 274
Leveaux, David, 19, 242, 428
Levenson, Rachel Beth, 320
Leventhal, Nathan, 343
Leverett, T. Doyle, 232
Levering, Kate, 240, 266
Levi, Nannette, 235
Levin, Kimberly, 361
Levine, Daniel C., 298, 313
Levine, Ilana, 248
Levine, Neil, 335
Levine, Robert, 305
Levy, Daniel, 345, 455
Levy, David, 420
Levy, Frank, 235

Levy, Joe, 427
Levy, Julia C., 236, 288, 451
Levy, Kate, 347
Levy, Lorie Cowen, 282
Levy, Steven M., 260, 273, 305, 450
Lewis, Carter W., 430
Lewis, Clea, 305
Lewis, Ellen M., 434
Lewis, Irene, 268, 403
Lewis, Liz, 266
Lewis, Marcia, 312
Lewis, Norm, 286
Lewis, R.W.B., 455
Lewis, Richard, 235
Lewis, Robin, 241
Lewis, Shannon, 245, 246
Lexington Group, 338
Ley, Pablo, 344
Leynse, James, viii
Li, Anna, 338
Li, Lisa, 433
Lianhua, Pan, 348
Liberatore, Lou, 358
Lichte, Richard, 339
Lichtenstein, Harvey, 290, 331, 337
Lichtenstein, Michael, 340
Lichtscheidl, Jim, 422
Liddy Plays, The, 331
Lieb, Dick, 235
Life and Adventures of Nicholas Nickleby, The, 330
Life, The, 222
Lifetime of Reasons, A, 332
Lifshey, Karen, 258, 259
Ligon, Tom, 436
Like Mean, *270*
Lillard, Toya Ane, 344
Lillian, 36, *268*, 456
Lillis, Padraic, 348
Lillo, Marie, 281
Lilly, Judlyne, 403
Lilly, T. Scott, 352
Lin, Ben, 349
Lin, Isabel, 352
Lin, Jodi, 349
Lin, Xiao, 348
Lina, Tess, 416
Lincoln Center Festival, 98, 224, 332, 343
Lincoln Center Theater, 18, 24, 30, 223, 243, 259, 269, 294, 343, 451
Lincoln, Juliet, 427
Lincoln, Michael, 230, 351
Linder, Ben, 335
Linderman, Donna, 343
Lindsay, Howard, 223

Lindsay-Abaire, David, 436
Lindstrom and Motambi, 420
Linklater, Hamish, 271, 353, 404
Linklater, Kristin, 351
Linney, Romulus, 331, 339, 351, 454
Linton, J.P., 249
Lioi, Margaret M., 267, 282, 340
Lion in Winter, The, 3, 4, 17, 18, *236*, *237*, 451
Lion King, The, 3, 24, 46, 222, 447, 453
Lionel, Stanley, 229
Lipitz, Ben, 412
Lippa, Andrew, 29, 248, 249
Lippard, Alex, 360
Lips, *349*
Lips Together, Teeth Apart, 454, 458
Lipton, Michael, 361
Lirio, Victor, 358
Lisanby, Charles, 235
Liscow, Wendy, 345
Lisher, Greg, 275
Little by Little, 36, 44, *265*
Little, Jennifer, 354
Little, Judy, 234
Little, Kyra, 402
Little Me, 3, 4, 30, 33, *236*, 246, 451, 452, 456
Little Prince, The, 246
Little, Stuart, 450
Little, Tara, 228
Little Theater of the Green Goose, The, *356*
Litvin, Mark, 237, 267, 282, 340
Litwin, Alicia, 273
Lively, DeLee, 320
Lively, Sarah, 363
Livent (U.S.) Inc., 24, 243, 245, 451
Lives of the Saints, *426*
Lives of the Saints, or Polish Joke, *426*
Living Nativity, The, 234
Livingston, Laura, 356
Livolsi-Stern, Katherine, 299
Liza With a Z, 246, 247
Lizcano, Rodney, 410
Lizhi, Zhao, 348
Lizzie Borden, *434*
Lizzie Borden's Tempest, *360*
Llana, Jose, 319
Lloyd, Christopher, 337
Lloyd, John Bedford, 349
Lobel, Adrianne, 238
Lobenhofer, Lee, 431

Lockett, Angela, 243, 244
Lockett, Jimmy, 311
Lockwood, Lois, 411
Lockwood, Sharon, 404
Lockyer, Peter, 315
Loco 7, 357
Lodato, Victor, 347
Loeb, Sally, 338
Loeffenholz, J., 313
Loesser, Emily, 356
Loesser, Frank, 256
Loewald, Kate, 345
Loewe, Frederick, 246
Loffredo, Charles, 359
Lofsnes, Martin, 229
Logan, Blainie, 355
Logan, Stacey, 309
Loggins, Kenny, 231, 451
L'Oiseau de Feu, 357
Lola, 436
Lolly, *335*
Lombard, Dirk, 260
Lomeka, Michael, 240
London, Becky, 256, 351
London, Daniel, 288
London, Frank, 357
London, Todd, 344
Lone Runner, The, *343*
Lonergan, Kenneth, 37, 289
Lonesome West, The, 4, 9, 12,
   13, *260*, 448, 450, 451, 452
**Long Day's Journey Into
   Night**, 14
Long, Jodi, 287
Long Wharf Theater, 279, 282,
   285, 424
Long, William Ivey, 241, 251,
   257, 280
Longbottom, Robert, 232, 235
Longendyke, Paula, 341
Lonzo, Tara, 249
Look What a Wonder, 428
Looking for Love, 427
Loomer, Lisa, 367, 435
Loomis, Mike, 273
Loose Ends, 454
Loot, *358*
Lopez, Alexandra, 339
Lopez, Carlos, 251
Lopez, Ignacio, 339
Lopez, Melinda, 457
Lopez, Priscilla, 298
Loquasto, Santo, 33, 246, 452
Lorca, Federico Garcia, 339,
   340
Lorca Festival, The, *340*
Lorca, Marcela K., 422
Lord, Charmaine, 342, 363

Lord, Sarah "Squid", 409
Lordan, John, 415
Lorentsen, Susan, 235
Loreque, Kevin, 311
Lortel Award Winners, 454
Lortel, Lucille, 273, 457
Lory, Alison, 232
Los Angeles Ovations, viii,
   458
Losing Weight, *411*
Loss of D-Natural, *359*
Lost Creek Township, *422*
Lost in Yonkers, 14, 456, 457
Lotito, Mark, 293, 425
Lotun, Martina, 351
Lotz, David, 225
Loudon, Dorothy, 401
Louiguy, 256
Louiselle, Bryan, 235
Louveau, Muriel, 337
Love, Brian, 318
Love Creek Productions, 358
Love, Edith H., 409
Love in the Age of Dion, *334*
Love, Mark, 361
**Love Song of Eleanor Purdy,
   The**, *362*
Love's Fire, 36, *270*
Lovejoy, Deirdre, 232
**Lovely Sunday for Creve
   Coeur, A**, *355*
Lovers and Executioners, 457
Lovett, Conor, 358
Lovett, Marjorie, 417
Lowe, Eva, 359
Lowe, Michele, 407
Lowenstein, David, 237
Lowery, David, 275
Lubetzky, Yael, 428
Lubin, Shellen, 361
Lucas, Craig, 11, 37, 279
Lucas, Josh, 285
Lucci, Derek, 360
Luce, William, 22
Luciano, Jason, 335
Lucille Lortel Awards, 453, 454
Lucille Lortel Debut Award,
   456
Luckinbill, Laurence, 310, 338
Lucy, Scott, 363
Ludlam, Charles, 47, 280
Ludwig, Avram, 360
Ludwig, Salem, 360
Luedtke, Wendy, 400
Luftig, Hal, 250, 303, 451
Luigs, Jim, 353
Luis, Marta Jiménez, 229
Luker, Rebecca, 320

Luker, Steve, 314
Lumbard, Dirk, 260, 458
Lunch Break, *335*
Lund, Julie, 281
Lundberg, Judith, 407
Lundeberg, Karl Fredrik, 417
Lundquist, Lori, 246
Lunetta, Larry, 237, 251
Luni, Yang, 348
Lunney, Robert Emmett, 279
Lunsford, Kate, 342
LuPone, Robert, 282, 344
Lurie, James, 342
Lurleen, *422*
Lustig, Joseph, 360
Lutken, David, 257, 359, 415
Luton, Jon, 344
Lyles, Leslie, 332
Lynch, Finbar, 7, 249, 414, 451
Lynch, Mark, 415
Lynch, Michelle, 235
Lynch, Thomas, 281, 288, 295,
   424, 428, 432, 435, 456
Lynching of Leo Frank, The,
   458
Lynd, David, 289
Lyon, Kimberly, 236
Lyons, Donald, 13, 448
Lyons, Thomas, 349, 417
Lysistrata, *361*
Lyz!, *361*

M, Lebo, 222
Ma, Jason, 359
Ma-Yi Theater Ensemble, 358
Maaske, Dee, 402
Mabe, Matthew, 255, 285, 349
Mabey, Rachel, 351
Mabou Mines, 344
Macbeth, *362*
MacCalla, Sylvia, 319
MacDevitt, Brian, 253, 284,
   286, 287, 407, 430
MacDonald, Bruce, 454
MacDonald, Don, 293
MacDonald, Karen, 405
MacDonald, Moira, 363
Macdonald, Robert David, 290
Macdonald, Sharman, 358
MacDonald, Tim, 292
MacDonnell, Christine, 248
MacDonnell, Theresa, 237
MacDougall, Delia, 404
MacDougall, Lee, 349
Macer-Story, E., 351
Maceyak, Dan, 237
Machado, Eduardo, 351, 352,
   355

Machaira, Frezi, 280
Machota, Joe, 314
Mack & Mabel, 225
Mack, Charles, 229
Mackay, Lizbeth, 349
Mackenzie, Doan, 248, 271
MacKenzie, J.C., 408
Mackey, Steve, 404
Mackie, Bob, 416
Mackintosh, Cameron, 23, 229,
    412
MacLeod, Charles R., 410
Macleod, Fiona, 422
Macleod, Mary, 245, 246, 292
MacNeil, Ian, 245
MacNichol, Katie, 337
MacPherson, Greg, 289, 337,
    338, 352
Macs (A Macaroni Requiem),
    363
MacSiacais, Jake, 354
Mad, *335*
Madden, Gloria, 355
Maddow, Ellen, 343, 344, 347
Maddow-Zimet, Isaac, 343
Maddox, David, 401, 457
Madera, Jason, 361
Madigan, Deirdre, 407
Madigan, Reese, 358
Madley, Billie, 352
Maeda, Jun, 342, 343
Magania, Alessandro, 360
Magee, Rusty, 355
Maggio, Frances, 407
Magic Theater, 432
Magicworks Entertainment,
    224, 259
Magid, Paul, 354
Magino, Troy, 235
Magno, Deedee Lynn, 316
Magnus, Jenny, 361
Maguire, Kate, 433
Maguire, Michael, 315
Maher, Matthew, 456
Mahl, Lori, 347
Mahon, Melissa Rae, 234
Mahowald, Joseph, 314
Maida, Muriel, 351
Maiden Lane, *338*, *339*
Maier, Jeanne, 235
Maifeld, Kevin, 422
Maika, Michele, 315
Maisel, David, 245
Maisel, Jennifer, 420
Major, Fred, 417
Majority of One, A, 331, *340*
Makin, Lisa, 255
Making Peter Pope, *363*
Making Tracks, *362*

Makkena, Wendy, 5, 223
Mako, Christopher, 354
Malcolm, Graeme, 353, 417
Maldonado, J., 313
Maleczech, Ruth, 344
Maleitzke, Peter, 431
Maleson, Leon, 236, 261
Malicote, Melanie, 235
Malik, Art, 431
Malkin, Seth, 252
Malle, William, 409
Mallet, Eric, 343
Malone, Michael, 425
Maloney, Aedin, 340
Maloney, Jacqueline, 410
Maloney, Peter, 339
Malouf, Jacqui, 282
Maltby, Jacquey, 323
Maltby, Richard, Jr., 24, 33,
    221, 245, 246, 358, 452, 455
Mamaloshen, 4, 20, 21, *229*
Mame, 224
Mamet, David, 9
**Man in the Brooks Brothers
    Shirt, The**, *361*
Man Who Was Death, The,
    358
Mancina, Mark, 222
Mancini, Linda, 361
Mandelbaum, Ken, 448, 453
Mandell, Alan, 288
Mandell, Michael, 269, 359
Mandvi, Aasif, 43, 272, 334,
    457
Maner, Tim, 356
Manglaras, Stephanie, 458
Manhattan Casanova, *436*
Manhattan Playhouse, 359
Manhattan Special, *335*
Manhattan Theater Club
    (MTC), 35, 36, 44, 255, 264,
    274, 285, 347
Manhunt, *358*
Maniactin Productions Inc., 304
Manifest, *427*
Manifesto, 420
Manley, Frank, 417
Mann, Emily, 428
Mann, Terrence, 307, 311, 315,
    319
Mann, Theodore, 455
Manning, Beth, 420
Manning, Jerry, 345
Manning, Joanne, 235
Manning, Peter, 223, 450
Manor, The, 351
Mansfield, Elizabeth, 400
Mansfield, Peter, 425
Mansur, Susan, 266

Mantello, Joe, 268, 286, 288,
    430
Mantle, Burns, vii
Mantle, Doreen, 292
Mantzke, Christia Leigh, 322,
    402
**Many a Good Hanging
    Prevents a Bad Marriage**,
    359
Manzi, Warren, 264
Mapa, Alec, 415
Maradudin, Peter, 404
Marano, Vincent, 361
Marans, Jon, 355, 432
Marat/Sade, *457*
Marathon '99, 339
Marber, Patrick, 9, 11, 12, 254,
    255, 447, 450
Marcante, Mark, 351, 352
Marcel, J. Russell, 359
March, Stephanie, 249
March Tale, *405*
Marchetti, Will, 433
Marchica, Ray, 297
Marchionda, Cindy, 261, 322,
    458
Marco, Natasha, 358
Marco Polo Sings a Solo, 329,
    350
Marcum, Brian J., 258
Marcus, Daniel, 240, 319
Marcus, Joan, viii
Marcus, Leslie, 268, 280
Marcus, Lisa, 277
Marcus, Steven, 359
Marder, Samuel, 235
Margolin, Deb, 340
Margolis, Robert, 360
Margoshes, Steve, 402
Margotta, Michael, 361
Margraff, Ruth, 344, 345, 356
Margulies, Donald, 41, 273, 367
Margulies, Ellen, 294
Marie, Jean, 234
Marineu, Barbara, 309
Marinoff, Judith, 255
Marinos, Peter, 225
Marioge, Philippe, 292
Marion, Martin, 410
Marion, Tom, 359
Marisol, *457*
Mark Taper Forum, 282, 330,
    416, 431, 459
Mark, Zane, 222
Markell, Denis, 264
Markell, Jodie, 303, 327, 359
Markert, Russell, 235
Markey, Shauna, 260, 261
Markham, Kika, 249

Markinson, Martin, 8, 232
Markle, Lois, 363, 431
Markoe, Gerald Jay, 334
Markowitz, Andrew, 358
Marks, I.W., 257
Marks, Jack R., 355
Marks, Ken, 278, 431
Marks, Peter, 447
Marlene, 3, 4, 22, 23, *256*, 451
Marley, Donovan, 409, 410
Marlin-Jones, Davey, 405
Marnich, Melanie, 340, 411, 416
Marques, David, 259
Marr, John, 275
Marren, Howard, 430
Marriage Play, The, 431
Marsh, Frazier W., 419
Marsh, Henry, 458
Marsh, Jonah, 270
Marshall, Donna Lee, 230, 231
Marshall, Kathleen, 245, 275, 298, 338
Marshall, Rob, 236, 452
Marta, Darcy, 360
Martin, Cary Patrick, 334
Martin, Eileen, 228
Martin, Greta, 300
Martin, Ivan, 361
Martin, Jane, 420, 454
Martin, Jesse L., 318
Martin, Julia, 343
Martin, Kamilah, 319
Martin, Kevin Mitchell, 351
Martin, Lourdes, 350
Martin, Lucy, 256, 358
Martin, Manuel, 350
Martin, Matt, 228
Martin, Michael X., 286, 300
Martin, Nicholas, 38, 270, 281, 350, 437, 456
Martin, Peter, 294, 295
Martin R. Kaufman Theater, 358
Martin, Steven, 424
Martinez, Antonio Gil, 343
Martinez, J. Preston, 270
Martinez, Rogelio, 339, 341, 345, 355
Marting, Kristin, 356
Martini, Richard, 259
Martling, Wendy, 359
Maruhashi, Setsuko, 234
Maruyama, Merv, 359
Marvel, Elizabeth, 362, 428
Marvel, Jonathan, 342
Marvin, Mel, 32, 258, 259, 404, 428
Marx, Bill, 457

Marx, Peter, 251
Mary and Myra, *345*
Mary-Arrchie Theater Company, 458
Marzullo, Frank, 351
Masamune, Tohoru, 437
Masenheimer, David, 318
Mashita, Nelson, 433
Masina, Giulietta, 19
Mason, Buck, 239
Mason, David, 437
Mason, Karla, 360
Mason, Luba, 314
Mason, Marsha, 430
Mason, Mindy, 234
Mason, Robert, 360
Mass, A.J., 356
Massey, Kenya Unique, 258, 402
Massie, Christina, 294
Mastascusa, Richie, 235
Master Builder, The, *405*
Masteroff, Joe, 222, 430
Mastro, Michael, 223
Mastrogiorgio, Danny, 358
Mastrosimone, William, 361
Mather, Ted, 434
Mathers, Craig, 358
Mathews, Tony, 259, 304
Mathias, Sean, 256
Mathis, Carmen, 351
Mathis, Stanley Wayne, 248, 315
Matricardi, Lisa, 232, 299
Matrone, Marissa, 223
Matson, R.J., 273
Matsumoto, Masahiro, 358
Matsuoka, Lisa, 234
Matsusaka, Tom, 348, 349
Matsuyama, Saeka, 21, 229
Mattei, Peter, 345
Mattern, Jennifer, 427
Matthew, Ed, 244
Matthews, Dakin, 280
Matthews, Justus, 408
Matz, Peter, 425
Mau, Les J.N., 349
Mauer, Gary, 315, 316
Maurer, Ingrid, 436
Maurer, Kelly, 277, 419
Mauro, Dana Lynn, 324
Mauro, Joseph, 273
Maust, Conrad, 427
Maxwell, Mitchell, 230
Maxwell, Richard, 349, 350, 456
Maxwell, Roberta, 358
Maxwell, Victoria, 230
May, Andrew, 421

May, Deven, 458
May, Elaine, 264, 317
Mayberry, Mariann, 406
Mayer, Michael, 18, 29, 223, 237, 248, 275, 353, 452
Mayo, Don, 402
Mayotte, Cliff, 404
Mayrhauser, Jennifer von, 428
Mazzie, Marin, 318
Mays, Jefferson, 277
McAdams, John, 361
McAllister, Elan, 255, 451
McArdle, Andrea, 309
McArthur, Sean, 360
McBoyle, Peter, 293
McBurney, Simon, 343
MCC Theater, 282, 327, 344
McCall, Nancy, 294, 295
McCallum, David, 274
McCamus, Tom, 292
McCann, Christopher, 288, 405
McCann, Mary, 336
McCarter Theater, 19, 242, 243, 270, 279, 286, 368, 428, 451
McCarthy, Dennis, 408
McCarthy, Elaine J., 433
McCarthy, Jeff, 307, 353
McCarthy, Mary, 361
McCarthy, Terry, 340
McCartney, Jesse, 240, 241
McCarty, Conan, 422
McCatty, Mary, 234
McCaul, Sorcha, 228
McCauley, Ann, 410
McCauley, Jim, 354
McCauley, Judith, 260
McClain, Saundra, 284
McClanahan, Rue, 430
McClarin, Curtis, 310
McClelland, Kay, 230
McClelland, Michael, 335
McClintock, Jodie Lynne, 351, 421
McClinton, Marion, 340
McCluggage, John, 432
McCoin, Mark, 337
McColgan, John, 228, 229
McColl, Ian, 413
McCollum, Kevin, 269, 430
McConachie, Patrice, 234
McConahay, Liz, 321
McConnell, Johnnie, 358
McCoo, Marilyn, 322
McCook, John, 416
McCormack, Andrea, 313
McCormack, Mary, 310
McCormick, Bradley, 275
McCormick, Carolyn, 337, 417
McCormick, Michael, 298, 319

McCourt, Frank, 295, 339
McCourt, Malachy, 295
McCourt, Sean, 359
McCoy Rigby Entertainment, 239, 451
McCrane, Deirdre, 255
McCulloh, Barbara, 239, 323
McCullough, Mark, 290
McCully, Emily Arnold, 411
McCurdy, Patricia, 334
McCutchen, Heather, 345
McDaniel, John, 251
McDermott, Colleen, 404
McDermott, Jim, 458
McDermott, Kate, 421
McDevitt, Brian, 280
McDiarmid, Ian, 290
McDonagh, Martin, 9, 12, 13, 223, 260, 450
McDonald, Audra, 318, 340
McDonald, Julie, 234
McDonald, Kirk, 243, 318
McDonald, Tanny, 282
McDonough, Marty, 235
McDormand, Frances, 337
McEachran, Michael, 236
McElroy, Andrew, 400, 401
McElroy, Michael, 318
McEowen, Michael, 239
McEwan, Adrienne, 316
McFadden, Corinne, 235
McFadden, Mary, 337
McGarty, Michael, 425
McGaugh, Jamey, 435
McGee, Kenneth J., 238
McGee, Noel, 354
McGeen, Donn, 261
McGillin, Howard, 299, 300, 338
McGillis, Joan, 415
McGinn, Andrew, 268, 306
McGinn/Cazale Theater, 359
McGinnis, Megan, 244
McGinty, Joe, 278
McGovern, Christopher, 434
McGowan, Julian, 292
McGowan, Tom, 312
McGrail, Brian, 355
McGrane, Paul, 339
McGrath, Bob, 405
McGrath, Mark, 232
McGrath, Matt, 298, 437
McGrath, Michael, 45, 236, 266
McGraw, Steve, 294, 295
McGuigan, A. Ryan, 358
McGuigan, Marcy, 351
McGuinness, Frank, 19, 242, 428
McGuire, Mitchell, 347

McGuire, Rose, 435
McGuire, William Biff, 432
McGurk, Michael, 410
McHugh, Bill, 335
McHugh, Jim, 361
McHugh, Joanne, 236
McIlvaine, Julia, 285
McInerney, Bernie, 284
McInerney, Jay, 277
McIntosh, Cameron, 416
McIntyre, Ronald L., 360
McKayle, Donald, 259, 304
McKechnie, Donna, 298
McKechnie, Garrett, 306
McKeever, Michael, 404, 415
McKenzie, Bruce, 417, 419
McKenzie, James B., 436
McKenzie, Julia, 416
McKeon, Johanna, 348
McKidd, Kevin, 291
McKinley, Philip William, 363, 420
McKinney, Sharon, 412
McKneely, Joey, 224, 436
McLane, Derek, 280, 286, 287, 294, 425
McLane, Judy, 420, 421
McLaughlin, Buzz, 420
McLaughlin, Ellen, 282, 457
Mclean, Anthony, 293
McLean, Devin, 334
McLeod, Dana, 335
McLeod, Donna-Claire, 293
McLeod, Kevin, 419
McMahon, Bridie, 354
McMahon, Caroline, 261
McMahon, Katie, 228
McMahon, Ryan E., 272, 289, 334
McMillan, Colleen, 427
McMorrow, Jonathan, 228
McMorrow, Thomas, Jr., 305
McMullen, Kenneth, 240
McNally, Terrence, 34, 35, 222, 285, 430
McNamara, Dyanne, 270
McNeely, Anna, 311
McNeil, Lonnie, 362
McNelis, Paula, 228
McNicholas, Jim, 273
McNicholas, Steve, 264
McNicholl, BT, 257, 436
McNitt, Dennis, 348
McNulty, William, 417
McPherson, Conor, 13, 255, 329, 349, 359
McQueen, Ellen, 419
McRobbie, Peter, 252, 286
McSweeney, Mary Ann, 248

McSweeny, Ethan, 404, 415
McVay, Marcelle, 407
McVety, Drew, 285, 286, 349
McVey, J. Mark, 323
Me and My Girl, 458
Meade, Craig, 351, 352
Meade, William, 224
Meadow, Lynne, 285, 286
Meadows, Carol Lee, 300
Meadows, Hannah, 235
Meadows, Jordan, 348
Meaney, Colm, 330, 337
Means, Charles, 277
Meanwhile on the Other Side of Mount Vesuvius, *354*
Meany, Kevin, 225
Meazza, Michela, 229
Mecchi, Irene, 222
Mechanics, The, 409
Meckler, Nancy, 290, 291
Medak, Susan, 404
Medcalf, Charlotte, 343
Medders, Katy, 358
Medea, 36, *279*, *280*, 416
Medeiros, Michael, 355
Medina, Aixa M. Rosario, 299
Medina, Wilfredo, 436
Medley, Cassandra, 338, 339
Medori, Michael, 334
Mee, Charles L., 406
Mee, Erin B., 344
Meeh, Gregory, 224, 260
Meehan, Thomas, 450
Meeks, Edith, 342
Megan Wanlass, 277
Megel, Joseph, 420
Mehler, Jack, 353, 421
Mehta, Ajay, 287
Mehta, Rishi, 287
Meinen, Thomas Owen, 409
Meisels, Annie, 358
Meisle, Kathryn, 277
Meisle, William, 353
Meister, Brian, 255
Melhem, D.H., 351
Melia, Careena, 430
Mello, Lori, 234
Mellom, Andie, 402
Mellon, James J., 411
Mellor, Stephen, 340
Meloni, Christopher, 437
Melrose, Ron, 232
Melting Pot Theater, 359
Melton, Heather, 351
Memoir for the Stage, A, *286*
Memory of Water, The, 36, *285*, *286*
Memran, Steven, 411, 430
Mena, Christian, 318

Menard, Mark, 229, 261
Mendel, Tom, 239
Mendes, Sam, 243
Mendillo, Stephen, 337
Mendoza, Jesus, 408
Mendus, Clive, 343
Menefee, Pete, 235
Menken, Alan, 221, 240
Menkharis, *360*
Mennier, Louise-Marie, 353
Mennuto, Tony, 351
Menopausal Gentlemen, 456
Menuhin, Valentine, 343
Menzel, Idina, 319
Meola, Tony, 231, 241, 269, 412
Mercado, Hector Jaime, 310
Mercer, Douglas, 334
Mercer, Johnny, 246
Merchandising, 420
Merchant of Venice, The, *356*, 456, 457
Merchant, Scott, 410
Mercier, G.W., 353
Mercy, *353*
Meredith, Sam, 229
Merkerson, S. Epatha, 457
Merlin, Joanna, 450
Merlin, Russ, 360
Merman, Ethel, 27, 251
Merner, George, 324
Merrick, David, 33, 456
Merritt, Kevin, 342
Merz, Jesse, 360
Meshugah, *428*
Messinger, Matt, 223
Messmer, Michele, 412
Meston, Paul M., 348
Metamorphoses, 416
Metamurphosis Minor, *347*
Metheny, Russell, 426
Methot, Christien, 338
Metropulos, Penny, 306, 402
Mettawee River Theater
    Company, 359
Metz, Stefan, 343
Metzgar, Bonnie, 267, 282
**Mexican Standoff at Fat Squaw
    Springs**, 435
Meyer, Johanna S., 350
Meyer, Marlane, 353
Meyer, Matt, 419
Meyer, Richard, 435
Meyer, Stanley A., 402
Meyers, Christianne, 351
Meyers, Janine, 230, 231
Meyers, John, 232
Meyers, Marc, 361
Meyersfield, Eric, 313
Meyman, Dottie Belle, 234

Meza, Vanessa, 289
Mezick, Matthew, 424
Michaels, Donna Lee, 335
Michaels, Jay, 273
Michaels, Lorne, 228
Michaelson, Roger, 342
Michels, Stephanie, 235
Mickelson, Gary, 237
Mickey, Susan, 422
Midgette, Monique, 257
Midsummer Night's Dream, A,
    355
Mierzejewski, William, 355
Migliore, Mike, 239
Miguel, Mayumi, 235
Milam, Wilson, 289
Milazzo, Annmarie, 278
Milburn, Rob, 287, 406, 421
Mileaf, Maria, 419
Miles, Julia, 353
Milk and Honey, 224
Millado, Chris B., 358
Millard, Karen, 335
Miller & Lyles, 253, 254, 296
Miller, Andrew Elvis, 359
Miller, Arthur, ix, 14, 41, 222,
    249, 282, 329, 452
Miller, Betty, 350
Miller, Caitlin, 417, 419
Miller, Claci, 311
Miller, Daniel D., 232
Miller, Donally, 335
Miller, Gene, 257, 415
Miller, Henry G., 436
Miller, Jason, 42, 289, 329
Miller, John, 230, 231, 232, 236,
    244, 257, 261
Miller, Josh, 334
Miller, Kelly, 334
Miller, Kenita, 429
Miller, Matthew Floyd, 249
Miller, Mindy, 400
Milligan, Tuck, 284
Millikan, Robert, 298
Millman, Gabriel, 240, 241
Mills, Danny, 427
Mills, David, 357
Mills, Mike, 275
Milne, Dan, 348
Milne, Karen, 244
Milwaukee Repertory Theater,
    421
Mimosa, 359
Minefee, Daryl, 416
Mineola Twins, The, viii, 36,
    38, *288*, 453, 455, 456
Minez, Adrienne, 413
Mingione, Ernest, 363
Minnaar, Dawid, 276

Minnelli, Vincente, 235
Minnick, Michele, 344
Minor, Judy, 339
Minskoff, Patricia, 358
Mint Theater, 359
Minyana, Philippe, 343
Miramontez, Rick, 248, 249,
    303
Miranda, Bobby, 311
Miranda, Sol, 339, 350
Miranda Theater Company,
    359
Mirette, *411*
Mirette on the High Wire, 411
Mirkurbanov, Igor, 343
Mirror, The, *356*
Misanthrope, The, 331, *337*,
    456
Miser, The, 36, *293*, *360*
Mishima, Yukio, 356
Mishkin, Chase, 273, 297
Mislaid Heaven, A, 458
**Miss Coco Peru's Liquid
    Universe**, *363*
Miss Saigon, 221, 316
**Misshapen Jack, the Nebraska
    Hunchback**, *359*
Missing Footage, *425*
Mistretta, Sal, 457
Mitani, Noboru, 361
Mitchell, Aleta, 359
Mitchell, Brian Stokes, 42, 300,
    301, 318
Mitchell, Craig, 411
Mitchell, Jerry, 248, 286
Mitchell, John Cameron, 264,
    314
Mitchell, Langdon, 355
Mitchell, Mark, 229, 241, 298,
    301
Mitchell, Tracey, 358
Mitchell, Tricia, 311
Mittelman, Arnold, 224
Mixon, Chris, 422
Miyagawa, Chiori, 341
Miyori, Kim, 433
Mizell, Kelly, 405
Mizzone, Vanessa, 437
Mockus, Jeff, 432
Modern, B., 432
Modr, Heidi, 261
Mogentale, David, 249
Mohn, Leslie, 344
Mohr, Jim, 430
Moinot, Michel, 353
Moira, Lissa, 351
Moja, I Made, 276, 277
Mokuami, Kawatake, 329, 355
Molaskey, Jessica, 243, 244, 353

Molière, 292, 305, 332, 337, 360
Molina, Alfred, 307
Molina, Renee, 303
Molla, Chris, 275
Mollicone, Henry, 432
Molloy, *358*
Molloy, Irene, 257, 414
Molly Sweeney, 454
Molossi, Robert, 349
Mom's Life, A, 21, *229, 354*
Moment of Aha, The, 332, *355*
Moment of Truth, *356*
Monaco, John, 251
Monda, Carol, 286
Monday, Dick, 361
Mones, Steve, 353
Monette, Richard, 292, 293
Monge, Julio, 224, 284
Monk, Debra, 430
Monro, Jonathan W., 293
Monster and Wife, *358*
Monsters of Grace, 331, *337*
Montague, Seána, 291
Montano, Robert, 237
Montecchi, Fabrizio, 357
Montel, Ginger, 255
Montel, Michael, 344, 354, 360, 361
Monteleone, Christopher, 324
Montelongo, Matthew, 288
Montes, Esperanza, 303
Montgomery, Barbara, 347
Montgomery, Hannah Rae, 410
Montgomery, J.C., 243, 244
Montgomery, Reggie, 414, 422
Montgomery, Samantha, 421
Month in the Country, A, 458
Moodey, David, 338
Moon, Hyo Jung, 225
Mooney, Debra, 232, 430
Mooney, Declan, 340
Mooney, Kirstin, 232
Moonlight, 40
Moonshine, *358*
Moor, Bill, 337
Moore, Benjamin, 432, 433
Moore, Charlotte, 255, 331, 339, 340
Moore, Christi, 261
Moore, Christopher, 360
Moore, Dana, 245, 246
Moore, Des, 228
Moore, F., 260, 304
Moore, Fleecie, 254, 297
Moore, Jennifer Rae, 271, 306
Moore, Karen, 297, 305
Moore, Larry, 411
Moore, Lou, 417
Moore, Maggie, 436

Moore, Oscar E., 404
Moore, Randy, 410
Moore, Ruth, 421
Moore, Tim, 360
Moore, Valerie, 293
Moorer, Margo, 406
Mooy, Brad, 416
Mora, Clara, 303
Morace, Eric, 363
Morales, Mio, 424
Morales, Rolando, 352
Moran, Martin, 321, 337
Moran, Michael, 343, 363
More Than Murder, *351*
More to Love, 3, 4, 7, 9, *230*
Moresco, Bobby, 228
Morfee, Scott, 288
Morfogen, George, 268
Morgan, Cass, 309
Morgan, Charlie, 400
Morgan, Ian, 347
Morgan, James, 265, 266, 290, 354
Morgan, Maggie, 426
Morgan, Robert, 350
Morgan, Roger, 228
Moriarty, Joe, 228
Moriber, Brooke Sunny, 243, 244
Morick, Jeanine, 310
Morin, Richard, 348
Moritz, Joel, 407, 458
Morning, Noon and Night, *349*
Morogiello, John, 403
Morrill, Paul S., 340
Morris, Haviland, 245, 280
Morris, Hurvey, 272
Morris, Kenny, 273
Morris, Pavlina Emily, 409
Morrison, Bill, 405
Morrison, Chris, 429
Morrison, James, 430
Morrison, James, LL, 243, 259, 275
Morrison, John, 361
Morrison, John-Andrew, 416
Morrissey, Steven, 275
Morrisson, Danny, 354
Morrow, Karen, 323
Morse, Barry, 233
Morse, Robin, 349, 358
Morse, Tom, 239
Mortimer, Isabel, 229
Mortimer, Terry, 422
Mortimer, Vicki, 255
Morton, Amy, 406
Morton, Joe, 307
Mosakowski, Susan, 341
Mosby, Josh, 245

Moscone, Jonathan, 409, 427
Moscow Folk Ballet Company, 228
Moseley, Robin, 286
Mosello, Joe, 251
Moses, 358
Moses, Burke, 309
Moses, My Love, *358*
Mosher, Gregory, 281
Moss, Alvin, 230
Moss, Barry, 231, 241, 261, 281
Moss, Karen, 230
Most Fabulous Story Ever Told, The, 35, 36, 38, 47, *277*, 327, *436*
Mother Hubbard, *360*
Mother's Day, *345*
Mount, Anson, 268, 285
Mountain, Michelle, 405
Mountain, Vince, 406
Mountebanks, 359
Moving Theater, 249, 414, 450
Mowatt, Joseph, 248
Mowers, David, 345
Moyer, Allen, 270, 279, 285, 290, 338, 437
Moynihan, Bobby, Jr., 457
Mozer, Elizabeth, 425
Mpls., St. Paul, *419*
Mr. Abbott Award, 455
Mr. Rebbetzin, *335*
Mrs. Santa Claus, 225
Mrozek, Slawomir, 356
MTC (see Manhattan Theater Club)
Much Ado About Nothing, 36, *292, 293*, 457
Mueller, Catherine, 355
Mufson, Lauren, 269
Mugleston, Linda, 237, 238
Muir, Heather, 360
Muir, Kevin, 293
Muir, Sandra, 343
Mujeres Y Hombres, 36, *303*
Mukulski, Rob, 229
Mula, Tom, 406
Mulcahy, Jack, 425
Mulheren, Michael, 286, 300, 301
Mullaney, Patrick, 311
Mullen, Deena Lynn, 459
Mullen, Marie, 309
Mullen, Patricia, 293
Mulligan, Niall, 228
Mullins, Carol, 343
Munch, Courtney, 335
Munday, Hugo, 252
Munderloh, Otts, 229, 286
Munger, Kendra, 356

Mungioli, Arnold J., 246
Munkacsi, Kurt, 337
Munoz, Gonzalo, 350
Munro, Jonathan W., 293
Munroe, Charles A., 415
Muraoka, Alan, 359
Murashkovsky, Sophia, 342
Murder in America, *359*
Murder, Madness and Lady Macbeth, *344*
Murillo, Carlos, 338, 340
Murin, David, 424, 433
Murmurs of California, *334*
Murney, Christopher, 357
Murphey, Mark, 402
Murphy, Bob, 347
Murphy, Brenda, 354
Murphy, Brittany, 321
Murphy, Case, 342
Murphy, Gregory, 356
Murphy, Jack, 256, 414, 451
Murphy, Joseph, 255
Murphy, Jy, 356
Murphy, Robert, 290, 338, 353
Murphy, Rosemary, 417
Murphy, Stephen Kennedy, 360
Murphy, Timothy, 359
Murphy, Tom, 309, 347
Murphy, Vincent, 417
Murray, Brian, 18, 19, 224, 331, 353
Murray, Diedre, 330, 344
Murray, Mary Gordon, 314
Murray, Rupert, 228
Murray, Tom, 458
Murray-Smith, Joanna, 223
Murrell, John, 356
Murtaugh, James, 425
Musgrove, Brad, 245, 246
Music Makers Inc., 258
Music-Theater Group, 330, 344
Musical Theater Works, 359
Musser, Tharon, 260, 297
Muzikar, Joe, 360
Mwine, Ntare, 432
My Quarrel with Hersh Rasseyner, 420
My Sister Eileen, 246
Myars, Mark, 230
Myers, Christianne, 337, 344
Myers, Eileen, 339
Myers, Elissa, 232
Myers, Jonathan Tipton, 338
Myers, Larry, 351
Myers, Mary, 338, 349
Myers, Nancy, 255
Myers, Robert, 458
Myers, Scott, 243, 256

Myler, Randal, 243, 259, 303, 304, 411, 451
Myopia, *340*
Mystery of Irma Vep, The, 36, 47, *280*, 453, 458
Mystery School, The, *347*
Myth, *416*
Mytholojazz, *348*

Nadal, Harry, 350
Nadeschkin, 359
Nadylam, William, 292
Nagel, Gil, 340
Nakagawa, Jon, 279, 450
Nakagawa, Todd, 348
Nakahara, Ron, 344, 348
Nakasone, Aiko, 362
Nakazawa, Keiji, 361
Naked Angels, 303, 327, 359
Nanjing Race, The, 454
Nankivell, Hugh, 276
Napier, Edward, 344, 353
Napier, John, 459
Naplin, Christy, 409
Naro, Thomas V., 238, 267, 282
Nash, J. Richey, 334
Nash, N. Richard, 359
Nason, Brian, 424, 425, 433, 437
Nason, Susanna, 235
Nassauer, Rebecca, 342
Natel, Jean-Marc, 221
Nathan, Hayley, 234
Nathanson, Lawrence, 337
National Actors Theater, 17, 252
National Asian American Theater, 359
National Black Touring Circuit, 289
National Endowment for the Arts, 455
National Medals of the Arts, 455
National Music Theater Conference, 436
National Playwrights Conference, 436
National Theater, 331
National Theater of Greece, 279
Natwora, Holly, 268
Nauffts, Geoffrey, 37, 303, 327, 359
Naughton, Amanda, 431
Naughton, Greg, 337
Naughton, James, 36, 297, 313
Naughton, Kiera, 338

Nayea, Star, 430
Neal, Rome, 360
Near, Timothy, 432, 433
Nederlander Organization, The, 239, 451
Nedostop, Tatiana, 228
Needles, *360*
Nees, Hugh, 401
Neil, Jim, 293
Neill, Erin, 404
Neill, Ross, 323
Neilson, Anthony, 363
Nelis, Tom, 412
Nellis, Jeff, 305
Nelson & O'Reilly Productions, 234
Nelson, Bruce, 401
Nelson, Evelyn, 347
Nelson, Fred, 348
Nelson, Jeff, 246
Nelson, Kenneth, 313
Nelson, Kris, 422
Nelson, Mark, 288, 424
Nelson, Novella, 267, 414
Nelson, Rebecca, 342
Nelson, Richard, 280, 281, 412
Nelson, Willie, 455
Nersisyan, Karen, 436
Nesbit, Pat, 344
Nesbitt, Vivian, 360
Ness, Robert, 407
Netanyahu, Benjamin, 10
Netzband, Auguste, 362
Neuhaus, Robert, 406
Neumann, David, 338
Neumann, Frederick, 344, 356
Neustadt, Ted, 338
Neuwirth, Bebe, 312
Never Been Anywhere, *357*
Never on Friday, *340*
Never the Sinner, 457
Neville, David, 430
Nevin, Carriene, 253, 296
New 42nd Street Inc, The, 259, 303
New America Playwrights Festival, 432
New Brain, A, 29, 36, 44, *269*, 448, 456
New Culture for a Country, *338*
New Directions Theater, 359
New Dramatists, 344
New Federal Theater, 347
New Girl in Town, 246, 247
New Group, The, 285, 289, 290, 347
New Shanghai Circus, The, *348*

New Victory Theater, The, 30, 347, 357

New Work Now!, 340

New York Drama Critics Circle, viii, 11, 447

New York Drama Critics Circle Awards, 25, 446

New York Gilbert and Sullivan Players, 359

New York Idea, The, *355*

New York International Fringe Festival, 359

New York Performance Works, 360

New York Public Library for the Performing Arts Reading Room Readings, 360

New York Shakespeare Festival (see Joseph Papp Public Theater)

New York Shakespeare Festival Shakespeare Marathon, 284

New York Theater Workshop, 44, 277, 327, 329

Newborn, Phineas, 402

Newer, David, 348

Newhard, Mari, 356

Newkirk, Dee Ann, 342

Newman, David, 222

Newman, Jim, 401

Newman, Karyl, 250, 414

Newman, Phyllis, 331, 340

Newman, Ralph, viii

Newport, Elaina, 46, 273

Newsome, Joel, 340

Newsome, Paula, 338

Newton, John, 245

Newton, Walter, 409

Next of Kin, *335*

Next Theater Company, The, 412

Nhan, Ngo Thanh, 352

Nicetown, *362*

Nicholls, Malcolm, 417, 419

Nichols, Alexander V., 404

Nichols, Mark, 362

Nichols, Mike, 297

Nicholson, Paul E., 402

Nickerson, Jay, 361

Nicklaus, Jill, 258, 259

Nielsen, Kristine, 281, 424, 456

Niesen, Jim, 351

Niewood, Gerard J., 235

Night Dance, *359*

Night in November, A, 36, 43, *280*

Night Must Fall, 3, 4, 15, 17, *252, 253*

Night of the Tribades, The, *361*

Night Remembers, The, *335*

Night They Burned Washington, The, *362*

Night Vision, *345*

Nightengale, Eric, 361

Nijinsky Speaks, *356*

Nijinsky's Last Dance, 457

Nikolessi, Betty, 280

Niles, Mary Ann, 247

Nine Scenes About Love, *345*

1933, *411*

1933 Was a Bad Year, 411

Nintzel, Ken, 348

Nipkow, Leslie, 332, 355

Nishii, Brian, 343

Nixon, Cynthia, 338

No Exit, *358*

Noah's Archives, *360*

Nobbs, Keith, 237, 275, 338, 353

Noble/Lohner and Beda, 252

Nobody Lonesome for Me, *424*

Nocciolino, Albert, 239, 451

Noel, Craig, 430

Noel, Todd, 323

Nolan, Jim, 358

Nolan, Susannah, 361

Noll, Christiane, 265, 314

Noone, James, 17, 232, 253, 286, 350, 430

Nooney, Tony, 354

Norby, Kate, 359

Norman, Ginger, 235

Norman, Marsha, 270, 331, 454

Norris, Bruce, 350

North, Alan, 350

North American Cultural Lab, 342

North, Dennis E., 405

North Shore Music Theater, 457

Norton, Jim, 13, 255

Norton Prize for Sustained Excellence, 457

Norworth, Jack, 230

Nosaty, Cathy, 276

Nostrand, Michael, 239

Not About Nightingales, 4, 6, 164–191, *249*, *414*, 448, 450, 451, 452, 456

Not Your Ordinary Tappers, 305

Notary, Rhonda, 234

Notes: A Love Story@www.com, *360*

Nothin's Easy and Nobody's Happy, *359*

Nowak, Michael, 458

Nunes-Ueno, Paulo, 339

Nunn, Bill, 284

Nunn, Emily, 453

Nunn, Trevor, 6, 221, 249, 250, 254, 256, 414, 452, 456

Nunsense, 272

Nunsense A-Men!, 36, 46, *271*

Nunsense Theatrical Company, The, 271

Nuremberg, 404

Nurick, Benjamin, 237

Nussbaum, Susan, 407

Nutt, Katie, 232

Nuyorican Poets Café, 360

Nyberg, Pamela, 344, 350

Nye, April Ann, 270

NYOTs, 305

O'Boyle, Sally, 415

O'Brian, Brian, 228

O'Brien, Adale, 419

O'Brien, Aoibheann, 228

O'Brien, Cubby, 251

O'Brien, Dan, 368

O'Brien, Erin, 350

O'Brien, Jack, 230, 430

O'Brien, Liam Christopher, 337

O'Brien, Paul, 224

O'Brien, Richard, 351

O'Brien, Stephen, 359

O'Byrne, Brian F., 260, 309, 451

O'Cain, Denise, 228

O'Carroll, Leslie, 410

O'Casey, Sean, 340

O'Connell, Deirdre, 340

O'Connell, Wanda, 335

O'Connor, David, 435

O'Connor, Francis, 260

O'Connor, Gregory, 335

O'Connor, Ian, 261

O'Connor, Mariann M., 415

O'Connor, Patrick, 417

O'Connor, Patricia W., 350

O'Connor, Susan, 352

O'Doherty, Cahir, 345

O'Donnell, Marc, 427

O'Donnell, Mark, 285

O'Dowd, Paulette, 360

O'Flaherty, Michael, 334, 411, 412

O'Gorman, Michael, 228

O'Gorman, Robert, 355

O'Grady, Kathleen, 252

O'Hanlon, Barney, 277, 419

O'Hara, John, 361

O'Hara, Kelli, 457
O'Hara, Robert, 340
O'Hare, Denis, 310
O'Hare, Fergus, 242, 428
O'Keefe, Laurence, 455
O'Keefe, Michael, 290
O'Keefe, Steve, 359
O'Keeffe, Paul, 347
O'Leary, Christine Friday, 430
O'Malley, Brendan, 356
O'Malley, Glyn, 431
O'Malley, Kerry, 278
O'Malley, Regina, 420
O'Neill, Denis, 340
O'Neill, Eoghan, 228
O'Neill, Eugene, vii, ix, 13, 255, 360, 455
O'Neill Society Medal, 455
O'Neill, Terence, 354
O'Neill, Vincent, 339
O'Quinn, Keith, 246
O'Reilly, Ciaran, 255, 339, 340
O'Reilly, Terry, 344
O'Rourke, Janice, 354
O'Shea, Mark, 354
O'Steen, Michelle, 234, 300
O'Sullivan, Anne, 426
O'Toole, Fintan, 448
Oakes, Brandon, 430
Oakley, Trace, 409
Oatts, Laura, 232
Oatts, Richard, 235
Obele, David, 352
Oberle, Michael, 417, 419
Oberman, Brett, 275
Obie Awards, 456
Obispo, Fabian, 306, 349, 353, 368, 424
Obolensky, Kira, 412
Ochoa, Steven, 224
Ockert, Carolyn, 235
Ockrent, Mike, 240, 241
Oddo, John, 297
Oddo, Lou, 261
Odell, Rich, 335
Odets, Marc, 435
Odiseo, Could You Stop and Pick Up Some Eggs and Milk on the Way Home?, *339*
Odland, Bruce, 337
Odorisio, Rob, 305, 344, 349, 424, 433
Odze, Warren, 257
Oedipus, *337*, 456
Oedipussy, *349*
Oesterling, Tanya, 335
Off-Book, *356*

Offending the Audience, *355*
Offner, Deborah, 354
Offspring of the Cold War, *340*
Ogawa, Aya, 350
Ogimi, Teruhiko, 361
Oh, Coward!, *339*
Oh, Sandra, 35, 284, 415, 456
Ohio Theater, 360
Oikonomou, Zacharoula, 280
Ojeda, Perry Laylon, 237, 298
Oka, Marc, 401, 402
Okada, Yutaka, 354
Okpokwasili, Okwuchukwu, 350
Okun, Alexander, 433
Olcott, Nick, 435
Olcott, Thomas B., 235
Old Globe Theater, 232, 430
Old Neighborhood, The, 9
Old Possum's Book of Practical Cats, 221
Old Settler, The, *349*, 456, 457
Old Wicked Songs, 459
Oldakowski, Thomas J., 235
Oldest Profession, The, *344*
Olds, Gabriel, 321
Olich, Michael, 433
Olin, Elissa, 354
Olinder, Laurie, 405
Olive, John, 433
Olle, Alex, 344
Olmstead, Dan, 427
Olsen, Robert, 270
Olshanetsky, Alexander, 229
Omilami, Elizabeth, 422
Oms, Alba, 339
On the Jump, *408*, 409
On the Town, 4, 29, 30, 44, *237*, *238*, 452
On the Twentieth Century, 457, 459
Once Attractive Woman, The, *339*
Once Vaudeville, *360*
One Dream Sound, 280
140, *270*, *271*
100 Variations on a Family Theme, *350*
1, 2, 3. Muerte, Muerte, Morte: Pressed, *339*
One-Eyed Man Is King, The, *430*
Only a Kingdom, *425*
Only in America, *338*
Onrubia, Cynthia, 236, 311
Ontological-Hysteric Theater, 331, 348
Oo-Bla-Dee, *406*

Ooms, Richard, 422
Opel, Nancy, 245, 424, 426
Open Couple, The, *356*
Open the Gate, *351*
Oppenheim, Jonas, 348
Oppenheimer, Alan, 408
Opsahl, Jason, 286
Orange, Phasaan, 335
Orbach, Jerry, 313, 453
Orbach, Ron, 312, 354
Orczy, Baroness, 222, 232, 233
Ordway Music Theater, 430
Oregon Shakespeare Festival, 402
Oreskes, Daniel, 19, 242, 428
Orfeh, 32, 230, 231, 258, 259
Origlio, Tony, 225
Orison, *356*
Orizondo, Carlos, 339
Orlandersmith, Dael, 42, 277, 279, 327, 424, 456
Orlin, Robyn, 276
Orloff, Rich, 359
Ornithology, *436*
Ornstein, Suzanne, 298, 299, 301
Oronato, Joseph, 235
Orr, Ashley Rose, 320
Orr, Christopher, 338
Ortese, Rebecca, 344
Orth, Sarah E., 362
Orth, Zak, 353
Orth-Pallavicini, Nicole, 404
Ortiz, John, 267
Orton, Joe, 330, 358
Oscar, Brad, 300
Oscar Hammerstein Award, 456
Oscar Wilde's Lover, *427*
Oshun: The Goddess of Love, *360*
Osian, Matte, 224
Ossola, Paul, 278
Other Side of Alice, The, 403
Other Side of Life, The, *335*
Ott, Sharon, 432, 433
Ottavino, John, 435
Otterson, Pamela Elaine, 234
Ou, Tina, 298
Ouellette, Wendy, 289
Ouimette, Stephen, 293
Oulianine, Anik, 224
Oustiougov, Iouri, 228
Out of Joint, 290
Outer Critics Circle Awards, 6, 9, 44, 456
Ouyoung, Juliet, 348
Ovenden, Holly, 235

Ovenden, Steve, 352
Over & Over, *401*
Over the River and Through the Woods, 36, 40, *281*
Overbey, Kellie, 38, 281
Overstreet, W. Benton, 248
Ovid, 416
Owen, Leah, 335
Owen, Molly, 356
Owen, Paul, 417, 419
Owens, Dan, 420
Owens, Destin, 313
Owens, Frederick B., 320
Owens, Geoffrey, 284
Owens, Jon, 239
Owens, Robert Alexander, 267, 268
Oxley, J. Leonard, 458
Oy!, *359*
OyamO (Charles Gordon), 428, 430, 436
Ozborne, Vinny, 228

P.S. 122, 357
P.S/M.S. 330 Glee Club, 241
Pabotoy, Orlando, 277
Pace, Michael, 335
Pace Theatrical Group, 224, 249, 256, 257, 451
Pacheco, Joe, 437
Pacific Overtures, 25, 459
Paciotto, Andrea, 343
Pacitti, Joanna, 322
Packard, William, 292
Padagat, Del, 432
Padla, Steven, 233
Padrissa, Carlos, 344
Pagés, Maria, 228
Pagano, Michael, 230
Page, Carolann, 340
Page, Ken, 311
Page, Patrick, 241, 309, 458
Pai, Liana, 287
Paige, Amanda, 298
Painting You, *270, 271*
Pajama Game, The, 247
Pak, Woody, 362
Pakledinaz, Martin, 288, 337, 432, 456
Palermo, Andrew, 251
Paley, Petronia, 347
Pallet, Marshall, 320
Palmer, Frank S., 355
Palmer, Gavan, 311
Palmer, Saxon, 270
Palmer, Sean, 235, 245, 246
Palmer, Tony, 292
Pan Asian Repertory Theater, 348

Panaro, Hugh, 316, 323
Panczyk, Jonathan, 334
Pang, Andrew, 348
Panson, Bonnie, 269
Pantelides, Manos, 337
Papadamaki, Apostolia, 337
Paper Mill Playhouse, 261, 420
Papoutsis, Alex, 359
Pappas, Evan, 25, 243, 358, 431
Paquin, Daniel, 335
Parade, 4, 24, 25, 26, 30, 122–153, *243*, 447, 448, 451, 452, 455, 456
Paradise Hotel, 331, *348*
Paradox of Authorship, *335*
Paraiso, Nicky, 358
Paramour, *430*
Pare, Michael, 334
Parent, Matthew L., 434
Parfitt, Judy, 17, 252
Parichy, Dennis, 286
Pariseau, Kevin, 314
Parisi, Constance, 335
Parisse, Annie, 362
Park Avenue, *362*
Park, Dong Woo, 225
Park, Kolleen, 225
Park, Michael, 236, 320
Park, Sang Ho, 225
Park, Yong, 225
Parke, Evan Dexter, 358, 428
Parker, Alecia, 251
Parker, Christina, 335
Parker, David, 425
Parker, Gloria, 295
Parker, Mary-Louise, 40, 274, 275
Parker, Scott, 335
Parker, Wayne David, 405
Parker, William, 342
Parkinson, Elizabeth, 245, 246
Parkman, Desiree, 251
Parks, Angela, 355
Parks, Brian, 456
Parks, Christine, 351
Parks, Suzan-Lori, 340
Parks, Trina, 347
Parlato, Dennis, 320
Parnell, Charles, 358
Parnell, Peter, 330, 337, 454
Parov, Nikola, 228
Parrish, Sally, 344
Parry, Chris, 6, 250, 414, 452, 456
Parry, Raphael, 409
Parson, Annie-B, 338
Parsons, Estelle, 450
Partington, Tom, 244
Partlan, William, 436

Parva, Michael, 355
Pasadena Playhouse, 425
Pascal, Adam, 318
Paschal Full Moon, *345*
Pasekoff, Marilyn, 240
Pashalinski, Lola, 267
Pasic, Ines, 276, 277, 357
Pask, Scott, viii, 38, 279, 288, 453, 455
Paska, Roman, 357
Paskandi, Geza, 356
Pasley, Thomas, 427
Pasquale, Steve, 316
Pass, Eric, 334
Passionate Women, *342*
Pastorelli, Robert, 437
Patch, Jerry, 409
Patel, Neil, 223, 277, 353, 408, 411, 424
Patellis, Anthony, 342
Paternostro, Michael, 245, 246
Paterson, David, 261
Patinkin, Mandy, 20, 21, 229, 330
Patsas, Yorgos, 280
Patterson, Chuck, 284
Patterson, Howard Jay, 354
Patterson, Jackie Jay, 253, 296
Patterson, Jay, 432
Patterson, Meredith, 240
Patterson, Sean, 335
Patton, Eva, 342
Patton, Will, 405
Paul Dresher Ensemble Electro-Acoustic Band, 404
Paul, Ngozi, 292, 293
Paul, Pamela, 358
Paul, Richard Joseph, 338
Paulding, Nathalie, 350
Pauley, Wilbur, 252
Paulsen, Jeanne, 432
Paulson, Sarah, 288
Paulus, Diane, 344
Pavilion, The, 427
Pavlopoulos, Lefteris, 280
Paw, Elizabeth, 316
Pawk, Michele, 310
Paxton, Jill, 361
Payankov, Yasen, 406
Paykin, Lanny, 298, 299, 301
Payne, Joe, 424, 458
Payne, Stephen, 359
Payton, Khary, 409
Payton, Larry, 239, 248, 451
Payton-Wright, Pamela, 353, 433
Peace, Josh, 294
Peakes, John, 416
Peakes, Judith, 416

Peanuts, 248
Pearce, Daniel, 271, 354
Pearl Theater Company, 360
Pearl, Tom, 348
Pearlstein, Noam, 354
Pearsall, Kerri, 234
Pearson, Glen, 284
Pebworth, Jason, 316
Peck, Erin Leigh, 314
Peck, Gregory, 455
Peck, Jonathan, 237
Peden, Margaret Sayers, 356
Peden, William, 360
Pederson, Chris, 275
Pedi, Christine, 236
Peer Gynt, 351, 457
Pegnato, Lisa, 413
Peil, Mary Beth, 338
Pelfrey, Matt, 419
Pell, Karren, 422
Pell, Stephen, 47
Pellegrino, Joe, 334
Pelletier, Carol Ann, 352
Pelty, Adam, 232
Pelzman, Richard, 402
Pemberton, Lenore, 362
Pemberton, Michael, 249
Pen, Polly, 450
Pendleton, Austin, 355, 356
Penhall, Joe, 347
Penitentiary of Love, *359*
Penlington, Neil, 229
Pennewell, Norwood, 429
Pennington, Gail, 240
People vs. Mona, The, 433
Pepe, Neil, 336
Pera, Denise, 305
Pera Palas, *358*
Perdiguès, Jacques, 292
peregriNasyon, *358*
Perez, Gary, 428
Perez, Lazaro, 355
Perez, Luis, 257
Perez, Mercedes, 410
Perfect Crime, 264
Performance Space 122, 349
Pericles, 36, *282*, *284*, *285*
Perilo, Josh, 285
Perishable Theater, 368
Perkins, Kathy, 347
Perkins, Wayashti, 430
Perkinson, Coleridge-Taylor, 406
Perloff, Carey, 417, 431
Permission To Be Nick, *334*
Pero, Victoria, 355
Perrier, Olivier, 348
Perry, Claudia, 356
Perry, Ernest, Jr., 406

Perry, Jennifer, 402
Perry, Lynette, 318
Perry, Robert, 337
Perry, Shauneille, 347
Perry-Lancaster, Renee, 234
Persson, Gene, 248, 451
Pesce, Vince, 300
Pete Sanders Group, The, 232, 239, 251, 272, 294
Peter and Wendy, 44, 457
Peter Ibbetson, 353
Peter Pan, 3, 4, *239*, 322, 451
Peters, Bernadette, 27, 28, 251, 451, 456
Peters, Clarke, 14, 255, 456
Peters, Roberta, 455
Peterson, Chris, 241
Peterson, Lisa, 285, 353, 433
Peterson, Patricia Ben, 300
Petit, Leonard, 348
Petkoff, Robert, 355, 424
Petrarca, David, 287
Petrick, John, 358
Petrilli, Stephen, 334
Petro, David, 311
Petrone, Mike, 407
Petrovich, Aaron, 350
Petti, Lori, 289
Pettiford, Valarie, 245, 246, 323, 452
Petty, Bart, 458
Petty, Dan, 234
Peyser, Lynne, 243
Peyser, Noah D., 421
Pfisterer, Sarah, 323
Phèdre, 36, *290*, *291*, *292*, 331
Phaedra, *405*, 456, 457
Phantom, 457
Phantom of the Opera, The, 221, 316
Phil Bosakowski Theater, 360
Philip Glass Ensemble, 337
Philadelphia Story, The, 223
Philadelphia Theater Company, 426
Philippi, Michael, 249, 434
Phillips, Angie, 424
Phillips, Arte, 425
Phillips, Bob, 349
Phillips, Clayton, 244
Phillips, Derek, 355
Phillips, J.P., 402
Phillips, Jessica, 232
Phillips, Paul, 272
Phillips, Siân, 23, 256, 451
Phoenix, Alec, 282, 344
Photographs From S-21, *344*
Pia, Al, 457
Piaf, Edith, 256

Piano Lesson, The, 454
Piano Store, The, 360
Piccinni, Angela, 241
Piccione, Nancy, 286, 287
Pick, Anthony, 351
Pick Up Performance Company, 431
Pickering, James, 421
Pickering, Rose, 421
Pickering, Steve, 15, 249, 412
Pickett, Helen Eve, 363
Pickup, Ronald, 256
Pidgeon, Eugene, 260, 261
Piech, Jennifer, 321
Piemme, Karen Altree, 432
Pierce, Matthew, 356
Piercy, Emily, 24, 229
Pietro, Dave, 297
Pietrowski, John, 420
Pigeon Hole, *334*
Pigott-Smith, Tim, 255
Pilbrow, Richard, 288
Pillow, Charlie, 257
Pimentel, Luz Aurora, 344
Pinchot, Bronson, 416
Pincus, Warren, 266, 412
Pinder, Craig, 414
Pine, Larry, 353
Pine, Margaret, 436
Pines, Jeff, 302
Pinsky, Robert, 360
Pintauro, Joe, 436
Pinter, Harold, 40, 41, 288, 330, 337, 453
Pinto, Keith, 432
Pioggia, Joe, 360
Piper, Nicholas, 400
Pippin, 34, 247
Pippin, Don, 235
Piro, Jacquelyn, 315
Pisco, Frank, 357
Pita, Arthur, 229
Pitcher, Rebecca, 316
Pitchford, Dean, 24, 230, 231, 451
Pitchfork Disney, The, 332, *337*
Pitoniak, Anne, 256
Pittelman, Ira, 255, 271, 451
Pittman, Demetra, 402
Pitts, Lisa Renee, 363
Pittu, David, 321
Pizzi, Joey, 236, 277
Pizzi, Paula, 282, 344
Place, Patricia, 458
Plank, Dean, 241
Platt, Howard, 295
Platt, Jon B., 294
Play On!, 458

Playboy of the Western World, The, 457
Playhouse 91, 360
Playhouse at St. Clement's, 360
Playstation Levels 1–4, *356*
Playwrights Horizons, 36, 268, 280, 353
Playwrights Theater of New Jersey, 420
Pleasants, Philip, 422
Plenty, 260
Plotkin, Tom, 230, 314
Pluess, Andre, 407, 458
Plummer, Amanda, 39, 288, 289
Podemski, Tamara, 319
Poe, Richard, 353
Polaha, Kristoffer, 360
Poland, Christine, 354
Polcsa, Juliet, 344
Polgar, Jonathan R., 358
Polites, Theo, 360
Pollard, Jonathan, 281
Polley, Nora, 293
Pollitt, Barbara, 276
Pollock, George, 334, 354
Polson, Judith J. K., 359
Pomerantz, Will, 343, 356, 361
Pomeroy, Chris, 400, 401
Poole, Richard, 310
Poor, Bray, 424
Pop, Iggy, 275
Pope, Manley, 318
Pope, Peggy, 355
Pope, Stephanie, 299, 312
Pope, Wes, 235, 237, 238, 299
Poppe, Kimberly, 363
Poppo and the GoGo Boys, 342
Porazzi, Arturo E., 299, 301
Porazzi, Debora, 252
Porches, *347*
Porretta, Matthew, 315
Porter, Adina, 337
Porter, Cole, 223, 252, 256
Porter, Gregory, 259, 304
Porter, Lisa, 284
Porterfield, Hayes, 427
Porterfield, Jim, 405
Portes, Lisa, 409
Portland Stage Company, 277, 427
Posner, Aaron, 427
Posner, Jeremy M., 338, 340
Posner, Kenneth, *223*, 236, 237, 248, 285, 290, 338, 415
Post, Vernon, 244
Potter, Kirsten, 421
Poulenc, Francis, 245

Poulos, Jim, 318
Poulos, Mitch, 351
Powell, Anthony, 410, 411
Powell, Chesley, 235
Powell, Dawn, 416
Powell, Linda, 363
Powell, Michael Warren, 342
Powell, Molly, 359
Powell, Sean, 358
Powell, Shaun, 298
Power, Gohnny, 342
Power Plays, 264
Power, Sean, 340, 342
Powers, Amy, 434
Powers, Brendan, 339
Powers, Dennis, 410
Poyrazoglu, Ali, 358
Prater Violet, *361*
Precia, Stacie, 322
Preface to the Alien Garden, A, *428*
Premium Bob, 358
Premsrirat, Michael, 348
Prendergast, Shirley, 347
Prentiss, Paula, 317
Presentment, The, *426*
President's Awards, 455
Presley, Doug, 400, 401
Press, Red, 298, 299, 301
Press, Seymour Red, 224, 238, 269, 286, 298, 299, 301
Press, Warren, 436
Preston, Carrie, 280
Preston, Corliss, 411
Preston, John, 361
Preston, Michael, 354
Preston, Simon, 357
Pretlow, Wayne, 257, 414
Prettyman, Lyndi, 335
Previn, Andre, 455
Price, Ben, 400, 401
Price, Jim, 257, 415
Price, Kevin, 347
Price, Mark, 248
Price, Michael P., 411, 412
Price, Reynolds, 359
Price, Taylor, 362
Price, The, 41
Price You Pay, The, *347*
Pride's Crossing, 447
Primary English Class, The, 36, *293*
Primary Stages, 13, 329, 349
Prince, Faith, 30, 236
Prince, Harold, 24, 243, 244, 447, 452
Prince, Josh, 236, 298, 300
Prince of Parthia, The, vii
Pritner, Juliet, 358

Prittie, David, viii
Private Battles, *358*
Private Life of Sir Isaac Newton, The, *360*
Producers' Club, 360
Proletarians, The, *351*
Proletti, Paolo, 337
Promise Keepers, Losers Weepers, 458
Proposals, 9
Prouse, Derek, 358
Provenza, Rosario, 430
Provincetown Playhouse, 360
Provost, Sarah, 343
Pryce, Jonathan, 316
Prymus, Ken, 334, 424
Public Domain, 360
Public Theater (see The Joseph Papp Public Theater)
Publicity Office, The, 229, 234, 275, 294
Pucci, Lou Taylor, 320
Pudenz, Steve, 411
Puente, Ricardo, 350
Puerto Rican Traveling Theater, 349
Pugh, Jim, 246, 248
Pugliese, Frank, 338, 347, 359
Pulido, Lacie Katrina, 351
Pulido, Marina Lisa, 351
Pulitzer Prize Winners, 448
Pulse Theater, 360
Punchline, *335*
Punsalan, Robin, 348
Purcell, Erin Quinn, 282, 354
Purl, Linda, 8, 232, 430
Purnell, Kimberly, 360
Purple Rose Theater Company, 367, 405
Purser, Reese Phillip, 422
Pursley, David, 431
Putman, Matthew, 360
Putting It Together, *416*, 458
Puyo, Magda, 344
Pyant, Paul, 242, 428
Pyatt, Larry, 239
Pyne, Linnea, 289

Qaiyum, Gregory J., 287
Qi, Wang, 348
Quade, Vicki, 264
Quarles, Robert, 409
Quarrel, The, *420*
Quasi Un Fantasia, 427
Queal, Allison, 261
Queen Esther, 359
Queen Esther: Unemployed Superstar, *359*

Queen of Hearts, *356*
Queen of the Sea, The, *404*
Queens, The, 353
Quesnel, Pooky, 291
Question of Loyalty: The Rise and Fall of Edward R. Murrow, A, *360*
Question of Water, A, 403
Queypo, Kalani, 430
Quiet Storms, *350*
Quigley, Pearce, 292
Quigley, Ursula, 228
Quijas, Vanessa, 410
Quilty, John, 356
Quindere, Maneco, 342
Quinn, Aileen, 239
Quinn, Colin, 7, 228
Quinn, Laura, 311
Quinn, Patrick, 309, 320
Quintero, Joe, 352, 353
Quintero, Wayland, 340, 342
Quinton, Everett, 47, 280

R & J, 264
Rabe, David, 361, 437
Rabke, Kelly, 421
Race of the Ark Tattoo, The, 456
Racey, Noah, 298, 300
Racine, Jean, 290, 405
Racine, Sylvain, 348
Racing Demon, 9, 10
Rada, Mirenda, 274
Radiant Baby, 436
Radio City Christmas Spectacular, 4, *234*
Radio City Entertainment, 232, 260
Radio City Productions, 228
Rafart, Carlos, 339
Rafferty, Colleen, 335
Rafferty, Sarah, 270
Raffio, Richard, 235
Raffio, Ron, 244
Rafter, Casey, 299
Ragno, Joseph, 334
Ragtime, 3, 24, 25, 222, 318, 455, 456, 457
Rahman, Aishah, 338
Rahming, Gregory Emanuel, 237
Raiter, Frank, 268
Raitt, Kathleen, 232, 256, 451
Raize, Jason, 315
Raja, Roxanne, 431
Rak, Rachelle, 245, 246
Ralabate, Maria Jo, 311
Rall, Tommy, 246

Ramamurthy, Sendhil, 287
Rambal, Virginia, 339
Ramblin, Lute, 344
Rambo, David, 417
Rame, Franca, 356
Rameau, Patrick, 292
Ramey, Aaron, 420
Ramicova, Dunya, 417
Ramirez, Frank, 304
Ramirez, Maria Elena, 267, 268
Ramirez, Sara, 258, 259
Ramona, Red, 287, 350, 459
Ramone, Ross, 324
Ramsey, Kenna J., 319
Ramsey, Sue, 354
Ramshur, Steve, 407
Rand, Jeb, 234
Rand, Randolph Curtis, 338
Randall, Tony, 252
Randell, Patricia, 359
Randich, Jean, 345, 359
Randle, Mary, 315
Rando, John, 301, 305, 424, 426, 433, 435
Randolph, Jim, 281
Randolph-Macon Woman's College, 294
Randolph-Wright, Charles, 363
Rankin, Steve, 224
Ranson, Malcolm, 250, 414, 422
Ranwez, Alain, 409
Rao, Dileep, 431
Rapp, Anthony, 29, 248, 318
Rasche, David, 232
Rashad, Phylicia, 284
Rashid, Mujahid Abdul, 432
Rashmi, 267, 268
Rashovich, Gordana, 428
Raskin, Kenny, 309
Rasmussen, Jens, 348
Rat Lab, *335*
Ratner, Bruce C., 290
Rattazzi, Steven, 362
Rattlestick Productions, 331, 361
Ravenshead, *404*
Ravin, Beth, 251
Raw Deals and Some Satisfaction, *345*
Raw Space, 361
Ray, Connie, 269
Rayne, Stephen, 250, 414
Rayzner, Joshua, 230
Razaf, Andy, 256
RCA Victor, 455
Real, *363*
Real Thing, The, 12
Reams, Lee Roy, 33, 224, 225, 247, 309

Reardon, Joe, 239
Reaves-Phillips, Sandra, 253, 254, 296, 297, 334
Rebeck, Theresa, 424
Rebel Women, *360*
Recht, Ray, 274
Reckless Moments, 347
Red, 36, *285*, *287*, *433*
Red Clay Ramblers, The, 24, 239
Red Corners, *407*
Red Room, 361
Red Sky Productions, 430
Redbird, Petur, 430
Redd, Randy, 243, 244
Redden, Nigel, 343
Reddin, Keith, 408
Reddy, Brian, 433
Redgrave, Corin, 7, 249, 414, 451
Redgrave, Vanessa, 249
Redhead, 246
Redish, A. David, 409
Redman, Angela, 356
Redmond, Amy, 339
Redmond, Lawrence, 401
Redmond, Marge, 353, 355, 415
Redsecker, John, 299
Redwood, John Henry, 349
Reed, Christopher Benson, 334, 335
Reed, G.W., 356
Reed, Ishmael, 360
Reed, Janet, 349
Reed, Larry, 276, 277
Reed, Robert, 229
Reed, Rondi, 435
Reed, Royal, 256, 257, 414
Reeder, Ana, 347
Reemtsma, Todd M., 351
Rees, Roger, 280, 332, 337
Reese, Charles, 347
Reeve, Dana, 7, 230.
References to Salvador Dali Make Me Hot, *340*
Refuge, 331, 455
Regan, Jennifer, 358
Regan, Katie, 228
Regan, Suzi, 405
Regeneration (Ex?), *345*
Reggio, Paul, 361
Regis, John, 361
Regni, Al, 299, 301
Rehac, Kevin, 266
Rehearsal, The, 18
Rehrmann, Alexis, 352
Reid, Chick, 292, 293
Reid, Keenah, 237, 238
Reid, Marci, 225

Reid, Tom, 334
Reidy, David, 338
Reiner, Alysia, 363
Reingold, Jacquelyn, 347
Reinis, Jonathan, 259, 451
Reinking, Ann, 33, 245, 246, 247, 312, 452
Reinle, Kim, 362
Reisch, Michele, 253, 296, 334
Reisman, Jane, 281
Reiss, Jay, 354
Reisz, Karel, 288
Rembert, Jermaine R., 235
Re/membering Aunt Jemima: A Menstrual Show, *338*
Remembrance of Things Present, The, *335*
Remigio, Kristine, 316
Remington, Ralph, 422
Remler, Pamela, 240
Rendell, Carolyn, 359
Renick, Kyle, 275, 353
Renn, Jeffrey, 293
Reno, 361
Reno, Don, 270
Reno Finds Her Mind, *361*
Reno, Philip, 269
Renschler, Eric, 229
Rent, 29, 44, 222, 318, 327, 458
Repicci, William, 303
Request Concert, 459
Resnick, Amy, 359, 432
Resnik, Hollis, 315
Rest Is Easy, The, *345*
Restrepo, Federico, 357
Retribution, 36, *289*
Return of the Chocolate-Smeared Woman, The, *355*
Reugg, Mark Allen, 426
Reunion: A Civil War Epic in Miniature, *334*
Reyes, Guillermo, 420
Reynolds, Desi, 228
Reynolds, Jennifer, 421
Reynolds, Kathleen, 360
Reynolds, Rebecca, 419
Reynolds, Samuel F., 359
Reynolds, Todd, 251
Reynolds, Vickilyn, 310
Reza, Yasmina, 223
Rhian, Glenn, 241, 269, 298
Rhinehart, JoAnna, 347
Rhinoceros, *358*
Rhodes, Josh, 245, 246
Rhodes, Norman, 334, 335
Rhythm, Charlie, 259, 304
Ribant, Alan, 405
Ricapito, Christie, 427
Ricci, Hector, Jr., 358

Rice, Michael, 239
Rice, Paul, 355
Rice, Tim, 221, 222, 402
Rich, Carl O'Neal, 405
Rich, James, 318
Rich, Rebecca, 400, 401
Rich, Shirley, 450
Richard, Ellen, 223, 236, 270, 288, 450, 451
Richard, Judine, 237, 238
Richard Kornberg & Associates, 248, 249, 269, 277
Richard Rodgers Awards, 455
Richard, Stephen, 435
Richards, Bryan, 419
Richards, David, 450
Richards, Gary, 404
Richards, Jamie, 339
Richards, Jeffrey, 273, 274, 282, 303, 305
Richards, Lloyd, 436
Richards, Sharon, 298
Richards, Tom, 425
Richardson, Anselm, 335
Richardson, Desmond, 245, 246, 451
Richardson, Drew, 288
Richardson, Karl, 232, 257, 414
Richardson, Natasha, 11, 12, 254, 310, 456
Richenthal, David, 249, 451
Richmond, Terry, 232
Richy, Allison, 234
Rickson, Ian, 243, 255
Riddell, Derek, 291
Ride Down Mt. Morgan, The, 36, 41, *282*, *284*, *285*
Ridge, John David, 245, 452
Ridiculous Theatrical Company, The, 47, 280
Ridley, Philip, 337
Riebling, Tia, 334
Riehle, Richard, 255, 298
Rieppi, Pablo, 229
Ries, Tim, 230
Riesman, Michael, 337
Rifkin, Jay, 222
Rifkin, Ron, 310
Rigby, Cathy, 27, 239, 323
Rigg, Diana, 291, 331
Riggs, Cornell H., 348
Riggs, Mitchell, 355
Riley, Ron, 352
Riley, Tiffany, 361
Rinaldi, Philip, 224, 244, 245, 250, 269, 293, 294, 295, 298
Ring Round the Moon, 4, 18, *243*, *245*, 451, 452, 456
Ringer, Jenifer, 299

Rinklin, Ruth E., 259
Riopelle, Paul, 361
Riopelle, Peter, 361
Riordan, James, 356
Ripley, Alice, 315
Ripley, Katherine Martinez, 412
Risser, Ivy, 234
Risso, Richard, 410
Rita, Rui, 295, 414, 436, 437
Ritchie, Michael, 436
Ritschel, Jack, 425
Rivera, Angelo, 311
Rivera, Carmen, 350
Rivera, Chita, 312
Rivera, Eileen, 359
Rivera, Jose, 340, 416
Rivera, Matt, 310
Riverdance, 4, *228*
Riverdance Irish Dance Troupe, 228
Rivkin, Dan, 302
Rizk, Joumana, 342
Rizner, Russ, 235
Rizzo, Jeff, 261
Rno, Sung, 344
Roach, Dan, 428, 430
Roach, Kevin Joseph, 342
Roach, Maxine, 261
Road Home: Stories of Children at War, The, *355*
Roark, Jeffrey, 410
Robards, Jason, 13, 256, 455
Robber Bridegroom, The, 25
Robbins, Carrie, 353
Robbins, Jerome, 237, 239
Robbins, Julie, 294
Robbins, Rex, 424
Robbins, Tom Alan, 315
Roberson, George, 351
Roberson, J., 313
Roberson, Ken, 275, 288, 353
Roberson, Rudy, 253, 296, 334
Roberts, Alexandra, 292
Roberts, Bill, 261
Roberts, Chapman, 253, 254, 296
Roberts, Christopher, 351, 415
Roberts, Dallas, 417
Roberts, Jennifer, 431
Roberts, Jimmy, 264, 281
Roberts, Joan, 432
Roberts, Jonathan, 222
Roberts, Marcia, 242, 252, 259
Roberts, Mark, 363
Roberts, Robin Sanford, 259, 304, 431
Robertson, Joel, 244
Robertson, Lanie, 424

Robertson, Scott, 422
Robin, Kate, 345
Robin, Leo, 246
Robinson, Andrew J., 409, 459
Robinson, Bill, 253, 296
Robinson, Bruce J., 411
Robinson, J.R., 342
Robinson, Janelle, 323
Robinson, Joe, 294
Robinson, Roger, 402
Robinson, Vicki Sue, 358
Robinson, Walter, 428
Robison, Heather, 271, 422
Roby, Elizabeth, 421
Rocco, Jamie, 261
Roché, Sebastian, 294
Rocha, Kali, 281, 284, 430
Roche, Christian, 409
Roche, Suzzy, 363
Rock and Roy, *345*
Rock, Michael, 356
Rocket Man, 368
Rockwood, Jerry, 362
Roddy, Buzz, 293
Roddy, Pat, 228
Roderick Peoples, 458
Rodgers, Andrew, 235
Rodgers, Mary, 424
Rodgers, Richard, 223, 297
Rodin, Gil, 247
Rodine, Eric, 252
Rodriguez, Frank, 363
Rodriguez, Jai, 319
Rodriguez, Jesusa, 344
Rodriguez, Naomi, 459
Rodriguez, Raymond, 402
Rodriguez, Robynn, 402
Rodriguez, Veronica Diaz, 339
Roe, James, 232
Roe, Libby, 359
Roeder, Peggy, 337
Roesch, Diana K., 303
Roethke, Linda, 412, 458
Rogan, Peter, 339, 340
Roger, Pascale, 334
Rogers, Anne, 425
Rogers, David, 432
Rogers, Duncan M., 355
Rogers, Jeff, 407
Rogers, Jimmie, 259, 304
Rogers, Mike, 361
Rogers, Natalie, 429
Rogers, Sally, 292
Rohlfing, Nicholas, 362
Rohn, Jennifer, 271
Roi, Natacha, 255
Roland, Richard, 321
Roles, Elizabeth, 303

Rolfsrud, Erika, 271, 435
Rollin' on the T.O.B.A., 4, 24, 31, 36, *253*, *296*, *333*
Rolon, Bill, 260, 261
Roman, Carmen, 362
Roman Fever, *339*
Roman Ruins, *343*
Romano, Christy Carlson, 243
Romano, Joe, 435
Romanovsky, Ron, 272
Romeo and Juliet, 264
Romeo, Mark, 363
Ron, Liat, 343
Ronan, Brian, 236
Ronceria, Alejandro, 430
Ronnie Burkett Theater of Marionettes, 276
Rooney, Mickey, 260
Roost, Alisa, 360
Rosanio, Rocco, 359
Rosario, Liana, 352
Rosario, Willie, 268
Rosato, Mary Lou, 337
Rose, Anika Noni, 404
Rose, Billy, 247
Rose, Bob, 230
Rose McClendon: Harlem's Gift to Broadway, *347*
Rose, Nick, 335
Rose, Peter Pamela, 417
Rose, Richard, 400
Rose, Sarah, 353
Rosegg, Carol, viii
Rosen, Benjamin, 427
Rosen by Any Other Name, A, 457
Rosen, Craig David, 335
Rosen, Eric, 458
Rosen, Sharon, 359
Rosenbaum, David, 407
Rosenberg, David, viii
Rosenberg, Deena, 258
Rosenberg, James L., 356
Rosenberg, Michael S., 338
Rosenberg, Misses, 232
Rosenberg, Roger, 237
Rosenberg, Sandy, 232
Rosenfels, Joan, 270
Rosenkranz, Ian, 348
Rosenthal, Mark, 290
Rosenthal, Thomas, 421
Rosenzweig, Richard, 261
Roseto, Joe, 343
Rosin, Jennifer, 340
Rosokoff, Daniel S., 298
Ross, Abby, 334
Ross, Blair, 266
Ross, Brad, 265, 266

Ross, Jamie, 324
Ross, Jane, 362
Ross, Jerry, 247
Ross, JoAnna, 230
Ross, Lisette Lecat, 432
Ross, Michael, 282, 285
Ross, Parisa, 311
Ross, Rusty, 359
Ross, Sandi, 292
Ross, Stuart, 436
Ross, Tom, 343
Ross-Waterson, Colin, 229
Rosser, Felice, 343
Rossetter, Kathryn, 355
Rossini, 252
Rostand, Edmond, 264
Rotella, Mary, 420
Roth, C.P., 352
Roth, Daryl, 269, 282, 303
Roth, Joanna, 291
Roth, Katherine, 339, 351, 353, 409
Roth, Mary Robin, 458
Roth, Michael, 232, 431, 433
Roth, Robert Jess, 402
Roth, Susan, 436
Rothchild, Kennon III, 351
Rothenberg, David, 270, 275, 294
Rothfield, Michael, 305
Rothman, Carole, 289, 328
Rothman, John, 281
Rothschild, Ami, 361
Rotter, Fritz, 256
Rotunda, Connie, 355
Round House Theater, 457
Roundabout Theater Company, 4, 5, 18, 36, 40, 222, 223, 236, 249, 270, 287, 288, 450, 451
Rouner, Christina, 347
Rouse, Brad, 244
Roussel, Daniel, 417
Rousselet, Yaneck, 292
Roussos, Tasos, 337
Routh, Marc, 255, 280, 453
Rovere, Craig, 355
Rowe, Stephen, 405
Rowell, Mary, 235, 256
Roy, Queen, 458
Royal Court Theater, 243, 255, 260, 287, 450
Royal National Theater, 6, 249, 254, 256, 414, 450
Royal Shakespeare Company, 268, 330
Royer, Judith, 347
Rozenblatt, David, 229

Roznowski, Robert, 314
Rubald, Mark, 410
Rubano, Craig, 232
Ruben, Daniel, 406, 412
Rubens, Herbert, 252, 281
Rubenstein, Gillian, 347
Rubin, Brian, 244, 245, 269, 294
Rubin, John Gould, 337
Rubin, Michael, 257
Rubin-Vega, Daphne, 319
Rubinstein, John, 318
Rubinstein, Madelyn, 261
Rubio, Isabel, 350
Ruby, Harry, 248
Rucker, Mark, 408
Rudall, Nicholas, 362, 458
Rudd, Paul, 18, 224
Ruddigore, *359*
Rudin, Scott, 243, 254, 256, 275, 450
Rudin, Stuart, 342
Rudnick, Paul, 35, 38, 277, 327, 436
Rudy, Sam, 265, 279, 302
Rue, John, 361
Ruede, Clay, 241, 251, 299, 301
Ruess, John, 323
Ruffalo, Mark, 37, 290, 453
Ruffelle, Frances, 315
Ruffin, Raun, 257
Ruggeri, Christopher A., 410
Ruggiero, Rob, 294
Ruivivar, Francis, 260
Rules of Charity, The, 428
Rum and Vodka, *359*
Rumi, Jalaluddin, 337
Runfola, Maggie, 339
Runnette, Sean, 355
Running Man, 330, *344*, 448, 456
Rupert, Michael, 318
Rupli, Erika Lynn, 401
Rusalka, the Little Rivermaid, *342*
Rush, Cindi, 289
Rusinek, Roland, 240
Russek, Jim, 230
Russell, Beth, 244
Russell, Bill, 235
Russell, Brian Keith, 431
Russell, Donnell A., 229
Russell, Henny, 407
Russell, John C., 275, 353
Russell, Mark, 349, 456
Russell, Reuven, 420
Rust, Kari Beth, 302
Rustin, Chris, 330, 344
Rutan, Bob, 358

Rutherford, Ivan, 314
Rutigliano, Danny, 315
Rutigliano, Peter, 275
Ruttman, Jim T., 235
Ruvolo, Mary, 260, 261
Ruyle, Bill, 268, 343
Ryall, William, 420
Ryan, Amy, 338
Ryan, Ann, 228
Ryan, Jim, 322
Ryan, Julia, 355
Ryan, Kate Moira, 345, 416
Ryan, Lisa, 228
Ryan, Roz, 240, 312, 322
Ryan, Samantha, 335
Ryan, Sheila, 228
Ryan, Steve, 255
Ryan, Tammy, 363, 420
Ryan-Peters, Colleen, 406
Rybolt, Peter, 412
Rydman, Christopher, 431
Ryland, Jack, 425
Ryu, Sang, 225
Ryu, Seok Yong, 225

S, David, 437
S, Silvia Gonzalez, 345, 347
S.D., Trav, 359
Sabella, D., 313
Sabella, Ernie, 312
Sabellico, Richard, 340
Sabin, Marc, 334
Sacharow, Lawrence, 355
Sack, Domonic, 297
Sacre, Antonio, 361
Sade, Niv, 343
Safan, Chris, 436
Safdie, Oren, 342
Safe as Houses, 368
Sagal, Peter, 411
Sagardia, Elisa, 239, 322
Sagona, Vincent, 361
Sahely, Ed, 359
Sahs, Kirsten, 40, 302, 458
Saidy, Fred, 360
Saietta, Robert, 350
Saini, Maninder K., 334
Saint, David, 424
Saint Francis Talks to the Birds, *426*
Saint, Joe, 350
Saire, David, 360
Saito, James, 351
Sajadi, Amir, 287
Sakakura, Lainie, 245, 246
Sakata, Jeanne, 431, 433
Sakina's Restaurant, 36, 43, *272*, *334*, 457

Saks, Eva, 345
Saks, Gene, 355
Salas, Hope, 342
Salata, Gregory, 435
Salazar, Mikael, 408
Saldivar, Matthew, 353, 424
Salem, Peter, 291
Sales, Hunt, 275
Sales, Tony, 275
Salguero, Sophia, 362
Salkin, Eddie, 237, 258, 261
Sallinger, Conrad, 299
Salmon, Scott, 235
Salom, Jaime, 350
Salome, *276*, *277*
Salomons, Ruthlyn, 229
Salon, The, 361
Salonga, Lea, 316
Saltz, Amy, 436
Salzman, Thomas, 404
Sampson, Darice, 430
Samson, Richard, 256
Samuel Beckett Theater, 361
Samuel, Peter, 243, 244, 315
Samuels, Bruce, 251
Samuels, Jason, 305, 310
San Diego Repertory Theater, 243, 259, 303, 451
San Filippo, Louniece, 409
San Jose Repertory Theater, 432, 433
San Jose, Sean, 432
Sanchez, Alex, 245, 246, 247
Sanchez, Edwin, 416, 436
Sanchez, Jose, 437
Sanctifying Grace, 228
Sand, George, 329, 355
Sanders, Erin, 359
Sanders, Gregory, 407, 410
Sanders, Myron Andrew, 410
Sanders, Pete, 232, 239, 251, 272, 294
Sanders, Sheri C., 412
Sanderson, Austin, 431
Sandglass Theater, 357
Sandhu, Rommy, 237, 238
Sandish, Dale, 321
Sandmann, Cindy, 361
Sandow, Nick, 347
Sandrow, Nahma, 340
Sanes, Camilia, 337
Sanford Meisner Theater, 361
Sanford, Tim, 268, 280
Sang, Christine, 344
Sanidas, Frieda, 409
Sanks, Winston Anton, 410
Santagata, Frank, 236, 258
Santaland Diaries, The, 457

Santana, Carlota, 303, 304
Santana, Julia, 319
Santiago, Paul, 404
Santiago-Hudson, Ruben, 357
Santis, Edmund De, 363
Santopietro, Michele, 358
Santoro, Michael, 359
Santos, Tim, 235
Santvoord, Van, 339
Sanville, Guy, 405, 406
Saporito, Jim, 246
Sarachu, Cesar, 343
Sardinia, Tom, 425
Sargeant, Greig, 342, 362
Sarnelli, Daniel, 282, 344
Sarno, Janet, 354
Saroyan, William, 355
Sarpola, Richard, 232
Sarter, Matt, 335
Sartre, Jean-Paul, 358
Sasanov, Catherine, 344
Satalof, Stu, 286, 301
Satchell, Amanda, 420
Saturday Night Live, 228
Saul, Christopher, 348
Saunders, A., 313
Savage, Anthony, 228
Savage, Fred, 436
Savage, Keith, 323
Savarese, John, 313
Savion Glover/Downtown, 264
Savion Glover: Downtown, 36, 44, *304*
Sawyer, John, 257, 415
Sayan, Levon, 230
Saypol, Ben, 298
Scalera, Niki, 314
Scanlan, Robert, 360
Scanlon, Richard, 342
Scarlet Pimpernel, The, 3, 4, 26, 222, *232*
Scarpa, Michelle, 426
Scarpulla, Stephen, 240, 241
Scent of the Roses, *432*
Schönberg, Claude-Michel, 221
Schübel, Wilbert, 276
Schachner, Dan, 358
Schaeffer, Eric D., 401, 416
Schaffer, Zack, 353
Schamir, Dan, 359
Schanker, Larry, 406
Scharnberg, Kim, 232, 257, 414
Schartner, Genevieve, 353
Schatz, Jack, 236, 301
Schechter, David, 360
Scheck, Frank, 15, 447
Schecter, Amy, 275, 280, 294
Schecter, Jeffrey, 309
Scheherazade, 454

Scheine, Raynor, 284
Schell, Moe, 330
Schellenbaum, Tim, 342, 347
Schenck, Joni Michelle, 235
Schenck, Megan, 234
Schenker, Diane, 348
Schertler, Nancy, 239, 433
Schifrin, Lalo, 247
Schilke, Raymond D., 223, 281, 294, 303, 337
Schiralli, Michael, 359
Schisgal, Murray, 356
Schlag, James, 360
Schlossberg, Julian, 297, 303
Schmetterer, Mark, 334
Schmidt, Douglas W., 252, 257, 414
Schmidt, Harvey, 264, 411
Schmidt, Lisa Lee, 409
Schmidt, Paul, 405
Schmidt, Peter, 426
Schmidt, Robert N., 422
Schmidt, Ryan, 354
Schmiedl, Eric, 422
Schmitt, Ann Margaret, 273
Schmitt, Eric-Emmanuel, 417
Schmittroth, Marc, 352
Schmitz, Peter, 422
Schmon, Lisa, 437
Schneid, Megan, 281
Schnirman, David, 252, 338
Schnitzler, Arthur, 11, 243, 356
Schnupp, John D., 235
Schnurr, Vikki, 240
Schoeffler, Paul, 239, 323
Schofield, Mary Anne, 361
School of Natural Philosophy, The, *426*
Schranz, Doran, 407
Schreiber, Liev, 42, 268, 456
Schreier, Dan Moses, 268, 284, 295
Schrier, David Moses, 353
Schroader, Darren, 409
Schroder, Wayne, 240
Schroeder, Charles, 270
Schroeder, Kate, 235
Schubert, Rene, 337
Schuck, John, 322
Schuette, James, 277, 406
Schuh-Turner, Gina, 313
Schulfer, Roche Edward, 249, 406
Schulman, Charlie, 436
Schulman, Susan L., 289
Schultz, Armand, 424
Schultz, Carol, 360
Schultz, Leip, Conner and Phillips, 256

Schultz, Matthew, 409
Schultz, Victor, 251
Schulz, Bruno, 343
Schulz, Charles M., 248
Schurkamp, Richard, 266
Schuster, Massimo, 357
Schutzman, Steve, 403
Schwartz, Andy, 301
Schwartz, Arthur, 247, 362
Schwartz, Craig, viii
Schwartz, Erica, 224, 284
Schwartz, Gary, 286, 358
Schwartz, Joel, 340
Schwartz, Murray, 259
Schwartz, Robert Joel, 347
Schwartz, Scott, 425
Schwartz, Stephen, 34, 247, 424
Schwartz, Tyagi, 305
Schwarz, Stephen, 433
Schweikardt, Michael, 294, 334
Schwerer, Jennifer Leigh, 234
Scientific Romances: H.G. Wells's The War of the Worlds and The Invisible Man, *412*
Scilla, Maryellen, 234
Sciotto, Eric, 251
Scofield, Pamela, 270, 281
Scolari, Peter, 299, 300
Score, Diedre Murray, 456
Scott, Christopher, 310, 334
Scott, Clark, 305
Scott, Eric Dean, 350
Scott, Harold, 349
Scott, Jason M., 351
Scott, Les, 251
Scott, Leslie, 342
Scott, Peggy, 284
Scott, Robyn, 273
Scott, Seret, 303
Scott, Sherie, 319, 401, 402
Scott, Steve, 406
Scott, Tamara, 362
Scott, Timothy, 311
Scrofani, Aldo, 294
Scrofano, Paula, 458
Scruggs, Sharon, 405
Scurfield, Matthew, 343
Seagull, The, *360, 362*, 458
Seaquist, Carla, 355
Searle, Tom, 229
Seascape, 431
Seat-of-Our-Pants Productions, 415
Seaton, Laura, 301
Seattle Repertory Theater, 330, 432, 433
Seawell, Brockman, 411
Sebek, Herman W., 311

Sebesky, Don, 244, 452, 456
Seboko, Louis, 276
Seckel, Danny, 275, 419
Second Stage Theater, 41, 289, 328
Second Summer, 404
Secret History of the Lower East Side: The Patron Saint of the Nameless Dead, The, *338*
Secret Machine, The, *345*
Secrets Every Smart Traveler Should Know, 264
Sedaris, Amy, 277
Sedgwick, Kyra, 18, 19, 224
Sedgwick, Rob, 361, 425
See, Sheena, 363
Seeger, Pete, 256
Seelbach, Michael, 324
Sefcovic, Tom, 229
Segal, David F., 430
Segal, George, 307
Segel, Jonathan, 275
Segrest, Diana, viii
Sei, Julie, 358
Seidman, John, 431
Seinfeld, Jerry, 3, 7, 225
Selbert, Marianne, 235
Selby, William, 294
Selden, Neil, 335
Seldes, Marian, 18, 245, 451
Self Defense, or Death of Some Salesman, *344*
Seligson, Gary, 259
Sell, Ronald, 241
Sella, Robert, 5, 223, 310, 455
Seller, Jeffrey, 269
Selvaratnam, Tanya, 363
Semmelman, Jim, 224
Senavinin, Shawn, 302
Senor, Andy, 319
Seo, Beom Seok, 225
Seo, Byung Goo, 225
Serbagi, Roger, 363
Serban, Andrei, 42, 268, 342, 343, 457
Serinian, Sebu, 241
Sermonia, Julius, 311
Serrand, Dominique, 454
Serva, David, 303
Sesma, Thom, 268, 316
Setterfield, Valda, 431
Sevan, Adriana, 431
Seven Angels Theater, 435, 457
1776, 222
78th Street Theater Lab, 361
Severson, Kelli Bond, 251
Severson, Sten, 403
Sex and Longing, 9, 38

Sexton, Jed, 363
Sexton, Michael, 345
Sexual Perversity in Chicago, 12
Seyd, Richard, 426
Seykell, Ron, 311
Sezman, Dan, 275
SFX Entertainment, 230, 256, 259, 451
Shabach Audio, 253, 296
Shadow of a Gunman, The, *340*
ShadowLight Productions, 276
Shafer, Cory, 412
Shakespeare, William, 18, 223, 264, 267, 270, 282, 292, 305, 334, 342, 343, 355, 356, 360, 362, 416
Shakin' the Mess Outta Misery, *338*
Shakir, Omari, 422
Shaklin, Alex, 407
Shalhoub, Tony, 331, 337
Shallat-Chemel, Lee, 409
Shalom, Shai, 340
Shalwitz, Howard, 281
Shamos, Jeremy, 268, 285
Shanahan, Mark, 358
Shane, Tracy, 316
Shange, Ntozake, 270, 327
Shanghai Moon, *351*
Shank, Adele, 416
Shankel, Lynne, 248
Shanklin, James, 282, 284
Shanley, John Patrick, 363
Shannon, Erika, 322
Shannon, Marguerite, 431
Shannon, Mike, 288
Shapiro, Mark R., 289
Shapiro, Mel, 350
Shapiro, Steve, 404
Shapley, Lois, 335
Sharar, Carol, 257
Shared Experience, 290
Sharif, Bina, 351
Sharkey, Anthony, 228
Sharkey, Dan, 286
Sharp, Alex, 323
Sharp, Frances McAlpin, 360
Sharp, Jonathan, 299, 300
Sharpe, Ron, 257, 414
Shatto, Bart, 257, 414
Shattuck, Scott, 358
Shaughraun (The Vagabond), 331, *339*
Shavzin, Richard, 458
Shaw, Arje, 340
Shaw, George Bernard, 270, 358, 360

Shaw, Jane, 338
Shaw, Jane Catherine, 343
Shaw, Jenifer, 334
Shaw, Joseph, 292, 293
Shaw, Kevin, 401
Shaw, Peggy, 456
Shaw, Terrence, 409
Shayne, Tracy, 425
Shea, Brian, 410
Shea, Ed, 239
Shea, Ingrid, 410
Shea, Jere, 270
Sheaffer, Ben, 285, 320
Shearer, Andy, 285
Shearing, Geoffrey, 252
Sheehan, Ciaran, 316
Sheffer, Jonathan, 455
Shell, Roger, 239
Shelley, Carole, 310
Shelley, Mary, 400
Shelton, Joel, 237
Shelton, Mark, 360
Shelton, Sloane, 404
Shengsheng, Gao, 348
Shepard, Brian, 239
Shepard, Holly, 293
Shepard, Matthew, 315
Shepard, Tina, 343
Shephard-Massat, S.M., 411
Shepherd, Ryan, 311
Shepherd, Tommy, 432
Sheppard, John, 229
Shepperd, Michael A., 334
Sher, Bartlett, 427
Sheridan, Jamey, 417
Sheridan, Ryan, 228
Sherin, Mimi Jordan, 268, 277, 284, 417, 419, 428
Sherman, Barry Del, 353
Sherman, Charley, 412
Sherman, Daniel, 288
Sherman, Gregory J., 355
Sherman, Guy, 341
Sherman, Jonathan Marc, 437
Sherman, Keith, 265, 266
Sherman, Kim D., 306, 345, 403
Sherman, Laura, 239
Sherman, Loren, 435
Sherman, Lori, 275, 353
Sherman, Mark, 230
Sherman, Richard M., 229
Sherman, Robert B., 229
Sherman-Morcelo, Rebecca, 235
Sherrard, Tudor, 419
Sherwood-Moss, Genia, 234
Shetty, Vishal, 429
Shevett, Anita & Steve, viii
Sheward, David, 448

Shibaoka, Mazakazu, 294
Shibley, Noah, 427
Shields, Cary, 318
Shields, Timothy J., 421
Shiffman, J. Fred, 457
Shigo, Allison, 335
Shimono, Sab, 433
Shimosato, Keiko, 404
Shin, Eddie, 406
Shiner, David, 24, 30, 239, 345
Shinick, Kevin, 253
Shipley, Sandra, 414
Shire, David, 24, 358
Shirley Herz Associates, 265, 279, 302
Shiskine, Iouri, 228
Shivers, John, 305
Shlag, James Joseph, 360
Shnec, Zachary, 235
Shoemaker, Michael, 228
Shoemaker's Prodigious Wife, The, *339*
Shook, Warner, 433
Shopkorn, Stanley, 282
Shore, Allen M., 232
Shore, Daniel J., 360
Short, Martin, 30, 236, 451, 456
Short Stories, *276*, *277*, *357*
Shortridge, Dominique, 409
Show Boat, vii, 323
Shriver, Lisa, 278
Shropshire, Noble, 249, 414
Shubert Organization, The, 243, 254, 256, 275, 450
Shubert Performing Arts Center, 457
Shue, James, 354
Shugrue, Martin, 253, 296
Shurak, Heidi, 335
Shusterman, Tamlyn, 234, 299, 300
Shutt, Christopher, 250, 343, 414, 456
Siberry, Michael, 320
Sibrava, Karin, 362
Sick Again, *345*
Side Man, 4, 5, 6, 18, 47, 81– 103, *223*, 327, 448, 450, 451, 453, 455, 456
Side Show, 46
Sidia, I Made, 276
Siedenberg, Charlie, 289
Siegel, Ed, 457
Siegel, Eric, 432
Siegel, Joshua, 235
Siegel, Ronnie, 334
Siegfried, Mandy, 275, 288, 353
Siff, Maggie, 354
Siford, Daniel, 286

Sighvats, Asta, 343
Signature Required, *361*
Signature Theater, 329, 350, 401, 457
Sikora, Megan, 235
Silane, Jane, 234
Silberman, Brian, 427
Silbert, Peter, 421
Silcott, Thomas, 310
Sills, Beverly, 343
Sills, Douglas, 232, 319
Silver, Gerry, 362
Silver, Matthew, 260
Silver, Morty, 251
Silver, Nicky, 353
Silverman, Adam, 337
Silvers, Gene, 358
Silverstein, Steven, 224
Silvis, David, 412
Simard, Jennifer, 314
Simeone, John, 334
Simmons, Bonnie, 311
Simmons, Godfrey L., Jr., 281, 349
Simmons, Gregory, 250
Simmons, Helen L., 347
Simmons, Lisa, 413
Simmons, Peter T., 286
Simmons, Shantell, 410
Simms, Aaron, 421
Simon, John, 19, 34, 447, 453
Simon, Lee, Jr., 342
Simon, Mark, 244
Simon, Neil, 9, 30, 222, 236, 426
Simon, Nina, 251
Simon, Paul, 20, 230
Simone, 319
Simons, Lorca, 273
Simonson, Eric, 428
Simpatico, David, 355, 363
Simple Heart, A, *338*
Simple Stories, The, 253, 296, 333
Simply the Thing She Is, 405
Simpson, Herb, 368
Simpson, Jim, 329, 355, 456
Simpson, Linda, 349
Simpson, Peter, 350
Simpson, Thomas Adrian, 401
Sims, Bill, Jr., 357
Sims, Michael Vaugh, 306
Sing Me to Sleep, 456, 457
Singer, Isaac Bashevis, 351, 428
Singer, Stephen, 255
Singing, The, *345*, 455
Singleton, J. Lynn, 239, 451
Sinha, Ashok, 361
Sinisterra, Jose Sanchis, 345
Sins of Sor Juana, The, 409

Siopsis, Norman, 363
Siravo, Joe, 425
Sirens, The, *363*
Sirtis, Marina, 427
Sisolak, Michael, 268, 290
Sissons, Narelle, 37, 284, 289, 337, 425
Sister Mary Ignatius Explains It All for You, 38
Sister Week, *345*
Sisters Matsumoto, *433*
Sisto, Rocco, 349
Siti Company, 277, 419
Six Degrees of Separation, 14
Six Figures Theater Company, 361
Sjoblom, Paula, 338
Skaff, Greg, 259
Skenazy, Lenore, 340
Skepple, Sharon, 429
Skin of Our Teeth, The, 36, 42, *267*, *268*, 401
Skinner, Emily, 424
Skinner, Kate, 288
Skinner, Randy, 301
Skipitares, Theodora, 343, 357, 455
Skipper, Michael, 257
Sklar, Dan, 309
Skowron, Jeff, 315
Skull in Connemara, A, 13
Sky Watching, *415*
Skybell, Stephen, 353
Skye, Robin, 243, 244
Skylight, 9, 447
Skylight Productions, 274
Slamp, Dana, 306
Slant, *340*, 342
Slap Head: Demon Barber, *357*
Slap 'Em Down, *361*
Slater, Christian, 6, 223
Slaughterhouse Five, 428
Slee, Paul A., 344
Slezak, Victor, 339
Slingsby, Chris, 228
Sloan, Amanda W., 281
Sloan, John, 354
Sloane, Amy, 360
Sloe, Jed, 415
Sloman, John, 240
Slop–Culture, *419*
Slover, Tim, 368, 405
Sluberski, Ted, 361
Smart, Annie, 433
Smell of the Kill, The, *407*
Smith, Aaryn, 410
Smith, Anna Deavere, 327
Smith, Brendan, 223

Smith, Charles, 345
Smith, Chris, 339
Smith, Cotter, 279
Smith, Craig, 358
Smith, Darren, 228
Smith, Debra, 234
Smith, Derek, 232, 245, 430
Smith, Don, 235
Smith, Evan, 280
Smith, Felton, 272
Smith, Geddeth, 339
Smith, J. Tucker, 255
Smith, Jacob, 268
Smith, Jacques C., 318
Smith, Jay, 348
Smith, Jessica Chandlee, 265, 334
Smith, JillAnne, 351
Smith, John David, 244
Smith, Lee, 422
Smith, Lois, 288
Smith, Martin, 276
Smith, Michael, 404, 422
Smith, Molly, 435
Smith, Novella, 348
Smith, Patti, 275
Smith, Paul J., 261
Smith, Rae, 255, 343
Smith, Rex, 232, 319
Smith, Robert G., 302
Smith, Roger Guenveur, 340
Smith, Roger Preston, 239
Smith, Rolt, 241, 255
Smith, Sara C., 410
Smith, Scott, 426, 427
Smith, T. Ryder, 362
Smith, Tim, 276, 355
Smith, Timothy Edward, 251
Smith-Cameron, J., 17, 286
Smitrovich, Bill, 294, 437
Smoke on the Mountain, 36, **269**, **270**
Smokey Joe's Cafe, 221, 320
Smolik, Cody, 342
Smoot, Gary, 459
Smother, Donna, 458
Smulyan, Jane, 273
Snakebit, 36, 37, 47, *303*, 327, *359*
Snapshots, *359*
Snapshots '98, *363*
Sneade, Valerie, 420
Snelson, Nicole Ruth, 251
Snider, Alisha, 335
Snider, David, 268
Snider, Peggy, 404
Snider-Stein, Teresa, 350
Snow, Amber, 234
Snow, Tom, 24, 230, 451

Snowdon, Ted, 303, 305
Snyder, Ted, 248
Sobel, Randi Jean, 335
Sobel, Shepard, 360
Soble, Stanley, 285
Sobol, James, 360
Sobol, Joshua, 343
Society of Stage Directors and Choreographers, 450
Sodman, Lisa, 405
Soelistyo, Julyana, 408
Soetaert, Susan L., 340
Soffer, Serena, 230
Sogliuzzo, Andre, 359
Soho Playhouse, 39
Soho Rep, 350
Soho Triptych, The, *361*
Soileau, Paul, 427
Sokol, Marilyn, 425
Sokufa, Busi, 276
Solimando, Dana, 239
Solimando, Elisa, 239
Solis, Cynthia, 354
Solis, Jeffrey, 353
Solis, Octavio, 344
Solomon, Alisa, 455, 456
Solomon, Joseph, 429
Solomon, Kayla, 335
Solomon-Glover, Andre, 323
Solomonson, H., 229
Soloway, Leonard, 273, 305
Some Voices, *347*
Someone's Comin' Hungry, *335*
Somerville, Phyllis, 355
Something, Something Uber Alles, *359*
Somma, Joseph, 335
Sommers, Allison, 248
Sommers, Avery, 312
Sommers, Michael, 447
Somogyi, Ilona, 282, 344, 353
Son, Diana, 35, 419
Sonata da Camera Obscura, *348*
Sondermeyer, Laurie, 420
Sondheim, Stephen, 24, 229, 416, 455
Songs for a New World, 25
Soni, Saket, 406
Sonnets for an Old Century, 416
Sony, Warrick, 276
Soper, Tom, 352
Sophiea, Cynthia, 232
Sophocles, 19, 242, 243, 355, 428
Sordelet, Rick, 232, 290, 294, 402, 421, 435

Soroko, April, 427
Sostillio, Troy, 281, 285
Soto, Jock, 299
Sottile, Michael, 362
Soul, Graham, 348
Soul, Kristofer, 435
Soules, Dale, 403
Sound of Music, The, 29, 223
Soursourian, Matthew, 267, 268
South Coast Repertory, 274, 281, 282, 408
South Side Middle School Select Chorus, 241
Southern Christmas, 420
Sowers, Scott, 351
Spaans, Rick, 251
Space, 458
Spacey, Kevin, 13, 14, 255, 451, 456
Spahr, Scott, 237, 238
Spanger, Amy, 319
Spangler, Walt, 336, 337, 349, 419
Sparks, Don Lee, 433
Sparks, Willis, 256
Spector, Daniel Nathan, 426
Speech Therapy, *419*
Speer, Alexander, 417
Speers, Holly, 416
Speiser, Marianne, 351
Spencer, Frank, 235
Spencer, J. Robert, 421
Spencer, M.E., 313
Spencer, Richard, 235
Spencer, Stanley, 23
Spencer, Stuart, 339
Spencer, Susan, 410
Sperling, Ted, 269, 340, 356
Spialek, Hans, 298, 299
Spicola, Sal, 271
Spigelgass, Leonard, 331, 340
Spillane, Bobby, 228
Spinella, Stephen, 242, 428
Spiner, Brent, 319
Spinoza, Tony, 239
Spinozza, David, 246
Spiro, Matthew, 404
Spitzer, Harriet, 334
Spivak, Alice, 275
Spletzer, Phil, 229
Spontaneous Broadway, *356*
Spoonamore, Stephen, 360
Spore, Richard, 337
Spranger, Amy, 312
Sprauer, Fred, 411
Spray, *349*
Spread Eagle, 331, *353*
Spring Awakening, *343*
Spring Fever: Tabletop, *355*

Spring Killing, 404
Springer, Ashton, 253, 296
Springer/Chicoine Public
  Relations, 223, 253, 271, 289,
  306
Springer, Gary, 223, 253, 271,
  272, 289, 306
Sprinkle, Annie, 349
Spybey, Dina, 255
Squadron, Anne, 259, 451
Squeezed Avocadoes, *347*
Squire, Theresa, 337
Squitero, Roger, 257
St. Juste, Steve, 429
St. Nicholas, 13, 329
St. Paule, Irma, 339
Stackell, Joe, 344
Stackpole, Dana, 237, 238
Stadlen, Lewis J., 300, 301
Stafford, Chris, 281, 421
Stafford, Maeliosa, 260
Stafford-Clark, Max, 292
Stage Directors and
  Choreographers Foundation
  Awards, 455
Stahl, Stephen, 356
Stamenov, Ivan, 242, 428
Stametz, Lee, 410, 411
Stamile, Lauren, 237, 360
Stamoulis, Gregory, 337
Stancari, Lou, 401
Stanek, Jim, 286
Stanley, 23
Stanley, Jeffrey, 338
Stanton, Robert, 268, 424
Stanzilis, Michael, 234
Staples, Deborah, 421
Stapleton, Jean, 431
Star Billing, 20, *356*
Star Keeper, The, *348*
Starbuck, Christina, 361
Stargazers, *341*
Starger, Ilene, 255, 256
Starlin, Drew, 303
Starobin, Michael, 241, 269
Starr-Levitt, Megan, 316
Starstruck, *361*
Stations of the Cross, *413*
Staudenmayer, Edward, 266,
  294
Stauffer, Jana, 289
Stauffer, Scott, 224
Stavrogin's Confession, *361*
Steady, Maduka, 256
Stear, Rick, 224
Stearns, David Patrick, 448
Stebbins, Michael, 341
Stec, Alyssa, 234
Steegmuller, Francis, 355

Steele, Ed, 358
Steele, Kameron, 361
Steele, Kevin, 261
Steers, Katherine, 234
Steffen, Robert, 360
Stehlin, Jack, 354
Steib, Laura, 284
Steiger, Rick, 257
Stein, Adam, 268
Stein, Andy, 340
Stein, Debra, 349
Stein, Douglas, 239
Stein, Edward, 335
Stein, Erik, 286
Stein, Gertrude, 363
Stein, James J., Jr., 359
Stein, Jean, 223
Stein, Joan, 260, 450
Stein, Joseph, 401
Stein, Saul, 284, 338
Steinberg, Alli, 282, 344
Steinberg, David, 260, 261
Steinberg, Joseph S., 252
Steinberg, Lori, 359
Steinberg, Stuart, 356
Steinem, Gloria, 303
Steiner, Marian, 435
Steinitz, Nadia, 342
Steinman, Barry, 415
Steinman, Jim, 231, 451
Steinmeyer, Jim, 232, 407
Steir, Judith Shubow, 425
Stenborg, Helen, 282, 344
**Step in and Stand Clear: A
  City Slam**, 331, *338*
Stepanek, Brian, 458
Stepanova, Elena, 343
Stephens, Claudia, 338, 349,
  407
Stephens, Toby, 18, 245, 291,
  456
Stephenson, Don, 243, 244, 321
Stephenson, Shelagh, 285
Stephenson, Thaddeus, 400,
  401
Steppenwolf Theater
  Company, 406, 455
Sterlin, Jenny, 287
Sterling Barn Theater, 457
Sterman, Andrew, 232
Stern, Adrienne, 274
Stern, Amy Patricia, 279
Stern, Cheryl, 314
Stern, Daniel, 289, 430
Stern, David, 406
Stern, Edward, 407
Stern, Eric, 229, 244
Stern, Henry J., 267
Stern, James D., 255, 274

Stern, Jenna, 289
Stern-Wolfe, Mimi, 351
Sternberg, Jennifer, 359
Sternhagen, Frances, 332, 353,
  450
Stetkevych, Julian, 406
Stetson, Ron, 339
Stetson, Wendy Rich, 268
Stevens, Anise Mouette, 335
Stevens, Leslie, 426
Stevens, Paula, 355
Stevens, Ronald "Smokey",
  253, 254, 296, 333, 334
Stevens, Susan Riley, 427
Stevenson, Isabelle, 452
Stevenson, Robert Louis, 222,
  420
Steward of Christendom, The,
  457
Stewart, Anita, 427
Stewart, Daniel, 414, 425
Stewart, Daniel Freedom, 249
Stewart, Ellen, 341
Stewart, Gwen, 319
Stewart, Jaye, 253, 296, 333
Stewart, Mark, 224
Stewart, Patrick, 41, 284, 455
Stewart, Stevens,, 253
Stieb, Corey Tazmania, 350
Stifelman, Leslie, 299
Stiles, George, 412
Stilgoe, Richard, 221
Still, Melly, 348
Still, Peter John, 427
Stillman, Greg, 265
Stills, *335*
Stimac, Marilyn, 425
Stimac, Tony, 425
Stinton, Matt, 302
Stites, Kevin, 237, 238
Stoeckle, Robert, 404
Stoklos, Denise, 342
Stolarsky, Paul, 289
Stoller, Mike, 221
Stomp, 264
Stone, *351*
Stone, Amber, 298, 402
Stone, Chris, 415
Stone, Danton, 426
Stone, Daryl, 282, 347
Stone, David, 297
Stone, Elise, 358
Stone, Greg, 316
Stone, Jessica, 298, 425
Stone, Michael, 360
Stone, Peter, vii, 27, 222, 250
Stookesberry, Sam, 410
Stop Kiss, 35, 36, 47, *282, 284,
  285*, 456

Stoppard, Tom, 431
Storm, Douglas, 232
Story Goes On: The Music of Maltby and Shire, The, *358*
Story, Kay, 322
Story Theater, 330
Stothart, Herbert, 260
Stout, Mary, 234, 359
Stoutenborough, Kate, 435
Strahs, Jim, 350
Straight as a Line, *350*, *406*
Stram, Henry, 321
Strand, John, 457
Strange Case of Dr. Jekyll and Mr. Hyde, The, 222
Stransky, Charles, 293
Strasser, Robin, 281
Stratford Festival, 36, 292
Strathairn, David, 40, 288
Stratton, Hank, 402
Straus, Robert V., 252
Strauss, Bill, 46, 273
Strauss, Kim, 415
Stravinsky, Igor, 357
Strawbridge, Stephen, 337
Strawdog Theater, 458
Street of Crocodiles, The, 332, *343*
Streltsov, Ilia, 228
Strickland, Laurie, 410
Strickland, Ted, 427
Stripling, Mitch, 360
Stroganov, Aleksandr, 436
Stroman, Susan, 241
Strong, Caroline, 360
Stroud, Leslie, 234
Struthers, Sally, 322
Stuart, Ian, 407
Stuart, Kelly, 359
Stuart, Vicki, 407
Stubner, Heidi, 239, 251
Stuck, 331, *361*
Studio Theater, 361
Stuffed Puppet Theater, 277
Stuffed Shirts, 420
Stuhlbarg, Michael, 310
Stuhlreyer, Paul A. III, 402
Stuhr, Greg, 408
Stump-Vanderpool, Leslie, 234
Stupid Kids, 36, *275*, *353*
Sturge, Tom, 284
Sturiale, Grant, 235
Stutts, Will, 427
Styles, Joy E., 360
Styne, Jule, 239, 246, 297, 354
Suarez, Hugo, 276, 277, 357
Subandi, I Made, 276
Subirana, Libert, 348

Substitute, The, *335*
Suckling, Jenny-Lynn, 251
Suddeth, Allen, 281
Suddeth, J. Allen, 268, 287
Sudduth, Skipp, 224, 255
Sueka, Seema, 458
Suga, Shigeko, 342
Sugarman, David, 236, 256
Sukadana, I Made, 276
Suleman, Adam, 431
Sullivan, Daniel, 295, 417, 437
Sullivan, John Carver, 265
Sullivan, Kim, 347
Sullivan, Lynn, 234, 235
Sullivan, Michael Gene, 431
Sullivan, Nick, 230, 231
Sullivan, Patrick Ryan, 309
Sullivan, Sean, 349
Sullivan Street Lounge, 361
Sult, Jeff, 334
Summa, Don, 248, 249, 269, 290, 303
Summer and Smoke, 332
Summer Camp 4, 350
Summer Moon, The, *433*
Summerford, Dennis, 324
Summers, Alison, 345, 359
Summers, Nicole, 430
Sun Always Rose, The, *345*
Sunjata, Daniel, 224
Sunny Morning, A, *356*
Sunset Boulevard, 324
Sunshine Boys, The, 222
Supple, Tom, 348
Supprian-Katsoulis, Timos, 337
Susan Hightower, 277
Susan Smith Blackburn Prize, 331, 455
Susilo, Emiko Saraswati, 276
Susko, Michael, 235
Sussman, Ben, 407, 458
Sussman, Darren Reid, 434
Sussman, David, 361
Sussman, Matthew, 406
Sutcliffe, Steven, 318
Sutherland, Donald, 417
Sutherland, Sean, 338, 354
Sutherland, The, 458
Sutzkever, Abraham, 229
Svich, Caridad, 339
Swaby, Donn, 428
Swados, Elizabeth, 268, 343
Swan Lake, 4, 23, 24, *229*, 451, 452, 455, 456
Swan, The, 457
Swartz, Burton, 335
Sweatshop, *354*
Sweatt, Davis, 400

Swee, Daniel, 224, 245, 256, 295
Sweet Charity, 246, 247
Sweet Jane Productions, 350
Sweet, Jeffrey, viii, 368, 458
Sweet Maggie Blues, 405
Swenson, Britt, 232
Swiderski, Jennifer, 401
Swift, Allen, 428
Swindley, Ted, 401
Swingler, Frank, 360
Sydney Prescott Show, The, *356*
Sylvia, Abe, 311
Sylvia and Danny Kaye Playhouse, 361
Symphonie Fantastique, 36, 44, *265*, 329, 457
Synchronicity Space, 361
Synchronized Swimming: The Dry Version, *359*
Synnott, Cathal, 228
Szobody, Bill, 244
Szor, Terry, 244
Szucs, Andrea, 351

Tabeek, James, 235, 298
Tabor, Phil, 270
Taccone, Tony, 404, 415
Tagano, Mia, 294
Taggart, Jack, 417
Tagliarino, Salvatore, 350
Tague, Eileen, 437
Tahmin, Mary, 275
Taipei Theater, 362
Takada, Mio, 340
Takahashi, Junichi, viii
Take It Like Amanda, *358*
Takematsu, Yuji, 351, 352
Taking in Open-Light, *345*
Taking Leave, 368
Talai, Amir, 431
Tales of Washington Irving, or The Old Dutch Bowling League, *427*
Talking Band, 343
Talking With, 454
Tamaki, Yasuko, 240
Tamano, Yuichi, 352
Taming of the Shrew, The, *342*
Tan, Amy, 348
Tanaka, Masako, 361
Tanaka, Miyuki, 361
Tanganyika, 428
Tangen, Rulan, 430
Tanji, Lydia, 433
Tanner, Jill, 422
Tanner, Lutin, 429

Tanner, Tony, 360
Tansley, Brooke, 435
Tapp, Kirsty, 229
Taranda, Marina, 228
Target Margin Theater, 362
Tartuffe, 36, *305*, *306*
Tasca, Jules, 368
Tate, Jimmy, 309, 310
Tate, Judy, 338
Tatum, Bill, 356
Taucher, Dean, 303
Taxi! Taxi! or The Equality of Life, *350*
Taylor, Andy, 310
Taylor, Bobby, 270
Taylor, James, 424
Taylor, Jane, 276
Taylor, Jean, 342
Taylor, Joseph Lyle, 223
Taylor, Markland, viii
Taylor, Meschach, 309
Taylor, Michael P., 235
Taylor, Myra Lucretia, 242, 428
Taylor, Nichola, 235
Taylor, Owen, 311
Taylor, Patricia, 353
Taylor, Paul, 225
Taylor, Rebecca, 340
Taylor, Regina, 406
Taylor, Robbie, 335
Taylor, Ron, 18, 31, *243*, 259, 260, 303, 304, 451
Taylor, Scott, 241
Taymor, Julie, 222
Tazewell, Paul, 238, 259, 457
Tchaikovsky, Pyotr Ilyich, 23, 229
Teale, Polly, 290
Teare, Nigel, viii
Teatro Gioco Vita, 357
Teatro Hugo and Ines, 277, 357
Teatron Theater, 357
Tees, John III, 425
Teeter, Lara, 425
Tellier, Jerry, 320
Telsey, Bernard, 249, 259, 271, 277, 278, 282, 286, 344
Telushkin, Joseph, 420
Tenenbom, Tuvia, 358
TenEyck, Karen, 407
Tennessee Williams Remembered, 332, *355*
Tenney, Jon, 288
Tennille, Toni, 324
Tennis, Anyone, *335*
Tepper, Arielle, 234, 281, 294
Tepper, Kirby, 436
Terkel, Studs, 424, 432
Terminal Exit, 427

Terminating, or Lass Meine Schmertzen Nicht Verloren Sein, or Ambivalence, *270*, *271*
Terra Prenyada, *357*
Terrill Middle School Broadway Chorus, 241
Terror as Usual, 357
Terry, Sonny, 259, 304
Tesla's Letters, *338*
Tesori, Jeanine, 19, 224, 330, 417, 431, 451, 456
Testa, Jim, 235
Testa, Mary, 30, 44, 237, 269, 299, 300, 452
Testani, Andrea J., 223
Tetreault, Paul R., 414
Thaler, Dan, 348
Thaler, Jordan, 238, 267, 284, 285
Thalken, Joseph, 298, 299, 425
Tharps, Lisa, 271, 282, 344
That Championship Season, 36, 41, *289*, *290*, 329
That's My Time, *361*
Thatcher, Kristine, 407
Theard, Sam, 254, 260, 297, 304
Theater 3, 362
Theater Development Fund, 455
Theater for a New Audience, 362
Theater for the New City, 350
Theater Hall of Fame, viii, 462
Theater Offensive, 457
Theater Row Theater, 362
Theater Royal, 291
Theater Ten Ten, 362
Theatersports, *356*
Theatre de Complicite, 332, 343
Thelen, Jodi, 353
Them, *419*
Therriault, Michael, 293
They Still Mambo in Havana, *355*
Thibodeau, Marc, 229, 234, 275
Thicke, Alan, 313
Thiel, Regan, 315
Thies, Howard, 341, 342
Things You Shouldn't Say Past Midnight, 36, 40, *305*
1348, *355*
30th Street Theater, 363
30 Years in the Life of Cleopatra Jackson, *351*
This Is Our Youth, 36, 37, *289*, *290*, 453

This Lime Tree Bower, 13, 329, *349*
This Property Is Condemned, 332
Thistle, Linda, 401
Thole, Cynthia, 241
Thomas, D. Paul, 426
Thomas, Dean, 244, 271
Thomas, Erica, 275
Thomas, Marc Anthony, 335
Thomas, Marie, 334
Thomas, Ray Anthony, 414
Thompson, Adrienne, 351
Thompson, Beth, 340
Thompson, Fisher Sr., 260, 304
Thompson, Jason, 359
Thompson, Jay, viii
Thompson, Jennifer Laura, 27, 230, 314
Thompson, John Douglas, 428
Thompson, John Leonard, 407
Thompson, Karl, 235
Thompson, Kent, 243, 259, 303, 422
Thompson, Malachi, 458
Thompson, Mark, 243
Thompson, R. Scott, 402
Thompson, Raphael Nash, 342, 362
Thompson, Regan, 422
Thompson, Richard, 15, 249
Thompson, Stuart, 249, 450
Thompson, Walter, 351
Thomson, Laurel, 292, 293
Thoreau, Henry David, 342
Thorell, Clarke, 321
Thorne, Francis, 455
Thorne, Joan Vail, 332, 345, 353
Thorne, Tracy, 353
Thornton, Carl, 318
Thornton, David, 347
Thornton, Mike, 273
Thrasher, Mark, 244, 261
Three Tall Women, 327, 431, 454
Threepenny Opera, The, 457
Throne, Tyr, 342
Thunder Knocking on the Door, 457
Thurber, Lucy, 339
Thurman, Uma, 332, 337
Thurston, Michael, 334
Thurston, Philip, 224, 230
Thwak, *363*
Thy Kingdom's Coming, *355*
Tichler, Rosemarie, 237, 267, 282, 340
Tidwell, Brian, 239

Tierney, Susan, 348, 356
Tiesler, Paul, 323
Tietz, Fred, 405
Tieze, Eric, 410
Tighe, Susanne, 231, 260
Tilford, Mike, 273
'Til the Rapture Comes, 353
Tillinger, John, 17, 232, 253, 286, 353, 430
Tillotson, John, 435
Tilly, David, 228
Tilt, 343
Time It Is, 351
Time of Your Life, The, 355
Timothy M. Thompson, 435
Timperman, Marisa, 437
Ting, Liuh-Wen, 232
Tinka's New Dress, 276, 457
Tiplady, Steve, 276
Tipton, Jennifer, 431
Tisdale, Christianne, 308
Titanic, 222, 320, 453
Titcomb, Caldwell, viii, 457
Titcomb, Gordon, 257
Titus, David, 46, 271
Tkacz, Virlana, 343
To Be a Turk, 342
To Mandela, 345
To T or Not to T, 420
Tobias, Frederick K., 247
Todaro, Mary Jo, 225
Todd, Chris, 282
Todd, Derek, 363
Todd Theater Troupe, 342
Todd, Tony, 286
Todd Under Mitleidgen, 403
Todorowski, Ron, 230
Tofani, David, 298, 301
Together Again, 334
Toibin, Fiana, 255
Tokyo Can Can 2, 354
Tolan, Cindy, 285
Tolan, Kathleen, 360
Tolins, Jonathan, 425
Tolk, Alexandra, 436
Tolstoy, Leo, 290
Tom Killen Award, 456
Tom, Tony, 331
Tomboulidou, Martha, 280
Tomei, Paula, 408
Tomita, Tamlyn, 433
Tomkins, Leslie, 232
Tomzak, Karyn, 234
Tondino, Guido, 293
Tonemah, 430
Tongue of a Bird, 36, 282, 285
Tony (Antoinette Perry) Awards, 25, 450, 452
Tony 'n' Tina's Wedding, 264

Tony Origlio Publicity, 225
Topdog/Underdog, 340
Topol, Richard, 359
Topsy on the Boardwalk, 343
Torcellini, Jamie, 309
Torke, Michael, 337
Torn, Angelica, 5, 223
Torn, Tony, 342, 348
Toro, Puli, 350
Torre, Maggie, 261
Torre, Roma, 448
Torres, Bill, 339
Torres, Maria, 267, 268
Torres, Marilyn, 339
Torres, Maximo, 298
Torsiglieri, Anne, 243, 244
Toser, David, 340
Total Fictional Lie, 349
Toth, Richard, 356
Tova, Theresa, 318
Towber, Chaim, 229
Towers, Charles, 422
Towey, Augustine, 339
Town, Johanna, 292
Townsend, Darby, 355
Townsend, Elizabeth Ann, 356
Toy Theater, 357
Traces of the Western Slopes, 409
Train Stories, 361
Trainspotting, 36, 294
Traister, Andrew J., 430
Tramway End, The, 355
Transit of Venus, 433
Tranter, Neville, 276, 277
Trapnell, Susan Baird, 432
Trapp Family Singers, The, 223
Trapp, Maria Augusta, 223
Trask, Stephen, 264
Trav S.D., 359
Traveling Companions, 360
Travelogue, 361
Traverse des Sioux, 420
Traversing Jacob, 339
Travis, David, 358
Tree, Brian, 293
Tremarello, Richard, 239
Trenet, Charles Louis, 256
Trese, Adam, 353
Trestle at Pope Lick Creek, The, 368
Trettentero, Patrick, 358
Trevino, Victor, 335
Trial of One Short-Sighted Black vs. Mammy Louise and Safreeta Mae, The, 347
Triantafyllopoulos, Kostas, 279
Tribbey, Amy, 421
Tribe, 430

Tribeca Playhouse, 363
Trigg, Richard, viii
Trigger Street Productions, 255, 451
Trigueros, Charles, 269
Trilogy Theater, 363
Trinity Repertory Company, 428
Trinneer, Connor, 38, 294
Trio, Annie, Kids, Ensemble, 251
Triptych, 359
Troilus and Cressida, 334
Troob, Danny, 231, 235
Tropicana, Carmelita, 456
Trousdale, Christopher, 320
Trovato, Vincent, 265
True West, 12
Truhn, Augie, 409
Trujillo, Raoul, 430
Trujillo, Sergio, 245, 246
Truro, Victor, 425
Trusits, Marie, 361
Trust Me, 335
Tsantili, Foteini, 280
Tsolakidou, Anni, 280
Tsotra, Irene, 337
Tsoutsouvas, Sam, 284
Tuan, Alice, 338, 340
Tuason, Miguel, 251, 280
Tubert, Susana, 353
Tubes, 264
Tucci, Louis, 337
Tucci, Maria, 41, 338
Tucci, Michael, 312
Tucker, Bethany, 422
Tucker, Julie, 270, 288
Tucker, Sarah, 412
Tudor, Kristin, 234
Tudyk, Alan, 277, 337, 436
Tullis, Dan, Jr., 323
Tully, Ann, 405
Tully, Edward, 358
Tunick, Jonathan, 235, 286, 416
Turco, Paige, 338
Turn of the Screw, The, 349, 456, 458
Turner, Cedric, 423
Turner, Christine, 356
Turner Entertainment Co., 285
Turner, Robert, 360
Turner, Stephen Barker, 349
Turnstyle/Ambassador Theater Group, 255
Turturro, John, 331, 337
Twari, Rookie, 351
Tweed, Angela, 355

Twelfth Night, 4, 18, 19, 36, *223*, *224*, *305*, *306*, *343*, 451, 452, 456
29th Street Repertory, 39, 288, 289, 363
Twins, 38
Twisden, Jane, 280
Twist, Basil, 44, 265, 329, 457
2, 454
2 1/2 Jews, 36, *305*
2B, *361*
2.5 Minute Ride, 36, 42, *282*, *285*, 457
Two Rooms, 458
Two Sisters and a Piano, *428*
Two Trains Running, 454
Two-Headed, *345*
Tyler, Jim, 235
Tynes, Antoinette, 347
Tyson, David A., 407

Ubu & the Truth Commission, *276*
Ubu Repertory Theater, 352
Ucedo, Maria, 269
Uchima, Teff, 412
Ueno, Watoku, 343, 352
Uesugi, Mikiko, 432
Uffelman, Jonathan, 306
Uggams, Leslie, 349
Uhry, Alfred, 25, 222, 243, 447, 451, 456
Ullian, Peter, 338
Ullian, Seth, 294
Ullrich, Mattie, 287, 343, 347
Ullyart, Kendra, 422
Ulmer, Harum, Jr., 359
Umbilical Brothers, 363
Underwood, David, 235
Undoing, The, *361*
Uneasy Chair, The, 36, *280*
Unel, Sinan, 358
Ungaro, Joan, 455
Unger, Michael, 289
United Scenic Artists, 450
Untitled Life, *345*
Unzippin' My Doodah and Other National Priorities, 36, 46, *273*
Up, Down, Strange, Charmed, Beauty and Truth, *339*
Up, Up and Away, *421*
Uphues, Patrick, 458
Urban, Kenneth, 345
Urban Stages, 363
Urbano, Maryann, 433
Urbinati, Rob, 360
Urcioli, Paul, 281

Uriarte, Sarah, 308
Urich, Tom, 260, 261
Ursus, 359
Usher, Claire, 228
Utah Shakespearean Festival, 405

Vaccariello, Patrick, 401
Vaccaro, Barbara H., 235
Vaccaro, Danny, 260, 261, 271
Vachlioti, Merope, 337
Vagias, James M., 434
Vail, Emily, 405
Valdes-Aran, Ching, 415, 416
Valdez, Carlos, 294, 428, 430
Valentin, Joel, 429
Valentine's Day, *347*
Valenzuela, Rocio, 410
Valiando, Christian, 240, 241
Valk, Kate, 363
Valley, Paul Michael, 319, 350
Vallone, Peter F., 267
Valois, Onni Johnson, 343
Valot, Antoine, 409
Valparaiso, 405, 457
Valsetz, 458
Vamvaka, Melina, 279
van Bergen, Jim, 349, 426, 433
Van Der Walt, Lulu, 286
Van Druten, John, 222
Van Dyk, Reed, 286
Van Dyke, Elizabeth, 289, 423
Van Grack, Brad, 273
van Griethuysen, Ted, 457
Van Grogingen, Chris, 409
van Hoven, Eric, 299, 300
Van Liew, Joel, 363
van Meerbeke, Luk, 276, 277
Van Patten, Joyce, 7, 18, 230, 245
Van Pelt, David, 351
Van Slyke, Anjel, 344
Van Tieghem, David, 279, 282, 284, 286, 288, 344, 349, 353, 424, 457
Van Treuren, James, 232
Van Vliet, Julia, 273, 341
Van Zandt, Ned, 255
vanden Heuvel, Wendy, 355
Vanstone, Hugh, 243, 255
Vargas, Frances, 361
Varjas, Grant James, 339
Varner, Kevin, 306
Vasen, Tim, 403
Vasquez, Chris, 240
Vasquez, Michael, 352
Vassallo, Ed, 352
Vasta, Stephen, 339

Vaudeville 2000, *342*
Vaughan, Melanie, 243, 244
Vaughn, Brian, 421
Vaughn, Kimberly, 256
Vega, Manuel, 334
Vegetable Love, *363*
Velde, Fred, 363
Vellela, Tony, 355, 360
Veloudos, Spiro, 457
Veneklase, J. Gregor, 354
Venetian Twins, The, *422*
VenJohnson, Genevieve, 362
Vennema, John C., 284
Verastique, Rocker, 299
Verderame, Frank, 361
Verdon, Gwen, 245, 247, 455
Vereen, Ben, 313
Vergara, Bob, viii
Verheyen, Mariann, 284
Vermeulen, James, 284, 347
Vernon Early, *422*
Verrett, LaTrice, 347
Verrett, Shirley, 347
Versalie, Elizabeth West, 342
Vest, Buddy, 247
Vest, Nancy Elizabeth, 285
Vetere, Richard, 363
Vettel, Christopher, 420
Via Dolorosa, 4, 9, *243*, *245*, 447, 456
Vichengrad, Kirk, 334
Vichi, Gerry, 300, 301
Vickery, John, 315
Vicki Sue Robinson . . . Behind the Beat, *358*
Victor/Victoria, 324
Victory Gardens Theater, 368, 407
Video Viagra, *351*
Viertel, Thomas, 255, 280, 453
View From the Bridge, A, 222
Villa Villa, 269
Villar-Hauser, Ludovica, 356
Villegas, Juan, 351
Villella, David, 251
Vimtrup, Brent, 360
Vincent, Alan, 229
Vincent, Irving, 339
Vincent, Maura, 426
Vineyard Theater, 37, 276, 279, 327, 330, 353
Vining, David, 335
Viola, Steve, 358
Violet, 447, 454
Virginia Stage Company, 424
Virta, Ray, 360
Virtual Reality, 264
Visiting Mr. Green, 264
Visitor From Philadelphia, *427*

Visitors From Forest Hills, *427*
Vistation, *419*
Vitale, Angela, 358
Viverito, Vince, 435
Vivian, Robert, 334
Vlastnik, Frank, 359
Vogel, Emma, 361
Vogel, Frederic B., 256
Vogel, Paula, 38, 288, 327, 449, 457
Vogels, Matthias, 277
Vogelstein, Cherie, 339
Voltulevich-Manor, Natalia, 343
Volunteer Firemen, *356*
Von Berg, Peter, 348
von Mayrhauser, Jennifer, 290, 428
von Tilzer, Albert, 230
Vonnegut, Kurt, 428
Vorwald, Terrance, 427
Voyce, Kaye, 284, 426
Vreeland, Diana, 277
Vroman, Lisa, 316
Vujcec, Carolyn, 362
Vukovic, Monique, 288
Vukovich, James, 425
Vulcano, Giancarlo, 352
Vuolo, Louis, 360

W-Wow! Radio, *358*
Wade, Joey, 458
Wade, John, 294
Wade, Mark, 363
Wadsworth, Stephen, 288
Wagenheim, Kal, 361
Wager, Douglas C., 435
Waggoner, Jamie, 261
Wagner, Chuck, 307
Wagner, Curt, 348
Wagner, Daniel MacLean, 457
Wahl, Karl, 235
Wait Until Dark, 223
Waite, Ralph, 350
Waiting for Godot, 331, *337*
Waiting for Philip Glass, *270*, *271*
Waiting for the Parade, *356*
Waiting Room, The, 458
Waiting To Be Invited, 411
Wake Baby, *347*
Wakefield, Scott, 349
Waldmann, Clem, 278
Waldrop, Mark, 264, 299
Walk in the Woods, A, 454
Walker, Chet, 33, 245, 246
Walker, Christopher, 405
Walker, Cindy, 270

Walker, Daniel C., 405
Walker, Diana, 359
Walker, Don, 299
Walker, Fredi, 319
Walker, George F., 361
Walker, Jay, 428
Walker, Jerry Jeff, 248
Walker, John Patrick, 341
Walker, Jollina, 345
Walker, Jonathan, 344
Walker, Lanier, 422
Walker, Liz, 276
Walker, Mia, 251
Walking off the Roof, *350*, *408*
Walkinshaw, Andrew, 229
Wallace, John, 260, 304
Wallace, Megan, 409
Wallace, Naomi, 368, 420
Wallach, Andy, 351
Wallach, Eli, 332, 355
Waller, Thomas "Fats", 256
Walnut Street Theater, 426
Walsh, Alice Chebba, 256
Walsh, Ellis, 253, 296
Walsh, Fiona, 339
Walsh, James A., 356
Walsh, Paul, 454
Walsh, Thommie, 298, 299
Walt Disney Productions, 458
Walters, Charles, 335
Walters, Godfrey, 348
Walton, Bob, 299, 300
Walton, Emma, 430
Walton, Jim, 299, 300
Walton, Tony, 28, 241, 251, 288, 425, 430
Waltz of the Toreadors, The, 430
Wan, Josephine, 352
Wanamaker, Zoë, 19, 242, 428, 451
Wands, Susan, 342
Wanetik, Ric, 256
Wang Dang Doodle, 458
Wang, Luoyong, 316
Wang, Nathan, 433
Wang, Wang Yingying, 348
Wang, Xinyi, 348
Wann, Jim, 433
War, *339*
War, Sex and Dreams, *343*
Ward, Beverly, 323
Ward, Caitlin, 427
Ward, Douglas Turner, 347
Ward, Elizabeth, 232
Ward, Kirby, 323
Ward, Lauren, 45, 266, 319
Ward, Leanda, 228
Ward, Matthew, 265, 294

Ward, Robert, 455
Ward, Tom, 229
Wardrop, Ewan, 229
Warga, Michael, 356
Warhawks & Lindberghs, 458
Warhol, Andy, 277
Waring, Wendy, 299
Warmbrunn, Erika, 362
Warren, David, 353
Warren, Harry, 246
Warren, Jennifer Leigh, 458
Warren, Joel, 425
Warrick, Brittani, 402
Warshawsky, Mark M., 230
Washington, Sharon, 414
Washington Theater Awards Society, 457
Washington-Sarajevo Talks, The, *355*
Wasserstein, Wendy, 9, 270, 420
Wasted, 454
Watanabe, Greg, 433
Waterbury, Marsha, 313
Waters, Daryl, 222
Waters, Harry Jr., 404, 431
Waters, Les, 433
Waterston, Sam, 455
Watkins, Amanda, 311, 411
Watkins, J. Kathleen, 245, 246
Watkins, Jonathan, 458
Watkins, Maurine Dallas, 222
Watkins, Sharon, 401
Watson, Donald, 356
Watson, Janet, 411
Watson, June, 292
Watt, Michael, 250, 451
Wattis, Phyllis, 250
Watts, Wendy, 260, 261
Waxdal, Peter D., 268
Waxman, Anita, 242, 259, 280, 451
Way Back to Paradise, *340*
Way of All Fish, The, 264
Wayang Listrik/Electric Shadows, *276*
Wayfarer, The, *356*
Waymire, Kellie, 408
Waysdorf, Matt, 410
We Beat Whitey Ford, *361*
Weatherbox, The, 331, *361*
Weathers, Danny, 415
Weaver, Fritz, 18, 245
Webb, Jimmy, 421
Webb, Nick, 409
Webber, Andrew Lloyd, 24, 46, 221
Webber, Stephen, 277, 419
Weber, Michael, 458.

Weber, Mick, 361, 363
Weber, Rod, 256
Weber-Miller, Angela, 412
Webster, Bryan, 284, 348
Webster, Joseph, 299, 300
Webster, Virginia, 305
Wechsler, David, 239
Wedekind, Frank, 343
Weeks, Todd, 337
Wehle, Brenda, 353
Wehr, Adrienne, 343
Weigert, Robin, 224, 281
Weikel, Chris, 420
Weil, Melissa, 314
Weil, Sean, 342
Weimar, Peter Martin, 261
Wein, Glenn, 264
Weinberg, Jason, 344
Weinstock, Stephen, 345
Weir, The, 3, 4, 13, *255*, 329, 448, 456
Weiskopf, Walt, 246, 248
Weiss, Arnold, 275
Weiss, David, 241
Weiss, Jeff, 255
Weiss, Marcus, 359
Weiss, Matthew, 359
Weissbard, A.J., 351
Weissberg, Franklin E., 450
Weissberger Theater Group, 5, 223
Weissler, Barry, 250, 289, 451
Weissler, Fran, 250, 289, 451
Weitz, Stephen, 335
Weitzman, Ira, 244, 269
Welch, Christopher Evan, 422
Welch, Jessica, 401
Welch, Laurie, 234
Welcome to the Club, 45
Welcome to the Moon, *363*
Welden, Bess, 427
Weldon, Duncan C., 428, 451
Weller, Lucy, 291
Weller, Michael, 328, 454
Wellman, Mac, 329, 330, 355, 420
Wells, Christopher, 321
Wells, Emily N., 243
Wells, H.G., 407
Wells, Melissa, 409
Wells, Michael Louis, 339
Wellwarth, George E., 356
Welsh, Irvine, 294
Welzer, Irving, 250, 451
Wember, Asa, 435
Wendell & Ben, *436*
Wendholt, Scott, 246
Wendland, Mark, 15, 249, 268, 284, 414, 428

Wendle, Brooke, 234
Wendt, Angela, 278
Wendt, George, 307
Wendt, Roger, 237, 251, 269
Wendy, Darlene, 234
Wentong, Yu, 348
Werder, Tom, 424
Werking, Jon, 246, 248
Werner, Howard, 336
Wertenbaker, Carlo, 343
Wesner, George, 235
West, Charles, 232
West, Cheryl, 289
West, Darron L., 277, 285, 337, 419
West, Matt, 402
West, Troy, 406
Westbeth Theater Center, 363
Westenberg, Robert, 410
Westhafer, Emily, 261
Weston, Jon, 238, 278
Weston, Michael, 37, 303, 359
Westport Country Playhouse, 436
Wet Spot, *342*
Wetzel, Patrick, 251
Wexler, Matthew, 357
Weynand, David, 419, 421
Whale, Toby, 291
Whalen, Peter, 351
Wharton, Edith, 339
What Are You Afraid Of, *419*
What Corbett Knew, *345*
What the Living Do, *340*
What We Don't Confess, *360*
Wheatley, Mark, 343
Wheaton, Donna, 409
Wheeldon, Christopher, 299
Wheeler, David, 405
Wheeler, Harold, 236, 452
Wheeler, Leslie, 361
Wheeler, Thad J., 286
Wheetman, Dan, 243, 259, 260, 303, 304, 337, 451
Whelan, Bill, 228, 229
When I Was a Girl, I Used to Scream and Shout, *358*
When Pigs Fly, 24, 264
When the Bough Breaks, *362*
Whinnett, Pete, 228
Whitacre, Bruce E., 350
Whitaker, Bill, 239
Whitaker, Liesl, 261
White, Alton Fitzgerald, 318
White, Bernard, 415, 416
White Black Man, The, 436
White, Cassandra, 257, 414
White, Dana, 406
White, David, 321, 410

White, George C., 436
White, Greg, 271
White, J. Steven, 268
White, Jennifer Dorr, 358
White, Jo Ann Hawkins, 323
White, Lillias, 313
White, Margot, 360
White Mimosa, The, *358*
White, Olevia, 437
White, Randy, 361
White, Richard, 420
White, Welker, 347
Whitehead, Sam, 447, 453
Whitehead, W.M., 436
Whitehill, B.T., 303, 351
Whitehouse, Amy, 281, 344
Whitelaw, Arthur, 248, 451
Whitfield, Michael J., 293
Whiting, Richard, 246
Whitlock, Isiah, 255, 349
Whitlow, Daryll, 259, 304
Whitner, Daniel, 293
Whitney, Delora, 354
Whitney, John Justin, 334
Whitney-Barratt, Belinda, 298, 299, 301
Whitton, Margaret, 22, 256
Whitty, Jeff, 280
Who Shall Live, Who Shall Die, 289
Who's Afraid of Virginia Woolf?, 431
Whoriskey, Kate, 405
Whyte, Elizabeth, 358
Wichert, David-Paul, 337
Widmann, Thom, 256
Widmer, Philip, 353
Wieloszynski, Daniel, 241
Wiener, Sally Dixon, viii, 358
Wierzel, Robert, 271, 417, 426
Wig Lady, The, *345*
Wiggins, Michael, 306, 437
Wiggins, N. Elaine, 311
Wigle, Christopher, 437
Wija, I Wayan, 276, 277
Wilborn, Kip, 323
Wilbur, Richard, 305
Wilcox, Larry, 261
Wild Dog Casino, *351*
Wilde, Oscar, 331, 359
Wilder, Andrew, 232
Wilder, Baakari, 309, 310
Wilder, Matthew, 338
Wilder, Susan, 294
Wilder, Thornton, 267, 268, 363, 401
Wildhorn, Frank, 23, 24, 26, 222, 232, 256, 414, 451
Wildman, Robert, 434

Wiley, Eric, 358
Wilkins, Lee, 273
Wilkins, Luke, 412
Wilkinson, Colm, 314
Wilkof, Lee, 300, 301, 359
Will, Ethyl, 246
Will You Accept the Charges, *419*
Willett, Richard, 359, 361
Willey, Charles, 363
William Inge Festival Award, 455
Williams, Allen, 431
Williams, Alon, 239
Williams, Alyson, 253, 296
Williams, Andy, 348
Williams, Bert, 254, 296
Williams, Caroline, 419
Williams, Cartier Anthony, 298
Williams, Cezar, 342
Williams, Clarence, 253, 254, 296, 297
Williams, Dana, 230
Williams, Delores King, 273
Williams, Don Clark, 359
Williams, Elizabeth, 242, 259, 280, 451
Williams, Elliott, 360
Williams, Emlyn, 15, 252
Williams, Hank Sr., 260, 304
Williams, Jacqueline, 406
Williams, Jason, 360
Williams, Jeff, 241
Williams, Julius P., 347
Williams, Kurt, 342, 350
Williams, Laurie, 419
Williams, Lenny, 273
Williams, Marion, 344, 436
Williams, Marsha Garces, 249, 450
Williams, Penny Koleos, 404
Williams, Robert, 339, 340, 350
Williams, Shelley, 404
Williams, Tennessee, ix, 6, 7, 249, 355, 414, 450
Williams, Teresa, 401, 422
Williams, Treat, 44, 286
Williams, William, 360
Williamson, Jill, 244
Williamson, Kirsten, 432
Williamson, Laird, 410
Williamson, Nance, 433
Williamson, Ruth, 236, 344
Williamstown Theater Festival, 277, 436
Williford, Steven, 347, 355, 358
Willinger, David, 351
Willis, Dan, 236
Willis, Gay, 323

Willis, Jack, 360, 362, 424
Willis, John, 453
Willis, Mervyn, 342
Willis, Micha, 429
Willis, Susan, 422
Willison, Walter, 358
Willner, Sarah, 276
Willoughby, Graham, 356
Willow Cabin Theater, 363
Wilmes, Gary, 348, 349
Wilner, Jon, 224
Wilner, Sheri, 419
Wilshusen, Carrie, 411
Wilson, Annie, Kids, Foster, 251
Wilson, August, 454
Wilson, Caleb, 400, 401
Wilson, Chandra, 237, 238
Wilson, Chuck, 244
Wilson, Darlene, 232
Wilson, Deborah Y., 261
Wilson, Elizabeth, 285
Wilson, Faith, 280
Wilson, Lanford, 328, 367, 405, 454
Wilson, Mary Louise, 310, 329, 350
Wilson, Michael, 404, 414
Wilson, Patrick, 258, 259, 278
Wilson, Rainn, 422
Wilson, Robert, 331, 337
Wilson, Steve, 404
Wilson, Virgil, 422
Wiltsie, Jennifer, 252
Wimbs, John, 228
Winant, Bruce, 312
Winder, John, 241
Winding the Ball, *359*
Windrow, Jaime, 234
Winds of God, The, *358*
Winer, Linda, 447, 453
Wing, Anna, 292
Wingate, William P., 428
Wingfield, Garth, 362
Wings, 454
Wink & a Smile, A, *361*
Winkler, Richard, 407
Winnick, Jay Brian, 340
Winslow, Elaine, 234
Winslow, Pamela, 309
Winston, Tarik, 228
Winterset, *358*
Wirth, Doug, 361
Wise, Birgit Rattenborg, 249
Wise, Blaine, 422
Wise Guise III: Getting It Up!, *351*
Wise, Scott, 245, 246
Wise, Steve, 415

Wise, William, 363
Wiseman, Elizabeth, 348
Wish You Were Here: Acapulco, *354*
Wishbones and Falling Stars, *335*
Wisniski, Ron, 457
Wit, ix, 8, 34, 35, 36, 47, 104–121, *282*, 327, *344*, 447, 448, 449, 453, 454, 455, 456
With Allison's Eyes, 416
Witt, Howard, 15, 249, 451
Witt, Ken, 409
Wittow, Frank, 422
Wizard of Oz, The, 4, *260*, 458
Wojnar, Dan, 288
Wolcz, Ulla, 342
Wolf, Dan, 432
Wolf, Eugene, 400
Wolf, Gary, 363
Wolf Lullaby, *336*
Wolf, Marc, 355
Wolf, Miky, 354
Wolf, Scott, 6, 223, 437
Wolfe, George C., 222, 237, 238, 267, *282*, 340
Wolfe, Gregory, 355
Wolfe, J.D., 363
Wolfe, James, 355
Wolfe, John Leslie, 243
Wolfe, Wayne, 246
Wolff, Jannie, 342
Wolfson, David, 340
Wolinsky, Robert, 252
Wolos-Fonteno, David, 423, 424
Wolpe, Lenny, 320
Woman Who Fell From the Sky, The, *359*
Women of Lockerbie, The, *345*
Women of Orleans, The, *356*
Women's Project and Productions, The, 353
Won, Allen, 246
Wondisford, Diane, 344
Wong, B.D., 29, 248, 338
Wong, Peter J., 348
Woo Art International, 415
Woo, Jung Hoon, 225
Wood, D.M., 341
Wood, Frank, 5, 223, 451
Wood, John, 360
Wood, Mark Dundas, 345
Woodbury, Richard, 249
Woodhouse, Sam, 243, 259, 303
Woodman, Liz, 250, 306
Woodruff, Virginia, 324
Woods, Carol, 312
Woods, Eileen, 234

Woods, Jeremy, 421
Woods-Nolan, Beth, 234
Woodward, Jeffrey, 428
Woodward, Jennifer, 356
Woodward, Jeremy, 427
Woody Guthrie's American Song, *359*
Woody, Jimmie D., 268
Woolard, David C., 256, 301, 353, 404, 424, 435
Woolley, Jim, 251
Woolly Mammoth Theater Company, 281
Woolsey, Wysandria, 244
Woolverton, Linda, 221, 222, 402
Wooster Group, The, 363, 456
Wooster, Nikki, 355
Wooten, Arthur, 415
Wooten, Jason, 411
Wooten, John, 368
Wopat, Tom, 28, 251, 451
Words, *335*
Worgelt Study, The, *345*
Working, *424*
Working Theater, The, 363
World Mysteries: The Mysteries of Eleusis, The, *337*
World of Statistics, The, *356*
Worley, JoAnne, 260
Worth, Irene, 18, 329, 337, 355
Woza Africa!, *454*
WPA Theater, 24, 275, 353
Wreghitt, Randall L., 242, 252, 260, 450, 451
Wright, Amy, 350, 355
Wright, Barbara, 356
Wright, Ben, 229
Wright, Craig, 427
Wright, David, 272, 347, 360
Wright, Ford, 350
Wright, Garland, 306
Wright, Jeffrey, 310
Wright, Max, 18, 19, 224
Wright, Miller, 269, 295
Wright, Sam Breslin, 437
Wright, Samuel E., 315
Wright, Sara, 409
Wright, Sheyvonne, 423
Wright, Valerie, 251
Wrightson, Ann G., 402
Wu, Jade, 293
Wu, Mia, 244, 271
Wu, Pamela A., 433
Wuthering Heights, *421*
Wyant, Shelley, 342
Wyatt, Kirsten, 248

Wycherly, William, 360
Wyman, Nick, 337
Wyman, Seana, 348
Wynkoop, Christopher, 421

Xenos, George, 289, 337
Xiroyanni, Caterina, 351

Y2K, *417*
Yablokoff, Herman, 229
Yada, Masanobu, 358
Yager, Jerry, 338, 437
Yager, Missy, 37, 290
Yaji, Shigeru, 239
Yajima, Mineko, 298, 299, 301
Yamamoto, Toshiro Akira, 294
Yamauchi, Wakako, 454
Yan, Xu, 348
Yang, In Ja, 225
Yang, Jo, 348
Yang, Lia, 348
Yang, Welly, 359, 362
Yang, Young Il, 225
Yannatou, Savina, 279, 280
Yara Arts Group, 343
Yassukovich, Tatyana, 351, 352
Yates, Christopher, 420
Yates, Deborah, 234, 299
Yavich, Anita, 284, 287, 341, 403, 412, 424, 428
Yeargan, Michael, 32, 259, 271, 287
Yeates, Ray, 355
Yeats, William Butler, 342
Yee, Dave, 236
Yeghiayan, Lori, 415, 416
Yellin, Harriet, 294
Yelusich, Andrew V., 410
Yeston, Maury, 222
Yew, Chay, 285, 345, 433
Yi, Jiang, 348
Yi, Mun Yol, 225
Yi Sang Counts to Thirteen, *344*
Yield of the Long Bond, 459
Ying, Xu, 348
Yionoulis, Evan, 338
YiYi, El, 303
Yoakum, Stephen, 422
Yong, William, 229
Yoo, Mia, 268, 343
Yoon, Eun Kyoung, 225
York, Rachel, 232, 319
York, Sandy, 428
York Theater Company, 29, 36, 44, 265, 354
York, Y, 432
Yorkey, Brian, 362

Yorra, Sarah, 355
Yoshida, Atsushi, 358
Yoshimura, Akira, 340
You Never Can Tell, 36, *270*
You're a Good Man, Charlie Brown, 4, 18, 29, *248*
You're a Good Man Charlie Brown, 248, 265, 451, 452, 455, 456
Youki-Za, , 357
Youmans/Caesar, 252
Youmans, James, 407, 414, 424
Youmans, William, 356
Young and Deadly, *335*
Young, B. Jason, 310
Young, Courtney, 236
Young, Han, 342
Young, John G., 360
Young, Keith, 238
Young, Neal, 265
Young Playwrights, Inc., 455
Young, Ric, 287
Young Vic Theater Company, The, 348
Youngblood, Shay, 338
Yowman, Deandrea, 414
Yu, Hee Sung, 225
Yu, Ryun, 433
Yulin, Harris, 349
Yun, Chan, 225
Yun, Ho Jin, 225
Yun, Zhang, 348
Yung, Perry, 340, 342, 343
Yung, Susan, 291
Yurich, Carmen, 311
Yurman, Lawrence, 229, 235
Yvon, Bernie, 318

Zabriskie, Nan, 406
Zacarías, Karen, 409
Zacek, Dennis, 407
Zachry, Anne Louise, 362
Zagier, Norman, 257
Zagnit, Stuart, 289
Zaks, Jerry, 257
Zaloom, Paul, 276
Zambri, Catherine, 357
Zane, Greg, 235
Zapata, Carmen, 339
Zaragoza, Gregory, 251
Zauderer, Illana, 358
Zavaglia, Richard, 436
Zayas, David, 355
Zbornik, Kristine, 294
ZDF Enterprises, 252
Zeisler, Ellen, 290

Zeisler Group, The, 273, 290
Zeisler, Mark, 361
Zeitounian, Chloe, 241
Zelinski, Scott, 348
Zeller, Sam, 239
Zemarel, Jamie, 273
Zemon, Matt, 430
Zemon, Tom, 232
Zerkle, Greg, 315
Zerlin, David, 458
Zerman, Melvyn B., vii
Zerva, Dimitra, 280
ZFX Inc., 239
Zhanbalov, Erzhena, 343
Zhang, Ruth, 348
Zhao, Xin, 299
Zhengjie, Chen, 348

Ziegfeld Follies of 1936, 36, 42, *297*, *299*
Ziegfeld Follies of 1936–37, 299
Zieglerova, Klara, 339, 425
Zielinski, Scott, 353, 406, 408, 458
Ziemba, Karen, 299, 300, 312
Ziemer, Paul, 282
Zien, Chip, 269
Ziman, Richard, 249, 414
Zimberg, Stuart, 265
Zimdahl, Catherine, 347
Zimet, Paul, 343, 344, 347
Zimmer, Hans, 222
Zimmer, Missy Lay, 311
Zimmerman, Pamela, 355
Zimmermann, Julie, 335

Zingaro Equestrian Theater, 337
Zinn, David, 337, 424
Zito, Joseph Jude, 359
Zittel, Dan, 289
Zmed, Adrian, 313
Zoglin, Richard, 448
Zohar, Rita, 428
Zola, Greg, 285
Zoo Story, The, 431
Zora Neale Hurston, 36, *289*
Zorker, Christopher, 416
Zuber, Catherine, 224, 286, 294, 405, 452, 457
Zubrycki, Robert, 229
Zuhlke, Edward, 237
Zuzuki, Kimmy, 293
Zweigbaum, Steven, 241, 255